EFFECTIVE MARKETING RESEARCH IN CANADA

EFFECTIVE MARKETING RESEARCH IN CANADA

FIRST CANADIAN EDITION

WILLIAM G. ZIKMUND
Oklahoma State University

H. ONUR BODUR
Concordia University

THOMSON

NELSON

Australia   Canada   Mexico   Singapore   Spain   United Kingdom   United States

THOMSON
★
NELSON

**Effective Marketing Research in Canada,
First Canadian Edition**
by William G. Zikmund and H. Onur Bodur

**Associate Vice President,
Editorial Director:**
Evelyn Veitch

Publisher:
Veronica Visentin

Marketing Manager:
Kathaleen McCormick

Senior Developmental Editor:
Joanne Sutherland

**Photo Researcher and Permissions
Coordinator:**
Susan Selby

**Senior Content Production
Manager:**
Natalia Denesiuk Harris

Production Service:
International Typesetting
& Composition

Copy Editor:
Wendy Thomas

Proofreader:
Wayne Herrington

Indexer:
Kevin Broccoli

**Senior Manufacturing
Coordinator:**
Joanne McNeil

Design Director:
Ken Phipps

Interior Design:
Ann Small Design

Interior Design Modifications:
Dianna Little

Cover Design:
New Design Group

Cover Image:
Topical Press Agency/Hulton
Archive/Getty Images

Compositor:
International Typesetting
& Composition

Printer:
Courier

**Library and Archives Canada
Cataloguing in Publication Data**

Zikmund, William G.
Effective marketing research in Canada / William G. Zikmund, H. Onur Bodur. — 1st Canadian ed.

Includes bibliographical references and index.
ISBN13: 978-0-17-625208-3
ISBN10: 0-17-625208-8

1. Marketing research—Canada—Textbooks. I. Bodur, H. Onur, 1972– II. Title.

HF5415.2.Z536 2007   658.8'3971
C2006-906669-8

BRIEF CONTENTS

CONTENTS

PART 2 DESIGNING RESEARCH STUDIES

PART 3 MEASUREMENT CONCEPTS

PART 4 SAMPLING AND DATA COLLECTION

PART 5   ANALYSIS AND INTERPRETATION OF DATA

PART 6 PRESENTATION OF THE RESEARCH REPORT

PART 7 COMPREHENSIVE CASE

The use of the Internet for marketing research has come of age. Technological developments and social diffusion of the Internet are dramatically shaping the future of marketing research. As the Internet becomes increasingly representative of the world's population, innovative techniques that can be administered online will become standard. In the 21st century, marketing research on the Internet has moved out of the introductory stage of its product life cycle into the growth stage.

Effective Marketing Research in Canada reflects the astonishing changes in information technology that have taken place in the last few years. I have worked diligently and carefully to make this a book that reflects the practice of marketing research in our new digital age. While the book's primary focus is on time-honoured, traditional marketing research methods, I have included extensive coverage of Internet research.

ORGANIZATION OF THE BOOK

The organization of *Effective Marketing Research in Canada* follows the logic of the marketing research process. The book is organized into seven parts. Each part presents the basic research concepts for one of the stages in the research process and discusses how these concepts relate to decisions about conducting specific projects.

Part 1: Introduction to Marketing Research Process discusses the scope of marketing research, provides an overview of the entire marketing research process, and explains how the Internet and globalization are changing the nature of information systems. It also addresses organizational and ethical issues in marketing research.

Part 2: Designing Research Studies covers problem definition, research proposals, exploratory research, and secondary data. It examines the concepts and issues related to designing and using surveys, observation studies, and experiments.

Part 3: Measurement Concepts discusses the logic of measurement and the practical issues involved in attitude measurement and questionnaire design.

Part 4: Sampling and Data Collection explains why sampling is required and how to design samples, conduct fieldwork, and determine sample size. A review of basic statistical concepts appears in this part of the book.

Part 5: Analysis and Interpretation of Data covers editing, coding, descriptive data analysis, and inferential statistical analysis.

Part 6: Presentation of the Research Report covers the communication of research results. It ends with a final note on the use of marketing research.

Part 7: Comprehensive Case provides materials that challenge students to apply and integrate the concepts they have learned.

FEATURES OF EFFECTIVE MARKETING RESEARCH IN CANADA

Effective Marketing Research in Canada builds on the very successful text by William G. Zikmund, which is currently in its ninth edition. The book places great emphasis on the power of the Internet to conduct marketing research. It was important to me that this material not be lumped into an added chapter at the end of the book or into a single chapter on survey research. There are unique aspects of Internet research that touch on information systems, gathering of secondary data, survey design, sample selection, questionnaire design, Web traffic monitoring, and many other topics. The placement of Internet issues was carefully thought out. These issues are integrated in the right place, surrounded by the right context.

An accessible, interesting writing style is another hallmark of this textbook. With a careful balance between theory and practice and a sprinkling of interesting examples, the writing style helps to clarify rather than mystify. In addition, the text offers comprehensive rather than superficial treatment of topics.

A wide variety of up-to-date cases and examples on Canadian and international topics appear throughout the text. These include discussion of timely topics such as these:

Chapter 1: The Role of Marketing Research begins with the interesting story of how McCain used marketing research to successfully introduce a new beverage into the highly competitive juice box market. Chapter 1 concludes with a forward-looking section entitled "Marketing Research in the 21st Century." It explains how two trends, globalization of business and growth of the Internet as a communication medium, have changed the way we think about marketing research.

Concerns about privacy have caught the attention of the public and the marketing research world. The impact of new technology on privacy is discussed in depth in **Chapter 3: Organizational and Ethical Issues in Marketing Research.**

The use of the Internet for qualitative exploratory research is growing rapidly. **Chapter 5: Exploratory Research and Qualitative Analysis** discusses the use of online focus groups, videoconferencing, and streaming media technologies.

Chapter 6: Secondary Data Research in a Digital Age discusses information technology and how it is rapidly changing how secondary data are acquired. The chapter contains up-to-date Census data and examines the changing face of secondary data in our Internet age. This chapter concludes with two unique and valuable appendices: Appendix 6A describes numerous Canadian and international sources for secondary data, while Appendix 6B explains how to effectively search databases and retrieve information using computers.

Chapter 7: Survey Research: An Overview and Chapter 8: Survey Research: Basic Methods of Communication with Respondents reflect the role of the Internet and other new technologies in survey research. Chapter 7 opens with a story about how KitchenAid's marketing team used marketing research to figure out how to transfer brand equity from its small-appliance division to large appliances without increasing its marketing budget. Chapter 8 includes a major section on the advantages and disadvantages of Internet surveys. It explains everything from the basics (defining an Internet survey) to sophisticated topics such as security concerns.

Chapter 9: Observation features coverage of monitoring Web site traffic. It uses relevant examples about companies—such as Media Metrix Canada and Nielsen// NetRatings—that specialize in monitoring Internet activity.

Chapter 13: Questionnaire Design has extensive material on writing questions and formatting Web pages for Internet surveys. It discusses why the layout and physical attractiveness of the questionnaire are crucial in Internet and other self-administered questionnaires. Going beyond a mere cursory description of the Internet questionnaire, it explains how graphical user interfaces allow the researcher to control the background, colours, fonts, and other visual features displayed on the computer screen. It discusses status bars, radio-button questions, drop-box questions, variable piping, and many other questionnaire design issues unique to Internet surveys.

Chapter 14: Sampling Designs and Sampling Procedures includes a section that describes the best methods of drawing Internet samples. The discussion ranges from drawing samples of Web site visitors to forming panels from opt-in sampling frames. It also covers sampling problems associated with surveys conducted on the Internet.

A review of statistical theory in **Chapter 15** provides students with an overview of the basic aspects of statistics. Because this managerially oriented textbook is a marketing research textbook and not a statistics monograph, students are given the tools needed to review and comprehend statistical theory. Even students with rusty statistical skills will benefit from a quick review of the basic statistical concepts in Chapter 15.

Chapters 16, 17, and 18 discuss data collection, data preparation, and basic data analyses. These chapters reflect the growing use of computer software in data preparation and analysis. In order to provide a hands-on experience to students, several exhibits and end-of-chapter questions display statistical menus and output from SPSS. More importantly, SPSS instructions at the end of each of these chapters provide an excellent reference for students in data preparation and analyses.

Chapter 19: Communicating Research Results: Research Report, Oral Presentation, and Research Follow-Up includes a discussion of real-time report distribution. Employees now have the ability to share data, executive summaries, and reports on their company intranet.

COMPREHENSIVE INSTRUCTOR RESOURCES

Materials to supplement the content of the textbook are available to help instructors perform their vital teaching function. The extensive learning package provided with *Effective Marketing Research in Canada* includes a Test Bank, a computerized Test Bank (ExamView Testing Software), a comprehensive Instructor's Manual, PowerPoint presentation slides, data sets for several cases, and online marketing resources (available on the Web at www.effectivemarketingresearch.nelson.com).

- **The Instructor's Resource CD-ROM** (ISBN: 0-17-644031-3) contains valuable instructor resources on one easy-to-use CD-ROM: the Test Bank, ExamView Testing Software, the Instructor's Manual, PowerPoint presentation slides, and data sets for cases.

- **The Test Bank** has been carefully written to provide a variety of questions, covering every major concept in the textbook. The questions have all been scrutinized to eliminate ambiguity and to provide varying levels of difficulty. Each question is identified with a page number from the textbook where the answer may be located.

- **ExamView** is an easy-to-use automated testing program that allows instructors to create exams by using provided questions, modifying questions, or adding new questions.

- **The Instructor's Manual** was designed to ease lecture presentation by offering detailed and comprehensive lecture outlines and solutions to all assignments. The solution to each case includes the objective of the case, a brief summary of the case, and recommended questions and solutions. The Instructor's Manual is available both on the Instructor's Resource CD-ROM and at www.effectivemarketingresearch.nelson.com, on the instructor's portion of the Web site.

- **PowerPoint Presentation Slides** summarize and illustrate key concepts in each chapter. These slides are available both on the Instructor's Resource CD-ROM and at www.effectivemarketingresearch.nelson.com, where they can be downloaded.

- **Excel and SPSS Data Sets** are available for several of the end-of-chapter cases and the comprehensive case at the end of the book. The comprehensive case presents an entire research project and includes a database useful for assignments dealing with statistical analysis. Students may download the data sets at www. effectivemarketingresearch.nelson.com. Data sets are also available on the Instructor's Resource CD-ROM.

- ■ **The Comprehensive Video Library** (ISBN: 0-324-18150-7) introduces students to marketing research challenges in a variety of interesting businesses. Video cases in this expanded library guide students through problem analysis, problem solving, and application of chapter concepts. Video cases, suggested solutions, and teaching notes are included in the Instructor's Manual.

- ■ **CBC Videos** are available on the *Effective Marketing Research* Web site. Nothing helps students master concepts like seeing them put into practice in the real world. This video package will add visual impact and current, real-world examples to your lectures.
- ■ **Web Resources** at **www.effectivemarketingresearch.nelson.com** provide the latest information about what's new and what's cool in marketing research. The site features links to other research-related sites, downloadable instructor resources, CBC video clips and cases, and much more.

RESOURCES FOR STUDENTS

In addition to coverage of the latest information technology (described above), *Effective Marketing Research in Canada* includes the following student resources:

- ■ **The Dedicated Web site www.effectivemarketingresearch.nelson.com** includes chapter quizzes that allow students to test and retest their knowledge of chapter concepts. In addition, the Web site features CBC video clips and cases, downloadable PowerPoint slides, flash cards of key terms, the very best online marketing research resources available, and much more.
- ■ **InfoTrac—College Edition** is packaged free with each new text. This fully searchable online database gives professors and students 24-hour access to full-text articles from a variety of well-known periodicals and scholarly journals.
- ■ **SPSS** brings affordable, professional statistical analysis and modelling tools to a student's own PC. Based on the professional version of one of the world's leading desktop statistical software packages, SPSS 14.0 for Windows Student Version (ISBN: 0-324-53741-7) includes an easy-to-use interface and comprehensive online help that lets students learn statistics, not software.

ACKNOWLEDGMENTS

Undoubtedly there are more people than modestly mentioned here that have helped in the development of this project. First, I would like to thank William G. Zikmund for all the efforts put into this textbook on previous editions. Without the solid structure improved over his numerous revisions, the project would not be where it is today.

I would like to thank Simla Barki, who has displayed great commitment and diligence in all her assistance during the preparation of the textbook and the instructor's resources. I also appreciate the support of my graduate students who assisted with this project or allowed me to focus on this project by helping on other projects.

The first Canadian edition could not be written or published without the expert assistance and support of the Thomson Nelson team. I am grateful to Joanne Sutherland, who helped me immensely from the start of the project to the end and motivated me to stay on schedule, to Veronica Visentin for her generous support and patience, to Ric Kitowski for initiating the project, and to all other Thomson Nelson team members who contributed to the project at different levels.

I have to admit that I owe greatly to my family members who tolerated the long nights, weekends, and holidays that I spent in front of my computer and helped me meet my schedule. Special thanks go to Sarman, LouLou, Charlie, and Elsa, who were forgiving, as always.

I would like to thank my mentors, Neeraj Arora and Kent Nakamoto, and all my marketing research students who have directly or indirectly contributed to my professional development.

Finally, I would like thank friends and colleagues who have generously contributed to the development of the book:

Richard Appleby, *Okanagan University College*
Simla Barki, *Concordia University*
Robert Duncan, *British Columbia Institute of Technology*
Victor Emerson, *Acuity Research Group Inc.*
Ray Friedman, *Lethbridge Community College*
Daniel Gardiner, *University of British Columbia*
Bianca Grohmann, *Concordia University*
Michael Guolla, *University of Ottawa*
Valerie Hill, *Algonquin College*
Vinay Kanetkar, *University of Guelph*
Philippe Laporta, *AC Nielsen Canada*
Gregg Levis, *Georgian College*
Ian MacLean, *etc.tv*
Ming Ouyang, *University of New Brunswick*
Sridhar Samu, *University of Manitoba*
Diana Serafini, *Dawson College*
Elena Skliarenko, *Seneca College*
Carol West, *Sheridan College*

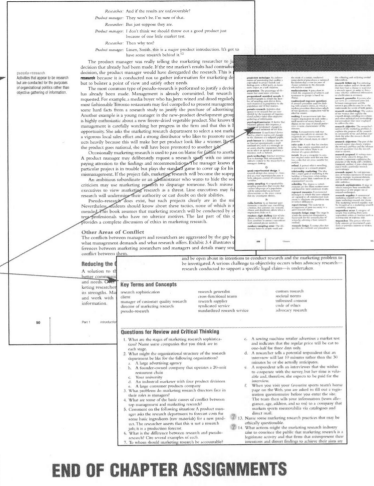

Key terms within the chapter and in the margins help students recognize and retain important marketing research and statistical terminology. Learning the vocabulary of marketing research is essential to understanding the topic, and *Effective Marketing Research in Canada* facilitates this in three ways. First, key concepts are boldfaced and completely defined when they first appear in the textbook. Second, all key terms and concepts are listed at the end of each chapter, and terms are highlighted in a marginal glossary. Third, a **glossary** summarizing all key terms and definitions appears at the end of the book for handy reference. A glossary of frequently used symbols is also included.

and be open about its intentions to conduct research and the marketing problem to be investigated. A serious challenge to objectivity occurs when advocacy research—research conducted to support a specific legal claim—is undertaken.

Key Terms and Concepts

research sophistication	research generalist	custom research
client	cross-functional teams	societal norms
manager of customer quality research	research supplier	informed consent
director of marketing research	syndicated service	code of ethics
pseudo-research	standardized research service	advocacy research

Questions for Review and Critical Thinking

1. What are the stages of marketing research sophistication? Name some companies that you think are in each stage.
2. What might the organizational structure of the research department be like for the following organizations?
   a. A large advertising agency
   b. A founder-owned company that operates a 20-unit restaurant chain
   c. Your university
   d. An industrial marketer with four product divisions
   e. A large consumer products company
3. What problems do marketing research directors face in their roles as managers?
4. What are some of the basic causes of conflict between top management and marketing research?
5. Comment on the following situation: A product manager asks the research department to forecast costs for some basic ingredients (raw materials) for a new product. The researcher asserts that this is not a research job; it is a production forecast.
6. What is the difference between research and pseudo-research? Cite several examples of each.
7. To whom should marketing research be accountable?
8. How can a marketing researcher help top management better understand the functions and limitations of research?
9. Identify a research supplier in your area, and determine what syndicated services and other functions are available to clients.
10. What do you think would be the best way to find work in marketing research?
11. Go to the library to learn the job titles and responsibilities for the various types of marketing research jobs. (*Hint:* One of the best sources is Thomas Kinnear and Ann Root, eds., *1994 Survey of Marketing Research* [Chicago: American Marketing Association, 1995].)
12. Comment on the ethics of the following situations:
   a. A food warehouse club advertises "savings up to 30 percent" after a survey showed a range of savings from 2 percent to 30 percent below average prices for selected items.
   b. A radio station broadcasts the following message during a syndicated rating service's rating period: "Please fill out your diary."

   c. A sewing machine retailer advertises a market test and indicates that the regular price will be cut to one-half for three days only.
   d. A researcher tells a potential respondent that an interview will last 10 minutes rather than the 30 minutes he or she actually anticipates.
   e. A respondent tells an interviewer that she wishes to cooperate with the survey, but her time is valuable and, therefore, she expects to be paid for the interview.
   f. When you visit your favourite sports team's home page on the Web, you are asked to fill out a registration questionnaire before you enter the site. The team then sells your information (team allegiance, age, address, and so on) to a company that markets sports memorabilia via catalogues and direct mail.
13. Name some marketing research practices that may be ethically questionable.
14. What actions might the marketing research industry take to convince the public that marketing research is a legitimate activity and that firms that misrepresent their intentions and distort findings to achieve their aims are not true marketing research companies?
15. Comment on the following interview:

   Interviewer: *Good afternoon, sir. My name is Mrs. Johnson and I am with Counselling Services. We are conducting a survey concerning Memorial Park. Do you own a funeral plot? Please answer yes or no.*

   Respondent: *(pauses)*

   Interviewer: *You do not own a funeral plot, do you?*

   Respondent: *No.*

   Interviewer: *Would you mind if I sent you a letter concerning Memorial Park? Please answer yes or no.*

   Respondent: *No.*

   Interviewer: *Would you please give me your address?*

16. Look through your local newspaper to find a story derived from survey research results. Does the newspaper article outline the study's methodology? Could this research have been considered advocacy research?

END OF CHAPTER ASSIGNMENTS

At the end of each chapter in *Effective Marketing Research in Canada*, there are a variety of assignments from which to choose. This gives instructors more choice in selecting just the right assignment for their classes. It also gives you a greater variety of activities, making it less likely that you'll repeat the same kind of assignment chapter after chapter.

Questions for Review and Critical Thinking promote student involvement in the classroom by prompting them to think about topics beyond the text's coverage. Review materials enhance students' understanding of key concepts.

Ethics questions, identified by a special icon, are included in each chapter. Among the compelling issues students are asked to explore is the redefining of the right to privacy in light of new technology.

Exploring the Internet activities provide considerable value for students of marketing research. A serious effort has been made to provide current URLs for numerous worthwhile educational Internet links.

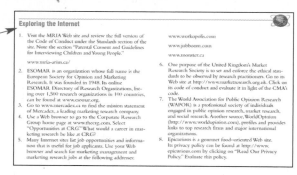

Extensive cases illustrate marketing research concepts and build knowledge and research skills. These cases present interesting, real-life research situations that require students to make thoughtful decisions. They offer the opportunity for active participation in the decision-making process, one of the most effective forms of learning.

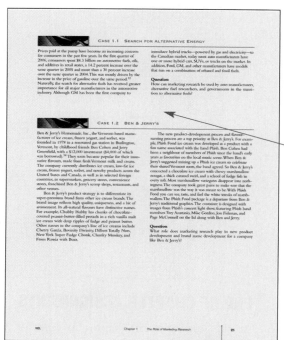

SPSS instructions appear at the end of Chapters 16, 17, and 18. SPSS data sets are available for several of the end-of-chapter cases.

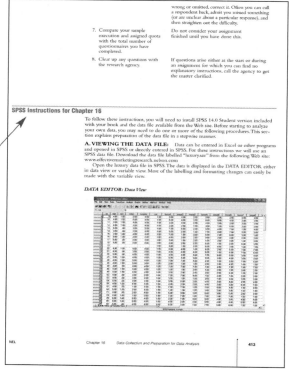

William G. Zikmund

A native of the Chicago area, William G. Zikmund now lives in Tulsa, Oklahoma. He is a professor of marketing at Oklahoma State University. He received a bachelor of science in marketing from the University of Colorado, a master of science in marketing from Southern Illinois University, and a Ph.D. in business administration with a concentration in marketing from the University of Colorado.

Before beginning his academic career, Professor Zikmund worked in marketing research for Conway/Millikin Company (a marketing research supplier) and Remington Arms Company (an extensive user of marketing research). Professor Zikmund also has served as a marketing research consultant to several business and nonprofit organizations. His applied marketing research experiences range from interviewing and coding to designing, supervising, and analyzing entire research programs.

During his academic career, Professor Zikmund has published dozens of articles and papers in a diverse group of scholarly journals ranging from the *Journal of Marketing* to the *Accounting Review* to the *Journal of Applied Psychology*. In addition to *Exploring Marketing Research*, Professor Zikmund has written *Essentials of Marketing Research, Business Research Methods, Marketing, Effective Marketing*, and a work of fiction, *A Corporate Bestiary*.

Professor Zikmund is a member of professional organizations including the American Marketing Association, the Academy of Marketing Science, the Association for Consumer Research, the Society for Marketing Advancement, the Marketing Educators' Association, and the Association of Collegiate Marketing Educators. He has served on the editorial review boards of the *Journal of Marketing Education, Marketing Education Review, Journal of the Academy of Marketing Science,* and *Journal of Business Research.*

Dr. H. Onur Bodur

H. Onur Bodur currently lives in Montreal, Quebec. He has earned his Master of Science in Business Administration with a concentration in marketing (1996) and Ph.D. in marketing from Virginia Tech (2000). Professor Bodur is currently an Associate Professor at Concordia University's John Molson School of Business.

Professor Bodur's research focuses primarily on consumer decision making and its marketing and public policy implications. His research has been published in highly regarded periodicals, including the *Journal of Marketing Research,* the *Journal of Consumer Psychology,* and *Psychology & Marketing.* Professor Bodur has presented his work and chaired sessions at internationally renowned academic conferences of the Association for Consumer Research (ACR), Marketing Science, Society for Consumer Psychology (SCP), European Marketing Academy Conference (EMAC), and INFORMS. He has served as a reviewer for international conferences and journals, contributed to supervision of Master's and Ph.D. theses, and received external research grants from industry and government institutions, such as Quebec's Fonds Québécois de la Recherche sur la Société et la Culture (FQRSC) and the Social Sciences and Humanities Research Council (SSHRC) of Canada.

Professor Bodur is a member of professional organizations that include the American Marketing Association (AMA), the Association for Consumer Research (ACR), the Society for Consumer Psychology (SCP), INFORMS, the Academy of Marketing Science (AMS), the Society for Judgment and Decision Making (SJDM), the Centre for Interuniversity Research and Analysis on Organizations (CIRANO), and the Administrative Sciences Association of Canada (ASAC). In addition to an array of other marketing courses, Professor Bodur has taught marketing research at the undergraduate and graduate levels in Canada, the United States, and Japan.

THE ROLE OF
MARKETING RESEARCH

McCain Foods Limited holds a 20 percent share of Canada's $303-million juice-box market but they are relative newcomers to this highly competitive sector, which is characterized by frequent price discounting and various private labels. Executives of McCain Foods Limited relied on marketing research for any new product introduction, but when the new product was a ready-to-serve beverage for *kids* it was especially important. The new beverage needed to appeal to the healthier preferences of parents (mostly mothers) and yet still be attractive in taste and packaging to the real consumers of their product: the kids.[1]

For McCain Foods, a giant in the food sector as the world's largest producer of French fries, aiming at 6- to 12-year-olds with ready-to-serve beverages was a first.[2] The company recognized that assuming that mothers would be the only target of their messages could be a costly mistake, given the important role kids played in determining what goes in the lunch box. The product was a healthy alternative to other drinks, with less sugar, no artificial flavours or colours, and 100 percent of the recommended daily serving of Vitamin C. All these features made it a relatively easier sell to mothers. However, in order to increase kids' "nag factor" to persuade parents to buy their product, it was essential that McCain increase the attraction for the new beverage among 6- to 12-year-olds.

More typical marketing research methods, such as surveys, could not be used to uncover the preferences of the under-12 market, and the focus groups had to involve kids. Some of the major decisions about the product's flavours, packaging, and promotion relied on the marketing research conducted with these target consumers. For instance, the name "Zwak" was chosen for the product because kids thought the letter "z" was cool; in addition, they usually sign off e-mails and chat lines with "SWAK" (sealed with a kiss). The decision to make the drink available in berry, grape, orange, peach, strawberry,

What you will learn in this chapter

1 To understand the importance of marketing research as a management decision-making tool.

2 To recognize that the essence of marketing research is to fulfill the marketing manager's need for knowledge of the market.

3 To define marketing research.

4 To understand the difference between basic and applied marketing research.

5 To explain that marketing research is a means for implementing the marketing concept and total quality management.

6 To discuss the various categories of marketing research activities.

7 To understand the managerial value of marketing research and its role in the development and implementation of marketing strategy.

8 To understand when marketing research is needed and when it should not be conducted.

and kiwi flavours also was an outcome of this research. The product was launched in English Canada and the United States first, with innovative TV spots starring a trio of cartoon characters—Kai, Celeste, and Zoomi—searching for Zwak drinks in their adventures. The Japanese-style cartoon characters each possesses different superpowers: Celeste has super vision, Zoomi has sonic speed, and Kai has the ability to shrink. They also appear on the packaging of the drink and in three online games: "Fruit Driver," "Cloud Hopping," and "Brain Puzzle."[3] Although many factors, such as product characteristics and integrated launch of the product, contributed to its success, marketing research was instrumental in determining the design and specifics of the product and promotion. ∎

The following examples demonstrate how marketing research can lead to new products, improvements in existing goods and services, and changes in marketing strategy. As you read these examples, imagine that you are a marketing manager and consider the importance of marketing research in providing information that is essential for good decision making.

Bell Mobility conducted research among the Canadian youth in order to understand what they want from their mobile phone provider. As a result of Bell's marketing research with more than 1,000 Canadian youths, the new Solo Mobile was offered with walkie-talkie capabilities, free text messages, and the choice of "no-contract" monthly or prepaid plans without any activation fees.[4]

Jelly Belly brand sells 40 varieties of jelly beans, with the number growing every year. Some of the flavours under development have come from suggestions from visitors to Jelly Belly's Web site. In return for filling out an interactive questionnaire, visitors get samples sent to them. One question the company asks is for input on new flavours. Jelly Belly gets a great response to this question, and marketers take all the suggestions seriously. Researchers categorize them and group them by similar flavours. Some of the suggestions are put back on the Web so that people can vote for their favourites. The company has received some really off-the-wall flavour ideas. Among the strangest are flavours such as Dill Pickle, Taco, Persimmon Pudding, Blackened Plantain, and Cream of Wheat.[5]

Altoids are a thumbnail-sized breath freshener packaged in a tin. The company's advertising agency did psychological testing with the brand's target market—young, single, urban males. Researchers gave Altoids users ten magazines and asked them to cut out pictures and paste them on paper to make a collage that represented their feelings about Altoids. The researchers' psychological interpretation of the collages suggested that there were three emotional dimensions associated with the brand. One was the feeling of freshness, which was portrayed by open space and outdoor scenes such as waterfalls. The second association was British, which was illustrated with pictures of British royalty. The third dimension was sex appeal, represented by images identified with young male fantasies, such as "hot" women dressed in red.[6]

Each of these examples illustrates a different aspect of marketing research. The Bell Mobility example shows how research findings can be directly translated into product and service offerings. The Altoids example points out the value of qualitative analysis to understand brand associations. The Jelly Belly example suggests that new technologies are changing the nature of marketing research. Researchers use techniques other than surveys to gain information. Government and trade association statistics, internal records, experiments, and test marketing are valuable tools for marketing research. The examples presented here illustrate only a few applications of marketing research. This chapter introduces marketing research and its role in marketing decision making.

Marketing research fulfills the marketing manager's need for knowledge of the market. Information acquired through research is used to identify and define marketing opportunities and problems; to generate, refine, and evaluate marketing actions; to monitor marketing performance; and to improve the understanding of marketing as a process.[7] The task of marketing research is to help specify and supply accurate information to reduce the uncertainty in decision making.

Information from a manager's experiences frequently is used in an intuitive manner because of the time pressures on business decisions or because the problem does not warrant more formal research methods. However, the primary task of marketing management is effective decision making. Relying on seat-of-the-pants decision making—decision making without systematic inquiry—is like betting on a long shot at the racetrack because the horse's name is appealing. Occasionally there are successes, but in the long run intuition without research can lead to disappointment. Marketing research helps decision makers shift from intuitive information gathering to systematic and objective investigating.

Marketing Research Defined

marketing research
The systematic and objective process of generating information to aid in making marketing decisions.

Marketing research is defined as the systematic and objective process of generating information to aid in making marketing decisions. This process includes specifying what information is required, designing the method for collecting information, managing and implementing the collection of data, analyzing the results, and communicating the findings and their implications.[8]

This definition suggests first that marketing research information is not intuitive or haphazardly gathered. Literally, *research* (re-search) means "to search again." The term connotes patient study and scientific investigation wherein the researcher takes another, more careful look at the data to discover all that is known about the subject.

Second, if the information generated or data collected is to be accurate, the marketing researcher must be objective. The need for objectivity was cleverly stated by the 19th-century American humorist Artemus Ward: "It ain't the things we don't know that gets us in trouble. It's the things we know ain't so." The researcher should be detached and impersonal rather than biased and attempting to support his or her preconceived ideas. If bias enters into the research process, the value of the research is considerably reduced.

As an example, a developer owned a large area of land and wished to build a high-prestige shopping centre. He wanted a research report to demonstrate to prospective retailers that there was a large market potential for such a centre. He conducted his survey exclusively in an elite neighbourhood. Not surprisingly, the findings showed that a large percentage of the respondents wanted a high-prestige shopping centre. Results of this kind are misleading and should be disregarded. In this example, had the prospective retailers discovered how the results had been obtained, the developer would have lost credibility. Had the retailers been ignorant of the bias in the research design and unaware that the researchers were not impartial, their decision may have had more adverse consequences than one made strictly on intuition. The importance of striving for objectivity cannot be overemphasized: Without objectivity, research is valueless.

This definition of marketing research is not restricted to any one aspect of the marketing mix. The objective of research is to facilitate the managerial decision-making process for all aspects of the firm's marketing mix: pricing, promotion, distribution, and product decisions. By providing the necessary information on which to base decisions, marketing research can reduce the uncertainty of a decision and thereby decrease the risk of making the wrong decision. However, research should be an aid to managerial judgment and not a substitute for it.

Management is more than conducting marketing research; applying the research remains a managerial art. For example, a few years ago research indicated that women who bought frozen dinners tended to lead hectic lives and had trouble coping with everyday problems. Using this information, an advertising agency developed an ad for a frozen-food company showing a run-down woman flopping into a chair just before her family was to arrive home for dinner. Suddenly realizing that she had a problem, the woman got the bright idea of cooking a frozen dinner. The beginning of the ad turned out to be a terrible mistake. The company quickly found out that the last thing women wanted to be reminded of was how tired they were. Research can suggest directions for changes in the marketing mix, but it cannot ensure correct marketing execution.

Finally, marketing research can be applied in various organizations or institutions and it should not be confused with market research. Market research is gathering, recording, and analysis of data with respect to a particular market, where market refers to a specific customer group in a specific geographic area.[9] The marketing research definition, however, is limited only by one's definition of *marketing*. Although research in the marketing area of a for-profit corporation is marketing research, a broader definition of marketing research includes non-profit organizations such as the Canadian Diabetes Association, the Toronto Zoo, and the Vancouver Symphony Orchestra. Each of these organizations exists to satisfy social needs, and each requires marketing skills to produce and distribute the products and services that people want. Hence, marketing research may be conducted by organizations that are not business organizations. The federal and provincial governments, for example, perform many functions that are similar, if not identical, to those of business organizations. Federal agencies may use research techniques for evaluative purposes in much the same way as managers at Bombardier or McCain Foods. This book explores *marketing research* as it applies to all types of organizations and institutions that engage in some form of marketing activity.

Basic Research and Applied Research

basic (pure) research
Research conducted to expand the limits of knowledge, to verify the acceptability of a given theory, or to learn more about a certain concept.

applied research
Research conducted when a decision must be made about a real-life problem.

One purpose of conducting marketing research is to develop and evaluate concepts and theories. **Basic** or **pure research** attempts to expand the limits of knowledge. It is not aimed at solving a particular pragmatic problem. It has been said that there is nothing so practical as a good theory. Although this is true in the long run, basic marketing research findings generally cannot be immediately implemented by a marketing executive. Basic research is conducted to verify the acceptability of a given theory or to learn more about a certain concept. **Applied research** is conducted when a decision must be made about a specific real-life problem. Our focus is on applied research—studies that are undertaken to answer questions about specific problems or to make decisions about particular courses of action or policies.

Applied research is emphasized in this discussion because most students will be oriented toward the day-to-day practice of marketing management, and most students and researchers will be exposed to short-term, problem-solving research conducted for businesses or non-profit organizations. However, the procedures and techniques used by applied and basic researchers do not differ substantially; both employ the scientific method to answer the question at hand. Broadly defined, the term **scientific method** refers to the techniques and procedures used to recognize and understand marketing phenomena. In the scientific method, empirical evidence (facts from observation or experimentation) is analyzed and interpreted to confirm or disprove prior conceptions. In basic research, testing these prior conceptions or hypotheses and then making inferences and conclusions about the phenomena lead to the establishment of general laws about the phenomena. Use of the scientific method in applied research ensures objectivity in gathering facts and testing creative ideas for alternative marketing strategies. The essence of research, whether basic or

scientific method
The techniques and procedures used to recognize and understand marketing phenomena.

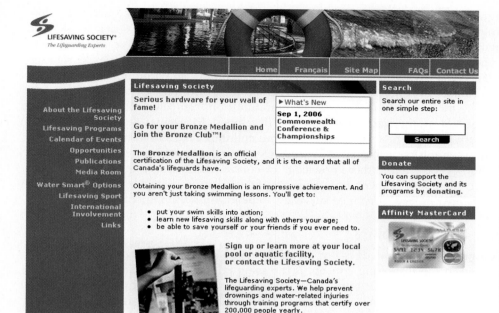

applied, lies in the scientific method. Much of this book deals with scientific methodology. Thus, the techniques of basic and applied research differ largely in degree rather than substance.

THE MARKETING CONCEPT

marketing concept
The most central idea in marketing thinking, which calls on managers to be consumer-oriented, to stress long-run profitability rather than sales volume, and to adopt a cross-functional perspective.

Although this book focuses on marketing research, marketing managers should understand how marketing research fits into the broader scope of marketing. Research is one of the primary tools that enables firms to implement the philosophical idea of the marketing concept.[11] The **marketing concept** is the most central idea in marketing thinking. It has evolved over time as production- and engineering-oriented firms have responded to changes in the economic environment to become marketing-oriented firms. The marketing concept is threefold, and it calls on managers to

1. be consumer oriented,
2. stress long-run profitability rather than sales volume, and
3. adopt a cross-functional perspective for the integration and coordination of marketing and other corporate functions.

Consumer Orientation

According to the marketing concept, the consumer is at the centre of the operation, the pivot point about which the business moves to achieve the balanced best interests of all concerned. According to this philosophy, the firm creates products and services with consumers' needs in mind. Many marketing theorists and operating marketing managers believe that the satisfaction of consumers' wants is the justification for a firm's existence.

The revitalization of Sun-Rype's Fruit to Go clearly illustrates a consumer orientation. Based on its marketing research, Sun-Rype found that mothers wanted Fruit to Go to be more appealing to their children, but wanted it to stay 100 percent fruit.

From the perspective of the kids, the product was not perceived as "junk food" like other common snacks and they accepted that a 100 percent fruit snack would give them the energy to get through their busy day. Armed with these insights, Sun-Rype hired Karacters Design Group in Vancouver to create a wholesale package redesign incorporating active imagery, vibrant colours, and a bold new personality for Fruit to Go to satisfy both its targets: mothers and kids. Once Sun-Rype had successfully upped the kid appeal, a communications campaign to get the word out to kids and mothers across Canada was developed. Magazines were used to target mothers, and advertisements geared toward children were run in magazines distributed in schools as well as on YTV and Teletoon television channels.

Sun-Rype realized that knowledge of consumers' needs, coupled with product research and development, leads to successful marketing strategies and that industry leadership—indeed, corporate survival—depends on satisfying consumers.[12]

Long-Run Profitability

Consumer orientation does not mean slavery to consumers' every fleeting whim. Implicit in the marketing concept is the assumption of the continuity of the firm, and the firm must make a profit to survive in the long run. Most consumers would prefer to have a Porsche priced under $15,000. However, the production costs of this car exceed that figure, and the firm surely would fail if it attempted to satisfy this desire.

The second aspect of the marketing concept argues against profitless volume or sales volume for the sake of volume alone. Marketing cost analysis has taught numerous firms that 20 percent of their customers have been responsible for 80 percent of their profits and that salespeople have spent too much time on unprofitable accounts. The marketing concept suggests that these firms should re-evaluate their efforts to sell to small, unprofitable accounts.

A Cross-Functional Effort

Marketing personnel do not work in a vacuum, isolated from other company activities. The actions of people in areas such as production, credit, and research and development may affect an organization's marketing efforts. Similarly, the work of marketers will affect activities in other departments. Problems are almost certain to arise from lack of an integrated, companywide effort. The marketing concept stresses a cross-functional perspective to achieve consumer orientation and long-term profitability.

When a firm lacks organizational procedures for communicating marketing information and coordinating marketing efforts, the effectiveness of its marketing programs will suffer. Marketing research findings produce some of the most crucial marketing information; thus, such research is management's key tool for finding out what customers want and how best to satisfy their needs. It is vital, then, that management conducts marketing research, that researchers produce valid and reliable results, and that those results be communicated to decision makers so that they can help shape the firm's marketing strategy.

Keeping Customers and Building Relationships

So far, we have talked about getting customers, but keeping customers is equally important. Marketers want customers for life. Effective marketers work to build long-term relationships with their customers. The term **relationship marketing** communicates the idea that a major goal of marketing is to build long-term relationships with the parties that contribute to the company's success.

Once an exchange is made, effective marketing stresses managing the relationships that will bring about additional exchanges. Effective marketers view making a sale not as the end of a process but as the start of the organization's relationship with

relationship marketing
The idea that a major goal of marketing is the building of long-term relationships with the parties that contribute to an organization's success.

a customer. Satisfied customers will return to a company that has treated them well if they need to purchase the same product in the future. If they need a related item, satisfied customers know the first place to look.

Total Quality Management

total quality management
A business philosophy that focuses on integrating customer-driven quality throughout an organization with continuous improvement of product quality and service.

Total quality management is a business philosophy that embodies the belief that the management process must focus on integrating customer-driven quality throughout the organization. Total quality management stresses continuous improvement of product quality and service.

The philosophy underlying the implementation of total quality management was clearly articulated by a Burger King executive: "The customer is the vital key to our success. We are now looking at our business through the customers' eyes and measuring our performance against their expectations, not ours."[13] A company that employs a total quality strategy must evaluate itself through the eyes of the customer.

Obviously, the marketing concept and total quality management are closely intertwined. In a company that practises total quality management, manufacturing's orientation toward lowest-cost productivity should harmonize with marketing's commitment to quality products at acceptable prices. For example, if Ford Motor Company advertises that "Quality Is Job One," the production department must make sure that every automobile that comes off the assembly line will meet consumers' quality specifications. The notion that quality improvement is every employee's job must be integrated throughout the organization so that marketing and production will be in harmony. If this notion conflicts with manufacturing's desire to allow for variations from quality standards, the firm must implement statistical quality controls and other improvements in the manufacturing operation to improve its systems and increase productivity.

Implementing a total quality management program requires considerable measurement. It involves routinely asking customers to rate a company against its competitors. It involves measuring employee attitudes. It involves monitoring company

H. J. Heinz knew that kids under 12 are the biggest ketchup consumers. So it conducted research among kids and mothers to see if it could increase customer satisfaction and enhance its relationship with its customers. Researchers observed kids and how they used Heinz's traditional ketchup bottles. They concluded that the bulky bottle made it difficult for kids to control the pour—ketchup was squirted in blobs, and messy spills were common. To make kids a lot happier, Heinz introduced EZ Squirt, vitamin C–fortified ketchup in an hourglass-shaped package designed especially for kids. The new plastic bottle is easy for kids to hold with two hands. Its narrow nozzle allows kids to apply (and draw) a ketchup stream on their food. Best of all, however, EZ Squirt ketchup is green. The green colour was also the result of research with kids, who said they would like to see ketchup in some colour other than red. Blue and other colours were investigated, but researchers concluded the green had more "kitchen logic."[14] Similarly, Burger King realized based on its research that kids have a preference for the "unexpected" when it comes to food. In a 2001 campaign, Burger King built on this idea in a four-week promotion involving Heinz EZ Squirt Blastin' Green ketchup, Gooey Green Apple Ooze, an apple-flavoured dipping sauce for chicken, and Frozen Green Minute Maid Cherry treats, a combination that served kids food and "entertainment." The campaign was complemented by the in-store promotion of merchandise involving Shrek, the green ogre from the swamp.[15]

Marketing research is a means to bridge the information gap between marketing executives and consumers. Wrangler's Bareback Jeans come without back pockets because women indicated that they wanted a slim fit and a button front, and that, unlike men, they had no need for back pockets.

performance against benchmark standards. These activities use marketing research extensively, so marketing research with external customers and with employees in the organization (internal customers) contributes much to a total quality management program.

Chapter 7 discusses the measurement of quality and customer satisfaction in detail. Throughout this book, however, we will explain how marketing research can help a company achieve customer-driven quality.

Marketing Research: A Means for Implementing the Marketing Concept

Satisfying the consumer is a major goal of marketing. One purpose of marketing research is to obtain information that identifies consumers' problems and needs, bridging the information gap between marketing executives and consumers. Researching consumer needs enables firms to fulfill the marketing concept.

Rubbermaid's new-product development process epitomizes this function.[16] Every new Rubbermaid product starts with research that asks one simple question: What's wrong with existing products? No consumer problem is considered too small, no concern too finicky. In research about children's lunch boxes, parents indicated they often worried about where to put milk money, allergy medicines, keys, and other small things their kids needed to take to school. When Rubbermaid came out with its backpack lunch box, which was designed to slip easily into a backpack, it built in a change holder.

Another company marketing backpacks to teenagers wanted to get feedback on a new pocket. Teenage subjects immediately pointed out that the pocket was too small for a Walkman. The new pocket did not satisfy its customers' needs, so the company changed the backpack design.

Measuring consumer satisfaction is another means of determining how well a company is fulfilling the marketing concept. Customer satisfaction research can

EXHIBIT 1.1 | MARKETING RESEARCH MAY MEASURE
CONSUMER SATISFACTION[17]

QUALITY OF SERVICE SURVEY

Please rate the service you recently received from GE Factory Service (product and date shown on the reverse side). Consider all service calls required for this particular problem. Indicate your answers by checking the appropriate box for each question.

1. When you called for service were you able to get through on the first call without getting a busy signal? .... YES ☐ NO ☐

2. When you called, were you placed on hold? .... YES ☐ NO ☐

3. Did the person you talked with on the phone give you the feeling that he/she really cared about your problem? .... YES ☐ NO ☐

4. What day was your appointment scheduled for? .... SAME DAY ☐ NEXT DAY ☐ 3RD DAY ☐ 4TH DAY ☐ LATER ☐

5. Was this the day you most preferred? .... YES ☐ NO ☐

6. If not, what day would you have most preferred? .... SAME DAY ☐ NEXT DAY ☐ 3RD DAY ☐ 4TH DAY ☐ LATER ☐

7. When was the technician scheduled to arrive? .... AM 8-12 ☐ PM 12-5 ☐ EVENING AFTER 5 ☐ ALL DAY 8-5 ☐

8. Was this time of day you most preferred? .... YES ☐ NO ☐

9. Did the technician come on the scheduled day? .... YES ☐ NO ☐

10. Did the technician arrive during the scheduled time period? .... YES ☐ NO ☐

11. Did the technician give you the feeling he/she really cared about your problem? .... YES ☐ NO ☐

12. Did the technician seem to be knowledgeable and competent about your product? .... YES ☐ NO ☐

13. Did the technician explain what was done to fix your problem? .... YES ☐ NO ☐

14. Were the charges on the invoice explained to you? .... YES ☐ NO ☐

15. Considering the service you received, how would you rate the charges for:

	NO CHARGE INVOLVED	VERY REASONABLE	REASONABLE	UNREASONABLE	VERY UNREASONABLE
LABOR (incl. home call)	☐	☐	☐	☐	☐
PARTS	☐	☐	☐	☐	☐
TOTAL CHARGE	☐	☐	☐	☐	☐

16. How many trips were required to complete the repair? .... 1 ☐ 2 ☐ 3 ☐ 4 ☐ MORE THAN 4 ☐

17. Overall, how would you rate our technician? .... EXCELLENT ☐ GOOD ☐ FAIR ☐ POOR ☐

18. If a part was needed to complete the repair, was the part: ..... AVAILABLE ON SERVICE TRUCK ☐ MAILED TO YOU ☐ BROUGHT BACK LATER BY A TECHNICIAN ☐ NO PART NEEDED ☐

19. If a part was ordered, how many days did it take for you to get the part? ..... NO PART ORDERED ☐ SAME DAY ☐ 1-4 DAYS ☐ 5-9 DAYS ☐ MORE THAN 9 DAYS ☐

20. Considering all these questions, how satisfied are you with the overall service you received? ..... VERY SATISFIED ☐ SATISFIED ☐ NEITHER SATISFIED/DISSATISFIED ☐ DISSATISFIED ☐ VERY DISSATISFIED ☐

21. If you needed to replace the product you had repaired, how likely would you be to buy the General Electric or Hotpoint brand? ..... DEFINITELY WOULD BUY GE/HOTPOINT ☐ PROBABLY WOULD BUY GE/HOTPOINT ☐ MIGHT OR MIGHT NOT BUY GE/HOTPOINT ☐ PROBABLY WOULD NOT BUY GE/HOTPOINT ☐ DEFINITELY WOULD NOT BUY GE/HOTPOINT ☐

22. Please add any comments you have about the service you received.

_____

_____

_____

ascertain whether an organization's total quality management program is meeting customer expectations and management objectives. General Electric's major-appliance division sends the questionnaire shown in Exhibit 1.1 to customers after repair calls to determine how well the company is accomplishing its objective of consumer satisfaction. The questionnaire asks whether the appointment was scheduled promptly, whether the repair person showed up on time and was polite, and if the customer was satisfied with the service. Customer satisfaction surveys such as this tend to be standardized and ongoing so that performance can be compared against previously established standards. These measures lead to the evaluation of managers according to consumers' perceptions of quality in addition to the evaluation of actual operational quality. Customer satisfaction research plays a major role in customer retention efforts, because it provides information about the likelihood that the organization will keep its existing customers.

Marketing research can also help prevent commercialization of products that are not consumer oriented. Sometimes ideas that look like technological breakthroughs in the laboratory fall flat when presented to consumers. For example, a powdered pain reliever was supposed to be a soothing remedy because it was to be mixed with milk. It did not soothe customers, however. Research showed that the public thought this great step forward was actually a step backward in convenience. Someone forgot to consider the consumer benefit.

By improving efficiency, research also facilitates profitability. For instance, during the introduction of a new product, accurate forecasting of the product's potential sales volume is an essential basis for estimating its profitability. A firm considering the introduction of a cat snack that contains hairball medicine might rely on a test market experiment to determine the optimal price for this new concept. Extensive testing should be done to ensure that the marketing program is fine-tuned to maximize the firm's profitability while satisfying consumers.

Because of the importance of integrating company efforts, a marketing researcher must be knowledgeable not only about marketing research but about the entire spectrum of marketing activities.

THE MANAGERIAL VALUE OF MARKETING RESEARCH FOR STRATEGIC DECISION MAKING

Effective marketing management requires research. Canada Post recently conducted a survey before launching its online birthday reminder service. This research was beneficial in further developing the program—it revealed that 70 percent of Canadians would prefer to receive a card in the mail for their birthday, instead of an e-mail greeting.[18] At Ford Motor Company, research is so fundamental that the company hardly makes any significant decision without the benefit of some kind of marketing research. The prime managerial value of marketing research comes from the reduced uncertainty that results from information and facilitates decision making about marketing strategies and tactics to achieve an organization's strategic goals.

Developing and implementing a marketing strategy involves four stages:

1. Identifying and evaluating opportunities
2. Analyzing market segments and selecting target markets
3. Planning and implementing a marketing mix that will satisfy customers' needs and meet the objectives of the organization
4. Analyzing marketing performance[19]

Identifying and Evaluating Opportunities

Before developing a marketing strategy, an organization must determine where it wants to go and how to get there. Marketing research can help answer these questions by investigating potential opportunities to identify attractive areas for company action.

Marketing research may provide diagnostic information about what is occurring in the environment. A mere description of some social or economic activity, such as trends in consumer purchasing behaviour, may help managers recognize problems and identify opportunities for enriching marketing efforts.

The use of such diagnostic information was instrumental in *Chatelaine*, a magazine targeting Canadian women, introducing an Internet games section on the magazine's Web site that features games targeted to adult women. Their research found that 80 percent of *Chatelaine* Web site members visit online gaming sites; online gaming was a frequently discussed topic on the magazine's online forums. Secondary research further revealed that "women over 40 spend nearly 50% more time each week playing online games than men [and that] they're also more likely than men or teens to play online games daily." Based on these findings, *Chatelaine* launched its games site, featuring games such as Mah-Jong Quest, Bejeweled, Scrabble, and Monopoly, which were geared toward women.[20]

Market opportunities may be evaluated using many performance criteria. For example, the performance criterion of market demand typically is estimated using marketing research techniques. Estimates of market potential or predictions about future environmental conditions allow managers to evaluate opportunities. Accurate sales forecasts are among the most useful pieces of planning information a marketing manager can have. Complete accuracy in forecasting the future is not possible, because change is constantly occurring in the marketing environment. Nevertheless, objective forecasts of demand or changing environments may be the foundations on which marketing strategies are built.

Analyzing and Selecting Target Markets

The second stage of marketing strategy development is to analyze market segments and select target markets. Marketing research is a major source of information for determining which characteristics of market segments distinguish them from the overall market.

Market segmentation studies by *Maclean's* provide a good example of this essential activity. Marketing research depicts the average *Maclean's* reader as a 43-year-old college graduate with an average household income of $72,310 who makes significant contributions to personal finances (mutual funds and RRSPs).[21]

Planning and Implementing a Marketing Mix

Using the information obtained in the two previous stages, marketing managers plan and execute a marketing mix strategy. However, marketing research may be needed to support specific decisions about virtually any aspect of the marketing mix. Often the research is conducted to evaluate an alternative course of action. For example, advertising research investigated whether an actress, one of Hollywood's most beautiful women, would make a good spokesperson for a specific brand of hair colouring. She was filmed in some test commercials to endorse the brand, but the commercials were never aired because, although viewers recognized her as an outstanding personality in the test commercials, they did not perceive her as a user of home hair colouring kits or as an authority on such products.

Managers face many diverse decisions about marketing mixes. The following examples highlight selected types of research that might be conducted for each element of the marketing mix.

Product Research

Product research takes many forms and includes studies designed to evaluate and develop new products and to learn how to adapt existing product lines. Concept testing exposes potential customers to a new product idea to judge the acceptance and feasibility of the concept. Product testing reveals a product prototype's strengths and weaknesses or determines whether a finished product performs better than competing brands or according to expectations. Brand-name evaluation studies investigate whether a name is appropriate for a product. Package testing assesses size, colour, shape, ease of use, and other attributes of a package. Product research encompasses all applications of marketing research that seek to develop product attributes that will add value for consumers.

When Crazy Plates meal kits were introduced, there was an air of excitement among grocers. The meal kits were an extension of two of the most successful Canadian cookbooks ever—*Looneyspoons* and *Crazy Plates*. Despite high expectations,

British Airways' marketing research revealed that many business travellers find air travel a frustrating experience—full of hassles from the office to the airport to a hotel or a meeting and back again. Air travellers want to know they're being cared for. With these findings in mind, executives at British Airways made a decision to alter its service. The airline relaunched its Club Europe business-class services to smooth business travellers' paths, providing them more time and space, and, above all, eliminating the hassles. The new Club Europe service, whose cost exceeded £70 million, includes new seats, more business lounges, limousines at taxi rates, and speedier service through security and customs at Heathrow's Terminal One.[22]

the Crazy Plates meal kits were not very successful in the freezer aisles. Retail sales were below expectations. Rather than creating a product for the frozen-food market, which desires a meal for two with a cooking time under 15 minutes, the *Looneyspoons* team had designed a product for themselves and families like their own containing a serving for five with a preparation time of up to 40 minutes. After the team conducted research, the Crazy Plates' servings and cooking times were reduced, resulting in a 400 percent increase in sales over those of the old product.[23]

Pricing Research

Most organizations conduct pricing research. A competitive pricing study is a typical marketing research project of this type. However, research designed to learn the ideal price for a product or to determine if consumers will pay a price high enough to cover cost is not uncommon. For example, a Bausch & Lomb survey of 5,000 contact lens wearers showed that more than 60 percent of them would be interested in one-day disposable lenses if the price came down to about a dollar a day. This led to the introduction of the Softlens brand, which proclaimed a significant price advantage over competitors. Pricing research may also investigate when discounts or coupons should be offered, explore whether there are critical product attributes that determine how consumers perceive value, or determine if a product category, such as soft drinks, has price gaps among national brands, regional brands, and private labels.[24]

A well-known consumer products company was mired in a key pricing threshold of 99 cents for one of its products. Since the company wasn't making money on the product at that price, executives wondered what would happen if they were to raise the price beyond that threshold. And how high should they go—$1.02, $1.09, $1.20? Results of their research accurately predicted that once the $1 threshold was surpassed, volume would not be significantly changed until the price reached $1.29. Consequently, the company raised the price of the product to $1.29, a 30 percent increase.[25]

Research may answer many questions about price. Is there a need for seasonal or quantity discounts? Are coupons more effective than price reductions? Is a brand price elastic or price inelastic? How much of a price difference is optimal to differentiate items in the product line?

Distribution Research

It is also very important to understand where consumers would like to make their purchases. Many factors, including convenience, distance, and retail atmosphere, can have an impact on the decision of where a consumer makes a purchase. The increase in

WHAT WENT RIGHT?

PROCTER & GAMBLE'S WETJET GAMBLE

Procter & Gamble markets 300 brands to nearly five billion people in 140 countries. In its introduction of Swiffer WetJet, a battery-operated cleaning appliance similar to its cousin Swiffer Sweeper, Procter & Gamble decided to test market the product before launching it worldwide.

Given the objectives of the company, Canada was chosen as the test-market country. One of the reasons for this choice was the enthusiastic response of Canadian consumers to the Swiffer Sweeper when it had been introduced a year earlier. The consumers were already familiar with the previous model that

looked and operated similar to the WetJet. They understood the benefits of the product. Test marketing for the new product included both television and print advertisements, in-store demonstrations, and other marketing tactics. The results from the test market were positive. The company's marketing executives felt more confident that such a unique product would receive acceptance from similar consumers around the world. Several years after its introduction, the Swiffer WetJet was still on the Canadian market and it had been introduced in the United States and Europe.

Internet usage and high rates of Internet accessibility has made the Internet a growing distribution channel in Canada. Seventy percent of Canadian households and 95 percent of Canadian businesses are online.[26] Mountain Equipment Co-op and Sears Canada are among the many major retailers that have researched and now offer home shopping services via the Internet. New interactive media and home delivery as a means of distribution have the potential to revolutionize channel-of-distribution systems, and retailers are spending millions of dollars to research this alternative. Although most distribution research does not have the dramatic impact of the results of the research on Internet shopping systems, research focused on developing and improving the efficiency of channels of distribution is important to many organizations.

A typical study in the distribution area may be conducted to select retail sites or warehouse locations. A survey of retailers or wholesalers may be conducted because the actions of one channel member can greatly affect the performance of other channel members. Distribution research often is needed to gain knowledge about retailers' and wholesalers' operations and to learn their reactions to a manufacturer's marketing policies.

The 3M Corporation surveys its industrial distributors anonymously to determine how they feel about doing business with each of their suppliers, including 3M. The purpose of the research is to investigate distributors' attitudes about relationships with sales representatives, ordering procedures, on-time delivery, training of distributor personnel, product quality, and many other activities that help build long-term relationships.

Promotion Research

Research that investigates the effectiveness of premiums, coupons, sampling deals, and other sales promotions is classified as promotion research. Promotion research includes buyer motivation studies to generate ideas for copy development, media research, and studies of advertising effectiveness. However, the most time, money, and effort are spent on advertising research.

Marketing research can be instrumental in determining whether coupons used as a price promotion tool would result in increased consumer responses across Canada. The 2003 results of the Nielsen Homescan Panel omnibus survey, based on nearly 10,000 respondents, suggest differences in coupon usage across Canadian consumers.

When the Insurance Corporation of B.C. and the broadcasters of British Columbia created public service announcements using violent car-crash imagery, they were targeting young men between the ages of 21 and 35. Their research had revealed that 80 percent of the drivers responsible for alcohol-related car accidents were males between these ages. In addition, it was clear from the results of their focus group research that ads with violent imagery would be effective in reminding the target group not to drink and drive. As a result, the new ads targeted young men in order to reduce the number of accidents related to drinking and driving.[27]

In general, 86 percent of the respondents said that they had used at least one coupon within the past year. Shoppers in Ontario and the West were more likely to have used coupons within the past week than those in the Atlantic region. However, shoppers from Quebec were more likely to have used coupons than those from Ontario and the West (65 percent more likely) and from those in the Atlantic region (46 percent more likely). These findings clearly illustrate the differences in coupon usage and the impact of coupon promotions on sales in different Canadian provinces and regions.[28]

Marketing research helps marketers in making promotion-related decisions. The findings of such research can influence decisions about whether to use coupons in a given region and media decisions (e.g., television, newspapers, magazines, or other media alternatives) to convey the advertiser's message. Choices among media alternatives may be based on research that shows how many people in the target audience each advertising vehicle can reach.

The Integrated Marketing Mix

The individual elements of the marketing mix do not work independently. Hence, many research studies investigate various combinations of marketing ingredients to gather information to suggest the best possible marketing program.

Analyzing Marketing Performance

After a marketing strategy has been implemented, marketing research may serve to inform managers whether planned activities were properly executed and are accomplishing what they were expected to achieve. In other words, marketing research may be conducted to obtain feedback for evaluation and control of marketing programs. This aspect of marketing research is especially important for successful total quality management.

performance-monitoring research
Research that regularly provides feedback for evaluation and control of marketing activity.

Performance-monitoring research refers to research that regularly, sometimes routinely, provides feedback for evaluation and control of marketing activity. For example, most firms continuously monitor wholesale and retail activity to ensure early detection of sales declines and other anomalies. In the grocery and drug industries,

MESSAGE NOT RECEIVED

Advertising is a hectic business with tight deadlines and rush jobs. In an effort to increase consumers' awareness of the agency and its services, the Financial Consumer Agency of Canada spent $300,000 on advertising. "The ad campaign per se was our first attempt in reaching all Canadians at the same time," spokesman Bruno Levesque said in an interview. The ad described the agency and provided a toll-free number and Web site address. The campaign consisted of a series of three ads placed in urban newspapers across Canada, as well as regional weeklies. However, the results of the polls commissioned by the agency before and after the campaign were alarming. Of the 4,300 Canadians surveyed by telephone prior to the campaign's launch date, 30 percent indicated that they had heard about "a federal agency created to ensure banks respect consumer protection laws and educate consumers." The results of a second survey of 2,001 Canadians after the campaign indicated that only 21 percent had heard of such an agency. The national ad campaign was a failure. Levesque acknowledges the agency's campaign coincided with the peak of the RRSP season and the message may have been crowded out. This is a time of year when many financial institutions are promoting their products in print and broadcast. "We were out there at the same time as a number of organizations, and some confusion may have arisen, " he said. "Maybe this was not the best time of year."[29]

sales research may use Universal Product Codes (UPC) on packages read by electronic cash registers and computerized checkout counts to provide valuable market-share information to store and brand managers interested in the retail sales volumes of their products. Market–share analysis and sales analysis are the most common forms of performance-monitoring research. Almost every organization compares its current sales with previous sales and with competitors' sales. However, analyzing marketing performance is not limited to the investigation of sales figures.

SportChek, with more than 100 sports equipment stores across Canada, employs performance-monitoring research using in-store kiosks. Customers can directly access SportChek.ca from the interactive kiosks to search for information. SportChek can get "real-time" customer feedback from the kiosks and can also conduct customer research to observe patterns over time. Kiosks also help SportChek identify the types of customer service issues to focus on.[30]

When analysis of marketing performance indicates that things are not going as planned, marketing research may be required to explain why something went wrong. Detailed information about specific mistakes or failures is frequently sought. If a general problem area is identified, breaking down industry sales volume and a firm's sales volume into different geographical areas may explain specific problems. Exploring problems in greater depth may indicate which managerial judgments were erroneous.

WHEN IS MARKETING RESEARCH NEEDED?

A marketing manager confronted with two or more alternative courses of action faces the initial decision of whether to conduct marketing research. The determination of the need for marketing research centres on (1) time constraints, (2) the availability of data, (3) the nature of the decision to be made, and (4) the value of the research information in relation to costs.

Time Constraints

Systematic research takes time. In many instances management believes that a decision must be made immediately, allowing no time for research. Decisions sometimes are made without adequate information or thorough understanding of market situations. Although making decisions without researching a situation is not ideal, sometimes the urgency of a situation precludes the use of research.

Availability of Data

Often managers already possess enough information to make sound decisions without marketing research. When they lack adequate information, however, research must be considered. Managers must ask themselves if the research will provide the information needed to answer the basic questions about a decision. Furthermore, if a potential source of data exists, managers will want to know how much it will cost to obtain the data.

If the data cannot be obtained, research cannot be conducted. For example, many African nations have never conducted a population census. Organizations engaged in international business often find that data about business activity or population characteristics that are readily available in Canada are nonexistent or sparse in developing countries. Imagine the problems facing marketing researchers who wish to investigate market potential in places like Uzbekistan, Yugoslavian Macedonia, and Rwanda.

Nature of the Decision

The value of marketing research will depend on the nature of the managerial decision to be made. A routine tactical decision that does not require a substantial investment may not seem to warrant a substantial expenditure for marketing research. For example, a computer company must update its operator's instruction manual when it makes minor product modifications. The research cost of determining the proper wording to use in the updated manual is likely to be too high for such a minor decision. The nature of the decision is not totally independent of the next issue to be considered: the benefits versus the costs of the research. In general, however, the more strategically or tactically important the decision, the more likely it is that research will be conducted.

Benefits versus Costs

There are both costs and benefits to conducting marketing research. Earlier we discussed some of the managerial benefits of marketing research. Of course, conducting research to obtain these benefits requires an expenditure of money. In any decision-making situation managers must identify alternative courses of action and then weigh the value of each alternative against its cost. Marketing research can be thought of as an investment alternative. When deciding whether to make a decision without research or to postpone the decision in order to conduct research, managers should ask three questions: (1) Will the payoff or rate of return be worth the investment? (2) Will the information gained by marketing research improve the quality of the marketing decision enough to warrant the expenditure? (3) Is the proposed research expenditure the best use of the available funds?

For example, *TV-Cable Week* was not test-marketed before its launch in the United States. Although the magazine had articles and stories about TV personalities and events, its main feature was program listings, channel by channel, showing the exact programs a particular subscriber could receive. To produce a custom magazine for each individual cable TV system in the United States required developing a costly computer system. Because that development necessitated a substantial expenditure, one that could not be scaled down for research, conducting research was judged to be an unwise investment. The value of the research information was not positive because

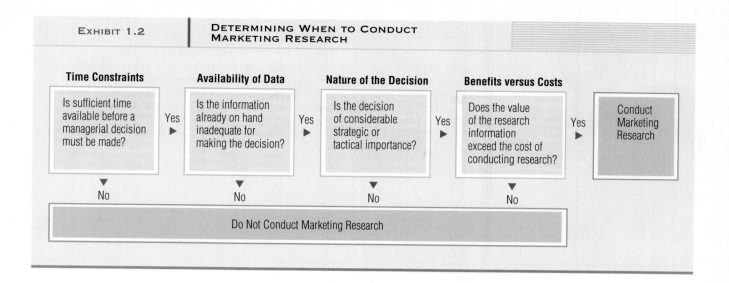

EXHIBIT 1.2 | DETERMINING WHEN TO CONDUCT MARKETING RESEARCH

Time Constraints

Is sufficient time available before a managerial decision must be made?

Yes ▶

Availability of Data

Is the information already on hand inadequate for making the decision?

Yes ▶

Nature of the Decision

Is the decision of considerable strategic or tactical importance?

Yes ▶

Benefits versus Costs

Does the value of the research information exceed the cost of conducting research?

Yes ▶

Conduct Marketing Research

No ▼   No ▼   No ▼   No ▼

Do Not Conduct Marketing Research

its cost exceeded its benefits. Unfortunately, pricing and distribution problems became so compelling after the magazine was launched that the product was a marketing failure. Nevertheless, without the luxury of hindsight, managers made a reasonable decision not to conduct research. They analyzed the cost of the information (that is, the cost of test marketing) relative to the potential benefits of the information. For larger companies, such as Procter & Gamble with many unique product introductions each year, marketing research costs may be affordable and justified. However, smaller companies may decide to not conduct marketing research or to choose less expensive methods. For instance, test marketing, given the launch-like expenses it involves and the sneak preview it provides to competitors, may be perceived as too heavy a cost when compared to other expenses the company faces. Exhibit 1.2 outlines the criteria for determining when to conduct marketing research.

MARKETING RESEARCH IN THE 21ST CENTURY

Marketing research, like all business activity, has been strongly influenced by two major trends in business: increased globalization and rapid growth of the Internet and other information technologies. These trends will continue, and likely accelerate, as the 21st century progresses. We consider their significance for marketing research here.

Global Marketing Research

Marketing research has become increasingly global and will become more so in the 21st century. Some companies have extensive international marketing research operations. One such company, Ipsos, conducts marketing research across five continents and has ten offices in Canada.[31] AC Nielsen International, known for its television ratings, is the world's largest marketing research company.

Companies that conduct business in foreign countries must understand the nature of those particular markets and judge whether they require customized marketing strategies. For example, although the 15 nations of the European Union share a single formal market, marketing research shows that Europeans do not share identical tastes for many consumer products. Marketing researchers have found no such thing as a typical European consumer; language, religion, climate, and centuries of tradition divide the nations of the European Union. Scantel Research, a British firm that advises companies on colour preferences, found inexplicable differences in Europeans' preferences in medicines. The French prefer to pop purple pills, but the English and Dutch favour

The world economy has become global, and corporations market products in many countries. People think of their home culture as the normal way of life, but consumers in other cultures often have different values, beliefs, and behaviours. Marketing research helps marketers understand cultural differences. Colgate-Palmolive is a progressive company that conducts marketing research around the world. Colgate-Palmolive used marketing research when it introduced a new and improved toothpaste in Colombia.

white ones. Consumers in all three countries dislike bright red capsules. This example illustrates that companies that do business in Europe must judge whether they need to adapt to local customs and buying habits.[32]

Although the nature of marketing research can differ around the globe, the need for marketing research is universal. Throughout this book, we will discuss the practical problems involved in conducting marketing research in Europe, Asia, Latin America, the Middle East, and elsewhere.

Growth of the Internet

Obtaining and communicating information is the essence of marketing research. Consider that a researcher seeking facts and figures about a marketing issue may find more extensive information on the Internet more quickly than by visiting a library. Another researcher who is questioning people from around the globe may do so almost instantaneously with an Internet survey and get responses 24 hours a day, 7 days a week. Visitors to an organization's Web site may find that online questions are personalized, because the site incorporates information technology that remembers the particular "click-stream" of the Web pages they visited. These few examples illustrate how the Internet and other information technologies are dramatically changing the face of marketing research.

In the 21st century, marketing research on the Internet is moving out of the introductory stage of its product life cycle into the growth stage. The rest of this book reflects this change. Throughout the book, we will discuss the latest information technologies and their application to marketing research. Marketing research via the Internet has come of age.

SUMMARY

Marketing research is a tool companies use to discover consumers' wants and needs so that they can satisfy those wants and needs with their product offerings. Marketing research is the marketing manager's source of information about market conditions. It covers topics ranging from long-range planning to near-term tactical decisions.

Marketing research is the systematic and objective process of generating information—gathering, recording, and analyzing data—to aid marketing decision making. The research must be conducted systematically, not haphazardly. It must be objective to avoid the distorting effects of personal bias. Applied marketing research seeks to facilitate managerial decision making. Basic or pure research seeks to increase knowledge of theories and concepts.

Marketing research is a means of implementing the marketing concept, the most central idea in marketing. The marketing concept says that a firm must be oriented toward both consumer satisfaction and long-run profitability (rather than short-run sales volume). Organizations need to focus on both creating and keeping customers. Furthermore, cross-functional activities need to be integrated to achieve these goals.

Marketing research can help implement the marketing concept by identifying consumers' problems and needs, improving efficiency, and evaluating the effectiveness of marketing strategies and tactics.

Total quality management is a business philosophy that has much in common with the marketing concept. Companies that have adopted the total quality management philosophy view employees as internal customers. Implementing a total quality management program requires considerable marketing research with external customers and with employees in the organization (internal customers).

The development and implementation of a marketing strategy consist of four stages: (1) identifying and evaluating opportunities, (2) analyzing market segments and selecting target markets, (3) planning and implementing a marketing mix that will satisfy customers' needs and meet the objectives of the organization, and (4) analyzing marketing performance. Marketing research helps in each stage by providing information for strategic decision making.

Managers use marketing research to define problems, identify opportunities, and clarify alternatives. They also use it to determine what went wrong with past marketing efforts, describe current events in the marketplace, or forecast future conditions.

Marketing managers determine whether marketing research should be conducted based on (1) time constraints, (2) availability of data, (3) the nature of the decision to be made, and (4) the benefit of the research information versus its cost.

Key Terms and Concepts

marketing research
basic (pure) research
applied research

scientific method
marketing concept
relationship marketing

total quality management
performance-monitoring research

Questions for Review and Critical Thinking

1. In your own words, define *marketing research* and describe its task.
2. Is it possible to make sound marketing decisions without marketing research? What advantages does research offer to the decision maker over seat-of-the-pants decision making?
3. Which of the following organizations are likely to use marketing research? Why? How?
   a. Manufacturer of breakfast cereals
   b. Manufacturer of nuts, bolts, and other fasteners
   c. A hospital
   d. A computer software producer
4. Name some products that logically might have been developed with the help of marketing research.
5. An automobile manufacturer is conducting research in an attempt to predict the type of car consumers will desire in the year 2020. Is this basic or applied research? Explain.

6. In what specific ways can marketing research influence the development and implementation of marketing strategy?
7. What is the relationship between marketing research and a total quality management program?
8. An advertising agency's slogan is "People listen to us because we listen to them." Has this firm integrated the marketing research function with the marketing concept?
9. The owner of 22 restaurants was asked how he does marketing research. He answered that he does it after midnight, driving around in a pickup truck: "I stay up late. If it's midnight and I don't have anything else to do, I drive around town and look at the lines in front of places. I'll look at the garbage and see if a guy's doing business. If he's got a real clean bunch of garbage cans and an empty dumpster, he's not doing any business. I find out a lot by talking to my vendors. I ask the bread guy how many

boxes of buns the drive-in down the street is buying. Very few restaurateurs do that. But that's the way I research my market." Is this marketing research?

10. Comment on the following statements:
   a. Marketing managers are paid to take chances with decisions. Marketing researchers are paid to reduce the risk of making those decisions.
   b. A marketing strategy can be no better than the information on which it is formulated.
   c. The purpose of research is to solve marketing problems.

Exploring the Internet: What Is Ahead?

Exploring the Internet is a feature that will give you an opportunity to use the Internet to gain additional insights about marketing research. Internet exercises are included in each of the remaining chapters.

The home page for this textbook is at

www.effectivemarketingresearch.nelson.com.

CASE 1.1   SEARCH FOR ALTERNATIVE ENERGY

Prices paid at the pump have become an increasing concern for consumers in the past few years. In the first quarter of 2006, consumers spent $8.3 billion on automotive fuels, oils, and additives in retail stores, a 14.2 percent increase over the same quarter in 2005 and more than a 30 percent increase over the same quarter in 2004. This was mostly driven by the increase in the price of gasoline over the same period.[33] Naturally, the search for alternative fuels has received greater importance for all major manufacturers in the automotive industry. Although GM has been the first company to introduce hybrid trucks—powered by gas and electricity—to the Canadian market, today most auto manufacturers have one or more hybrid cars, SUVs, or trucks on the market. In addition, Ford, GM, and other manufacturers have models that run on a combination of ethanol and fossil fuels.

Question

How can marketing research be used by auto manufacturers, alternative fuel researchers, and governments in the transition to alternative fuels?

CASE 1.2   BEN & JERRY'S

Ben & Jerry's Homemade, Inc., the Vermont-based manufacturer of ice cream, frozen yogurt, and sorbet, was founded in 1978 in a renovated gas station in Burlington, Vermont, by childhood friends Ben Cohen and Jerry Greenfield, with a $12,000 investment ($4,000 of which was borrowed).[34] They soon became popular for their innovative flavours, made from fresh Vermont milk and cream. The company currently distributes ice cream, low-fat ice cream, frozen yogurt, sorbet, and novelty products across the United States and Canada, as well as in selected foreign countries, in supermarkets, grocery stores, convenience stores, franchised Ben & Jerry's scoop shops, restaurants, and other venues.

Ben & Jerry's product strategy is to differentiate its super-premium brand from other ice cream brands. The brand image reflects high quality, uniqueness, and a bit of amusement. Its all-natural flavours have distinctive names. For example, Chubby Hubby has chunks of chocolate-covered peanut-butter-filled pretzels in a rich vanilla malt ice cream with deep ripples of fudge and peanut butter. Other names in the company's line of ice creams include Cherry Garcia, Bovinity Divinity, Dilbert Totally Nuts, New York Super Fudge Chunk, Chunky Monkey, and From Russia with Buzz.

The new product-development process and flavour-naming process are a top priority at Ben & Jerry's. For example, Phish Food ice cream was developed as a product with a fun name associated with the band Phish. Ben Cohen had been a neighbour of members of Phish since the band's early years as favourites on the local music scene. When Ben & Jerry's suggested mixing up a Phish ice cream to celebrate their shared Vermont roots, the band agreed. So Ben & Jerry's concocted a chocolate ice cream with chewy marshmallow nougat, a thick caramel swirl, and a school of fudge fish in every tub. Most marshmallow variegates disappear into nothingness. The company took great pains to make sure that the marshmallow was the way it was meant to be. With Phish Food you can see, taste, and feel the white streaks of marshmallow. The Phish Food package is a departure from Ben & Jerry's traditional graphics. The container is designed with images from Phish's concert light show, featuring Phish band members Trey Anastasio, Mike Gordon, Jon Fishman, and Page McConnell on the lid along with Ben and Jerry.

Question

What role does marketing research play in new product development and brand name development for a company like Ben & Jerry's?

2

THE MARKETING RESEARCH PROCESS

What you will learn in this chapter

1. To classify marketing research as either exploratory research, descriptive research, or causal research.

2. To list the stages in the marketing research process.

3. To identify and briefly discuss the various decision alternatives available to the researcher during each stage of the research process.

4. To explain the difference between a research project and a research program.

Suppose you are assigned to take charge of the marketing research effort when a tobacco company is developing a smokeless cigarette. You are told that the smokeless cigarette does not burn tobacco and greatly reduces the production of harmful substances linked to health concerns; in addition, it is approved by government agencies. Company executives believe it will be the world's cleanest cigarette. It is consumed like a cigarette but is not lit and does not emit any smoke, tar, or carbon monoxide. The best part is that it does not affect others and can be consumed even in No Smoking areas. Users do not need to worry about tar stains on teeth; because there is no smoke, there are no odours on breath, clothes, hair, or furniture.

Here is how the new product works. A special sealed plastic tube preserves the freshness of the tobacco inside. When the tube ends are cut, tobacco extract vapours, including nicotine and tobacco flavour, are released with each puff. The nicotine and tobacco flavours are invisible. No tar is released. After each use (one to ten puffs), the "cigarette" renews itself through a capillary action that acts on the tobacco. This regeneration takes about 20 minutes. Smokers can carry two or more tubes and alternate their use. The same plastic tube can be used again and again, each time seeming like a fresh new cigarette. One new smokeless cigarette can last one to three days, one pack as long as 600 old-style cigarettes.

This product has already been introduced in the United States (visit aerosinfo.com). However, will a smokeless cigarette appeal to smokers? Will non-smokers be more tolerant of a smokeless cigarette? In what situations will a smokeless cigarette be preferred to a regular cigarette? The research process can help answer questions such as these, but what form should the research take? Should a laboratory taste test be conducted? Should a survey of non-smokers be part of the research strategy?

This chapter discusses how managers make decisions about planning research strategies and tactics. It also presents an overview of the types of research designs and briefly discusses the stages in the research process. ■

DECISION MAKING

decision making
The process used to resolve a problem or to choose from alternative opportunities.

Formally defined, **decision making** is the process of resolving a problem or choosing from alternative opportunities. A decision maker must recognize the nature of the problem or opportunity, identify how much information is available, and determine what information is needed. Every marketing problem or decision-making situation can be classified on a continuum ranging from complete certainty to absolute ambiguity as displayed in Exhibit 2.1.[1] This classification is based on (i) the clarity of the marketing problem or opportunity and (ii) the information needs to address the marketing problem or opportunity. For example, an advertising agency may need to know the demographic characteristics of subscribers to magazines in which it may place a client's advertisements. So the marketing problem is clear. Under complete certainty, the agency knows exactly what information it needs and the information is available. Under uncertainty, the adverting agency may not know exactly what information it needs and/or this information is not available. Under complete ambiguity, however, the agency may not even define the nature of the marketing problem or opportunity to be addressed. This is the most difficult decision situation. The more ambiguous a situation is, the more likely it is that additional time must be spent on marketing research.

TYPES OF MARKETING RESEARCH

 Marketing research provides information to reduce uncertainty. It helps focus decision making. Sometimes marketing researchers know exactly what their marketing problems are and design careful studies to test specific hypotheses. For example, a soft drink company introducing a new clear cola might want to know whether a gold or a silver label would make the packaging more effective. This problem is fully defined and an experiment may be designed to answer the marketing question with little preliminary investigation.

In more ambiguous circumstances, management may be totally unaware of a marketing problem. For example, McDonald's may notice that Mo's Burgers, a competitor in the Japanese market, introduced Mo's Roast Katsu Burger, a roast pork cutlet drenched in traditional Japanese katsu sauce and topped with shredded cabbage. The managers may not understand much about Japanese consumers' feelings about this menu item. Some exploratory research may be necessary to gain insights into the nature of such a problem. To understand the variety of research activity, it is beneficial to categorize types of marketing research.

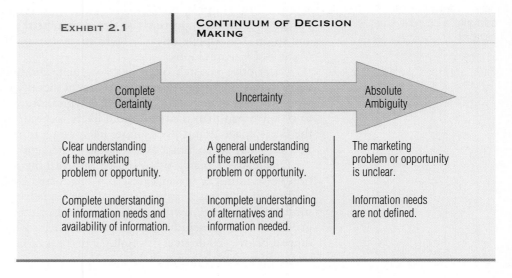

EXHIBIT 2.1 | **CONTINUUM OF DECISION MAKING**

Complete Certainty	Uncertainty	Absolute Ambiguity
Clear understanding of the marketing problem or opportunity.	A general understanding of the marketing problem or opportunity.	The marketing problem or opportunity is unclear.
Complete understanding of information needs and availability of information.	Incomplete understanding of alternatives and information needed.	Information needs are not defined.

POETRY AND RESEARCH: AN ODD COUPLE?

I keep six honest serving men,
(they taught me all I knew).
Their names are What, and Why, and When,
and How, and Where, and Who.

—*Rudyard Kipling*

Kipling's words can be helpful to the marketing researcher. Those who ask the *what, why, when, how, where,* and *who* questions will start on the right road to solving their marketing research problems.

Marketing research can be classified on the basis of either technique or function. Experiments, surveys, and observational studies are just a few common research techniques. Classifying research by its purpose or function shows how the nature of the marketing problem influences the choice of methods. The nature of the problem will determine whether the research is (1) exploratory, (2) descriptive, or (3) causal.

Exploratory Research

exploratory research
Initial research conducted to clarify and define a problem.

Exploratory research is conducted to clarify ambiguous problems. Management may have discovered a general problem, but it may need research to gain a better understanding of the dimensions of the problem and to aid analysis. Exploratory research is *not* intended to provide conclusive evidence from which to determine a particular course of action. Usually exploratory research is conducted with the expectation that subsequent research will be required to provide such conclusive evidence. Rushing into detailed surveys before less expensive and more readily available sources of information have been exhausted can lead to serious mistakes.

For example, suppose a Chinese fast-food restaurant chain, based in Vancouver, is considering expanding its hours and product line with a breakfast menu. Exploratory research with a small number of current customers might find a strong negative reaction to eating a spicy vegetable breakfast at a Chinese fast-food outlet. Thus, exploratory research might help crystallize a problem and identify information needed for future research.

Descriptive Research

descriptive research
Research designed to describe characteristics of a population or phenomenon.

The major purpose of **descriptive research,** as the name implies, is to describe characteristics of a population. Marketing managers frequently need to determine who purchases a product, portray the size of the market, identify competitors' actions, and so on. Descriptive research seeks to determine the answers to *who, what, when, where,* and *how* questions.

Descriptive research often helps segment and target markets. For example, surveys conducted by the Alberta Government identify the characteristics of consumers who purchase organic food products. A typical organic food purchaser is more likely to be a woman than man and more likely to be in the 25-to-34 age group than in the over-55 age group. She is more likely to be from British Columbia (30 percent) and less likely to be from Saskatchewan (7 percent) or Alberta (12 percent).[2]

Descriptive research often is used to reveal the nature of shopping or consumption behaviour. For instance, research conducted by Leger Marketing revealed that cold weather is not a major deterrent for Canadian grill owners. Among the consumers who already own a grill, 50 percent of the respondents reported that they grill year-round, including 19 percent who have grilled when the thermometer dipped below –20 degrees. Overall, 72 percent of Canadians surveyed would like to own a luxury barbecue grill.[3]

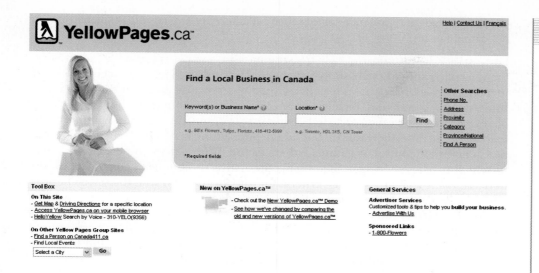

Accuracy is of paramount importance in descriptive research. Although they cannot completely eliminate errors, good researchers strive for descriptive precision. Suppose a study seeks to describe the market potential for portable satellite radios. If the study does not precisely measure sales volume, it will mislead the managers who are making production scheduling, budgeting, and other decisions based on it.

Unlike exploratory research, descriptive studies are based on some previous understanding of the nature of the research problem. Although the researcher may have a general understanding of the situation, the conclusive evidence that answers questions of fact necessary to determine a course of action has yet to be collected. Many circumstances require descriptive research to identify the reasons consumers give to explain the nature of things. In other words, a *diagnostic analysis* is performed when consumers are asked questions such as "Why do you feel that way?" Although they may describe why consumers feel a certain way, the findings of a descriptive study such as this, sometimes called *diagnostics,* do not provide causal evidence. Frequently, descriptive research attempts to determine the extent of differences in needs, attitudes, and opinions among subgroups.

Causal Research

causal research
Research conducted to identify cause-and-effect relationships among variables.

The main goal of **causal research** is to identify cause-and-effect relationships among variables. Exploratory and descriptive research normally precede cause-and-effect relationship studies. In causal studies, researchers typically have an expectation about the relationship to be explained, such as a prediction about the influence of price, packaging, advertising, and the like on sales. Thus, researchers must be quite knowledgeable about the subject. Ideally, the manager wants to establish that one event (say, a new package) is the means for producing another event (an increase in sales). Causal research attempts to establish that when we do one thing, another thing will follow. The word *cause* is common in everyday conversation, but from a scientific research perspective, identifying a causal relationship requires the following:

1. Establish the appropriate causal order or sequence of events
2. Measure the association between the presumed cause and the presumed effect

3. Recognize the presence or absence of alternative plausible explanations or causal factors[6]

For instance, in investigating whether the increase in sales is caused by advertising, the researcher should establish that changes in advertising spending occurred before increases in sales. Next, the researcher should observe an association between advertising spending and sales. Finally, the researcher should eliminate alternative plausible explanations or causal factors. For instance, a competitor withdrawing from the market or income increases in the target population may also increase sales. The researcher must control or eliminate these factors. Within the complex environment in which managers operate, identifying alternative or complex causal facts can be difficult. Even when these three criteria for causation are present, the researcher can never be certain that the causal explanation is adequate.

Most basic scientific studies in marketing (for example, the development of consumer behaviour theory) ultimately seek to identify cause-and-effect relationships. One often associates science with experiments. To predict a relationship between, say, price and perceived quality of a product, causal studies often create statistical experiments with controls that establish contrast groups. A number of marketing experiments are conducted by both theory developers and pragmatic business people. More will be said about experiments and causal research in Chapter 10.

Uncertainty Influences the Type of Research

The uncertainty of the research problem is related to the type of research project. Exhibit 2.2 illustrates that exploratory research is conducted during the early stages of decision making, when the decision situation is ambiguous and management is very uncertain about the nature of the problem. When management is aware of the problem but lacks some knowledge, descriptive research is usually conducted. Causal research requires sharply defined problems.

STAGES IN THE RESEARCH PROCESS

 As previously noted, marketing research can take many forms, but systematic inquiry is a common thread. Systematic inquiry requires careful planning of an orderly investigation. Marketing research, like other forms of scientific inquiry, involves a sequence of highly interrelated activities. The stages of the research process overlap continuously, and it is somewhat of an oversimplification to state

EXHIBIT 2.2	RELATIONSHIP OF UNCERTAINTY TO TYPES OF MARKETING RESEARCH		
	Exploratory Research (Ambiguous Problem)	**Descriptive Research (Partially Defined Problem)**	**Causal Research (Problem Clearly Defined)**
Possible situation	"Our sales are declining and we don't know why."	"What kind of people are buying our product? Who buys our competitor's products?"	"Will buyers purchase more of our product in a new package?"
	"Would people be interested in our new product idea?"	"What features do buyers prefer in our product?"	"Which of two advertising campaigns is more effective?"

Note: The degree of uncertainty of the research problem determines the research methodology.

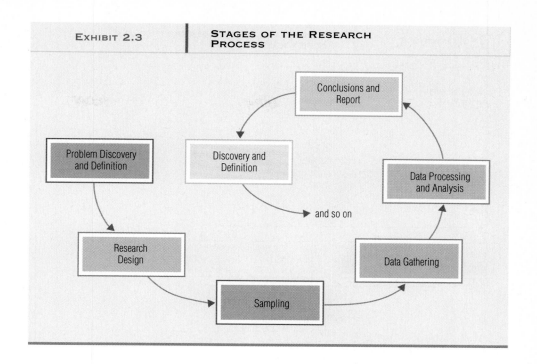

EXHIBIT 2.3 | STAGES OF THE RESEARCH PROCESS

that every research project has exactly the same ordered sequence of activities. Nevertheless, marketing research often follows a general pattern. The stages are (1) defining the problem, (2) planning a research design, (3) planning a sample, (4) collecting the data, (5) analyzing the data, and (6) formulating the conclusions and preparing the report.

Exhibit 2.3 portrays these six stages as a cyclical, or circular-flow, process. The circular-flow concept is used because the conclusions from research studies usually generate new ideas and problems that need to be investigated. In practice, the stages overlap chronologically and are functionally interrelated; sometimes the later stages are completed before the earlier ones. If it is known that the data will be analyzed by computer, then computer coding requirements will be included in the questionnaire design. The professional researcher should anticipate executives' needs for information in the planning process and considers these needs during the analysis and tabulation stages.

Alternatives in the Research Process

The researcher must choose among a number of alternatives during each stage of the research process. The research process can be compared to a map. On a map some paths are better charted than others; some are difficult to travel and some are more interesting and beautiful than others. Rewarding experiences may be gained during the journey. It is important to remember that there is no single right or best path for all journeys. The road one takes depends on where one wants to go and the resources (money, time, labour, and so on) available for the trip. The map analogy is useful for the marketing researcher because at each stage of the research process there are several paths to follow. In some instances, the quickest path will lead to appropriate research because of time constraints. In other circumstances, when money and human resources are plentiful, the appropriate path may be quite different. Exploration of the various paths of marketing research decisions is the primary purpose.

The following sections briefly describe the six stages of the research process. (Each stage is discussed in greater depth in later chapters.) Exhibit 2.4 shows the decisions that researchers must make in each stage. This discussion of the research

EXHIBIT 2.4 | FLOWCHART OF THE MARKETING RESEARCH PROCESS

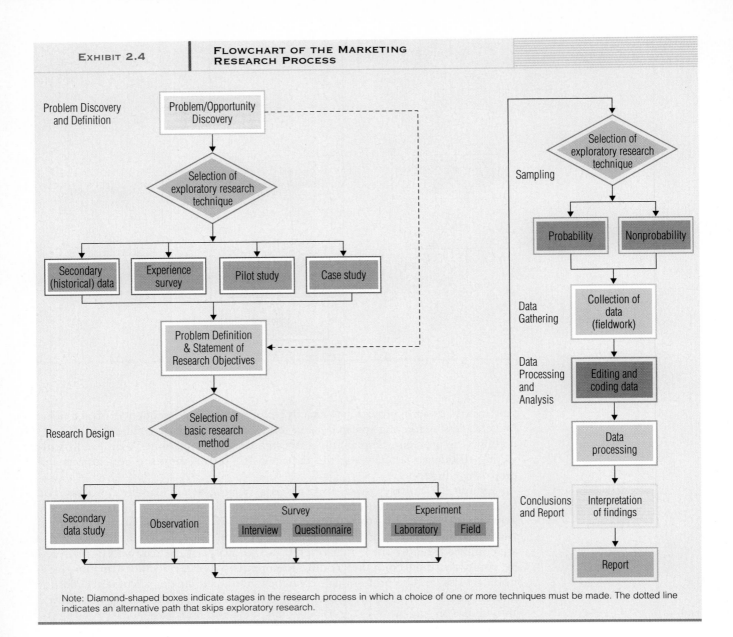

Note: Diamond-shaped boxes indicate stages in the research process in which a choice of one or more techniques must be made. The dotted line indicates an alternative path that skips exploratory research.

process begins with problem discovery and definition, because most research projects are initiated to remedy managers' uncertainty about some aspect of the firm's marketing program.

Discovering and Defining the Problem

Exhibit 2.4 shows that the research process begins with *problem discovery*. Identifying the problem is the first step toward its solution. In general usage, the word *problem* suggests that something has gone wrong. Actually, the research task may be to clarify a problem, define an opportunity, or monitor and evaluate current operations. The concept of problem discovery and definition must encompass a broader context that includes analysis of opportunities. It should be noted that the initial stage is problem *discovery* rather than *definition*. The researcher may not have a clear-cut statement of the problem at the outset of the research process; often, only symptoms of the problem are apparent at that point. Sales may be declining, but management may not know the exact nature of the problem. Thus, the problem statement often is made only in general terms; what is to be investigated is not yet specifically identified.

Defining the Problem

In marketing research, the adage "a problem well defined is a problem half solved" is worth remembering. This adage emphasizes that an orderly definition of the research problem lends a sense of direction to the investigation. Careful attention to the **problem definition stage** allows the researcher to set the proper research objectives. If the purpose of the research is clear, the chances of collecting necessary and relevant information and not collecting surplus information will be much greater.

Albert Einstein noted that "the formulation of a problem is often more essential than its solution."[7] This is good advice for marketing managers. Too often they concentrate on finding the right answer rather than asking the right question. Many managers do not realize that defining a problem may be more difficult than solving it. In marketing research, if the data are collected before the nature of the marketing problem is carefully thought out, they probably will not help solve the problem.

To be efficient, marketing research must have clear objectives and definite designs. Unfortunately, little or no planning goes into the formulation of many research problems. Consider the case of the Ha–Pah–Shu–Tse brand of Indian fried bread mix (from the Pawnee Indian word for red corn). The owner of the company, Mr. Ha–Pah–Shu–Tse, thought that his product, one of the few Native American food products available in the United States, was not selling because it was not widely advertised. He wanted a management consulting group to conduct some research concerning advertising themes. However, the management consultants pointed out to the Ha–Pah–Shu–Tse family that using the family name on the bread mix might be a foremost source of concern. They suggested that consumer behaviour research to investigate the brand image might be a better initial starting point, rather than advertising copy research. Family management agreed.

It should be emphasized that the word *problem* refers to the managerial problem (which may be a lack of knowledge about consumers or advertising effectiveness) and the information needed to help *solve* the problem. Defining the problem must precede determination of the purpose of the research. Frequently the marketing researcher will not be involved until line management has discovered that some information about a particular aspect of the marketing mix is needed. Even at this point the exact nature of the problem may be poorly defined. Once a problem area has been discovered, the marketing researcher can begin the process of precisely defining it.

Although the problem definition stage of the research process probably is the most important one, it frequently is a neglected area of marketing research. Too many researchers forget that the best place to begin a research project is at the end. Knowing what is to be accomplished determines the research process. An error or omission in problem definition is likely to be a costly mistake that cannot be corrected in later stages of the process. Chapter 4 discusses problem definition in greater detail.

Exploratory Research

Exploratory research usually is conducted during the initial stage of the research process. The preliminary activities undertaken to refine the problem into researchable form need not be formal or precise. The purpose of the exploratory research process is to progressively narrow the scope of the research topic and transform ambiguous problems into well-defined ones that incorporate specific research objectives. By investigating any existing studies on the subject, talking with knowledgeable individuals, and informally investigating the situation, the researcher can progressively sharpen the concepts. After such exploration, the researcher should know exactly which data to collect during the formal phases of the project and how to conduct the project. Exhibit 2.4 indicates that managers and researchers must decide whether to use one or more exploratory research techniques. As Exhibit 2.4 indicates, this stage is optional.

The marketing researcher can employ techniques from four basic categories to obtain insights and gain a clearer idea of the problem: secondary data analysis, pilot studies, case studies, and experience surveys.

Secondary Data Analysis *Secondary data,* or *historical data,* are data previously collected and assembled for some project other than the one at hand. (*Primary data* are data gathered and assembled specifically for the project at hand.) Secondary data often can be found inside the company, at a public or university library, or on the Internet. In addition, some firms specialize in providing various types of information, such as economic forecasts, that are useful to many organizations. The researcher who gathers data from Statistics Canada publications and Web sites or from the *Survey of Current Business* is using secondary sources. Investigating secondary data sources has saved many a researcher from "reinventing the wheel" in primary data collection.

pilot study
A collective term for any small-scale exploratory research technique that uses sampling but does not apply rigorous standards.

Pilot Studies The term **pilot study** covers a number of diverse research techniques. Pilot studies collect data from the ultimate consumers or the actual subjects of the research project to serve as a guide for a larger study. When the term *pilot study* is used in the context of exploratory research, it refers to a study whose data collection methods are informal and whose findings may lack precision.[8] A popular exploratory pilot study that has become increasingly popular in application is focus group research. The focus group session brings together six to ten people in a loosely structured format; the technique is based on the assumption that individuals are more willing to share their ideas when they are able to hear the ideas of others. Information obtained in these studies is qualitative and serves to guide subsequent quantitative study. For example, Toronto Crime Stoppers used focus groups to determine how to target children and teenagers. Interestingly, the teenagers perceived Crime Stoppers as a "snitch line" and "totally run by the police." Consequently, Toronto Crime Stoppers decided to work with DDB Canada, an advertising agency experienced in youth marketing, in order to implement a rebranding strategy.[9]

Case Study Method The case study method is a close examination of one or a few situations similar to the problem being investigated to obtain information. For example, a ski resort in Banff may intensively investigate the marketing activities of a few innovative and popular ski resorts in Austria. The primary advantage of the case study is that an entire organization or entity can be investigated in depth with meticulous attention to detail. However, conducting a case study often requires the cooperation of the party whose history is being studied. This method does not follow standard procedures, and the success of any case study is highly dependent on the alertness, creativity, intelligence, and motivation of the individual performing the case analysis.

A typical focus group session brings together six to ten people to explore consumer opinions and behaviours. Focus groups, like other pilot studies, use sampling but do not apply rigorous standards.

Experience Survey   An experience survey is an exploratory technique by which a small number of interviews are conducted with carefully selected people who have insight, knowledge, or experience in the area to be investigated. For example, a dog food producer that is ready to launch a new all-natural dog food may discuss the general product characteristics with some of the retailers and some members of the company's own salespeople. The purpose of such discussions is to exhaust the information available from relatively inexpensive sources before gathering expensive primary data. While the interviews with knowledgeable individuals may reveal nothing conclusive, they may help define the problem more formally.

The above four basic methods of exploratory research are explained in greater detail in Chapter 5. Because the purpose of exploratory research is to gain insights and discover new ideas, researchers may use considerable creativity and flexibility. Data generally are collected using several exploratory techniques. Exhausting these sources usually is worth the effort because the expense is relatively low. Furthermore, insights into how and how not to conduct research may be gained from activities during the problem definition stage. If the conclusions made during this stage suggest marketing opportunities, the researcher is in a position to begin planning a formal, quantitative research project.

Statement of Research Objectives

A researcher must initially decide precisely what to research. After identifying and clarifying the problem, with or without exploratory research, the researcher should make a formal statement of the problem and the *research objectives*. This statement delineates the type of information that should be collected and provides a framework for the scope of the study.

A typical research objective might seek to answer a question such as "To what extent did the new pricing program achieve its objectives?" In this sense the statement of the problem is a research question.

The best expression of a research objective is a well-formed, testable research hypothesis. A *hypothesis* is a statement that can be refuted or supported by empirical data. For example, an exploratory study might lead to the hypothesis that a market share decline recognized by management is occurring predominantly among households in which the head of the household is 45 to 65 years old with an income of $45,000 per year or less. Another hypothesis might be that concentrating advertising efforts in monthly waves (rather than conducting continuous advertising) will cause an increase in sales and profits. Once the hypothesis has been developed, the researcher is ready to select a research design.

Planning the Research Design

After the researcher has formulated the research problem, he or she must develop the research design as part of the **research design stage**. A **research design** is a master plan that specifies the methods and procedures for collecting and analyzing the needed information; it is a framework for the research plan of action. The objectives of the study determined during the early stages of the research are included in the design to ensure that the information collected is appropriate for solving the problem. The researcher also must determine the sources of information, the design technique (survey or experiment, for example), the sampling methodology, and the schedule and cost of the research.

Selection of the Basic Research Method

Here again, the researcher must make a decision. Exhibit 2.4 shows the four basic design techniques for descriptive and causal research: secondary data, observation, surveys, and experiments. The objectives of the study, the available data sources, the urgency of the decision, and the cost of obtaining the data will determine which method should be chosen. The managerial aspects of selecting the research design will be considered later.

research design stage
The stage in which the researcher determines a framework for the research plan of action by selecting a basic research method.

research design
A master plan that specifies the methods and procedures for collecting and analyzing needed information.

Secondary Data   Like exploratory research studies, descriptive and causal studies use previously collected data. Although the terms *secondary* and *historical* are interchangeable, we will use the term *secondary data* here. An example of a secondary data study is the use of a mathematical model to predict sales on the basis of past sales or a correlation with related variables. Manufacturers of digital cameras may find that sales are highly correlated with discretionary personal income. To predict future market potential, projections of disposable personal income may be acquired from the government or a university. This information can be manipulated mathematically to forecast sales. Formal secondary data studies have benefits and limitations similar to those of exploratory studies that use secondary data, but generally the quantitative analysis of secondary data is more sophisticated.

Observation   The objective of many research projects is merely to record what can be observed—for example, the number of automobiles that pass by a proposed site for a gas station. This can be mechanically recorded or observed by humans. Research personnel known as *mystery shoppers* may act as customers to observe actions of sales personnel or do comparative shopping to learn prices at competing outlets.

The main advantage of the observation technique is that it records behaviour without relying on reports from respondents. Observational data are often collected unobtrusively and passively without a respondent's direct participation. For instance, in 2004 BBM Research of Canada started using a "portable people meter" (PPM), introduced by Arbitron, a media and marketing research firm, that measures how many people are exposed to or are listening to individual radio stations and television stations, including cable TV. The PPM, the size of a mobile phone, is worn like a pager and detects hidden audio tones within a station or network's audio stream, logging each time it finds such a signal. With PPM, the audience numbers suddenly increased in all categories by 8 percent. Rather than a sudden change in audience numbers, this increase was due to the superior accuracy of totally passive, less intrusive PPMs compared to the old handwritten logs or "people meter" instruments that sat on top of the TV set and required some input from the participants (such as pushing a button or keeping a log).[10]

Direct marketers often conduct experiments to determine how to increase response to pamphlets, catalogues, or Internet offerings. Experiments have shown that the wording of headline copy and prices can greatly influence the success of direct marketing.

The smaller size and less intrusive nature of the portable people meter improved accuracy of audience numbers across Canada.

Observation is more complex than mere "nose counting," and the task is more difficult than the inexperienced researcher would imagine. Several things of interest, such as attitudes, opinions, motivations, and other intangible states of mind, simply cannot be observed.

Surveys   The most common method of generating primary data is the survey. Most people have seen the results of political surveys by Leger Marketing or Ipsos Reid, and some have been respondents (members of a sample who supply answers) to marketing research questionnaires. A *survey* is a research technique by which information is gathered from a sample of people using a questionnaire. The task of writing a list of questions and designing the format of the printed or written questionnaire is an essential aspect of the development of a survey research design.

Research investigators may choose to contact respondents by telephone or mail, on the Internet, or in person. An advertiser spending $30,000 to $40,000 for 30 seconds of commercial time during the Stanley Cup playoffs on CBC's *Hockey Night in Canada* may telephone people to quickly gather information concerning their responses to the advertising.[11] A manufacturer of a birth control device for men might determine the need for a versatile survey method wherein an interviewer can ask a variety of personal questions in a flexible format. Although personal interviews are expensive, they are valuable because investigators can use visual aids and supplement the interviews with

Movie marketers often use survey research. Gauging audiences' responses to three or four versions of trailers or television commercials is a typical research project designed to bring more people in on opening night. Audience previews have been responsible for the decisions about the final version of many films.

Many managers view consumer research as a necessary precursor to product introduction.[12] Unfortunately, innovative products that lack much in common with existing products often prove this attitude to be wrong. When the telephone answering machine was consumer tested, it faced an almost universally negative reaction, since most individuals felt that using a mechanical device to answer a phone was rude and disrespectful. Today, of course, many people regard their answering machines as indispensable and would dread scheduling daily activities without them. In the same vein, the computer mouse flunked its initial testing. Surveys indicated that potential customers found it awkward and unnecessary.

Surveys about new food products face terrible problems. For one, a person's desire for food is powerfully influenced by the ambiance of the meal, dining companions, and what foods were eaten recently, all of which confound and confuse the results of survey research. Even more erratic results come from studies of children's food, like a new cereal or snack. Kids' responses are strongly swayed by how well they like the people doing the test and the playthings available. Worse, kids quickly change their minds, and in a taste test of several foods a child can judge one food the best but an hour later proclaim the same food "icky."

Marketing researchers must be aware of the potential problems when deciding exactly what research design will best solve their research problems.

observations. Each of these survey methods has advantages and disadvantages. A researcher's task is to find the most appropriate way to collect the needed information.

Experiments   Marketing *experiments* hold the greatest potential for establishing cause-and-effect relationships. Experimentation allows investigation of changes in one variable, such as sales, while manipulating one or two other variables, perhaps price or advertising, under controlled conditions. Ideally, experimental control provides a basis for isolating causal factors by eliminating outside, or exogenous, influences.

For instance, experiments can help in understanding effectiveness of different promotional methods, advertisements, or media alternatives. In 2004, Nestlé launched a test campaign for two food category brands, brands A and B, using radio and magazine ads in Toronto and Montreal. The campaign targeted busy adults who potentially needed an alternative to home cooking that was convenient, easy to prepare, and great tasting. Following the campaign, a sample of adults who made a Nestlé or a similar product purchase in the past six months were interviewed over the Internet. Respondents were a mix of consumers exposed to the radio campaign and those who were not. When comparing the brands, there was no difference in the percentage of participants who reported that the ad made the brand more appealing. However, a higher percentage of participants enjoyed listening to Brand B's ad than Brand A's (47 percent and 44 percent respectively). Nestlé also found out that the recognition of the radio ads in the campaign was significantly higher than the average in both cities.[13]

An experiment controls conditions so that one or more variables can be manipulated in order to test a hypothesis. In the Nestlé example, there was a comparison of different ads and an observation of brand evaluations and ad recognition. Other experiments—laboratory experiments, for example—are deliberate modifications of an environment created for the research itself. One example of a laboratory experiment is a toy company showing alternative versions of a proposed TV commercial to groups of children and observing which one keeps their attention longest.

Ice.com, a Montreal-based online jewellery store, had to face one of the common problems of online retailing: abandoned shopping carts on the virtual aisles of the online store.[14] Although customers browse through the pages of the store and start an online order, some never complete the transaction, referred to as the abandonment rate. The online jewellery store, offering merchandise from $40 to $45,000, had shopping cart abandonment rates hovering around 75 percent.

Realizing the extent of the problem through their webtracking data, Ice.com started processing the data from its monthly sweepstakes at www.ice.com to build an e-mail database of potential customers who browsed the online store but never made a purchase. The sweepstakes offered various prizes from luxury cruises to luggage sets and resulted in a permission-based e-mail database of 1.5 million people, from both the United States and Canada. To convert the browsers to buyers, Ice.com sent tailored e-mails with attractive offers to members of the database. Particularly, the e-mail offers were e-commerce enabled, allowing customers to complete a transaction in just three steps. Compared to mass e-mails, this solution resulted in a 550 percent increase in conversion rates according to Pinny Gniwisch, the company's executive vice-president of marketing. Once familiar with the online store's purchase environment, customers did come back, increasing the repeat buyers to 25 percent. Abandonment rates dropped to 52 percent and annual sales increased to $10 million.

TO THE POINT

You cannot put the same shoe on every foot.

PUBLIUS SYRUS

The "Best" Research Design

It is argued that there is no single best research design and there are no hard-and-fast rules for good marketing research. This does not mean, however, that the researcher faces chaos and confusion. It means that the researcher can choose among many alternative methods for solving a problem. Consider the researcher who must forecast sales for the upcoming year. Some commonly used forecasting methods are surveying executive opinion, collecting sales–force composite opinions, surveying user expectations, projecting trends, and analyzing market factors.

The ability to select the most appropriate research design develops with experience. Inexperienced researchers often jump to the conclusion that the survey method is the best design because they are most familiar with this method. When Chicago's Museum of Science and Industry wanted to determine the relative popularity of its exhibits, it could have conducted a survey. Instead, a creative researcher familiar with other research designs suggested a far less expensive alternative: an unobtrusive observation technique. The researcher suggested that the museum merely keep track of the frequency with which the floor tiles in front of the various exhibits had to be replaced, indicating where the heaviest traffic occurred. When this was done, the museum found that the chick-hatching exhibit was the most popular. This method provided the same results as a survey but at a much lower cost.

After determining the proper design, the researcher moves on to the next stage—planning the sample.

Sampling

sampling stage
The stage in which the researcher determines who is to be sampled, how large a sample is needed, and how sampling units will be selected.

Although the sampling plan is outlined in the research design, the **sampling stage** is a distinct phase of the research process. For convenience, however, we will treat the sample planning and the actual sample generation processes together in this section.

If you take your first bite of a steak and conclude that it needs salt, you have just conducted a sample. *Sampling* involves any procedure that uses a small number of items or a portion of the population to make a conclusion regarding the whole population. In other words, a sample is a subset from a larger population. If certain statistical procedures are followed, a researcher need not select every item in a population because the results of a good sample should have the same characteristics as the population as a whole. Of course, when errors are made, samples do not give reliable estimates of the population. A famous example of error due to sampling is the 1936 *Literary Digest* fiasco in the United States. The magazine conducted a survey and predicted that Republican Alf Landon would win over Democrat Franklin D. Roosevelt by a landslide in that year's presidential election. This prediction was wrong—and the error was due to sample selection. The post-mortems showed that *Literary Digest* had sampled its readers as well as telephone subscribers. In 1936 these people were not a representative cross-section of voters, because in those days, people who could afford magazine subscriptions and phone service were generally well-to-do—and a disproportionate number of them were Republicans.

This famous example suggests that the first sampling question to ask is "Who is to be sampled?" The answer to this primary question requires the identification of a *target population*. Defining this population and determining the sampling units may not be so easy. If, for example, a savings and loan association surveys people who already have accounts for answers to image questions, the selected sampling units will not represent *potential* customers. Specifying the target population is a crucial aspect of the sampling plan.

The next sampling issue concerns *sample size*. How big should the sample be? Although management may wish to examine every potential buyer of a product or service, doing so may be unnecessary as well as unrealistic. Typically, larger samples are more precise than smaller ones, but proper probability sampling can allow a small proportion of the total population to give a reliable measure of the whole. A later discussion will explain how large a sample must be in order to be truly representative of the universe or population.

The final sampling decision concerns choosing how to select the sampling units. Students who have taken a statistics course generally understand simple random sampling, in which every unit in the population has an equal and known chance of being selected. However, this is only one type of sampling. For example, a cluster sampling procedure may reduce costs and make data gathering procedures more efficient. If members of the population are found in close geographical clusters, a sampling procedure that selects area clusters rather than individual units in the population will reduce costs. Rather than selecting 1,000 individuals throughout Canada, it may be more economical to first select 25 cities or towns and then sample within those cities or towns. This will substantially reduce travel, hiring, and training costs. In determining the appropriate sampling plan, the researcher will have to select the most appropriate sampling procedure for meeting the established study objectives.

There are two basic sampling techniques: probability sampling and nonprobability sampling. A *probability sample* is a sample in which every member of the population has a known, non-zero probability of selection. If sample units are selected on the basis of personal judgment (for example, a test-market city is selected because it appears to be typical), the sample method is a *nonprobability sample*. In reality, the sampling decision is not a simple choice between two methods. Simple random samples, stratified samples, quota samples, cluster samples, and judgmental samples are some of the many methods for drawing a sample. Chapter 14 gives a full discussion of these techniques.

Gathering Data

data gathering stage
The stage in which the researcher collects the data.

Once the research design (including the sampling plan) has been formalized, the process of gathering or collecting information, the **data gathering stage,** may begin. Data may be gathered by humans or recorded by machines. Scanner data illustrate electronic data collection by machine.

Obviously, the many research techniques involve many methods of *data gathering*. The survey method requires some form of direct participation by the respondent. The respondent may participate by filling out a questionnaire or by interacting with an interviewer. If an unobtrusive method of data gathering is used, the subjects do not actively participate. For instance, a simple count of motorists driving past a proposed franchising location is one kind of data gathering method. However the data are collected, it is important to minimize errors in the process. For example, the data gathering should be consistent in all geographical areas. If an interviewer phrases questions incorrectly or records a respondent's statements inaccurately (not verbatim), major data collection errors will result.

Often there are two phases to the process of gathering data: pre-testing and the main study. A *pre-testing phase* using a small subsample may determine whether the data gathering plan for the *main study* is an appropriate procedure. Thus, a small-scale pre-test study provides an advance opportunity for an investigator to check the data collection form to minimize errors due to improper design, such as poorly worded or organized questions. There is also a chance to discover confusing interviewing instructions, learn if the questionnaire is too long or too short, and uncover other such field errors. Tabulation of data from the pre-tests provides the researcher with a format for the knowledge that may be gained from the actual study. If the tabulation of the data and statistical results does not answer the researcher's questions, the investigator may need to redesign the study.

Processing and Analyzing Data

Editing and Coding

After the fieldwork has been completed, the data must be converted into a format that will answer the marketing manager's questions. This is part of the **data processing and analysis stage.** Data processing generally begins with editing and coding the data. *Editing* involves checking the data collection forms for omissions, legibility, and consistency in classification. The editing process corrects problems such as interviewer errors (an answer recorded on the wrong portion of a questionnaire, for example) before the data are transferred to the computer.

Before data can be tabulated, meaningful categories and character symbols must be established for groups of responses. The rules for interpreting, categorizing, recording, and transferring the data to the data storage media are called *codes.* This coding process facilitates computer or hand tabulation. If computer analysis is to be used, the data are entered into the computer and verified. Computer-assisted (online) interviewing is an example of the impact of technological change on the research process. Telephone interviewers, seated at computer terminals, read survey questions displayed on the monitor. The interviewer asks the questions and then types in the respondents' answers. Thus, answers are collected and processed into the computer at the same time, eliminating intermediate steps that could introduce errors.

Analysis

Analysis is the application of reasoning to understand the data that have been gathered. In its simplest form, analysis may involve determining consistent patterns and summarizing the relevant details revealed in the investigation. The appropriate analytical technique for data analysis will be determined by management's information requirements, the characteristics of the research design, and the nature of the data gathered. Statistical analysis may range from portraying a simple frequency distribution to very complex multivariate analyses, such as multiple regression. Later chapters will discuss three general categories of statistical analysis: univariate, bivariate, and multivariate analyses.

data processing and analysis stage
The stage in which the researcher performs several interrelated procedures to convert the data into a format that will answer management's questions.

Drawing Conclusions and Preparing a Report

As mentioned earlier, most marketing research is applied research aimed at making a marketing decision. An important but often overlooked aspect of the marketing researcher's job is to look at the analysis of the information collected and ask, "What does this mean to management?" The final stage in the research process, the **conclusions and report preparation stage**, consists of interpreting the information and making *conclusions* for managerial decisions.

conclusions and report preparation stage
The stage in which the researcher interprets information and draws conclusions to be communicated to decision makers.

The research *report* should effectively communicate the research findings. All too many reports are complicated statements of technical aspects and sophisticated research methods. Frequently, management is not interested in detailed reporting of the research design and statistical findings, but wishes only a summary of the findings. If the findings of the research remain unread on the marketing manager's desk, the study will have been useless. The importance of effective communication cannot be overemphasized. Research is only as good as its applications.

Marketing researchers must communicate their findings to a managerial audience. The written report serves another purpose as well: It is a historical document that will be a record that may be referred to later if the research is to be repeated or if further research is to be based on what has come before.

Now that we have outlined the research process, note that the order of topics in this book follows the flowchart of the research process presented in Exhibit 2.4. Keep this flowchart in mind while reading later chapters.

THE RESEARCH PROGRAM STRATEGY

 Our discussion of the marketing research process began with the assumption that the researcher wished to gather information to achieve a specific marketing objective. We have emphasized the researcher's need to select specific techniques for solving one-dimensional problems, such as identifying market segments, selecting the best packaging design, or test-marketing a new product.

However, if you think about a firm's marketing mix activity in a given period of time (such as a year), you'll realize that marketing research is not a one-shot activity—it is a continuous process. An exploratory research study may be followed by a survey, or a researcher may conduct a specific research project for each aspect of the marketing mix. If a new product is being developed, the different types of research might include market potential studies to identify the size and characteristics of the market; product usage testing to record consumers' reactions to prototype products; brand name and packaging research to determine the product's symbolic connotations; and test marketing the new product. Because research is a continuous process, management should view marketing research at a strategic planning level. The **program strategy** refers to a firm's overall plan to use marketing research. It is a planning activity that places a series of marketing research projects in the context of the company's marketing plan.

program strategy
The overall plan to conduct a series of marketing research projects; a planning activity that places each marketing project in the context of the company's marketing plan.

The marketing research program strategy can be likened to a term insurance policy. Conducting marketing research minimizes risk and increases certainty. Each research project can be seen as a series of term insurance policies that makes the marketing manager's job a bit safer.

SUMMARY

Decision making is the process by which managers resolve problems or choose among alternative opportunities. Decision makers must recognize the nature of the problem or opportunity, identify how much information is available, and recognize what information they need. Every marketing decision can be classified on a continuum ranging from complete certainty to absolute ambiguity.

Exploratory, descriptive, and causal research are three major types of marketing research projects. The clarity with which the research problem is defined determines whether exploratory, descriptive, or causal research is appropriate. Exploratory research is appropriate when management knows only the general nature of a problem; it is used not to provide conclusive evidence but to clarify problems. Descriptive research is conducted when there is some understanding of the nature of the problem; such research is used to provide a more specific description of the characteristics of a problem. Causal research identifies cause-and-effect relationships when the research problem has been narrowly defined.

Research proceeds in a series of six interrelated phases. The first is problem definition, which may include exploratory research using secondary data, experience surveys, or pilot studies. Once the problem is defined, the researcher selects a research design. The major designs are surveys, experiments, secondary data analysis, and observation. Creative research design can minimize the cost of obtaining reliable results. After the design has been selected, a sampling plan is chosen, using a probability sample, a nonprobability sample, or a combination of the two.

The design is put into action in the data gathering phase. This phase may involve a small pre-test before the main study is undertaken. In the analysis stage the data are edited and coded, then processed, usually by computer. The results are interpreted in light of the decisions that management must make. Finally, the analysis is presented to decision makers in a written or oral report. This last step is crucial, because even an excellent project will not lead to proper action if the results are poorly communicated.

Quite often research projects are conducted together as parts of a research program. Such programs can involve successive projects that monitor an established product or a group of projects undertaken for a proposed new product to determine the optimal form of various parts of the marketing mix.

A major problem facing students of marketing research is that they must consider each stage in the research process separately. However, without concentrated emphasis on the total process, understanding the individual stages is difficult. Thus, learning marketing research is like walking a tightrope between too broad and too narrow a focus.

Key Terms and Concepts

decision making
exploratory research
descriptive research
causal research
problem definition stage

pilot study
research design stage
research design
sampling stage
data gathering stage

data processing and
  analysis stage
conclusions and report preparation
  stage
program strategy

Questions for Review and Critical Thinking

1. For each of the following situations, decide whether the research should be exploratory, descriptive, or causal:
   a. Establishing the functional relationship between advertising and sales
   b. Investigating consumer reactions to the idea of a new laundry detergent that prevents shrinkage in hot water
   c. Identifying target market demographics for a shopping centre
   d. Estimating sales potential for concrete vibrators in a western sales territory

2. Describe a research situation that allows one to infer causality.

3. A researcher is interested in knowing the answer to a *why* question, but does not know beforehand what sort of answer will satisfy. Will answering this question involve exploratory, descriptive, or causal research? Explain.

4. Do the stages in the research process follow the scientific method?

5. Why is the problem definition stage of the research process probably the most important stage?

6. The Government of Canada is conducting technological research into the feasibility of creating a plastic-like substance on which currency notes can be printed. Using this substance for printing banknotes would increase the circulation life of lower-value notes and enhance their utility in vending machines. What type of consumer research should be conducted?

7. Which research design seems appropriate for the following studies?
   a. The manufacturer and marketer of flight simulators and other pilot training equipment wish to forecast sales volume for the next five years

   b. A local chapter of the Canadian Cancer Society wishes to identify the demographic characteristics of individuals who donate more than $500 per year
   c. A major petroleum company is concerned with the increased costs of marketing regular leaded gasoline and is considering dropping this product
   d. A food company researcher wishes to know what types of food are carried in brown-bag lunches to learn if the company can capitalize on this phenomenon
   e. A researcher wishes to identify who plays bingo

8. Should the marketing research program strategy be viewed as a strategic planning activity?

Exploring the Internet

1. Use a Web browser to go to the Ipsos Canada Polls & Research section of its Web site at http://www.ipsos.ca/pa/polls.cfm. The page is updated regularly. Click on "Canada" to read the results of one of the polls. Then review the privacy policy.
2. Use a Web browser to access Lycos (http://www.lycos.com). What keyword topics can be investigated? How can you use the information you find using these keywords in designing a research project?
3. Go to the Advertising Research Foundation's home page at http://www.arfsite.org. What research information can you access?

Anthony Cox, president and founder of Dark Beans Coffee Company, was meeting Mike Goldberg, his marketing manager. Cox and Goldberg were discussing the need to develop a marketing plan for the company's Equal Share Ice Coffee, the proposed brand name for a new product line of Fair Trade cold coffees. The line was to include five flavours: standard coffee, Swiss chocolate, mocha, espresso, and amaretto. The use of the Fair Trade Certified logo meant a lot to customers: It was a signal of social responsibility—a company would share more of the profits with farmers growing the coffee, thus improving their lives. The number of companies that wanted to be responsible corporate citizens had increased among the coffee chains. Two of the biggest chains, Starbuck's and Timothy's, had already introduced Fair Trade Certified coffee over the past few years. Fair Trade coffee sales had increased in Canada in the past few years to more than $19 million annually.

Another trend that Cox had noticed was an increase in the popularity of cold coffee drinks and the tendency of younger consumers to opt for soft drinks instead of hot beverages for breakfast. Goldberg believed that the way to market the canned iced-coffee line was similar to the marketing strategies used by most soft drink marketers. As Goldberg indicated, soft drink consumption was substantially higher among preteens and teenagers than in other age groups. Both trends were obvious; however, would the marriage of Fair Trade coffee with ice be successful? Would the same preteen and teenage group be attracted to the "social responsibility" of the company's product line?

Cox saw Fair Trade iced coffee as an opportunity to compete in the soft drink market. He also thought it was a product that would bring Dark Beans Coffee into the socially responsible soft drink age. However, he was unsure whether there was adequate demand for the product line.

Questions

1. If you were a marketing research staff member attending this meeting, how would you define the research problem? Write a detailed statement of the research objectives for the Equal Share Ice Coffee project.
2. What type of information might be acquired using primary data sources? Using secondary data sources?
3. Outline a program strategy.

Note: The names used in this case are fictitious.[15]

3

ORGANIZATIONAL AND ETHICAL ISSUES IN MARKETING RESEARCH

What you will learn in this chapter

1 To understand the role and the degree of marketing research sophistication in organizations.

2 To explain pseudo-research and discuss the often conflicting relationship between marketing management and researchers.

3 To understand the role that research suppliers and research contractors play in the marketing research industry.

4 To identify the criteria for determining when outside research suppliers are needed.

5 To describe the three parties involved in most research situations and how interaction among them may identify ethical questions.

6 To discuss selected issues such as deception, privacy, and advocacy research from the perspective of each of the three parties.

7 To discuss the role of codes of ethics in marketing research.

As with other functional areas of business, marketing has been the target of organizational and ethical concerns. In particular, the area of marketing research has been affected by such organizational and ethical concerns.[1] Canadians, however, are historically receptive to marketing research activities. According to a 2005 survey conducted by the Marketing Research and Intelligence Association (MRIA), 87 percent of Canadians believe that market and survey research serves a valuable societal purpose. However, of the 2006 participants in this study, 53 percent reported being contacted for a survey that turned out to be an attempt to sell a product or service and 27 percent received survey calls whose true purpose was to raise funds for a charity or similar organization.[2] In Canada, as in many developed countries, *MUGGING* (Marketing Under the Guise of Interviewing) and *SUGGING* (Soliciting Under the Guise of Interviewing) are illegal. In fact, research conducted with 475 marketing research professionals in Canada and the United States suggests that Canadian marketing research professionals are a few steps ahead of the game. Only 3 percent of the Canadian marketing researchers who participated indicated that their company "had no code of ethics," whereas this was true for 16 percent of the U.S. respondents. In addition, while both U.S. and Canadian respondents claim to be familiar or extremely familiar with the company's code of ethics, this percentage is higher for Canada (United States 55 percent, Canada 70 percent).[3]

How can marketing researchers maintain certain standards of conduct and do what is morally right? This chapter discusses a variety of ethical issues that face managers and marketing researchers. The chapter also explores researchers' human side by discussing the place of research in the organization, some sources of the conflicts between marketing researchers and managers, and ways to reduce these conflicts. ∎

THE MISSION OF THE RESEARCH DEPARTMENT

A mission statement identifies the marketing research department's purpose within the organization. It explains what the department hopes to accomplish.

Exhibit 3.1 presents the mission statement of Mayer, Bourbonnais & Aube, a marketing research company based in Montreal. It shows the importance of a complete program of research that meets the needs of decision makers.

The most successful research departments are those whose mission is directly linked to the decision makers' needs. In most cases this means the research department must be valued, integrated, and an active part of the company's marketing process.

Conversely, those research departments that have not been successful seem to be independent of the decision makers' needs. Such departments tend to be isolated and operate within a vacuum. Their output may be technically precise, but it is rarely put to use because research is independent of the decision makers.[4]

DEGREE OF MARKETING RESEARCH SOPHISTICATION

research sophistication
A stage in which managers have considerable experience in the proper use of research techniques.

As business people have come to recognize that marketing research is a useful decision-making tool, its use has become more widespread. An organization's willingness to use research generally parallels its acceptance of the marketing concept. Just as some firms remain in the production-oriented stage, some ignore or are ignorant of marketing research. In some companies, the use of marketing research has evolved from a stage in which managers made decisions intuitively to a stage of **research sophistication,** in which managers have considerable experience in the proper use of research techniques. Marketing management's attitudes toward research methodology can range along a continuum from ignorance of research and intuition-centred decision making to sophisticated, research-centred decision making; see Exhibit 3.2. For purposes of discussion, we can identify three levels of marketing research sophistication.

Stage of Intuitive Decision Making

Marketing managers in this stage may be ignorant about marketing research or they may believe that research methodology should be confined to the ivory tower of academia or, at best, to technical research conducted elsewhere in the organization. These managers depend heavily on intuition and experience and obtain their information informally.

Stage of Sophistication

In this stage, marketing research has become a proactive force to identify decision makers' information needs. Marketing managers in this advanced stage recognize the potential of research to improve the decision-making process. They recognize

EXHIBIT 3.1	MISSION STATEMENT OF MAYER, BOURBONNAIS AND AUBE[5]

- To offer marketing research services grounded in the realities of the national marketplace.

- To provide precise data-gathering services to help you successfully carry out research projects.

- To establish a relationship of trust by delivering concrete strategies suited to your needs.

(www.mbarecherche.com)

EXHIBIT 3.2 | CONTINUUM OF MARKETING RESEARCH SOPHISTICATION

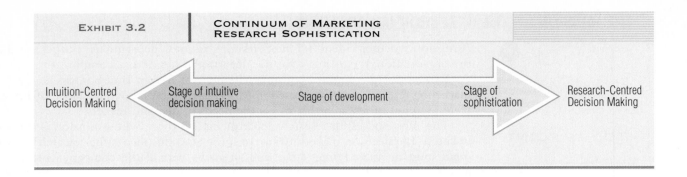

| Intuition-Centred Decision Making | Stage of intuitive decision making | Stage of development | Stage of sophistication | Research-Centred Decision Making |

that a fortune teller is probably a better bargain than poor research. They also recognize that while good research does not completely eliminate uncertainty, it can be an economically warranted means of at least reducing that uncertainty.

Stage of Development

Most companies are neither completely ignorant nor completely informed about what marketing research can and cannot do. Companies may use marketing research for the first few times on blind faith. Marketing managers in this stage naively believe that the result of the application of research methodology is the decision itself, rather than the information on which to base a good decision. They fail to see that good research can only reduce uncertainty; it cannot eliminate it. Over time managers gain experience and become increasingly familiar with marketing research. They begin to use research more often and to recognize occasions when it should be applied. This is a learning stage. Companies employ marketing research, but they do not exploit its full potential. Gradually, they increase their research sophistication.

At General Motors the goal of the marketing research department is to provide cost-effective market understanding that will allow General Motors to beat competitors to opportunities for existing and new products. The marketing research department's primary mission is to provide relevant, accurate, usable, and timely market information. The director of research says, "Our added value is found when we participate as an active and equal member of the decision-making team. This active role must be accomplished by being perceived as coming to the team without a personal point of view, as that perception could negatively affect the credibility of our primary mission."[6]

An American Marketing Association survey found that 76 percent of the companies surveyed reported having formal marketing research departments. Formal research departments are most common among consumer products companies, manufacturers, and retailers.[7] Larger companies are more likely to have marketing research departments.

The place of marketing research in an organization and the structure of the research department vary substantially, depending on the firm's acceptance of the marketing concept and its stage of marketing research sophistication. Improper placement of the marketing research department can isolate it. Researchers may lack a voice in executive committees when they have no continuous relationship with marketing management. Sometimes the research department is positioned at an inappropriately low level.

> Given that research and the decision makers are linked together, the best organization structure is to report as high up in the senior management ranks as possible—at least to the senior marketing vice president and preferably higher. The research department should also be able to have as broad a perspective across the company as possible. This is because of the information flow, which the research department manages, interprets, and communicates.[8]

Marketing Research as a Staff Function

Research departments that perform a staff function must wait for management to request assistance. Often the term **client** is used by the research department to refer to line management for whom services are being performed.

The research department responds to clients' requests and is responsible for the design and execution of all research. It should function like an internal consulting organization that develops action-oriented, data-based recommendations.

In a small firm the vice-president of marketing may be in charge of marketing research. This officer generally will have the sales manager collect and analyze sales histories, trade association statistics, and other internal data. If a survey needs to be conducted, an advertising agency or a firm that specializes in marketing research will be contracted to do the job.

As marketing research departments grow, they tend to specialize by product or strategic business unit. With this in mind, Cara created a central "branding team" to fully evaluate each brand (including Second Cup, Swiss Chalet, and Harvey's), research consumers' needs, and develop marketing to support their efforts.[9] Each business unit's research director reports to the vice-president of corporate marketing services. Many large organizations have **managers of customer quality research,** who specialize in conducting surveys to measure consumers' satisfaction with product quality.

A large company like Johnson & Johnson may staff its research departments with more than 100 people. Exhibit 3.3 illustrates the organization of the marketing research department of a major firm. Within this organization the centralized marketing research department conducts research for all of the division's product groups. This is typical of a large research department that conducts much of its own research, including fieldwork. The director of marketing research reports to the vice-president of marketing.

Director of data collection (field supervisor), manager of quantitative research, focus group moderator, and manager of data processing are other positions in the marketing research industry. These are not shown in Exhibit 3.3. Some large organizations use outside marketing research contractors for this type of work; others conduct it in-house. We will discuss fieldwork, focus groups, and data processing elsewhere in the book. For now, we turn our attention to the job of director of marketing research and the interface between the marketing research department and other departments.

client
Term often used by the research department to refer to line management for whom services are being performed.

manager of customer quality research
A research staff person who specializes in conducting surveys to measure consumer's satisfaction with product quality.

WHAT WENT WRONG?

GETTING THE JOB DONE

Many years ago, I discovered what my role was when I was just learning how to run a market research department.[10] I was in a company where the chief executive officer took it upon himself to get to know his young managers. Periodically he would invite me to have lunch with him. Conversation ranged from topics that were on his mind to questions about what we were learning in market research that would help the company grow.

As a shrewd man, he'd learned the value of developing alternative channels of communication about what was going on in the organization and about pros and cons of decisions that would sooner or later reach his desk. He was also a very shrewd and demanding motivator of people.

At lunch once he asked me, "How many people do we have in this market research department now?" I mumbled something to the effect that we were overworked and didn't have enough people. He continued and asked me, "About how much money do we spend on market research totally—both the people and the project costs?"

I'd tell him and then explain that we weren't spending as much per sales dollar as our principal competitors and that we had very rigid controls on costs and on project approvals. He'd nod and explain to me how many dollars' worth of merchandise a salesperson

had to sell in a year simply to pay the expense of my department.

After catching my attention, he'd proceed with the topic that was on his mind. Some major marketing-oriented project had failed—I can't remember now whether it was a new product, a new advertising campaign, a new promotion, or just what it was. In any case the failure was clear and visible in the organization.

Then he asked me, "With all these people and all this money we spend in market research, how come we didn't have the marketing intelligence to tell us that this project wasn't going to succeed?" I said that the research we had done had raised serious questions about whether the project should go ahead. His response was, "Well, if we had reason to believe that this project wasn't going to succeed, why did we go ahead?"

My reply was, "Well, we tried to tell the brand group that it wasn't going to succeed, but they really believed in the project and they wanted to go ahead and so they ignored us and went ahead."

Then followed a long, deathly silence. Then he looked me straight in the eye, smiled, and said, "Well, you didn't get your job done, did you?" And that's how I learned what the role of market research should be in a corporation.

The Director of Marketing Research as a Manager

director of marketing research
The person who plans, executes, and controls the marketing research function.

The **director of marketing research** plans, executes, and controls the marketing research function. This person typically serves on executive committees that identify competitive opportunities and formulate marketing strategies for the organization. The director's responsibility is to provide the research point of view on these strategic issues.

Directors of marketing research must remember that they are managers rather than researchers. Marketing research directors tend to face several typical problems:

1. Skilled professionals find greater allure in conducting research than in managing people. They pride themselves on being hands-on researchers.
2. Operating managers perceive managers as chief project directors and expect them to do the work themselves. The research management role is not recognized.
3. Many able practitioners have trouble delegating responsibility. They may secretly fear the loss of control, or they may genuinely feel "I can do it better myself." Some may be loath to surrender the plaudits that often go to those who actually work on a project.
4. Some research managers view their staffs as mere extensions of their own capabilities, as extra arms and legs. Because managers cannot possibly do everything

EXHIBIT 3.3

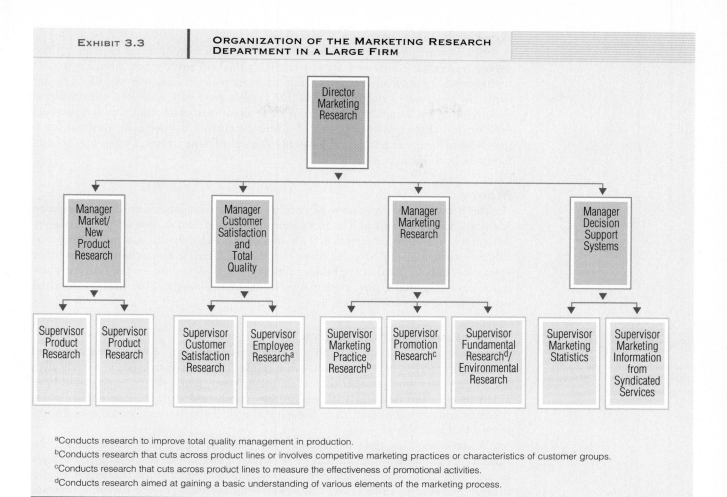

aConducts research to improve total quality management in production.

bConducts research that cuts across product lines or involves competitive marketing practices or characteristics of customer groups.

cConducts research that cuts across product lines to measure the effectiveness of promotional activities.

dConducts research aimed at gaining a basic understanding of various elements of the marketing process.

well themselves, this practice is bound to create problems. They may produce shoddy work, or they will be unable to attract or retain able staff.

5. Finally, research is often seen as a hodgepodge of techniques available to answer individual, unrelated questions. According to this view, a research operation encompasses an array of more or less equal projects, each handled by a project director. Hence, a full-time leader seems unnecessary.[11]

Many organizations have an infrequent need for marketing research. They may conduct little research in-house. Rather, their marketing research managers may rely heavily on outside research suppliers or consultants when the need for a study arises. In these organizations the marketing research manager's primary responsibilities involve communicating research needs to outside research suppliers and evaluating research proposals. The role of marketing research suppliers is discussed later in this chapter. Chapter 4 discusses problem definition and research proposals.

Sources of Conflict Between Marketing Management and Marketing Research

In principle the functions of marketing research should merge harmoniously with the objectives of marketing management for the benefit of both parties. In practice the relationship between the marketing research department and the users of marketing research frequently is characterized by misunderstanding and conflict.

Research That Implies Criticism

A product manager who requests a survey of dealer loyalty will not be happy if the survey finds that the dealers are extremely critical of him or her. Similarly, a sales manager who informally projects a 5 percent increase in sales will not like hearing from the research department that the market potential indicates sales volume should be up by 20 percent. In each of these situations, marketing research presents information that implies criticism of a line executive's decision. In personal life a sure way to lose a friend is to be openly critical of him or her. Things are no different in business.

Money

Research budgets are a source of conflict between management and researchers. Many managers see research as an expenditure rather than an investment. Managers who have had little experience with marketing research do not understand the valuable contributions of good research. Most marketing researchers contend that research is only as good as the budget allocated for it. A researcher can become frustrated knowing that a project that initially had laudable goals has become focused instead on how to save money.

Time: Emergency Research

If research programs are not systematically planned, marketing researchers will encounter emergency requests. Too often researchers are asked to begin a study after something goes wrong rather than at an earlier stage, when the research could have aided in effective decision making. Studies conducted after trouble occurs often produce unfavourable data that disparage the decision makers, making managers leery of all research projects.

When something goes wrong, managers want the research results immediately. Researchers believe, however, that good research takes time. Marketing researchers occasionally must endure lapses from good practice because of the urgency of a project. Sometimes a marketing researcher will have to submit to the time pressure and do a quick-and-dirty study. A sudden event can make it necessary to acquire data quickly—but most rush jobs could be avoided with proper planning of the research program. If it is necessary to conduct a study under severe time limitations, the researcher should be sure to point this out to management. Overuse of such precautions, on the other hand, can cause managers to see researchers as unnecessarily cautious and to mistrust their conclusions.

Intuitive Decision Making

So far the discussion has implied that managers are decision oriented and researchers generally are not. Many line marketing managers regard marketing as an art. They enjoy flying by the seat of their pants—though you will never get them to admit it. They revel in chaos, abhor facts, and fear research. They may see research as taking the fun out of their jobs. They are action-oriented. Some executives have an image of themselves as people of action. They pride themselves on their ability to reach decisions quickly and in a crisp, authoritative manner. Thirsting for action, they become impatient with what seems to them the plodding tempo of research. Some managers may complacently believe that intuitive decisions have brought them to their present positions, so why waste time waiting for research?

DeLorean Motor Company's decision to market an expensive sports car illustrates this phenomenon. Porsche and Corvette provided competing alternatives, and few people could afford cars in this class. Yet John Z. DeLorean overestimated demand for the DMC-12 because in his mind there was nothing quite like it on the road. DeLorean's confidence and sense that he could not fail became a major problem. His own marketing research showed that perhaps 12,000 DMC-12s at most could be sold in a year, yet production was scheduled at the equivalent of 20,000 cars per year. Today, except for its role as a "time machine" in the *Back to the Future* movies, the DeLorean is barely remembered.

If managers do use research, they often request simple projects that will provide concrete results with certainty. Researchers tend to see problems as complex questions that can be answered only within probability ranges. One aspect of this conflict is the fact that a research report provides findings, but cannot make decisions. Decision-oriented executives may unrealistically expect research to make decisions for them or provide some type of guarantee that the action they take will be correct. While research provides information for decision making, it does not always remove all the uncertainties involved in complex decisions. Certain alternatives may be eliminated, but the research may reveal new aspects of a problem. Although research is a valuable decision-making tool, it does not relieve the executive of the decision-making task.

Presentation of the right facts can be extremely useful. However, decision makers often believe that researchers collect the wrong facts. Many researchers view themselves as technicians who generate numbers using sophisticated mathematical and statistical techniques; they may spend more time on technical details than on satisfying managerial needs. Each person who has a narrow perspective of another's job is a partial cause of the problem of generating limited or useless information.

A typical example is a researcher who disagrees with a marketing executive's simplified conception that all research is survey research. Without a careful definition of the problem, the executive might request that the researcher conduct a telephone survey to measure advertising effectiveness. The researcher, who sees the measurement of advertising effectiveness as a complex and expensive task, may feel pressured to deliver more than the survey promises. The researcher knows the technique is inadequate for the request and therefore may focus on more elaborate techniques.

A comparison has been made between weather reporters and marketing researchers. The average person watching a TV weather report wants to know whether he or she needs to take an umbrella to work the next day. The weather reporter provides enormous amounts of information: It's snowing in Montreal, sunny in Toronto, and raining in Vancouver. Maps full of lines showing fronts, high- and low-pressure areas, and other weather facts are extraneous information to the person who simply does not want to risk getting wet. Fortunately, most weather reporters eventually let us know if rain is in the forecast. In a similar vein, the marketing researcher may be overly technical with clients.

Future Decisions Based on Past Experience

Managers wish to predict the future, but researchers measure only current or past events. In 1957 Ford introduced the Edsel, one of the classic marketing failures of all time. One reason for the Edsel's failure was that the marketing research conducted several years before the car's introduction indicated a strong demand for a medium-priced car for the "man on his way up." By the time the car was introduced, however, consumer preference had shifted to two cars, one being a small import for the suburban wife. Not all research information is so dated, but all is based on what people have done in the past rather than what they will do in the future.

Pseudo-Research and Organizational Politics

A product manager once demanded a market test for a new product. The marketing researcher had reason to suspect that the product manager was really interested in a countrywide introduction of the product but needed a confidence booster to take this step. The exchange between them went something like this:

> *Researcher:* What if the test results are favourable?
>
> *Product manager:* Why, we'll launch the product nationally, of course.

> *Researcher:* And if the results are unfavourable?
>
> *Product manager:* They won't be. I'm sure of that.
>
> *Researcher:* But just suppose they are.
>
> *Product manager:* I don't think we should throw out a good product just because of one little market test.
>
> *Researcher:* Then why test?
>
> *Product manager:* Listen, Smith, this is a major product introduction. It's got to have some research behind it.[12]

pseudo-research
Activities that appear to be research but are conducted for the purposes of organizational politics rather than objective gathering of information.

The product manager was really telling the marketing researcher to justify a decision that already had been made. If the test market's results had contradicted the decision, the product manager would have disregarded the research. This is **pseudo-research** because it is conducted not to gather information for marketing decisions but to bolster a point of view and satisfy other needs.

The most common type of pseudo-research is performed to justify a decision that has already been made. Management is already committed, but research is still requested. For example, a media buyer who has been wined and dined regularly at the most fashionable Toronto restaurants may feel compelled to present management with some hard facts from a research study to justify the purchase of advertising space. Another example is a young manager in the new-product development groups who is highly enthusiastic about a new freeze-dried vegetable product. She knows that top management is carefully watching her progress in the firm and that this is her big opportunity. She asks the marketing research department to select a test market with a vigorous local sales effort and a strong distributor who likes to promote new products heavily because this will make her pet product look like a winner. By the time the product goes national, she will have been promoted to another job.

Occasionally marketing research is used to pass on blame for failure to another area. A product manager may deliberately request a research study with no intention of paying attention to the findings and recommendations. The manager knows that the particular project is in trouble but plays the standard game to cover up for his or her mismanagement. If the project fails, marketing research will become the scapegoat.

An ambitious subordinate or an administrator who wants to hide the source of criticism may use marketing research to disparage someone. Such misuse causes executives to view marketing research as a threat. Line executives may fear that research will undermine their authority or cast doubt on their abilities.

Pseudo-research does exist, but such projects clearly are in the minority. Nevertheless, students should know about these tactics, none of which is recommended. This book assumes that marketing research will be conducted by competent professionals who have no ulterior motives. The last part of this chapter provides a complete discussion of ethics in marketing research.

Other Areas of Conflict

The conflicts between managers and researchers are aggravated by the gap between what management demands and what research offers. Exhibit 3.4 illustrates the differences between marketing researchers and managers and details many sources of conflict between them.

Reducing the Conflict Between Management and Researchers

A solution to the conflict between managers and researchers revolves around better communication so that each will grow to understand the other's activities and needs. Over the years there has been a gradual process of education by marketing researchers to apprise management of the limitations of research as well as its strengths. Marketing managers need to better assess their information needs and work with researchers to plan the research activities that will supply this information.

Area of Potential Conflict	Top Management's Position	Marketing Researcher's Position
Research responsibility	Marketing researchers lack a sense of accountability. The sole function of the marketing researcher is to provide information.	The responsibility for research should be explicitly defined, and this responsibility should be consistently followed. The researcher should be involved with top management in decision making.
Research personnel	Marketing researchers are generally poor communicators who lack enthusiasm, skills, and imagination.	Top managers are anti-intellectual. Researchers should be hired, judged, and compensated on the basis of their research capabilities.
Budget	Research costs too much. Since the marketing research department's contribution is difficult to measure, budget cuts in the department are defensible.	"You get what you pay for." Research must have a continuing, long-term commitment from top management.
Assignments	Projects tend to be over-engineered and not executed with a sense of urgency. Researchers have a ritualized, staid approach.	Top managers make too many non-researchable or emergency requests and do not allocate sufficient time or money.
Problem definition	The marketing researcher is best equipped to define the problem; it is sufficient for the top manager to give general direction. Top managers cannot help it if circumstances change. The marketing researcher must appreciate this and be willing to respond to changes.	Researchers are often not given all the relevant facts about situations, which often change after research is under way. Top managers are generally unsympathetic to this widespread problem.
Research reporting	Most reports are dull, use too much jargon and too many qualifiers, and are not decision-oriented. Reports too often are presented after a decision has been made.	Top managers treat research reports superficially. Good research demands thorough reporting and documentation. Top managers give insufficient time to prepare good reports.
Use of research	Top managers should be free to use research as they see fit. Changes in the need for and timing of research are sometimes unavoidable.	Top managers' use of research to support a predetermined position or to confirm or excuse past decisions represents misuse. Also, it is wasteful to request research and then not use it after it has been conducted.

Just as users need education on the benefits of research, researchers need an understanding of and some experience in the areas they are researching. Better communication makes both parties more competent. Perhaps most important is more effective communication of the research findings and research designs. The researchers must understand the interests and needs of the users of the research. If the researchers are sensitive to the decision–making orientation of management and can translate research performance into management language, organizational conflict will diminish.

A **research generalist** can effectively serve as a link between management and the research specialist. The research generalist acts as a problem definer, an educator, a liaison, a communicator, and a friendly ear. This intermediary could work with specialists who understand management's needs and demands. The student of marketing research who has a business degree seems most suited for this coordinating function.

Cross-Functional Teams

As more companies awaken to the challenge of the global information age and the need to act quickly, old forms of organizational structure are fading fast. Today everyone in a progressive organization, from accountants to engineers, engages in a unified effort to consider all issues related to the development, production, or marketing of new products.

Cross-functional teams are composed of individuals from various organizational departments such as engineering, production, finance, and marketing who share a common purpose. Current management thinking suggests that cross-functional teams help organizations focus on a core business process, such as customer service or new-product development. Working in teams reduces the tendency for employees to focus single-mindedly on an isolated functional activity. The use of cross-functional teams to help employees improve product quality and increase customer value is a major trend in business today.

At trend-setting organizations many marketing research directors are members of cross-functional teams. New-product development, for example, may be done by a cross-functional team of engineers, finance executives, production personnel, marketing managers, and marketing researchers who take an integrated approach to solve a problem or exploit opportunities. In the old days marketing research may not have been involved in developing new products until long after many key decisions about product specifications and manufacturing had been made. Now marketing researchers' input is part of an integrated team effort. Researchers act both as business consultants and as providers of technical services. Researchers working in teams are more likely to understand the broad purpose of their research and less likely to focus exclusively on research methodology.

The effective cross-functional team is a good illustration of the marketing concept in action. It reflects an effort to satisfy customers by using all the organization's resources. Cross-functional teams are having a dramatic impact on views of the role of marketing research within the organization.

RESEARCH SUPPLIERS AND CONTRACTORS

The marketing research manager (in smaller firms, the marketing manager) must also interact with **research suppliers**, or commercial marketing research services. Although a great deal of marketing research activity is conducted in private companies' marketing research departments, much of it is also carried out by firms that may be variously classified as marketing research consulting companies (for example, Market Facts, Inc.), advertising agencies (such as J. Walter Thompson), suppliers of syndicated research services (such as Roper Starch Worldwide), interviewing agencies, universities, and government agencies. And with the growth of global business and the trend among firms to be "right-sized" organizations focusing on core competencies, there is more emphasis on working with research suppliers as partners.

No matter how large a firm's marketing research department is, some projects are too expensive to undertake in-house. A **syndicated service** is a marketing research supplier that provides standardized information for many clients. For example, Ipsos-Reid Canada sells research on a variety of subjects, including consumers' purchasing behaviour in the food and beverage industry. Marketers and advertisers in this sector may wish to purchase this study as it provides both basic information and strategic insight into the marketing and positioning of products.[14]

Syndicated services can provide expensive information economically to numerous clients because the information is not specific to one client but interests many. Such suppliers offer standardized information to measure media audiences, wholesale and retail distribution data, and other forms of data. For instance, AC Nielsen Canada's Internet Planner Study measures attitudes and behaviours of a large representative sample of Canadians online. The service provides relevant information to clients such as information about online purchases, online advertising, and Internet usage patterns.[15]

A number of organizations supply **standardized research services** at the request of individual clients. Typically the research organization has developed a unique methodology for investigating a specialty area, such as advertising effectiveness or brand-name evaluation. These research suppliers will conduct studies for individual clients using the same methods they use for other clients. AC Nielsen BASES is an organization that collects information throughout the new-product development process, from initial concept screening through test marketing. The BASES system can evaluate initiatives compared to other products in the competitive environment. For example, a client can compare its Day-After Recall scores with average scores for a product category.[16]

Even when a firm could perform the research task in-house, research suppliers may be able to conduct the project at a lower cost, faster, and from a completely objective perspective. A company that wishes to quickly evaluate a new advertising strategy may find an ad agency's research department is able to provide technical expertise on copy development research that is not available within the company itself.

Limited-service research suppliers specialize in particular research activities, such as syndicated service, field interviewing, or data processing. Full-service research suppliers contract for entire ad hoc marketing research projects. The client usually controls these marketing research agencies or management consulting firms, but the

standardized research service
A research organization that has developed a unique methodology for investigating a specialty area, such as advertising effectiveness.

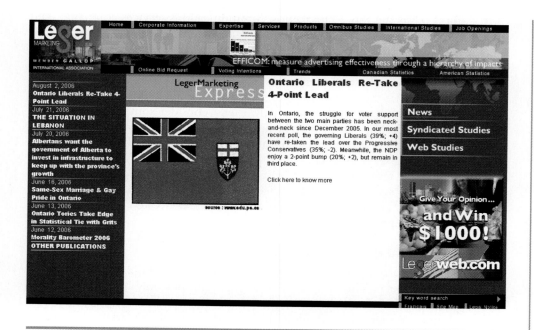

Leger Marketing is the largest independent research firm in Canada. As a research supplier, Leger Marketing conducts custom research tailored to clients' needs.[17]

Rank in 2003	Company	Head Office	Gross Revenues in 2003 (millions)
1	Cossette Communication Group	Quebec City, QC	$145.7
2	MDC Partners	Toronto, ON	65.6
3	Maritz Canada	Mississauga, ON	49.3
4	Carlson Marketing Group Canada	Toronto, ON	39.9
5	Nurun	Montreal, QC	24.5
6	Marketel	Montreal, QC	20.0
7	Allard Johnson Communications	Toronto, ON	18.3
8	Blast Radius	Vancouver, BC	16.4
9	Sharpe Blackmore Euro RSCG	Toronto, ON	12.8
10	Beauchesne, Ostiguy & Simard	Montreal, QC	12.0
11	Palm Publicité Marketing	Montreal, QC	11.9
12	Bristol Group	St. John's, NL	11.8
13	Marketing Communication Group	London, ON	11.2
14	Gee Jeffery & Partners Advertising	Toronto, ON	9.3
15	Diesel Marketing	Montreal, QC	8.7
16	DCC Communications	Toronto, ON	8.4
17	Capital C Communications	Toronto, ON	8.2
18	Ambrose Carr Linton Carroll	Toronto, ON	6.9
19	Venture Communications	Calgary, AB	6.9
20	Wasserman & Partners Advertising	Vancouver, BC	6.4

custom research
A marketing research study designed for an individual client and tailored to the client's unique needs.

research supplier handles most of the operating details of the **custom research** projects, tailoring them to the client's unique needs. A custom research supplier may employ individuals with titles that imply relationships with clients, such as *account executive* or *account group manager,* as well as functional specialists with titles such as *statistician, librarian, director of field services, director of tabulation and data processing,* and *interviewer.*

Exhibit 3.5 lists the top 20 marketing communications services companies and their revenues in 2003. In Canada, Ipsos Canada, AC Nielsen Canada, TNS Canadian Facts, Pollara, and Leger Marketing are large marketing research companies with offices in major Canadian cities. Most of these firms provide a variety of services, ranging from design activities to fieldwork. Their services are not covered in detail here because they are discussed throughout the book, especially in the sections on fieldwork. However, here we will briefly consider some managerial and human aspects of dealing with research suppliers.

In many cases the marketing research manager's job is primarily administrative: hiring interviewing services, data processing services, and so on. When it is necessary to hire outside research suppliers or contractors, the marketing researcher must be able to evaluate such specialized services. An analogy is the make-or-buy decision in the factory: The researcher can hire a research service to conduct the project or conduct the project with in-house personnel.

Considerations in Hiring Outside Suppliers

Expertise acquired from experience in similar situations may be a major reason for hiring outside suppliers. This consideration is important not only in the purchase of syndicated services but also in hiring an organization for a custom study. For example, Name Lab has considerable methodological expertise to help a marketer evaluate a brand name for a new product or service. Outside researchers may be experts in the latest statistical procedures or other complex techniques with which someone within the organization may be unfamiliar. On the other side of the coin, especially for marketers of technically complex industrial products, research suppliers often lack sufficient familiarity with a product or its customers to do an adequate job. The urgency of the decision and the company's own personnel resources influence the decision to use outside suppliers. When there are time pressures and the internal staff is busy with other projects, managers may decide to buy rather than make research. Of course, obtaining data quickly may be costly; economic factors are always important. The need for objectivity is another consideration. Outside consultants may be able to look objectively at a problem without concern for internal politics. If two internal interest groups espouse different solutions to a particular problem, the research consultant may provide answers without fear of reprisal from within the organization. The consultant is able to look at a problem with a fresh perspective rather than the possibly biased point of view of an internal employee.

A dramatic, innovative change in an organization's marketing plan may require secrecy. If confidentiality is a prime consideration, it may be best to have internal personnel conduct the research. The need for quality control is still another consideration that may influence the make-or-buy decision.

A major problem with research suppliers is the high variability of their performances. Suppliers may range from highly qualified, full-service agencies to hustlers, charlatans, and thieves. On rare occasions, an unethical or unqualified researcher will even misrepresent findings. Identifying unqualified research suppliers before the contract is signed is not always easy. Managers should be wary of contractors who offer research at unusually low prices. The technical specifications of a study (such as sample size and data collection procedure) should be carefully scrutinized and the reputation of the firm thoroughly checked. Many marketing research books depict the researcher as a knight in shining armour who exposes the truth. The low-cost research agency that skips some of the details of research may be more like the dragon than the knight. However, most marketing researchers are highly competent professionals. Most students of marketing research will become managers who must evaluate researchers. The following chapters provide information that will enable managers to make selection decisions that bypass or eliminate from serious consideration inept or unethical marketing research suppliers.

ETHICAL ISSUES IN MARKETING RESEARCH

As in all human interactions, there are ethical issues in marketing research. Our earlier discussion of organizational politics and the use of pseudo-research to bolster one's position within the organization illustrated situations where ethics come into play. This book considers various ethical issues concerning fair business dealings, proper research techniques, and appropriate use of research results in other chapters. The remainder of this chapter addresses society's and managers' concerns about the ethical implications of marketing research.

Ethical Questions Are Philosophical Questions

Ethical questions are philosophical questions. There is no general agreement among philosophers about the answers to such questions. However, the rights and obligations of individuals generally are dictated by the norms of society. **Societal norms** are codes of behaviour adopted by a group; they suggest what a member of the group ought to do under given circumstances. This section reflects the authors' perceptions of the norms of our society (and undoubtedly their own values to some extent).[19]

societal norms
Codes of behaviour adopted by a group that suggest what a member of the group ought to do under given circumstances.

EXHIBIT 3.6 | INTERACTION OF RIGHTS AND OBLIGATIONS

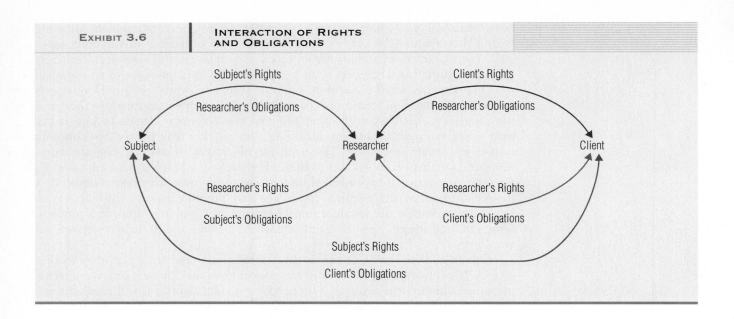

General Rights and Obligations of Concerned Parties

Most research situations involve three parties: the researcher, the sponsoring client (user), and the respondent (or subject). The interaction of each party with one or both of the other two identifies a series of ethical questions. Consciously or unconsciously, each party expects certain rights and feels certain obligations toward the other parties. Exhibit 3.6 diagrams this relationship. Every society imposes a set of normatively prescribed expectations of behaviour (including rights and obligations) associated with a social role, such as researcher, and another, reciprocal role, such as respondent. Certain ethical behaviours may be expected only in specific situations, while other expectations may be more generalized. Conflicting perspectives about behavioural expectations may create ethical problems. For instance, several ethical issues concern the researcher's expected rights versus those of the respondent/subject. A number of questions arise because researchers believe they have the right to seek information, but subjects believe they have a right to privacy. A respondent who says, "I don't care to answer your question about my income" believes that he or she has the right to refuse to participate. Yet some researchers will persist in trying to get that information. In general, a fieldworker is expected not to overstep the boundary society places on consumer privacy.

For each of the subject's rights there is a corresponding obligation on the part of the researcher. For example, the individual's right to privacy dictates that the researcher has an obligation to protect the anonymity of the respondent. When that respondent discloses information about personal matters, it is assumed that such information will be guarded from all people other than the researcher.

Rights and Obligations of the Respondent

The ethical issues vary somewhat depending on whether the participant has given willing and informed consent. The notion of **informed consent** means that the individual understands the reason for the research and waives his or her right to privacy when he or she agrees to participate in the research study. (The rights of a participant in an unobtrusive observation study differ from a survey respondent's rights because he or she has not willingly consented to be a subject of the research.)

informed consent
Notion that the individual understands the reason for the research and waives his or her right to privacy when he or she agrees to participate in the research study.

The Obligation to Be Truthful

When a subject willingly consents to participate, it is generally expected that he or she will provide truthful answers. Honest cooperation is the main obligation of the respondent or subject. In return for being truthful, the subject has the right to expect confidentiality and anonymity. (*Privacy* refers to the issue of whether a respondent chooses to answer a researcher's questions; a person may choose to protect her privacy by not answering. *Confidentiality* refers to the obligation on the part of the researcher not to reveal the identity of an individual research subject. A person who waives her right to privacy by agreeing to answer a researcher's questions nonetheless has a right to expect that her answers and her identity will remain confidential.) Privacy and confidentiality are profound ethical issues in marketing research.

Privacy

Most North Americans relish their privacy. Hence, the right to privacy is an important issue in marketing research. This issue involves the subject's freedom to choose whether to comply with the investigator's request. Traditionally, researchers have assumed that individuals make an informed choice. However, critics have argued that the old, the poor, the poorly educated, and other underprivileged individuals may be unaware of their right to choose. They have further argued that an interviewer may begin with some vague explanation of a survey's purpose, initially ask questions that are relatively innocuous, and then move to questions of a highly personal nature. It has been suggested that subjects be informed of their right to be left alone or to break off the interview at any time. Researchers should not follow the tendency to "hold on" to busy respondents. However, this view definitely is not universally accepted in the research community.

Another aspect of the privacy issue is illustrated by this question: "Is a telephone call that interrupts someone's favourite television program an invasion of privacy?" The answer to this issue—and to most privacy questions—lies in the dilemma of where the rights of the individual end and the needs of society for better scientific information on consumer preference take over. Generally, certain standards of common courtesy have been set by interviewing firms, for example, not to interview late in the evening and at other inconvenient times. However, several critics may never be appeased. The computerized interview (sometimes called a *junk phone call*) has stimulated increased debate over this aspect of the privacy issue. As a practical matter, respondents may feel more relaxed about privacy issues if they know who is conducting the survey. Thus it is generally recommended that field interviewers indicate that they are legitimate researchers by passing out business cards, wearing name tags, or in other ways identifying the names of their companies.

In an observation study the major ethical issues concern whether the observed behaviour is public or private. Generally it is believed that unobtrusive observation of public behaviour in places such as stores, airports, and museums is not a serious invasion of privacy. However, recording private behaviour with hidden cameras and the like represents a violation of this right. For example, in a survey almost all research directors and line marketing executives disapproved of the practice of observing women through a one-way mirror as they tried on bras.

Deception

In a number of situations the researcher creates a false impression by disguising the purpose of the research. The researcher, at least at the outset of the research, is not open and honest. Bluntly stated, to avoid biased reactions, the researchers lie to subjects. Deception or concealment may be used if a researcher would otherwise be unable to observe or straightforwardly ask about the phenomena of interest and hold all other factors constant. Generally, such deception is justified under two conditions: (1) The researcher ensures that no physical danger or psychological harm will result from the deception, and (2) the researcher takes personal responsibility for informing the respondent of the concealment or deception after the research project ends.

The issue of deception is interrelated with the subject's right to be informed and with the means-to-an-end philosophical issue. The primary question is, does a minor deception substantially increase the value of the research? Suppose a survey research project involves contacting busy executives. Pretending to be calling long distance might improve the response rate, but is this a justifiable means to this end?

A distinction has been made between deception and discreet silence. The ethical question concerning the manifest content of a questionnaire versus the true purpose of the research has been cleverly stated as follows:

> Must we really explain, when we ask the respondent to agree or disagree with the statement, "prison is too good for sex criminals; they should be publicly whipped or worse," it is really the authoritarianism of his personality we are investigating, and not the public opinion on crime and punishment?[20]

The Right to Be Informed

It has been argued that subjects have a right to be informed of all aspects of the research. This includes information about its purpose and sponsorship. The argument for the researcher's obligation to protect this right is based on the academic tradition of informing and enlightening the public.

A pragmatic argument for providing respondents with information about the nature of the study concerns the long-run ability of researchers to gain cooperation from respondents. If the public understands why survey or experimental information has been collected and that the researchers may be trusted with private information, it may be easier in the long run to conduct research. Several research suppliers have suggested that public relations work is needed to convince consumers of the integrity of the research industry.

Rights and Obligations of the Researcher

(7)

General business ethics should be a standard for marketing research firms and marketing research departments. Our concern is not with issues such as bribery or the welfare and safety of one's employees, but with ethical issues that are specifically germane to marketing research practices.

More has been written about the ethics of researchers than about those of the other two parties because this group's purpose is clearly identifiable. Researchers have obligations to both subjects and clients as well as corresponding rights. A number of professional associations have developed standards and operating procedures for ethical practices by researchers. Exhibit 3.7 presents the **code of ethics** for the Canadian Marketing Association.

code of ethics
A set of guidelines that states the standards and operating procedures for ethical practices by researchers.

The Purpose of Research Is Research

It is considered unacceptable to misrepresent a sales tactic as marketing research. The use of schemes or misrepresenting the purpose as research to gain admission to a prospect's home, office, or other establishment is unethical and hurts the public as well as the research agencies. Founded in 2004 as a merger of the Canadian Association of Market Research Organizations (CAMRO), the Canadian Survey Research Council (CSRC), and the Professional Marketing Research Society (PMRS), the Marketing Research and Intelligence Association (MRIA) is an important Canadian not-for-profit association that monitors the marketing research activities of its more than 1,500 members. MRIA provides a large number of services to the marketing research sector and the general public in Canada, including the establishment of strict standards for marketing research professionals, ethical and practice standards, accreditation and audit services, publications, and conferences. For instance, the Survey Registration System of MRIA allows the public to verify

B. PURPOSE OF CMA CODE OF ETHICS AND STANDARDS OF PRACTICE

The CMA Code of Ethics and Standards of Practice (the "Code") is designed to establish and maintain standards for the conduct of marketing in Canada. Marketers acknowledge that the establishment and maintenance of high standards of practice are a fundamental responsibility to the public, essential to winning and holding consumer confidence, and the foundation of a successful and independent marketing industry in Canada. Members of the Canadian Marketing Association recognize an obligation – to the consumers and the businesses they serve, to the integrity of the discipline in which they operate and to each other – to practice to the highest standards of honesty, truth, accuracy, fairness and professionalism.

H. OVERARCHING ETHICAL PRINCIPLES

H1 Personal Information Practices

Marketers must promote responsible and transparent personal information management practices in a manner consistent with the provisions of the Personal Information Protection and Electronic Documents Act (Canada) and/or applicable provincial legislation and the 10 privacy principles detailed in <u>Section J</u> of this Code.

H2 Truthfulness

Marketing communications must be clear and truthful. Marketers must not knowingly make a representation to a consumer or business that is false or misleading.

H3 Campaign Limitations

H3.1: Marketers must not participate in any campaign involving the disparagement or exploitation of any person or group on the grounds of race, colour, ethnicity, religion, national origin, gender, sexual orientation, marital status or age.

H3.2: Marketers must not participate in the dissemination of unsolicited material that is sexually explicit, vulgar or indecent in nature, except where required to do so by law, such as a common carrier.

H3.3: Marketers must not participate in the dissemination of any material that unduly, gratuitously and without merit exploits sex, horror, mutilation, torture, cruelty, violence or hate, except where required to do so by law, such as a common carrier.

H3.4: Marketers must not knowingly exploit the credulity, lack of knowledge or inexperience of any consumer, taking particular care when dealing with vulnerable consumers. The term "vulnerable consumer" includes, but is not limited to children, teenagers, people with disabilities, the elderly and those for whom English or French is not their first language.

I. UNIVERSAL MARKETING PRACTICES

These practices apply regardless of industry sector, sub-discipline or marketing medium employed.

I1 Accuracy of Representation

I1.1: Marketers must not misrepresent a product, service or marketing program and must not mislead by statement or manner of demonstration or comparison

I1.2: Photography, artwork, type size, colour, contrast, style, placement, verbal description and audio-visual portrayal must accurately and fairly describe the product or service offered.

I1.3: Marketers must ensure that the general impression of the communication does not deceive by omission or commission.

I2 Clarity: Marketing communications must be executed in a manner that is simple and easy to understand.

I3 Disclaimers: Disclaimers in any medium must be prominent and easily accessible, in close proximity to the representations to which they relate. Disclaimers must not be used to contradict claims but to provide additional information.

I4 Support for Claims: Test or survey data referred to in any marketing communication must be reliable, accurate and current and must support the specific claim being made. Marketers must be able to substantiate the basis for any performance claim or comparison and must not imply a scientific, factual or statistical basis where none exists.

I5 Disguise: Marketers must not claim to be carrying out a survey or research when their real purpose is to sell a product or service, or to raise funds.

I6 Testimonials: Testimonials and endorsements must be: a) authorized by the person or organization quoted; b) genuine and related to the experience of the person or organization quoted, both at the time made and at the time of the marketing communication; c) positioned as opinion, not fact, unless supported by valid research; and d) not taken out of context so as to distort the opinion or experience of the person or organization quoted.

I7 Timeliness: Descriptions and promises must reflect actual conditions, situations and circumstances existing at the time of the promotion.

(For more information and to view the complete code, visit: http://www.the-cma.org/regulatory/codeofethics.cfm)

the legitimacy of a survey and to register a complaint against a member company through a toll-free number. In addition to public benefits, the service also helps the research agencies in enhancing their credibility and differentiating their services from practices that hurt the industry, such as telemarketing.[21]

Objectivity

The need for objective scientific investigation to ensure accuracy is stressed throughout this book. Researchers should maintain high standards to ensure that their data are accurate. Furthermore, they must not intentionally try to prove a particular point for political purposes.

Misrepresentation of Research

Research companies (and clients) should not misrepresent the statistical accuracy of their data, nor should they overstate the significance of the results by altering the findings. Basically, the researcher has the obligation to both the client and the subjects to analyze the data honestly and to report the actual data collection methods correctly. For example, the failure to report a variation from a technically correct probability sampling procedure is ethically questionable. Likewise, any major error that has occurred during the course of the study should not be kept secret from management or the sponsor. Hiding errors or variations from the proper procedures tends to distort or shade the results. A more blatant breach of the researcher's responsibilities would be the outright distortion of data, such as excluding or changing neutral responses.

Protecting the Right to Confidentiality of Both Subjects and Clients

A number of clients might desire a list of favourable industrial sales prospects generated from a research survey. It is the researcher's responsibility to ensure that the privacy and anonymity of the respondents are preserved. If the respondent's name and address are known, this information should not be forwarded to the sponsoring organization under any circumstances.

Information that a research supplier obtains about a client's general business affairs should not be disseminated to other clients or third parties. The client or user of marketing research has a number of rights and obligations. The primary right is to expect objective and accurate data from the research supplier. The client should also be able to expect respect for any instructions of confidentiality.

Dissemination of Faulty Conclusions

The Canadian Marketing Association's Code of Ethics states that "test or survey data referred to shall be competent, reliable and must support the specific claim for which it is cited. No claim shall imply—by statement, illustration or presentation—a scientific, factual or statistical basis where none exists."[22] A dramatic example of a violation of this principle occurred in an advertisement of a cigarette smoker study. The advertisement compared two brands and stated that "of those expressing a preference, over 65 percent preferred" the advertised brand to a competing brand. The misleading portion of this reported result was that most of the respondents did *not* express a preference; they indicated that both brands tasted about the same. Thus only a very small percentage of those studied actually revealed a preference, and the results were somewhat misleading. Such shading of results violates the obligation to report accurate findings.

The Marketing Research and Intelligence Association's (MRIA) Code of Conduct for members provides detailed coverage of some of the issues discussed. See Exhibit 3.8 for the core principles of MRIA's Code of Conduct for members.

EXHIBIT 3.8 | TEN CORE PRINCIPLES OF MRIA'S CODE OF CONDUCT[23]

PRINCIPLE 1: CONSENT

Contact with members of the public is at all times to be undertaken with their consent and with observance of their right to withdraw at any time.

PRINCIPLE 2: PUBLIC CONFIDENCE

Members should act in a manner that serves to promote and augment, not diminish, the confidence of the public in research in general.

PRINCIPLE 3: PUBLIC'S RIGHT TO PRIVACY

The use of research data should extend only to those purposes for which consent was received. The public's desire for privacy and anonymity is to be respected.

PRINCIPLE 4: ACCURACY

Members agree to recommend those research methods which are appropriate to the research goals, and to avoid conducting research which would be inaccurate or misleading. Members must be accurate in all aspects of research and refrain from purporting or suggesting levels of accuracy which are greater than is warranted by the nature of the research. Members shall report and interpret their results in a manner that represents these results accurately and acknowledges such limitations on the research which, in the absence of such acknowledgement, might mislead.

PRINCIPLE 5: ETHICAL PRACTICE

Members shall at all times act honestly, ethically and fairly in their dealings with all members of the public, clients, employers, sub-contractors and each other. They will refrain from activities which show disrespect or otherwise unjustifiably demean, criticize or disparage others.

PRINCIPLE 6: CLIENT RIGHTS

Members shall protect the interests of their clients and clients' rights to confidentiality. Members shall ensure that records of research will be held for the appropriate periods and that these will be protected from theft, misuse and inadvertent destruction.

PRINCIPLE 7: LAWFULNESS

Members, in their conduct of research, shall abide by the prevailing provincial, national and international legislation which applies to the research they conduct.

PRINCIPLE 8: COMPETENCY

Members agree to uphold high standards of general competency in the design, execution, analysis, reporting, interpretation and consulting phases of all research.

PRINCIPLE 9: FAMILIARITY

Members will undertake to keep themselves, their co-workers and clients informed about the code of conduct to avoid breaches of it, and will undertake also to inform themselves of any recent changes made by assessing, where necessary, such sources as the MRIA website or other material.

PRINCIPLE 10: PROFESSIONALISM

Members commit themselves to the goal of seeking to continuously improve themselves in their chosen profession.

AIR CANADA IN TROUBLE

In 2001, Air Canada mailed out brochures to its Aeroplan customers, titled "All about your privacy." The brochure explained, in detail, why Air Canada wanted to collect certain information and how Aeroplan members could benefit from its collection by being offered tailored products and services from the airline and its allied business partners. The company also explained to its customers how they could, if they wished, opt out of having the information collected and shared with other companies.

However, Canada's privacy commissioner, George Radwanski, started an investigation into whether Air Canada was violating the Personal Information Protection and Electronic Documents Act (PIPEDA) and asked Air Canada to suspend its direct mail and data collection program immediately.

Radwanski's concern was that the brochure placed the responsibility on the customers to "opt out" of having their information collected and shared. Although the collection and sharing of information is not always against the law, legislation dictates that customers should be asked to "opt in" if the information collected is of a sensitive nature (e.g., health, finances). Air Canada, however, indicated on the brochure that it would gather information and share that information with its business allies unless customers notified Air Canada otherwise. More interestingly, Air Canada did not include this statement on half of the 60,000 brochures sent out in an attempt simply to compare the consumer reactions to the "opt-out" format. Nevertheless, Air Canada immediately agreed to the privacy commissioner's requests and agreed not to collect or to process the data.[24]

Competing Research Proposals

Consider a client who has solicited several bids for a marketing research project. The client asks the research supplier that wins the bid to appropriate ideas from the proposal of a competing research supplier and include them in the research study. This generally is regarded as unethical.

Rights and Obligations of the Client Sponsor (User)

Ethical Behaviour Between Buyer and Seller

The general business ethics expected between a purchasing agent and a sales representative should hold in the marketing research situation. For example, if the purchasing agent has already decided to purchase a product (or research proposal) from a friend, it would be unethical for that person to solicit competitive bids that have no chance of being accepted just to fulfill a corporate purchasing policy stating that a bid must be put out to some number of competitors.

An Open Relationship with Research Suppliers

The client sponsor has the obligation to encourage the research supplier to objectively seek out the truth. To encourage this objectivity, a full and open statement of the problem, explication of constraints in time and money, and any other insights that may help the supplier anticipate costs and problems should be provided. In other words, the research sponsor should encourage efforts to reduce bias and to listen to the voice of the public.

An Open Relationship with Interested Parties

Conclusions should be based on the data. A user of research should not knowingly disseminate conclusions from a research project or service that are inconsistent with or not warranted by the data. Violation of this principle is perhaps the greatest transgression that a client can commit. Justifying a self-serving or political position that is not supported by the data poses serious ethical questions. Indicating that the data show something in order to make a sale is also ethically questionable.

advocacy research
Research undertaken to support a
specific claim in a legal action.

Advocacy research—research undertaken to support a specific claim in a legal action—puts a client in a unique situation. Advocacy research, such as a survey conducted to show that a brand name is not a generic name, differs from research that traditionally has been intended for internal use only. The conventional factors, such as sample size, people to be interviewed, and questions to be asked, are weighed against cost when making an internal decision. A court's opinion of the value of advocacy research may be based exclusively on sampling design or some methodological issue. Thus the slightest variation from technically correct sampling procedures may be magnified by a lawyer until a standard marketing research project no longer appears adequate in the judge's eye. How open should the client be in the courtroom?

The question of advocacy research is one of objectivity: Can the researcher seek out the truth when the sponsoring client wishes to support its position at a trial? The ethical question stems from a conflict between legal ethics and research ethics. Although the courts have set judicial standards for marketing research methodology, perhaps only the client and individual researcher can resolve this question.

Privacy

People believe the collection and distribution of personal information without their knowledge is a serious violation of their privacy. The privacy rights of subjects create a privacy obligation on the part of the client. Suppose a database marketing company is offering a mailing list compiled by screening millions of households to obtain brand usage information. The information would be extremely valuable to your firm, but you suspect those individuals who filled out the information forms were misled into thinking they were participating in a survey. Would it be ethical to purchase the mailing list? If respondents have been deceived about the purpose of a survey and their names subsequently are sold as part of a user mailing list, this practice is certainly unethical. The client and the research supplier have the obligation to maintain respondents' privacy.

Consider another example. Sales managers know that a marketing research survey of their business-to-business customers' buying intentions includes a means to attach a customer's name to each questionnaire. This confidential information could be of benefit to a sales representative calling on a specific customer. A client wishing to be ethical must resist the temptation to identify those accounts (that is, those respondents) who are the hottest prospects.

Privacy on the Internet

Privacy on the Internet is a controversial issue. A number of groups question whether Web site questionnaires, registration forms, and other means of collecting personal information are legitimate. Many marketers argue that their organizations don't need to know who the user is because the individual's name is not important for their purposes. However, they do want to know certain information (such as demographic characteristics or product usage) associated with an anonymous profile. For instance, a Web advertiser could reach a targeted audience without having access to identifying information. Of course, unethical companies may violate anonymity guidelines.

AOL Canada's privacy policy states that the company "will not use or disclose information about [a customer's] individual visits to AOL.CA or information [given] such as [the customer's] name, address, E-mail address or telephone number, to any outside companies. [AOL Canada will] not specifically collect information about children and believe that children should get their parents' consent before giving out any personal information."[25] Research shows that people are more willing to disclose sensitive information if they know the Web site's privacy policy.[26]

For this reason, many high-traffic Web sites such as Yahoo and Lycos have privacy statements that visitors can easily access. Organizations such as the Electronic Frontier Foundation and the Online Privacy Alliance are involved in developing privacy guidelines.

TRUSTe (http://www.truste.org) is a third-party organization that evaluates Web sites' privacy policies, certifies Web sites, and issues a seal of trust to organizations that meet its privacy standards.[27] TRUSTe classifies sites into three categories: "no exchange" sites, where no personal user data are collected; "one-to-one exchange" sites that collect user data for their own purposes but do not share them with third parties; and "third-party exchange" sites that share the information with others. "One-to-one exchange" sites are permitted to share user data—such as credit card numbers, names, and addresses—with business partners in order to complete transactions as long as the business partners agree not to collect the user data themselves.[28]

Commitment to Research

Some potential clients have been known to request research proposals from research suppliers when there is a low probability that the research will be conducted. A research consultant's opinion may be solicited even though management is not really planning research and funds have not been allocated for the project. For example, obtaining an outsider's opinion of a company problem via a research proposal provides an inexpensive consultation. If the information supports a given manager's position in an ongoing debate within the company, it could be used politically rather than as a basis for research. Most research practitioners believe that because the research supplier must spend considerable effort planning a custom-designed study, the client has the obligation to solicit proposals only for seriously considered projects.

Pseudo-Pilot Studies

Clients should be open about the marketing problem to be investigated. However, there is a special case of this problem that should be explained. Sometimes a client suggests that a more comprehensive study is in the planning stages and the proposal the research supplier is bidding on is a pilot study. The research consultant is told that if his or her company does a good job during the pilot study stages, there will be an additional major contract down the line. Too often such pilot studies lead to nothing more; the comprehensive study never materializes, and the consultant must absorb a loss.

A Final Note on Ethics

There are certainly unethical researchers in the world and a number of shady dealings do occur. But marketing researchers are no different from other business people—or from people in general, for that matter. One may occasionally run across a researcher who produces a report on fabricated findings. Likewise, interviewers occasionally cheat by filling out the questionnaires themselves. (In pre-Castro Cuba there was at least one firm that, for a fee, would provide a handsomely engraved certificate attesting that the Court of Public Opinion held the client or his products in whatever kind of high esteem might be desired—with no extra charge for percentages.) Under some circumstances even honest researchers take shortcuts, some of which may be ethically questionable. However, researchers, like most business people, generally are ethical. The answer to the question "What is ethical?" is not easy—only one's conscience can prevent any questionable practice.

SUMMARY

1 Different firms have varying degrees of marketing research sophistication. In the first stage of such sophistication, firms ignore research and rely on intuition. In the second stage, they are naively impressed with marketing research and expect it to remove all risk from marketing decisions. During this stage managers may become disillusioned with research because they have made costly mistakes based on poor research findings. A firm in the last stage has a realistic appreciation for marketing research and uses it as a tool to reduce risk rather than as a way to foretell the future.

A marketing research function may be organized in any number of ways depending on a firm's size, business, and stage of research sophistication. Marketing research managers must remember they are managers, not just researchers.

2 There are several sources of conflict between marketing managers and marketing researchers. Managers may be unhappy if research shows they are doing a poor job, or they may use research to pass the buck when they encounter difficulty. Managers with narrow conceptions of research may expect it to deliver sophisticated results with overly simplified procedures. In addition, managers may resent attempts to reduce intuitive decision making, or they may commission pseudo-research for political reasons rather than for discovering facts. Finally, unrealistic time and money constraints may preclude effective research.

There are many ways to reduce the conflict between researchers and managers. Mutual education, improved planning, emphasis on effective communication, and use of research generalists as go-betweens may all be helpful.

3 **4** Research suppliers and contractors can augment the research staff of a small firm, or they can provide services impossible for even large firms to handle internally. However, some of these firms are unreliable, do a sloppy job, or even falsify results. Managers need to exercise care in using such services, especially when they offer research at unrealistically low prices.

5 **6** **7** There is no general agreement about the answers to ethical questions that surround marketing research. However, societal norms suggest codes of conduct that are appropriate in given circumstances. There are three concerned parties in marketing research situations: the researcher, the sponsoring client (user), and the respondent (subject). Each party has certain rights and obligations. The respondent's rights include the right to privacy and the right to be informed about all aspects of the research; his or her main obligation is to give honest answers to research questions. The researcher is expected to adhere to the purpose of the research; maintain objectivity; avoid misrepresenting research findings; protect subjects' and clients' right to confidentiality; and avoid shading research conclusions. The client is obligated to observe general business ethics when dealing with research suppliers; avoid misusing research findings to support its aims; respect research respondents' privacy;

and be open about its intentions to conduct research and the marketing problem to be investigated. A serious challenge to objectivity occurs when advocacy research—research conducted to support a specific legal claim—is undertaken.

Key Terms and Concepts

research sophistication
client
manager of customer quality research
director of marketing research
pseudo-research

research generalist
cross-functional teams
research supplier
syndicated service
standardized research service

custom research
societal norms
informed consent
code of ethics
advocacy research

Questions for Review and Critical Thinking

1. What are the stages of marketing research sophistication? Name some companies that you think are in each stage.
2. What might the organizational structure of the research department be like for the following organizations?
   a. A large advertising agency
   b. A founder-owned company that operates a 20-unit restaurant chain
   c. Your university
   d. An industrial marketer with four product divisions
   e. A large consumer products company
3. What problems do marketing research directors face in their roles as managers?
4. What are some of the basic causes of conflict between top management and marketing research?
5. Comment on the following situation: A product manager asks the research department to forecast costs for some basic ingredients (raw materials) for a new product. The researcher asserts that this is not a research job; it is a production forecast.
6. What is the difference between research and pseudo-research? Cite several examples of each.
7. To whom should marketing research be accountable?
8. How can a marketing researcher help top management better understand the functions and limitations of research?
9. Identify a research supplier in your area, and determine what syndicated services and other functions are available to clients.
10. What do you think would be the best way to find work in marketing research?
11. Go to the library to learn the job titles and responsibilities for the various types of marketing research jobs. (*Hint:* One of the best sources is Thomas Kinnear and Ann Root, eds., *1994 Survey of Marketing Research* [Chicago: American Marketing Association, 1995].)
12. Comment on the ethics of the following situations:
    a. A food warehouse club advertises "savings up to 30 percent" after a survey showed a range of savings from 2 percent to 30 percent below average prices for selected items.
    b. A radio station broadcasts the following message during a syndicated rating service's rating period: "Please fill out your diary."

c. A sewing machine retailer advertises a market test and indicates that the regular price will be cut to one-half for three days only.
d. A researcher tells a potential respondent that an interview will last 10 minutes rather than the 30 minutes he or she actually anticipates.
e. A respondent tells an interviewer that she wishes to cooperate with the survey, but her time is valuable and, therefore, she expects to be paid for the interview.
f. When you visit your favourite sports team's home page on the Web, you are asked to fill out a registration questionnaire before you enter the site. The team then sells your information (team allegiance, age, address, and so on) to a company that markets sports memorabilia via catalogues and direct mail.
13. Name some marketing research practices that may be ethically questionable.
14. What actions might the marketing research industry take to convince the public that marketing research is a legitimate activity and that firms that misrepresent their intentions and distort findings to achieve their aims are not true marketing research companies?
15. Comment on the following interview:

Interviewer: *Good afternoon, sir. My name is Mrs. Johnson and I am with Counselling Services. We are conducting a survey concerning Memorial Park. Do you own a funeral plot? Please answer yes or no.*

Respondent: *(pauses)*

Interviewer: *You do not own a funeral plot, do you?*

Respondent: *No.*

Interviewer: *Would you mind if I sent you a letter concerning Memorial Park? Please answer yes or no.*

Respondent: *No.*

Interviewer: *Would you please give me your address?*

16. Look through your local newspaper to find a story derived from survey research results. Does the newspaper article outline the study's methodology? Could this research have been considered advocacy research?

Exploring the Internet

1. Visit the MRIA Web site and review the full version of the Code of Conduct under the Standards section of the site. Note the section "Parental Consent and Guidelines for Interviewing Children and Young People."

   www.mria-arim.ca/

2. ESOMAR is an organization whose full name is the European Society for Opinion and Marketing Research. It was founded in 1948. Its online ESOMAR Directory of Research Organizations, listing over 1,500 research organizations in 100 countries, can be found at www.esomar.org.

3. Go to www.mercadex.ca to find the mission statement of Mercadex, a leading marketing research company.

4. Use a Web browser to go to the Corporate Research Group home page at www.thecrg.com. Select "Opportunities at CRG." What would a career in marketing research be like at CRG?

5. Many Internet sites list job opportunities and information that is useful for job applicants. Use your Web browser and search for marketing management and marketing research jobs at the following addresses:

   www.workopolis.com

   www.jobboom.com

   www.monster.ca

6. One purpose of the United Kingdom's Market Research Society is to set and enforce the ethical standards to be observed by research practitioners. Go to its Web site at http://www.marketresearch.org.uk. Click on its code of conduct and evaluate it in light of the CMA's code.

7. The World Association for Public Opinion Research (WAPOR) is a professional society of individuals engaged in public opinion research, market research, and social research. Another source, WorldOpinion (http://www.worldopinion.com), profiles and provides links to top research firms and major international organizations.

8. Epicurious is a gourmet food–oriented Web site. Its privacy policy can be found at http://www.epicurious.com by clicking on "Read Our Privacy Policy." Evaluate this policy.

Marc Fortin, director of marketing research for a large consumer packaged goods corporation, has a B.Comm. in marketing from Concordia University. He joined the firm nine years ago after a one-year stint as a marketing research trainee in the corporate headquarters of a western packing corporation. Four years ago, he received his MBA from a Montreal university in the night program. Marc has a wife and two children. He earns $100,000 a year and owns a home in the suburbs. He is typical of a marketing research director, except that he keeps a diary. At the end of every working day, he faithfully records the day's events. Several entries that describe his interactions with his firm's product and marketing managers are excerpted here.

January 7
Vincent Bernard, the brand manager for the cereal group, appeared to be under considerable pressure to get out a new product this year. He told me that the in-house usage tests were going to be the most important factor in the go/no-go decision for "his baby." He mentioned that the six-week test period was too long, and he wanted to shorten it to three weeks by placing the product with heavy users.

January 9
I presented Vincent with the negative results from our advertising copy testing. Just like a brand manager, he said to me, "You research guys are just like doctors. Every once in a while you make the wrong diagnosis and lose the patient. Marc, eight out of ten products fail even with good research. You and I know it's hard to measure a truly creative advertising campaign before it has been run for several months in the marketplace. Charlie down at the agency and I think this is one of our best ideas. We jointly came up with it. I would like you to think about how to test this ad after we produce it and run it in the marketplace for several months."

January 30
Elsa Marchand came into my office all flustered. People in sales had come up with a forecast that looked substantially different from hers. She wanted me to come up with a sales forecast that confirmed her forecasts. She needed the information in two weeks. She had to cover herself with the vice-president of marketing.

January 31
Joan Mendez, my top young research analyst, resigned today. She said she was taking a position at an advertising agency where working conditions were a little bit better.

February 12
The president called and said that the shaving lotion research study was extremely interesting. She said she was surprised that marketing research could gather so many facts in such a short period of time.

February 14
I called Quality Field Service Enterprises. I told them I had a rush job for 300 door-to-door interviews. Margaret said she was too busy with a home placement study and she couldn't do the job for several weeks. I called Atlantic Field Information Services and made a deal with Shirley. I told her I owed her one.

March 9
The executive vice-president of marketing said he liked my presentation of the results from the distributor survey. He said that we should do a distributor survey on a regular basis to keep Ralph down in sales on his toes.

March 18
Bob Brown, the assistant brand manager for shampoo products, came to me and said he had been working on an idea in his spare time. He said that he would like me to do some exploratory research, but that he didn't want his boss to know until the results looked favourable.

March 20
A head-hunter from an executive personnel service called and said that a top ad agency was looking for a marketing research manager. I told him I would think about it.

March 21
Love Fridays! Paul Langley from Optimex Data Processing took me out to lunch.

March 26
Ross said he had a frozen-hamburger survey that showed exactly what he wanted to present to management. He asked me to present an executive summary in "just about 10 minutes. Then I take over. Remember, I don't want to have comments about statistical significance—whatever that means." He indicated he thought my report was great— "long and hard to read, but great." It made my day.

March 29
In our new-product meeting the sales manager reported that sales volume in our western test market for product X had slowed down considerably. He explained that he thought the regional sales manager may have been too enthusiastic about the product. He thought that the western sales force may have persuaded the distributors to buy a four-month supply. Nevertheless, the overstocking problem would take care of itself as soon as the product got off the ground. It's too bad I had to follow that act. The product manager blew his stack when I told him about the results at the consumer level. Everything I came up with indicated that the trial rate was low and the repurchase rate was extremely low. The meeting ended when we decided to revise our marketing strategy quickly, before the introductory period of the test market was completed.

April 1
I had a meeting with the shampoo product manager today. She said that we were having some budget problems. She had to cut either advertising or marketing research. She said that she thought we could cut the focus group interviews with teenagers. "Just do the interviews with adults and we will eliminate some of our budget problems," she said.

April 2

I tried to meet with the executive vice-president of marketing today. I wanted to discuss the upcoming test market. He told me he was too busy. Told me to check with the assistant brand manager for the product group about the reformulation taste test.

April 3

I called the head-hunter today.

Question

What organizational and human relations problems does this diary reveal?

CASE 3.2   MARKETING RESEARCH INVOLVING CHILDREN AND TEENAGERS

A sensitive topic that has received attention around the world is marketing to children. With the development of the Broadcast Code for Advertising to Children in the 1970s, Canada had an early start in dealing with this issue compared to most other countries, including the United States. The mandatory code applies to the language, content, and positioning of Canadian advertising. Concerned Children's Advertisers (CCA), a non-profit organization comprising 26 Canadian companies, has the goal of creating and delivering socially responsible programs to Canadian children. CCA's TV commercials address issues ranging from managing peer pressure and building self-esteem to media literacy, supported by CCA's classroom and home-based programs for teachers and parents.[29]

How do we address concerns when conducting marketing research with children? Academic research that is funded and administered by universities undergoes strict reviews by the internal committees based on the Tri-Council Policy Statement. For instance, informed consent of the parents or the legal guardian is a must in conducting research with children.[30]

The Marketing Research and Intelligence Association's (MRIA) *Standards and Rules of Practice for Corporate Members of the Marketing Research and Intelligence Association* outlines how marketing research with children should be conducted. For example, it is essential to safeguard the welfare of the children and young people themselves and avoid any harm or disturbance in the interview process. The Canadian Marketing Association's Special Considerations in Marketing to Children and Teenagers, from *its* Code of Ethics and Standards of Practice (www.the-cma.org/consumer/ethics.cfm), and existing Canadian laws (see www.justice.gc.ca) provide additional guidance.[31]

Question

Assume that you will be conducting a study with children between the ages of 6 and 11 to understand their cereal preferences. This study is sponsored by a packaged goods company. Explain what type of ethical issues would be relevant and how you would address these issues.

4

DEFINING MARKETING PROBLEMS OR OPPORTUNITIES AND THE RESEARCH PROCESS

What you will learn in this chapter

1. To discuss the nature of decision makers' objectives and their role in formulating the research problem or opportunity.

2. To understand that proper problem or opportunity formulation is essential for effective marketing research.

3. To explain the iceberg principle.

4. To understand the importance of identifying key variables.

5. To discuss how formulation of research questions and hypotheses clarifies problem or opportunity formulation.

6. To discuss the influence of the statement of the marketing problem or opportunity on the specific research objectives.

7. To state research problems in terms of clear and precise research objectives.

8. To explain the purpose of the research proposal.

9. To outline a research proposal.

Once upon a time, a Sea Horse gathered up his seven pieces of eight and cantered out to find his fortune.[1] Before he had travelled very far he met an Eel, who said, "Psst. Hey, bud. Where ya goin'?"

"I'm going out to find my fortune," replied the Sea Horse proudly.

"You're in luck," said the Eel. "For four pieces of eight you can have this speedy flipper, and then you'll be able to get there a lot faster."

"Gee, that's swell," said the Sea Horse, and paid the money and put on the flipper, and slithered off at twice the speed. Soon he came upon a Sponge, who said, "Psst. Hey, bud. Where ya goin'?"

"I'm going out to find my fortune," replied the Sea Horse.

"You're in luck," said the Sponge. "For a small fee I will let you have this jet-propelled scooter so that you will be able to travel a lot faster."

So the Sea Horse bought the scooter with his remaining money and went zooming through the sea five times as fast. Soon he came upon a Shark, who said, "Psst. Hey, bud. Where you goin'?"

"I'm going out to find my fortune," replied the Sea Horse.

"You're in luck. If you'll take this shortcut," said the Shark, pointing to his open mouth, "you'll save yourself a lot of time."

"Gee, thanks," said the Sea Horse, and zoomed off into the interior of the Shark, there to be devoured.

The moral of this fable is that if you're not sure where you're going, you're liable to end up someplace else—and not even know it.

All researchers should keep in mind the lesson contained in the fable about the sea horse's journey during the beginning stages of the marketing research process. Marketing research is conducted to solve managerial problems. Before a research design is chosen, managers and researchers need a sense of direction for the investigation. An adage reminds us that if you do not know where you are going, any road will take you there. This suggests some good advice to managers and researchers: Defining the marketing problem carefully is extremely important because the definition determines the purpose of the research and, ultimately, the research design. This chapter explains how to define a marketing problem or opportunity and how to prepare a research proposal. ■

THE REST IS ARITHMETIC

The late Bob Keith, then president of the Pillsbury Company, was once persuaded by Pillsbury's researchers to review one of his major marketing decisions using a sophisticated, mathematical technique that required some input from him.[2] He agreed to the outcomes, their values, and their probabilities, and chose the decision rule he felt most appropriate. The computer then calculated the expectations, compared them, and reported the alternative that should be chosen according to that rule. Keith disagreed, noting that another alternative was obviously the only correct choice—indeed, it was the choice that had been made not long before. "How can that be?" the researchers asked. "You accepted all the values and probabilities and chose the decision rule yourself. The rest is arithmetic." "That's fine," Keith replied, "but you forgot to ask me about a few other things that were more important."

THE NATURE OF MARKETING PROBLEMS AND OPPORTUNITIES

Chapter 2 indicated that a decision maker's degree of uncertainty influences decisions about the type of research that will be conducted. In this chapter we elaborate on the conditions under which decision making occurs and the process by which managers clearly define marketing problems and opportunities.

Remember that a marketing manager may be completely certain about a business situation. For example, a retail store that has been recording and analyzing optical scanner data for years knows exactly what information its scanners need to record every day. Routine research techniques are regularly used to investigate routine problems that have already been defined.

At the other extreme, a manager or researcher may face an absolutely ambiguous decision-making situation. The nature of the problem to be solved is unclear. The objectives are vague, and the alternatives are difficult to define. This is by far the most difficult decision situation.

Most marketing decision situations fall between these two extremes. Managers usually grasp the general nature of the objectives they wish to achieve, but they often remain uncertain about the full details of the problem. Important information is missing. Ambiguity or uncertainty needs to be cleared up before making a formal statement of the marketing problem.

THE IMPORTANCE OF PROPER PROBLEM OR OPPORTUNITY FORMULATION

The formal quantitative research process should not begin until the problem or the opportunity has been clearly defined. However, properly and completely defining a marketing problem or opportunity is easier said than done. When a problem or opportunity is discovered, managers may have only vague insights about a complex situation. For example, suppose market share is declining on the west coast and management does not know the reason. If quantitative research begins before the manager learns exactly what is important, the investigation may yield false conclusions. The right answer to the wrong question may be absolutely worthless—indeed, it may even be harmful.

A well-known example is the Betamax–VHS battle in videotape recording technology. Although Sony's Betamax technology was superior in picture quality compared to VHS technology, consumers preferred to have the longer recording times that VHS was able to deliver (up to six hours). RCA discovered this through marketing research and was able to provide a delayed but more preferred alternative. This was one of several factors that contributed to the downfall of the Betamax format.[3]

Misinterpreting existing marketing research results may be just as harmful as having no marketing research at all. In promoting their Real cigarettes, R. J. Reynolds's marketing research indicated that consumers were shifting to natural products of all kinds. Executives interpreted the marketing research to mean that smokers did not want flavourings or additives in cigarettes. This led to advertising themes that stressed benefits like "nothing artificial added" and "all natural." Unfortunately, although methodologically sound, the research missed a crucial point: Smokers really did not care about flavourings and additives until they were asked. The research was based on a fundamental misconception that was not uncovered in the problem or opportunity formulation stage of the research. The real marketing problem was to find a way to appeal to smokers who actually were interested in low-tar cigarettes.

Consider what happened when Coca-Cola made the decision to change its Coke formula. Management's problem or opportunity formulation of the problem focused on a need to improve Coke's taste because its competitor's "Pepsi Challenge" advertising campaign touted Pepsi's superior taste. The research question was to investigate the ultimate consumer reaction to the taste of reformulated Coke. The results of the taste test led to the introduction of "new" Coke and the withdrawal from the market of regular Coke. As soon as consumers learned the company's original formula was no longer available, there were emotional protests from Coca-Cola loyalists. The consumer protests were so passionate and determined that the original formula was quickly brought back as Coca-Cola Classic. Later, the company learned that the consumer protests associated with dropping the original formula for Coke indicated a larger problem: Coke's marketing research was too narrow in scope and the problem was inadequately defined. The company had carried out a series of taste tests in shopping malls. No take-home taste tests were conducted, nor were consumers asked if the new Coke should replace the original. The marketing research failed to identify consumers' emotional attachment and loyalty to the brand as a problem for investigation. The Coca-Cola mistake teaches a valuable lesson: Do not ignore investigating the emotional aspects of buying behaviour.

THE PROCESS OF PROBLEM OR OPPORTUNITY FORMULATION

problem or opportunity formulation
The crucial first stage in the research process—determining the problem to be solved or the opportunity to be studied and the objectives of the research.

Just because a problem has been discovered or an opportunity recognized does not mean that the problem has been defined. A **problem or opportunity formulation** indicates a specific marketing decision to be clarified or problem to be solved. It specifies research questions to be answered and the objectives of research.

The process of defining the problem involves several interrelated steps, as shown in Exhibit 4.1:

1. Ascertain the decision maker's objectives
2. Understand the background of the problem

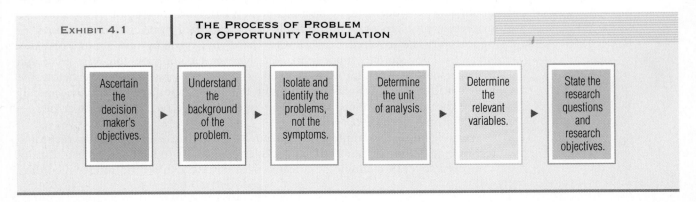

EXHIBIT 4.1 | THE PROCESS OF PROBLEM OR OPPORTUNITY FORMULATION

Ascertain the decision maker's objectives. → Understand the background of the problem. → Isolate and identify the problems, not the symptoms. → Determine the unit of analysis. → Determine the relevant variables. → State the research questions and research objectives.

3. Isolate and identify the problem, not the symptoms
4. Determine the unit of analysis
5. Determine the relevant variables
6. State the research questions (hypotheses) and research objectives

Ascertain the Decision Makers' Objectives

decision makers' objectives
Managerial goals expressed in measurable terms.

As a staff person, the research investigator must attempt to satisfy the **decision makers' objectives**—those of the brand manager, sales manager, and others who requested the project. Management and organizational theorists suggest that the decision maker should express goals to the researcher in measurable terms. Unfortunately, expecting this to happen is overly optimistic:

> Despite a popular misconception to the contrary, objectives are seldom clearly articulated and given to the researcher. The decision maker seldom formulates his objectives accurately. He is likely to state his objectives in the form of platitudes which have no operational significance. Consequently, objectives usually have to be extracted by the researcher. In so doing, the researcher may well be performing his most useful service to the decision maker.[4]

Researchers who must conduct investigations when a marketing manager wants the information "yesterday" usually get little assistance when they ask, "What are your objectives for this study?" Nevertheless, even decision makers who have only a gut feeling that marketing research might be a good idea benefit greatly if they work with the marketing researcher to articulate precise research objectives.[5] Both parties should attempt to gain a clear understanding of the purpose for undertaking the research.

One effective technique for uncovering elusive research objectives is to present the marketing manager with each possible solution to a problem and ask whether he or she would follow that course of action. A "no" can prompt further questioning to determine why the course of action is inappropriate; this usually will help formulate objectives. By illuminating the nature of the marketing opportunity or problem, exploratory research also helps managers clarify their research objectives.

iceberg principle
The idea that the dangerous part of many marketing problems is neither visible to nor understood by marketing managers.

Why do so many marketing research projects begin without clear objectives or adequate problem definitions? Marketing managers are logical people, and it seems logical that defining the problem is the starting point for any enterprise. Frequently, however, marketing researchers and managers cannot discover problems because they lack sufficiently detailed information. The **iceberg principle** serves as a useful analogy (see Exhibit 4.2). A sailor on the open sea notices only the 10 percent of an iceberg that extends above the surface of the water, while 90 percent is submerged. The dangerous part of many marketing problems, like the submerged

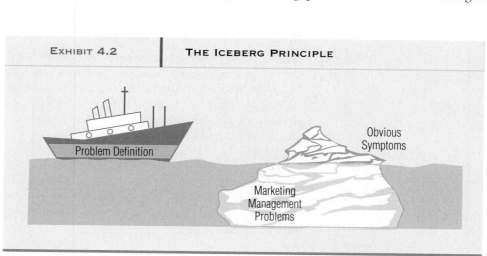

EXHIBIT 4.2 | THE ICEBERG PRINCIPLE

Problem Definition

Obvious Symptoms

Marketing Management Problems

portion of the iceberg, is neither visible to nor understood by marketing managers. If the submerged portions of the problem are omitted from the problem or opportunity formulation (and subsequently from the research design), the decisions based on the research may be less than optimal. The example of new Coke is a case in point. Omission of important information or faulty assumptions about the situation can be extremely costly.

Understand the Background of the Problem

Although no textbook outline for identifying a marketing problem exists, the iceberg principle illustrates that understanding the background of the problem is vital. Often experienced managers know a great deal about a situation and can provide researchers with considerable background information about previous events and why they occurred. Under these circumstances, when the decision maker's objectives are clear, the problem may be diagnosed exclusively by exercising managerial judgment. On other occasions, when information about what has happened before is inadequate or when managers have trouble identifying the problem, a situation analysis is the logical first step in defining the problem. A **situation analysis** involves the informal gathering of background information to familiarize researchers or managers with the decision area. Gaining an awareness of marketplace conditions and an appreciation of the situation often requires exploratory research. The many exploratory research techniques developed to help formulate clear definitions of the problem are covered in Chapter 5.

Isolate and Identify the Problem, Not the Symptoms

Anticipating the many influences and dimensions of a problem is impossible for any researcher or executive. For instance, a firm may have a problem with its advertising effectiveness. The possible causes of this problem may be low brand awareness, the wrong brand image, use of the wrong media, or perhaps too small a budget. Management's job is to isolate and identify the most likely causes. Certain occurrences that appear to be the problem may be only symptoms of a deeper problem. Exhibit 4.3 illustrates how symptoms may be mistaken for the true problem.

Other problems may be identified only after gathering background information and conducting exploratory research. How does one ensure that the fundamental problem has been identified, rather than its symptoms? There is no easy answer to this question. Executive judgment and creativity must be exercised. The archaeological puzzle in Exhibit 4.4 shows that good researchers must be creative in developing problem or opportunity formulations by investigating situations in new ways.

Determine the Unit of Analysis

Defining the problem requires that the researcher determine the unit of analysis for the study. The researcher must specify whether the investigation will collect data about individuals, households, organizations, departments, geographical areas, or objects. In studies of home buying, for example, the husband–wife dyad typically is the unit of analysis rather than the individual because many purchase decisions are made jointly by husband and wife.

Researchers who think carefully and creatively about situations often discover that a problem may be investigated at more than one level of analysis. Determining the unit of analysis, although relatively straightforward in most projects, should not be overlooked during the problem or opportunity formulation stage of the research. It is a fundamental aspect of problem or opportunity formulation.

situation analysis
A preliminary investigation or informal gathering of background information to familiarize researchers or managers with the decision area.

EXHIBIT 4.3 | SYMPTOMS CAN BE CONFUSING

Organization	Symptoms	Problem or Opportunity Formulation Based on Symptom	True Problem
Twenty-year-old neighbourhood swimming association in a major city	Membership has been declining for years. New water park with wave pool and water slides moved into town a few years ago.	Neighbourhood residents prefer the more expensive water park and have a negative image of swimming pool.	Demographic changes: Children in this 20-year-old neighbourhood have grown up; older residents no longer swim.
Manufacturer of palm-sized computer with wireless Internet access	Distributors complain prices are too high.	Investigate business users to learn how much prices need to be reduced.	Sales management: Distributors do not have adequate product knowledge to communicate product's value.
Microbrewery	Consumers prefer the taste of competitor's brand.	What type of reformulated taste is needed?	Package: Old-fashioned package influences taste perception.

EXHIBIT 4.4 | A PUZZLE[6]

What language is written on this stone found by archaeologists?

TOTI
EMUL
ESTO

Answer (turn book upside down):

The language is English: TO/TIE/MULES/TO. A great deal of time and effort is spent looking at familiar problems. Managers often do not look at these problems in a new light, however. Too often they see what they want to see or what they expect. They give stereotyped answers to problems. A good researcher creatively develops a hypothesis by looking at problems in a new way.

Determine the Relevant Variables

variable
Anything that may assume different numerical or categorical values.

Another aspect of problem or opportunity formulation is identification of key variables. The term *variable* is important in research. A **variable** is anything that varies or changes in value. Because a variable represents a quality that can exhibit differences in value, usually in magnitude or strength, it may be said that a variable generally is anything that may assume different numerical or categorical values. For example, attitudes toward airlines may be a variable ranging from positive to negative. Each attribute of airlines' services, such as safety, seat comfort, and baggage handling, is a variable.

In statistical analysis, a variable is identified by a symbol, such as X. Categories or numerical values may then be associated with this symbol. The variable "gender" may be categorized as male or female; gender is a **categorical variable**, since it has a limited number of distinct values. On the other hand, "sales volume" may encompass an infinite range of numbers; it is a **continuous variable**, one that can have an infinite number of values.

categorical variable
A variable that has a limited number of distinct values.

continuous variable
A variable that has an infinite number of possible values.

dependent variable
A criterion or variable to be predicted or explained.

independent variable
A variable that is expected to influence a dependent variable.

In causal research, the terms *dependent variable* and *independent variable* are frequently encountered. A **dependent variable** is a criterion or a variable that is to be predicted or explained. An **independent variable** is a variable that is expected to influence the dependent variable. For example, average sales compensation may be a dependent variable that is influenced or predicted by an independent variable such as number of years of experience. These terms are discussed in greater detail in the chapters on experimentation and data analysis.

Managers and researchers must be careful to identify all relevant variables necessary to define the managerial problem. Likewise, variables that are superfluous (not directly relevant to the problem) should not be included.

The process of identifying the relevant variables overlaps with the process of determining the research objectives. Typically, each research objective will mention a variable or variables to be measured or analyzed.

State the Research Questions and Research Objectives

Both managers and researchers expect problem or opportunity formulation efforts to result in statements of research questions and research objectives. At the end of the problem or opportunity formulation stage, the researcher should prepare a written statement that clarifies any ambiguity about what the research hopes to accomplish.

Defining the unit of analysis is an important aspect of the problem or opportunity formulation process. In many marketing research studies, the family rather than the individual is the appropriate unit of analysis.

THEY MAY WANT TO STRANGLE YOU!

Hugh Dubberly, a manager with the Times-Mirror Company, advocates the following step-by-step process to help clearly define the problem to be solved:[7]

"How do we define the problem? Begin by assembling all the relevant players in a room. Ask each player to describe the unmet need, or in other words, to suggest the cause of the problem. Write down each suggestion. Nothing you will do on the project will be more important. With each suggestion, ask in turn for its cause. And then the cause of the cause. And then

the cause of the cause of the cause. Keep at it like a 2-year-old. By the time everyone in the room wants to strangle you, you will very likely have found the root cause of the problem.

"After you've developed the problem statement, you need to be sure to gain consensus on it from all the relevant parties. Failure to get 'buy-in' from all the right people at this stage creates the potential for trouble later in the process. Someone who hasn't agreed on the definition up front is likely to want to change it later."

CLARITY IN RESEARCH QUESTIONS AND HYPOTHESES

Formulating a series of research questions and hypotheses adds clarity to the statement of the marketing problem. A personal computer company made the following statement about an advertising problem: In the broadest sense, the marketing problem is to determine the best ways [name of the company] can communicate with potential purchasers of laptop computers.

■ How familiar are consumers with the various brands of computers?

■ What attitudes do consumers have toward these brands?

■ How important are the various factors for evaluating the purchase of a laptop computer?

■ How effective are the communications efforts of the various competitive marketers with regard to message recognition?

Research questions make it easier to understand what is perplexing managers and to indicate what issues have to be resolved. A research question is the researcher's translation of the marketing problem into a specific inquiry.

A research question can be too vague and general if stated in terms such as "Is advertising copy X better than advertising copy Y?" Advertising effectiveness can be variously measured by sales, recall of sales message, brand awareness, intention to buy, and so on. Asking a more specific research question (e.g., "Which advertisement has a higher day–after recall score?") helps the researcher design a study that will produce pertinent information. The answer to the research question should be a criterion that can be used as a standard for selecting alternatives. The stage of the research obviously is related to problem or opportunity formulation. The goal of defining the problem is to state the research questions clearly and to develop well-formulated hypotheses.

A **hypothesis** is an unproven proposition or possible solution to a problem. Hypothetical statements assert probable answers to research questions. A hypothesis is a statement about the nature of the world; in its simplest form it is a guess. A sales manager may hypothesize that salespeople who show the highest job satisfaction will be the most productive. An advertising manager may believe that if consumers' attitudes toward a product are changed in a positive direction, consumption of the product will increase. Problem statements and hypotheses are similar. Both state

hypothesis

An unproven proposition or supposition that tentatively explains certain facts or phenomena; a probable answer to a research question.

"THE SLACKS DON'T FIT!"

A major catalogue retailer was experiencing a large number of returns of its boys' slacks.[8] Mothers were indicating on the return forms that they were returning the slacks because they didn't fit properly. Management thus defined the research problem as determining how to redesign the catalogue's diagrams and rewrite the instructions to help consumers place their mail orders for slacks. However, when interviewers from Oxtoby-Smith, a survey research company, brought the catalogues with the diagrams and instructions to consumers' homes, they found out that the boys' slacks actually fit perfectly. They also learned the mothers had ordered several pairs of slacks for their teenage sons in the hope that the teenagers would find at least one pair they would be willing to wear;

then the mothers returned the other pairs of slacks. The mothers felt uncomfortable with this buying situation, but did not wish to reveal the true reasons for returning the slacks. It was less trouble to provide the explanation of poor fit. The diagrams were not the problem. The instructions were not the problem.

The researcher at Oxtoby-Smith stated, "The lesson I learned from this discovery was that sometimes assumptions about the nature of the problem can be mistaken. That's okay if the research we do to investigate the problem we think we have enables us to identify the real problem. Very often, a major job of the researcher is to find out what the problem is. Frankly, sometimes that means not assuming that the client knows what the problem is."

relationships, but problem statements are interrogative, whereas hypotheses are declarative. Sometimes the two types of statements are almost identical in substance. An important difference, however, is that hypotheses usually are more specific than problem statements; typically, they are closer to the actual research operations and testing. Hypotheses are statements that can be empirically tested.

A formal statement of a hypothesis has considerable practical value in planning and designing research. It forces researchers to be clear about what they expect to find through the study, and it raises crucial questions about the data that will be required in the analysis stage. When evaluating a hypothesis, researchers should ensure that the information collected will be useful in decision making. Notice how the following hypotheses express expected relationships between variables:

- There is a positive relationship between buying on the Internet and the presence of younger children in the home.

- Sales are lower for salespeople in regions that receive less advertising support.

- Consumers will experience cognitive dissonance after the decision to purchase a TiVo personal video recorder.

- Opinion leaders are more affected by mass media communication sources than are non-leaders.

- Among non-exporters, the degree of perceived importance of overcoming barriers to exporting is related positively to general interest in exporting (export intentions).[9]

research objective
The researcher's version of the marketing problem; it explains the purpose of the research in measurable terms and defines standards for what the research should accomplish.

DECISION-ORIENTED RESEARCH OBJECTIVES

The **research objective** is the researcher's version of the marketing problem. After the research questions or hypotheses have been stated, the research project objectives are derived from the problem or opportunity formulation. They explain the purpose of the research in measurable terms and define standards for what the research should accomplish. In addition to explaining the reasons for conducting the project, research objectives help ensure that the research project will be manageable in size.

Exhibit 4.5 illustrates how the marketing problem of a retail chain store—whether it should offer an in-home shopping service using Internet ordering—is translated into research objectives.

In some instances the marketing problem and the project's research objectives are identical. However, the objectives must specify the information needed to make a decision. Identifying the needed information may require that managers or researchers be extremely specific, perhaps even listing the exact wording of the question in a survey or explaining exactly what behaviour might be observed or recorded in an experiment. Statements about the required precision of the information or the source of information may be required to clearly communicate exactly what information is needed. Many product buying decisions, for example, are made by both husband and wife. If this is the case, the husband–wife decision-making unit is the unit of analysis. The objective of obtaining X information about research questions from this unit should be specifically stated.

Exhibit 4.5 translates the broad research objective—to determine consumers' perceived need for a home shopping service—into specific objectives—namely, to determine consumer awareness, obtain ranked preferences for alternative forms of the service, compare the needs of various market segments, and so on. The specific objectives influence decisions about the research design because they indicate the type of information needed.

EXHIBIT 4.5	MARKETING PROBLEM TRANSLATED INTO RESEARCH OBJECTIVES

Marketing Management Problem / Questions	Research Questions	Research Objectives
Should the retail chain store offer in-home shopping via the Internet?	Are consumers aware of Internet home shopping systems? What are consumers' reactions to Internet shopping?	To determine consumer awareness with aided recall To measure consumer attitudes and beliefs about home shopping systems
In which of several possible forms should the service be offered?	How do consumers react to service form A? B? C? What are the perceived benefits of each form of service?	To obtain ratings and rankings of each form of service To identify perceived benefits of and perceived objections to the system
What market segment should be the target market?	Will consumers use the service? How often? Do the answers to the above questions differ depending on demographic group? Who are the best prospects?	To measure purchase intentions; to estimate likelihood of usage To compare—using cross-tabulations—levels of awareness, evaluations, purchasing intentions, etc., of men versus women, high-income versus low-income groups, young consumers versus older consumers, etc.
What pricing strategy should we follow?	How much do prospective customers think the service will cost? Do prospective customers think this product will be priced higher or lower than competitive offerings? Is the product perceived as a good value?	To ascertain consumers' knowledge and expectations about prices To learn how the price of this service is perceived relative to competitors' pricing To determine the perceived value of the service

Note: For simplicity, hypotheses are omitted from the exhibit.

The research objectives should be limited to a manageable number. Fewer study objectives make it easier to ensure that each will be addressed fully.

Exhibit 4.6 shows how the statement of a marketing problem influences the research objectives. The specific objectives, in turn, become the basis for the research design. Exhibit 4.6 also shows how exploratory research can help managers in the overall problem or opportunity formulation of the marketing problem. However, in routine situations or when managers are quite familiar with the background information, it is quite likely that the problem or opportunity formulation will be based exclusively on the decision maker's objectives.

Once the research has been conducted, the results may show an unanticipated aspect of the problem and suggest a need for additional research to satisfy the main objective. Accomplished researchers who have had the experience of uncovering additional aspects of a marketing problem after finishing fieldwork recommend designing studies that include questions crafted to reveal the unexpected.

HOW MUCH TIME SHOULD BE SPENT DEFINING THE PROBLEM?

Budget constraints usually influence the amount of effort that will be spent defining the problem. Most marketing situations are complex, and numerous variables may have some influence. Searching for every conceivable cause and minor influence is impractical. The importance of the recognized problem will dictate a reasonable amount of time and money to spend determining which possible explanations are most likely. Marketing managers, being responsible for decision making, may wish the problem or opportunity formulation process to proceed quickly. Researchers, who can take a long time to carefully define problems, may frustrate managers. However, the time taken to identify the correct problem is time well spent.

THE RESEARCH PROPOSAL

research proposal
A written statement of the research design that includes a statement explaining the purpose of the study and a detailed, systematic outline of procedures associated with a particular research methodology.

The **research proposal** is a written statement of the research design. It always includes a statement explaining the purpose of the study (research objectives) or a definition of the problem or the opportunity. It systematically outlines the particular research methodology and details the procedures that will be followed during each stage of

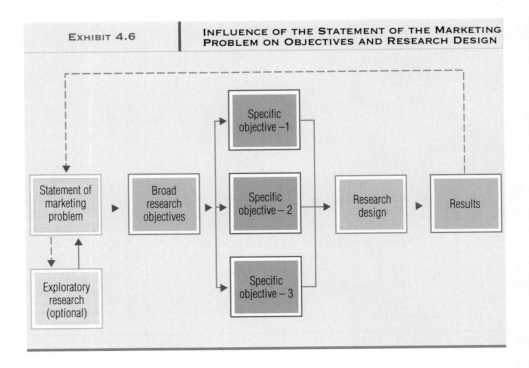

| EXHIBIT 4.6 | INFLUENCE OF THE STATEMENT OF THE MARKETING PROBLEM ON OBJECTIVES AND RESEARCH DESIGN |

the research process. Normally a schedule of costs and deadlines is included in the research proposal. Exhibit 4.7 illustrates an exemplary proposal for a short research project, exploring public attitudes toward a variety of tax–related issues. This research proposal could potentially be used by provincial or federal tax agencies (e.g., Canada Revenue Agency).

| EXHIBIT 4.7 | A SAMPLE RESEARCH PROPOSAL FOR REVENUE CANADA[10] |

Purpose of the Research

The general purpose of the study is to determine the taxpaying public's perceptions of the role of Revenue Canada in administering the tax laws. In defining the limits of this study, a careful review of the study areas that the client raised led to the identification of the following specific research objectives:

1. To identify the extent to which taxpayers cheat on their returns, their reasons for doing so, and approaches that can be taken to deter this kind of behaviour
2. To determine taxpayers' experience and level of satisfaction with various Revenue Canada services
3. To determine what services taxpayers need
4. To develop an accurate profile of taxpayers' behaviour relative to the preparation of their income tax returns
5. To assess taxpayers' knowledge and opinions about various tax laws and procedures

Research Design

The survey research method will be the basic research design. Each respondent will be interviewed in his or her home. The personal interviews are generally expected to last between 35 and 45 minutes, although the length will vary depending on the previous tax-related experiences of the respondent. For example, if a respondent has never been audited, questions on audit experience will not be addressed. Or if a respondent has never contacted Revenue Canada for assistance, certain questions concerning reactions to Revenue Canada services will be skipped.

Some sample questions that will be asked are

Did you or your spouse prepare your federal tax return for (year)?
☐ Self
☐ Spouse
☐ Someone else

Did the federal income tax package you received in the mail contain all the forms necessary for you to fill out your return?
☐ Yes
☐ No
☐ Didn't receive one in the mail
☐ Don't know

If you were calling Revenue Canada for assistance and someone were not able to help you immediately, would you rather get a busy signal or be asked to wait on hold?
☐ Busy signal
☐ Wait on hold
☐ Neither
☐ Don't know

During the interview a self-administered questionnaire will be given to the taxpayer to ask certain sensitive questions, such as

Have you ever claimed a dependent on your tax return that you weren't really entitled to?
☐ Yes
☐ No

Sample Design

A survey of approximately 5,000 individuals located in all provinces throughout Canada will provide the database for this study. The sample will be selected on a probability basis from all households in each province.

Eligible respondents will be adults over the age of 18. Within each household an effort will be made to interview the individual who is most familiar with completing the federal tax forms. When there is more than one taxpayer in the household, a random process will be used to select the taxpayer to be interviewed.

Data Gathering

The fieldworkers of a consulting organization will conduct the interviews.

Data Processing and Analysis

Standard editing and coding procedures will be utilized. Simple tabulation and cross-tabulations will be utilized to analyze the data.

Report Preparation

A written report will be prepared, and an oral presentation of the findings will be made by the research analyst at the convenience of Revenue Canada.

Budget and Time Schedule

Any complete research proposal should include a schedule of how long it will take to conduct each stage of the research and a statement of itemized costs.

Preparation of a research proposal forces the researcher to think critically about each stage of the research process. Vague plans, abstract ideas, and sweeping generalizations about problems or procedures must become concrete and precise statements about specific events. Information to be obtained and research procedures to be implemented have to be clearly specified so others may understand their exact implications. All ambiguities about why and how the research will be conducted must be clarified before the proposal is complete.

Because the proposal is a clearly outlined plan submitted to management for acceptance or rejection, it initially performs a communication function; it serves as a mechanism that allows managers to evaluate the details of the proposed research design and determine if alterations are necessary. The proposal helps managers decide if the proper information will be obtained and if the proposed research will accomplish what is desired. If the marketing problem has not been adequately translated into a set of specific research objectives and a research design, the client's assessment of the proposal will help ensure that the researchers revise it to meet the client's information needs.

The proposal must communicate exactly what information will be obtained, where it will be obtained, and how it will be obtained. For this reason, it must be explicit about sample selection, measurement, fieldwork, and so on. For instance, most survey proposals will include a copy of the proposed questionnaire (or at least some sample questions) to ensure that managers and researchers agree on the information to be obtained and on the wording of questions.

The format for the Revenue Canada research proposal in Exhibit 4.7 follows the six stages in the research process outlined in Exhibit 2.4. At each stage, one or more questions must be answered before the researcher can select one of the various alternatives. For example, before a proposal can be completed, the researcher needs to know what is to be measured. A simple statement like "market share" may not be enough; market share may be measured by auditing retailers' or wholesalers' sales, using trade association data, or asking consumers what brands they buy. What is to be measured is just one of many important questions that must be answered before setting the research process in motion. This issue will be addressed in greater detail in Chapter 11; for now, Exhibit 4.8 presents an overview of some of the basic questions that managers and researchers typically must answer when planning a research design.

Review the sample research proposal in Exhibit 4.7 to see how some of the questions in Exhibit 4.8 were answered in a specific situation.[11] However, you will have to read the entire book before you can fully understand these issues.

In business, one often hears the adage "Don't say it, write it." This is wise advice for the researcher who is proposing a research project to management. Misstatements and faulty communication may occur if the parties rely only on each individual's memory of what occurred at a planning meeting. Writing a proposal for a research design, specifying exactly what will be done, creates a record to which everyone can refer and eliminates many problems that might arise after the research has been conducted. With a written proposal, management and researchers alike are less likely to discover after completion of the research that information related to a particular variable was omitted or that the sample size was too small for a particular subgroup. Furthermore, as a statement of agreement between marketing executives and researchers, the formal proposal will reduce the tendency for someone reading the results to say, "Shouldn't we have had a larger sample?" or "Why didn't you do it this way?" As a record of the researcher's obligation, the proposal also provides a standard for determining whether the research was conducted as originally planned.

When the research will be conducted by a consultant or an outside research supplier, the written proposal serves as that person's bid to offer a specific service. Typically, a client solicits several competitive proposals, and these written offers help management judge the relative quality of alternative research suppliers.

Decisions to Make	Basic Questions
Problem or opportunity formulation	What is the purpose of the study?
	How much is already known?
	Is additional background information necessary?
	What is to be measured? How?
	Can the data be made available?
	Should research be conducted?
	Can a hypothesis be formulated?
Selection of basic research design	What types of questions need to be answered?
	Are descriptive or causal findings required?
	What is the source of the data?
	Can objective answers be obtained by asking people?
	How quickly is the information needed?
	How should survey questions be worded?
	How should experimental manipulations be made?
Selection of sample	Who or what is the source of the data?
	Can the target population be identified?
	Is a sample necessary?
	How accurate must the sample be?
	Is a probability sample necessary?
	Is a national sample necessary?
	How large a sample is necessary?
	How will the sample be selected?
Data gathering	Who will gather the data?
	How long will data gathering take?
	How much supervision is needed?
	What procedures will data collectors need to follow?
Data analysis and evaluation	Will standardized editing and coding procedures be used?
	How will the data be categorized?
	Will computer or hand tabulation be used?
	What is the nature of the data?
	What questions need to be answered?
	How many variables are to be investigated simultaneously?
	What are the criteria for evaluation of performance?

(continued)

EXHIBIT 4.8	(CONTD.)
Type of report	Who will read the report?
	Are managerial recommendations requested?
	How many presentations are required?
	What will be the format of the written report?
Overall evaluation	How much will the study cost?
	Is the time frame acceptable?
	Is outside help needed?
	Will this research design attain the stated research objectives?
	When should the research begin?

One final comment needs to be made about the nature of research proposals: Not all proposals follow the same format. The researcher must adapt his or her proposal to the target audience. An extremely brief proposal submitted by an organization's internal marketing research department to its own marketing executives bears little resemblance to a complex proposal submitted by a university professor to a federal government agency to research a basic consumer issue.

SUMMARY

 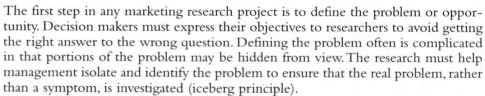 The first step in any marketing research project is to define the problem or opportunity. Decision makers must express their objectives to researchers to avoid getting the right answer to the wrong question. Defining the problem often is complicated in that portions of the problem may be hidden from view. The research must help management isolate and identify the problem to ensure that the real problem, rather than a symptom, is investigated (iceberg principle).

 A variable is anything that changes in value. Variables may be categorical or continuous. One aspect of problem or opportunity formulation is the identification of the key dependent and independent variables.

 Research questions and hypotheses are translations of the marketing problem into marketing research terms. A hypothesis is an unproven proposition or a possible solution to the problem. Hypotheses state relationships between variables that can be tested empirically. Research objectives specify information needs. For the research project to be successful, the research problem must be stated in clear and precise research objectives.

 The research proposal is a written statement of the research design that will be followed in addressing a specific problem. The research proposal allows managers to evaluate the details of the proposed research and determine if alterations are needed. Most research proposals include the following sections: purpose of the research, research design, sample design, data gathering and/or fieldwork techniques, data processing and analysis, budget, and time schedule.

Key Terms and Concepts

problem or opportunity formulation	variable	independent variable
decision makers' objectives	categorical variable	hypothesis
iceberg principle	continuous variable	research objective
situation analysis	dependent variable	research proposal

Questions for Review and Critical Thinking

1. In its broadest context, what is the task of problem or opportunity formulation?
2. In the following nine-dot square, connect all nine dots using no more than four straight lines and without lifting the pencil from the paper. What does the solution of this problem imply about the solutions of problem formulation situations?

$$\begin{matrix} \bullet & \bullet & \bullet \\ \bullet & \bullet & \bullet \\ \bullet & \bullet & \bullet \end{matrix}$$

3. What is the iceberg principle?
4. State a problem in your field of interest, and list some variables that might be investigated to solve this problem.
5. Evaluate the following statement of marketing problems:
   a. A farm implement manufacturer: Our objective is to learn the most effective form of advertising so we can maximize product line profits.
   b. An employees' credit union: Our problem is to determine the reasons that employees join the credit union, determine members' awareness of credit union services, and measure attitudes and beliefs about how effectively the credit union is operated.
   c. The producer of a television show: We have a marketing problem. The program's ratings are low. We need to learn how we can improve our ratings.
   d. A soft-drink manufacturer: The marketing problem is that we do not know if our bottlers are more satisfied with us than our competitors' bottlers are with them.
   e. A women's magazine: Our problem is to document the demographic changes that have occurred in recent decades in the lives of women and to put them in historical perspective; to examine several generations of Canadian women through most of this century, tracking their roles as students, workers, wives, and mothers and noting the changes in timing, sequence, and duration of these roles; to examine at what age and for how long a woman enters various stages of her life: school, work, marriage, childbearing, divorce. This will be accomplished by analyzing demographic data over several generations.
   f. A manufacturer of fishing boats: The problem is to determine sales trends over the past five years by product category and to determine the seasonality of unit boat sales by quarters and by region of the country.
   g. The inventor of a tension headache remedy (a cooling pad that is placed on the forehead for up to four hours): The purpose of this research is (1) to identify the market potential for the product, (2) to identify what desirable features the product should possess, and (3) to determine possible advertising strategies/channel strategies for the product.
6. Go the library, find business journals, and record and evaluate some hypotheses that have been investigated in recent years. Identify the key independent and dependent variables.
7. What purpose does a research proposal serve?
8. What role should managers play in the development of the research proposal?
9. Comment on the following statements:
   a. "The best marketing researchers are prepared to rethink and rewrite their proposals."
   b. "The client's signature is an essential element of the research proposal."
10. You have been hired by a group of hotel owners, restaurant owners, and other people engaged in businesses that benefit from tourism in Sutton, Quebec. They wish to learn how they can attract a large number of college students to their town during winter vacation. Define the marketing research problem.
11. You have been hired by a local Big Brothers and Big Sisters of Canada organization to learn how they can increase the number of males who volunteer to become Big Brothers to fatherless boys. Define your research objectives.
12. You have solicited research proposals from several firms. The lowest bidder has the best questionnaire and proposal. However, there is one feature in the proposal submitted by a firm that will not receive the job that you particularly like. How should you handle this situation?

Exploring the Internet

1. How could the Internet help define a marketing problem that needs to be researched?
2. Could e-mail be used to solicit research proposals from marketing research suppliers? What would be the advantages and disadvantages of using this method of distribution?

Initially, Jeff Matthews began working on an air filter system to eliminate odours and allergens caused by his dogs, Oscar and Mozart, at the Matthews home. The current model he has developed, Pure-Blue Air Cleaner, does more than eliminate pet odours. Pure-Blue is a high-tech air filtering system that is portable, economic, and efficient.

Jeff believes that he has developed an air cleaner with unique benefits. One way to measure efficiency of an air cleaner is to compare the Clean Air Delivery Rate (CADR) to electrical energy (in watts) it consumes. The CADR/watts ratio for Pure-Blue Air Cleaner is 16.73, better than HEPA air filters and any other model in the market. Pure-Blue is also very silent. With the long winter season in Canada and the long hours spent indoors, Jeff is looking forward to high sales for Pure-Blue. Jeff has contacted Mark-IQ, a Canadian marketing research company, to understand whether there is a market for his product. Julie Carter, president of Mark-IQ, meets with Jeff a number of times and examines the product. She prepares the project description and sends it to Jeff. Exhibit 4.1.1 shows the research project description.

Questions
1. Evaluate the problem definition.
2. If this research proposal were submitted to you, how would you react?

Note: The names of the people and organizations are fictitious.

CASE EXHIBIT 4.1.1 | **RESEARCH PROJECT DESCRIPTION**

Product: Pure-Blue is an electrostatic precipitator air cleaner. It is quiet, energy-efficient, and easy to maintain, as there are no filters to replace. It eliminates bacteria and mould. The current model is suitable for rooms up to 80 square metres. Additional models can be developed to cover larger areas without a significant loss of efficiency. Estimated price: $600.

Foreseen Uses: Pure-Blue is suitable for residential use, especially for homes that do not have a central filtration system. It also is suitable for office use with its sleek design, small size, and quiet operation. For consumers with allergies or respiratory problems and/or pets, Pure-Blue should be very attractive.

Marketing Issue: To acquire the technology to produce this product, our client must buy a production company at a substantial cost. This research should identify whether the market potential for the product will justify the capital expenditure.

Research Objectives
A. Among residential consumers, determine
   1. Basic reactions to product concept
   2. Foreseen applications by consumers
   3. Price sensitivity/expectations
   4. Willingness to buy
   5. Likelihood of foreseen use

B. Among business consumers (e.g., hospitals, businesses, kindergartens), determine
   1. Basic reactions to product concept
   2. Foreseen applications
   3. Reaction to cost/price sensitivity
   4. Willingness to buy/use

Research Audience
A. Residential consumers
   1. Consumers with allergies and other chronic respiratory problems
   2. Consumers with pets
   3. Consumers at homes without central filtering systems

B. Business consumers
   1. Hospitals and health clinics
   2. Small to large-scale businesses

EXPLORATORY RESEARCH AND QUALITATIVE ANALYSIS

The woman chose a story that she remembered from her childhood.[1] One Christmas she waited in giddy excitement to find out what was in the biggest package under the tree. It had the best wrapping paper. She could hardly imagine what it might be. But after she unwrapped the gift, it turned out to be something so ordinary that she hardly remembers what it was, only the disappointment that it didn't live up to the promise of its package.

The short story, written by a woman who had just finished looking at an early version of Chrysler's PT Cruiser, was the impetus that prompted designers to take another look at the interior. They redesigned it from standard, fixed seating to the more adaptable, unexpected interior that appears in the production car.

The team studying the design of the PT Cruiser read through hundreds of similar stories, looking for clues they could translate into action. . . . But rather than relying on focus groups, as they might have in the past, the team used a different type of qualitative research. Consumers met for three hours to look at the vehicle, discuss it, and then write stories. The environment is more relaxed than a focus group and the goal is not to get people to recommend changes but to get them to tap into less tangible feelings via their creative writing. "Sometimes people just don't know how to say what they really think about a vehicle." Creative writing often draws it out.

Exploratory research serves as a source for developing ideas that are then subjected to further research investigation. At Chrysler, exploratory research helped reduce some of the risks of introducing a new, unconventional vehicle in the ever-changing automobile industry. This chapter discusses the various exploratory research techniques used in marketing research. ■

What you will learn in this chapter

1. To understand the differences between qualitative research and quantitative research.

2. To explain the purposes of exploratory research.

3. To identify the four general categories of exploratory research.

4. To explain the advantages and disadvantages of experience surveys, case study methods, focus group interviews, projective techniques, depth interviews, and other exploratory research techniques.

5. To understand how technology is changing the nature of exploratory research.

6. To understand when exploratory techniques are appropriate and to understand their limitations.

exploratory research
Initial research conducted to clarify and define the nature of a problem.

When a researcher has a limited amount of experience with or knowledge about a research issue, **exploratory research** is a useful preliminary step. It helps ensure that a more rigorous, conclusive future study will not begin with an inadequate understanding of the nature of the marketing problem.

Conclusive research answers questions of fact necessary to determine a course of action. Exploratory research, on the other hand, never has this purpose. Most, but certainly not all, exploratory research designs provide qualitative data. Usually, exploratory research provides greater understanding of a concept or crystallizes a problem rather than providing precise measurement or quantification. The focus of qualitative research is not on numbers but on words and observations: stories, visual portrayals, meaningful characterizations, interpretations, and other expressive descriptions. A researcher may search for numbers to indicate economic trends but exploratory research does not involve rigorous mathematical analysis. Any source of information may be informally investigated to clarify which qualities or characteristics are associated with an object, situation, or issue.

Alternatively, the purpose of quantitative research is to determine the quantity or extent of some phenomenon in the form of numbers. Most exploratory research is not quantitative. This chapter discusses exploratory research under the assumption that its results are qualitative. Exploratory research may be a single investigation or a series of informal studies intended to provide background information. Researchers must be creative in the choice of information sources to be investigated. They must be flexible enough to investigate all inexpensive sources that may provide information to help managers understand a problem. This flexibility does not mean that researchers need not be careful and systematic when designing exploratory research studies. Most of the techniques discussed in this chapter have limitations. Researchers should be keenly aware of the proper and improper uses of the various techniques.

Exploratory researchers can be creative in their search for ideas. Researchers who conduct beeper studies provide consumers or business subjects with a questionnaire and instruct them to record their actions, interactions, moods, and stress levels every time the beeper goes off. Asking subjects to use disposable cameras, video cameras, and tape recorders is a variation of the beeper study.

The purpose of exploratory research is intertwined with the need for a clear and precise statement of the recognized problem. Researchers conduct exploratory research for three interrelated purposes: (1) diagnosing a situation, (2) screening alternatives, and (3) discovering new ideas.

Diagnosing a Situation

Much has already been said about the need for situation analysis to clarify a problem's nature. Exploratory research helps diagnose the dimensions of problems so that successive research projects will be on target; it helps set priorities for research. In some cases exploratory research helps orient management by gathering information on an unfamiliar topic. A research project may not yet be planned, but information about an issue will be needed before the marketing strategy can be developed.

For example, when an advertising agency got an account for a new coffee containing chicory, the firm began the research process with exploratory research to diagnose the situation. The researchers learned that almost nobody had heard of chicory. It wasn't being used, and nobody seemed to know how to use it. This led to the hypothesis that the advertising could portray the chicory ingredient any way the client wanted.

Screening Alternatives

When several opportunities, such as new product ideas, arise at once, but budgets don't allow trying all possible options, exploratory research may be used to determine the best alternatives. Exploratory research can help reveal which of several new product ideas are the best ones to pursue. Many good products are not on the market because a company chose to market something better. Exploratory research may indicate that some new product ideas are unworkable. An exploratory look at market data (size, number, and so on) may depict a product alternative as not feasible because the market of buyers is too small. This aspect of exploratory research is not a substitute for conclusive research; however, certain evaluative information can be gained from such studies.

Concept testing is a frequent reason for conducting exploratory research. **Concept testing** is a general term for many different research procedures, all of which have the same purpose: to test some sort of stimulus as a proxy for a new, revised, or repositioned product or service. Typically consumers are presented with a written statement or filmed representation of an idea and asked if they think it is new and different, if they would use it, whether they like it, and so on. Concept testing is a means of evaluating ideas by providing a feel for their merits prior to the commitment of any research and development, manufacturing, or other company resources.

For instance, exploratory research conducted by Pine-Sol revealed that younger working women in Canada wanted a different level of strength from the product, not the strength Pine-Sol stood for. Younger working women brought up two different types of clean: (a) the clean when a friend drops by and (b) the clean when your mother-in-law is visiting. Out of this came the idea for a new level of clean: the "thorough clean."[2]

Researchers look for trouble signals in consumer evaluations of concepts to reduce the number of concepts under consideration or improve them to avoid future problems. Concept testing portrays the functions, uses, and possible applications for the proposed good or service. For example, marketers scrapped a concept for a men's shampoo that claimed to offer a special benefit to hair damaged by overexposure to the sun, heat from a hair dryer, or heavy perspiration after exploratory research showed that consumers thought the product was a good idea for someone

concept testing
Any exploratory research procedure that tests some sort of stimulus as a proxy for an idea about a new, revised, or repositioned product, service, or strategy.

with an outdoor lifestyle, but not for themselves.[3] Early research indicated that although the product was seen as unique, the likelihood of persuading men that it matched their self-images was low.

If a concept is flawed, but the product has not been evaluated negatively, researchers may learn that the product concept needs to be refined or repositioned. For example, Procter & Gamble marketed Enviro-Paks—soft plastic refill pouches of detergents, fabric softeners, and other cleaning products—in Europe and Canada before concept-testing them in the United States. Concept testing with U.S. consumers indicated that Americans preferred refill packaging that was different from what was available in Canada and Europe—packaging that would be more convenient to use.

Exhibit 5.1 shows excellent concept statements for two seafood products made from squid. The statements portraying the intangibles (brand image, product appearance, name, and price) and a description of the product simulate reality. The product idea is clearly conveyed to the subject.

| Exhibit 5.1 | CONCEPT STATEMENTS FOR TWO SEAFOOD PRODUCTS[4] |

Squid Concept Alternative 1: CALAMARIOS

CALAMARIOS[a] are a new and different seafood product made from tender, boneless North Atlantic squid. The smooth white body (mantle) of the squid is thoroughly cleaned, cut into thin, bite-sized rings, then frozen to seal in their flavour. To cook CALAMARIOS, simply remove them from the package and boil them for only 8 minutes. They are then ready to be used in a variety of recipes.

For example, CALAMARIOS can be combined with noodles, cheese, tomatoes, and onions to make "Baked CALAMARIOS Cacciatore." Or CALAMARIOS can be marinated in olive oil, lemon juice, mint, and garlic and served as a tasty squid salad. CALAMARIOS also are the prime ingredient for "Calamari en Casserole" and "Squid Italienne." You may simply want to steam CALAMARIOS, lightly season them with garlic, and serve dipped in melted butter. This dish brings out the fine flavour of squid. A complete CALAMARIOS recipe book will be available free of charge at your supermarket.

CALAMARIOS are both nutritious and economical. Squid, like other seafood, is an excellent source of protein. CALAMARIOS can be found at your supermarket priced at $6.50 per package of 500 g. Each package you buy is completely cleaned and waste-free.

Because of their convenient versatility, ample nutrition, and competitive price, we hope you will want to make CALAMARIOS a regular item on your shopping list.

[a]Calamari is the Italian word for squid.

Squid Concept Alternative 2: SCLAM CHOWDER

SCLAM CHOWDER is a delicious new seafood soup made from choice New England clams and tasty, young, boneless North Atlantic squid. Small pieces of clam are combined with bite-sized strips of squid and boiled in salted water until they are soft and tender. Sautéed onions, carrots, and celery are then added together with thick, wholesome cream, a dash of white pepper, and a sprinkling of fresh parsley. The entire mixture is then cooked to perfection, bringing out a fine, natural taste that will make this chowder a favourite in your household.

SCLAM CHOWDER is available canned in your supermarket. To prepare, simply combine SCLAM CHOWDER with 750 mL of milk in a saucepan, and bring to a boil. After the chowder has reached a boil, simmer for 5 minutes and then serve. One can makes two to three servings of this hearty, robust seafood treat. Considering its ample nutrition and delicious taste, SCLAM CHOWDER is quite a bargain at $3.89 per can.

Both clams and squid are high in protein, so high in fact that SCLAM CHOWDER makes a healthy meal in itself, perfect for lunches as well as with dinner. Instead of adding milk, some will want to add a cup of sour cream and use liquid chowder as an exquisite sauce to be served on rice, topped with grated Parmesan cheese.

However you choose to serve it, you are sure to find SCLAM CHOWDER a tasty, nutritious, and economical seafood dish.

Researchers conducting concept testing ask consumers to react to a stimulus and indicate what they like and dislike. Automobile marketers have consumers design their dream cars using computerized design systems similar to those used by automotive designers.

Discovering New Ideas

Marketers often conduct exploratory research to generate ideas for new products, advertising copy, and so on. For example, automobile marketers have consumers design their dream cars using computerized design systems similar to those used by automotive designers. This exploratory research might generate ideas that would never have occurred to the firms' own designers.[5]

Uncovering consumer needs is a great potential source of product ideas. One goal of exploratory research is to first determine what problems consumers have with a product category. When research has to determine what kinds of products people will buy, there is a difference between asking people about what they want or need and asking them about their problems. When you ask a customer what he or she wants in a dog food, the reply likely will be "Something that is good for the dog." If you ask what the problems with dog food are, you may learn that "the dog food smells bad when it is put into the refrigerator." Once problems have been identified through research, the marketing job is to find how to solve them.

CATEGORIES OF EXPLORATORY RESEARCH

3 There are many techniques for investigating undefined research problems. Several of the most popular qualitative techniques are discussed in the next section. However, the purpose, rather than the technique, determines whether a study is exploratory, descriptive, or causal. For example, telephone surveys (discussed in Chapter 7) are sometimes used for exploratory purposes, although they are used mainly for descriptive research. The versatile qualitative techniques discussed in this chapter tend to be used primarily—but not exclusively—for exploratory purposes.

A manager may choose from four general categories of exploratory research methods: (1) experience surveys, (2) secondary data analysis, (3) case studies, and (4) pilot studies. Each category provides various alternative ways to gather information.

EXPERIENCE SURVEYS

experience survey
An exploratory research technique in which individuals who are knowledgeable about a particular research problem are questioned.

If management decides that an idea is worthwhile, the decision maker may personally spend some time analyzing the situation. In attempting to gain insight into the problems at hand, researchers may discuss the concepts with top executives and knowledgeable individuals, both inside and outside the company, who have had personal experience in the field. This constitutes an informal **experience survey.** People who are knowledgeable about the area to be investigated often are willing to share their experiences with others (competitors excluded, of course). For example, a firm that is ready to launch a new product may discuss the general nature of the product with some of its key retailers and wholesalers. Members of the company's sales force also may be a valuable source of information. The purpose of such discussions is to exhaust the information available from relatively inexpensive sources before gathering expensive primary data. While the interviews with knowledgeable individuals may reveal nothing conclusive, they may help define the problem more formally.

Exploratory research during situation analysis may be quite informal. Input from knowledgeable people both inside and outside the company may come from little more than informal conversations. Just to get ideas about the problem, the marketing manager, rather than the research department, may conduct an experience survey. An experience survey may constitute a small number of interviews with some carefully selected people. Some formal questions may be asked, but the respondents generally will be allowed to discuss the questions with few constraints. Knowledgeable people should be selected because they are articulate on a particular subject; the researcher is not trying to establish a representative probability sample. The purpose is to help formulate the problem and clarify concepts rather than to develop conclusive evidence.

SECONDARY DATA ANALYSIS

Another economical and quick source of background information is trade literature. Searching through such material is exploratory research with secondary data. Basic theoretical research rarely is conducted without extensive reviews of the literature or reviews of similar research reports.

A chain saw manufacturer received from its Japanese distributor a recommendation to modify its product with a drilling attachment on the sprocket (replacing the chain and guide bar) so that the chain saw could be used as a mushroom-planting device. The distributor indicated that many such units had been sold in Japan. However, an experience survey with only one individual, the president of the Mushroom Growers Association, indicated that the product was not feasible in the United States. Most Americans favour a white, cultured mushroom grown in enclosed areas or caves rather than the variety of mushrooms grown on wood in Japan. The mushroom expert indicated that Americans believe too many superstitious tales about poisonous mushrooms and would not change their eating habits to include the Japanese variety.

Using secondary data may be equally important in applied research. Suppose the brand manager of a company that manufactures dental hygiene products is contacted by an inventor of a tongue cleaner. The inventor states that her stainless steel device cleans the tongue deposits that cause bad breath. Shortly thereafter, the brand manager finds information in the library that explains the practice of tongue cleaning: It began centuries ago and is a common practice among certain Asian people. If the problem had concerned an existing product, the manager's situational analysis might have begun with an analysis of sales records by region and by customer or some other source of internal data.

Investigating data that have been compiled for some purpose other than the project at hand, such as accounting records or trade association data, is one of the most frequent forms of exploratory research. Because this is also a technique for conclusive research (both descriptive and causal research), a separate chapter (Chapter 6) is devoted to the investigation of secondary sources.

Marketing managers often conduct situation analysis using experience surveys and secondary data studies without a need for assistance from marketing research specialists. Informal situation analysis can indicate projects that still need clarification and may warrant further exploratory investigation. In that case, the marketing research specialist is called in to design a more elaborate exploratory study.

CASE STUDIES

case study method
The exploratory research technique that intensively investigates one or a few situations similar to the problem situation.

The purpose of the **case study method** is to obtain information from one or a few situations that are similar to the researcher's problem situation. For example, a bank in Montreal may intensively investigate the marketing activities of an innovative bank in Vancouver. A shirt manufacturer interested in surveying retailers may first look at a few retail stores to identify the nature of any problems or topics that a larger study should investigate.

A marketing research manager for Schwinn bicycles used observation techniques to conduct an exploratory case study. Here is a description of the case situation in his own words:

> We had a very successful dealer on the West Coast. He sold a lot of bicycles. So it occurred to me that we'd go out and find out how he's doing it. We'll use a tape recorder and get in the back room where we'll hear these magic words that he says to people to make them buy bicycles. We'll take that tape back to the factory. We'll have it all typed out. We'll print it in the *Reporter* [a dealer newsletter]. We'll send it to all the other dealers and everybody can say the same words. And, boy, we'll need another factory! Right? So we go out. The guy's got a nice store. We sit in the back room and we listen. The first customers come in, a man and a woman with a boy about nine or ten years old. The dad says, "Which one is it?" The son says, "This one over here." Dad looks at it. He says to the clerk, "How much is it?" The clerk says, "$179.95." The father says, "Okay, we'll take it." It blew the whole bit. So we stand there and we listen to some of these conversations going on like this. Suddenly it dawned on us that it was not what they say, it's the atmosphere of the store. Here was not Joe's old, dirty bike shop—it was a beautiful store on the main street. A big sign was in front, "Valley Cyclery," inside [were] fluorescent lights, carpeting on the floor, stereo music, air-conditioning, a beautiful display of bicycles. It was like a magnet. People came in. So, maybe this is the catch. We tried to introduce that idea to other dealers. Put a bigger investment into your store and see what happens. Some of them did, and it happened.[6]

This observational case study serendipitously led to a discovery that would change Schwinn's entire channel of distribution strategy in the United States. The opportunity was a direct result of being open-minded in the problem discovery stage of marketing research.

The primary advantage of the case study is that an entire organization or entity can be investigated in depth with meticulous attention to detail. This highly focused attention enables the researcher to carefully study the order of events as they occur or to concentrate on identifying the relationships among functions, individuals, or entities. A fast-food restaurant may test a new menu item or a new store design in a single location before launching the change throughout the chain to learn about potential operating problems that could hinder service quality.

Conducting a case study often requires the cooperation of the party whose history is being studied. A successful franchisee may be willing to allow the franchisor access to records and reports. Intensive interviews or long discussions with the franchisee and his or her employees may provide an understanding of a situation. The researcher has no standard procedures to follow; he or she must be flexible and attempt to glean information and insights wherever possible. This freedom to search for whatever data an investigator deems important makes the success of any case study highly dependent on the alertness, creativity, intelligence, and motivation of the individual performing the case analysis.

TGI Friday's, a U.S. restaurant chain, used a case study in its efforts to build smaller restaurants with the same number of seats as its older restaurant designs (5,700 square feet with 210 seats, compared to 9,200 square feet with 240 seats). With the cooperation of the U.S. Navy, the company executives studied the food-handling operations in a nuclear submarine with a crew of 155 people. With crew on duty 24 hours per day, the Navy served four meals daily, resulting in 620 meals per day for a crew of 155 in an extremely confined space. The executives of Friday's could gather important information in redesigning their restaurants and the Navy was pleased to let Friday's use its operations as a case study.[7]

As with all exploratory research, the results from case studies should be seen as tentative. Generalizing from a few cases can be dangerous, because most situations are atypical in some sense. The bank in Montreal may not be in a market comparable to the one in Vancouver. Even if situations are not directly comparable, however, a number of insights can be gained and hypotheses suggested for future research.

Obtaining information about competitors may be very difficult, because they generally like to keep the secrets of their success to themselves. The exact formula of Coca-Cola, for example, is known by only a few top executives in the firm; they feel that confidentiality is a definite competitive edge in their product strategy. Thus researchers may have limited access to information from other firms.

PILOT STUDIES

pilot study
A collective term for any small-scale exploratory research project that uses sampling but does not apply rigorous standards.

The term *pilot study* covers a number of diverse research techniques. Within the context of exploratory research, the term indicates that some aspect of the research (for example, fieldwork) will be on a small scale. Thus a **pilot study** is a research project that involves sampling, but it relaxes the rigorous standards used to obtain precise, quantitative estimates from large, representative samples.

In one kind of pilot study, researchers or managers try to experience what consumers experience to gain inexpensive and valuable insight. Without indicating their real positions with the company, researchers or managers may wait on customers, ride in repair trucks, and answer telephones. For example, the chairperson of a major car rental company occasionally gets in line with airport customers waiting for cars or works behind the counter to get customer reactions. This form of pilot study may yield true comprehension of the situation to be investigated.

A pilot study generates primary data, but usually for qualitative analysis. This characteristic distinguishes pilot studies from research that gathers background information using secondary data. Some researchers refer to pilot studies that generate qualitative information as *qualitative research*. The primary data usually come from

consumers or other subjects of ultimate concern rather than from knowledgeable experts or case situations. This distinguishes pilot studies from experience surveys and case studies. Major categories of pilot studies include focus group interviews, projective techniques, and depth interviews.

Focus Group Interviews

focus group interview
An unstructured, free-flowing interview with a small group of people.

The focus group interview has become so popular that many advertising and research agencies consider it the only qualitative research tool. As noted in Chapter 2, a **focus group interview** is an unstructured, free-flowing interview with a small group of people. It is not a rigidly constructed question-and-answer session but a flexible format that encourages discussion of a brand, advertisement, or new-product concept. The group meets at a central location at a designated time; typically, it consists of a moderator or interviewer and six to ten participants, although larger groups are sometimes used. The participants may range from consumers talking about hair colouring, petroleum engineers talking about problems in the "oil patch," or children talking about toys. The moderator introduces the topic and encourages group members to discuss the subject among themselves. Ideally, the discussion topics emerge at the group's initiative. Focus groups allow people to discuss their true feelings, anxieties, and frustrations, as well as the depth of their convictions, in their own words. The primary advantages of focus group interviews are that they are relatively fast, easy to execute, and inexpensive. In an emergency situation, three or four group sessions can be conducted, analyzed, and reported in less than a week at a cost substantially lower than that of other attitude-measurement techniques. Remember, however, that a small group of people will not be a representative sample no matter how carefully they are recruited. Focus group interviews cannot take the place of quantitative studies.

The flexibility of focus group interviews has some advantages, especially when compared with the rigid format of a survey. Numerous topics can be discussed and many insights can be gained, particularly with regard to the variations in consumer behaviour in different situations. Responses that would be unlikely to emerge in a survey often come out in group interviews: "*If* it is one of the three brands I sometimes use and *if* it is on sale, I buy it; otherwise, I buy my regular brand" or "*If* the day is hot and I have to serve the whole neighbourhood, I make Kool-Aid; otherwise, I give them Dr Pepper or Coke."

If a researcher is investigating a target group to determine who consumes a particular beverage or why a consumer purchases a certain brand, situational factors must be taken into account. If the researcher does not realize the impact of the occasion on which the particular beverage is consumed, the results of the research may be general rather than portraying the consumer's thought process. A focus group elicits situationally specific responses: On a hot day the whole neighbourhood gets Kool-Aid; but if there are just a few kids, they get Dr Pepper or Coke.

When research showed that milk consumption levels dropped dramatically among young people between the ages of 16 and 23, the B.C. Dairy Foundation decided to target this age group. The foundation executed further research in order to understand how best to target this age group. Focus groups were conducted and participants expressed their desire to be surprised by milk; they said they'd like to see it behave in a non-traditional way. So the creative strategy drew from what was learned in the focus groups and what was already known of the teen target: Younger consumers did not have overly negative things to say about milk. While words like "boring," "old-fashioned," and "fattening" did arise, for the most part milk was associated with positive attributes like "nutritional," "comforting," and even "cleansing." Perhaps most importantly, when asked where these consumers felt milk could stretch as a brand, participants encouraged the foundation to push the boundaries by using words and images that conveyed empowerment, confidence, and, not surprisingly, humour. Based on these insights a "Cold Crew" street team was introduced; this subtly branded team of sexy, urban young people created "milk mayhem" at major teen-targeted events throughout British Columbia.[10]

Focus groups often are used for concept screening and concept refinement. The concept may be continually modified, refined, and retested until management believes it is acceptable.

The specific advantages of focus group interviews have been categorized as follows:[11]

Synergy: The combined effort of the group will produce a wider range of information, insights, and ideas than will the accumulation of separately secured responses from a number of individuals.

Snowballing: A bandwagon effect often operates in a group interview situation. A comment by one individual often triggers a chain of responses from the other participants. Brainstorming of ideas frequently is encouraged in focus group sessions.

Serendipity: It is more often the case in a group than in an individual interview that some idea drops out of the blue. The group also affords a greater opportunity to develop an idea to its full potential.

Stimulation: Usually, after a brief introductory period, the respondents want to express their ideas and expose their feelings as the general level of excitement over the topic increases.

Security: In a well-structured group, the individual usually can find some comfort in the fact that his or her feelings are similar to those of others in the group and that each participant can expose an idea without being obliged to defend it or follow through and elaborate on it. One is more likely to be candid because the focus is on the group rather than on the individual; the participant soon realizes that the things said are not necessarily being identified with him or her.

Spontaneity: Because no individual is required to answer any given question in a group interview, the individual's responses can be more spontaneous and less conventional. They should provide a more accurate picture of the person's position on some issue. In the group interview, people speak only when they have definite feelings about a subject, not because a question requires a response.

Specialization: The group interview allows the use of a more highly trained interviewer (moderator) because certain economies of scale exist when a number of individuals are interviewed simultaneously.

Structure: The group interview affords more control than the individual interview with regard to the topics covered and the depth in which they are treated. The moderator has the opportunity to reopen topics that received too shallow a discussion when initially presented.

Speed: The group interview permits securing a given number of interviews more quickly than does interviewing individual respondents.

Scientific scrutiny: The group interview allows closer scrutiny in several ways. First, the session can be observed by several people; this affords some check on the consistency of the interpretations. Second, the session can be tape-recorded or videotaped. Later, detailed examination of the recorded session can offer additional insight and help clear up disagreements about what happened.

Group Composition

The ideal size of the focus group is six to ten relatively similar people. If the group is too small, one or two members may intimidate the others. Groups that are too large may not allow for adequate participation by each group member. Homogeneous groups seem to work best, because they allow researchers to concentrate on consumers with similar lifestyles, experiences, and communication skills. The session does not become rife with too many arguments and different viewpoints stemming from diverse backgrounds.

When the Centers for Disease Control and Prevention in Atlanta tested public service announcements about AIDS through focus groups, it discovered that single-race groups and multicultural groups reacted differently. By conducting separate focus groups, the organization was able to gain important insights about which creative strategies were most appropriate for targeted versus broad audiences.

For example, a typical homogeneous group might be made up of married, full-time homemakers with children at home; the group would not include unmarried, working women. Having first-time mothers in a group with women who have three or four children reduces the new mothers' participation; they look to the more experienced mothers for advice. Although they may differ in their opinions, they defer to the more experienced mothers; thus first-time mothers and experienced mothers would be in separate groups.

Researchers who wish to collect information from different types of people should conduct several focus groups; for example, one focus group might consist only of men and another only of women. Thus a diverse sample may be obtained even though each group is homogeneous. Most focus group experts believe that four focus group sessions (often in different cities) can satisfy the needs of exploratory research.

Environmental Conditions

The group session may take place at the research agency, the advertising agency, a hotel, or one of the subjects' homes. Research suppliers that specialize in conducting focus groups operate from commercial facilities that have videotape cameras in observation rooms behind one-way mirrors and microphone systems connected to tape recorders and speakers to allow observation by others who aren't in the room. Some researchers suggest that a "coffee klatch" or "bull session" atmosphere can be established in the commercial research facility to ensure that the mood of the sessions will be as relaxed and natural as possible. They expect more open and intimate reports of personal experiences and sentiments to be obtained under these conditions.

The Moderator

moderator
The person who leads a focus group discussion.

The moderator's job is to develop a rapport with the group and to promote interaction among its members. The **moderator** should be someone who is really interested in people, who listens carefully to what others have to say, and who can readily establish rapport and gain people's confidence and make them feel relaxed and eager to talk. Careful listening is especially important because the group interview's purpose is to stimulate spontaneous responses. The moderator's role is also to focus the discussion on the areas of concern. When a topic is no longer generating fresh ideas, the effective moderator changes the flow of discussion. The moderator does not give the group total control of the discussion, but normally has prepared questions on topics that concern management. However, the timing of these questions in the discussion and the manner in which they are raised are left to the moderator's discretion. The term *focus group* thus stems from the moderator's task: He or she starts out by asking for a general discussion but usually focuses in on specific topics during the session.

Planning the Focus Group Outline

discussion guide
A document prepared by the focus group moderator that contains remarks about the nature of the group and outlines the topics or questions to be addressed.

Effective focus group moderators prepare discussion guides to help ensure that the groups cover all topics of interest. The **discussion guide** begins with a written statement of the prefatory remarks to inform the group about the nature of the focus group; it then outlines topics or questions to be addressed in the group session.

Exhibit 5.2 displays the discussion guide for the focus group research that was used by a cancer centre based in the United States. The cancer centre wanted to warn the public about the effects of the sun. The marketing researchers had several objectives for this question guide:

- The first question, asking participants to describe their feelings about being out in the sun, was intended to elicit the range of views present in the group, given that some individuals might view being out in the sun as a healthful practice while others would view it as dangerous. It seemed important to have group members see the extent to which others held views different from their own. Furthermore, this was the only question asked of every participant in turn. As no one could fail to be able to answer, it gave each individual a non-threatening chance to talk and thus broke the ice.

ARE BROOMS AND MOPS ONLY "WOMEN'S TOOLS"?

Sometimes the best ideas pop into people's minds just as they're drifting off to sleep.[12] About an hour into one of Rubbermaid Inc.'s drowsier focus groups on housewares, a woman frustrated by the pace shattered the calm by accusing the industry of sexism.

"Why do companies continue to treat brooms and mops like they were 'women's tools'?" she complained. "They're poorly designed and second-class to hammers and saws, which are balanced and moulded to fit men's hands. Brooms and mops make housework more miserable, not easier."

The outburst sent Rubbermaid executives scrambling for notepads. The company didn't make cleaning products at the time, but it was more than willing to listen to reasons why it should. The woman's remarks not only made sense but eventually convinced the company to enter a product category it had avoided for so long.

After five years of research and development, Rubbermaid's housewares products division introduced a line of about 50 cleaning products and brushes. They ranged from a $1.29 sink brush to a $15.99 push broom, and while you can't saw wood or hammer a nail with them, each has been specially designed to make cleaning easier. Handles are supposed to fit comfortably in consumers' hands, and bristles are angled to reach tight spaces. Focus groups helped Rubbermaid identify areas of the house that need cleaning, right down to the spaces between banister supports. The company identified what people use to clean those spaces (most people use a dust rag for banisters). Rubbermaid employees also called consumers at home and asked them what cleaning products they owned and what they expected to pay for them. The company even researched the product line's colour. All of the products are blue, because consumers associate blue most closely with freshness and cleanliness.

- The second question, asking whether participants could think of any reason to be warned about exposure to the sun, was simply designed to introduce in question form the idea of a warning.

- Succeeding questions were asked, first on an open-ended basis, about possible formats of warnings of danger from the sun. Respondents were asked to react to any formats that participants suggested on an open-ended basis, and then to react to formats the cancer centre personnel had in mind.

- Finally, the "bottom line" question asked which format would be most likely to induce participants to take protective measures, and then a catch-all question asked for any comments they wanted to pass along to the sponsor, which was revealed as the particular cancer centre.

Notice that the researchers who planned the outline established certain objectives for each part of the focus group. The initial effort was to break the ice and establish rapport within the group. The logical flow of the group session then moved from general discussion about sunbathing to more focused discussion of types of warnings about danger from sun exposure.

Focus Groups as Diagnostic Tools

Researchers predominantly use focus groups as a means of conducting exploratory research. Focus groups can be helpful in later stages of a research project, but the findings from surveys or other quantitative techniques raise more questions than they answer. Managers who are puzzled about the meaning of survey research results may use focus groups to better understand what consumer surveys indicate. In such a situation, the focus group supplies diagnostic help after quantitative research has been conducted.

EXHIBIT 5.2 | **DISCUSSION GUIDE FROM A U.S. CANCER CENTRE FOCUS GROUP**[13]

Thank you very much for agreeing to help out with this research. We call this a focus group; let me explain how it works, and then please let me know if something isn't clear.

This is a discussion, as though you were sitting around just talking. You can disagree with each other, or just comment. We do ask that just one person talk at a time, because we tape-record the session to save me from having to take notes. Nothing you say will be associated with you—this is just an easy way for us to get some people together.

The subject is health risk warnings. Some of you may remember seeing a chart in a newspaper that gives a pollen count or a pollution count. And you've heard on the radio sometimes a hurricane watch or warning. You've seen warnings on cigarette packages or cigarette advertising, even if you don't smoke. And today we're going to talk about warnings about the sun. Before we start, does anybody have a question?

1. OK, let's go around and talk about how often you spend time in the sun, and what you're likely to be doing. (FOR PARENTS): What about your kids—do you like them to be out in the sun?

2. OK, can you think of any reason that somebody would give you a warning about exposure to the sun?

(PROBE: IS ANY SUN EXPOSURE BAD, OR ONLY A CERTAIN DEGREE OF EXPOSURE, AND IF SO, WHAT IS IT? OR IS THE SUN GOOD FOR YOU?)

3. What if we had a way to measure the rays of the sun that are associated with skin problems, so that you could find out which times of the day or which days are especially dangerous? How could, say, a radio station tell you that information in a way that would be useful?

4. Now let me ask you about specific ways to measure danger. Suppose somebody said, "We monitored the sun's rays at noon, and a typical fair-skinned person with unprotected skin will burn after 40 minutes of direct exposure." What would you think?

5. Now let me ask you about another way to say the same kind of thing. Suppose somebody said, "The sun's rays at noon today measured 10 times the 8 a.m. baseline level of danger." What would you think?

6. OK, now suppose that you heard the same degree of danger expressed this way: "The sun's rays at noon today measured 8 on a sun danger scale that ranges from 1 to 10." What would you think?

7. What if the danger scale wasn't numbers, but words? Suppose you heard "The sun's rays at noon showed a moderate danger reading," or "The sun's rays showed a high danger reading." What would you think?

8. And here's another possibility: What if you heard "Here's the sun danger reading at noon today—the unprotected skin of a typical fair-skinned person will age the equivalent of 1 hour in a 10-minute period."

9. OK, what if somebody said today is a day to wear long sleeves and a hat, or today is a day you need sunscreen and long sleeves. What would you think?

10. OK, here's my last question. There are really three things you can do about sun danger: You can spend less time in the sun, you can go out at less dangerous times of day, like before 10 in the morning or after 4 in the afternoon, and you can cover your skin by wearing a hat, or long sleeves, or using protective sunscreen lotion. Thinking about yourself listening to the radio, what kind of announcement would make you likely to do one or more of those things? (PARENTS: WHAT WOULD MAKE YOU BE SURE THAT YOUR CHILD WAS PROTECTED?)

11. And what would you be most likely to do to protect yourself? (YOUR CHILD?)

12. Before we break up, is there anything else you think would be useful for our cancer centre's people to know?

OK, thank you very much for your help.

Videoconferencing and Streaming Media

The videoconferencing industry has grown dramatically in recent years. And as the ability to communicate via telecommunications and videoconferencing links has improved in quality, the number of companies using these systems to conduct focus groups has increased. With traditional focus groups, marketing managers and creative personnel often watch the moderator lead the group from behind one-way mirrors. If the focus group is being conducted out of town, the marketing personnel usually have to spend more time in airplanes, hotels, and taxis than they do watching the group session. With videoconferenced focus groups, marketing managers can stay home.

streaming media
Multimedia content, such as audio or video, that can be accessed on the Internet without being downloaded first.

Streaming media consist of multimedia content such as audio or video that is made available in real time over the Internet or a corporate intranet, with no download wait and no file to take up space on a viewer's hard disk.[14] This new technology for digital media delivery allows researchers to "broadcast" focus groups that can be viewed online. The offsite manager uses RealPlayer or Microsoft Media Player to view a focus group on a computer rather than at a remote location. Except for a decrease in quality of the video when there are bandwidth problems, the effect is similar to videoconferencing.

Pollara, a national marketing research company based in Montreal, offers the option of television-quality focus group webcasting. Clients can view focus groups online from home or office, as long as there is a high-speed connection, eliminating the need to travel to focus group facilities in person. Three remotely operated cameras track the conversation, capturing the expressions on the faces of the participants. Clients can see what is on a participant's monitor so they can follow the discussion better.[15]

Interactive Media and Online Focus Groups

online focus group
A focus group whose members use Internet technology to carry on their discussion.

The use of the Internet for qualitative exploratory research is growing rapidly. The term **online focus group** refers to a qualitative research effort in which a group of individuals provides unstructured comments by entering their remarks into a computer connected to the Internet. The group participants keyboard their remarks either during a chat-room format or when they are alone at their computers. Because respondents enter their comments into the computer, transcripts of verbatim responses are available immediately after the group session. Online groups can be quick and cost-efficient. However, because there is less interaction between participants, group synergy and snowballing of ideas may be diminished.

A research company may set up a private chat room on its company Web site for focus group interviews. Participants in these chat rooms feel that their anonymity is very secure. Often they will make statements or ask questions they would never pose under other circumstances.[16] This can be a major advantage for a company investigating sensitive or embarrassing issues.

Many focus groups using the chat-room format involve a sample of participants who are online at the same time, typically for about 60 to 90 minutes. Because participants do not have to be together in the same room at a research facility, the number of participants in these online focus groups can be much larger than in traditional focus groups. Twenty-five participants or more is not uncommon for the simultaneous chat-room format. Participants can be at widely separated locations, even in different time zones, because the Internet does not have geographical restrictions. Of course, a major disadvantage is that only individuals with Internet access can be selected for an online group. (The nature of Internet samples will be discussed in depth in Chapters 8 and 14.)

The job of an online moderator resembles that of an in-person moderator. However, the online moderator should possess fast and accurate keyboard skills or be willing to hire an assistant who does. Ideally, the discussion guide is downloaded directly onto the site so the moderator can, with one click, enter a question into the dialogue stream.[17]

A problem with online focus groups is that the moderator cannot see body language and facial expressions (bewilderment, excitement, interest, etc.) to interpret how people are reacting. Also, the moderator's ability to probe and ask additional questions on the spot is reduced in online focus groups, especially those in which group members are not participating simultaneously.[18] Research that requires focus group members to actually touch something (such as a new easy-opening packaging design) or taste something cannot be performed online.

TO THE POINT

Necessity, mother of invention.
WILLIAM WYCHERLEY

The complexity of the subject will determine the exact nature and length of an online focus group. For many online projects, the group discussion can continue for 24 or 48 hours or even longer. Cross Pen Computing Group tested the appeal of an advertising campaign for a new product called CrossPad with an online brainstorming group that ran for five days.[19]

As the session's time expands, so may the number of participants. Some sessions involve quite a large number, perhaps as many as 200 participants. Whether these online chat sessions are true focus groups or not is a matter of some minor debate. However, these online research projects do have their purpose. For example, YTV has a kids' advisory panel known as SWAT (Stay Weird All the Time), plus focus group research and the annual YTV Kid and Tween Report. The annual Tween Report collects information every year on a wide variety of key topics such as leisure activities, amount of regular allowance, and media habits. YTV also conducts Web polls and surveys through its Web site, www.ytv.com.[20]

Although we have not yet discussed Internet surveys, it is important to make a distinction between online focus groups, which provide qualitative information, and Internet surveys, which provide quantitative findings. Chapter 8 discusses technological challenges and how to administer Internet surveys. (Much of that discussion is also relevant for researchers wishing to conduct online focus groups.)

Shortcomings

The shortcomings of focus groups are similar to those of most qualitative research techniques, as discussed later in this chapter. However, here we must point out two specific shortcomings of bringing people together for focus groups. First, focus groups require sensitive and effective moderators; without a good moderator, self-appointed participants may dominate a session, giving somewhat misleading results. If participants react negatively toward the dominant member, a "halo effect" on attitudes toward the concept or topic of discussion may occur. This situation should be carefully avoided. Second, some unique sampling problems arise with focus groups. Researchers often select focus group participants because they have similar backgrounds and experiences or because screening indicates that the participants are more articulate or gregarious than the typical consumer. Such participants may not be representative of the entire target market. (The Exploring Research Ethics box on the next page addresses this issue.)

Projective Techniques

There is an old story about asking a man why he purchased a Mercedes. When asked directly why he purchased a Mercedes, he responds that the car holds its value and does not depreciate much, that it gets better gas mileage than you'd expect, or that it has a comfortable ride. If you ask the same person why a neighbour purchased a Mercedes, he may well answer, "Oh, that status seeker!" This story illustrates that individuals may be more likely to give true answers (consciously or unconsciously) to disguised questions. Projective techniques seek to discover an individual's true attitudes, motivations, defensive reactions, and characteristic ways of responding.

The assumption underlying these methods can be summed up in Oscar Wilde's observation: "A man is least himself when he talks in his own person; when he is given a mask he will tell the truth." In other words, advocates of projective techniques assume that when directly questioned, respondents do not express their true feelings because they are embarrassed about answers that reflect negatively on their self-concept; they wish to please the interviewer with the "right" answer, or they cannot reveal unconscious feelings of which they are unaware. However, if respondents are presented with unstructured, ambiguous stimuli, such as cartoons or inkblots, and are allowed considerable freedom to respond, they will express their true feelings.

Although reaching major generalizations about the target population when using focus groups is a common error that various marketing research textbooks warn about, another issue that is related to focus group research is how the researchers have recruited participants.

When focus groups are populated by individuals who are focus group addicts to increase their financial gain, the information that is gathered may be useless—even, in fact, harmful. Roger, a 27-year-old from Toronto, has responded to classified ads for focus

groups and has participated in about a dozen focus groups. He claims that, after the first few focus groups, companies have called him back to recruit him even when he did not fit the target market, such as when his age, product usage, or brand preferences did not match the target market.

To prevent such instances, marketing research companies often inform their employees that their recruits will be contacted by the supervisors to verify their personal information and fit with the target group.[21]

---

projective technique
An indirect means of questioning that enables a respondent to project beliefs and feelings onto a third party, an inanimate object, or a task situation.

A **projective technique** is an indirect means of questioning that enables respondents to project beliefs and feelings onto a third party, an inanimate object, or a task situation. Respondents are not required to provide answers in any structured format. They are encouraged to describe a situation in their own words with little prompting by the interviewer. Individuals are expected to interpret the situation within the context of their own experiences, attitudes, and personalities and to express opinions and emotions that may be hidden from others and possibly themselves. The most common projective techniques in marketing research are word association tests, sentence completion methods, third-person techniques, and thematic apperception tests.[22]

Word Association Tests

word association test
A projective technique in which the subject is presented with a list of words, one at a time, and asked to respond with the first word that comes to mind.

During a **word association test,** the subject is presented with a list of words, one at a time, and asked to respond with the first word that comes to his or her mind. Both verbal and nonverbal responses (such as hesitation in responding) are recorded. For example, a researcher who reads a list of job tasks to sales employees expects that the word association technique will reveal each individual's true feelings about the job tasks. A sales representative's first thought presumably is a spontaneous answer because the subject does not have enough time to think about and avoid making admissions that reflect poorly on himself or herself.

Word association frequently is used to test potential brand names. For example, a liquor manufacturer attempting to market a clear-coloured light whiskey tested the brand names Frost, Verve, Ultra, and Master's Choice. Frost was seen as upbeat, modern, clean, and psychologically right; Verve was too modern, Ultra was too common, and Master's Choice was not upbeat enough.

Interpreting word association tests is difficult, and the marketing researcher should make sure to avoid subjective interpretations. When there is considerable agreement in the free-association process, the researcher assumes that the test has revealed the consumer's inner feelings about the subject. Word association tests are also analyzed by the amount of elapsed time. For example, if the researcher is investigating alternative advertising appeals for a method of birth control, a hesitation in responding may indicate that the topic arouses some sort of emotion (and the person may be seeking an "acceptable" response). The analysis of projective technique results takes into account not only what consumers say, but also what they do not say.

Word association tests can also be used to pre-test words or ideas for questionnaires. This enables the researcher to know beforehand whether and to what degree the meaning of a word is understood in the context of a survey.

Sentence Completion Method

The **sentence completion method** is also based on the principle of free association. Respondents are required to complete a number of partial sentences with the first word or phrase that comes to mind. For example:

People who drink beer are _____.

A man who drinks a dark beer is _____.

Imported beer is most liked by _____.

The woman in the commercial _____.

Answers to sentence completion questions tend to be more extensive than responses to word association tests. The intent of sentence completion questions is more apparent, however.

Third-Person Technique and Role Playing

An example illustrates the value of the third-person technique. When the poll, which was taken in Iowa, asked, "Will you wind up in heaven or hell?" nearly all participants reported that they would be saved, but one-third described a neighbour as a "sure bet" for hell.

Almost literally, providing a mask is the basic idea behind the **third-person technique.** Respondents are asked why a third person (for example, a neighbour) does what he or she does or what he or she thinks about a product. For example, male homeowners might be told: "We are talking to a number of homeowners like you about this new type of lawn mower. Some men like it the way it is; others believe that it should be improved. Please think of some of your friends or neighbours, and tell us what they might find fault with on this new type of lawn mower." Respondents can transfer their attitudes to neighbours, friends, or co-workers. They are free to agree or disagree with an unknown third party.

The best-known and certainly a classic example of a study that used this indirect technique was conducted in 1950, when Nescafé Instant Coffee was new to the market. Two shopping lists, identical except for the brand of coffee, were given to two groups of women:

- Pound and a half of hamburger
- 2 loaves of Wonder bread
- Bunch of carrots
- 1 can of Rumford's Baking Powder
- Nescafé Instant Coffee [or Maxwell House Coffee, drip grind]
- 2 cans Del Monte peaches
- 5 pounds potatoes

The instructions were

> Read the shopping list. Try to project yourself into the situation as far as possible until you can more or less characterize the woman who bought the groceries. Then write a brief description of her personality and character. Whenever possible indicate what factors influenced your judgment.

CIGARETTE SMOKING—ARE SMOKERS BEING HONEST WITH THEMSELVES?

Cigarette smoking in public spaces is an emotionally charged and hotly debated issue.[23] Direct, undisguised questioning may not be the best way to uncover people's view on the topic, because cigarette smoking seems to trigger ego defence mechanisms. Marketing researchers directly questioned why 179 smokers who believed cigarettes to be a health hazard continued to smoke. The majority answered, "Pleasure is more important than health," "Moderation is okay," "I like to smoke." Such responses suggest that smokers are not dissatisfied with their habit. However, in another portion of the study, researchers used the sentence completion method. Respondents were asked to give the first thing that came to mind after hearing the sentence "People who never smoke are _____."

The answers were "better off," "happier," "smarter," "wiser," "more informed." To "Teenagers who smoke are _____," smokers responded with "foolish," "crazy," "uninformed," "stupid," "showing off," "immature," "wrong." The sentence completion test indicated that smokers are anxious, uncomfortable, dissonant, and dissatisfied with their habit. The sentence completion test elicited responses that the subjects would not have given otherwise.

Forty-eight percent of the housewives given the list that included Nescafé described the Nescafé user as lazy and a poor planner. Other responses implied that the instant coffee user was not a good wife and spent money carelessly. The Maxwell House user, however, was thought to be practical, frugal, and a good cook.

Role playing is a dynamic re-enactment of the third-person technique in a given situation. The **role-playing technique** requires the subject to act out someone else's behaviour in a particular setting. For example, a child in a role-playing situation might use a pretend telephone to describe the new cookie she has just seen advertised. She projects herself into a mother role. Many researchers who specialize in research with children believe the projective play technique can be used to determine a child's true feelings about a product, package, or commercial. Young children frequently have their own meaning for many words. A seemingly positive word such as good, for example, can be a child's unflattering description of the teacher's pet in his class. In a role-playing game, the child can show exactly what he thinks "good" means.

Role-playing is particularly useful in investigating situations in which interpersonal relationships are the subject of the research—for example, salesperson–customer, husband–wife, or wholesaler–retailer relationships.

Thematic Apperception Test (TAT)

A **thematic apperception test (TAT)** presents subjects with a series of pictures in which consumers and products are the centre of attention. The investigator asks the subject to tell what is happening in the pictures and what the people might do next. Hence, themes (thematic) are elicited on the basis of the perceptual-interpretive (apperception) use of the pictures. The researcher then analyzes the contents of the stories that the subjects relate.

The picture or cartoon stimulus must be sufficiently interesting to encourage discussion but ambiguous enough not to disclose the nature of the research project. Clues should not be given to the character's positive or negative predisposition. A pre-test of a TAT investigating why men might purchase chain saws used a picture of a man looking at a very large tree. The subjects of the research were homeowners and weekend woodcutters. When confronted with the picture of the imposing

role-playing technique
A projective technique that requires the subject to act out someone else's behaviour in a particular setting.

thematic apperception test (TAT)
A projective technique that presents a series of pictures to research subjects and asks them to provide a description of or a story about the pictures.

A child placed in a role-playing situation may be better able to express her true feelings. A child may be told to pretend she is a parent talking to a friend about toys, food, or clothing. Thus the child does not feel pressure to express her own opinions and feelings directly.

tree, they almost unanimously said that they would get professional help from a tree surgeon. Thus early in the pre-testing process, the researchers found out that the picture was not sufficiently ambiguous for the subjects to identify with the man in the picture. If subjects are to project their own views into the situation, the environmental setting should be a well-defined, familiar problem, but the solution should be ambiguous.

Frequently, the TAT consists of a series of pictures with some continuity so that stories may be constructed in a variety of settings. The first picture might portray two women discussing a product in a supermarket; in the second picture, a person might be preparing the product in the kitchen; the final picture might show the product being served at the dinner table.

Cartoon Tests

picture frustration
A version of the TAT that uses a cartoon drawing for which the respondent suggests dialogue the characters might engage in.

The **picture frustration** version of the TAT uses a cartoon drawing in which the respondent suggests a dialogue in which the characters might engage. Exhibit 5.3 is a purposely ambiguous illustration of an everyday occurrence. The two office workers are shown in a situation and the respondent is asked what the woman might be talking about. This setting could be used for discussions about products, packaging, the display of merchandise, store personnel, and so on.

Several other projective techniques apply the logic of the TAT. Construction techniques request that consumers draw a picture, construct a collage, or write a short story to express their perceptions or feelings. For example, children hold in their heads many pictures that they are unable to describe in words. Asking a child to "draw what comes to your mind when you think about going shopping" enables the child to use his or her visual vocabulary to express feelings.[24]

Depth Interviews

depth interview
A relatively unstructured, extensive interview in which the interviewer asks many questions and probes for in-depth answers.

Motivational researchers who want to discover reasons for consumer behaviour may use relatively unstructured, extensive interviews during the primary stages of the research process. A **depth interview** is similar to a client interview conducted by a clinical psychologist or psychiatrist. The researcher asks many questions and probes for additional elaboration after the subject answers. In depth interviews, in contrast to projective techniques, the subject matter is generally undisguised. The interviewer's

EXHIBIT 5.3   PICTURE FRUSTRATION VERSION OF TAT

role is extremely important in the depth interview. He or she must be a highly skilled individual who can encourage the respondent to talk freely without influencing the direction of the conversation. Probing questions such as "Can you give me an example of that?" and "Why do you say that?" stimulate the respondent to elaborate on the topic. An excerpt from a depth interview is given in Exhibit 5.4.

International marketing researchers find that in certain cultures, depth interviews work far better than focus groups. They provide a quick means to assess buyer behaviour in foreign lands.

The depth interview may last more than an hour and requires an extremely skilled interviewer; hence, it is expensive. In addition, the topic for discussion is largely at the discretion of the interviewer, so the success of the research depends on the interviewer's skill—and, as is so often the case, good people are hard to find. A third major problem stems from the necessity of recording both surface reactions and subconscious motivations of the respondent. Analysis and interpretation of such data are highly subjective, and it is difficult to settle on a true interpretation.

An example of conflicting claims is illustrated by a study of prunes done by two organizations. One study used projective techniques to show that people considered prunes shrivelled, tasteless, and unattractive; symbolic of old age and parental authority (thus disliked); and associated with hospitals, boarding houses, peculiar people, and the Army. The other study stated that the principal reason people did not like prunes was the fruit's laxative property.

Finally, alternative techniques, such as focus groups, can provide much the same information as depth interviews.

EXHIBIT 5.4 | EXCERPTS FROM A DEPTH INTERVIEW[25]

An interviewer (I) talks with Marsha (M) about furniture purchases. Marsha indirectly indicates she delegates the buying responsibility to a trusted antique dealer. She has already said that she and her husband would write the dealer telling him the piece they wanted (e.g., bureau, table). The dealer would then locate a piece that he considered appropriate and would ship it to Marsha from his shop in another city.

M: . . . We never actually shopped for furniture since we state what we want and (the antique dealer) picks it out and sends it to us. So we never have to go looking through stores and shops and things.

I: You depend on his (the antique dealer's) judgment?

M: Um, hum. And, uh, he happens to have the sort of taste that we like and he knows what our taste is and always finds something that we're happy with.

I: You'd rather do that than do the shopping?

M: Oh, much rather, because it saves so much time and it would be so confusing for me to go through stores and stores looking for things, looking for furniture. This is so easy that I just am very fortunate.

I: Do you feel that he's a better judge than . . .

M: Much better.

I: Than you are?

M: Yes, and that way I feel confident that what I have is very, very nice because he picked it out and I would be doubtful if I picked it out. I have confidence in him, (the antique dealer) knows everything about antiques, I think. If he tells me something, why I know it's true—no matter what I think. I know he is the one that's right.

This excerpt is most revealing of the way in which Marsha could increase her feeling of confidence by relying on the judgment of another person, particularly a person she trusted. Marsha tells us quite plainly that she would be doubtful (i.e., uncertain) about her own judgment, but she "knows" (i.e., is certain) that the antique dealer is a good judge, "no matter what I think." The dealer once sent a chair that, on first inspection, did not appeal to Marsha. She decided, however, that she must be wrong, and the dealer right, and grew to like the chair very much.

SOME ISSUES IN USING EXPLORATORY RESEARCH

Exploratory research cannot take the place of conclusive, quantitative research. Nevertheless, firms often use what should be exploratory studies as final, conclusive research projects. This can lead to incorrect decisions. The most important thing to remember about exploratory research techniques is that they have limitations. Most of them provide qualitative information, and interpretation of the findings typically is judgmental. For example, the findings from projective techniques can be vague. Projective techniques and depth interviews were frequently used decades ago by practitioners who categorized themselves as motivational researchers. They produced some interesting and occasionally bizarre hypotheses about what was inside a buyer's mind, such as the following:

A woman is very serious when she bakes a cake because unconsciously she is going through the symbolic act of giving birth.

A man buys a convertible as a substitute mistress.

Men who wear suspenders are reacting to an unresolved castration complex.[26]

Unfortunately, bizarre hypotheses cannot be relegated to history as long-past events. Several years ago researchers at the McCann-Erickson advertising agency interviewed low-income women about their attitudes toward insecticides. The women indicated that they strongly believed a new brand of roach killer sold in little plastic trays was far more effective and less messy than traditional bug sprays. Rather than purchase the new brand, however, they remained stubbornly loyal to their old bug sprays. Baffled by this finding, the researchers did extensive qualitative research with female consumers. After reviewing the women's drawings and in-depth descriptions of roaches, the researchers concluded that women subconsciously identified roaches with men who had abandoned them. Spraying the roaches and watching them squirm and die was enjoyable—so by using the spray, the women both gained control over the roaches and vented their hostility toward men.[27] Conclusions based on qualitative research may be subject to considerable interpreter bias.

Findings from focus group interviews likewise may be ambiguous. How should a facial expression or nod of the head be interpreted? Have subjects fully grasped the idea or concept behind a nonexistent product? Have respondents overstated their interest because they tend to like all new products? Because of such problems in interpretation, exploratory findings should be considered preliminary.

Another problem with exploratory studies deals with the ability to make projections from the findings. Most exploratory techniques use small samples, which may not be representative because they have not been selected on a probability basis. Case studies, for example, may have been selected because they represent extremely good or extremely bad examples of a situation rather than the average situation.

In 2004, Playland, an amusement park in Vancouver, ran an advertisement picturing a girl with vomit, relish, and milkshake stains on her clothing. The text read: "Vomit print by Hell's Gate; Relish motif by Drop Zone; Milkshake design by Crazy Beach Party." A TV spot also showed a scene changing from family day at the beach to an out-of-focus blur leaving the visitors dizzy and barfing. Kai Clemen, associate creative director at Wasserman & Partners Advertising, which created the advertisement, said, "The ads were meant to appeal to families and teens. In fact, they were extensively focus group tested." The ads tested were designed to emphasize the rides at Playland. However, when a mother of three showed the ad to her children and their friends they disliked it immensely. After watching the television commercial, one child asked, "What kind of stupid ad is that?" Another simply said, "Bad," and the oldest of the children thought that Playland's attendance numbers would drop.[28]

Before making a scientific decision, the researcher should conduct a quantitative study with an adequate sample to ensure that measurement will be precise. This is not to say that exploratory research lacks value; it simply means that such research cannot deliver what it does not promise. The major benefit of exploratory research is that it generates insights and clarifies the marketing problems for hypothesis testing in future research. One cannot determine the most important attributes of a product until one has identified those attributes. Thus exploratory research is extremely useful, but it should be used with caution.

SUMMARY

1. Qualitative research is subjective in nature. Much of the measurement depends on evaluation by the researcher rather than vigorous mathematical analysis. Quantitative research determines the quantity or extent of an outcome in numbers. It provides an exact approach to measurement.

2. This chapter focused on qualitative exploratory research. Exploratory research may be conducted to diagnose a situation, screen alternatives, or discover new ideas. It may take the form of gathering background information by investigating secondary data, conducting experience surveys, scrutinizing case studies, or utilizing pilot studies. The purpose of the research, rather than the technique, determines whether a study is exploratory, descriptive, or causal. Thus the techniques discussed in this chapter are primarily but not exclusively used for exploratory studies.

3. There are four general categories of exploratory research methods: (1) experience surveys, (2) secondary data analysis, (3) case studies, and (4) pilot studies. Each category provides various alternative ways to gather information. Secondary data analysis is an exploratory research method covered in greater detail in the next chapter.

4 Experience survey is a research technique in which individuals who are knowledgeable about a particular research problem are questioned.

The case study method involves intensive investigation of one particular situation that is similar to the problem under investigation.

Focus group interviews are unstructured, free-flowing group sessions that allow individuals to initiate and elaborate on the topics of discussion. Interaction among respondents is synergistic and spontaneous, characteristics that have been found to be highly advantageous.

Projective techniques are an indirect means of questioning respondents. Some examples are word association tests, sentence completion tests, the third-person technique, the role-playing technique, and thematic apperception tests.

Depth interviews are unstructured, extensive interviews that encourage a respondent to talk freely and in depth about an undisguised topic.

5 As the ability to communicate via the Internet, telecommunications, and video-conferencing links improves, a number of companies are using these new media to conduct focus group research.

6 Although exploratory research has many advantages, it also has several shortcomings and should not take the place of conclusive, quantitative research. Knowing where and how to use exploratory research is important. Many firms make the mistake of using an exploratory study as a final, conclusive research project. This can lead to decisions based on incorrect assumptions. Exploratory research techniques have limitations: The interpretation of the findings is based on judgment, samples are not representative, the techniques rarely provide precise quantitative measurement, and the ability to generalize the qualitative results is limited.

Key Terms and Concepts

exploratory research
concept testing
experience survey
case study method
pilot study
focus group interview

moderator
discussion guide
streaming media
online focus group
projective technique
word association test

sentence completion method
third-person technique
role-playing technique
thematic apperception test (TAT)
picture frustration
depth interview

Questions for Review and Critical Thinking

1. Comment on the following remark by a marketing consultant: "Qualitative exploration is a tool of marketing research and a stimulant to thinking. In and by itself, however, it does not constitute market research."

2. What type of exploratory research would you suggest in the following situations?
   a. A product manager suggests development of a non-tobacco cigarette blended from wheat, cocoa, and citrus.
   b. A research project has the purpose of evaluating potential brand names for a new insecticide.
   c. A manager must determine the best site for a convenience store in an urban area.
   d. An advertiser wishes to identify the symbolism associated with cigar smoking.

3. What benefits can be gained from case studies? What dangers, if any, do they present? In what situations are they most useful?

4. What is the function of a focus group? What are its advantages and disadvantages?

5. If a researcher wanted to conduct a focus group with teenagers, what special considerations might be necessary?

6. A focus group moderator plans to administer a questionnaire before starting the group discussion about several new product concepts. Is this a good idea? Explain.

7. Discuss the advantages and disadvantages of the following focus group techniques:
   a. A videoconferencing system that allows marketers to conduct focus groups in two different locations with participants who interact with each other
   b. A system that uses telephone conference calls for group sessions

8. A packaged goods manufacturer receives many thousands of customer letters a year. Some are complaints,

some are compliments. They cover a broad range of topics. Are these letters a possible source for exploratory research? Why or why not?

9. Evaluate the following concept statement for a new frozen food product:

INTRODUCING CHICKEN MARINADE MEALS FROM CREATE-A-MEAL!

Now you can quickly and easily make delicious, marinated chicken and serve the perfect side dish too, with new Chicken Marinade Meals from Create-A-Meal! It comes with both a highly flavoured marinade for your chicken and a pasta/vegetable medley to complete the meal—a delicious traditional dinner has never been easier. Simply add your chicken to the special two-minute marinade and broil. Cook the combination of flavoured pasta or potatoes and crisp, colourful Green Giant vegetables, and serve with the chicken for a delicious home-cooked meal.

Varieties:
- Roasted Garlic Herb with Pasta Primavera
- Teriyaki with Oriental Pasta/Vegetable Medley
- Mesquite Chicken with Roasted Potatoes and Vegetables
- Lemon Pepper Chicken with White Cheddar Rotini and Broccoli
- Honey Mustard Chicken with Garden Herb Pasta and Vegetables
- Red Wine Chicken with Roasted Potatoes and Vegetables

Found in your grocer's freezer case
Suggested Retail Price, $4.99
Servings: 4
Size: 600 gram bag

10. How might exploratory research be used to screen various ideas for advertising copy in television commercials?

11. Most projective techniques attempt to assess a respondent's true feelings by asking indirect questions rather than using direct questions that could give the respondent a good idea about the researcher's true motives. Does the use of this technique constitute deception?

Exploring the Internet

1. How might the following organizations use an Internet chat room for exploratory research?
   a. A zoo
   b. A computer software manufacturer
   c. A video game manufacturer
2. Connect with a special-interest Internet bulletin board such as one for college students. Conduct an online focus group exploring what criteria students use to choose destinations for spring break.

3. The Bristol Group Inc. and the Consumer Research Centre are marketing research companies with focus group facilities. Go to http://www.bristolgroup.ca and http://www.consumerresearch.ca to view these facilities.

4. To learn about streaming media, go to

   http://www.videostreamingservices.com.

Hamilton Power Tools had been marketing industrial products by catering to the construction and industrial tool markets. One of its products, the gasoline-powered chain saw, was somewhat different from traditional construction and industrial tools. The chain saw line had been added in 1949 when John Hamilton Sr. had the opportunity to acquire a small chain saw manufacturer. Hamilton believed that construction workers would have a need for gasoline-powered chain saws. He acquired the business to diversify the company into other markets.

During the 1990s the chain saw market was rapidly changing, and Hamilton Power Tool executives began to realize they needed some expert marketing advice. Reports from trade publications, statistics from the Chain Saw Manufacturers' Association, and the personal experience of Mr. Campagna, marketing manager of Hamilton Power Tools, had led them to believe that the current chain saw industry was composed of roughly the following markets: professionals (lumberjacks), farmers, institutions, and casual users (home or estate owners with many trees on their lots). The casual user segment was considered to be the future growth market. Campagna wished to ensure that Hamilton would not make any mistakes in marketing its product to this segment of weekend woodcutters who once or twice a year used a chain saw to cut firewood or prune trees in the backyard.

In March 2005, when chain saw sales began to slow down, Campagna persuaded the aging John Hamilton Sr. that some consumer research was necessary. Consumer Touch of Toronto was hired to perform two research projects. The first was a thematic apperception test (TAT). In the second week of July, the TAT was completed. Dale Conway and Frank Baggins, from Consumer Touch, presented the results of the survey of chain saw users.

The TAT respondents had been shown a series of pictures and were asked to express their feelings about the people in the pictures. Conway told Campagna that although the study was exploratory, it could be used to gain insights into the reasons people make certain purchases. He also suggested that the test would be a means of gaining the flavour of the language people use in talking about chain saws, and it could be a source of new ideas for copywriting.

The TAT was conducted in British Columbia and Alberta. Case Exhibit 5.1.1 shows the TAT used by the researchers. The findings of this study were based on those respondents who either planned to purchase a chain saw in the next 12 months, already owned a chain saw, or had used a chain saw in the past. The findings were as follows:

The first picture (Exhibit A in Case Exhibit 5.1.1) shown to the respondent was of a man standing looking at a tree. The interviewer asked the respondent the following question:

> I have a problem which you may find interesting. Here's a picture of a man who is thinking about the purchase of a chain saw. Suppose that such a man is your neighbour. What do you suppose he is thinking about?

After the respondent's initial answer, the following probing question was asked:

> Now, if he came to you for advice and you really wanted to help him, what would you tell him to do? Why do you think this would be the best thing for him to do?

Initial responses seemed to centre on what the man would do with the tree. Many respondents expressed an interest in the tree and were concerned with preservation. It seemed that pride in having a tree that added beauty to

---

CASE EXHIBIT 5.1.1 | HAMILTON TAT STUDY[29]

Exhibit A

Exhibit B

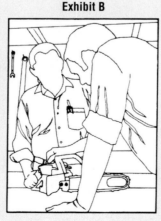

Exhibit C

Exhibit D

one's property was important to some respondents. Some of the typical responses were as follows:

> He's thinking about cutting the tree down.

> Why cut a whole tree when you can save part of it?

> He could trim out part of those trees and save some of them.

> We lose trees due to disease and storm damage.

> Trees beautify property and make it more valuable.

> I don't like to destroy trees.

Considering the alternatives to buying and using a chain saw was the next step many of the respondents took. Basically, the ultimate consumer sees the alternatives to the purchase of a chain saw as

1. Using a hand saw
2. Hiring a tree surgeon
3. Renting or borrowing a chain saw

These alternatives were in the respondents' minds partly because they were concerned about the cost of doing the job. They seemed to be worried about the investment in a chain saw, about whether it paid to buy one for a small, one-time job. (Another reason for the alternatives came out in responses to a later picture.) Some quotations illustrate this line of thinking:

> He's thinking how to go about it. He will use his hand saw.

> He doesn't have to invest in a chain saw for only one tree.

> He's thinking about how to get the tree down—the cost of doing it himself versus having someone else do it. Have him cut it down himself, it's not too big a tree. He'll save the cost.

> He's thinking whether it pays for a couple of trees.

> If it would be worth it. How much longer with an axe.

> He's thinking whether he should do it himself or get someone else do it for him. Get someone who knows what he is doing.

> He's thinking he'll rent a chain saw for a small area and would buy one for a large area.

> The best way to get a job done. Chain saw is faster, but a hand saw is cheaper. Depends on how much work he has to do.

An interesting comment made by two respondents was "He's thinking about Dutch elm disease." There had been publicity about the fatal Dutch elm disease in Canada a few years earlier. The respondents were projecting their situations into the TAT pictures.

Other statements were made concerning the ease and speed of using a chain saw. Some questions regarding the characteristic performance of a chain saw were raised in response to this question; however, Exhibit B covered this area more adequately. This picture showed two men standing in a chain saw store looking at a chain saw. The question asked went as follows:

> Here is a picture of the same man in a chain saw store. Suppose he's a friend of yours—your next-door neighbour, perhaps. Tell me what you think he will talk about with the store clerk.

The issue most frequently raised was how the chain saw worked. An equal number of respondents wanted to know first how much it cost. Weight (lightness) was the next most frequently raised issue. Horsepower was of concern to many of the respondents. Other subjects they thought the man would talk about with the clerk were maintenance and availability of repair, performance (what size tree the chain saw would cut), durability and expected life, safety (what safety features the chain saw had), and ease of starting the chain saw. In relation to price, respondents had the following types of comments:

> Well, price is the most important, of course.

> He's wondering how he will pay for it.

One respondent said, "He's not considering price; price means nothing compared to safety." One individual was concerned whether the chain would come off the "blade" (respondents referred to the guide bar as a "blade" rather than a "guide bar").

Various other issues were raised by respondents, including

> Ease of handling

> Length of blade

> Which was the best brand?

> Whether it had direct drive

> Whether it had a gas protector

> Self-lubrication

> The warranty (guarantee)

> Ease of controls

> Specifications

> Availability of credit

> Possibility of mixing oil and gas

Exhibit C showed a man cutting a felled tree with the chain saw. Respondents were asked:

> The man in the picture is the same man as in the last picture. He purchased the chain saw he was looking at. Knowing that he purchased the chain saw, what can you tell me about him? Can you tell me anything about the character and personality of this man?

A follow-up question was

What do you suppose this man is thinking about while he's using his chain saw?

A common response was that the man was satisfied. Typical responses were "He's pleased," "He's happy he bought the chain saw," "Lots of time saved," and "He's happy with the chain saw, he made the right decision." Many favourable overtones to using a chain saw were given—for example,

Sure beats bucking with an axe.

He's thinking about speed of getting through, time saved.

How much easier it is to cut a tree down with a chain saw than a hand saw.

He seems to be saying "Why didn't I buy a chain saw sooner?"

Respondents in general seemed to think the man was using the chain saw for the first time.

Very prominent in many respondents' answers was the fear of using a chain saw—it seemed to be a major reason that people would not purchase one. Some typical comments were

He's a little frightened. He doesn't know how to go about it, but he's willing to learn.

If he gets caught in that blade . . .

He's watching what he's doing—he could lose a limb.

He might be somewhat apprehensive about the use of it.

He looks scared of it.

He better think safety.

In general, the test, as it is designed to do, made the respondents project their own personalities and backgrounds onto the character of the man in the pictures. Respondents described the man in a variety of ways. He was described as a blue-collar worker, an office worker labouring after hours and on weekends, a somewhat wealthy man able to afford a chain saw, and a homeowner. A number of responses indicated that he was a do-it-yourselfer, a man who liked to "do his own thing." "Farmer" was another more than scattered response. Associations with an outdoorsman, a man who liked to keep in shape, were also indicated. One quotation seems to sum it all up:

This seems to be his first job. He seems to be happy about it. He seems to think the chain saw will lighten his workload. He looks like he has not owned many power tools. He looks excited. He seems like he will be able to do a lot of cleanup work that he would not have been able to do without the chain saw. The chain saw is sure an improvement over the hand saw. It's faster, easier to use.

The fourth picture (Exhibit D) showed a man and woman seated before a fireplace. The question read,

Here's a picture of the same man as in the previous pictures, sitting and talking with a woman. What do you suppose they're talking about?

An analysis of the fourth picture in the projection test showed that respondents felt the man and woman in the picture were happy, content, cozy, and enjoying the fireplace. The man was "enjoying the fruits of his labour." It came out very strongly that a man who uses a chain saw is proud of himself after he cuts the wood; he thinks his cutting of wood with a chain saw is a job well done. Some typical comments:

He's very happy to cut his own wood for his fireplace—real proud of himself.

He's telling her how much he saved by cutting it himself.

They're talking about the logs, how pleased he is with himself.

He's thinking about the beauty of the fire, fire logs he himself sawed from their property.

The people projecting onto the picture seemed to think that because the job was well done, purchasing a chain saw was worthwhile:

The man in the picture is saying, "The chain saw pays for itself. There's a $300 job, and you will be able to use the chain saw afterwards."

Work's done, and there's enough for winter, and he has trees for winters to come.

What a good buy that chain saw was. Cut wood costs, save money.

The woman in the picture was also very happy; she was satisfied and probably thinking about the future. But most of all she was very proud of her husband. This came out very strongly. For example,

The woman is looking to the enjoyment of the fireside and of the money saved because they cut their own wood. She might have questioned the investment before this, before sitting in front of the fireplace.

She is proud of her husband.

She is pleased the tree is down.

The woman is probably proud of the fireplace and starting the fire. He's probably thinking about the wood he sawed.

The man and woman are congratulating each other on finally getting around to buying a chain saw and cutting firewood.

She is complimenting him on his ability and on how handy it is to have a man around the house.

She is also thinking that possibly it was easier for her husband to use a chain saw.

The woman didn't care about the chain saw, but she was satisfied. The husband's concern over his wife's approval of this investment was also brought out by this picture—evidently men were worried that their wives would not see the value of a chain saw purchase. Also, there were implications that the man should be tired after using the chain saw—"and he had to work hard in the afternoon to get the logs for the fireplace."

After the presentation, Campagna was reasonably impressed. He asked Hamilton what his opinion was.

Hamilton said, "This is all very interesting, but I don't see how it can lead to greater profits in our chain saw division."

Questions

1. How should Conway and Baggins respond to Hamilton's final comment?
2. Is Hamilton investigating the casual user market segment correctly?
3. What conclusions would you draw from the thematic apperception test? Do you feel this is a valid and reliable test?
4. What specific recommendations would you make to Campagna concerning the casual user chain saw market?

CASE 5.2   TODAY'S MAN

David Feld, founder of Today's Man, a $204-million (U.S.) retailer based in Moorestown, New Jersey, guessed that many men equated buying clothes with going to the dentist, but he didn't know why.[30] Feld paid for focus groups to uncover the truth, but he never met a focus group he trusted.

Finally, Feld's advertising agency recommended he talk to a company of professional hypnotists based in New York. Feld was sceptical, but he was desperate and curious enough to commission a study focused on why men feel uncomfortable in clothing stores. "The results really shook us up," Feld reports. The comments the men made under hypnosis had the ring of authenticity for which he had been searching.

Hypnotized men revealed that they often hated the way their clothes fit but didn't know how to complain. "One guy told us that the last time he bought a suit, it didn't fit right—but he didn't say anything," Feld says. "He then told the hypnotist how insecure and dopey he felt when he wore that suit." Furthermore, some of the groggy men admitted to a sense of powerlessness—they felt ganged up on by both their wives and pushy salespeople. "We had never gotten that answer before," Feld says.

Question

Evaluate the research methods used by Today's Man.

6

SECONDARY DATA RESEARCH IN A DIGITAL AGE

What you will learn in this chapter

1 To discuss the advantages and disadvantages of secondary data.

2 To give typical examples of secondary data analysis conducted by marketing managers.

3 To understand the nature of model building with secondary data.

4 To discuss and give examples of the various internal and proprietary sources of secondary data.

5 To discuss the channels of distribution for external sources of secondary data.

6 To identify and give examples of various external sources of secondary data.

According to Statistics Canada, Canada's population has grown from 31,021,300 people in 2001 to 32,270,500 people in 2005. Within these four years, Ontario had the strongest population growth from 11,897,600 to 12,541,400 people, followed by Quebec, whose population grew from 7,397,000 to 7,598,100 people. Conversely, Newfoundland and Labrador's and Saskatchewan's populations decreased from 522,000 and 1,000,100 people to 516,000 and 994,100 people respectively.[1]

Canada is also a multicultural society as shown by Statistics Canada's findings that 13.4 percent of the country's population is made up of Chinese, South Asians, Blacks, and Filipinos. In 2001, British Columbia had the highest number of visible minorities (in ratio to its population); approximately 21.6 percent of the province's population was made up of visible minorities. Ontario had the second-largest visible minority population with 2,153,045 people falling into that category. Newfoundland and Labrador and Nunavut had the smallest number of visible minorities, making up only 0.8 percent of the province's and territory's populations. Among the visible minorities, South Asians are expected to be the largest visible minority group in Canada by 2017, with the vast majority living in Toronto and Vancouver. With their spending power, the South Asian market is worth $12.6 billion a year in Toronto alone. Needless to say, tracking and responding to such trends is important for Canadian businesses. For instance, Telus, a telecommunication company, has formed a South Asian advisory panel that meets twice a year with senior executives to assess the new products and services in the communications field that will be attractive to the community. IKEA Canada is also taking a closer look at its South Asian customers. For instance, IKEA decided to run print ads during Diwali, the Indian festival of lights, in the Toronto area using the Hindi expressions "Yeh Kea" (done this) and "Who Kea" (done that) followed by "IKEA."[2]

These facts about the population of Canada and reactions of firms illustrate the richness and value of secondary data. They also illustrate that analysis and interpretation are important activities. This chapter discusses how to conduct research with secondary data in a digital age. It examines many of the diverse sources for secondary data. It also includes two appendixes: Appendix 6A, Selected Sources for Secondary Data, and Appendix 6B, Database Searching and Retrieving with Computers. ■

SECONDARY DATA RESEARCH

secondary data
Data that have been previously collected for some purpose other than the one at hand.

Secondary data are gathered and recorded by someone else prior to (and for purposes other than) the current project. Secondary data usually are historical and already assembled. They require no access to respondents or subjects.

Advantages

The primary advantage of secondary data comes from their availability. Obtaining them is almost always faster and less expensive than acquiring primary data. This is particularly true when electronic retrieval is used to access data that are stored digitally. In many situations, collecting secondary data is instantaneous.

Consider the money and time saved by researchers who obtained updated population estimates for a town during the interim between the 2000 and 2010 censuses. Instead of doing the fieldwork themselves, researchers could acquire estimates from a firm dealing in demographic information or from sources such as Statistics Canada. Many of the activities normally associated with primary data collection (for example, sampling and data processing) are eliminated by using secondary data.

In some instances data cannot be obtained using primary data collection procedures. For example, a manufacturer of farm implements could not duplicate the information in the *Census of Agriculture* because much of the information there (for example, amount of taxes paid) might not be accessible to a private firm.

Disadvantages

An inherent disadvantage of secondary data is that they were not designed specifically to meet the researchers' needs. Thus researchers must ask how pertinent the data are to their particular project. To evaluate secondary data, researchers should ask questions such as these:

- Is the subject matter consistent with our problem definition?

- Do the data apply to the population of interest?

- Do the data apply to the time period of interest?

- Do the secondary data appear in the correct units of measurement?

- Do the data cover the subject of interest in adequate detail?

Consider the following typical situations:

- A researcher interested in forklift trucks finds that the secondary data on the subject are included in a broader, less pertinent category encompassing all industrial trucks and tractors. Furthermore, the data were collected five years earlier.

- An investigator who wishes to study individuals earning more than $100,000 per year finds the top category in a secondary study reported at $75,000 or more per year.

- A brewery that wishes to compare its per-barrel advertising expenditures with those of competitors finds that the units of measurement differ because some report point-of-purchase expenditures with advertising whereas others do not.

- Data from a previous warranty card study show where consumers prefer to purchase the product but provide no reasons.

Each of these situations shows that even when secondary information is available, it can be inadequate. The most common reasons that secondary data do not adequately satisfy research needs are (1) outdated information, (2) variation in definition of terms, (3) different units of measurement, and (4) lack of information to verify the data's accuracy.

Information quickly becomes outdated in our rapidly changing environment. Because the purpose of most studies is to predict the future, secondary data must be timely to be useful.

Every primary researcher has the right to define the terms or concepts under investigation to satisfy the purpose of his or her primary investigation. This is little solace, however, to the investigator of the South Asian market in Canada who finds secondary data reported as "percent non-white." Variances in terms or variable classifications should be scrutinized to determine if differences are important. The populations of interest must be described in comparable terms. Researchers frequently encounter secondary data that report on a population of interest that is similar but not directly comparable to their population of interest. For example, for firms interested in expanding to the United States, secondary data sources may not be perfectly comparable between commercial and government sources. Arbitron, a radio audience research company based in the United States, reports its television audience estimates by geographical areas known as ADI (Areas of Dominant Influence). An ADI is a geographic area consisting of all counties in which the home market commercial television stations receive a preponderance of total viewing hours. This unique population of interest is used exclusively to report television audiences. However, the geographic areas used in the U.S. census of population, such as Metropolitan Statistical Areas, are not comparable to ADIs.

Units of measurement may cause problems if they do not conform exactly to a researcher's needs. For example, lumber shipments in millions of board-feet are quite different from billions of ton-miles of lumber shipped on freight cars. Head-of-household income is not the same unit of measure as total family income. Often the objective of the original primary study may dictate that the data are summarized, rounded, or reported so that, although the original units of measurement were comparable, aggregated or adjusted units of measurement are not suitable in the secondary study.

data conversion
The process of changing the original form of the data to a format suitable to achieve the research objective, also called data transformation.

When secondary data are reported in a format that does not exactly meet the researcher's needs, data conversion may be necessary. **Data conversion** (also called *data transformation*) is the process of changing the original form of the data to a format suitable to achieve the research objective. For example, sales for food products may be reported in kilograms, cases, or dollars. An estimate of dollars per kilogram may be used to convert dollar volume data to kilograms or another suitable format.

Another disadvantage of secondary data is that the user has no control over their accuracy. Although timely and pertinent secondary data may fit the researcher's requirements, the data could be inaccurate. Research conducted by other persons may be biased to support the vested interest of the source. For example, media often publish data from surveys to identify the characteristics of their subscribers or viewers, but they will most likely exclude derogatory data from their reports. If the possibility of bias exists, the secondary data should not be used.

Investigators are naturally more prone to accept data from reliable sources such as the Government of Canada. Nevertheless, the researcher must assess the reputation of the organization that gathers the data and critically assess the research design to determine whether the research was correctly implemented. Unfortunately, such evaluation may not be possible if the manager lacks information that explains how the original research was conducted.

cross-checks
The comparison of data from one source with data from another source to determine the similarity of independent projects.

Researchers should verify the accuracy of the data whenever possible. **Cross-checks** of data from multiple sources—that is, comparison of the data from one source with data from another—should be made to determine the similarity of independent

EXHIBIT 6.1 | EVALUATING SECONDARY DATA[3]

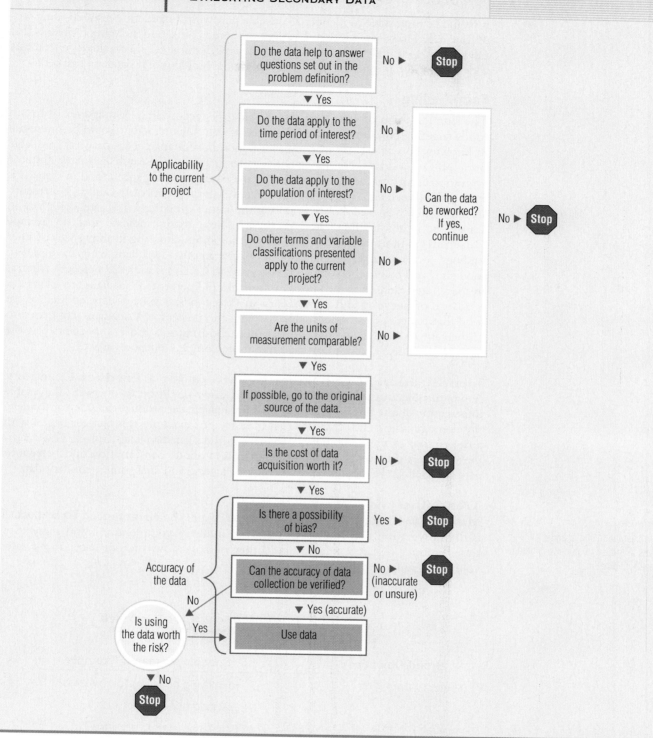

projects. When the data are not consistent, researchers should attempt to identify reasons for the differences or to determine which data are most likely to be
correct. If the accuracy of the data cannot be established, the researcher must
determine whether using the data is worth the risk. Exhibit 6.1 illustrates a
series of questions that should be asked to evaluate secondary data before they
are used.

It would be impossible to identify all possible purposes of marketing research using secondary data. However, it is useful to illustrate some common marketing problems that can be addressed with secondary research designs. Exhibit 6.2 shows three general categories of research objectives: fact-finding, model building, and database marketing.

Fact-Finding

The simplest form of secondary data research is fact-finding. A marketer of health foods targeting consumers in both Canada and the United States would be interested in knowing the differences in consumer trends. For instance, secondary data available from NPD Canada, a consumer and retailer marketing research company (http://www.npd.com/canada.html), reveals that the fastest-growing snack food in Canada is fresh fruit (40 percent), whereas in the United States it is chocolate candy (35 percent). In the United States chocolate is among the fastest-growing snack categories, and in Canada it is among the fastest declining. These results indicate that on average Canadians are more concerned than Americans about choosing healthy snacks. Other findings corroborate a higher level of concern among Canadians when it comes to food choices. The number-one lunch beverage in Canada is milk (29 percent), whereas in the United States it is carbonated soft drinks (30 percent). Canadians are asking for a balance of nutrition and convenience in their foods; it is no longer enough to eat food that just tastes and smells good. Twenty-one percent of Canadians, compared to 15 percent of Americans, disagree that how food tastes is more important than the nutritional value.[4] Fact-finding can serve more complex purposes as well.

Identification of Consumer Behaviour for a Product Category

A typical objective for a secondary research study might be to uncover all available information about consumption patterns for a particular product category or to identify demographic trends that affect an industry. For example, this chapter began with a description of the demographic changes in the Canadian marketplace. This example illustrates the wealth of factual information about consumption and behaviour patterns that can be obtained by carefully collecting and analyzing secondary data.

Trend Analysis

market tracking
The observation and analysis of trends in industry volume and brand share over time.

Marketers watch for trends in the marketplace and the environment. **Market tracking** is the observation and analysis of trends in industry volume and brand share over time. Scanner research services and other organizations provide facts about sales volume to support this work.

EXHIBIT 6.2	COMMON RESEARCH OBJECTIVES FOR SECONDARY DATA STUDIES
Broad Objective	**Specific Research Example**
Fact-finding	Identifying consumption patterns
	Tracking trends
Model building	Estimating market potential
	Forecasting sales
	Selecting trade areas and sites
Database marketing	Enhancing customer databases
	Developing prospect lists

EXHIBIT 6.3

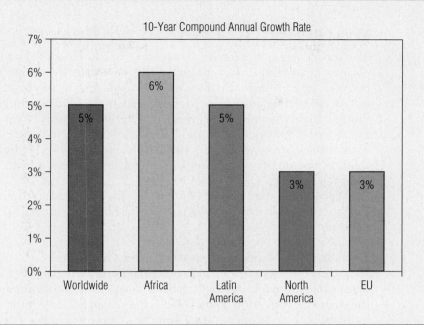

Almost every large consumer goods company routinely investigates brand and product category sales volume using secondary data. This type of analysis typically involves comparisons with competitors' sales or with the company's own sales in comparable time periods. It also involves industry comparisons among different geographic areas. Exhibit 6.3 shows the trend in cola market share relative to the total carbonated soft drink industry.

Environmental Scanning

In many instances, the purpose of fact-finding is simply to study the environment to identify trends. **Environmental scanning** entails information gathering and fact-finding designed to detect indications of environmental changes in their initial stages of development. The Internet can be used for environmental scanning; however, there are other less recurrent means, such as periodic review of contemporary publications and reports. For example, environmental scanning for information about members of the Millennium Generation (also called Generation Y) showed them to be enthusiastic about activities that their parents or grandparents enjoyed during their leisure time, especially if the older Generation-X cohort sneered at it. In particular, it showed that today's teens find bowling and swing dancing appealing. As a result of scanning the environment, Brunswick, which operates a chain of family entertainment centres, began promoting Cosmic Bowling—bowling in a darkened alley lit only by glow-in-the-dark lanes, pins, and balls and flashing laser lights.[6]

A number of online information services routinely collect news stories about industries, product lines, and other topics of interest that have been specified by the researcher. Other Internet-based tools, such as **push technology** that automatically delivers content to the researcher's or manager's desktop, can help in environmental scanning.[7] Push technology uses "electronic smart agents" to find information without the researcher having to do the searching. The smart agent, which is a custom software program, filters, sorts, prioritizes, and stores information for later viewing.[8] This frees the researcher from doing the searching. The true value of push

environmental scanning
Information gathering and fact-finding that is designed to detect indications of environmental changes in their initial stages of development.

push technology
Internet information technology that automatically delivers content to the researcher's or manager's desktop.

technology is that the researcher who is scanning the environment can specify the kinds of news and information he or she wants, have it delivered to his or her computer quickly, and view it at leisure.

Model Building

model building
The use of secondary data to help specify relationships between two or more variables. Model building can involve the development of descriptive or predictive equations.

The second general objective for secondary research, model building, is more complicated than simple fact-finding. **Model building** involves specifying relationships between two or more variables, perhaps extending to the development of descriptive or predictive equations. Models need not include complicated mathematics, though. In fact, decision makers often prefer simple models that everyone can readily understand over complex models that are difficult to comprehend. For example, market share is company sales divided by industry sales. Although some may not think of this simple calculation as a model, it represents a mathematical model of a basic relationship.

We will illustrate model building by discussing three common objectives that can be satisfied with secondary research: estimating market potential, forecasting sales, and selecting sites.

Estimating Market Potential for Geographic Areas

Marketers often estimate market potential using secondary data. In many cases exact figures may be published by a trade association or another source. However, when the desired information is unavailable, the researcher may estimate market potential by transforming secondary data from two or more sources. For example, managers may find secondary data about market potential for a country or other large geographic area, but this information may not be broken down into smaller geographical areas, such as by metropolitan area, or in terms unique to the company, such as sales territory. In this type of situation, researchers often need to make projections for the geographic area of interest.

Many companies provide smart agent software; Nortel, a world-renowned Ontario-based company, provides such software.[9]

EXHIBIT 6.4 | MARKET POTENTIAL FOR CRACKERS IN EUROPE

Country	(1) Population in 2005 (Thousand)	(2) Population Projection for 2010 (Thousand)	(3) Annual Per-Capita Cracker Consumption (U.S. Dollars)	(4) Market Potential Estimate (Thousand U.S. Dollars)
United Kingdom	60,441	61,292	9.48	581,047
Germany	82,431	82,431	1.91	157,443
Italy	58,103	58,307	4.33	252,468
France	60,656	61,786	3.56	219,960
Spain	40,342	40,645	0.62	25,200

An extended example will help explain how secondary data can be used to calculate market potential. A marketer of crackers is contemplating building a processing plant in Europe. Managers wish to estimate market potential for the United Kingdom, Germany, Spain, Italy, and France. Secondary research uncovered data for per-capita cracker consumption and population projections for the year 2010. The data for the five European countries appear in Exhibit 6.4. (The per-capita cracker consumption data were obtained from AC Nielsen Company.[10] The population estimates are based on information from the *CIA Factbook* database: http://www.cia.gov/cia/publications/factbook/index.html.)

To calculate market potential for Italy in the year 2010, multiply that country's population (in thousands) in the year 2010 (column 2 in Exhibit 6.4) by its per-capita cracker consumption (column 3 in Exhibit 6.4):

$$58,307 \times \$4.33 = \$252,468$$

In Italy the market potential for crackers is $252,468 thousand, or $252,468,000. As Exhibit 6.4 reveals, although Germany's population is much higher, it has a much lower market potential.

Forecasting Sales

Marketing managers need information about the future. They need to know what company sales will be next year and in future time periods. Sales forecasting is the process of predicting sales totals over a specific time period.

Accurate sales forecasts, especially for products in mature, stable markets, frequently come from secondary data research that identifies trends and extrapolates past performance into the future. Marketing researchers often use internal company sales records to project sales. A rudimentary model would multiply past sales volume by an expected growth rate. A researcher might investigate a secondary source and find that industry sales are expected to grow by 10 percent; multiplying company sales volume by 10 percent would give a basic sales forecast.

Exhibit 6.5 illustrates trend projection using a moving average projection of growth rates. Average annual operating revenues for spectator sports are secondary data from Statistics Canada.[11] The moving average is the sum of growth rates for the past three years divided by 3 (number of years). The resulting number is a forecast of the percentage increase in ticket price for the coming year.

Using the three-year average growth rate of 1 percent for the 2001, 2002, and 2003 revenue periods, we can forecast the average operating revenue for 2004 as follows:

$$\$2,181.7 + (\$2,181.7 \times .01) = \$2,203.5$$

SEARCHING FOR *THE* ANSWER

Even at the secondary data collection stages, one of the currents that a market researcher has to move against is the management's tendency to request answers that are already developed internally to the decision problem at hand—in other words, to support decisions that the management is intending to make or has already made.

Deborah Sawyer, president of Information Plus, a company that retrieves secondary information and conducts custom research primarily for business-to-business marketers, agrees research is all too often used to support decisions that have already been made. Sawyer tells the story of a trust company that

wanted to introduce an investment product aimed at pension plan sponsors. Although well-established in the U.S. and Britain, the money management technique was relatively new to Canada. Research showed the Canadian market was not ready for the product. The technique had low recognition and the brand name the client had chosen had the lowest recognition of the three names proposed. Convinced it could overcome any obstacles, the trust company ignored the research and went ahead with its plans. In the end, the vice-president pulled the plug on the project, having failed to convince pension plan sponsors the product was a "worthwhile investment."

Source: Adapted from an article by Barbara Smith, Published in **strategy** September 6, 1993. Brunico Communications Inc. Reproduced by permission.

Moving average forecasting is best suited to a static competitive environment. More dynamic situations make other sales forecasting techniques more appropriate.

Statistical trend analysis using secondary data can be much more advanced than this simple example. Many statistical techniques build forecasting models using secondary data. This chapter emphasizes secondary data research rather than statistical analysis. Data collection chapters later in this text explain more sophisticated statistical model building techniques for forecasting sales.

Analysis of Trade Areas and Sites

site analysis techniques
Techniques that use secondary data to select the best location for retail or wholesale operations.

Marketing managers examine trade areas and use **site analysis techniques** to select the best locations for retail or wholesale operations. Secondary data research helps managers make these site selection decisions. Some organizations, especially franchisers,

EXHIBIT 6.5	SALES FORECAST USING SECONDARY DATA AND THE MOVING AVERAGE METHOD		
Year	Average Operating Revenue (in millions) ($)	Percentage Rate of Growth (Decline) from Previous Year	3-Year Moving Average Rate Rate of Growth (Decline)
1997	1,366.5	—	—
1998	1,773.6	+29.8	—
1999	1,708.0	−3.7	—
2000	2,160.7	+26.5	+17.5
2001	1,860.2	−13.9	+2.9
2002	2,148.9	+15.5	+9.4
2003	2,181.7	+1.5	+1

Forecast of average operating revenue for 2004: $2,181.7 + ($2,181.7 × .01) = $2,203.5

Exhibit 6.6	Secondary Data for the Calculation of an Index of Retail Saturation
1. Population	261,785
2. Annual per capita shoe sales	$54.43
3. Local market potential (line 1 × line 2)	$14,249,000
4. Square feet of retail space used to sell shoes	94,000 sq. ft.
5. Index of retail saturation (line 3/line 4)	152

have developed special computer software based on analytical models to select sites for retail outlets. The researcher must obtain the appropriate secondary data for analysis with the computer software.

index of retail saturation
A calculation that describes the relationship between retail demand and supply.

The **index of retail saturation** offers one way to investigate retail sites and to describe the relationship between retail demand and supply.[12] It is easy to calculate once the appropriate secondary data are obtained:

$$\text{Index of retail saturation} = \frac{\text{Local market potential (demand)}}{\text{Local market retailing space}}$$

For example, Exhibit 6.6 shows the relevant secondary data for shoe store sales in a defined radius surrounding a shopping centre. These types of data can be purchased from vendors of market information such as Claritas in the United States and Environics Analytics in Canada. First, local market potential (demand) is estimated by multiplying population times annual per capita shoe sales. The index of retail saturation is

$$\text{Index of retail saturation} = \frac{\$14,249,000}{94,000} = 152$$

This index figure can be compared with those of other areas to determine which sites have the greatest market potential with the least amount of retail competition. An index value above 200 is considered to indicate exceptional opportunities.

Data Mining

Large corporations' decision support systems often contain millions or even hundreds of millions of records of data. These complex data volumes are too large to be understood by managers. Consider, for example, a credit card company collecting data on customer purchases. Each customer might make an average of ten transactions in a month, or 120 per year. With 3 million customers and five years of data, it's easy to see how record counts quickly grow beyond the comfort zone for most humans.[13]

data mining
The use of powerful computers to dig through volumes of data to discover patterns about an organization's customers and products. It is a broad term that applies to many different forms of analysis.

neural network
A form of artificial intelligence in which a computer is programmed to mimic the way that human brains process information.

Two points about data volume are important to keep in mind. First, relevant marketing data are often in independent and unrelated files. Second, the number of distinct pieces of information each data record contains is often large. When the number of distinct pieces of information contained in each data record and data volume grow too large, end users don't have the capacity to make sense of it all. Data mining helps clarify the underlying meaning of the data.

The term **data mining** refers to the use of powerful computers to dig through volumes of data to discover patterns about an organization's customers and products. It is a broad term that applies to many different forms of analysis. For example, **neural networks** are a form of artificial intelligence in which a computer is programmed to mimic the way that human brains process information. One computer expert put it this way:

Chapter 6   *Secondary Data Research in a Digital Age*

A neural network learns pretty much the way a human being does. Suppose you say "big" and show a child an elephant, and then you say "small" and show her a poodle. You repeat this process with a house and a giraffe as examples of "big" and then a grain of sand and an ant as examples of "small." Pretty soon she will figure it out and tell you that a truck is "big" and a needle is "small." Neural networks can similarly generalize by looking at examples.[14]

Wal-Mart uses data mining. Wal-Mart's information system houses more than 7 terabytes of data on point of sale, inventory, products in transit, market statistics, customer demographics, finance, product returns, and supplier performance. The data are mined to develop "personality traits" for each of Wal-Mart's 3,000-plus outlets, which Wal-Mart managers use to determine product mix and presentation for each store. Wal-Mart's data-mining software looks at individual items for individual stores to decide the seasonal sales profile of each item. The data-mining system keeps a year's worth of data on the sales of 100,000 products and predicts which items will be needed in each store.[15]

Data mining can also be used for social marketing purposes. The Toronto-based Foster Parent Plan of Canada (FPP) supports children and families in 45 developing countries using the support provided by foster parents in Canada and other countries. FPP matched the survey research conducted by Market Facts to its in-house database to identify foster parents with higher commitment levels. By being able to predict whether a given foster parent would continue his or her support, FPP had the opportunity to plan for the future in addition to taking actions to retain the support of a foster parent with low commitment.[16]

Market basket analysis is a form of data mining that analyzes anonymous point-of-sale transaction databases to identify coinciding purchases or relationships between products purchased and other retail shopping information.[17] Consider this example about patterns in customer purchases: Osco Drugs, a drugstore chain in the United States, mined its databases provided by checkout scanners and found that when men go to its drugstores to buy diapers in the evening between 6:00 p.m. and 8:00 p.m., they sometimes walk out with a six-pack of beer as well. Knowing this behavioural pattern, it's possible for store managers to change the layout of their stores so that these items are closer together.[18]

The example of a credit card company with large volumes of data illustrates a data-mining application known as *customer discovery*. The credit card company will probably track information about each customer: age, gender, number of children, job status, income level, past credit history, and so on. Very often the data about these factors will be mined to find the patterns that make a particular individual a good or bad credit risk.[19]

This advertisement's copy says "To our data mining system, they're twins. Because both order milk with their hamburgers." It provides an example of market basket analysis.

Marriott Vacation Club International, the largest seller of vacation time-share condos in the United States, has slashed the amount of junk mail it has to send out to get a response.[20] How? With a computer, a database, and some help from Acxiom Corporation, which specializes in data processing of secondary data for marketers.

What Marriott is doing is called data mining. This is the science of combing through digitized customer files to detect patterns. Marriott starts with names, mostly of hotel guests. Digging into a trove of motor vehicle records, property records, warranty cards, and lists of people who have bought by mail, Acxiom

enriches the prospect list. It adds such facts as the customers' ages, estimated incomes, what cars they drive, and if they golf. Then Marriott uses complex computer programs (neural networks) to figure out who is most likely to respond to a mailed flyer.

Using these clues, Marriott is able to cast its net a little more narrowly and catch more fish. Data mining has increased the response rate to Marriott's direct-mail, time-share pitches to certain hotel guests from 0.75 percent to 1 percent. That seems like a slim gain, but it makes a big difference to a company that sent out 3 million glossy solicitations at a cost of up to $1.50 each in a single year.

When a company knows the identity of the customer who makes repeated purchases from the same organization, an analysis can be made of sequences of purchases. *Sequence discovery,* the use of data mining to detect sequence patterns, is a popular application among direct marketers, such as catalogue retailers. A catalogue merchant has information for each customer, revealing the sets of products that the customer buys in every purchase order. A sequence discovery function can then be used to discover the set of purchases that frequently precedes the purchase of, say, a microwave oven. As another example, sequence discovery used on a set of insurance claims could lead to the identification of frequently occurring medical procedures performed on patients, which in turn could be used to detect cases of medical fraud.

Data mining requires sophisticated computer resources and it is expensive. That's why companies like Angoss Software, IBM, Oracle Canada, Environics Analytics, and Information Builders offer data-mining services. Customers send the databases they want analyzed and let the data-mining company do the "number crunching."

Database Marketing and Customer Relationship Management

As we have already mentioned, a CRM (customer relationship management) system is a decision support system that manages the interactions between an organization and its customers. A CRM maintains customer databases containing customers' names, addresses, phone numbers, past purchases, responses to past promotional offers, and other relevant data such as demographic and financial data. **Database marketing** is the practice of using CRM databases to develop one-to-one relationships and precisely targeted promotional efforts with individual customers. For example, a fruit catalogue company CRM contains a database of previous customers, including what purchases they made during the Christmas holidays. Each year the company sends last year's gift list to customers to help them send the same gifts to their friends and relatives.

Because database marketing requires vast amounts of CRM data compiled from numerous sources, secondary data are often acquired for the exclusive purpose of developing or enhancing databases. The transaction record, which often lists the item purchased, its value, customer name, address, and postal or zip code, is the

database marketing
The use of customer databases to promote one-to-one relationships with customers and create precisely targeted promotions.

building block for many databases. This may be supplemented with data customers provide directly, such as data on a warranty card, and by secondary data purchased from third parties. For example, credit services may sell databases about applications for loans, credit card payment history, and other financial data. Several companies, such as Donnelley Marketing (with its BusinessContentFile and ConsumerContentFile services), Claritas (with PRIZM NE), and Environics Analytics (with PRIZM Canadian Edition), collect primary data and then sell demographic data that can be related to small geographic areas, such as those with a certain postal code. BBM Canada, a non-profit broadcast research organization, collects primary data on TV station reach and share information in Canada for six standard demographics in all measured areas. Demographic information about adults, men (ages 18 to 49) and women (ages 25 to 54), is also collected.[21] (Remember that when the vendor collects the data, they are primary data, but when the database marketer incorporates the data into his or her database, they are secondary data.)

Now that some of the purposes of secondary data analysis have been addressed, it is appropriate to discuss sources of secondary data.

SOURCES OF SECONDARY DATA

Chapter 2 classified secondary data as either internal to the organization or external. Modern information technology makes this distinction seem somewhat simplistic. For instance, the data that appear in a book published by the federal government may also be purchased from an online information vendor for instantaneous access and subsequently stored in a company's decision support system.

Internal data should be defined as data that originated in the organization, or data created, recorded, or generated by the organization. **Internal and proprietary data** is perhaps a more descriptive term.

internal and proprietary data
Secondary data that originate inside the organization.

Internal and Proprietary Data Sources

Most organizations routinely gather, record, and store internal data to help them solve future problems. Routine documents such as sales invoices allow external financial reporting, which in turn can be a source of data for further analysis. If the data are properly coded into a modular database, the researcher may be able to conduct more detailed analysis using the decision support system. Sales information can be broken down by account or by product and region; information related to orders received, back orders, and unfilled orders can be identified; sales can be forecast on the basis of past data.

Researchers frequently aggregate or disaggregate internal data. Other useful sources of internal data include salespeople's call reports, customer complaints, service records, warranty card returns, and other records. For example, a computer service firm used internal secondary data to analyze sales over the previous three years, categorizing business by industry, product, purchase level, and so on. The company discovered that 60 percent of its customers represented only 2 percent of its business and that nearly all these customers came through telephone directory advertising. This simple investigation of internal records showed that, in effect, the firm was paying to attract customers it did not want.

External Data: The Distribution System

external data
Data created, recorded, or generated by an entity other than the researcher's organization.

External data are generated or recorded by an entity other than the researcher's organization. The government, newspapers and journals, trade associations, and other organizations create or produce information. Traditionally, this information has been in published form, perhaps available from a public library, trade association, or government agency. Today, however, computerized data archives and

electronic data interchange make external data as accessible as internal data. Exhibit 6.7 illustrates some traditional and some modern ways of distributing information.

Information as a Product and Its Distribution Channels

Because secondary data have value, they can be bought and sold like other products. And just as bottles of perfume or plumbers' wrenches may be distributed in many ways, secondary data also flow through various channels of distribution.

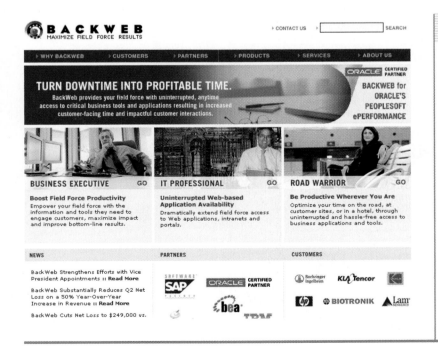

BackWeb (http://www.backweb.com) mobilizes critical web applications and content for mobile workforces and remote offices. This empowers companies to take their existing web applications and make them available to their mobile employees when they are disconnected or intermittently connected to the network. Companies can take web applications that are content and media rich as well as transactional and enable them for offline use on a mobile employees' laptop. BackWeb's web and polite synchronization mobile solution is commonly deployed to sales forces, field employees, mobile managers and remote operations.

EXHIBIT 6.7 | INFORMATION AS A PRODUCT AND ITS DISTRIBUTION CHANNELS

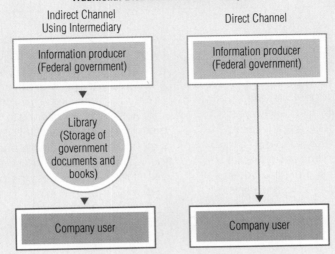

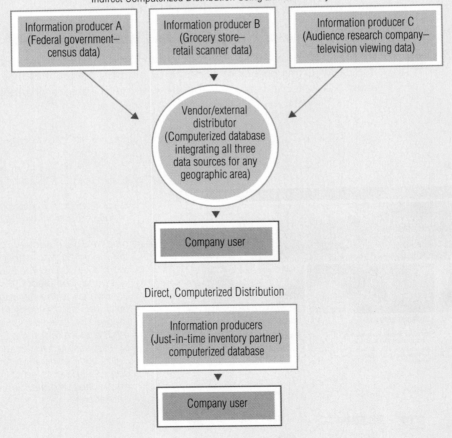

Traditional Distribution of Secondary Data

Indirect Channel Using Intermediary

Information producer (Federal government)

Library (Storage of government documents and books)

Company user

Direct Channel

Information producer (Federal government)

Company user

Modern Distribution of Secondary Data

Indirect Computerized Distribution Using an Intermediary

Information producer A (Federal government—census data)

Information producer B (Grocery store—retail scanner data)

Information producer C (Audience research company—television viewing data)

Vendor/external distributor (Computerized database integrating all three data sources for any geographic area)

Company user

Direct, Computerized Distribution

Information producers (Just-in-time inventory partner) computerized database

Company user

Many users, such as the Fortune 500 corporations, purchase documents and computerized census data directly from the government. However, many small companies get census data from a library or another intermediary or vendor of secondary information.

Libraries

Traditionally, libraries' vast storehouses of information have served as a bridge between users and producers of secondary data. The library staff deals directly with the creators of information, such as the federal government, and intermediate distributors of information, such as abstracting and indexing services. The user need only locate the appropriate secondary data on the library shelves. Libraries provide collections of books, journals, newspapers, and so on for reading and reference. They also stock many bibliographies, abstracts, guides, directories, and indexes, as well as offering access to basic databases.

The Internet

The Internet is, of course, a growing source of distribution of much secondary data. Its creation has added an international dimension to the acquisition of secondary data. For example, the Library and Archives Canada Web site (http://www.collections canada.ca/) provides access to online resources, services, and the collection of Library and Archives Canada. Most public libraries across Canada can also be accessed online. Exhibit 6.8 lists some of the more popular Internet addresses where secondary data may be found.

EXHIBIT 6.8	SELECTED INTERNET SITES FOR SECONDARY DATA	
Name	**Description**	**URL**
Yahoo!	Portal that serves as a gateway to all kinds of sites on the Web.	http://www.yahoo.ca
CEOexpress	The 80/20 rule applied to the Internet. A series of links designed by a busy executive for busy executives.	http://www.ceoexpress.com
The Ottawa Public Library	Library resources and links.	http://www.library.ottawa.on.ca
Statistics Canada	Statistical information about Canada, including the Census.	http://www.statcan.ca/
Government of Canada	A comprehensive source of Canadian government information.	http://www.canada.gc.ca/
Marketing Magazine	Provides content on marketing, advertising, and media.	http://www.marketingmag.ca/
Advertising Age magazine	Provides content on marketing media, advertising, and public relations (focus on USA).	http://www.adage.com
Small Business	The Globe and Mail's resources for running a small business.	http://www.theglobeandmail.com/partners/adp/sbr/
Wall Street Journal Interactive	Provides a continually updated view of business news around the world.	http://www.wsj.com
CBC Archives	A comprehensive source of news items dating back to the 1930s.	http://archives.cbc.ca/

(continued)

EXHIBIT 6.8 | (CONTD.)

NAICS—North American Industry Classification System	Describes the new classification system that replaced the SIC system.	http://www.census.gov/epcd/www/naics.html
MapQuest	Allows users to enter a postal code and see a map.	http://www.mapquest.ca
Business Europe	Provides links to obtain information about European countries.	http://www.businesseurope.com
Brint.com: The BizTech Network	Business and technology portal and global network for e-business, information, technology, and knowledge management.	http://www.brint.com

Vendors

Many external producers make secondary data available directly from the organizations that produce the data or through intermediaries, which are often called *vendors*. Vendors such as the Dow Jones News Retrieval Service allow managers to access thousands of external databases via desktop computers and telecommunications systems. Hoovers (http://www.hoovers.com) specializes in providing information about thousands of companies' financial situations and operations.

Producers

External secondary data can be classified by the nature of the producer of information: publishers of books and periodicals, government sources, media sources, trade association sources, and commercial sources. Exhibit 6.9 provides further examples of each source. Also, see Appendix 6A for references to secondary data producers and other sources.

Many firms specialize in computerized census and demographic data.

EXHIBIT 6.9 | PRODUCERS OF SECONDARY DATA

Nature of Producer	Examples
Books and Periodicals	Professional journals (Journal of Marketing, Journal of Marketing Research, Marketing Science), commercial business periodicals (Commerce, Canadian Business, Profit, Wall Street Journal, Fortune, Business Week).
Government Sources	Statistics Canada and Government of Canada provide a wealth of data on the Internet.
	Provincial, municipal, and local governments provide data about the population, economy, and transportation systems, structured to suit local needs.
Media Sources	Broadcast or print media, such as Canadian Business magazine, commissioned research studies on a broad range of topics and readership (e.g., Opera Canada describing readers of the magazine to potential advertisers).
Trade Association Sources	Canadian Health Food Association, Canadian Plastics Industry Association, Newspaper Advertising Bureau.
Commercial Sources	**Market Share and Industry Trends:** Information Resources, Inc., AC Nielsen Canada, Polk Canada.
	Demographic, Geodemographic, and Census Updates: Optima Marketing, Environics Analytics.
	Consumer Attitude and Public Opinion Research: Pollara, Compas, IPSOS Canada.
	Consumption and Purchase Behaviour Data: NPD Canada (e.g., National Eating Trends), National Family Opinion (NFO), Marketing Research Corporation of America (MRCA).
	Advertising Research: BBM Canada, The Radio Marketing Bureau, Nielsen Media Research, Leger Marketing.

Brochure for Effipub, Leger Marketing's service for measuring the impact of advertising campaigns

SINGLE-SOURCE DATA—INTEGRATED INFORMATION

AC Nielsen Company offers data from both its television meters and scanner operations. The integration of these two types of data helps marketers investigate the impact of television advertising on retail sales. In other ways as well, users of data find that merging two or more diverse types of data into a single database offers many advantages.

PRIZM NE by Claritas Corporation in the United States and the Canadian edition, PRIZM CE by Environics Analytics, and many other syndicated databases report product purchase behaviour, media usage, demographic characteristics, lifestyle variables, and business activity by geographic area. Canada's large immigrant population (18 percent of the population) and multi-ethnic diversity of the population make it a unique country and result in interesting segments for geodemographic analyses.[23] The two database systems, PRIZM NE and PRIZM CE, share 16 segments (groups of customers) that are similar between the United States and Canada. However, Canada has 50 distinct segments, including the 15 francophone segments. For instance, "Mini Van & Vin Rouge" is a francophone cluster mostly located in Quebec. Customers in this group are mostly families and couples who are homeowners and enjoy ice skating, skiing, backyard pools, radio comedy programs, and dress-up occasions. They have an annual income between $75,000 and $85,000, use ATMs heavily, and often own two vehicles. Although such data are often called *geodemographic,* they cover such a broad range of phenomena that no one name is a good description. These data use small geographic areas, such as dissemination areas, as the unit of analysis.

single-source data
Diverse types of data offered by a single company. The data are usually integrated on the basis of a common variable such as geographic area or store.

The marketing research industry uses the term **single-source data** for diverse types of data offered by a single company. Exhibit 6.10 identifies several major marketers of single-source data.

SOURCES FOR GLOBAL RESEARCH

As business has become more global, so has the secondary data industry. The Japan Management Association Research Institute, Japan's largest provider of secondary research data to government and industry, maintains an office in San Diego. The office in San Diego provides translators and acts as an intermediary between Japanese researchers and U.S. clients.

EXHIBIT 6.10	EXAMPLES OF SINGLE-SOURCE DATABASES
Print Measurement Bureau http://www.pmb.ca/	Canada's leading syndicated study for single-source data on print readership, non-print media exposure, product usage, and lifestyles.
ProQuest Business Databases http://www.proquest.com/	The ProQuest online information service provides access to thousands of current periodicals and newspapers, many updated daily and containing full-text articles from 1986.
Global Market Information Database http://www.gmid.euromonitor.com	Euromonitor International's Global Market Information Database is an online business information system providing business intelligence on countries, consumers, and industries. It offers integrated access to statistics, market reports, company profiles, and information sources.

Secondary data compiled outside Canada have the same limitations as domestic secondary data. However, international researchers should watch for certain pitfalls that frequently are associated with foreign data and cross-cultural research. First, data may simply be unavailable in certain countries. Second, the accuracy of some data may be called into question. This is especially likely with official statistics that may be adjusted for the political purposes of foreign governments. Finally, although economic terminology may be standardized, various countries use different definitions and accounting and recording practices for many economic concepts. For example, different countries may measure disposable personal income in radically different ways. International researchers should take extra care to investigate the comparability of data among countries.

Other organizations besides the Canadian government compile databases that may aid international marketers. For example, *The European Union* (http://europa. eu.int/ index_en.htm) reports on historical and current activity in the European Union. It is a comprehensive reference guide that provides information about laws and regulations, a detailed profile of each European Union member state, investment opportunities, sources of grants and other funding, and other information about business resources. The appendix to this chapter lists many secondary data sources, including some that offer information about countries around the world.

A number of U.S.-based organizations offer a wealth of data about foreign countries. For instance, as part of the U.S. government, *The CIA Factbook* and the *National Trade Data Bank* are especially useful and both can be accessed using the Internet. Particularly, the National Trade Data Bank (NTDB) has been published monthly on CD-ROM since 1990 and includes information on demographic, political, and socioeconomic conditions in hundreds of countries.

SUMMARY

Secondary data are data that have been gathered and recorded previously by someone else for purposes other than those of the current researcher. Secondary data usually are historical and do not require access to respondents or subjects. Primary data are data gathered for the specific purpose of the current researcher.

The chief advantage of secondary data is that they are almost always less expensive to obtain than primary data. Generally they can be obtained rapidly and may provide information not otherwise available to the researcher. The disadvantage of secondary data is that they were not intended specifically to meet the researcher's needs. The researcher must examine secondary data for accuracy, bias, and soundness. One way to do this is to cross-check various available sources.

Secondary research designs address many common marketing problems. There are three general categories of secondary research objectives: fact-finding, model building, and database marketing. A typical fact-finding study might seek to uncover all available information about consumption patterns for a particular product category or to identify business trends that affect an industry. Model building is more complicated; it involves specifying relationships between two or more variables. Model building need not involve a complicated mathematical process, but it can help marketers to estimate market potential, forecast sales, select sites, and accomplish many other objectives. The practice of database marketing, which involves maintaining customer databases with customers' names, addresses, phone numbers, past purchases, responses to past promotional offers, and other relevant data such as demographic and financial data, is increasingly being supported by marketing research efforts.

Managers often get data from internal proprietary sources such as accounting records. On the other hand, external data are generated or recorded by another entity. The government, newspaper and journal publishers, trade associations, and other organizations create or produce information. Traditionally this information has been distributed in published form, either directly from producer to researcher, or indirectly through intermediaries such as public libraries. Modern computerized data archives, electronic data interchange, and the Internet have changed the distribution of external data, making them almost as accessible as internal data. Push technology is a term referring to an Internet information technology that automatically delivers content to the researcher's or manager's desktop. This helps in environmental scanning.

Data mining is the use of powerful computers to dig through volumes of data to discover patterns about an organization's customers and products. It is a broad term that applies to many different forms of analysis.

The marketing of multiple types of related data by single-source suppliers has radically changed the nature of secondary data research.

As business has become more global, so has the secondary data industry. International researchers should watch for certain pitfalls that can be associated with foreign data and cross-cultural research.

Key Terms and Concepts

secondary data	push technology	neural network
data conversion	model building	database marketing
cross-checks	site analysis techniques	internal and proprietary data
market tracking	index of retail saturation	external data
environmental scanning	data mining	single-source data

Questions for Review and Critical Thinking

1. Secondary data have been called the first line of attack for marketing researchers. Discuss this description.
2. Identify some typical research objectives for secondary data studies.
3. Over the past five years, a manager has noted a steady growth in sales and profits for her division's product line. Does she need to use any secondary data to further evaluate her division's condition?
4. Suppose you wish to learn about the size of the soft-drink market, particularly root beer sales, growth patterns, and market shares. Indicate probable sources for these secondary data.
5. How might a retailer such as La Senza use data mining?
6. What would be the best source for the following data?
   a. Population, average income, and employment rates for Alberta
   b. Maps of Canadian cities
   c. Trends in automobile ownership
   d. Divorce trends in Canada
   e. Median weekly earnings of full-time, salaried workers for the previous five years

   f. Annual sales of the top ten fast-food companies
   g. Top ten Web sites ranked by number of unique visitors
   h. Attendance at professional sports events
7. Suppose you are a marketing research consultant and a client comes to your office and says, "I must have the latest information on the supply of and demand for Quebec potatoes within the next 24 hours." What would you do?
8. Use Statistics Canada to find the total population, median age, and total retail sales for (a) your hometown and (b) the town in which your school is located.
9. Use secondary data to learn the size of the Canadian golf market and to profile who golfs.
10. A newspaper reporter reads a study that surveyed children and then reports that a high percentage of children recognize Joe Camel, cigarette spokescharacter, but fails to report that the study also found that a much higher percentage of children indicated very negative attitudes toward smoking. Is this a proper use of secondary data?

Exploring the Internet

1. The home page for BRINT Research Initiative (Business Research, Management Research & Information Technology Research) is at http://www.brint.com/. It contains links to hundreds of information-based Web sites. Visit this site and identify several interesting sources you can go to from there.

2. Go to the Census section of the Statistics Canada Web site (http://www12.statcan.ca/english/census01/home/index.cfm) and navigate to the population section. Find today's estimate of the Canadian population.
3. Use the Internet to learn what you can about Indonesia.

a. Use a Web browser to go to http://www.asiadragons.com/ and click on Indonesia.

b. Visit the *CIA World Factbook* (http://www.cia.gov/cia/publications/factbook/).

c. Go to Infoseek or Google and use "Indonesia" as a search word.

What kinds of information are available from these sources?

4. FIND/SVP is a company that provides information about many different industries worldwide, working with associates in 36 countries (Compass North Inc. in Canada). Go to the FIND/SVP home page at http://www.findsvp.com. Select an industry. What industry information is available?

5. Go to Statistics Norway at http://www.ssb.no/. What data, if any, can you obtain in English? What languages can be used to search this Web site? What databases might be of interest to the business researcher?

6. Go to the Statistical Abstract of the United States at http://www.census.gov/compendia/statab/. What government statistics might be of interest to the business researcher interested in the U.S. market?

7. Going to the University of Waterloo's library Web site at http://www.lib.uwaterloo.ca/ and clicking on Resources for Research will lead you to many hyperlinks for a vast number of sources for secondary information.

8. Go to the Concordia University library's Database resources on the Web at http://www.library.concordia.ca/research/databases/. You will find links to many databases. Visit the site and report what you find.

Dennis Middlemist was a weekend do-it-yourselfer. A hobby he particularly enjoyed was building furniture for his own home. After many years of frustration with trial-and-error adjustment of his radial arm saw using a T-square and trial cuts, Middlemist decided that he needed to invent an alignment device.

Before long, Middlemist had designed a solution. A custom prototype was built at a local engineering shop. When Middlemist tested the device, it seemed to work perfectly for his needs. The proud inventor sought out a lawyer to patent the device, and it looked as if a patent would be available. At this point, Middlemist started to dream about the possibility of the Middlemist Precision Tool Company and the vast empire he would leave to his children. In reality, however, he knew little about marketing and wondered what market information he would need,

such as what the market potential would be, before getting serious about manufacturing the device. He thought the best place to start would be to determine the number of radial arm saws in Canada and the number of prospective customers for his invention.

Questions
1. If you were a research consultant called in to help Dennis Middlemist define his marketing problem, what information do you think would be most important to him?
2. Middlemist has decided to see what information about the radial arm saw market can be found in secondary data sources. Go to your library and find what you can on radial arm saws and/or any related information that might be of value to Middlemist.

SELECTED SOURCES FOR SECONDARY DATA

This appendix briefly describes numerous valuable sources for secondary data. Most are available on CD-ROM and online. Many require subscription fees. However, most college and university libraries allow students to use these sources free of charge.

MAJOR INDEXES AND REFERENCE GUIDES

ABI/INFORM Database. A much-used database abstracting by subject significant articles that are published in more than 1,000 leading business and management publications, including nearly 1,800 worldwide business periodicals. Full text is available for more than 600 of the most popular and important sources.

ABI/INFORM Trade & Industry. Search more than 750 business periodicals and newsletters with a trade or industry focus. Provides users with the latest industry news, product and competitive information, marketing trends, and a wide variety of other topics. Contains publications on every major industry, including finance, insurance, transportation, construction, and many more.

Canadian Business and Current Affairs Complete. A source for Canadian business information made up of *CBCA Business, CBCA Current Events, CBCA Education,* and *CBCA Reference. CBCA Business* indexes over 450 Canadian business periodicals, many with full text, including trade journals, general business publications, academic journals, topical journals, and professional publications. *CBCA Education* focuses on Canadian information in the field of education; currently over 130 journals are indexed, covering both research and practice-oriented publications; 24 journals are currently available in full-text format. *CBCA Complete* also indexes articles in over 600 Canadian newspapers, magazines, and journals in all subject areas from 1982 onward. Includes full-text articles from over 150 of the indexed Canadian periodicals starting in 1993.

PAIS International in Print (New York: Public Affairs Information Service; monthly with periodic cumulations). A subject index to public policy literature published in 60 countries. Business topics emphasize economic factors, industry surveys, and business-societal interactions rather than details of business operations. Besides selectively indexing articles written in English and in five other languages, it covers some books, government publications, and pamphlets.

Reader's Guide to Periodical Literature (New York: H. W. Wilson Company; published partly monthly and partly semimonthly, with periodic cumulations). Indexes nearly 200 general-interest U.S. and Canadian magazines by subject and author. Does not cover business, academic, or other scholarly magazines, and thus is of greater interest to general audiences.

Canadian Foreign Relations Index. CFRI is a compilation of the print series *A Bibliography of Works on Canadian Foreign Relations,* published in six volumes by the various staff at the John Holmes Library. It contains Canadian and foreign material on Canada's foreign relations, defence, economic relations, foreign aid, international law, and international environmental concerns.

Canadian Newsstand. Canadian Newsstand offers unparalleled access to the full text of Canadian newspapers.

Canada Newswire. The largest news release database in Canada. Searchable by keyword, date, organization name, stock symbol, industry, and so on. (http://www.newswire.ca)

Canadian Research Index (CRI). Also known as Microlog Index, indexes a selection of Canadian federal, provincial, and municipal government documents.

Canadian Trade Index. Provides detailed information regarding over 26,000 Canadian companies, including 20,000 manufacturers, 11,500 active exporters, 7,000 distributors of products in Canada, and 3,700 service companies for manufactured products. Includes a comprehensive list of over 50,000 products and services.

Encyclopedia of Consumer Brands (Detroit: Gale Group Inc., 1993). The three volumes present the origin, evolution, and current market status of some of the world's most recognizable consumer brands.

North American Industry Classification System (NAICS). Statistics Canada, the Economic Classification Policy Committee (ECPC) of the United States, and Mexico's Instituto Nacional de Estadística, Geografía e Informática (INEGI) have agreed upon the limited industry revisions for NAICS 2002. This revision of the 1997 industry classification system extends the three-country agreement level for the Construction sector and recognizes the important changes in the Information sector that have occurred since the introduction of NAICS. Also available at: http://www.statcan.ca/english/Subjects/Standard/naics/2002/naics02-index.htm.

Canadian Business Patterns. This CD-ROM contains tables at the 1-, 2-, 3-, and 4-digit Standard Industrial Classification 1980 levels; tables at the 2-, 3-, 4-, and 6-digit North

American Industrial Classification System (as of December 1998); eight employment size categories, including "indeterminate" (as of December 1998); and data produced on a semi-annual basis beginning with June 1990 for provincial, national data, December 1990 for census metropolitan areas data, and December 1996 for agglomeration, census division, and census sub-division area data. It also offers graphic capabilities, varied data manipulation and worksheet features, compatibility with many software packages, as well as step-by-step user documentation and background methodology.

Scott's Directories. Annually lists manufacturers, their products, and their standard industrial classification (SIC) codes, alphabetically as well as by city and region. The directory also provides the names and telephone and fax numbers of chief executives, as well as corporate information such as annual sales. Directories come in four volumes: Ontario, Quebec, Atlantic Canada, and Western Canada.

Government Publications

The Government of Canada generates a vast array of publications through its various departments and agencies. Two services are useful in keeping track of these publications. The *Weekly Checklist of Canadian Government Publications* put out by the Depository Services Program, Public Works and Government Services Canada, lists the book and serial titles that have been released during the week by the Parliament of Canada, federal departments, and Statistics Canada. The second service is the Canadian Government Publishing's Internet site. The *Weekly Checklist* is also available at this location.

Government of Canada

All departments, agencies, and branches of the federal and provincial government(s) can be accessed through the government's Web site at http://www.canada.gc.ca.

Statistics Canada

Statistics Canada publishes extensive statistical information that is gathered through various sources. Statistics Canada produces statistics that help Canadians better understand their country—its population, resources, economy, society, and culture. Statistics Canada, Demography Division, provides summary data on demographic, economic, social, and other aspects of the Canadian economy and society.

Statistics Canada's Web Site

A wealth of information can be found on the Statistics Canada Web site. The Canadian Statistics section presents free tabular data on all aspects of Canada's economy, land, people, and government. This free data can be retrieved from CANSIM II, Statistics Canada's online statistical database. This database also allows access to more detailed data for a small fee. As previously mentioned, however, most college and university libraries allow students to use CANSIM II free of charge.

Canadian Economic Observer

Published monthly, the *Canadian Economic Observer* is the most readily available Statistics Canada publication. It is made up of two parts: a journal with feature articles and economic analysis, and a statistical summary. The journal provides commentary on Canadian and international economic trends, analysis of current economic conditions, and a monthly feature article. The statistical summary provides a complete range of hard data on critical economic indicators, prices, markets, trade, and demographics.

Canada Year Book

The *Canada Year Book* records in narrative and statistical format the developments in Canada's economic, social, and political life. (The *Canada Year Book* is a publication of Statistics Canada.)

Market Research Handbook

Published annually, the *Market Resource Handbook* delivers first-hand results from more than 20 specialized Statistics Canada surveys in one practical resource that is very useful for locating target markets. The *Handbook*'s data are divided into a number of categories, including population, employment and earnings, expenditures, industry statistics, and projections.

Census of Canada

Census statistics can be of great value to marketing researchers because the figures are quoted in such detail, both by subject and by geographic location. The data can be used as a starting point even when they are somewhat out of date.

Census of Agriculture. The Census of Agriculture collects a wide range of data on the agriculture industry, such as number and type of agricultural operations, farm operator characteristics, business operating arrangements, land management practices, crop areas, numbers of livestock and poultry, farm business capital, operating expenses and receipts, and farm machinery and equipment. These data provide a comprehensive picture of the agriculture industry across Canada every five years, at the national and provincial levels, as well as at lower levels of geography.

Census of Population. Conducted every five years, the Census of Population provides the population and dwelling counts not only for Canada but also for each province and territory, and for smaller geographic units such as cities or districts within cities. The census also provides information about Canada's demographic, social, and economic characteristics. (http://www12.statcan.ca/english/census01/home/index.cfm)

Industry Canada. Strategis, Industry Canada's Internet site, is the federal government's major initiative in providing information on business, trade, and investment in Canada as well as on the international business environment. The Strategis site contains over 50,000 reports. (http://www.strategis.ic.gc.ca)

STATISTICAL DATA

Bank of Canada Review. Published quarterly, the *Bank of Canada Review* combines articles and news items on monetary policy with extensive charts and tables on the major financial and economic statistical indicators collected and analyzed by the bank. Most of the articles from the *Review*, other publications, and selected financial statistics are available at the Bank of Canada's Web site.

Canadian Business Patterns. This CD-ROM contains tables at the 1-, 2-, 3-, and 4-digit Standard Industrial Classification 1980 levels; tables at the 2-, 3-, 4-, and 6-digit North American Industrial Classification System (as of December 1998); eight employment size categories, including "indeterminate" (as of December 1998); and data produced on a semi-annual basis beginning with June 1990 for provincial, national data, December 1990 for census metropolitan areas data, and December 1996 for agglomeration, census division, and census sub-division area data. It also offers graphic capabilities; varied data manipulation and worksheet features, compatibility with many software packages, as well as step-by-step user documentation and background methodology.

Canadian Financial Markets Research Centre. Includes daily and monthly Toronto Stock Exchange trading information about specific securities; information on "price adjustments" such as dividends, stock splits, and recapitalizations; information on daily and monthly index levels; as well as selected other financial markets information. The database is divided into two parts: common equities and preferred equities.

Canadian Outlook: Economic Forecast. Published quarterly, the *Economic Forecast* features forecasts on the major components of the Canadian economy, including consumer expenditures, housing, government, business, international trade, energy, employment, labour force, costs and prices, and the financial markets.

Historical Statistics of Canada. Historical Statistics of Canada contains approximately 1,088 statistical tables on the social, economic, and institutional conditions of Canada from 1867 to the mid-1970s. The tables are arranged in sections with an introduction explaining the content of each section, the principal sources of data for each table, and general explanatory notes regarding the statistics. The electronic version of *Historical Statistics of Canada* is accessible for free on the Web site of Statistics Canada.

Income Trends in Canada. This annual publication presents highlights and summary statistics on the income of families. The income concepts covered are market income, government transfers, total income, income tax, income after tax, and low income. Cross-sectional estimates of these income concepts are reported for both current and historical years. Historical estimates are derived from the Survey of Consumer Finances (SCF). Beginning with 1996, the Survey of Labour and Income Dynamics (SLID) provides the data. Key tables are tabulated for Canada and the provinces. Some of the tables are also cross-classified by family type and number of earners in the family. The publication contains detailed tables on low income defined by the low-income cut-offs (LICOs). Estimates on depth of low income (measured as average income gap from the cut-offs) are presented for families by various characteristics. There are also data showing the number of years (persistence) that people have remained in low income. In addition to summary statistics, the publication provides analysis of income trends, charts, notes and definitions, information on survey methodology, and data quality.

Industry Norms and Key Business Ratios (Dun & Bradstreet Canada). Provides financial information and ratios for key industries in Canada. The data is presented by SIC codes for approximately 800 different lines of business and is based on the analysis of over 55,000 public and private companies. Users can also enter the financial statement of a given company and produce a comparative report.

Labour Force Historical Review. Produced annually, the Labour Force Historical Review is a comprehensive database of Labour Force Survey estimates, containing thousands of cross-classified data series and spanning over two decades from 1976 onward. Monthly and annual average series are available on a wide range of subjects, including labour force status by demographic, education and family characteristics, trends in the labour markets of metropolitan cities, economic regions, industry and occupation estimates, and much more.

Small Business Profiles. Free service that provides statistical information on the performance of small businesses in Canada. Standard Industrial Classification (SIC) codes are used throughout Small Business Profiles. The CD-ROM is cumulative for 1993, 1995, and 1997. It provides more options and flexibility than the Web version when searching for data in each year.

MARKET DATA

Canadian Markets. Produced by the Financial Datagroup, provides annual demographic and retail data for more than 700 Canadian urban and regional markets.

Canadian Advertising Rates and Data. Published monthly, provides addresses, advertising rates, circulation, mechanical requirements, and personnel and branch office information for radio and TV stations, newspapers, magazines, and Web advertising sites for all of Canada.

FP Markets, Canadian Demographics. Published annually, it is one of the most extensive sources for demographics on Canadian urban markets. Provides data and projections for population, households, retail sales, and personal income for markets nationwide.

Print Measurement Bureau (PMB). Prepares product category reports that provide information about the users of more than 1,000 products and services. Compares the demographic profiles of users versus non-users, and heavy users versus light users on dimensions such as age, education, marital status, income, occupation, employment status, region and city, household size, residence ownership, sex, and language. Data are also matched to location where main grocery shopping occurs and are usually gathered over two years.

Survey of Buying Power: Canadian Data (New York: *Sales & Marketing Management;* annual constitutes an extra August issue of *S&MM*). *Sales & Marketing Management* publishes a separate issue for subscribers focusing on Canada. This report provides geographical variations of population, income, and retail sales.

INDUSTRY DATA

FP Survey of Industrials. Published annually, it covers all publicly traded Canadian manufacturing and service companies. Describes the companies' operations and highlights of events over the past year, plus financial data and ratios that are useful for investment purposes. The companies are also listed by North American Industrial Classification System codes.

Fraser's Canadian Trade Dictionary. Published annually in four volumes, it provides a comprehensive listing of manufacturers by product classification, as well as an alphabetical listing. Trade names and their manufacturers, and international firms who have agents or distributors in Canada, also have their own specific listings.

There are many other possible sources for information on industries, several of which are listed elsewhere in this appendix. Dun & Bradstreet's *Industry Norms & Key Business Ratios*, for instance, provides financial information and ratios for key industries in Canada. Industry Canada, of course, provides a wealth of information regarding business, trade, and investment in Canada.

INDUSTRY REFERENCE GUIDES

Findex (Bethesda, MD: Cambridge Scientific Abstracts; annual, with midyear supplement). Available online. A descriptive U.S. directory of approximately 13,000 market research reports, studies, and surveys on specific products or industries available from over 500 U.S. and foreign research publishers. They are arranged by subject categories, and for each there is a brief description, publisher, date, paging, and price. Selected company reports are described at the end. Companion indexes covering Europe and other countries are *Predicasts F&S Index Europe* and *Predicasts F&S Index International* (both are monthly, with quarterly and annual cumulations). These are online in *PTS F&S Indexes*.

PTS PROMPT Database (Cleveland: Predicasts, Inc.; monthly, with quarterly and annual cumulations). PROMPT is an acronym for "Predicasts Overview of Market and Technology." This database provides quick access to abstracts (and some full text) on industries, companies, products, markets, and applied technology from a wide range of worldwide journals and other sources, such as investment analysts' reports, research studies, and government publications. It can be useful for identifying articles on such subjects as competitive activities, new products and technologies, market size and share, financial trends, mergers and acquisitions, contracts, joint ventures, and new facilities.

Gale Group Trade and Industry Index Database (Foster City, CA: Gale Group). A multi-industry database covering international company, industry, product, and market information, with strong coverage of such areas as management techniques, financial earnings, economic climate, product evaluations, and executive changes. It provides strong coverage of over 65 major international industries, including automotive, defence, chemicals, electronics, advertising and marketing, retailing, telecommunications, insurance, metals, and oil.

CORPORATE DIRECTORIES

Canadian National Services Directory. Published annually by D&B Companies of Canada Ltd. (Mississauga, ON), it contains listings of Canadian businesses in the service industry only. These businesses have to have 20 or more employees, annual revenue of $1 million or more, and a North American Industrial Classification System code in the service industry sector. Address and company-specific information are provided. Also contains a business by NAICS code and geographic index.

Blue Book of Canadian Business. An online business directory compiled by Canadian Newspaper Services International (Toronto). Includes profiles of Canada's top-performing companies, including executive biographies, sales, assets, net income, and stock trading volume. It can be a very useful resource for business-to-business marketing activities.

Guide to Market Research Services. Published annually in the May issue of *Marketing Magazine*. Lists by Canadian city firms that are involved in market research. Provides a description of the services offered along with addresses.

The Fortune 500 (annual, in *Fortune,* second issue in April). Each year *Fortune* (Time, Inc. Chicago) publishes four ranked lists of largest companies. This one ranks the largest U.S. industrial corporations by sales, assets, profits, and so forth, and also by industry. *Fortune* publishes several other ranked lists:

- *The Fortune Service 500* (first issue in June) with separate rankings for the 100 largest (each) diversified service companies, commercial banks, and diversified financial companies, and 50 largest (each) savings institutions, life insurance companies, retailing companies, transportation companies, and utilities

- *The Fortune Global 500* (first issue in July), ranking the largest industrial companies in the world, and the largest banks

- *The Fortune Global 500* (last issue in July), with separate rankings of worldwide service companies in the same categories as in the U.S. ranked list

Greenbook: International Directory of Marketing Research Companies and Services (New York Chapter, American Marketing Association, Chicago; annual). A descriptive list of marketing research companies, arranged alphabetically with four indexes, including one by geographic location.

To identify the numerous published business and industrial directories, buyer's guides, and rosters, consult a guide such as *Directories in Print* (Detroit: Gale Group Inc.; annual with supplements) and its companion guide, *City & State Directories in Print.*

SELECTED INTERNATIONAL SOURCES
Statistics

Business & Industry. Provides business information (news, facts, figures, events, and market information) at an international level. Sources include over 1,000 trade publications; national, international, and regional newspapers; business dailies and newsletters. Over 60 percent of the records are full-text, with the remainder including informative abstracts that contain key facts.

Monthly Bulletin of Statistics Online (Washington, DC: United Nations Statistics Division, http://esa.un.org/unsd/mbs/mbssearch.asp). Presents current monthly economic statistics for most of the countries and areas of the world. Each month a different selection of special tables is presented showing annual and/or quarterly data on a variety of subjects illustrating important long-term economic trends and developments.

OECD Statistics Brief (Paris: Organization for Economic Cooperation and Development, http://www.oecd.org). Presents important statistical issues to the international community of statisticians, economists, policy makers, and researchers each month.

The 1988 Industrial Commodity Statistics Yearbook (New York: United Nations Publications). Provides statistics on the production in physical quantities of about 530 industrial commodities by country, geographical region, and economic grouping, and for the world. It includes data for a 10-year period (1989–1998 in the current edition) for about 200 countries.

United Nations Common Database. The UNCD provides selected series from 30 specialized international data sources for all available countries and areas. UNCD is a comprehensive database compiled by the United Nations and covers economic, social, financial, and development topics. The database can be accessed through the UN Statistics Division Web site (http://unstats.un.org/unsd/cdb/).

The World Development Indicators (Washington, DC: World Bank, annual). Compilation of data about development. WDI 2001 includes approximately 800 indicators organized in six sections: World View, People, Environment, Economy, States and Markets, and Global Links. The data cover 148 economies and 14 country groups with basic indicators for another 59 economies.

Statistical Abstract of the United States (Washington, DC: U.S. Bureau of the Census; annual, http://www.census.gov/compendia/statab/). One of the most valuable statistical reference books, consisting of many social, political, and economic statistical tables, each taken from original government reports. It also serves as a reference for more detailed information because it gives the source at the foot of each table and also includes guides to statistics, state statistical abstracts, and some foreign statistics at the end.

Reference Guides

Europa World Year Book (London: Europa Publications; two volumes). Important source for brief information about countries, such as recent history, economic statistics, government, political organizations, and holidays; also lists important newspapers, periodicals, radio and TV stations, banks, insurance companies, trade associations, railroads, and much more. Some data on international organizations are at the front of Volume 1.

European Directory of Marketing Information Sources (biennial) and *International Directory of Marketing Information Sources* (biennial) (London: Euromonitor Plc). These two guides describe the following types of information available for each country: official sources and publications (including statistical publications); libraries and information sources; leading market research companies; information databases; abstracts and indexes; major business and marketing journals; leading business and marketing associations; and European business contacts (such as embassies and chambers of commerce).

Global Market Information Database. Business information resource available from Euromonitor International, Inc. Provides key business information on countries, companies, markets, and consumers. Country statistics contain demographic, economic, and marketing statistics for countries worldwide. Market reports contain international market performance, important developments in the product sector, and competition strategy. Also included are country reports of sales trends, new products, and marketing developments worldwide. Company reports offer strategic profiles of the leading multinationals in the industry. Consumer lifestyle analysis and statistics by country examine indicators, choices, and factors to compare market conditions around the world.

Statistical Yearbook. A comprehensive source of international data for socioeconomic indicators, published by the United Nations. Other publications by the United Nations include the *Demographic Yearbook* and the *International Trade Statistics Yearbook*.

Corporate Directories and Investment Data

Disclosure/Worldscope: Industrial Company Profiles and *Disclosure/Worldscope: Financial & Service Company Profiles* (Bridgeport, CT: D/W Partners; eight unnumbered volumes; annual). There are five volumes in the first title. Four volumes contain concise (one-page) statistical profiles for more than 3,000 leading industrial companies in 24 countries and 18 industries. Statistics, usually for a six-year period, cover financial statement data, financial ratios and growth rate, per-share data, and more. The fifth volume is a User's Guide. Two of three volumes of the second title give similar data for over 1,000 major financial, transportation, and utilities companies in 24 countries. The third volume is a User's Guide.

Moody's International Manual (New York: Moody's Investors Service; two volumes, annual, with supplements). A financial manual covering major corporations in some 100 countries and arranged by country. Data given for each corporation usually include a brief financial history, a description of business and property, officers, and financial statement figures, plus more. Centre blue pages contain comparative international statistics.

Primary International Businesses (New York: Dun & Bradstreet Information Services; annual). Directory-type information for approximately 50,000 leading companies in 140 countries; arranged by country, with indexes by SIC industries and by company.

Standard Directory of International Advertisers & Agencies (Wilmette, IL: National Register Publishing Company; annual). Describes both large companies that advertise and advertising agencies outside the United States. Besides the usual directory information for each company, this directory often gives names of sales personnel, the name of the ad agency, advertising appropriations, and media used. Noted elsewhere in this appendix are two indexes that are good sources for locating current articles and news about companies and industries outside the United Sates: *Predicasts F&S Index Europe* and *Predicasts F&S Index International*. Both are accessible online as *PTS F&S Indexes*.

DATABASE SEARCHING AND RETRIEVING WITH COMPUTERS

Developments in information technology have had a major impact on the retrieval and use of published data. Many manual retrieval methods are being replaced by computerized database retrieval systems.

A large organization might subscribe to the Lexis system, for example. A business executive could use the computer retrieval system to search for articles related to new laws pertaining to, say, Canada Revenue Agency policy for deduction for an office at home. If an executive needed a broader search to look for material not found in Lexis, the computer may be asked to search all the databases offered by an online vendor such as the Dow Jones News Retrieval Service. Searching more databases is possible, but of course this increases the cost of the research.

A STEP-BY-STEP SEARCH FOR A COMPUTERIZED BIBLIOGRAPHY

To illustrate the database searching process, consider an example of one online information service. ProQuest is found in many public and university libraries. ProQuest Direct allows the user to create a computerized bibliography efficiently by collecting information stored in commercial databases. Three examples follow:

Periodical Abstracts Research II accesses over 1,800 publications covering general reference, health, social sciences, humanities, education, general business, communications, law, general sciences, and medicine. Full text is available for over 800 titles.

ABI/INFORM Global accesses nearly 1,500 publications covering accounting, finance, marketing, management, international business, real estate, taxation, investment and banking, business trends, and new technologies and products. Full text is available for over 800 titles.

National Newspapers accesses national newspapers, such as the *National Post* or *Globe and Mail* and regional newspapers. Full text is available for most titles.

The typical search begins at the ProQuest Search-by-word screen illustrated in Exhibit 6B.1 and progresses through various screens that present titles of articles. (Before you get to the Search-by-word screen, several simple menu options may have to be turned on or off. However, because the system is menu-driven, advancing to this screen is very simple.) Database searching requires that the researcher initiate either a controlled vocabulary search by entering specific descriptive terms or names, such as a company name, or a subject list search.

An article can be available in any or all of the following five formats.

- *Citation* format displays bibliographic information, such as author, title, source, and date.

- *Abstract* format displays a citation plus a brief summary of the article.

- *Full Text* format displays the citation, abstract, and the complete text of the article in ASCII format.

- *Text 1 Graphics* format displays the citation, abstract, and the complete text of the article in ASCII format, plus originally published images in thumbnail size but adjustable for size.

- *Page Image* format displays scanned images of the article as it was originally published. Adobe Acrobat Reader is needed to display Page Image format. It can be downloaded for free from the ProQuest Direct site.

An on-screen icon indicates the available formats for each article.

Exhibit 6B.2 shows the results of a ProQuest® search on "e-mail surveys."

Exhibit 6B.3 shows an abstract obtained in a ProQuest/ABI/INFORM search for articles on "e-mail surveys."

A controlled vocabulary search relies on standard search terms (specific descriptors or vocabulary code names) in the search list; a free-text search finds matches for user-specified keywords. Standard search terms provide a common language for describing key topics in articles. In Exhibit 6B.1, "e-mail surveys" is a standard search term (vocabulary code) that indicates the primary focus of the article. A free-text search identifies articles on the basis of words in the abstract. Articles that mention e-mail surveys but do not have that topic as a primary focus may be found in this way.

Perhaps the major advantage of computerization is the computer's ability to merge or delete references to obtain precisely what is needed. A researcher interested in e-mail surveys may also use the descriptor "market research," which, with a simple change of options in the menu, would restrict the search to articles that discuss e-mail surveys used in market research. Most systems offer several search options, such as an *and* option to merge two descriptive search terms or a *not* option to eliminate certain references. For example, a researcher studying survey research may wish to exclude political polls. The *not* option allows for this. If a search does

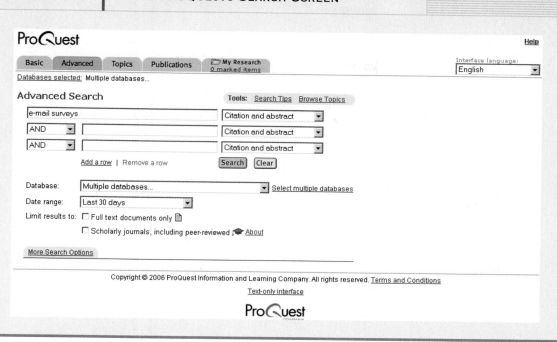

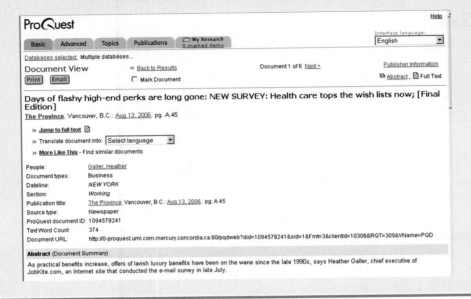

not retrieve enough abstracted articles, the *or* option can broaden the search, so instead of the limited search term "cars," a researcher might enter "cars or automobiles." You will have to study the individual search and retrieval system to investigate all the options it offers.

CD-ROM (Compact Disk—Read Only Memory) systems provide an alternative technology for storing data and database searching. Large amounts of data (the equivalent of 275,000 printed pages or 1,500 floppy disks) can be stored on a single compact disk. Many libraries have CDs that contain bibliographic indexes and databases. The CD-ROM can be inserted into a computer at the library or elsewhere. CD-ROM systems are also widely used for the storage of financial, statistical, and market databases.

Although KitchenAid is best known for its Stand Mixer, the company markets a full line of small and large kitchen appliances, including dishwashers and refrigerators.[1] A couple of years ago, the counter-top appliance division was doing fine, but sales for the company's larger appliances were declining. The KitchenAid team had to figure out a way to transfer brand equity from its small-appliance division to its large appliances—and they had to do it without increasing their marketing budget.

Researchers started with an analysis of data from eight years of warranty card surveys for all of KitchenAid's products and with an analysis of the database from the 40,000 households who participate in consumer panel surveys conducted by NFO Worldwide, a global marketing research company that is now part of Taylor Nelson Sofres (TNS). The KitchenAid researchers learned that across all products, their brand signified "high quality" to customers, but that only their counter-top line of appliances had the reputation for innovation. In a subsequent exploratory research study, researchers discovered consumers weren't interested in the appliance for the appliance's sake. They were interested in what the appliance could do for them—help them to prepare delicious foods and be able to entertain friends and family while serving their culinary creations. To confirm and quantify these preliminary findings, KitchenAid conducted a segmentation study. Based on the survey results, management decided to focus on "the culinary-involved," a segment of consumers who were heavy users of kitchen appliances and who believed in having the best

What you will learn in this chapter

1. To understand the terms *survey*, *sample survey*, and *respondent*.

2. To understand the advantages of using surveys.

3. To recognize that few surveys are error-free.

4. To distinguish between random sampling error and systematic error.

5. To classify the various types of systematic error and give examples of each type.

6. To discuss how response error may be an unconscious misrepresentation or a deliberate falsification.

7. To classify surveys according to method of communication, according to the degree of structure and disguise in questionnaires, and on a temporal basis.

8. To distinguish between cross-sectional and longitudinal studies.

products for their homes. These household chefs were passionate about cooking, and most important to KitchenAid, the segment cut across all demographic groups: It wasn't confined to upper-income households.

Past research had shown that consumers actively use magazines to plan their major appliance purchases, often tearing pages out of home and lifestyle magazines to file away for ideas and inspiration, so KitchenAid planned a print-only campaign. One magazine ad featured a picture of lemon soufflé pancakes dominating more than three-quarters of one page. The pancakes are drizzled in a creamy lemon sauce and topped with raspberries. On the page facing the picture, beneath the smaller images of the large and small appliances that helped to prepare the dish, the text invited the reader to visit the company's Web site for the recipe. These ads ran in 59 publications, ranging from *Architectural Digest* to *People*.

What was the payoff of this research and advertising effort? After the first six months of 2000, when the campaign started, sales for both counter-top and major appliances were showing "double-digit growth." In the first two months of the campaign, contacts to KitchenAid's 800 number and its Web site were more than three times what they had been over the previous year, and hit rates to the site were up nearly 60 percent. Most satisfying: The marketing team produced these results using 64 percent of its budget from the previous year—and without use of a television advertising presence. Much of KitchenAid's success can be attributed to the quality of its surveys.

The purpose of survey research is to collect primary data—data gathered and assembled specifically for the project at hand. This chapter, the first of two on survey research, defines the subject. It also discusses typical research objectives that may be accomplished with surveys and various advantages of the survey method. It explains many potential errors that researchers must be careful to avoid. Finally, it classifies the various survey research methods. ■

THE NATURE OF SURVEYS

respondent
The person who verbally answers an interviewer's questions or provides answers to written questions.

sample survey
A more formal term for a survey.

survey
A method of collecting primary data in which information is gathered by communicating with a representative sample of people.

Surveys require asking people—called **respondents**—for information using either verbal or written questions. Questionnaires or interviews collect data through the mail, on the telephone, or face to face. The more formal term, **sample survey**, emphasizes that the purpose of contacting respondents is to obtain a representative sample of the target population. Thus a **survey** is defined as a method of collecting primary data based on communication with a representative sample of individuals.

Survey Objectives: Type of Information Gathered

The type of information gathered in a survey varies considerably depending on its objectives. Typically, surveys attempt to describe what is happening or to learn the reasons for a particular marketing activity.

Identifying characteristics of target markets, measuring consumer attitudes, and describing consumer purchasing patterns are common survey objectives. Most marketing surveys have multiple objectives; few gather only a single type of factual information. For example, a snowmobile manufacturer might conduct a survey to determine whether consumers are aware of the brand name and learn what purchasers like and dislike about various product features. Demographic information

Dentyne Ice's survey research objective was to understand what goes on in the hearts and minds of young men and women in the 15–24 age range when they're at that crucial moment before the first kiss.[2] The research showed that, without question, there is the nervous anticipation of one's first kiss with a new love interest. Marketing research helped develop a series of ads to put 15–24-year-old characters in humorous situations that illustrate variations of using gum to freshen their breath before a first kiss. One commercial features a young man closing in for a kiss with an attractive someone. At that moment, he imagines himself surrounded by every guy she's ever kissed before—all of them issuing taunts and generally undermining his resolve. Happily, there's a quick confidence-booster available, in the form of Dentyne Ice.

and information on media exposure might also be collected in the survey to help plan a market segmentation strategy. Although consumer surveys are a common form of marketing research, not all survey research is conducted with the ultimate consumer. Frequently studies focus on wholesalers, retailers, or industrial buyers.

Because most survey research is descriptive research, the term *survey* is most often associated with quantitative findings. Although it is true that most surveys are conducted to quantify certain factual information, some aspects of surveys may also be qualitative. In new product development, a survey often has a qualitative objective of testing and refining new product concepts or promotions. Stylistic, aesthetic, or functional changes may be made on the basis of respondents' suggestions.

In the case of Kraft Canada, survey research identified consumers' lack of knowledge about Kraft products and helped in the development of new advertisements. Two years after shifting ad dollars from its Shake'n Bake products to its new products, Kraft Canada experienced a 4 percent loss in the market share of its Shake'n Bake line. Kraft hired a marketing research company and sent out 2,300 questionnaires to discover that most consumers thought the product was only used for chicken when in fact it also comes in flavours for pork and other poultry. Armed with this information, Kraft Canada developed new advertisements to communicate to the consumers that there are other flavours of Shake'n Bake besides chicken. The new TV advertisements, designed by BBDO Canada, featured two pigs named Wilbur and Arthur who are horrified to discover that Shake'n Bake makes a coating for pork. Following the first eight weeks of the new advertising, the sales increased by 54 percent compared to the previous 52 weeks.[3]

Although most marketing surveys are descriptive, they can also be designed to provide insights about causal explanations or to explore ideas.

Advantages of Surveys

Surveys provide a quick, inexpensive, efficient, and accurate means of assessing information about a population. The examples given earlier illustrate that surveys are quite flexible and, when properly conducted, extremely valuable to the manager.

As we discussed in Chapter 1, marketing research has proliferated since the general adoption of the marketing concept. The growth of survey research is related to the simple idea that to find out what consumers think, you need to ask them.[4]

Survey research reveals that the lunch hour isn't what it used to be. According to a poll conducted in 2003, more than half (54 percent) of the respondents under the age of 35 admitted to consuming fast food or junk food instead of a complete meal once a week or more. Younger Canadians were also twice as likely as their older counterparts to skip meals once a day.[5]

Over the last 50 years and particularly during the last two decades, survey research techniques and standards have become quite scientific and accurate. When properly conducted, surveys offer managers many advantages. However, they can also be used poorly.

It may be no exaggeration to say that the greater number of surveys conducted today are a waste of time and money. Many are simply bad surveys. Samples are biased; questions are poorly phrased; interviewers are not properly instructed and supervised; and results are misinterpreted. Such surveys are worse than none at all because the sponsor may be misled into a costly area. Even well-planned and neatly executed surveys may be useless if, as often happens, the results come too late to be of value or are converted into a bulky report which no one has time to read.[6]

The disadvantages of specific forms of survey data collection (personal interview, telephone, mail, Internet, and other self-administered formats) are discussed in Chapter 8. However, errors are common to all forms of surveys, so it is appropriate to describe them generally.

ERRORS IN SURVEY RESEARCH

3

A manager who is evaluating the quality of a survey must estimate its accuracy. Exhibit 7.1 outlines the various forms of survey error. The two major sources of survey error are random sampling error and systematic error.

Random Sampling Error

4

Most surveys try to portray a representative cross-section of a particular target population. Even with technically proper random probability samples, however, statistical errors will occur because of chance variation in the elements selected for the sample. Without increasing sample size, these statistical problems are unavoidable. However, such **random sampling errors** can be estimated; Chapters 14 and 15 will discuss these in greater detail.

random sampling error
A statistical fluctuation that occurs because of chance variation in the elements selected for a sample.

EXHIBIT 7.1 | CATEGORIES OF SURVEY ERRORS

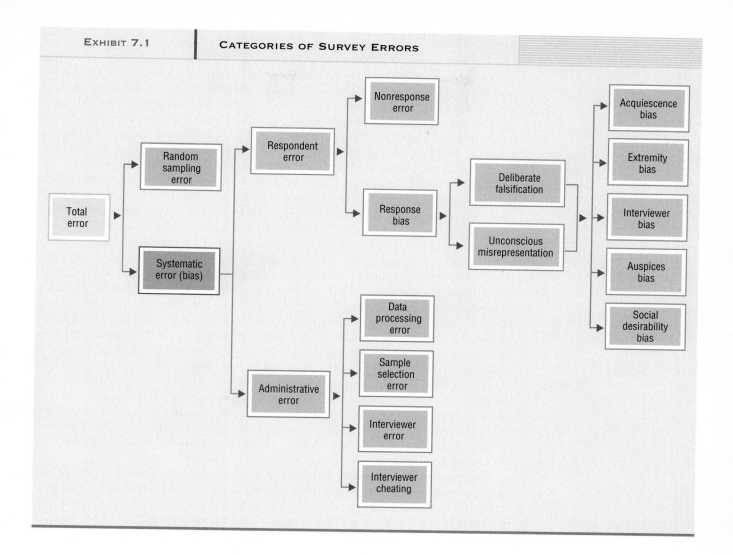

Systematic Error

systematic error
Error resulting from some imperfect aspect of the research design that causes respondent error or from a mistake in the execution of the research.

sample bias
A persistent tendency for the results of a sample to deviate in one direction from the true value of the population parameter.

Systematic error results from some imperfect aspect of the research design or from a mistake in the execution of the research. Because all sources of error rather than those introduced by the random sampling procedure are included, these errors or biases are also called *nonsampling errors*. A **sample bias** exists when the results of a sample show a persistent tendency to deviate in one direction from the true value of the population parameter. The many sources of error that in some way systematically influence answers can be divided into two general categories: respondent error and administrative error. These are discussed in the following sections.

RESPONDENT ERROR

respondent error
A category of sample bias resulting from some respondent action or inaction such as nonresponse or response bias.

Surveys ask people for answers. If people cooperate and give truthful answers, a survey will likely accomplish its goal. If these conditions are not met, nonresponse error or response bias, the two major categories of **respondent error**, may cause a sample bias.

Nonresponse Error

Few surveys have 100 percent response rates. A researcher who obtains an 11 percent response to a five-page questionnaire concerning various brands of spark plugs may face a serious problem. To use the results, the researcher must be sure that those who did respond to the questionnaire were representative of those who did not.

The statistical differences between a survey that includes only those who responded and a perfect survey that would also include those who failed to respond are referred to as **nonresponse error.** This problem is especially acute in mail and Internet surveys, but it also threatens telephone and face-to-face interviews.

People who are not contacted or who refuse to cooperate are called **nonrespondents.** A nonresponse occurs if someone is not at home at the time of both the initial call and a subsequent callback. The number of **no contacts** in survey research has been increasing because of the proliferation of answering machines and growing use of caller ID to screen telephone calls.[7] A parent who must juggle the telephone and a half-diapered child and refuses to participate in the survey because he or she is too busy is also a nonresponse. When Levi Strauss & Company (Canada) tested a card-based rewards program in 1997, the company also created a product registration program that asked buyers of Levi's products to fill out a survey and mail it back. However, most of the buyers did not respond. According to Wayne Alguire of Levi's, part of the reason for the nonresponse was that consumers did not understand the incentive to participate.[8] **Refusals** occur when people are unwilling to participate in the research. No contacts and refusals can seriously bias survey data.

Arbitron, an international media and market research firm, had problems getting people to record their radio-listening habits in diaries every day; in one period only 28 percent of a sample filled in the diary. Arbitron conducted a survey to find differences between people who were willing and unwilling to keep diaries. The diary keepers were found to favour middle-of-the-road, "beautiful" music and news/talk stations; nonrespondents favoured contemporary and rap stations.

Comparing the demographics of the sample with the demographics of the target population is one means of inspecting for possible biases in response patterns. If a particular group, such as older citizens, is underrepresented or if any potential biases appear in a response pattern, additional efforts should be made to obtain data from the underrepresented segments of the population. For example, personal interviews may be used instead of telephone interviews for the underrepresented segments.

nonresponse error
The statistical differences between a survey that includes only those who responded and a perfect survey that would also include those who failed to respond.

nonrespondent
A person who is not contacted or who refuses to cooperate in the research.

no contact
A person who is not at home or who is otherwise inaccessible on the first and second contact.

refusal
A person who is unwilling to participate in a research project.

Nonresponse error can be high when conducting international marketing research. People in many cultures do not share Canadians' views about providing information. In Mexico citizens are reluctant to provide information over the phone to strangers. In many Middle Eastern countries many women would refuse to be interviewed by a male interviewer.

YOU ARE WHAT YOU EAT?

Survey respondents saying one thing and doing another is a response bias problem.[9] In a survey conducted by Angus Reid Group, 71 percent of Canadians polled rated their own personal eating habits as good from a nutritional standpoint, and 94 percent rated nutrition (second only to taste) as an important factor when choosing their groceries. However, when polled on the four food groups and the recommended daily servings adults should include from each food group, there appeared to be a lack of understanding of what makes up healthy eating. This was especially true of the "Grain Products" category. Only 7 percent correctly identified the recommended daily amount as 5 to 12 servings. Further, less than half correctly identified 5 to 10 as the correct servings of "Vegetables and Fruit." Clearly, the respondents wanted to eat healthfully, yet whether they would be able to do so is not clear given their level of nutritional knowledge. Results from an independent survey suggest that only 43 percent of Canadians get their daily 5 to 10 servings of vegetables and fruit frequently, as recommended by Canada's Food Guide to Healthy Eating.[10]

After receiving a refusal from a potential respondent, an interviewer can do nothing other than be polite. The respondent who is not at home when called or visited should be scheduled to be interviewed at a different time of day or on a different day of the week.

With a mail survey the researcher never really knows whether a nonrespondent has refused to participate or is just indifferent. Researchers know that those who are most involved in an issue are more likely to respond to a mail survey. **Self-selection bias** is a problem that frequently plagues self-administered questionnaires. In a restaurant, for example, a customer on whom a waiter spilled soup, a person who was treated to a surprise dinner, or others who feel strongly about the service are more likely to complete a self-administered questionnaire left at the table than individuals who are indifferent about the restaurant. Self-selection biases distort surveys because they overrepresent extreme positions while underrepresenting responses from those who are indifferent. Several techniques will be discussed later for encouraging respondents to reply to mail and Internet surveys.

self-selection bias
A bias that occurs because people who feel strongly about a subject are more likely to respond to survey questions than people who feel indifferent about it.

Response Bias

A **response bias** occurs when respondents tend to answer questions with a certain slant. People may consciously or unconsciously misrepresent the truth. If a distortion of measurement occurs because respondents' answers are falsified or misrepresented, either intentionally or inadvertently, the resulting sample bias will be a *response bias*.

Consider the following examples from U.S. elections. In a New York City mayoral election, all the polls showed the black candidate leading the white candidate by 12 to 16 percentage points, but the black candidate won by just 2 percentage points. On the same day, a black candidate in a Virginia gubernatorial election was 9 to 11 percentage points ahead of the white candidate in the polls but won the Virginia governorship by only 0.3 percentage point. After these elections, research experts explained that whites who say they are undecided in a black–white race nevertheless usually vote overwhelmingly for the white candidate. People who plan to vote against a black candidate, for whatever reason, seem reluctant to admit their true intentions. Perhaps they fear being labelled "racists" or they want the interviewer to think they are socially progressive. But the result is that in elections with candidates of different races, the survey results are likely to show response bias. Thus, to estimate the true vote, researchers should include a corrective measure to allow for this response bias.

response bias
A bias that occurs when respondents either consciously or unconsciously tend to answer questions with a certain slant that misrepresents the truth.

Deliberate Falsification

Occasionally people deliberately give false answers. It is difficult to assess why people knowingly misrepresent answers. A response bias may occur when people misrepresent answers to appear intelligent, to conceal personal information, to avoid embarrassment, and so on. For example, respondents may be able to remember the total amount of money spent grocery shopping, but they may forget the exact prices of individual items that they purchased. Rather than appear ignorant or unconcerned about prices, they may provide their best estimate and not tell the truth—namely, that they cannot remember. Sometimes respondents become bored with the interview and provide answers just to get rid of the interviewer. At other times respondents provide the answers they think are expected of them to appear well informed. On still other occasions, they give answers simply to please the interviewer.

One explanation for conscious and deliberate misrepresentation of facts is the so-called average man hypothesis. Individuals may prefer to be viewed as average so they alter their responses to conform more closely to their *perception* of the average person. Average man effects have been found to exist in response to questions about such topics as savings account balances, car prices, voting behaviour, and hospital stays.

Unconscious Misrepresentation

Even when a respondent is consciously trying to be truthful and cooperative, response bias can arise from the question format, the question content, or some other stimulus. For example, bias can be introduced by the situation in which the survey is administered. The results of two in-flight surveys concerning aircraft preference illustrate this point. Passengers flying on B-747s preferred B-747s to L-1011s (74 percent versus 19 percent), while passengers flying on L-1011s preferred L-1011s to B-747s (56 percent versus 38 percent). The difference in preferences appears to have been largely a function of the aircraft the respondents were flying on when the survey was conducted, although sample differences may have been a factor. A potential influence was the respondent's satisfaction with the plane on which he or she was flying when surveyed. In other words, in the absence of any strong preference, the respondent may simply have identified the aircraft travelled on and indicated that as his or her preference.[11]

A recent survey conducted by Campbell Company of Canada and Decima Research revealed that while 68 percent of Canadians say they are eating healthier today than they were three years ago, only 43 percent are frequently getting their daily 5 to 10 servings of vegetables and fruit, as recommended by Canada's Food Guide to Healthy Eating.[12] When it comes to diet, similar response biases are reported for Americans as well. In response to survey questions conducted by the National Restaurant Association, Americans say they intend to be virtuous in their eating (fresh fruit and bran muffins), but what they actually eat (many hamburgers) doesn't reflect what they say.

Sometimes it is just a matter of how you ask the question.[13] When Burger King sent a survey company into the field to query fast-food fanciers on which they preferred, flame-broiled or fried hamburgers, they found a three-to-one preference for the open flame, or flame-broiled method—Burger King's own. The company and its agency immediately incorporated that finding into a comparative advertising campaign.

But when Leo Shapiro, president of a marketing research company, conducted his own survey, he rephrased the question and came up with distinctively different answers. "If you have two methods of cooking and it's a verbal survey, the choice of words could influence the outcome," Shapiro said in explaining why he decided to conduct his own survey of 308 fast-food customers. An interviewer asked: "Do you prefer a hamburger that is grilled on a hot stainless-steel grill or cooked by passing the raw meat through an open gas flame?" Shapiro's researchers found that 53 percent preferred their burgers from a stainless-steel grill. This means they opted for McDonald's fried over Burger King's open flame. The interviewer then added another dimension:

"The chain that grills on a hot stainless-steel griddle serves its cooked hamburgers at the proper temperature without having to use a microwave oven. The chain that uses the flame puts the hamburgers into a microwave oven after they are cooked and before serving them. Just knowing this, from which of these two chains would you prefer to buy a hamburger?"

McDonald's hot stainless-steel griddles and microwaveless restaurants won again. This time they pulled in a 5 1⁄2-to-1 margin over Burger King. The Burger King hamburgers do come off one at a time, so in rush periods the microwave is used to preserve the serving temperature and to melt the cheese. Burger King refuses to provide details on its survey beyond saying it was national, done by a nationally known public opinion company, that the question asked was "Do you prefer your hamburgers flame-broiled or fried?" and that they are completely satisfied with the survey.

"We found the word 'fried' was unappetizing," Shapiro said. "You don't eat fried foods. The word 'cooked' is neutral, and 'open-gas' is more precise but less appetizing [than Burger King's 'flame-broiled' description]." Shapiro stated that the most significant finding of this survey is how important the methods of cooking and serving were to the hamburger consumer.

Respondents who misunderstand questions may unconsciously provide biased answers. Or they may be willing to answer but unable to do so because they have forgotten the exact details. Asking "When was the last time you attended a concert?" may result in a best-guess estimate because the respondent has forgotten the exact date.

A bias may also occur when a respondent has not thought about an unexpected question. Many respondents will answer questions even though they have given them little thought. For example, in most investigations of consumers' buying intentions, the predictability of the intention scales depends on how close the subject is to making a purchase. The intentions of subjects who have little knowledge of the brand or the store alternatives being surveyed and the intentions of subjects who have not yet made any purchase plans cannot be expected to predict purchase behaviour accurately.

Asking respondents how spicy they like their chilli is unlikely to produce well-articulated answers. In many cases consumers cannot adequately express their feelings in words; there is an unconscious communication breakdown. An international marketing research survey provides a classic example of a communication breakdown. A survey in the Philippines found that despite seemingly high toothpaste usage only a tiny percentage of people responded positively when asked, "Do you use toothpaste?" As it turned out, the brand name Colgate is a generic name for toothpaste in the Philippines. When researchers returned and asked, "Do you use Colgate?" the positive response rate soared.

As the time between a purchase or a shopping event and the survey contact increases, the tendency for underreporting information about that event increases. Time lapse influences people's ability to precisely remember and communicate specific factors. Unconscious misrepresentation bias may also occur because consumers unconsciously avoid facing the realities of a future buying situation. Housing surveys record that Americans overwhelmingly continue to aspire to owning detached, single-family dwellings (preferably single-level, ranch-type structures that require two to five times the amount of land per unit required for attached homes). However, builders know that *attached* housing purchases by first buyers are higher than respondents expect.

Types of Response Bias

There are five specific categories of response bias: acquiescence bias, extremity bias, interviewer bias, auspices bias, and social desirability bias. These categories overlap and are not mutually exclusive. A single biased answer may be distorted for many complex reasons, some distortions being deliberate and some being unconscious misrepresentations.

acquiescence bias
A category of response bias that results because some individuals tend to agree with all questions or to concur with a particular position.

Acquiescence Bias Some respondents are very agreeable; these yea-sayers accept all statements they are asked about. This tendency to agree with all or most questions is known as **acquiescence bias**, and it is particularly prominent in new product research. Questions about a new product idea generally elicit some acquiescence bias because respondents give positive connotations to most new ideas. For example, sporting goods manufacturers Spalding, Rawlings, and Mizuno found that consumers responded favourably when they were asked about pump baseball gloves (with a mechanism similar to those in pump basketball shoes). However, when these expensive gloves hit the market, they sat on the shelves. When conducting new product research, researchers should recognize the high likelihood of acquiescence bias.

Another form of acquiescence is evident in some people's tendency to disagree with all questions. Thus acquiescence bias is a response bias due to the respondents' tendency to concur with a particular position.

extremity bias
A category of response bias that results because some individuals tend to use extremes when responding to questions.

Extremity Bias Some individuals tend to use extremes when responding to questions; others always avoid extreme positions and tend to respond more neutrally. Response styles vary from person to person, and extreme responses may cause an **extremity bias** in the data.[14] This issue is dealt with in Chapter 12 on attitude research.

interviewer bias
A response bias that occurs because the presence of the interviewer influences respondents' answers.

Interviewer Bias Response bias may arise from the interplay between interviewer and respondent. If the interviewer's presence influences respondents to give untrue or modified answers, the survey will be marred by **interviewer bias**. Many

In Asia, cultural values about survey research differ from those in Canada. Asians have less patience with the abstract and rational question wording commonly used in Canada. Researchers must be alert for culture-bound sources of response bias in international marketing research. For example, the Japanese do not wish to contradict others, leading to a bias toward acquiescence and yea-saying.

homemakers and retired people welcome an interviewer's visit as a break in routine activities. Other respondents may give answers they believe will please the interviewer rather than the truthful responses. Respondents may wish to appear intelligent and wealthy—of course they read *Canadian Geographic* rather than *Playboy*.

The interviewer's age, gender, style of dress, tone of voice, facial expressions, or other nonverbal characteristics may have some influence on a respondent's answers. If an interviewer smiles and makes a positive statement after a respondent's answers, the respondent will be more likely to give similar responses. In a research study on sexual harassment against saleswomen, male interviewers might not yield as candid responses as female interviewers would.

Many interviewers, contrary to instructions, shorten or rephrase questions to suit their needs. This potential influence on responses can be avoided to some extent if interviewers receive training and supervision that emphasize the necessity of appearing neutral.

If interviews go on too long, respondents may feel that time is being wasted. They may answer as abruptly as possible with little forethought.

Auspices Bias   Suppose that ING Canada, a financial institution with a niche in online banking, is conducting a study on perceived security of online financial transactions. The answers to the survey may be deliberately or subconsciously misrepresented because respondents are influenced by the organization conducting the study. If an independent marketing research company is conducting the same study, respondents' answers might vary from those in an ING survey because of **auspices bias**.

Social Desirability   A **social desirability bias** may occur either consciously or unconsciously because the respondent wishes to create a favourable impression or save face in the presence of an interviewer. Answering that one's income is only $35,000 a year might be difficult for someone whose self-concept is that of an upper-middle-class person "about to make it big." Incomes may be inflated, education overstated, or perceived respectable answers given to gain prestige. In contrast, answers to questions that seek factual information or responses about matters of public knowledge (postal code, number of children, and so on) usually are quite accurate. An interviewer's presence may increase a respondent's tendency to give inaccurate answers to sensitive questions such as "Did you vote in the last election?" "Do you have termites or roaches in your home?" or "Do you colour your hair?"

auspices bias
Bias in the responses of subjects caused by their being influenced by the organization conducting the study.

social desirability bias
Bias in responses caused by respondents' desire, either conscious or unconscious, to gain prestige or appear in a different social role.

ADMINISTRATIVE ERROR

administrative error
An error caused by the improper administration or execution of the research task.

The results of improper administration or execution of the research task are **administrative errors**. They are caused by carelessness, confusion, neglect, omission, or some other blunder. Four types of administrative error are data processing error, sample selection error, interviewer error, and interviewer cheating.

Data Processing Error

data processing error
A category of administrative error that occurs because of incorrect data entry, incorrect computer programming, or other procedural errors during data analysis.

Processing data by computer, like any arithmetic or procedural process, is subject to error because data must be edited, coded, and entered into the computer by people. The accuracy of data processed by computer depends on correct data entry and programming. **Data processing errors** can be minimized by establishing careful procedures for verifying each step in the data-processing stage.

Sample Selection Error

sample selection error
An administrative error caused by improper sample design or sampling procedure execution.

Sample selection error is systematic error that results in an unrepresentative sample because of an error in either the sample design or the execution of the sampling procedure. Executing a sampling plan free of procedural error is difficult. A firm that selects its sample from the phone book will have some systematic error, because unlisted numbers are not included. Stopping female respondents during daytime

When asked in surveys, parents with children in diapers gave socially desirable answers, saying that they did not want the diapers they used to stereotype their children in male or female roles. However, when one company introduced gender-specific diapers, parents bought pink diapers for girls and would not put pink diapers on boys.

hours in shopping centres excludes working people who shop by mail, Internet, or telephone. In other cases, the wrong person may be interviewed. Consider a political pollster who uses random-digit dialling to select a sample rather than a list of eligible voters. Although 17-year-olds may be willing to give their opinions, they are the wrong people to ask because they cannot vote.

Interviewer Error

Interviewers' abilities vary considerably. **Interviewer error** is introduced when interviewers record answers but check the wrong response or are unable to write fast enough to record answers verbatim. Or selective perception may cause interviewers to misrecord data that do not support their own attitudes and opinions.

Interviewer Cheating

Interviewer cheating occurs when an interviewer falsifies entire questionnaires or fills in answers to questions that have been intentionally skipped. Some interviewers cheat to finish an interview as quickly as possible or to avoid questions about sensitive topics.

If interviewers are suspected of faking questionnaires, they should be told that a small percentage of respondents will be called back to confirm whether the initial interview was actually conducted. This should discourage interviewers from cheating.

RULE-OF-THUMB ESTIMATES FOR SYSTEMATIC ERROR

Sampling errors due to random or chance fluctuations may be estimated by calculating confidence intervals with the statistical tools presented in Chapters 14, 15, 17, and 18.

The techniques for estimating systematic, or nonsampling, error are less precise. Many researchers have established conservative rules of thumb based on experience to estimate systematic error. They have found it useful to have some benchmark figures or standards of comparison to understand how much error can be expected. For example, according to some researchers in the consumer packaged-goods field, approximately one-half of those who say they "*definitely* will buy" or "*probably* will buy" within the next three months actually do make a purchase.[15] For consumer durables, however, the figures are considerably lower; only about one-third of those who say they definitely will buy a certain durable within the next three months will actually do so. Among those who say they *probably* will buy, the number who actually purchase durables is so much lower that it is scarcely worth including it in the early purchase estimates for new durables. Thus researchers often present actual survey findings *and* their interpretations of estimated purchase response based on estimates of nonsampling error. For example, one pay-per-view cable TV company surveys geographic areas it plans to enter and estimates the number of people who indicate they will subscribe to its service. The company knocks down the percentage by a "ballpark 10 percent" because experience in other geographic areas has indicated that there is a systematic upward bias of 10 percent on this intentions question.

WHAT CAN BE DONE TO REDUCE SURVEY ERROR?

Now that we have examined the sources of error in surveys, you may have lost some of your optimism about survey research. Don't be discouraged! The discussion emphasized the bad news because it is important for marketing managers to realize that surveys are not a panacea. There are, however, ways to handle and reduce survey errors. For example, Chapter 13 on questionnaire design discusses the reduction of response bias; Chapters 14 and 15 discuss the reduction of sample selection and random sampling error. Indeed, much of the remainder of this book discusses various techniques for reducing bias in marketing research. The good news lies ahead!

CLASSIFYING SURVEY RESEARCH METHODS

 Now that we have discussed some advantages and disadvantages of surveys in general, it is appropriate to classify surveys according to several criteria. Surveys may be classified based on the method of communication, the degrees of structure and disguise in the questionnaire, and the time frame in which the data are gathered (temporal classification).

Chapter 8 classifies surveys according to method of communicating with the respondent, covering topics such as personal interviews, telephone interviews, mail surveys, and Internet surveys. The classifications based on structure and disguise and on time frame will be discussed in the remainder of this chapter.

Structured and Disguised Questions

In designing a questionnaire (or an *interview schedule*), the researcher must decide how much structure or standardization is needed.[16] A **structured question** limits the number of allowable responses. For example, the respondent may be instructed to choose one alternative response such as "under 18," "18–35," or "over 35" to indicate his or her age. **Unstructured questions** do not restrict the respondent's answers. An open-ended, unstructured question such as "Why do you shop at Canadian Tire?" allows the respondent considerable freedom in answering.

The researcher must also decide whether to use **undisguised questions** or **disguised questions.** A straightforward, or undisguised, question such as "Do you have dandruff problems?" assumes that the respondent is willing to reveal the information. However, researchers know that some questions are threatening to a person's ego, prestige, or self-concept. Therefore, they have designed a number of indirect techniques of questioning to disguise the purpose of the study.

Questionnaires can be categorized by their degree of structure and degree of disguise. For example, interviews in exploratory research might use *unstructured-disguised* questionnaires. The projective techniques discussed in Chapter 5 fall into this category. Other classifications are *structured-undisguised, unstructured-undisguised,* and *structured-disguised.* These classifications have two limitations. First, the degree of structure and the degree of disguise vary; they are not clear-cut categories. Second, most surveys are hybrids, asking both structured and unstructured questions. Recognizing the degrees of structure and disguise necessary to meet survey objectives will help in the selection of the appropriate communication medium for conducting the survey.

structured question
A question that imposes a limit on the number of allowable responses.

unstructured question
A question that does not restrict the respondents' answers.

undisguised question
A straightforward question that assumes the respondent is willing to answer.

disguised question
An indirect question that assumes the purpose of the study must be hidden from the respondent.

Chapter 7   *Survey Research: An Overview*

Temporal Classification

Although most surveys are for individual research projects conducted only once over a short time period, other projects require multiple surveys over a long period. Thus surveys can be classified on a temporal basis.

Cross-Sectional Studies

A countrywide survey was taken to examine the different attitudes of cross-sections of the Canadian public toward grilling of food. People from central Canada were more likely to grill sausages than those in western Canada (81 percent in Ontario and 82 percent in Quebec versus 55 percent in western Canada), and Atlantic Canadians grilled more clams, oysters, calamari, and mussels (12 percent) than the national average of 4 percent.[17] This was a **cross-sectional study** because it collected the data at a single point in time. Such a study samples various segments of the population to investigate relationships among variables by cross-tabulation. Most marketing research surveys fall into this category, particularly those that deal with market segmentation. The typical method of analyzing a cross-sectional survey is to divide the sample into appropriate subgroups. For example, if a winery expects income levels to influence attitudes toward wines, the data are broken down into subgroups based on income and analyzed to reveal similarities or differences among the income subgroups.

Longitudinal Studies

In a **longitudinal study** respondents are questioned at two or more different times. The purpose of longitudinal studies is to examine continuity of response and to observe changes that occur over time. Many syndicated services, such as Ipsos Canada, conduct regular surveys. For instance, the Ipsos Trend Report Canada identifies and monitors shifts in Canadians' values, behaviours, and perceptions about marketplace, social, economic, and political issues affecting them and has been doing so since 1986. It is an example of a longitudinal study that uses successive samples; its researchers survey several different samples at different times. Longitudinal studies of this type are sometimes called *cohort studies,* because similar groups of people who share a certain experience during the same time interval (cohorts) are expected to be included in each sample.

In applied marketing research, a longitudinal study that uses successive samples is called a **tracking study** because successive waves are designed to compare trends and identify changes in variables such as consumer satisfaction, brand image, or advertising awareness. These studies are useful for assessing aggregate trends but do not allow for tracking changes in individuals over time.

Conducting surveys in waves with two or more sample groups avoids the problem of response bias resulting from a prior interview. A respondent who was interviewed in an earlier survey about a certain brand may become more aware of the brand or pay more attention to its advertising after being interviewed. Using different samples eliminates this problem. However, researchers can never be sure whether the changes in the variable being measured are due to a different sample or to an actual change in the variable over time.

Consumer Panel   A longitudinal study that gathers data from the same sample of individuals or households over time is called a **consumer panel.** Consider the packaged-goods marketer that wishes to learn about brand-switching behaviour. A consumer panel that consists of a group of people who record their purchasing habits in a diary over time will provide the manager with a continuous stream of information about the brand and product class. Diary data that are recorded regularly over an extended period enable the researcher to track repeat-purchase behaviour and changes in purchasing habits that occur in response to changes in price, special promotions, or other aspects of marketing strategy.

---

cross-sectional study
A study in which various segments of a population are sampled and data are collected at a single moment in time.

longitudinal study
A survey of respondents at different times, thus allowing analysis of response continuity and changes over time.

TO THE POINT

Time is but the stream I go a-fishing in.

HENRY DAVID THOREAU

tracking study
A type of longitudinal study that uses successive samples to compare trends and identify changes in variables such as consumer satisfaction, brand image, or advertising awareness.

consumer panel
A longitudinal survey of the same sample of individuals or households to record their attitudes, behaviour, or purchasing habits over time.

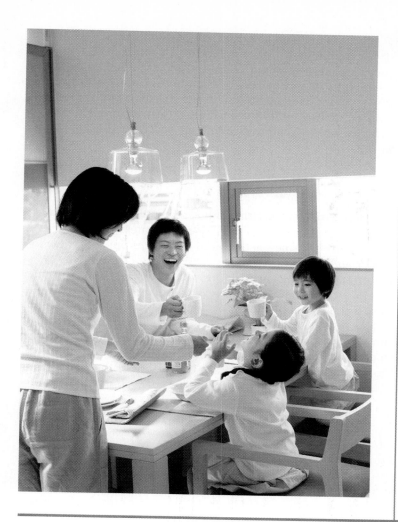

Consumer panels provide longitudinal data. Most established commercial panels allow researchers to break panel data down by demographics. For example, researchers interested in Asian-Canadian families can track how this demographic group's purchasing behaviour changes over time.

Panel members may be contacted by telephone, in a personal interview, by mail questionnaire, or by e-mail. Typically respondents complete media exposure or purchase diaries and mail them back to the survey organization. If the panel members have agreed to field-test new products, face-to-face or telephone interviews may be required. The nature of the problem dictates which communication method to use.

Because establishing and maintaining a panel is expensive, they often are managed by contractors who offer their services to many organizations. A number of commercial firms, such as AC Nielsen, Ipsos Canada, and Consumer Research, specialize in maintaining consumer panels. In recent years Internet panels have grown in popularity. Because clients of these firms need to share the expenses with other clients to acquire longitudinal data at a reasonable cost, panel members may be asked questions about a number of product classes.

The first questionnaire a panel member is asked to complete typically includes questions about product ownership, product usage, pets, family members, and demographic data. The purpose of such a questionnaire is to gather the behavioural and demographic data that will be used to identify heavy buyers, difficult-to-reach customers, and so on for future surveys. Individuals who serve as members of consumer panels usually are compensated with cash, attractive gifts, or the chance to win a sweepstakes.

Marketers whose products are purchased by few households find panels an economical means of reaching respondents who own their products. A two-stage process typically is used. A panel composed of around 15,000 households can be screened with a one-question statement attached to another project. For example, a question in an NFO Worldwide questionnaire screens for ownership of certain uncommon products, such as motorcycles. This information is stored in a database. Then households with the unusual item can be sampled again with a longer questionnaire.

TOTAL QUALITY MANAGEMENT AND CUSTOMER SATISFACTION SURVEYS

total quality management
A business philosophy that emphasizes market-driven quality as a top organizational priority.

As Chapter 1 described, **total quality management** is a business strategy that emphasizes market-driven quality as a top priority. Total quality management involves implementing and adjusting the firm's business activities to ensure customers' satisfaction with the quality of goods and services.

For many years North American corporations failed to keep pace with the product quality strategies of a number of overseas competitors.[18] For example, Xerox Corporation lost a substantial portion of its market share to Ricoh, Canon, and other Japanese copier makers. Xerox's internal audit concluded that Xerox had lost sight of "an axiom as old as business itself . . . focusing on quality that meets the customer's requirements."[19] Today, however, Xerox and many other organizations recognize the need to get customer feedback about the quality of their goods and services. This emphasizes the important role of marketing research.

What Is Quality?

Today, quality is not only defined by engineering standards. Effective executives who subscribe to a total quality management philosophy believe that the product's quality must go beyond acceptability for a given price range. Rather than merely being relieved that nothing went wrong, consumers should experience some delightful surprises or reap some unexpected benefits. In other words, quality assurance is more than just meeting minimum standards. The level of quality is the degree to which a good or service corresponds to buyers' expectations.

Obviously, an Audi A8 does not compete with a Honda Civic. Buyers of these automobiles are in different market segments, and their expectations of quality differ widely. Nevertheless, managers at Jaguar and Nissan try to establish the quality levels their target markets expect and then to produce and market products and services that continually surpass expectations.

Internal and External Customers

Organizations like GfK Arbor LLC, a marketing research and consulting firm, that have adopted the total quality management philosophy believe a focus on customers must include more than external customers. They believe that everyone in the organization has customers:

> Every person, in every department, and at every level, has a customer. The customer is anyone to whom an individual provides service, information, support, or product. The customer may be another employee or department (internal) or outside the company (external).[20]

Total quality management programs work most effectively when every employee knows exactly who his or her customers are and what output internal and external customers expect. Also, it is important to know how customers perceive their needs are being met. All too often differences between perceptions and reality are not understood.

Implementing Total Quality Management

This chapter began by describing KitchenAid. The firm's success is due in part to its ability to satisfy its customers' needs for high-quality kitchen appliances. Implementing a total quality management program requires considerable survey research. A firm must routinely ask customers to rate it against its competitors. It must periodically measure employee knowledge, attitudes, and expectations. It must monitor company performance against benchmark standards. It must determine whether customers found any delightful surprises or major disappointments. In other words, a total quality management strategy expresses the conviction that to improve quality, an organization must regularly conduct surveys to evaluate quality improvement.

Exhibit 7.2 illustrates the total quality management process. The exhibit shows that overall tracking of quality improvement requires longitudinal research. The process begins with a *commitment and exploration stage,* during which management makes a commitment to total quality assurance and marketing researchers explore external and internal customers' needs and beliefs. The research must discover what product features customers value, what problems customers are having with the product, what aspects of product operation or customer service have disappointed customers, what the company is doing right, and what the company may be doing wrong.

One case in point is Clairol Canada. Clairol Canada performs extensive marketing research involving cosmeticians and consumers. A survey in 1993 asked cosmeticians how effective they felt themselves as sales influencers, how they perceived Clairol's role, and how they saw consumers. Clairol also asked their consumers about the effectiveness of cosmeticians as sales influencers and their perceptions of cosmeticians. The findings from this survey provided Clairol with insights about what cosmeticians and consumers really want, how they differ, and what Clairol can do to serve both groups.[22]

After internal and external customers' problems and desires have been identified, the *benchmarking stage* begins. Research must establish quantitative measures that can serve as benchmarks or points of comparison against which to evaluate future efforts. The surveys must establish initial measures of overall satisfaction, of the frequency of customer problems, and of quality ratings for specific attributes. It is essential to identify the company's or brand's position relative to competitors' quality positions.

EXHIBIT 7.2 | LONGITUDINAL RESEARCH
FOR TOTAL QUALITY MANAGEMENT

	Marketing Research Activity with External Consumers (Customers)	Marketing Management Activity	Marketing Research Activity with Internal Consumers (Employees)
Time 1 **Commitment and exploration stage**	Exploratory study to determine the quality the customer wants, discover customer problems, and identify the importance of specific product attributes.	Establish marketing objective that the customer should define quality.	Exploratory study to determine (1) whether internal customers, such as service employees, are aware of the need for service quality as a major means to achieve customer satisfaction and (2) whether they know the quality standards for their jobs. Establish whether employees are motivated and trained. Identify road blocks that prevent employees from meeting customer needs.
Time 2 **Benchmarking stage**	Benchmarking study to measure overall satisfaction and quality ratings of specific attributes.	Identify brand's position relative to competitors' satisfaction and quality rating; establish standards for customer satisfaction.	Benchmarking to measure employees' actual performance and perceptions about performance.
Time 3 **Initial quality improvement stage**	Tracking wave 1 to measure trends in satisfaction and quality ratings.	Improve quality; reward performance.	Tracking wave 1 to measure and compare what is actually happening with what should be happening. Establish whether the company is conforming to its quality standards.
Time 4 **Continuous quality improvement**	Tracking wave 2 to measure trends in satisfaction and quality ratings.	Improve quality; reward performance.	Tracking wave 2 to measure trends in quality improvement.

Time (vertical axis label)

The *initial quality improvement* stage establishes a quality improvement process within the organization. Management and employees must translate quality issues into the internal vocabulary of the organization. The company must establish performance standards and expectations for improvement.

After managers and employees have set quality objectives and implemented procedures and standards, the firm continues to track satisfaction and quality ratings in successive waves. The purpose of tracking wave 1 is to measure trends in satisfaction and quality ratings. Marketing researchers determine whether the organization is meeting customer needs as specified by quantitative standards.

The next stage, *continuous quality improvement*, consists of many consecutive waves with the same purpose—to improve over the previous period. Continuous quality improvement requires that management allow employees to initiate problem solving without a lot of red tape. Employees should be able to initiate proactive communications with consumers. In tracking wave 2, management compares results with those of earlier stages. Quality improvement management continues. For example, Clairol Canada implements quality control in real life. Clairol Canada employees have the authority to establish an ad hoc group to explore a problem that they have observed. Furthermore, if the group determines that this is indeed a real problem, Clairol Canada employees can work on the problem to come up with a solution. The company encourages this collective problem-solving behaviour with awards and support from higher management.[23]

Exhibit 7.2 shows that total quality management programs measure performance against *customers'* standards—not against standards determined by quality engineers within the company. All changes within the organization are oriented toward improvement of customers' perceptions of quality. The exhibit indicates the need for integration of establishing consumer requirements, quantifying benchmark measures, setting objectives, conducting marketing research studies, and making adjustments in the organization to improve quality. Continuous quality improvement is an ongoing process. Considerations in the actual measurement of quality of goods and service delivery are further addressed in Chapters 11, 12, and 13.

SUMMARY

The survey is a common tool for asking respondents questions. Surveys can provide quick, inexpensive, and accurate information for a variety of objectives. The typical survey is a descriptive research study with the objective of measuring awareness, product knowledge, brand usage behaviour, opinions, and so on. The term *sample survey* is often used because a survey is expected to obtain a representative sample of the target population.

Two major forms of error are common in survey research. The first, random sampling error, is caused by chance variation and results in a sample that is not absolutely representative of the target population. Such errors are inevitable, but they can be predicted using the statistical methods discussed in later chapters on sampling. The second major category of error, systematic error, takes several forms. Nonresponse error is caused by subjects' failing to respond to a survey. This type of error can be reduced by comparing the demographics of the sample population with those of the target population and making a special effort to contact underrepresented groups.

Response bias occurs when a response to a questionnaire is falsified or misrepresented, either intentionally or inadvertently. There are five specific categories of response bias: acquiescence bias, extremity bias, interviewer bias, auspices bias, and social desirability bias. An additional source of survey error comes from administrative problems such as inconsistencies in interviewers' abilities, cheating, coding mistakes, and so forth.

Surveys may be classified according to methods of communication, by the degrees of structure and disguise in the questionnaires, and on a temporal basis. Questionnaires may be structured, with limited choices of responses, or unstructured, to allow open-ended responses. Disguised questions may be used to probe sensitive subjects. Surveys may consider the population at a given moment or follow trends over a period of time. The first approach, the cross-sectional study, usually is intended to separate the population into meaningful subgroups. The second type of study, the longitudinal study, can reveal important population changes over time. Longitudinal studies may involve contacting different sets of respondents or the same ones repeatedly. One form of longitudinal study is the consumer panel. Consumer panels are expensive to conduct, so firms often hire contractors who provide services to many companies, thus spreading costs over many clients.

Total quality management is the process of implementing and adjusting a firm's business strategy to ensure customers' satisfaction with the quality of goods or services. The level of quality is the degree to which a good or service corresponds to buyers' expectations. Marketing research provides companies with feedback about the quality of goods and services.

Implementing a total quality management program requires considerable survey research, conducted routinely, to ask customers to rate a company against its competitors. It also measures employee attitudes and monitors company performance against benchmark standards. After identifying customer problems and desires, the firm tracks satisfaction and quality ratings in successive waves. Total quality management research is an ongoing process for continuous quality improvement that works for both marketers of goods and service providers.

Key Terms and Concepts

respondent	self-selection bias	interviewer cheating
sample survey	response bias	structured question
survey	acquiescence bias	unstructured question
random sampling error	extremity bias	undisguised question
systematic error	interviewer bias	disguised question
sample bias	auspices bias	cross-sectional study
respondent error	social desirability bias	longitudinal study
nonresponse error	administrative error	tracking study
nonrespondent	data processing error	consumer panel
no contact	sample selection error	total quality
refusal	interviewer error	management

Questions for Review and Critical Thinking

1. Name several nonbusiness applications of survey research.
2. A major petroleum corporation markets its gasoline under a national brand name through a franchise dealer organization. The corporation is considering building a number of company-owned stations with a new brand name to market a low-priced gasoline product to compete with independent dealers. Would survey research be useful? If so, how?
3. What survey research objectives might Nissan Canada develop to learn about car buyers?
4. Give an example of each type of error listed in Exhibit 7.1.
5. In a survey, chief executive officers (CEOs) indicated that they would prefer to relocate their businesses in Victoria (first choice), Calgary, Edmonton, Montreal, or Halifax. The CEOs who said they were going to build the required office space in the following year were asked where they were going to build. They indicated they were going to build in Toronto, Montreal, Vancouver, or Ottawa. Explain the difference.
6. What potential sources of error might be associated with the following situations?
   a. In a survey of frequent flyers age 50 and older, researchers concluded that price does not play a significant role in airline travel because only 25 percent of the respondents check off price as the most important consideration in determining where and how they travel, while 35 percent rate price as being unimportant.

   b. A survey of voters finds that most respondents do not like negative political ads—that is, advertising by one political candidate that criticizes or exposes secrets about the opponent's "dirty laundry."
   c. Researchers who must conduct a 45-minute personal interview decide to offer $25 to each respondent because they believe that people who will sell their opinions are more typical than someone who will talk to a stranger for 45 minutes.
   d. A company's sales representatives are asked what percentage of the time they spend making presentations to prospects, travelling, talking on the telephone, participating in meetings, working on the computer, and engaging in other on-the-job activities. What potential sources of error might be associated with asking such a question?
   e. A survey comes with a Water Hardness Packet to test the hardness of the water in a respondent's home. The packet includes a colour chart and a plastic strip to dip into hot water. The respondent is given instruction in six steps on how to compare the colour of the plastic strip with the colour chart that indicates water hardness.
7. What topics about consumer behaviour might be extremely sensitive issues about which to directly question respondents?
8. A survey conducted by the Canadian Authors Association asked, "Have you read a book within the last year?" What response bias might arise from this question?

9. How might survey results for buying intentions be adjusted to account for consumer optimism?
10. Name some common objectives of cross-sectional surveys.
11. Give an example of a political situation in which longitudinal research might be useful. Name some common objectives for a longitudinal study in a business situation.
12. What are the advantages and disadvantages of using consumer panels?
13. Scan through your local newspaper to find some stories derived from survey research results. Was the study's methodology appropriate? Could the research have been termed *advocacy research*?

14. Suppose you are the marketing research director for your province's tourism bureau. Assess the province's information needs, and identify the information you will collect in a survey of tourists who visit your province.
15. A researcher sends out 200 questionnaires, but 50 are returned because the addresses are inaccurate. Of the 150 delivered questionnaires, 50 are completed and mailed back. However, 10 of these respondents wrote that they did not want to participate in the survey. The researcher indicates the response rate was 33.3 percent. Is this the right thing to do?

Exploring the Internet

1. Compas publishes the results of many of its opinion polls. Go to www.compas.ca, click on Compas Library, and then Policy and Opinion to find the latest poll or an archive of past polls.
2. Located at the University of Connecticut, the Roper Center is the largest library of public opinion data in the world. An online polling magazine and the methodology and findings of many surveys may be found at www.ropercenter.uconn.edu. Report on an article or study of your choice.
3. Go to the Ipsos Canada Web site (www.ipsos.ca/) to learn what type of survey research services the firm offers. What links to other survey research services can be accessed through Ipsos Canada's Web site?
4. The National Population Health Survey (NPHS), available from Statistics Canada (www.statcanada.ca), is a longitudinal survey covering 17,276 individuals across all ten provinces, and has been providing unique information about the health of Canadians since 1994–95. It provides information at the provincial and national levels on a wide range of health determinants and risk factors, such as alcohol consumption, smoking, chronic conditions, health care utilization, self-perceived health status, height, weight, restriction of activities, and stress. Go to http://www.statcanada.ca to learn about the objectives and methodology for this study.
5. The Princeton University Survey Research Center is located at

   www.wws.princeton.edu/psrc/.

   Review the studies that are listed.

CASE 7.1   THE GREETING CARD STUDY

Selected adult members of a consumer panel were sent the following cover letter and a questionnaire referred to as a *purchase diary* (the green purchase diary form is not shown here).

We are presently conducting a study for a greeting card manufacturer who, in order to be able to provide the "right card for the right person," would like to know the type of cards being purchased now and to whom they are being sent. We are asking our members to participate in this project by keeping a record of the greeting cards they purchase and receive during the next month.

As a participant, here is what we would like you to do.

1. Please record all purchases of greeting cards made by you and members of your household in the green purchase diary form provided for July. It is most important for this study that we have the information on *all* cards purchased by *everyone* in your household. Please make it known that as soon as someone in your household purchases a greeting card, he or she should either show you the card or give you the appropriate information so you can make the diary entry as soon after the purchase as possible.

Section 1 is for entries of individual greeting cards; Section 2 is to record the purchase of boxes or packages of cards.

2. Here is the very unusual part of this study. Please save all of the greeting cards you and other members of your household receive during the month of July and follow "Instructions for Cards Received" (blue page).

Accurate reporting is very important, so please read the instruction page for each form carefully. Your report will be for the month of July, so on July 31 or as soon after as possible, please return the appropriate materials. (We've enclosed a postage-paid envelope for your convenience.)

Your cooperation is deeply appreciated. We are sending you a loonie, as a token of our sincere thanks for your time and effort. Thank you very much!

Questions
1. Evaluate the cover letter. What type of appeal is used? Does the format of the cover letter follow the pattern indicated in the textbook? (See also Chapter 8.)
2. In your opinion, will respondents comply with the researcher's request? Why or why not?
3. What sources of survey error are most likely in a study of this type?

CASE 7.2   TURNER'S DEPARTMENT STORE

Turner's had been in business for 47 years. The first store was located downtown, but the organization had been expanding over the years. The local department store chain operated ten department stores and junior department stores, ranging in size from 10,000 to 60,000 square feet. All stores were located in a single metropolitan area with a population of approximately 600,000 people. The firm's volume strength was in soft goods, although it also handled housewares and small appliances in all stores as well as major appliances in some stores. Price savings on name brands were the primary emphasis of Turner's merchandising strategy.

Turner's was considering its first major venture into survey research. Clay Turner, executive vice-president, had

indicated that "we want to find out what customers and noncustomers think about us and to learn what directions we may take to gain a bigger share of the market." He sent a list of research needs (see Case Exhibit 7.2.1) to several marketing research consultants.

Questions
1. Has the marketing research problem been adequately defined?
2. What type of survey would you recommend?
3. What sources of survey error are most likely in this project?
4. Prepare a brief research proposal for this project.

Note: Names are fictitious to ensure confidentiality.

CASE EXHIBIT 7.2.1	RESEARCH NEEDS FOR TURNER'S DEPARTMENT STORES

We're not looking for praise or compliments but as honest an appraisal as possible. The questions contained here are merely suggestions and may be amplified, condensed, or changed as need be to arrive at a summary that can be acted on.

What Turner's wants to know is "How do people look upon Turner's, and what should we do to merit more of their patronage?" We will appreciate having from you the following:

1. Your suggested questionnaire
2. Sampling size or sizes
3. Degree of expected accuracy
4. Cost or costs
5. Time frame in which the study may be completed
6. Type of summary or summaries to be presented on completion
7. Recommendations for action

Perhaps the study should encompass all or part of the following:

1. A sampling sufficient to give an overall picture
2. The sampling to be divided as equally as possible among people who shop frequently at Turner's and those who shop at Turner's occasionally, seldom, or never
3. The sampling to be done at various income levels, as equitably as possible in relationship of the specific income levels to the total, perhaps

   $8,000–$14,999
   $15,000–$34,999
   $35,000–$54,999
   $55,000–$75,000
   Over $75,000

4. The sampling to be done by age level breakdown: under 25, 25–35, 36–44, over 44
5. The sampling to include family composition: ages of children, if any, and number of boys and girls
6. To determine from those who shop often or occasionally at Turner's what departments they depend on. (Examples: men's apparel; women's apparel, sportswear, hosiery, accessories; cosmetics and fragrances; men's, women's, and children's shoes; costume jewellery; fabrics, linens, sheets, towels, bedspreads, draperies; small appliances; major appliances; housewares; giftware; china; glassware; lamps; radios and televisions; boys', girls', infants' wear)
7. Some idea of readership of Turner's newspaper advertising, preferably among various income levels

8. How people perceive us in relation to other local retail firms (Sears, The Bay, Zeller's, Canadian Tire):

   Turner's merchandise is most like_____
   Turner's fashions are most like_____
   Turner's prices are most like_____
   Turner's stores look most like_____
   Turner's advertising is most like_____
   Turner's prices are as low as or lower than___

9. Turner's salespeople are helpful _____ courteous _____ discourteous _____ not helpful _____
10. Of those who do not shop at Turner's: "I would shop more at Turner's if _____ ."
11. Turner's advertising is informative _____ not informative _____ sometimes honest _____ not accurate _____
12. Do you think Turner's carries a large number of well-known brands?
13. Among those who shop often at Turner's: Do you shop most at the nearest Turner's store? Or do you go to another Turner's? Which one?
14. When you go to Turner's with a specific purchase in mind, do you usually find it in stock? (This applies particularly to everyday items such as hosiery, underwear, jeans, housewares, small appliances, etc.)
15. If the respondent has a Turner's charge account: Is charge authorization prompt?
16. When did you last shop at Turner's? (A week ago, a month ago, 3 months ago)
17. If the respondent has previously shopped at Turner's but no longer does so, is it because of a bad experience? Credit? Exchange, refund, or adjustment of a merchandise purchase?
18. Turner's values are _____ excellent _____ good _____ fair _____ poor
19. Turner's carries some irregulars and seconds _____ many irregulars and seconds _____ all first quality _____
20. I believe seconds and irregulars offer excellent value: yes _____ no _____

SURVEY RESEARCH:
Basic Methods of Communication with Respondents

What you will learn in this chapter

1. To understand when personal interviews, telephone interviews, or self-administered surveys should be conducted.

2. To discuss the advantages and disadvantages of personal interviews.

3. To explain when door-to-door personal interviews should be used instead of mall intercept interviews.

4. To discuss the advantages and disadvantages of telephone surveys.

5. To discuss the advantages and disadvantages of mail, the Internet, and other means of distributing self-administered questionnaires.

6. To understand how to increase response rates to mail surveys.

7. To provide examples of the influence of modern technology on survey research.

8. To select the appropriate survey research design.

9. To discuss the importance of pre-testing questionnaires.

The Ford Motor Company conducts style research clinics to appraise consumer reactions to the exterior and interior styling of new automotive designs. First, fibreglass prototypes or mock-ups of proposed models are made. Then respondents are recruited, usually after short telephone interviews, brought to a showroom, and shown the test mock-up and asked to compare it with competing models from the world market. Personal interviewers ask about every detail of the car as the prospects pore over it. Ultimately the results are fed back to designers in Detroit. Millions were spent on such surveys during the design of the Ford Taurus and the S-type Jaguar.

Chrysler also conducts research to learn consumers' reactions to its cars, both on and off the road.[1] Chrysler researchers give each survey participant a device called a Gridpad to improve the accuracy and speed of data collection. The Gridpad, a flat 8-by-10-inch box with a penlike wand, looks a little bit like an Etch-a-Sketch, but it is more sophisticated. While the survey respondent inspects new car models, multiple-choice questions are displayed on a screen. To respond, the individual simply touches the appropriate box on the Gridpad with the wand. Another gadget has a computerized touch screen showing a version of the car. Respondents specifically identify sections of the vehicle that they really like or really hate. The result is that survey researchers have a computerized map of a car's hot spots. When all the questions have been answered, the information is downloaded onto a desktop computer. Previously, survey participants used pencils to fill out the questionnaires, which then had to be sorted, boxed, and shipped to processing centres. The manager of business/research for Chrysler estimates that using the Gridpad saves about 100,000 sheets of paper on each research project. ∎

During most of the 20th century, survey data were obtained when individuals responded to questions asked by human interviewers (interviews) or to questions they read (questionnaires). Interviewers communicated with respondents face to face or over the telephone or respondents filled out self-administered paper questionnaires, which were typically distributed by mail. These media for conducting surveys remain popular with marketing researchers.

However, as we mentioned in Chapters 2 and 6, digital technology is having a profound impact on society in general and on marketing research in particular. Its greatest impact is in the creation of new forms of communications media.

Human Interactive Media and Electronic Interactive Media

When two people engage in a conversation, human interaction takes place. Human interactive media are a personal form of communication. One human being directs a message to and interacts with another individual (or a small group). When they think of interviewing, most people envision two people engaged in a face-to-face dialogue or a conversation on the telephone. Electronic interactive media allow marketers to reach a large audience, to personalize individual messages, and to interact using digital technology. To a large extent electronic interactive media are controlled by the users themselves. No other human need be present. In the context of surveys, respondents are not passive audience members. They are actively involved in a two-way communication when electronic interactive media are utilized.

The Internet, a medium that is radically altering many organizations' research strategies, provides a prominent example of the new electronic interactive media. Consumers determine what information they will be exposed to, and for how long they will view or hear it. Electronic interactive media also include CD-ROM and DVD materials, touch-tone telephone systems, touch-screen interactive kiosks in stores, and other forms of digital technology.

Non-Interactive Media

The traditional questionnaire received by mail and completed by the respondent does not allow a dialogue or an exchange of information providing immediate feedback. Hence, from our perspective, self-administered questionnaires printed on paper are non-interactive. This does not mean that they are without merit. It only means that this type of survey is not as flexible as surveys using interactive communication media.

Each technique for conducting surveys has its merits and shortcomings. The purpose of this chapter is to explain when different types of surveys should be used. The chapter begins with a discussion of surveys that use live interviews. It next turns to non-interactive, self-administered questionnaires. It then explains how the Internet and digital technology are dramatically changing survey research.

USING INTERVIEWS TO COMMUNICATE WITH RESPONDENTS

Interviews can be categorized based on the medium the researcher uses in communicating with individuals and recording data. For example, interviews may be conducted door to door, in shopping malls, or on the telephone. Traditionally interview results have been recorded using paper and pencil, but computers are increasingly supporting survey research.

The discussion about interviews begins by examining the general characteristics of face-to-face personal interviews. It then looks at the unique characteristics of door-to-door personal interviews, personal interviews conducted in shopping malls, and telephone interviews.

Although the history of marketing research is sketchy, the gathering of information through face-to-face contact with individuals has a long history. Periodic censuses were used to set tax rates and aid military conscription in the ancient empires of Egypt and Rome.[2] During the Middle Ages, the merchant families of Fugger and Rothschild prospered in part because their far-flung organizations enabled them to get information before their competitors could.[3]

A **personal interview** is a form of direct communication in which an interviewer asks respondents questions face-to-face. This versatile and flexible method is a two-way conversation between interviewer and respondent.

personal interview
Face-to-face communication in which an interviewer asks a respondent to answer questions.

The Advantages of Personal Interviews

Marketing researchers find that personal interviews offer many unique advantages. One of the most important is the opportunity for feedback.

The Opportunity for Feedback

Personal interviews provide the opportunity to give feedback to the respondent. For example, in a personal interview a consumer who is reluctant to provide sensitive information may be reassured by the interviewer that his or her answers will be strictly confidential. Personal interviews offer the lowest chance of misinterpretation of questions because the interviewer can clarify any questions respondents have about the instruction or questions. Circumstances may dictate that at the conclusion of the interview, the respondent be given additional information concerning the purpose of the study. This is easily accomplished with the personal interview.

Probing Complex Answers

probing
A method used in personal interviews in which the interviewer asks the respondent for clarification of answers to standardized questions.

An important characteristic of personal interviews is the opportunity to follow up by probing. If a respondent's answer is too brief or unclear, the researcher may *probe* for a more comprehensive or clearer explanation. In **probing** the interviewer asks for clarification of answers to standardized questions such as "Can you tell me more about what you had in mind?" (See Chapter 16 on data collection for an expanded

Marketing managers at Marriott Corporation know that people want a hotel room to feel residential because they see a hotel room as a home away from home. Customers prefer a clearly marked place to sit down, straight furniture legs, light walls, big bathrooms, spacious desk areas, and a long telephone cord. How did Marriott Corporation, the largest operator of hotels in the United States, learn about its customers' preferences? Simple! Marketing researchers have built an assortment of fake hotel rooms modelled on the competition and conducted surveys to test consumers' reactions. Customers walk through and rate the rooms.

discussion.) Although interviewers are expected to ask questions exactly as they appear on the questionnaire, probing allows them some flexibility. Depending on the research purpose, personal interviews vary in the degree to which questions are structured and in the amount of probing required. The personal interview is especially useful for obtaining unstructured information. Skilled interviewers can handle complex questions that cannot easily be asked in telephone or mail surveys.

Length of Interview

If the research objective requires an extremely lengthy questionnaire, personal interviews may be the only option. Generally telephone interviews last less than 10 minutes, whereas a personal interview can be much longer, perhaps 1 1/2 hours. A general rule of thumb on mail surveys is that they should not exceed six pages.

Completeness of Questionnaire

The social interaction between a well-trained interviewer and a respondent in a personal interview increases the likelihood that the respondent will answer all the items on the questionnaire. The respondent who grows bored with a telephone interview may terminate the interview at his or her discretion simply by hanging up the phone. Self-administration of a mail questionnaire requires more effort by the respondent. Rather than write lengthy responses, however, the respondent may fail to complete some of the questions. **Item nonresponse**—failure to provide an answer to a question—is least likely to occur when an experienced interviewer asks questions directly.

Props and Visual Aids

Interviewing respondents face to face allows the investigator to show them new product samples, sketches of proposed advertising, or other visual aids. In a survey to determine whether a super-lightweight chain saw should be manufactured, visual props were necessary because the concept of weight is difficult to imagine. Two small chain saws currently on the market and a third, wooden prototype disguised and weighted to look and feel like the proposed model were put in the back of a station wagon. Respondents were asked to go to the car, pick up each chain saw, and compare them. This research could not have been done in a telephone interview or mail survey.

Marketing research that uses visual aids has become increasingly popular with researchers who investigate film concepts, advertising problems, and moviegoers' awareness of performers. Research for movies often begins by showing respondents videotapes of the prospective cast. After the movie has been produced, film clips are shown and interviews conducted to evaluate the movie's appeal, especially which scenes to emphasize in advertisements.

High Participation

Although some people are reluctant to participate in a survey, the presence of an interviewer generally increases the percentage of people willing to complete the interview. Respondents typically are required to do no reading or writing—all they have to do is talk. Many people enjoy sharing information and insights with friendly and sympathetic interviewers.

Disadvantages of Personal Interviews

Personal interviews also have some disadvantages. Respondents are not anonymous and therefore may be reluctant to provide confidential information to another person. Suppose a survey asked top executives, "Do you see any major internal instabilities or threats (people, money, material, and so on) to the achievement of your marketing objectives?" Many managers may be reluctant to answer this sensitive question honestly in a personal interview in which their identities are known.

Entryware data collection software from Techneos Systems (www.techneos.com) can be used on Palm handheld computers to automate personal interviews. Using easy-to-carry handheld computers increases the time efficiency of interviewers and eliminates the need for later data entry.

Interviewer Influence

Some evidence suggests that demographic characteristics of the interviewer influence respondents' answers. For example, one research study revealed that male interviewers produced larger amounts of interviewer variance than female interviewers in a survey in which 85 percent of the respondents were female. Older interviewers who interviewed older respondents produced more variance than other age combinations, whereas younger interviewers who interviewed younger respondents produced the least variance.

Differential interviewer techniques may be a source of bias. The rephrasing of a question, the interviewer's tone of voice, and the interviewer's appearance may influence the respondent's answer. Consider the interviewer who has conducted 100 personal interviews. During the next one, he or she may lose concentration and either selectively perceive or anticipate the respondent's answer. The interpretation of the response may differ somewhat from what the respondent intended. Typically the public thinks of the person who does marketing research as a dedicated scientist. Unfortunately, some interviewers do not fit that ideal. Considerable interviewer variability exists. Cheating is possible; interviewers may cut corners to save time and energy, faking parts of their reports by dummying up part or all of the questionnaire. Control over interviewers is important to ensure that difficult, embarrassing, or time-consuming questions are handled in the proper manner.

Lack of Anonymity of Respondent

Because a respondent in a personal interview is not anonymous and may be reluctant to provide confidential information to another person, researchers often spend considerable time and effort to phrase sensitive questions to avoid social desirability bias. For example, the interviewer may show the respondent a card that lists possible answers and ask the respondent to read a category number rather than be required to verbalize sensitive answers.

Cost

Personal interviews are expensive, generally substantially more costly than mail, Internet, or telephone surveys. The geographic proximity of respondents, the length and complexity of the questionnaire, and the number of people who are nonrespondents because they could not be contacted (not-at-homes) will all influence the cost of the personal interview.

Door-to-Door Interviews and Shopping Mall Intercepts

Personal interviews may be conducted at the respondents' homes or offices, or in many other places. Increasingly, personal interviews are being conducted in shopping malls. Mall intercept interviews allow many interviews to be conducted quickly. Often respondents are intercepted in public areas of shopping malls and then asked to come to a permanent research facility to taste new food items or to view advertisements. The locale for the interview generally influences the participation rate, and thus the degree to which the sample represents the general population.

Door-to-Door Interviews

door-to-door interview
Personal interview conducted at respondents' doorsteps in an effort to increase the participation rate in the survey.

The presence of an interviewer at the door generally increases the likelihood that a person will be willing to complete an interview. **Door-to-door interviews** provide a more representative sample than mail surveys because of higher participation. It may also make it easier to reach people who do not have telephones, who have unlisted telephone numbers, or who are otherwise difficult to contact. Such interviews can help solve the nonresponse problem; however, they may underrepresent some groups and overrepresent others. For instance, high-rise apartment dwellers with security systems or executives who are too busy to grant personal interviews during business hours may be underrepresented. However, older, retired people may be more likely to be overrepresented.

Callbacks

callback
An attempt to recontact individuals selected for a sample who were not available initially.

When a person selected to be in the sample cannot be contacted on the first visit, a systematic procedure is normally initiated to call back at another time. **Callbacks,** or attempts to recontact individuals selected for the sample, are the major means of reducing nonresponse error. Calling back a sampling unit is more expensive than interviewing the person the first time around, because subjects who initially were not at home generally are more widely dispersed geographically than the original sample units. Callbacks in door-to-door interviews are important because not-at-home individuals (for example, working parents) may systematically vary from those who *are* at home (nonworking parents, retired people, and the like).

Mall Intercept Interviews

mall intercept interview
Personal interview conducted in a shopping mall.

Personal interviews conducted in shopping malls are referred to as **mall intercept interviews,** or *shopping centre sampling.* Interviewers typically intercept shoppers at a central point within the mall or at an entrance. The main reason mall intercept interviews are conducted is because their costs are lower. No travel is required to the respondent's home; instead, the respondent comes to the interviewer, and many interviews can be conducted quickly in this way.

A major problem with mall intercept interviews is that individuals usually are in a hurry to shop, so the incidence of refusal is high—typically around 50 percent. Nevertheless, the commercial marketing research industry conducts more personal interviews in shopping malls than it conducts door to door.

In a mall interview, the researcher must recognize that he or she should not be looking for a representative sample of the total population. Each mall will have its own target market's characteristics, and there is likely to be a larger bias than with careful household probability sampling. However, personal interviews in shopping malls are appropriate when the target group is a special market segment such as the parents of children of bike-riding age. If the respondent indicates that he or she has a child of this age, the parent can then be brought into a rented space and shown several bikes. The mall intercept interview allows the researcher to show large, heavy, or immobile visual materials, such as a television commercial. A mall interviewer can give an individual a product to take home to use and obtain a commitment that the respondent will cooperate when recontacted later by telephone. Mall intercept interviews are also valuable when activities such as cooking and tasting of food must be closely coordinated and timed to follow each other. They may also be appropriate when a consumer durable product must be demonstrated. For example, when videocassette recorders and DVD players were innovations in the prototype stage, the effort and space required to set up and properly display these units ruled out in-home testing.

Global Considerations

Willingness to participate in a personal interview varies dramatically around the world. For example, in many Middle Eastern countries women would never consent to be interviewed by a man. And in many countries the idea of discussing grooming behaviour and personal-care products with a stranger would be highly offensive. Few people would consent to be interviewed on such topics.

The norms about appropriate business conduct also influence business people's willingness to provide information to interviewers. For example, conducting business-to-business interviews in Japan during business hours is difficult because managers, strongly loyal to their firm, believe that they have an absolute responsibility to oversee their employees while on the job. In some cultures when a business person is reluctant to be interviewed, it may be possible to get a reputable third party to intervene so an interview may take place.

TELEPHONE INTERVIEWS

Good evening, I'm with a national marketing research company. Are you watching television tonight?

A: Yes.

Did you see the made-for-television movie on CBC?

telephone interview
Personal interview conducted by telephone, the mainstay of commercial survey research.

For several decades, **telephone interviews** have been the mainstay of commercial survey research. The quality of data obtained by telephone may be comparable to the quality of the data collected in personal interviews. Respondents are more willing to provide detailed and reliable information on a variety of personal topics over the telephone than with personal interviews. Telephone surveys can provide representative samples of the general population in Canada but may be a problem in less developed countries.

The Characteristics of Telephone Interviews

Telephone interviews have several distinctive characteristics that set them apart from other survey techniques. The advantages and disadvantages of these characteristics are discussed in this section.

Speed

One advantage of telephone interviewing is the speed of data collection. Whereas data collection with mail or personal interviews can take several weeks, hundreds of

BELL CANADA'S CALL PRIVACY SERVICE

Bell Canada's phone service Call Privacy is intended to screen annoying sales calls from telemarketers.[4] However, it is also sure to have an impact on researchers using telephone surveys.

For a monthly fee, the service allows the user to see who's calling every time, even if calls come from unknown or private numbers. Every caller is prompted to enter a number before the call can go through. This number then appears on the users' caller ID box and allows them to decide whether to take the call. The service also allows you to set a three-digit pass code to let those you know get through quickly.

telephone interviews can be conducted literally overnight. When the interviewer enters the respondents' answers directly into a computerized system, the data processing speeds up even more.

Cost

As the cost of personal interviews continues to increase, telephone interviews are becoming relatively inexpensive. It is estimated that the cost of telephone interviews is less than 25 percent of the cost of door-to-door personal interviews. Travel time and costs are eliminated. However, the typical Internet survey is less expensive than a telephone survey.

Telephone interviews can provide representative samples. However, willingness to cooperate with telephone surveys has declined in recent years. In addition, the widespread use of answering machines and caller ID systems makes it increasingly difficult to contact individuals.

One of the major problems in telephone interviewing is to convince consumers to pick up the phone and participate in a phone interview. The cooperation of consumers has dwindled over the years partly due to the negative reputation of some telemarketers who do not bother to check voluntary do-not-call lists, make phone calls outside of allowed hours, and use automated predictive diallers that call a large amount of numbers simultaneously.[5]

In June 2001, the U.S. Federal Trade Commission (FTC) established a "Do Not Call Registry" and invited U.S. consumers to sign up (visit http://www.donotcall. gov/ for further information).[6] The FTC requires marketers to delete consumers who have their phone numbers registered on the Do-Not-Call-Registry from their own lists and update this process every three months. By 2003, as much as 10 percent of the U.S. population (almost equivalent to the entire Canadian population) had registered. This regulation has affected telemarketers in Canada and overseas that are serving the U.S. market. In Canada, similar national do-not-call-list (DNCL) legislation is being developed by the Canadian Radio-television and Telecommunications Commission (CRTC). Although the Canadian Marketing Association (CMA) already has a do-not-call service mandatory for its members (visit www.the-cma.org/consumer/index.cfm), for non-member companies there was no legislation in place.[7] According to John Gustavsson, CEO of CMA, enforcement of the legislation is very important as well.[8]

How telephone interviewing will be influenced by the introduction of DNCL legislation in the long term still remains to be seen. Canadian companies and marketing researchers, however, are obliged to comply with the Personal Information Protection and Electronic Documents Act (PIPEDA), which affects every organization in Canada that collects personal information. The general hope in compliance with PIPEDA and privacy codes of the Canadian Association of Marketing Research Organizations (CAMRO) or Professional Marketing Research Society (PMRS) is that Canadians will understand their privacy rights and will be more likely to participate in marketing research.[9]

Absence of Face-to-Face Contact

Telephone interviews are more impersonal than face-to-face interviews. Respondents may answer embarrassing or confidential questions more willingly in a telephone interview than in a personal interview. However, mail and Internet surveys, although not perfect, are better media for gathering extremely sensitive information because they can be completely anonymous. There is some evidence that people provide information on income and other financial matters only reluctantly, even in telephone interviews. Such questions may be personally threatening for a variety of reasons, and high refusal rates for this type of question occur with each form of survey research.

Although telephone calls may be less threatening because the interviewer is not physically present, the absence of face-to-face contact can also be a liability. The respondent cannot see that the interviewer is still writing down the previous comment and may continue to elaborate on an answer. If the respondent pauses to think about an answer, the interviewer may not realize this and may go on to the next question. Hence, there is a greater tendency for interviewers to record no answers and incomplete answers in telephone interviews than in personal interviews.

Cooperation

In some neighbourhoods, people are reluctant to allow a stranger to come inside the house or even stop on the doorstep. The same people, however, may be perfectly willing to cooperate with a telephone survey request. Likewise, interviewers may be somewhat reluctant to conduct face-to-face interviews in certain neighbourhoods, especially during the evening hours. Telephone interviewing avoids these problems. However, some individuals refuse to participate in telephone interviews, and the researcher should be aware of potential nonresponse bias. Finally, there is some evidence that the likelihood that a call will go unanswered because a respondent is not at home varies by the time of day, the day of the week, and the month.

The poor reputation of telemarketing activities has contributed to the establishment of "Do Not Call" lists and stricter regulation of telemarketing by the CRTC (Canadian Radio-television and Telecommunications Commission). One trend is very clear. Telephone response rates are declining, according to studies done by the Response Rate Committee of MRIA.[10] Willingness to cooperate with telephone interviewing has declined over the years. In addition, it is increasingly difficult to establish contact with potential respondents, for three major reasons: (1) the proliferation of telephone numbers dedicated exclusively to fax machines and/or computers, (2) the widespread use of a non-dedicated phone line to access the Internet, and (3) the use of call-screening devices to avoid unwanted calls.[11]

Many people who own telephone answering machines will not return a call to help someone conduct a survey. Some researchers argue that leaving the proper message on an answering machine will produce return calls. The message left on the machine should explicitly state that the purpose of the call is not sales related.[12] Others believe no message should be left because researchers will reach respondents when they call back. The logic is based on the fact that answering machines are usually not turned on 100 percent of the time. Thus, if enough callbacks are made at different times and on different days, most respondents will be reached.[13] Caller ID services can have the same effect as answering machines if respondents do not pick up the phone when the display reads "out of area" or when an unfamiliar survey organization's name and number appear on the display.

Refusal to cooperate with interviews is directly related to interview length. A major study of survey research found that interviews of 5 minutes or less had a refusal rate of 21 percent; interviews of between 6 and 12 minutes had 41 percent refusal rates; and interviews of 13 minutes or more had 47 percent rates. In unusual cases a few highly interested respondents will put up with longer interviews. A good rule of thumb is to keep telephone interviews approximately 10 to 15 minutes long. In general, 30 minutes is the maximum amount of time most respondents will spend unless they are highly interested in the survey subject.

Representative Samples

Practical difficulties complicate obtaining representative samples based on listings in the telephone book. Comparable to the United States, 96.3 percent of households in Canada have telephones. Unlisted phone numbers and numbers too new to be printed in the directory are a greater problem. People have unlisted phone numbers for two reasons: because of mobility and by choice. Individuals whose phone numbers are unlisted because of a recent move differ slightly from those with published numbers. The unlisted group tends to be younger, more urban, and less likely to own a single-family dwelling. Households that maintain unlisted phone numbers by choice tend to have higher incomes. And, as previously mentioned, a number of low-income households are unlisted by circumstance. Researchers conducting surveys in areas where the proportion of unlisted phone numbers is high should be aware of this situation.

The problem of unlisted phone numbers can be partially resolved through the use of random digit dialling. **Random digit dialling** eliminates the counting of names in a list (for example, calling every fiftieth name in a column) and subjectively determining whether a directory listing is a business, institution, or legitimate household. In the simplest form of random digit dialling, telephone exchanges (prefixes) for the geographic areas in the sample are obtained. Using a table of random numbers, the last four digits of the telephone number are selected. Telephone directories can be ignored

random digit dialling
Use of telephone exchanges and a table of random numbers to contact respondents with unlisted phone numbers.

entirely or used in combination with the assignment of one or several random digits. Random digit dialling also helps overcome the problem due to new listings and recent changes in numbers. Unfortunately, the refusal rate in commercial random digit dialling studies (approximately 40 percent) is higher than the 25 percent refusal rate for telephone surveys that use only listed telephone numbers.

Callbacks

An unanswered call, a busy signal, or a respondent who is not at home requires a callback. Telephone callbacks are much easier to make than callbacks in personal interviews. However, as mentioned, the ownership of telephone answering machines is growing, and their effects on callbacks need to be studied.

Limited Duration

Respondents who run out of patience with the interview can merely hang up. To encourage participation, interviews should be relatively short. The length of the telephone interview is definitely limited.

Lack of Visual Medium

Because visual aids cannot be used in telephone interviews, packaging research, copy testing of television and print advertising, and concept tests that require visual materials cannot be conducted by phone. Certain attitude scales and measuring instruments, such as the semantic differential (see Chapter 12), cannot be used easily because they require the respondent to see a graphic scale.

Central Location Interviewing

central location interviewing
Telephone interviews conducted from a central location using WATS lines at fixed charges.

Research agencies or interviewing services typically conduct all telephone interviews from a central location. They contract for WATS (Wide-Area Telecommunications Service) lines from long-distance telephone services at fixed rates, which allow them to make unlimited telephone calls throughout the entire country or within specific geographic areas. Such **central location interviewing** allows firms to hire a staff of professional interviewers and to supervise and control the quality of interviewing more effectively. When telephone interviews are centralized and computerized, an agency or business can benefit from additional cost economies.

Computer-Assisted Telephone Interviewing

computer-assisted telephone interview (CATI)
Technology that allows answers to telephone interviews to be entered directly into a computer for processing.

Advances in computer technology allow responses to telephone interviews to be entered directly into the computer in a process known as **computer-assisted telephone interviewing (CATI)**. Telephone interviewers are seated at computer terminals. Monitors display the questionnaires, one question at a time, along with pre-coded possible responses to each question. The interviewer reads each question as it appears on the screen. When the respondent answers, the interviewer enters the response directly into the computer, and it is automatically stored in the computer's memory. The computer then displays the next question on the screen. Computer-assisted telephone interviewing requires that answers to the questionnaire be highly structured. If a respondent gives an unacceptable answer (that is, one not pre-coded and programmed), the computer will reject it.

Computer-assisted telephone interviewing systems include telephone management systems that select phone numbers, dial the numbers automatically, and perform other labour-saving functions. These systems can automatically control sample selection by randomly generating names or fulfilling a sample quota. A computer can generate an automatic callback schedule. A typical call management system might schedule recontact attempts to recall no answers after two hours and busy numbers after ten minutes and allow the interviewer to enter a more favourable time slot (day and hour) when a respondent indicates that he or she is too busy to be interviewed. Software systems also allow researchers to request daily status reports on the number of completed interviews relative to quotas.

Computerized Voice-Activated Telephone Interview

Technological advances have combined computerized telephone dialling and voice-activated computer messages to allow researchers to conduct telephone interviews without human interviewers. However, researchers have found that computerized voice-activated telephone interviewing works best with very short, simple questionnaires. One system includes a voice-synthesized module controlled by a microprocessor. With it the sponsor is able to register a caller's single response such as "true/false," "yes/no," "like/dislike," or "for/against." This type of system has been used by television and radio stations to register callers' responses to certain issues. One system, Telsol, begins with an announcement that the respondent is listening to a recorded message. Many people are intrigued with the idea of talking to a robot or a computer, so they stay on the line. The computer then asks questions, leaving blank tape in between to record the answers. If respondents do not answer the first two questions, the computer disconnects and goes to the next call.

Global Considerations

Different cultures often have different norms about proper telephone behaviour. For example, business-to-business researchers have learned that Latin American business people will not open up to strangers on the telephone. Hence, researchers in Latin America usually find personal interviews more suitable than telephone surveys. In Japan, respondents consider it ill-mannered if telephone interviews last more than 20 minutes.

SELF-ADMINISTERED QUESTIONNAIRES

Many surveys do not require an interviewer's presence. Marketing researchers distribute questionnaires to consumers through the mail and in many other ways (see Exhibit 8.1). They insert questionnaires in packages and magazines. They may place questionnaires at points of purchase or in high-traffic locations in stores or malls. They may even fax questionnaires to individuals. Questionnaires are usually printed on paper, but they may be posted on the Internet or sent via e-mail. No matter how the **self-administered questionnaires** are distributed, they are different from interviews because the respondent takes responsibility for reading and answering the questions.

Self-administered questionnaires present a challenge to the marketing researcher because they rely on the clarity of the written word rather than on the skills of the interviewer. The nature of self-administered questionnaires is best illustrated by explaining mail questionnaires.

self-administered questionnaire
Survey in which the respondent takes the responsibility for reading and answering the questions.

Mail Questionnaires

A **mail survey** is a self-administered questionnaire sent to respondents through the mail. This paper-and-pencil method has several advantages and disadvantages.

mail survey
A self-administered questionnaire sent to respondents through the mail.

Geographic Flexibility

Mail questionnaires can reach a geographically dispersed sample simultaneously because interviewers are not required. Respondents (such as farmers) who are located in isolated areas or those (such as executives) who are otherwise difficult to reach can easily be contacted by mail. For example, a pharmaceutical firm may find

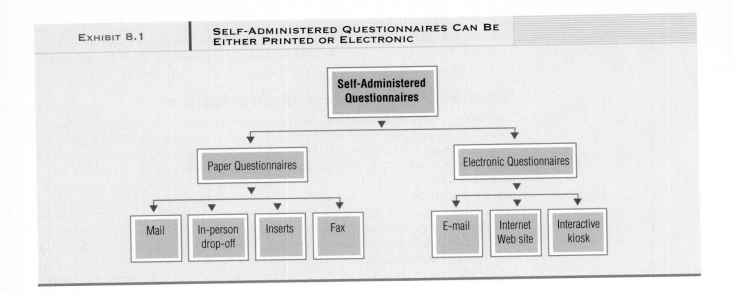

that doctors are not available for personal or telephone interviews. However, a mail survey can reach both rural and urban doctors who practise in widely dispersed geographic areas.

Cost

Mail questionnaires are relatively inexpensive compared to personal interviews and telephone surveys, though they are not cheap. Most include follow-up mailings, which require additional postage and printing costs.

Respondent Convenience

Mail surveys and other self-administered questionnaires can be filled out when the respondents have time; thus there is a better chance that respondents will take time to think about their replies. Many hard-to-reach respondents place a high value on convenience and thus are best contacted by mail. Particularly in business-to-business marketing research, mail questionnaires allow respondents to collect facts, such as sales statistics, that they may not be able to recall without checking. Being able to check information by verifying records or, in household surveys, by consulting with other family members should provide more valid, factual information than either personal or telephone interviews would allow.

Anonymity of Respondent

In the cover letter that accompanies a mail or self-administered questionnaire, marketing researchers almost always state that the respondents' answers will be confidential. Respondents are more likely to provide sensitive or embarrassing information when they can remain anonymous.

For example, personal interviews and a mail survey conducted simultaneously asked the question "Have you borrowed money at a regular bank?" Researchers noted a 17 percent response rate for the personal interviews and a 42 percent response rate for the mail survey. The results suggest that for research on personal and sensitive financial issues mail surveys are more confidential than personal interviews.

Anonymity can also reduce social desirability bias. People are more likely to agree with controversial issues, such as extreme political candidates, when completing self-administered questionnaires than when speaking to interviewers on the phone or at their doorsteps.

Absence of Interviewer

Although the absence of an interviewer can induce respondents to reveal sensitive or socially undesirable information, it can also be a disadvantage. Once the respondent receives the questionnaire, the questioning process is beyond the researcher's control. The respondent does not have the opportunity to ask questions to the interviewer. Problems that might be clarified in a personal or telephone interview can remain misunderstandings in a mail survey. There is no interviewer to probe for additional information or clarification of an answer, and the recorded answers must be assumed to be complete.

Respondents have the opportunity to read the entire questionnaire before they answer individual questions. Often the text of a later question will provide information that affects responses to earlier questions.

Standardized Questions

Mail questionnaires typically are highly standardized, and the questions are quite structured. Questions and instructions must be clear-cut and straightforward; if they are difficult to comprehend, the respondents will make their own interpretations, which may be wrong. With a mail survey, once the questionnaires are mailed, it is difficult to change the format or the questions.

Time Is Money

If time is a factor in management's interest in the research results, or if attitudes are rapidly changing (for example, toward a political event), mail surveys may not be the best communication medium. A minimum of two or three weeks is necessary for receiving the majority of the responses. Follow-up mailings, which usually are sent when the returns begin to trickle in, require an additional two or three weeks. The time between the first mailing and the cut-off date (when questionnaires will no longer be accepted) normally is six to eight weeks. In a regional or local study, personal interviews can be conducted more quickly. However, conducting a national study by mail might be substantially faster than conducting personal interviews across the nation.

Length of Mail Questionnaire

Mail questionnaires vary considerably in length, ranging from extremely short, postcard questionnaires to lengthy, multipage booklets that require respondents to fill in thousands of answers. A general rule of thumb is that a mail questionnaire should not exceed six pages in length. When a questionnaire requires a respondent to expend a great deal of effort, an incentive is generally required to induce the respondent to return the questionnaire. The following sections discuss several ways to obtain high response rates even when questionnaires are longer than average.

Response Rates

Questionnaires that are boring, unclear, or too complex get thrown in the wastebasket. A poorly designed mail questionnaire may be returned by only 15 percent of those sampled; thus it will have a 15 percent response rate. The basic calculation for obtaining a **response rate** is to count the number of questionnaires returned or completed, and then divide the total by the number of eligible people who were contacted or requested to participate in the survey. Typically, the number in the denominator is adjusted for faulty addresses and similar problems that reduce the number of eligible participants.

response rate
The number of questionnaires returned or completed divided by the number of eligible people who were asked to participate in the survey.

The major limitations of mail questionnaires relate to response problems. Respondents who complete the questionnaire may not be typical of all people in the sample. Individuals with a special interest in the topic are more likely to respond to a mail survey than those who are indifferent.

A researcher has no assurance that the intended subject will be the person who fills out the questionnaire. The wrong person answering the questions may be a problem when surveying corporate executives, physicians, and other professionals, who may pass questionnaires on to subordinates to complete.

There is some evidence that cooperation and response rates rise as home value increases. Also, if the sample has a high proportion of retired and well-off householders, response rates will be lower. Mail survey respondents tend to be better educated than nonrespondents. If they return the questionnaire at all, poorly educated respondents who cannot read and write well may skip open-ended questions to which they are required to write out their answers. Rarely will a mail survey have the 80 to 90 percent response rate that can be achieved with personal interviews. However, the use of follow-up mailings and other techniques may increase the response rate to an acceptable percentage. If a mail survey has a low response rate, it should not be considered reliable unless it can be demonstrated with some form of verification that the nonrespondents are similar to the respondents.

Increasing Response Rates for Mail Surveys

Nonresponse error is always a potential problem with mail surveys. Individuals who are interested in the general subject of the survey are more likely to respond than those with less interest or little experience. Thus people who hold extreme positions on an issue are more likely to respond than individuals who are largely indifferent to the topic. To minimize this bias, researchers have developed a number of techniques to increase the response rate to mail surveys. For example, almost all surveys include postage-paid return envelopes. Forcing respondents to pay their own postage can substantially reduce the response rate. Using a stamped return envelope instead of a business reply envelope increases response rates even more.[14] Designing and formatting attractive questionnaires and wording questions so that they are easy to understand also help ensure a good response rate. However, special efforts may be required even with a sound questionnaire. Several of these are discussed in the following subsections.

Cover Letter

cover letter
Letter that accompanies a questionnaire to induce the reader to complete and return the questionnaire.

The **cover letter** that accompanies a questionnaire or is printed on the first page of the questionnaire booklet is an important means of inducing a reader to complete and return the questionnaire. Exhibit 8.2 illustrates a cover letter and some of the points considered by a marketing research professional to be important in gaining respondents' attention and cooperation. The first paragraph of the letter explains why the study is important. The basic appeal alludes to the social usefulness of responding. Two other frequently used appeals are asking for help ("Will you do us a favour?") and the egotistical appeal ("Your opinions are important!"). Most cover letters promise confidentiality, invite the recipient to use an enclosed postage-paid reply envelope, describe any incentive or reward for participation, explain that answering the questionnaire will not be difficult and will take only a short time, and describe how the person was scientifically selected for participation.

A personalized letter addressed to a specific individual shows the respondent that he or she is important. Including an individually typed cover letter on letterhead rather than a printed form is an important element in increasing the response rate in mail surveys.[15]

Incentives Help

The respondent's motivation for returning a questionnaire may be increased by offering monetary incentives or premiums. Although pens, lottery tickets, and a variety of premiums have been used, monetary incentives appear to be the most effective and least biasing incentive. Although money may be useful to all respondents, its

| EXHIBIT 8.2 | EXAMPLE OF COVER LETTER FOR HOUSEHOLD SURVEY[16] |

Official letterhead	**CONCORDIA UNIVERSITY** **MONTREAL, PQ** Department of Marketing
Date mailed	April 19, 20XX
Inside address in matching type	John Doe 2190 Fontane Road Dorval, PQ
What study is about; its social usefulness	Proposals have been introduced in Parliament to encourage the growth of rural and small-town areas and slow down that of large cities. These proposals could greatly affect the quality of life provided in both rural and urban places. However, no one really knows in what kinds of communities people like you want to live or what is thought about these proposed programs.
Why recipient is important (and, if needed, who should complete the questionnaire)	Your household is one of a small number in which people are asked to give their opinion on these matters. It was drawn in a random sample of the entire province. In order that the results will truly represent the thinking of the people of Quebec, it is also important that we have about the same number of men and women participating in this study. Thus we would like the questionnaire for your household to be completed by an adult female. If none is present, then it should be completed by an adult male.
Promise of confidentiality; explanation of identification number	You may be assured of complete confidentiality. The questionnaire has an identification number for mailing purposes only. This is so that we may check your name off the mailing list when your questionnaire is returned. Your name will never be placed on the questionnaire.
Usefulness of study Token reward for participation	The results of this research will be made available to officials and representatives in our provincial government, members of Parliament, and all interested citizens. You may receive a summary of results by writing "copy of results requested" on the back of the return envelope, and printing your name and address below it. Please do not put this information on your questionnaire itself.
What to do if questions arise	I would be most happy to answer any questions you might have. Please write or call. The telephone number is (555) 123-4567.
Appreciation	Thank you for your assistance.
Pressed blue ballpoint signature Title	Sincerely, *H. Onur Bodur* H. Onur Bodur Project Director

primary advantage may be that it attracts attention and creates a sense of obligation. It is perhaps for this reason that monetary incentives work for all income categories. Often cover letters try to boost response rates with messages such as "We know that the attached dollar [or coin] cannot compensate you for your time. It is just a token of our appreciation." Response rates increase dramatically when the monetary incentive is to be sent to a charity of the respondent's choice rather than directly to the respondent.

Interesting Questions

The topic of the research and thus the point of the questions cannot be manipulated without changing the definition of the marketing problem. However, certain interesting questions can be added to the questionnaire, perhaps at the beginning, to stimulate respondents' interest and to induce cooperation. Questions that are of little concern to the researchers, but which the respondents want to answer, may provide respondents who are indifferent to the major portion of the questionnaire with a reason for responding.[17]

Follow-Ups

Exhibit 8.3 shows graphic plots of cumulative response rates for two mail surveys. The curves are typical of most mail surveys: The response rates start relatively high for the first two weeks (as indicated by the steepness of each curve), then gradually taper off.

After responses from the first wave of mailings begin to trickle in, most studies use a follow-up letter or postcard reminder. These request that the questionnaire be returned because a 100 percent return rate is important. A follow-up may include a duplicate questionnaire or may merely be a reminder to return the original questionnaire. Multiple contacts almost always increase response rates. The more attempts made to reach people, the greater the chances of their responding.[18]

Both of the studies in Exhibit 8.3 used follow-ups. Notice how the cumulative response rates picked up around week four.

Advance Notification

Advance notification, by either letter or telephone, that a questionnaire will be arriving has been successful in increasing response rates in some situations. For example, AC Nielsen has used this technique to ensure a high cooperation rate in filling out diaries of television watching. Advance notices that go out closer to the questionnaire mailing time produce better results than those sent too far in advance. The optimal lead time for advance notification is three days before the mail survey is to arrive.

Survey Sponsorship

Auspices bias may result from the sponsorship of a survey. One business-to-business marketer wished to conduct a survey of its wholesalers to learn their stocking policies and their attitudes concerning competing manufacturers. A mail questionnaire sent on the corporate letterhead very likely would have received a much lower response rate than the questionnaire actually sent, which used the letterhead of a commercial marketing research firm. Sponsorship by well-known and prestigious organizations such as universities or government agencies may also significantly influence response rates. A mail survey sent to members of a consumer panel will receive an exceptionally high response rate because panel members have already agreed to cooperate with surveys.

Other Techniques

Numerous other devices have been used for increasing response rates. For example, the type of postage (commemorative versus regular stamp), envelope size, colour of the questionnaire paper, and many other factors have been varied in efforts to increase response rates. Each has had at least limited success in certain situations;

EXHIBIT 8.3 | PLOTS OF ACTUAL RESPONSE PATTERNS FOR TWO COMMERCIAL SURVEYS

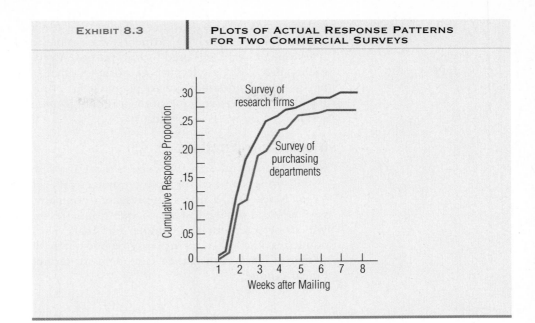

unfortunately, under other conditions each has failed to increase response rates significantly. The researcher should consider his or her particular situation. For example, the researcher who is investigating consumers faces one situation; the researcher who is surveying corporate executives faces quite another.

Keying Mail Questionnaires with Codes

A marketing researcher planning a follow-up letter or postcard should not disturb respondents who already have returned the questionnaires. The expense of mailing questionnaires to those who already have responded is usually avoidable. One device for eliminating those who have already responded from the follow-up mailing list is to mark the questionnaires so that they may be keyed to identify members of the sampling frame who are nonrespondents. Blind keying of questionnaires

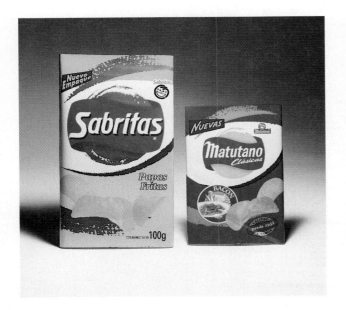

PepsiCo Foods International, marketer of Lay's potato chips, unified its market-leading potato chip brands worldwide with Walkers Crisps in the United Kingdom, Papas Sabritas in Mexico, and Matutano chips in Spain, using the Lay's name and a new global package design highlighted by a bold new icon called the Banner Sun.[19]

This initiative followed the most comprehensive market research program in food product history. Over 100,000 consumers in 30 countries were interviewed in an effort to describe, understand, and develop the worldwide potato chip market. PepsiCo learned that potato chips are "the cola of snacks." In country after country, potato chips are consumers' favourite snack. The company's international marketing approach enables Lay's to communicate and enhance the concept of potato chips as a timeless, simple pleasure to consumers around the world.

on a return envelope (systematically varying the job number or room number of the marketing research department, for example) or a visible code number on the questionnaire has been used for this purpose. Visible keying is indicated with statements such as "The sole purpose of the number on the last page is to avoid sending a second questionnaire to people who complete and return the first one." Ethical researchers key questionnaires only to increase response rates, thereby preserving respondents' anonymity.

Global Considerations

Researchers conducting surveys in more than one country must recognize that postal services and cultural circumstances differ around the world. For example, Leger Marketing, a marketing research company, has conducted numerous surveys in 42 countries. In Canada, questionnaires may be delivered directly to individuals selected for the sample, but mail may not be used in several other countries. The questionnaire may be personally delivered to respondents because of fear of letter bombs, unreliable delivery service, or low literacy rates in a particular country.[20]

Samsonite inserts this product registration questionnaire into all luggage and business case products. The chance to win a sweepstakes prize encourages consumers to respond to the questionnaire. The results of the questionnaire become key elements of Samsonite's consumer database and its direct-marketing programs.

Many forms of self-administered, printed questionnaires are very similar to mail questionnaires. Airlines frequently pass out questionnaires to passengers during flights. Restaurants, hotels, and other service establishments print short questionnaires on cards so that customers can evaluate the service. *Tennis Magazine, Advertising Age, Wired,* and many other publications have used inserted questionnaires to survey current readers inexpensively, and often the results provide material for a magazine article.

Many manufacturers use their warranty or owner registration cards to collect demographic information and data about where and why products were purchased. Using owner registration cards is an extremely economical technique for tracing trends in consumer habits. Again, problems may arise because people who fill out these self-administered questionnaires differ from those who do not.

Extremely long questionnaires may be dropped off by an interviewer and then picked up later. The **drop-off method** sacrifices some cost savings because it requires travelling to each respondent's location.

drop-off method
A survey method that requires the interviewer to travel to the respondent's location to drop off questionnaires that will be picked up later.

Fax Surveys

With fax surveys, potential survey respondents receive and/or return questionnaires via fax machines.[21] A questionnaire inserted in a magazine may instruct the respondent to clip out the questionnaire and fax it to a certain phone number. In a mail survey, a prepaid-postage envelope places little burden on the respondent. But faxing a questionnaire to a long-distance number requires that the respondent pay for the transmission of the fax. Thus a disadvantage of **fax surveys** is that only respondents with fax machines who are willing to exert the extra effort will return questionnaires. Again, people with extreme opinions will be more likely to respond.

Questionnaires can also be distributed via fax machine. These fax surveys reduce the sender's printing and postage costs and can be delivered and returned faster than

fax survey
A survey that uses fax machines as a way for respondents to receive and return questionnaires.

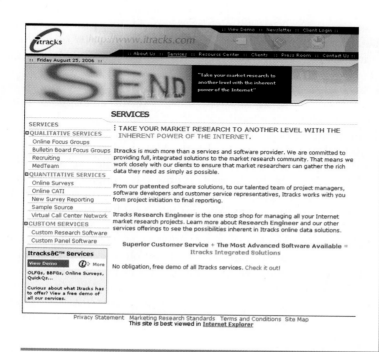

Itracks (www.itracks.com/) is an online data collection company that delivers quality data to professional market researchers. This image shows that the company offers a variety of services such as online surveys.[22]

traditional mail surveys. Questionnaires distributed via fax can deal with timely issues. Although most households do not have fax machines, when the sample consists of organizations that are likely to have fax machines, the sample coverage may be adequate.

E-Mail Surveys

e-mail survey
Surveys distributed through electronic mail.

Questionnaires can be distributed via e-mail. E-mail is a relatively new method of communication, and many individuals cannot be reached this way. However, certain projects lend themselves to **e-mail surveys**, such as internal surveys of employees or satisfaction surveys of retail buyers who regularly deal with an organization via e-mail. The benefits of incorporating a questionnaire in an e-mail include the speed of distribution, lower distribution and processing costs, faster turnaround time, more flexibility, and less handling of paper questionnaires. The speed of e-mail distribution and the quick response time can be major advantages for surveys dealing with time-sensitive issues.

Not much academic research has been conducted on e-mail surveys. Nevertheless, it has been argued that many respondents feel they can be more candid in e-mail than in person or on the telephone, for the same reasons they are candid on other self-administered questionnaires. However, in many organizations employees know that their e-mails are not secure and "eavesdropping" by a supervisor could possibly occur. Further, maintaining respondents' anonymity is difficult, because a reply to an e-mail message typically includes the sender's address. Researchers designing e-mail surveys should assure respondents that their answers will be confidential.

Not all e-mail systems have the same capacity: Some handle colour and graphics well; others are limited to text. The extensive differences in the capabilities of respondents' computers and e-mail software limit the types of questions and the layout of the e-mail questionnaire. For example, the display settings for computer screens vary widely, and wrap-around of lines may put the questions and the answer choices into strange and difficult-to-read patterns.[23] Many novice e-mail users find it difficult to mark answers in brackets on an e-mail questionnaire and/or to send a completed questionnaire using the e-mail Reply function. For this reason, some researchers give respondents the option to print out the questionnaire, complete it in writing, and return it via regular mail. Unless the research is an internal organizational survey, this, of course, requires the respondent to pay postage.

In general, the guidelines for printed mail surveys apply to e-mail surveys. However, there are some differences, because the cover letter and the questionnaire appear in a single e-mail message. A potential respondent who is not immediately motivated to respond, especially one who considers an unsolicited e-mail survey to be "spam," can quickly hit the Delete button to remove the e-mail. This suggests that e-mail cover letters should be brief and the questionnaires relatively short. The cover letter should explain how the company got the recipient's name. It should include a valid return e-mail address in the "FROM" box and reveal who is conducting the survey. Also, if the e-mail lists more than one address in the "TO" or "CC" field, all recipients will see the entire list of names. This has the potential to cause response bias and nonresponse error. When possible, the e-mail should be addressed to a single person. (The blind carbon copy, or BCC, field can be used if the same message must be sent to an entire sample.)[24]

E-mail has another important role in survey research. E-mail letters can be used as cover letters asking respondents to participate in an Internet survey. Such e-mails typically provide a password and a link to a Web site location that requires a password for access.

Technological innovation can change more than the way business is done in an industry—it can change entire cultures. The mechanical clock made regular working hours possible. The invention of railroads and the mass production of automobiles changed the way people thought about distance. Television changed the way we think about news and entertainment. And, because the Internet is the most important communication medium since the introduction of television, it is having a profound impact on marketing research. Self-administered polls will increasingly become electronic transactions between people and machines.[25]

Internet Surveys

Internet survey
A self-administered questionnaire posted on a Web site.

An **Internet survey** is a self-administered questionnaire posted on a Web site. Respondents provide answers to questions displayed onscreen by highlighting a phrase, clicking an icon, or keying in an answer. Many in the survey research community believe Internet surveys are the wave of the future. Like every other type of survey, Internet surveys have both advantages and disadvantages.

Speed and Cost-Effectiveness

Internet surveys allow marketers to reach a large audience (possibly a global one), to personalize individual messages, and to secure confidential answers quickly and cost-effectively. These computer-to-computer self-administered questionnaires eliminate the costs of paper, postage, and data entry, as well as other administrative costs. Once an Internet questionnaire has been developed, the incremental cost of reaching additional respondents is marginal. Hence, samples can be larger than with interviews or other types of self-administered questionnaires. Even with larger samples, surveys that used to take many weeks can be conducted in a week or less.

Visual Appeal and Interactivity

Surveys conducted on the Internet can be interactive. The researcher can use more sophisticated lines of questioning based on the respondents' prior answers. Many of these interactive surveys utilize colour, sound, and animation, which may help to increase respondents' cooperation and willingness to spend time answering the questionnaires. The Internet is an excellent medium for the presentation of visual materials, such as photographs or drawings of product prototypes, advertisements, and movie trailers. Innovative measuring instruments that take advantage of the ability to adjust backgrounds, fonts, colour, and other features have been designed and applied with considerable success.

Digital Marketing Services' Video E-Val is a proprietary technique combining a CD-ROM that is mailed to potential respondents and Internet software that controls the playing of high-quality video clips from the disk.[26] This technique allows

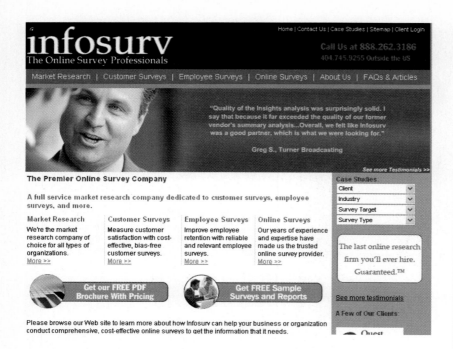

researchers to evaluate television commercials, television programs, and other large video files without being restricted by the small percentage of potentially qualified respondents who have access to broadband communications.

Respondent Participation and Cooperation

Participation in some Internet surveys occurs because computer users intentionally navigate to a particular Web site where questions are displayed. For example, a survey of over 10,000 visitors to the Ticketmaster Web site helped Ticketmaster better understand its customer purchase patterns and evaluate visitor satisfaction with the site. In some cases individuals expect to encounter a survey at a Web site; in other cases it is totally unexpected. In some instances the visitor cannot venture beyond the survey page without providing information for the organization's "registration" questionnaire. When the computer user does not expect a survey on a Web site and participation is voluntary, response rates are low. And, as with other questionnaires that rely on voluntary self-selection, participants tend to be more interested in or involved with the subject of the research than the average person.

For many other Internet surveys, respondents are initially contacted via e-mail. Often they are members of consumer panels who have previously indicated their willingness to cooperate. When individuals receive an e-mail invitation to participate, they are given a password or a PIN number. The e-mail invitation also provides a link to a URL or instructs a user to visit a certain Web site that contains a welcome screen. Like a cover letter in a mail survey, the **welcome screen** on an Internet survey serves as a means to gain respondents' cooperation and provides brief instructions. Experienced researchers require a respondent to provide a password or PIN to move from the welcome page to the first question. This prevents access by individuals who are not part of the scientifically selected sample. Assigning a unique password code also allows the researchers to track the responses of each respondent, thereby identifying any respondent who makes an effort to answer the questionnaire more than once.

Ideally, the welcome screen contains the name of the research company and information about how to contact the organization if the respondent has a problem or concern. A typical statement might be "If you have any concerns or questions

welcome screen
The first Web page in an Internet survey, which introduces the survey and requests that the respondent enter a password or PIN.

about this survey or if you experience any technical difficulties, please contact [name of research organization]."

Representative Samples

The population to be studied, the purpose of the research, and the sampling methods determine the quality of Internet samples, which varies substantially. If the sample consists merely of those who visit a Web page and voluntarily fill out a questionnaire, it is not likely to be representative of the entire Canadian population, because of self-selection error. However, if the purpose of the research is to evaluate how visitors feel about a Web site, randomly selecting every 100th visitor may accomplish the study's purpose. Scientifically drawn samples from a consumer panel or samples randomly generated in other ways can also be representative.[27]

Of course, a major disadvantage of Internet surveys is that many individuals in the general population cannot access the Internet. And all people with Internet access do not have the same level of technology. Many people with low-speed Internet connections (low bandwidth) cannot quickly download high-resolution graphic files. Many lack powerful computers or software that is compatible with advanced features programmed into many Internet questionnaires. Some individuals have minimal computer skills. They may not know how to navigate through and provide answers to an Internet questionnaire. For example, the advanced audio and video streaming technology of RealPlayer or Windows Media Player software can be used to incorporate a television commercial and questions about its effectiveness into an Internet survey. However, some respondents might find downloading the file too slow or even impossible; others might not have the RealPlayer or Windows Media Player software; and still others might not know how to use the streaming media software to view the commercial.

It appears that for the foreseeable future, Internet surveys sampling the general public should be designed with the recognition that problems may arise for the reasons just described. Thus photographs, animation, or other cutting-edge technological features created on the researcher's/Web designer's powerful computer may have to be simplified or eliminated so that all respondents can interact at the same level of technological sophistication.

Because Internet surveys can be accessed anytime (24/7) from anywhere, they can reach certain hard-to-reach respondents, such as doctors. Chapter 14 discusses sampling techniques for Internet surveys.

Accurate Real-Time Data Capture

The computer-to-computer nature of Internet surveys means that each respondent's answers are entered directly into the researcher's computer as soon as the questionnaire is submitted. In addition, the questionnaire software may be programmed to reject improper data entry. For example, on a paper questionnaire a respondent might incorrectly check two responses even though the instructions call for a single answer. In an Internet survey, this mistake can be interactively corrected as the survey is taking place. Thus the data capture is more accurate than when humans are involved.

Real-time data capture allows for real-time data analysis. A researcher can review up-to-the-minute sample size counts and tabulation data from an Internet survey in real time.

Callbacks

When the sample for an Internet survey is drawn from a consumer panel, it is easy to recontact those who have not completed the survey questionnaire. It is often a simple matter of having computer software automatically send e-mail reminders to panel members who did not visit the welcome page. Computer software can also identify the passwords of respondents who completed only a portion of the questionnaire and send those people customized messages. Sometimes such e-mails offer additional incentives to those individuals who terminated the questionnaire with only a few additional questions to answer, so that they are motivated to comply with the request to finish the questionnaire.

Personalized and Flexible Questioning

Computer-interactive Internet surveys are programmed in much the same way as computer-assisted telephone interviews. That is, the software that is used allows questioning to branch off into two or more different lines depending on a respondent's answer to a filtered question. The difference is that there is no interviewer. The respondent interacts directly with software on a Web site. In other words, the computer program asks questions in a sequence determined by the respondent's previous answers. The questions appear on the computer screen, and answers are recorded by simply pressing a key or clicking an icon, thus immediately entering the data into the computer's memory. Of course, these methods avoid labour costs associated with data collection and processing of paper-and-pencil questionnaires.

This ability to sequence questions based on previous responses is a major advantage of computer-assisted surveys. The computer can be programmed to skip from question 6 to question 9 if the answer to question 6 is no. Furthermore, responses to previous questions can lead to questions that can be personalized for individual respondents. (For example, "When you cannot buy your favourite brand, Revlon, what brand of lipstick do you prefer?") Often the respondent's name appears in questions to personalize the questionnaire. Fewer and more relevant questions speed up the response process and increase the respondent's involvement with the survey.

Use of a variety of **dialogue boxes** (windows that prompt the respondent to enter information) allows designers of Internet questionnaires to be creative and flexible in the presentation of questions. Chapter 13 discusses software issues, the design of questions, and questionnaire layouts for Internet surveys.

Respondent Anonymity

Respondents are more likely to provide sensitive or embarrassing information when they can remain anonymous. The anonymity of the Internet encourages respondents to provide honest answers to sensitive questions.

Response Rates

As mentioned earlier, with a password system, people who have not participated in a survey in a predetermined period of time can be sent a friendly e-mail reminder asking them to participate before the study ends. This kind of follow-up, along with preliminary notification, interesting early questions, and variations of most other techniques for increasing response rates to mail questionnaires, is recommended for Internet surveys.

Unlike mail surveys, Internet surveys do not offer the opportunity to send a physical incentive, such as a loonie, to the respondent. Incentives to respond to a survey must be in the form of a promise of a future reward—for example, "As a token of appreciation for completing this survey, the sponsor of the survey will make a sizable contribution to a national charity. You can vote for your preferred charity at the end of the survey." While some researchers have had success with promising incentives, academic research about Internet surveys is sparse, and currently there are few definitive answers about the most effective ways to increase response rates.

Security Concerns

Many organizations worry that hackers or competitors may access Web sites in order to discover new product concepts, new advertising campaigns, and other top-secret ideas. Respondents may worry whether personal information will

dialogue box
A window that opens on a computer screen to prompt the user to enter information.

remain private. No system can be 100 percent secure. However, many research service suppliers specializing in Internet surveying have developed password-protected systems that are very secure. One important feature of these systems restricts access and prevents individuals from filling out a questionnaire over and over again.

Kiosk Interactive Surveys

A computer with a touch screen may be installed in a kiosk at a trade show, at a professional conference, in an airport, or in any other high-traffic location to administer an interactive survey. Because the respondent chooses to interact with an on-site computer, self-selection often is a problem with this type of survey. Computer-literate individuals are most likely to complete these interactive questionnaires. At temporary locations such as conventions, these surveys often require a fieldworker to be at the location to explain how to use the computer system. This is an obvious disadvantage.

Survey Research That Mixes Modes

For many surveys, research objectives dictate the use of some combination of telephone, mail, e-mail, Internet, and personal interview. For example, the researcher may conduct a short telephone screening interview to determine whether respondents are eligible for recontact in a more extensive personal interview. Such a **mixed-mode survey** combines the advantages of the telephone survey (such as fast screening) and those of the personal interview. A mixed-mode survey can employ any combination of two or

mixed-mode survey
Study that employs any combination of survey methods.

more survey methods. Conducting a research study in two or more waves, however, creates the possibility that some respondents will no longer cooperate or will be unavailable in the second wave of the survey.

Several variations of survey research use cable television channels. For example, a telephone interviewer calls a cable subscriber and asks him or her to tune in to a particular channel at a certain time. An appointment is made to interview the respondent shortly after the program or visual material is displayed. NBC uses this type of mixed-mode survey to test the concepts for many proposed new programs.

SELECTING THE APPROPRIATE SURVEY RESEARCH DESIGN

Earlier discussions of research design and problem definition emphasized that many research tasks may lead to similar decision-making information. There is no best form of survey; each has advantages and disadvantages. A researcher who must ask highly confidential questions may use a mail survey, thus sacrificing speed of data collection to avoid interviewer bias. If a researcher must have considerable control over question phrasing, central location telephone interviewing may be appropriate.

To determine the appropriate technique, the researcher must ask several questions: Is the assistance of an interviewer necessary? Are respondents interested in the issues being investigated? Will cooperation be easily attained? How quickly is the information needed? Will the study require a long and complex questionnaire? How large is the budget? The criteria—cost, speed, anonymity, and so forth—may differ for each project.

Exhibit 8.4 summarizes the major advantages and disadvantages of typical door-to-door, mall intercept, telephone, mail, and Internet surveys. It emphasizes the typical types of surveys. For example, a creative researcher might be able to design highly versatile and flexible mail questionnaires, but most researchers use standardized questions. An elaborate mail survey may be far more expensive than a short personal interview, but generally this is not the case.

PRE-TESTING

9

pre-testing
Screening procedure that involves a trial run with a group of respondents to iron out fundamental problems in the survey design.

A researcher who is surveying 3,000 consumers does not want to find out after the questionnaires have been completed or returned that most respondents misunderstood a particular question, skipped a series of questions, or misinterpreted the instructions for filling out the questionnaire. To avoid problems such as these, screening procedures, or *pre-tests,* are often used. **Pre-testing** involves a trial run with a group of respondents to iron out fundamental problems in the instructions or design of a questionnaire. The researcher looks for such things as the point at which respondent fatigue sets in and whether there are any particular places in the questionnaire where respondents tend to terminate. Unfortunately, this stage of research may be eliminated because of costs or time pressures.

Broadly speaking, there are three basic ways to pre-test. The first two involve screening the questionnaire with other research professionals; and the third—the one most often called pre-testing—is a trial run with a group of respondents. When screening the questionnaire with other research professionals, the investigator asks them to look for such things as difficulties with question wording, problems with leading questions, and bias due to question order. An alternative type of screening might involve a client or the research manager who ordered the research. Often managers ask researchers to collect information, but when they see the questionnaire, they find that it does not really meet their needs. Only by checking with the individual who has requested the questionnaire does the researcher know for sure that the information needed will be provided. Once the researcher has decided on the final questionnaire, data should be collected with a small number of respondents (perhaps 100) to determine whether the questionnaire needs refinement.

EXHIBIT 8.4 | ADVANTAGES AND DISADVANTAGES OF TYPICAL SURVEY METHODS

	Door-to-Door Personal Interview	Mall Intercept Personal Interview	Telephone Interview	Mail Survey	Internet Survey
Speed of data collection	Moderate to fast	Fast	Very fast	Slow; researcher has no control over return of questionnaire	Instantaneous; 24/7
Geographic flexibility	Limited to moderate	Confined, possible urban bias	High	High	High (worldwide)
Respondent cooperation	Excellent	Moderate to low	Good	Moderate; poorly designed questionnaire will have low response rate	Varies depending on Web site; high from consumer panels
Versatility of questioning	Quite versatile	Extremely versatile	Moderate	Not versatile; requires highly standardized format	Extremely versatile
Questionnaire length	Long	Moderate to long	Moderate	Varies depending on incentive	Moderate; length customized based on answers
Item non-response rate	Low	Medium	Moderate	High	Software can assure none
Possibility for respondent misunderstanding	Low	Low	Average	High; no interviewer present for clarification	High
Degree of interviewer influence on answers	High	High	Moderate	None; interviewer absent	None
Supervision of interviewers	Moderate	Moderate to high	High, especially with central-location WATS interviewing	Not applicable	Not applicable
Anonymity of respondent	Low	Low	Moderate	High	Respondent can be either anonymous or known
Ease of callback or follow-up	Difficult	Difficult	Easy	Easy, but takes time	Difficult, unless e-mail address is known
Cost	Highest	Moderate to high	Low to moderate	Lowest	Low
Special features	Visual materials may be shown or demonstrated; extended probing possible	Taste tests, viewing of TV commercials possible	Fieldwork and supervision of data collection are simplified; quite adaptable to computer technology	Respondent amy answer questions at own convenience; has time to reflect on answers	Streaming media software allows use of graphics and animation

Note: The emphasis is on typical surveys. For example, an elaborate mail survey may be far more expensive than a short personal interview, but this generally is not the case.

ETHICAL ISSUES IN SURVEY RESEARCH

Chapter 3 mentioned that the Canadian Marketing Association's code of ethics expresses researchers' obligation to protect the public from misrepresentation and exploitation under the guise of marketing research. Many ethical issues apply to survey research, such as respondents' right to privacy, the use of deception, respondents' right to be informed about the purpose of the research, the need for confidentiality, the need for honesty in collecting data, and the need for objectivity in reporting data. You may wish to re-examine Chapter 3's coverage of these issues now that various survey research techniques have been discussed.[29]

SUMMARY

1 Interviews and self-administered questionnaires are used to collect survey data. Interviews can be categorized based on the medium used to communicate with respondents. Interviews may be conducted door-to-door, in shopping malls, or on the telephone. Traditionally, interviews have been recorded using paper and pencil, but survey researchers are increasingly using computers.

2 3 Personal interviews are a flexible method that allows researchers to use visual aids and various kinds of props. Door-to-door personal interviews can get high response rates, but they are also more costly to administer than other types of surveys. The presence of an interviewer may also influence subjects' responses. When a sample need not represent the entire country, mall intercept interviews may reduce costs.

4 Telephone interviewing has the advantage of providing data fast and at a lower cost per interview. However, not all households have telephones, and not all telephone numbers are listed in directories. This causes problems in obtaining a representative sample. Absence of face-to-face contact and inability to use visual materials also limit telephone interviewing. Computer-assisted telephone interviewing from central locations can improve the efficiency of certain kinds of telephone surveys.

5 6 7 8 Traditionally, self-administered questionnaires have been distributed by mail. Today, however, self-administered questionnaires may be dropped off to individual respondents, distributed from central locations, or administered via computer. Mail questionnaires generally are less expensive than telephone or personal interviews, but they also introduce a much larger chance of nonresponse error. Several methods can be used to encourage higher response rates. Mail questionnaires must be more structured than other types of surveys and cannot be changed if problems are discovered in the course of data collection.

The Internet and other interactive media provide convenient ways for organizations to conduct surveys. Internet surveys are quick and cost-effective, but not everyone has Internet access. Because the surveys are computerized and interactive, questionnaires can be personalized and data can be captured in real time. There are some privacy and security concerns, but the future of Internet surveys looks promising.

9 Pre-testing a questionnaire on a small sample of respondents is a useful way to discover problems while they can still be corrected.

Key Terms and Concepts

personal interview
probing
item nonresponse
door-to-door interview
callback
mall intercept interview
telephone interview
random digit dialling

central location interviewing
computer-assisted telephone interview (CATI)
self-administered questionnaire
mail survey
response rate
cover letter
drop-off method

fax survey
e-mail survey
Internet survey
welcome screen
dialogue box
mixed-mode survey
pre-testing

Questions for Review and Critical Thinking

1. What type of communication medium would you use to conduct the following surveys? Why?
   a. Survey of the buying motives of industrial engineers
   b. Survey of the satisfaction levels of rental-car users
   c. Survey of television commercial advertising awareness
   d. Survey of top corporate executives
2. A publisher offers college professors one of four best-selling mass-market books as an incentive for filling out a 10-page mail questionnaire about a new textbook. What advantages and disadvantages does this incentive have?
3. "Individuals are less willing to cooperate with surveys today than they were 15 years ago." Comment on this statement.
4. What do you think should be the maximum length of a self-administered questionnaire?
5. Do most surveys use a single communication mode (for example, the telephone), as most textbooks suggest?
6. A survey researcher reports that "205 usable questionnaires out of 942 questionnaires delivered in our mail survey converts to a 21.7 percent response rate." What are the subtle implications of this statement?
7. Evaluate the following survey designs:
   a. A researcher suggests mailing a small safe (a metal file box with a built-in lock) without the lock combination to respondents, with a note explaining that respondents will be called in a few days for a telephone interview. During the telephone interview, the respondent is given the combination and the safe may be opened.
   b. A shopping mall that wishes to evaluate its image places packets including a questionnaire, cover letter, and stamped return envelope in the mall where customers can pick them up if they wish.
   c. An e-mail message is sent to individuals who own computers, asking them to complete a questionnaire on a Web site. Respondents answer the questions and then have the opportunity to play a slot-machine game on the Web site. Each respondent is guaranteed a monetary incentive but has the option to increase it by playing the slot-machine game.
   d. A mall intercept interviewing service is located in a regional shopping centre. The facility contains a small room for television and movie presentations. Shoppers are used as sampling units. However, mall intercept interviewers recruit additional subjects for television commercial experiments by offering them several complimentary tickets for special sneak previews. Individuals contacted at the mall are allowed to bring up to five guests. In some cases the complimentary tickets are offered through ads in a local newspaper.
   e. *Maclean's* magazine opts to conduct a mail survey rather than a telephone survey for a study to determine the demographic characteristics and purchasing behaviour of its subscribers.
8. What type of research studies lend themselves to the use of e-mail for survey research? What are the advantages and disadvantages of using e-mail?

9. Comment on the ethics of the following situations:
   a. A researcher plans to use invisible ink to code questionnaires to identify respondents in a distributor survey.
   b. A political action committee conducts a survey about its cause. At the end of the questionnaire, it includes a request for a donation.
   c. A telephone interviewer calls at 1 p.m. on Sunday and asks the person who answers the phone to take part in an interview.
   d. An industrial marketer wishes to survey its own distributors. It invents the name "Prairie View Marketing Research" and sends out a mail questionnaire under this name.
   e. A questionnaire is printed on the back of a warranty card included inside the package of a food processor. The questionnaire includes a number of questions about shopping behaviour, demographics, and customer lifestyles. At the bottom of the warranty card is a short note in small print that says "Thank you for completing this questionnaire. Your answers will be used for marketing studies and to help us serve you better in the future. You will also benefit by receiving important mailings and special offers from a number of organizations whose products and services relate directly to the activities, interests, and hobbies in which you enjoy participating on a regular basis. Please indicate if there is some reason you would prefer not to receive this information."
10. How might the marketing research industry take action to ensure that the public believes that telephone surveys and door-to-door interviews are legitimate activities and that firms that misrepresent and deceive the public using marketing research as a sales ploy are not true marketing researchers?
11. A research company in the Netherlands offers a free computer to a sample of citizens who agree to answer questions downloaded every week in exchange for the computer. Comment on the ethics of this situation.
12. The American Testing Institute (also known as the U.S. Testing Authority) mails respondents what it calls a television survey. A questionnaire is sent to respondents, who are asked to complete it and mail it back along with a cheque for $14.80. In return for answering eight questions on viewing habits, the institute promises to send respondents one of 20 prizes ranging in value from $200 to $2,000—among which are video recorders, diamond watches, a lifetime supply of film, colour televisions, and two nights of hotel accommodations at a land development resort community. The institute lists the odds of winning as 1 in 150,000 on all prizes except the hotel stay, for which the odds are 149,981 out of 150,000. During a three-month period, the institute sends out 200,000 questionnaires. What are the ethical issues in this situation?

Exploring the Internet

1. Go to the Pew Internet and American Life page at www.pewinternet.org/. Several reports based on survey research will be listed. Select one of the reports. What were the research objectives? What were the first three questions on the survey?

2. Go to the Itracks Web site (www.itracks.com), click on Demo then Online Surveys, and go through the demonstration provided of what the company's online surveys look like. Write a short report about your experience.

3. Go to the NPD Canada Group Web site (www.npdcanada.com) and click on NPD Store. What types of custom and syndicated survey research services does the company offer?

4. Go to the MRIA (Marketing Research and Intelligence Association) home page (www.mria-arim.ca). Select About the MRIA, then Objectives/Mission.

5. Go to the CASRO (Council of American Survey Research Organizations) home page (www.casro.org). Select About CASRO. What are the key aspects of this research organization's mission?

6. Use a search engine such as Yahoo, Google, or MSN to see what you find if you enter "telephone survey" as keywords.

7. SurveyOnline is located at www.surveyonline.com. What unique service does this company offer?

8. Go to the National Quality Institute's Web site (www.nqi.ca), click on Assessment Services then Survey and e-Assessment Tools, and download the Customer Satisfaction Survey.

9. Go to Infopoll's Web site (http://infopoll.com) and click on Guided Tours to see how Internet surveys are made and executed.

10. For links to several Web sites demonstrating online surveys, go to

    www.effectivemarketingresearch.nelson.com.

Royal Barton started thinking about an electric fishing reel when his father had a stroke and lost the use of an arm. To see that happen to his dad, who had taught him the joys of fishing and hunting, made Barton realize what a chunk a physical handicap could take out of a sports enthusiast's life. Being able to cast and retrieve a lure and experience the thrill of a big bass trying to take your rig away from you were among the joys of life that would be denied Barton's father forever.

Barton was determined to do something about it, if not for his father, then at least for others who had suffered a similar fate. So, after tremendous personal expense and years of research and development, Barton perfected what is sure to be the standard bearer for all future freshwater electric reels. Forget those saltwater jobs, which Barton refers to as "winches." He has developed something that is small, is compact, and has incredible applications.

He calls it the Royal Bee. The first word is obviously his first name. The second word refers to the low buzzing sound the reel makes when in use.

The Royal Bee system looks simple enough and probably is if you understand the mechanical workings of a reel. A system of gears ties into the gears of the spool, and a motor in the back drives the gears attached to the triggering system.

All gearing of the electrical system can be disengaged so that you can cast normally. But pushing the button for "Retrieve" engages two gears. After the gears are engaged, the trigger travels far enough to touch the switch that tightens the drive belt, and there is no slipping. You cannot hit the switch until the gears are properly engaged. This means that you cast manually, just as you would normally fish, then you re-engage the reel for the levelwind to work. And you can do all that with one hand!

The system works on a 6-volt battery that you can attach to your belt or hang around your neck if you are wading. If you have a boat with a 6-volt battery, the reel can actually work off the battery. There is a small connector that plugs into the reel, so you could easily use more than one reel with the battery. For instance, if you have two or three outfits equipped with different lures, you just switch the connector from reel to reel as you use it. A reel with the Royal Bee system can be used in a conventional manner. You do not have to use it as an electric reel unless you choose to do so.

Barton believes the Royal Bee may not be just for handicapped fishermen. Ken Cook, one of the leading professional anglers in the country, is sold on the Royal Bee. After he suffered a broken arm, he had to withdraw from some tournaments because fishing with one hand was difficult. By the time his arm healed, he was hooked on the Royal Bee because it increased bassing efficiency. As Cook explains, "The electric reel has increased my efficiency in two ways. One is in flipping, where I use it all the time. The other is for fishing topwater, when I have to make a long cast. When I'm flipping, the electric reel gives me instant control over slack line. I can keep both hands on the rod. I never have to remove them to take up slack. I flip, engage the reel, and then all I have to do is push the lever with my thumb to take up slack instantly."

Cook's reel (a Ryobi 4000) is one of several that can be converted to the electric retrieve. For flipping, Cook loads his reel with 20-pound test line. He uses a similar reel with lighter line when fishing a surface lure. "What you can do with the electric reel is eliminate unproductive reeling time," Cook says.

A few extra seconds may not mean much if you are out on a neighbourhood pond just fishing on the weekend. But it can mean a lot if you are in tournament competition, where one extra cast might keep you from going home with $50,000 tucked in your pocket. "Look at it this way," Cook explains. "Let's suppose we're in clear water and it's necessary to make a long cast to the cover we want to fish with a topwater lure. There's a whole lot of unproductive water between us and the cover. With the electric reel, I make my long cast and fish the cover. Then, when I'm ready to reel in, I just press the retrieve lever so the battery engages the necessary gears, and I've got my lure back ready to make another cast while you're still cranking."

When Royal Barton retired from his veterinary supply business, he began enjoying his favourite pastimes: hunting, fishing, and developing the Royal Bee system. He realized he needed help in marketing his product, so he sought professional assistance to learn how to reach the broadest possible market for the Royal Bee system.

Questions

1. What marketing problem does Royal Barton face? What are his information needs? Outline some survey research objectives for a research project on the Royal Bee system.
2. What type of survey—personal interview, telephone interview, or mail survey—should be selected?
3. What sources of survey error are most likely to occur in a study of this type?
4. What means should be used to obtain a high response rate?

Although direct communication with consumers may explain a number of factors regarding consumer behaviour, valuable information can be gained from observations. Observations can lead to identification of consumer needs and introduction of new products. As part of its marketing research process in the laundry detergents and kitchen cleaner categories, Procter & Gamble had researchers visit individuals' homes to observe how they deal with their laundry. Typically, individuals piled their laundry into three categories: whites, colours, and delicates. The delicates pile had items that people strongly cared about and was dropped at the drycleaners. Results of the study led Procter & Gamble to develop Dryel, a product used in dryers at home to clean delicate items.[1]

Observation can be used to understand shopping patterns and behaviour and improvements of different aspects of the product, such as packaging. Reviewing videorecordings of shoppers at the meat section of the grocery stores and preparation of the meat at home cost around $60,000 yet revealed important information for the National Cattlemen's Beef Association (NCBA) in the United States. Although a typical shopper, usually a woman, would not admit to having little information about beef when asked, observation revealed that the typical items purchased were boneless chicken breast, ground beef, and sometimes a steak. Although round cuts and chucks were examined, they were usually not added to the shopping basket. Combined with the results of further qualitative research, NCBA learned that shoppers had little information about different cuts and the cooking methods each required. Many U.S. and Canadian grocery stores have revamped the meat section to include displays of beef arranged by cooking methods and added cooking instructions on packages.[2]

What you will learn in this chapter

1. To distinguish between scientific observation and casual observation.

2. To discuss the characteristics of observation research.

3. To give examples of nonverbal behaviour that can be observed.

4. To discuss the various situations in which direct observation studies may take place.

5. To discuss scientifically contrived observation.

6. To discuss some ethical issues in observation studies.

7. To define physical-trace evidence.

8. To define content analysis and explain the purposes of content analysis.

9. To describe the various types of mechanical observation.

10. To discuss the techniques for measuring physiological reactions.

Today, many other companies, such as Intel, Unilever, Bissell, and Colgate-Palmolive, use observations to understand their consumers. For instance, under their "Superbranding Ambition" initiative, Mark's Work Wearhouse wanted to reposition its brand. Its marketing team used observation as one method. In order to understand how Canadians choose and use their clothes, members of the marketing team went out and sat in the closets of cooperating customers and observed their clothing choices.[3]

In this chapter, we discuss the scientific methodology in data collection with observations. ■

WHEN IS OBSERVATION SCIENTIFIC?

 Observation becomes a tool for scientific inquiry when it

- Serves a formulated research purpose,

- Is planned systematically,

- Is recorded systematically and related to general propositions rather than simply reflecting a set of interesting curiosities, and

- Is subjected to checks or controls on validity and reliability.[4]

observation
The systematic process of recording the behavioural patterns of people, objects, and occurrences as they are witnessed.

In marketing research, **observation** is the systematic process of recording the behavioural patterns of people, objects, and occurrences as they are witnessed. No questioning or communicating with people occurs. The researcher who uses the observation method of data collection witnesses and records information as events occur or compiles evidence from records of past events.

WHAT CAN BE OBSERVED?

 A wide variety of information about the behaviour of people and objects can be observed. Exhibit 9.1 outlines seven kinds of observable phenomena: physical actions, such as shopping patterns or television viewing; verbal behaviour, such as sales conversations; expressive behaviour, such as tone of voice or facial expressions; spatial relations and locations, such as traffic patterns; temporal patterns, such as amount of time spent shopping or driving; physical objects, such as the amount of newspapers recycled; and verbal and pictorial records, such as the content of advertisements. (Although investigation of secondary data uses observation—see Chapter 6—it is not extensively discussed in this chapter.)

The observation method may be used to describe a wide variety of behaviour, but cognitive phenomena such as attitudes, motivations, and preferences cannot be observed. Thus observation research cannot provide an explanation of why a behaviour occurred or what actions were intended. Another limitation is that the observation period generally is of short duration. Behaviour patterns that occur over a period of several days or weeks generally are either too costly or impossible to observe.

THE NATURE OF OBSERVATION STUDIES

Marketing researchers can observe people, objects, events, or other phenomena using either human observers or machines designed for specific observation tasks. Human observation best suits a situation or behaviour that is not easily predictable in advance of the research. Mechanical observation, as performed by supermarket

EXHIBIT 9.1 | WHAT CAN BE OBSERVED

Phenomenon	Example
Physical action	A shopper's movement pattern in a store
Verbal behaviour	Statements made by airline travellers while waiting in line
Expressive behaviour	Facial expressions, tones of voices, and other forms of body language
Spatial relations and locations	How close visitors at an art museum stand to paintings
Temporal patterns	How long fast-food customers wait for their orders to be served
Physical objects	What brand-name items are stored in consumers' pantries
Verbal and pictorial records	Bar codes on product packages

scanners or traffic counters, can very accurately record situations or types of behaviour that are routine, repetitive, or programmatic.

Human or mechanical observation may be *unobtrusive;* that is, it may not require communication with a respondent. For example, rather than asking customers how much time they spend shopping in the store, a supermarket manager might observe and record the intervals between when shoppers enter and leave the store. The unobtrusive or nonreactive nature of the observation method often generates data without a subject's knowledge. A situation in which an observer's presence is known to the subject involves **visible observation;** a situation in which a subject is unaware that observation is taking place is **hidden observation.** Hidden, unobtrusive observation minimizes respondent error. Asking subjects to participate in the research is not required when they are unaware that they are being observed.

The major advantage of observation studies over surveys, which obtain self-reported data from respondents, is that the data do not have distortions, inaccuracies,

visible observation
Observation in which the observer's presence is known to the subject.

hidden observation
Observation in which the subject is unaware that observation is taking place.

Domain Stores, a chain of 23 furniture stores headquartered in Norwood, Massachusetts, hired Grid II, a market research firm, to videotape consumers in one of the furniture stores. Analysis of the videotapes revealed that people shop for furniture in twos. Of the 1,034 customers who entered the store, 954 came in pairs. In addition, facial expressions and other nonverbal behaviour indicated that many male customers were visibly ill at ease amid fluffed pillows and floral duvets. "The typical customer needs to be in the store at least nine minutes to feel comfortable enough to buy," says the company's CEO. "But if the spouse or boyfriend pulls her away too soon, we lose out on the sale." As a result of the observation research, the company remodelled its 23 stores with entertainment centres where sports fans can watch live events via cable.[5]

or other response biases due to memory error, social desirability bias, and so on. The data are recorded when the behaviour takes place.

OBSERVATION OF HUMAN BEHAVIOUR

Surveys emphasize verbal responses, while observation studies emphasize and allow for the systematic recording of nonverbal behaviour. Toy manufacturers such as Fisher Price use the observation technique because children often cannot express their reactions to products. By observing children at play with a proposed toy, doll, or game, marketing researchers may be able to identify the elements of a potentially successful product. Toy marketing researchers might observe play to answer the following questions: How long does the child's attention stay with the product? Does the child put the toy down after 2 minutes or 20 minutes? Are the child's peers equally interested in the toy?

Behavioural scientists have recognized that nonverbal behaviour can be a communication process by which meanings are exchanged among individuals. Head nods, smiles, raised eyebrows, and other facial expressions or body movements have been recognized as communication symbols. Observation of nonverbal communication may hold considerable promise for the marketing researcher. For example, with regard to customer–salesperson interactions it has been hypothesized that in low-importance transactions, where potential customers are plentiful and easily replaced (for example, a shoe store), the salesperson may show definite nonverbal signs of higher status than the customer. When customers are scarce, as in big-ticket purchase situations (for example, real estate sales), the opposite should be true: The salesperson might show many nonverbal indicators of deference. An observation study using the nonverbal communication measures shown in Exhibit 9.2 could test this hypothesis.

Of course, verbal behaviour is not ignored—indeed, in certain observation studies it is very important.

EXHIBIT 9.2	NONVERBAL COMMUNICATION: STATUS AND POWER GESTURES[6]					
	BETWEEN PEOPLE OF EQUAL STATUS		BETWEEN PEOPLE OF UNEQUAL STATUS		BETWEEN MEN AND WOMEN	
Behaviour	**Intimate**	**Nonintimate**	**Used by Superior**	**Used by Subordinate**	**Used by Men**	**Used by Women**
Posture	Relaxed	Tense (less relaxed)	Relaxed	Tense	Relaxed	Tense
Personal space	Closeness	Distance	Closeness (optional)	Distance	Closeness	Distance
Touching	Touch	Don't touch	Touch (optional)	Don't touch	Touch	Don't touch
Eye gaze	Establish	Avoid	Stare, ignore	Avert eyes, watch	Stare, ignore	Avert eyes
Demeanour	Informal	Circumspect	Informal	Circumspect	Informal	Circumspect
Emotional expression	Show	Hide	Hide	Show	Hide	Show
Facial expression	Smile	Don't smile	Don't smile	Smile	Don't smile	Smile

Paco Underhill runs Envirosell, a New York consumer research company that conducts observation research. He became interested in using cameras to analyze the flow of human traffic through public places after hearing a lecture by urban geographer William Whyte. Envirosell's clients now include large U.S. companies such as Staples, Quaker Foods, Bloomingdale's, Revlon, and Hallmark Cards (see www.envirosell.com for more details). The following is one reporter's account of what he learned about the value of observation research.

Underhill's research in retail settings led him to develop a body of observations he calls aisle theory.[7] Among his seminal findings is something we'll call the derriere-brush factor, although he calls it by another name. At his offices in New York, he showed me a film clip shot with a time-lapse camera aimed at a tie display in a narrow, heavily travelled aisle of the Bloomingdale's department store in Manhattan. Such aisles, meant to carry shoppers from store entrances onward into the store, are known in the retail industry as "driveways" or "power aisles."

Shoppers entered and dispersed; most zipped right by the tie display. Underhill stopped the projector.

"Stand up," he commanded.

I stood.

"Okay, you are standing at a counter. You are looking at ties. One of the most sensitive parts of your anatomy is your tail."

He began brushing my tail with his hand. Derriere-brush factor, he told me, "is simply the idea that the more likely you are to be brushed from the rear while you shop, the less likely you'll be converted from browser to buyer." In retail-speak, the "conversion ratio" of that display or counter will be low.

Underhill's stop-action film showed how few people stopped to examine the ties in the rack. Traffic swept past the few browsers in disconcerting volume.

When Bloomingdale's chairman saw the video, he called the clerk in charge of that department and had him move the tie rack out of the driveway. Later, a Bloomingdale's vice-president called Underhill and told him the chairman had personally had the sales tracked from that lone tie rack and discovered that within six weeks the increase had paid for Underhill's services. "That told me two things," Underhill said.

"One, I wasn't charging enough, and two, the mark-up on ties was even more obscene than I thought."

"He picks up common sense things," said Judith Owens, vice-president, marketing, of the National Retail Federation in New York, who periodically invites Underhill to show his stop-action films to the federation's many members. She watched one film of an audio store that drew mostly teenage clientele, yet placed its racks of CDs so high the kids couldn't reach them. "You watch that happen, then you hear Paco say if you drop your display by 18 inches you'll increase your productivity. Everybody says, my God, I never thought of that."

He showed AT&T that almost 20 percent of the people who came into its Phone Center stores were under 10 years old, and how salespeople spent a lot of their time simply protecting expensive phone systems displayed too close to the ground. His films showed how most people who entered a Revco drugstore failed to pick up a shopping basket and thus were automatically limited to buying only what they could carry.

Early in 1991 the Woolworth Corporation asked Underhill to study several of its Champs Sports stores to help figure out which layouts and designs worked best. Woolworth was planning a huge national expansion of the chain. It knew that sales from the rear section of each store—the hard goods section displaying such items as weights and basketballs—lagged far behind sales from other sections, but it didn't know why.

John Shanley, director of research for Woolworth, remembers how Underhill's stop-action film instantly solved the mystery. During peak sales periods, a line of customers would form from the cash register to the opposite wall of the store. "It literally prevented people from going from the front to the back," Shanley recalls. "They walked up to this line, turned and walked away." As a result, all of Champs' 500 stores were redesigned to feature a checkout area (known in the industry as the "cash-wrap") designed so that lines form along an axis from front to back. "All of a sudden the sales in the back of the store picked up," Shanley recalled.

But, I asked, shouldn't that barrier effect have been obvious without Underhill's help? "The obvious," Shanley answered, "isn't always that apparent."

Complementary Evidence

The results of observation studies may amplify the results of other forms of research by providing *complementary evidence* concerning individuals' "true" feelings. Focus group interviews often are conducted behind one-way mirrors from which marketing executives observe as well as listen to what is occurring. This allows for interpretation of nonverbal behaviour such as facial expressions or head nods to supplement information from interviews.

For example, in one focus group session concerning hand lotion, researchers observed that all the women's hands were above the table while they were casually waiting for the session to begin. Seconds after the women were told that the topic was to be hand lotion, all hands were placed out of sight. This observation, along with the group discussion, revealed the women's anger, guilt, and shame about the condition of their hands. Although they felt they were expected to have soft, pretty hands, their housework obligations required them to wash dishes, clean floors, and do other chores that were hard on their hands.

When focus group behaviour is videotaped, observation of the nonverbal communication symbols can add even more to marketers' knowledge of the situation.

DIRECT OBSERVATION

direct observation
A straightforward attempt to observe and record what naturally occurs; the investigator does not create an artificial situation.

Direct observation can produce a detailed record of events that occur or what people actually do. The observer plays a passive role. That is, there is no attempt to control or manipulate a situation—the observer merely records what occurs. Many types of data can be obtained more accurately through direct observation than by questioning. For example, recording traffic counts and/or observing the direction of traffic flows within a supermarket can help managers design store layouts that maximize the exposure of departments that sell impulse goods. A manufacturer can determine the number of facings, shelf locations, display maintenance, and other characteristics that make for better store conditions. If directly questioned in a survey, most shoppers would be unable to accurately portray the time they spent in each department. The observation method could, however, determine this without difficulty.

With the direct observation method, the data consist of records of events made as they occur. An observation form often helps keep the observations consistent and ensures that all relevant information is recorded. A respondent is not required to

Focus groups observed behind one-way mirrors are often videotaped. The ability to replay video records allows researchers to perform detailed analysis of physical actions.

When questioned in a survey, doctors answered that they spent about nine times more time informing patients than they actually did.[8] The physicians who were directly questioned answered that they spent about 12 minutes giving information to the average patient, but videotapes of the doctor–patient encounters indicated that the doctors spent only 1.3 minutes giving information. Furthermore, the doctors underestimated how much the patients wanted to know about their illnesses. When doctors' answers were compared with patients' answers about how much patients wanted to know, doctors underestimated the amount of information two out of three times.

recall—perhaps inaccurately—an event after it has occurred; instead, the observation is instantaneous.

In many cases, direct observation is the most straightforward form of data collection (or the only form possible). The produce manager at a Loblaws grocery store may periodically gather competitive price information at the Maxi and IGA stores in the neighbourhood. In other situations, observation is the most economical technique. In a common type of observation study, a shopping centre manager may observe the licence plate numbers on cars in its parking lot. These data, along with automobile registration information, provide an inexpensive means of determining where customers live.

Certain data may be obtained more quickly or easily using direct observation than by other methods. Sex, race, and other respondent characteristics can simply be observed. Researchers investigating a diet product may use observation when selecting respondents in a shopping mall. Overweight people may be prescreened by observing pedestrians, thus eliminating a number of screening interviews.

In a quality-of-life survey, respondents were asked a series of questions that were compiled into an index of well-being. Direct observation was also used by the interviewers because the researchers wanted to investigate the effect of weather conditions on people's answers. The researchers quickly and easily observed and recorded outside weather conditions on the day of the interviews, as well as the temperature and humidity in the building in which the interviews were conducted.[9]

Recording the decision time necessary to make a choice between two alternatives is a relatively simple, unobtrusive task that can be done through direct observation. **Response latency** refers to the choice time recorded as a measure of the strength of the preference between alternatives. It is hypothesized that the longer a decision maker takes to choose between two alternatives, the closer the two alternatives are in preference. A quick decision is assumed to indicate that the psychological distance between alternatives is considerable. The response latency measure is gaining popularity now that computer-assisted data collection methods are becoming more common (because the computer can record decision times).

response latency
The amount of time it takes to make a choice between two alternatives; used as a measure of the strength of preference.

Errors Associated with Direct Observation

Although no interaction with the subject occurs in direct observation, the method is not error-free; the observer may record events subjectively. The same visual cues that may influence the interplay between interviewer and respondent (e.g., the subject's age or sex) may come into play in some types of direct observation settings. For example, the observer may subjectively attribute a particular economic status or educational background to a subject. A distortion of measurement resulting from

Direct observation of consumers of juices and juice beverages revealed that many of them poured their beverages from large bottles they had purchased into smaller empty water bottles, the kind with a push-up top. This led to the conclusion that juices packaged in smaller, convenient-to-transport bottles would find a market.[10]

observer bias
A distortion of measurement resulting from the cognitive behaviour or actions of a witnessing observer.

contrived observation
Observation in which the investigator creates an artificial environment in order to test a hypothesis.

the cognitive behaviour or actions of the witnessing observer is called **observer bias.** For example, in a research project using observers to evaluate whether sales clerks are rude or courteous, fieldworkers may be required to rely on their own interpretations of people or situations during the observation process.

If the observer does not record every detail that describes the persons, objects, and events in a given situation, accuracy may suffer. As a general guideline, the observer should record as much detail as possible. However, the pace of events, the observer's memory, the observer's writing speed, and other factors will limit the amount of detail that can be recorded.

Interpretation of observation data is another major source of potential error. Facial expressions and other nonverbal communication may have several meanings. Does a smile always mean happiness? Does the fact that someone is standing or seated in close proximity to the president of a company necessarily indicate the person's status?

Scientifically Contrived Observation

Most observation takes place in a natural setting. Observation in which the investigator intervenes to create an artificial environment in order to test a hypothesis is called **contrived observation.** Contrived observation can increase the frequency of occurrence of certain behaviour patterns. For example, an airline passenger complaining about a meal or service from the flight attendant may actually be a researcher recording that person's reactions. If situations were not contrived, the research time spent waiting and observing a situation would expand considerably. A number of retailers use observers called *mystery shoppers* to come into a store and pretend to be interested in a particular product or service; after leaving the store, the "shopper" evaluates the salesperson's performance.

COMBINING DIRECT OBSERVATION AND INTERVIEWING

Some research studies combine visible observation with personal interviews. Researchers in these *ethnographic studies,* as they are called in anthropology, closely observe individual consumers' behaviour in everyday situations. During or after the in-depth observations, the individuals are asked to explain the meaning of their actions.[11] For example, direct observation of women applying hand and body lotion identified two kinds of users. Some women slapped on the lotion, rubbing it briskly into their skin. Others caressed their skin as they applied the lotion. When the women were questioned about their behaviour, the researchers discovered that women who slapped the lotion on were using the lotion as a remedy for dry skin. Those who caressed their skin were more interested in making their skin smell nice and feel soft. In a different study, men who are shopping for clothes have very distinct behaviours and reactions. Observation revealed that men will often become embarrassed and angry and leave a clothing store quickly rather than ask "Where is the men's section?" When asked about their behaviours, men are often unable to fully articulate their behaviours (e.g., "I don't exactly know how to explain it") or they simply may not have critically examined their own views (e.g., "Yeah, I guess I do do that, I never really thought about it"). Research combining observation and interviews can provide more detailed account of consumer behaviours.[12]

ETHICAL ISSUES IN THE OBSERVATION OF HUMANS

Observation methods introduce a number of ethical issues. Hidden observation raises the issue of the respondent's right to privacy. For example, a firm interested in acquiring information about how women put on their bras might persuade some retailers to place one-way mirrors in dressing rooms so that this behaviour may be observed unobtrusively. Obviously, there is an ethical question to be resolved in such a situation. Other observation methods, especially contrived observation, raise the possibility of deception of subjects.

Some people might see contrived observation as entrapment. To *entrap* means to deceive or trick into difficulty, which clearly is an abusive action. The problem is one of balancing values. If the researcher obtains permission to observe someone, the subject may not act in a typical manner. Thus the researcher must determine his or her own view of the ethics involved and decide whether the usefulness of the information is worth telling a white lie.

OBSERVATION OF PHYSICAL OBJECTS

Physical phenomena may be the subject of observation study. Physical-trace evidence is a visible mark of some past event or occurrence. For example, the wear on library books indirectly indicates which books are actually read (handled most) when checked out. A classic example of physical-trace evidence in a non-profit setting was erosion traces on the floor tiles around the hatching-chick exhibit at Chicago's Museum of Science and Industry. These tiles had to be replaced every six weeks; tiles in other parts of the museum did not need to be replaced for years. The selective erosion of tiles, indexed by the replacement rate, was a measure of the relative popularity of exhibits.

Clearly, a creative marketing researcher has many options available for determining the solution to a problem. The story about Charles Coolidge Parlin, generally recognized as one of the founders of commercial marketing research, counting garbage cans at the turn of the 20th century illustrates another study of physical traces.

Parlin designed an observation study to persuade Campbell's Soup Company to advertise in the *Saturday Evening Post*. Campbell's was reluctant to advertise because they believed that the *Post* was read primarily by working people who would prefer to make soup from scratch, peeling the potatoes and scraping the carrots, rather than paying 10¢ for a can of soup. To demonstrate that rich people weren't the target market, Parlin selected a sample of Philadelphia garbage routes. Garbage from each specific area of the city that was selected was dumped on the floor of a local National Guard Armory. Parlin had the number of Campbell's soup cans in each pile counted. The results indicated that the garbage from the rich people's homes didn't contain many cans of Campbell's soup. Although they didn't make soup from scratch themselves, their servants did. The garbage piles from the blue-collar area showed a large number of Campbell's soup cans. This observation study was enough evidence for Campbell's. They advertised in the *Saturday Evening Post*.[13]

The method used in this study is now used in a scientific project at the University of Arizona in which aspiring archaeologists sift through modern garbage; they examine soggy cigarette butts, empty milk cartons, and half-eaten Big Macs. Investigation of Arizona household garbage has revealed many interesting findings. For example, in Hispanic households the most popular baby food is squash.[14] It accounts for 38 percent of the baby food vegetables Hispanic babies consume. By contrast, in Anglo households peas account for 29 percent of all baby vegetables; squash ranks above only spinach, which is last. (Squash has been a dietary staple in Mexico and Central America for more than 9,000 years.) Sorting through fast-food restaurants' garbage reveals that wasted food from chicken restaurants (not counting bones) accounts for 35 percent of all food bought. This is substantially greater than the 7 percent of wasted food at fast-food hamburger restaurants.

What is most interesting about the garbage project is the comparison between the results of surveys about food consumption and the contents of respondents' garbage—garbage does not lie.[15] The University of Arizona project indicates that people consistently under-report the quantity of junk food they eat and over-report the amount of fruit and diet soda they consume. Most dramatically, however, studies show that alcohol consumption is under-reported by 40 to 60 percent.

Garbage is even more revealing in Buenos Aires, Argentina. The research company Garbage Data Dynamics analyzes discarded containers, newspapers, and other garbage in that city. Because garbage is collected daily in Buenos Aires and people typically dispose of garbage in small bags with grocery store names printed on them, certain types of data that cannot be collected in Canada or the United States can be obtained. The results are so specific that they can show what brand of soft drink was consumed with a certain meal.

Counting and recording physical inventories by means of retail or wholesale audits allows researchers to investigate brand sales on regional and national levels, market shares, seasonal purchasing patterns, and so on. Marketing research suppliers offer audit data at both the retail and the wholesale levels.

An observer can record physical-trace data to discover things that a respondent could not recall accurately. For example, actually measuring the number of millilitres of a liquid bleach used during a test provides precise physical-trace evidence without relying on the respondent's memory. The accuracy of respondents' memories is not a problem for the firm that conducts a pantry audit. The pantry audit requires an inventory of the brands, quantities, and package sizes in a consumer's home rather than responses from individuals. The problem of untruthfulness or some other form of response bias is avoided. For example, the pantry audit prevents the possible problem of respondents erroneously claiming to have purchased prestige brands. However, gaining permission to physically check consumers' pantries is not easy, and the fieldwork is expensive. Furthermore, the brand in the pantry may not reflect the brand purchased most often if it was substituted because of a cents-off coupon, because the subject's normal brand was out of stock, or for another reason.

CONTENT ANALYSIS

content analysis
The systematic observation and quantitative description of the manifest content of communication.

Content analysis obtains data by observing and analyzing the contents or messages of advertisements, newspaper articles, television programs, letters, and the like. It involves systematic analysis as well as observation to identify the specific information content and other characteristics of the messages. Content analysis studies the message itself; it involves the design of a systematic observation and recording procedure for quantitative description of the manifest content of communication. This technique measures the extent of emphasis or omission of a given analytical category. For example, the content of advertisements might be investigated to evaluate their use of words, themes, characters, or space and time relationships. The frequency of appearance of women, blacks, or other minorities in mass media has been a topic of content analysis.

Content analysis may be used to investigate questions such as whether some advertisers use certain types of themes, appeals, claims, or deceptive practices more than others. A cable television programmer might do a content analysis of network programming to evaluate its competition. For example, every year researchers analyze the Super Bowl to see how much of the visual material is live-action play and how much is replay, or how many shots focus on the cheerleaders and how many on spectators. The information content of television commercials directed at children can be investigated, as can company images portrayed in advertising, and numerous other aspects of advertising.

Study of the content of communications is more sophisticated than simply counting the items; it requires a system of analysis to secure relevant data. After one employee role-playing session involving leaders and subordinates, videotapes were analyzed to identify categories of verbal behaviours (e.g., positive reward statements, positive comparison statements, and self-evaluation requests). Trained coders, using a set of specific instructions, then recorded and coded the leaders' behaviour into specific verbal categories.

MECHANICAL OBSERVATION

In many situations the primary—and sometimes the only—means of observation is mechanical rather than human. Videotape cameras, traffic counters, and other machines help observe and record behaviour. Some unusual observation studies have used motion picture cameras and time-lapse photography. An early application of this observation technique photographed train passengers and determined their levels of comfort by observing how they sat and moved in their seats. Another time-lapse study filmed traffic flows in an urban square and resulted in a redesign of the streets. Similar techniques may help managers design store layouts and resolve problems in moving people or objects through spaces over time.

Television Monitoring

television monitoring
Computerized mechanical observation used to obtain television ratings.

Perhaps the best-known marketing research project globally involving mechanical observation and computerized data collection is AC Nielsen's **television monitoring** system for estimating national television audiences. Nielsen uses a consumer panel and sophisticated monitoring devices to obtain ratings for television programs in 18 countries.[16] In Canada, BBM Canada obtains both diary-based and mechanical observations of radio and TV viewership from panels. PeopleMeter, used by BBM, is an electronic box hooked up to television sets to capture important information on program choices, the length of viewing time, and the identity of the viewer.

Knowing who in the family is watching allows executives to match television programs with demographic profiles. When the panel household's television set is turned on, a question mark appears on the screen to remind viewers to indicate who is watching. The viewer then uses a handheld electronic device that resembles a television remote control to record who is watching. A device attached to the television automatically sends the observed data—the viewer's age and sex and what programs are being watched—over telephone lines to BBM's computers. A total sample of 3,150 households is distributed across Canada, representing the national Canadian TV viewership.[17] A more recent introduction, Portable People Meter (PPM), a pager-sized device that is carried by a panel member, automatically detects and records programming that the panel member is exposed to. The participating

When Steelcase, an office furniture manufacturer, decided there was an opportunity for a new product specifically designed for work teams, researchers believed that observation was the best research method. Steelcase placed video cameras at various companies so its staff could observe firsthand how teams operate. After the recording period ended, the researchers exhaustively analyzed the tapes, looking for the patterns of behaviour and motion that workers don't even notice themselves. The main observation was that people in teams function best if they can do some work collaboratively and some privately. These findings were utilized to design the Personal Harbor brand of modular office units. The units are similar in shape and size to a phone booth and can be arranged around a common space where a team works, fostering synergy but also allowing a person to work alone when necessary.[18]

broadcasters embed inaudible codes in the audio portion of their programming using encoders provided by BBM and Arbitron. The Portable People Meter can measure exposure to any electronic media that have audio that can be encoded—television, cable, and radio, even cinema advertising and in-store media.[19]

Monitoring Web Site Traffic

Most organizations record how many people visit their Web sites. A *hit* occurs when a user clicks on a single page of a Web site. If the visitor clicks on many places to access graphics or the like, that page receives multiple hits.[20] Organizations with Web sites consisting of multiple pages find it useful to track *page views,* or single, discrete clicks on individual pages. Page views more conservatively indicate how many users visit each individual page on the Web site and may also be used to track the path or sequence of pages that each visitor follows. A variety of information technologies are used to measure Web traffic and to maintain access logs.

Nielsen//NetRatings and comScore Networks are marketing research companies that specialize in monitoring Internet activity. The typical Internet monitoring company installs a special tracking program on the personal computers of a sample of Internet users who agree to participate in the research effort. Nielsen//NetRatings has its software installed in 225,000 computers in homes and workplaces in 26 countries. Internet monitoring enables these companies to identify the popularity of Web sites (AOL.com and Yahoo.com are among the most popular), measure the effectiveness of advertising banners, and provide other audience information. For example, a Media Metrix Canada study conducted with Canadian consumers indicated that online and retail store consumers are similar for four major multichannel retailers in Canada (Chapters, HMV, Sears, Futureshop).[21]

Scanner-Based Research

Lasers performing optical character recognition and bar-code technology like the universal product code (UPC) have accelerated the use of mechanical observation in marketing research. Chapter 6 noted that a number of syndicated services offer secondary data about product category movement generated from retail stores using scanner technology.

This technology now allows researchers to investigate more demographically or promotionally specific questions. For example, scanner research has investigated the different ways consumers respond to price promotions and how those differences

scanner-based consumer panel
A type of consumer panel in which participants' purchasing habits are recorded with a laser scanner rather than a purchase diary.

affect a promotion's profitability. One of the primary means of implementing this type of research is through the establishment of a **scanner-based consumer panel** to replace consumer purchase diaries. In a typical scanner panel, each household is assigned a bar-coded card that members present to the clerk at the register. The household's code number is coupled with the purchase information recorded by the scanner. Furthermore, as with other consumer panels, background information about the household obtained through answers to a battery of demographic and psychographic survey questions can also be coupled with the household code number.

Aggregate data, such as actual store sales as measured by scanners, are also available. These data parallel data provided by a standard mail diary panel, with some important improvements:

1. The data measure observed (actual) purchase behaviour rather than reported behaviour (recorded later in a diary).
2. Substituting mechanical for human record-keeping improves accuracy.
3. Measures are unobtrusive, eliminating interviewing and the possibility of social desirability or other bias on the part of respondents.
4. More extensive purchase data can be collected, because all UPC categories are measured. In a mail diary respondents could not possibly reliably record all items they purchased. Because all UPC-coded items are measured in the panel, users can investigate many product categories to determine loyalty, switching rates, and so on for their own brands as well as for other companies' products and locate product categories for possible market entry.
5. The data collected from computerized checkout scanners can be combined with data about advertising, price changes, displays, and special sales promotions. Researchers can scrutinize them with powerful analytical software provided by the scanner data providers.

Scanner data can show a marketer week by week how a product is doing, even in a single store, and track sales in response to local ads or promotions. Furthermore, several organizations, such as Information Resources Inc. Behaviour Scan System, have developed scanner panels and expanded them into electronic test market systems. These are discussed in greater detail in Chapter 10.

Advances in bar-code technology have led to **at-home scanning systems** that use handheld wands to read UPC symbols. Consumer panellists perform their own scanning *after* they have taken home the products. This advance makes it possible to investigate purchases made at stores that do not have in-store scanning equipment.

at-home scanning system
A system that allows consumer panellists to perform their own scanning after taking home products, using handheld wands that read UPC symbols.

Measuring Physiological Reactions

Marketing researchers have used a number of other mechanical devices to evaluate consumers' physical and physiological reactions to advertising copy, packaging, and other stimuli. Researchers use such means when they believe that consumers are unaware of their own reactions to stimuli such as advertising or that consumers will not provide honest responses. There are four major categories of mechanical devices used to measure physiological reactions: (1) eye-tracking monitors, (2) pupilometers, (3) psychogalvanometers, and (4) voice pitch analyzers.

A magazine or newspaper advertiser may wish to grab readers' attention with a visual scene and then direct it to a package or coupon. Or a television advertiser may wish to identify which selling points to emphasize. Eye-tracking equipment records how the subject reads a print ad or views a TV commercial and how much time is spent looking at various parts of the stimulus. In physiological terms, the gaze movement of a viewer's eye is measured with an **eye-tracking monitor,** which measures unconscious eye movements. Originally developed to measure astronauts' eye fatigue, modern eye-tracking systems need not keep a viewer's head in a stationary position. The devices track eye movements through invisible infrared light

eye-tracking monitor
A mechanical device used to observe eye movements. Some eye monitors use infrared light beams to measure unconscious eye movements.

beams that lock onto a subject's eyes. The light reflects off the eye, and eye-movement data are recorded while another tiny video camera monitors which magazine page is being perused. The data are analyzed by computer to determine which components in an ad (or other stimuli) were seen and which were overlooked.

The other physiological observation techniques are based on a common principle:

> Physiological research depends on the fact that adrenalin is produced when the body is aroused. When adrenalin goes to work, the heart beats faster and more strongly, and even enlarges.
>
> Blood flows to the extremities and increases capillary dilation at the fingertips and earlobes. Skin temperature increases, hair follicles stand up, skin pores emit perspiration, and the electrical conductivity of skin surfaces is affected. Eye pupils dilate, electrical waves in the brain increase in frequency, breathing is faster and deeper, and the chemical composition of expired air is altered. This process offers a choice of about 50 different measures—the question of which measure to use is to some extent irrelevant since they are all measuring arousal.[22]

A **pupilometer** observes and records changes in the diameter of a subject's pupils. A subject is instructed to look at a screen on which an advertisement or other stimulus is projected. When the brightness and distance of the stimulus from the subject's eyes are held constant, changes in pupil size may be interpreted as changes in cognitive activity that result from the stimulus (rather than from eye dilation and constriction in response to light intensity, distance from the object, or other physiological reactions to the conditions of observation). This method of research is based on the assumption that increased pupil size reflects positive attitudes toward and interest in advertisements.

A **psychogalvanometer** measures galvanic skin response (GSR), a measure of involuntary changes in the electrical resistance of the skin. This device is based on the

pupilometer
A mechanical device used to observe and record changes in the diameter of a subject's pupils.

psychogalvanometer
A device that measures galvanic skin response, a measure of involuntary changes in the electrical resistance of the skin.

How This Advertisement Was Read

% Noting Each Element

★ Most Common Starting Point

⬇ Most Common Viewing Pattern

*Measurements with an eye-tracking monitor of subject's response to this ad for Purina Puppy Chow showed that only 24 percent of consumers **took the time to view** the body copy message and that 95 percent of the viewers **looked** at the boy at the top of the ad. The red arrows show the most common viewing pattern—**began with the boy followed by a downward link at the dog.***

assumption that physiological changes, such as increased perspiration, accompany emotional reactions to advertisements, packages, and slogans. Excitement increases the body's perspiration rate, which increases the electrical resistance of the skin. The test is an indicator of emotional arousal or tension.

Voice pitch analysis is a relatively new physiological measurement technique that measures emotional reactions as reflected in physiological changes in a person's voice. Abnormal frequencies in the voice caused by changes in the autonomic nervous system are measured with sophisticated, audio-adapted computer equipment. Computerized analysis compares the respondent's voice pitch during warm-up conversations (normal range) with verbal responses to questions about his or her evaluative reaction to television commercials or other stimuli. This technique, unlike other physiological devices, does not require the researcher to surround subjects with mazes of wires or equipment.

All these devices assume that physiological reactions are associated with persuasiveness or predict some cognitive response. This has not yet been clearly demonstrated, however. There is no strong theoretical evidence to support the argument that a physiological change is a valid measure of future sales, attitude change, or emotional response. Another major problem with physiological research is the *calibration,* or sensitivity, of measuring devices. Identifying arousal is one thing, but precisely measuring *levels* of arousal is another. In addition, most of these devices are expensive. However, as a prominent researcher points out, physiological measurement is coincidental: "Physiological measurement isn't an exit interview. It's not dependent on what was remembered later on. It's a live blood, sweat, and tears, moment-by-moment response, synchronous with the stimulus."[23]

Each of these mechanical devices has another limitation, in that the subjects are usually placed in artificial settings (watching television in a laboratory rather than at home) and they know that they are being observed.

Following the more recent developments in neuroscience, marketing has started to adopt some of the physiological measures of neuroscience to understand consumer choices, such as functional magnetic resonance imaging (fMRI), magnetoencephalography (MEG), and electroencephalography (EEG). In a recent study, researchers observed brain scans (functional magnetic resonance imaging) of participants who were given a blind taste test of Coca-Cola and Pepsi. There were no differences in the percentage of participants that chose Coca-Cola and Pepsi. However, when the brand names were revealed, three out of four subjects preferred Coca-Cola. What is more interesting is that the bran scan revealed that the blind preferences and brand-based preferences activated different areas of the brain. Future research with physiological measures may provide a better understanding of consumer choices.[24]

voice pitch analysis
A physiological measurement technique that records abnormal frequencies in the voice that are supposed to reflect emotional reactions to various stimuli.

SUMMARY

Observation is a powerful tool for the marketing researcher. Scientific observation is the systematic process of recording the behavioural patterns of people, objects, and occurrences as they are witnessed. Questioning or otherwise communicating with subjects does not occur. A wide variety of information about the behaviour of people and objects can be observed. Seven kinds of phenomena are observable: physical actions, verbal behaviour, expressive behaviour, spatial relations and locations, temporal patterns, physical objects, and verbal and pictorial records. Thus both verbal and nonverbal behaviour may be observed.

A major disadvantage of the observation technique is that cognitive phenomena such as attitudes, motivations, expectations, intentions, and preferences are not observable. Furthermore, only overt behaviour of short duration can be observed. Nevertheless, many types of data can be obtained more accurately through direct observation than by questioning respondents. Observation is often the most direct or the only method for collecting certain data.

Marketing researchers employ both human observers and machines designed for specific observation tasks. Human observation is commonly used when the situation or behaviour to be recorded is not easily predictable in advance of the research. Mechanical observation can be used when the situation or behaviour to be recorded is routine, repetitive, or programmatic. Human or mechanical observation may be unobtrusive. Human observation brings the possibility of observer bias, even though the observer does not interact with the subject.

Observation can sometimes be contrived by creating the situations to be observed. This can reduce the time and expense of obtaining reactions to certain circumstances. Contrived observation, hidden observation, and other observation research designs that might use deception often raise ethical concerns about subjects' right to privacy and right to be informed.

Physical-trace evidence serves as a visible record of past events. Content analysis obtains data by observing and analyzing the contents of the messages in written and/or spoken communications. Mechanical observation uses a variety of devices to record behaviour directly. Mechanical observation takes many forms. National television audience ratings are based on mechanical observation and computerized data collection. Scanner-based research provides product category sales data recorded by laser scanners in retail stores. Many syndicated services offer secondary data collected through scanner systems. Physiological reactions, such as arousal or eye movement patterns, may be observed using a number of mechanical devices.

Key Terms and Concepts

observation
visible observation
hidden observation
direct observation
response latency

observer bias
contrived observation
content analysis
television monitoring
scanner-based consumer panel

at-home scanning system
eye-tracking monitor
pupilometer
psychogalvanometer
voice pitch analysis

Questions for Review and Critical Thinking

1. What are the advantages and disadvantages of observation studies compared to surveys?
2. Under what conditions are observation studies most appropriate?
3. Suggest some new uses for observation studies. Be creative.
4. A multinational fast-food corporation plans to locate a restaurant in La Paz, Bolivia. Secondary data for this city are outdated. How might you determine the best location using observation?
5. Discuss how an observation study might be combined with a personal interview.
6. The lost-letter technique has been used to predict voting behaviour. Letters addressed to various political groups are spread throughout a city. The "respondent" finds an envelope, reads the address of a group supporting (or opposing) a candidate, and mails back (or throws away) the envelope. It is assumed that the respondent's action indicates a favourable (or unfavourable) attitude toward the organization. Would this technique be appropriate in marketing research?
7. Outline a research design using observation for each of the following situations:
   a. A bank wishes to collect data on the number of customer services and the frequency of customer use of these services.

   b. A provincial government wishes to determine the driving public's use of seat belts.
   c. A researcher wishes to know how many women have been featured on *Maclean's* covers over the years.
   d. A fast-food franchise wishes to determine how long a customer entering a store has to wait for his or her order.
   e. A magazine publisher wishes to determine exactly what people see and what they pass over while reading one of its magazines.
   f. A food manufacturer wishes to determine how people use snack foods in their homes.
   g. An overnight package delivery service wishes to observe delivery workers beginning at the moment when they stop the truck, continuing through the delivery of the package, and ending when they return to the truck.
8. Watch the nightly news on a major network for one week. Observe how much time is devoted to national news, commercials, and other activity. (*Hint:* Think carefully about how you will record the contents of the programs.)
9. Comment on the ethics of the following situations:
   a. During the course of telephone calls to investors, a stockbroker records respondents' voices when they are answering sensitive investment questions and then

conducts a voice pitch analysis. The respondents do not know that their voices are being recorded.

b. A researcher plans to invite consumers to be test users in a simulated kitchen located in a shopping mall and then to videotape their reactions to a new microwave dinner from behind a one-way mirror.

c. A marketing researcher arranges to purchase the trash from the headquarters of a major competitor. The purpose is to sift through discarded documents to determine the company's strategic plans.

Exploring the Internet

1. The University of Arizona Department of Anthropology houses the Bureau of Applied Research in Anthropology. The garbage project is one of the bureau's research activities. Use a search engine to find the University of Arizona's home page and then navigate to the garbage project. What information is available?

2. You can review BBM Canada's website (www.bbm.ca) to learn more about radio and TV viewership studies.

Basically it looks like a desk lamp with a chunky smoked-glass body.[25] In fact, it is Lee Weinblatt's People Reader, a device designed to surreptitiously monitor the way people react to magazine advertising. Behind the smoked glass are two tiny remote-controlled video cameras, one that tracks eye movements and another that monitors which page is being perused. In a nearby office, technicians measure each dismissive glance and longing gaze.

Will a middle-aged man linger over an automobile ad featuring leggy female models? The People Reader was intended to answer questions like this for companies that spend millions of dollars on advertising and, in the past, have had to depend on the accuracy of a test subject's memory.

Weinblatt, 43 years old, is founder of the Pretesting Company, a 15-year-old concern in Englewood, New Jersey, that has become the leader in sleight-of-hand advertising research. He has developed an extensive bag of tricks, some of them incorporating technology originally developed for espionage. The People Reader is one; another is a mock car radio that plays prerecorded material and measures the speed with which a driver silences a commercial. There is also a television system that measures the tendency of viewers armed with remote-control devices to "zap" a particular commercial, and a computer-simulated supermarket to measure the allure of a new package. Weinblatt has hidden video cameras in a fake bar of Ivory soap, a box of cereal ("old hat," now, he says), and a ceiling sprinkler.

The unifying theme of Weinblatt's technology is eliciting responses consumers may not be aware of. Typically, people being tested are given only a limited idea—and often the wrong one—about what is actually being measured.

Since starting his company in 1985, Weinblatt has worked on projects for an impressive list of brands, including Purina pet food, Planter's peanuts, Raid insecticide, and *Sports Illustrated* magazine. Although Pretesting remains small, with revenues of $5.5 million, clients say Weinblatt offers them insights unlike those generated by any other advertising researchers. "I've recommended his tests many times," said Sue Le Barron, a project manager for pet food marketing research at Ralston Purina.

Traditionally, advertising research has been based on fairly overt approaches. To test a proposed television ad, for example, companies arrange to transmit the commercials to television sets of test subjects during normal programming and then interview them the next day on their ability to remember the ad and on their reactions. Similarly, the traditional method of pre-testing a new package or design is to expose it to a focus group of consumers who examine and react to it. Weinblatt argues that such techniques provide at best a murky picture, often failing to measure the impact of subliminal messages or, in the case of focus groups, prompting judgments in situations that don't mirror real life.

"Diagnostic research can be very useful for understanding what the problem is with a product, but it can never tell you what people are going to do in the real world," said Weinblatt. "Do people read *Newsweek* from the front or the back? How do you time the sequence of television ads? How does print stack up against TV? The questions have been piling up."

Weinblatt has been tinkering with attention-measuring devices since 1971. Armed with a master's degree in industrial psychology (and, later, in photography), he started out with the research subsidiary of the Interpublic Group of Companies Inc., which owns several major advertising agencies.

At the time, many advertising researchers were experimenting with "pupilmetrics," the measurement of pupil dilation, by filming people who were strapped into chairs and whose heads were anchored into wax moulds. Weinblatt designed equipment that was less intrusive. His first assignment came from Philip Morris, which he said wanted to find the least noticeable place to mount warning labels required by the U.S. Surgeon General on a pack of cigarettes. "We found that it didn't make any difference," said Weinblatt. "Smokers don't want to see."

In 1976, Weinblatt started Telcom Research, a manufacturer of portable eye movement recorders, which he sold in 1982, just before it was about to go bankrupt. But he continued inventing increasingly unobtrusive measurement devices and founded the Pretesting Company in 1985. Today he holds 28 patents.

To measure the chances that consumers will be attracted to a new package on crowded supermarket shelves, Weinblatt developed a computer-simulated shopping spree. Researchers evaluating a new line of dog food, for example, begin by recreating a supermarket rack in the dog food section that contains the new package. They then photograph the shelf as a whole and take close-ups of each quadrant of the shelf. This material is mixed in with similar sequences depicting the store entrance and several other supermarket sections.

People being tested are then told to "walk" through the store by reviewing slides of these images on a screen. Pressing buttons on a controller, they can move forward or backward between shelves and move in for close-ups. At each section they are asked to pick out what, if anything, they would like to buy. Their answers, however, constitute only a small part of the test. The key measurements, according to Weinblatt, are based on the way they move through the slides. Unknown to the customers, a computer linked to the controller logs the amount of time spent at each picture and provides an instant tabulation of how long a person lingered at the dog food rack and at a particular part of it containing the new product. Those data, in turn, can be compared with data for the rest of the supermarket and for competing products.

Weinblatt concedes there have been instances in which he incorrectly predicted that a commercial would fail. Nevertheless, he argues, his measurements offer crucial information in a world of cluttered store shelves, where nine out of ten new products fail. "The typical person spends 22 minutes shopping in a supermarket that contains 18,000 products," said Weinblatt. "What we're saying is, before you bet all that money on a new product, let's do the ideal and see if people are even going to notice it."

Question

Evaluate each observation technique used by the Pretesting Company. What possible applications might each technique have?

EXPERIMENTAL
RESEARCH AND TEST
MARKETING

The recent consumer focus on healthier diets has led a number of fast-food restaurants, packaged goods manufacturers, and even beer companies to develop products to support the healthier trend in food preferences. Although not as strongly influential in Canada, Atkins and similar low-carb diets were blamed for the 6 percent decrease in bread sales in the United States in 2003. According to a Print Measurement Bureau (PMB) survey in the same year, 10.8 percent of Canadians aged 25 to 54 were dieting.[1] Subway's own survey results revealed that 36 percent of their respondents were following a diet, and 34 percent of those were following a low-carb diet. To appeal to dieting consumers, Subway introduced "Atkins-friendly" menu items. Burger King also introduced low- or no-carb items. Even two major Canadian breweries, Molson and Labatt, introduced Molson Ultra and Labatt Sterling to capture the carb-sensitive segment.

Among fast-food restaurants, McDonald's Canada was one of the first to respond to changes in customer preferences for healthier food. According to Neil Everett, VP marketing, McDonald's own tracking studies revealed the preference for a healthier, more balanced lifestyle. However, would the consumers actually opt for salads instead of Big Macs with fries? McDonald's had already tried and failed with a healthier item, McLean Deluxe. Interviews and focus groups with 3,000 people across Canada revealed preferences for meat alternatives, whole wheat breads, low-fat desserts, and other low-fat options. Most importantly, respondents were not willing to sacrifice taste.[2]

In light of these findings, McDonald's developed new food entries and decided to test-market the new entries for three to four months at selected markets across Canada. Sales figures were observed for test markets with and without advertising support. The insights gained from the test markets were further used to modify the products, pricing, and positioning, and in the summer of 2002 Lighter Choices Menu was launched nationally. Although there were regional

What you will learn in this chapter

1. To define experimentation and discuss the requirements for making a true experiment.

2. To understand the terminology of experimentation.

3. To compare and contrast the two basic types of experimental error.

4. To discuss how to control extraneous variables in experimental situations.

5. To distinguish between internal and external validity.

6. To outline the various quasi-experimental designs and alternative, better experimental designs.

7. To discuss the useful functions that test marketing performs for marketing management.

8. To understand what factors to consider in selecting a test market.

differences in preference between the west coast, the Prairies, and Quebec, the initial launch did include different menu items across regions in the Lighter Choices Menu.

Past experience and the need to continue to introduce new products has led McDonald's to develop structured and standard procedures that include experiments and test marketing when it introduces these new products. The Lighter Choices Menu was adopted in the United States a year after it was introduced in Canada, resulting in a 6 percent increase in sales within a couple of months.[3] In 2003, the sales of new menu items in Canada had increased, mostly by the 58 percent boost in salad sales.[4] Increasing the number of more healthful menu items and changing public perception of the restaurant's offerings may be a long-term project for McDonald's and its competitors.

Lab experiments, field experiments, and test marketing are tools companies use in the development and introduction of new products. In this chapter, we discuss the role of experiments and test marketing in marketing research. ■

THE NATURE OF EXPERIMENTS

Most students are familiar with the concept of experimentation in the physical sciences. The term *experiment* typically conjures up an image of a chemist surrounded by bubbling test tubes and Bunsen burners. Behavioural and physical scientists have been far ahead of marketing researchers in the use of experimentation. Nevertheless, the purpose of experimental research is the same.

Experimental research allows the investigator to control the research situation so that *causal* relationships among variables may be evaluated. The marketing experimenter manipulates a single variable in an investigation and holds constant all other relevant, extraneous variables. Events may be controlled in an experiment to a degree not possible in a survey.

The researcher's goal in conducting an experiment is to determine whether the experimental treatment is the cause of the effect being measured. If a new marketing strategy (for example, new advertising) is used in a test market and sales subsequently increase in that market, but not in markets where the new strategy is not employed, the experimenter can feel confident that the new strategy caused the increase in sales.

Experiments differ from other research methods in degree of control over the research situation. In an **experiment,** one variable (the *independent variable*) is manipulated and its effect on another variable (the *dependent variable*) is measured, while all other variables that may confound the relationship are eliminated or controlled. The experimenter either creates an artificial situation or deliberately manipulates a real-life situation.

For example, a famous marketing experiment investigated the influence of brand-name identification on consumers' taste perceptions. The experimenter manipulated whether consumers tasted beer in labelled or unlabelled bottles. One week respondents were given a six-pack containing bottles labelled only with letters. The following week, respondents received another six-pack with brand labels. Thus respondents did not actually purchase beer from a store, but they drank the beer at home at their leisure. The experimenter measured reactions to the beers after each tasting. The beer itself was the same in each case, so differences in taste perception were attributed to label (brand) influence. This example illustrates that once an experimenter manipulates the independent variable, he or she measures changes in the dependent variable. The essence of an experiment is to do something to an individual and observe the reaction under conditions that allow this reaction to be measured against a known baseline.

experiment
A research method in which conditions are controlled so that one or more independent variables can be manipulated to test a hypothesis about a dependent variable. Experimentation allows evaluation of causal relationships among variables while all other variables are eliminated or controlled.

Decisions must be made about several basic elements of an experiment. These issues are (1) manipulation of the independent variable, (2) selection and measurement of the dependent variable, (3) selection and assignment of subjects, and (4) control over extraneous variables.[5]

Manipulation of the Independent Variable

The experimenter has some degree of control over the **independent variable.** The variable is independent because its value can be manipulated by the experimenter to whatever he or she wishes it to be. Its value may be changed or altered independently of any other variable. The independent variable is hypothesized to be the causal influence.

Experimental treatments are the alternative manipulations of the independent variable being investigated. For example, prices of $3.99, $4.49, and $4.99 might be the treatments in a pricing experiment. Price changes, advertising strategy changes, taste formulation, and so on are typical treatments.

In marketing research the independent variable often is a *categorical* or *classificatory variable* that represents some classifiable or qualitative aspect of marketing strategy. To determine the effects of point-of-purchase displays, for example, the experimental treatments that represent the independent variable are themselves the varying displays. Alternative advertising copy is another example of a categorical or classificatory variable. In other situations the independent variable is a *continuous variable.* The researcher must select the appropriate levels of that variable as experimental treatments. For example, the number of dollars that can be spent on advertising may be any number of different values.

Experimental and Control Groups

In the simplest type of experiment, only two values of the independent variable are manipulated. For example, consider measuring the influence of advertising on sales. In the experimental condition (treatment administered to the **experimental group**), the advertising budget may be $200,000. In the control condition (treatment administered to the **control group**), advertising may remain at zero or without change. By holding conditions constant in the control group, the researcher controls for potential sources of error in the experiment. Sales (the dependent variable) in the two treatment groups are compared at the end of the experiment to determine whether the level of advertising (the independent variable) had any effect.

Several Experimental Treatment Levels

The advertising/sales experiment with one experimental and one control group may not tell the advertiser everything he or she wishes to know about the advertising/sales relationship. If the advertiser wished to understand the functional nature of the relationship between sales and advertising at several treatment levels, additional experimental groups with advertising expenditures of $200,000, $500,000, and $1 million might be studied. This type of design would allow the experimenter to get a better idea of an optimal advertising budget.

More Than One Independent Variable

It is possible to assess the effects of more than one independent variable by using more complex experimental designs (such as full factorial or randomized block designs). For example, a restaurant chain might investigate the combined effects of increased advertising and a change in prices on sales volume. The purpose of most marketing research experimentation is to measure and compare the effects of experimental treatments on the dependent variable.

independent variable
In an experimental design, the variable that can be manipulated, changed, or altered independently of any other variable.

experimental treatments
Alternative manipulations of the independent variable being investigated.

experimental group
The group of subjects exposed to the experimental treatment.

control group
The group of subjects exposed to the control condition in an experiment—that is, not exposed to the experimental treatment.

Experimental treatments are alternative manipulations of the independent variable. Variations of advertising copy, graphic designs, and levels of prices charged are typical independent variables in marketing experiments.

Selection and Measurement of the Dependent Variable

dependent variable
The criterion or standard by which the results of an experiment are judged; a variable expected to be dependent on the experimenter's manipulation of the independent variable.

The **dependent variable** is so named because its value is expected to be dependent on the experimenter's manipulation of the independent variable; it is the criterion or standard by which the results are judged. Changes in the dependent variable are presumed to be a consequence of changes in the independent variable.

Selection of the dependent variable is a crucial decision in the design of an experiment. If researchers introduce a new pink grapefruit tea mix in a test market, sales volume is most likely to be the dependent variable. However, if researchers are experimenting with different forms of advertising copy appeals, defining the dependent variable may be more difficult. For example, measures of advertising awareness, recall, changes in brand preference, or sales might be used as the dependent variable, depending on the purpose of the ads. In the unit pricing experiment the dependent variable was the average price paid per unit. However, the dependent variable might have been the preference for either format of pricing information (a cognitive variable), brand-switching behaviour expressed as a percentage of consumers, or attitudes toward the store.

Often the dependent variable selection process, like the problem definition process, is considered less carefully than it should be. The experimenter's choice of a dependent variable determines what type of answer is given to the research question.

In a test market the amount of time needed for the effects to become evident should be considered in choosing the dependent variable. Sales may be measured several months after the experiment to determine if there were any carryover effects. Changes that are relatively permanent or longer lasting than changes generated only during the period of the experiment should be considered; repeat purchase behaviour may be important. Consumers may try a "loser" once, but they may not rebuy. The introduction of the original Crystal Pepsi illustrates the need to think beyond consumers' initial reactions. When Crystal Pepsi, a clear cola, was introduced, the initial trial rate was high, but only a small percentage of customers made repeat purchases. The brand never achieved high repeat sales within a sufficiently large market segment. Brand awareness, trial purchase, and repeat purchase are all possible dependent variables in an experiment. The dependent variable therefore should be considered carefully. Thorough problem definition will help the researcher select the most important dependent variable(s).

Selection and Assignment of Test Units

test units
Subjects or entities whose responses to experimental treatments are observed or measured.

Test units are the subjects or entities whose responses to the experimental treatment are measured or observed. Individuals, organizational units, sales territories, or other entities may be the test units. People are the most common test units in most marketing and consumer behaviour experiments. In our unit pricing example, supermarkets were the test units.

Sample Selection and Random Sampling Errors

As in other forms of marketing research, random sampling errors and sample selection errors may occur in experimentation. For example, experiments sometimes go awry even when a geographic area is specially chosen for a particular investigation. A case in point was the experimental testing of a new lubricant for outboard motors by Dow Chemical Company. The lubricant was tested in a warm- and a cold-weather area. In the warm-weather area, the product would have to stand up under continuous use and this test would prove the most demanding test. In the warm-weather area, the lubricant was a success. However, the story was quite different in the cold-weather area. Although the lubricant sold well and worked well during the summer, the following spring Dow discovered that in the colder northern climate it had congealed, allowing the outboard motors, idle all winter, to rust. The rusting problem never came to light in the warm-weather area, where the motors were in year-round use. Thus some *sample selection error* may occur because of the procedure used to assign subjects or test units to either the experimental or the control group.

random sampling error
An error that occurs because of chance; statistical fluctuations in which repetitions of the basic experiment sometimes favour one experimental condition and sometimes the other.

Random sampling error may occur if repetitions of the basic experiment sometimes favour one experimental condition and sometimes the other on a chance basis. An experiment dealing with charcoal briquettes may require that the people in both the experimental and the control groups be identical with regard to level of product usage and barbecuing habits. However, if subjects are randomly assigned to conditions without knowledge of their product usage, errors resulting from differences in that usage will be random sampling errors. Suppose a potato chip manufacturer that wishes to experiment with new advertising appeals wants the groups to be identical with respect to advertising awareness, media exposure, and so on. The experimenter must decide how to place subjects in each group and which group should receive treatment. Researchers generally agree that the random assignment of participants to groups and experimental treatments to groups is the best procedure.

randomization
A procedure in which the assignment of subjects and treatments to groups is based on chance.

Randomization

Randomization—the random assignment of subject and treatments to groups—is one device for equally distributing or scattering the effects of extraneous variables to all conditions. Thus the chance of unknown nuisance effects piling up in particular experimental groups can be identified. The effects of the nuisance variables will not be eliminated, but they will be controlled. Randomization assures the researcher that overall repetitions of the experiment under the same conditions will show the true effects, if those effects exist. Random assignment of conditions provides "control by chance."[6] Random assignment of subjects allows the researcher to assume that the groups are identical with respect to all variables except the experimental treatment.

Matching

Random assignment of subjects to the various experimental groups is the most common technique used to prevent test units from differing from each other on key variables; it assumes that all characteristics of the subjects have been likewise randomized. If the experimenter believes that certain extraneous variables may affect the dependent variable, he or she can make sure that the subjects in each group are matched on these characteristics. **Matching** the respondents on the basis of pertinent background information is another technique for controlling assignment errors. For example, in a taste test experiment for a dog food, it might be important to match the dogs in various experimental groups on the basis of age or breed. Similarly, if age is expected to influence savings behaviour, a bank conducting an experiment may have greater assurance that there are no differences among subjects if subjects in all experimental conditions are matched according to age.

Although matching assures the researcher that the subjects in each group are similar on the matched characteristics, the researcher cannot be certain that subjects have been matched on all characteristics that could be important to the experiment.

Repeated Measures

Experiments in which the same subjects are exposed to all experimental treatments are said to have **repeated measures.** This technique eliminates any problems due to subject differences, but it causes some other problems that we will discuss later.

Control over Extraneous Variables

The fourth decision about the basic elements of an experiment concerns control over extraneous variables. To understand this issue, it is important to understand the various types of experimental error.

In Chapter 7 we classified total survey error into two basic categories: random sampling error and systematic error. The same dichotomy applies to all research designs, but the terms *random (sampling) error* and *constant (systematic) error* are more frequently used when discussing experiments.

Constant Experimental Error

We have already discussed random error in the context of experimental selection and assignment of test units. **Constant error** (bias) occurs when the extraneous variables or the conditions of administering the experiment are allowed to influence the dependent variables every time the experiment is repeated. When this occurs, the results will be confounded because the extraneous variables have not been controlled or eliminated.

For example, if subjects in an experimental group are always administered treatment in the morning and subjects in the control group always receive the treatment in the afternoon, a constant, systematic error will occur. In such a situation the time of day—an uncontrolled extraneous variable—is a cause of constant error. In a training experiment the sources of constant error might be the persons who do the training (line or external specialists) or whether the training is conducted on the employees' own time or on company time. These and other characteristics of the training may have an impact on the dependent variable and will have to be taken into account.

---

matching
A procedure for the assignment of subjects to groups that ensures each group of respondents is matched on the basis of pertinent characteristics.

repeated measures
Experimental technique in which the same subjects are exposed to all experimental treatments to eliminate any problems due to subject differences.

constant error
An error that occurs in the same experimental condition every time the basic experiment is repeated; a systematic bias.

A number of extraneous variables may affect the dependent variable, thereby distorting the experiment. An example shows how extraneous variables may have an impact on results.[7] Suppose a television commercial for brand Z gasoline shows two automobiles on a highway. The announcer states that one car has used brand Z *without* the special additive and the other has used it *with* the additive. The car without the special additive comes to a stop first, and the car with it comes to a stop 10 to 15 metres farther down the road. (We will assume that both cars used the same quantity of gasoline.) The implication of this commercial is that the special additive (the independent variable) results in extra mileage (the dependent variable). As experimenters who are concerned with extraneous variables that could affect the result, we can raise the following questions:

1. Were the *engines* of the same size and type? Were the conditions of the engines the same (tuning and so on)?
2. Were the *cars* of the same condition (gear ratios, fuel injector settings, weight, wear and tear, and so on)?
3. Were the *drivers* different? Were there differences in acceleration? Were there differences in the drivers' weights?

Because an experimenter does not want extraneous variables to affect the results, he or she must control or eliminate such variables.

Demand Characteristics

The term **demand characteristics** refers to experimental design procedures that unintentionally hint to subjects about the experimenter's hypothesis. Demand characteristics are situational aspects of the experiment that demand that the participants respond in a particular way; hence, they are a source of constant error (see Exhibit 10.1). If participants recognize the experimenter's expectation or demand, they are likely to act in a manner consistent with the experimental treatment; even slight nonverbal cues may influence their reactions.

In most experiments the most prominent demand characteristic is the person who actually administers the experimental procedures. If an experimenter's presence, actions, or comments influence the subjects' behaviour or sway the subjects to slant their answers to cooperate with the experimenter, the experiment has *experimenter bias.* When subjects slant their answers to cooperate with the experimenter, they in effect are acting as guinea pigs and tend to exhibit behaviours that might not represent their behaviour in the marketplace. For example, if subjects in an advertising experiment understand that the experimenter is interested in whether they changed their attitudes in accord with a given advertisement, they may answer in the desired direction to please him or her. This attitude change reflects a **guinea pig effect** rather than a true experimental treatment effect.

A famous management experiment illustrates a common demand characteristic. Researchers were attempting to study the effects on productivity of various working conditions, such as hours of work, rest periods, lighting, and methods of pay, at the Western Electric Hawthorne plant in Cicero, Illinois. The researchers found that workers' productivity increased whether the work hours were lengthened or shortened, whether lighting was very bright or very dim, and so on. The surprised investigators realized that the workers' morale was higher because they were aware of being part of a special experimental group. This totally unintended effect is now known as the **Hawthorne effect** because researchers realize that people will perform differently when they know they are experimental subjects.[8]

If subjects in a laboratory experiment interact (i.e., are not relatively isolated), their conversations may produce joint decisions rather than a desired individual decision. For this reason, social interaction generally is restricted in laboratory experiments.

demand characteristics
Experimental design procedures or situational aspects of an experiment that provide unintentional hints about the experimenter's hypothesis to subjects.

TO THE POINT

We are never deceived; we deceive ourselves.

JOHANN WOLFGANG
VON GOETHE

guinea pig effect
An effect on the results of an experiment caused by subjects changing their normal behaviour or attitudes in order to cooperate with an experimenter.

Hawthorne effect
An unintended effect on the results of a research experiment caused by the subjects knowing that they are participants.

blinding effect
A technique used to control subjects' knowledge of whether or not they have been given a particular experimental treatment.

To reduce demand characteristics, the researcher typically takes steps to make it difficult for subjects to know what he or she is trying to find out. **Blinding** is used to control subjects' knowledge of whether they have been given a particular experimental treatment. In a cola taste test, one group of subjects might be exposed to the new formulation and the other exposed to the regular cola. If the subjects were blinded, all may have been told they had not been given the new formulation (or all may have been told they had received the new formulation). This technique frequently is used in medical research when subjects are given chemically inert pills (*placebos*) rather than medication. It may also be used in marketing experiments. For example, if the researchers themselves do not know which toothpastes are in the tubes marked with triangles, circles, or squares, they will not unconsciously influence the subjects. In these circumstances, neither the subjects nor the experimenter knows which are the experimental and which are the controlled conditions. Both parties are blinded; hence, such experiments are called **double-blind designs.**

double-blind design
A technique in which neither the subjects nor the experimenter knows which are the experimental and which the controlled conditions.

Establishing Control

The major difference between experimental research and other research is an experimenter's ability to hold conditions constant and to manipulate the treatment. To conclude that A causes B, a brewery experimenting with a new clear beer's influence on beer drinkers' taste perceptions must determine the possible extraneous variables other than the treatment that may affect the results and attempt to eliminate or control those variables. We know that brand image and packaging are important factors in beer drinkers' reactions, so the experimenter may wish to eliminate the effects associated with them. He or she may eliminate these two extraneous variables by packaging the test beers in plain packages without brand identification.

constancy of conditions
A situation in which subjects in experimental groups and control groups are exposed to situations identical except for differing conditions of the independent variable.

When extraneous variables cannot be eliminated, experimenters may strive for **constancy of conditions;** that is, they make efforts to expose all subjects in each experimental group to situations that are exactly alike except for the differing conditions of the independent variable. For example, a supermarket experiment involving four test products required that all factors other than shelf space (the treatment) be kept constant throughout the testing period. In all stores the shelf level that had existed before the tests began was maintained throughout the test period; only the amount of shelf space was changed. One problem involved store personnel accidentally changing shelf level when stocking the test products. This deviation from the constancy of conditions was minimized by auditing each store four times a week. The experimenter personally stocked as many of the products as possible, and the cooperation of stock clerks also helped reduce treatment deviations.

If the experimental method requires that the same subjects be exposed to two or more experimental treatments, an error may occur due to the *order of presentation*. If a soft-drink company plans to test consumers' comparison of a high-caffeine, extra-sugar version of its cola to its regular cola, one of the drinks must be tasted before the other. Consumers might tend to prefer the first drink they taste if they cannot tell any difference between the drinks. Another example is an electronic games manufacturer that has subjects perform an experimental task requiring some skill (that is, playing a game). Subjects might perform better on the second task simply because they have had some experience with the first task. *Counterbalancing* attempts to eliminate the confounding effects of order of presentation by requiring that half the subjects be exposed to treatment A first and then to treatment B while the other half receive treatment B first and then treatment A.

The random assignment of subjects and experimental treatments to groups is an attempt to control extraneous variations that result from chance. If certain extraneous variations cannot be controlled, the researcher must assume that the confounding effects will be present in all experimental conditions with approximately the same influence. (This assumption may not hold true if the assignments were not random.) In many experiments, especially laboratory experiments, interpersonal contact between members of the various experimental groups and/or the control group must be eliminated or minimized. After the subjects have been assigned to groups, the various individuals should be kept separated so that discussion about what occurs in a given treatment situation will not become an extraneous variable that contaminates the experiment.

ETHICAL ISSUES IN EXPERIMENTATION

Experimental researchers address privacy, confidentiality, deception, accuracy of reporting, and other ethical issues common to other research methods. The question of subjects' right to be informed, however, tends to be very prominent in experimentation. Research codes of conduct often suggest that the experimental subjects should be fully informed and receive accurate information. Yet experimental researchers who know that demand characteristics can invalidate an experiment may not give subjects complete information about the nature and purpose of the study. Simply put, experimenters often intentionally hide the true purpose of their experiments from the subjects. **Debriefing** is the process of providing subjects with all the pertinent facts about the nature and purpose of the experiment after the experiment has been completed.

debriefing
The process of providing subjects with all pertinent facts about the nature and purpose of an experiment after its completion.

Debriefing subjects involved in the experiment by communicating the purpose of the experiment and the researcher's hypotheses about the nature of consumer behaviour is expected to counteract negative effects of deception, relieve stress, and provide an educational experience for the subject.

> Proper debriefing allows the subject to save face by uncovering the truth for himself. The experimenter should begin by asking the subject if he has any questions or if he found any part of the experiment odd, confusing, or disturbing. This question provides a check on the subject's suspiciousness and effectiveness of manipulations. The experimenter continues to provide the subject cues to the deception until the subject states that he believes there was more to the experiment than met the eye. At this time the purpose and procedure of the experiment [are] revealed.[9]

Researchers debrief subjects when there has been clear-cut deception or when they fear subjects may have suffered psychological harm in participating in an experiment (a rarity in marketing research). However, if the researcher does not foresee potentially harmful consequences in participation, he or she may omit debriefing because of time and cost considerations.

AN EXTREME EXAMPLE OF LACK OF DEBRIEFING

In an experiment conducted in a natural setting, independent food merchants in a number of Dutch towns were brought together for group meetings, in the course of which they were informed that a large organization was planning to open up a series of supermarkets in the Netherlands.[10] Subjects in the High Threat condition were told that there was a high probability that their town would be selected as a site for such markets and that the advent of these markets would cause a considerable drop in their business. On the advice of the executives of the shopkeepers' organizations, who had helped to arrange the group meetings, the investigators did not reveal the experimental manipulations to their subjects.

One cannot help but worry about the Dutch merchants involved in the study. Did some of them go out of business in anticipation of the heavy competition? Do some of them have an anxiety reaction every time they see a bulldozer?

Chances are that they soon forgot about this threat (unless, of course, supermarkets actually did move into town) and that it became just one of the many little moments of anxiety that must occur in every shopkeeper's life.

Do we have a right, however, to add to life's little anxieties and to risk the possibility of more extensive anxiety purely for the purposes of our experiments, particularly since deception deprives the subjects of the opportunity to choose whether they wish to expose themselves to the risks that might be entailed?

Another issue that may—but typically does not—arise in marketing experiments is the subject's right to safety from physical and mental harm. Most researchers believe that if the subject's experience may be stressful or cause physical harm, the subject should receive adequate information about this aspect of the experiment *before* agreeing to participate.

FUNDAMENTAL QUESTIONS IN EXPERIMENTATION

Basic versus Factorial Experimental Designs

In *basic experimental designs* a single independent variable is manipulated to observe its effect on a single dependent variable. However, we know that complex marketing dependent variables such as sales, product usage, and preference are influenced by several factors. The simultaneous change in independent variables such as price and advertising may have a greater influence on sales than if either variable is changed alone. *Factorial experimental designs* are more sophisticated than basic experimental designs; they allow for an investigation of the interaction of two or more independent variables.

Field and Laboratory Experiments

A marketing experiment can be conducted in a natural setting (a field experiment) or in an artificial setting—one contrived for a specific purpose (a laboratory experiment). In a **laboratory experiment** the researcher has almost complete control over the research setting. For example, subjects are recruited and brought to an advertising agency's office, a research agency's office, or perhaps a mobile unit designed for research purposes. They are exposed to a television commercial within the context of a program that includes competitors' ads, and they are not interrupted as they view the commercials. They are then allowed to purchase either the advertised

laboratory experiment
An experiment conducted in a laboratory or other artificial setting to obtain almost complete control over the research setting.

product or one of several competing products in a simulated store environment. Trial purchase measures are thus obtained. A few weeks later, subjects are contacted again to measure their satisfaction and determine repeat purchasing intention. This typical laboratory experiment gives the consumer an opportunity to "buy" and "invest." In a short time span, the marketer is able to collect information on decision making.

Another variation of a simulated shopping experiment involves using a representative panel of homemakers who receive a weekly visit at home from a salesperson in a mobile shopping van. This allows the researcher to measure trial, repeat purchase, and buying rates. Prior to the salesperson's visit the subjects are mailed a sales catalogue and an order form that features the products being tested along with all the leading brands and any promotional support that is either current or being tested.

Other laboratory experiments may be more controlled or artificial. For example, a **tachistoscope** allows a researcher to experiment with the visual impact of advertising, packaging, and so on by controlling the amount of time a subject is exposed to a visual image. Each stimulus (for example, package design) is projected from a slide to the tachistoscope at varying exposure lengths (1/10 of a second, 3/10, and so on). The tachistoscope simulates the split-second duration of a customer's attention to a package in a mass display.

Field experiments generally are used to fine-tune marketing strategies and to determine sales volume. For example, Betty Crocker's Squeezit (a 10 percent fruit juice drink in a squeeze bottle) could not keep up with demand in test marketing. The research showed the product's introduction needed to be postponed until production capacity could be increased.

McDonald's conducted a field experiment to test-market Triple Ripple, a three-flavour ice cream product. The product was dropped because the experiment revealed distribution problems reduced product quality and limited customer acceptance. In the distribution system the product would freeze, defrost, and refreeze. Solving the problem would have required each McDonald's city to have a local ice cream plant with special equipment to roll the three flavours into one. A naturalistic setting for the experiment helped McDonald's executives realize the product was impractical.

These examples illustrate that experiments vary in their degree of artificiality. Exhibit 10.2 shows that as experiments increase in naturalism, they begin to approach the pure field experiment, and as they become more artificial, they approach the laboratory type. The degree of artificiality in experiments refers to the amount of manipulation and control of the situation that the experimenter creates to ensure that the subjects will be exposed to the exact conditions desired.

tachistoscope
A device that controls the amount of time a subject is exposed to a visual image.

field experiment
An experiment conducted in a natural setting, where complete control of extraneous variables is not possible.

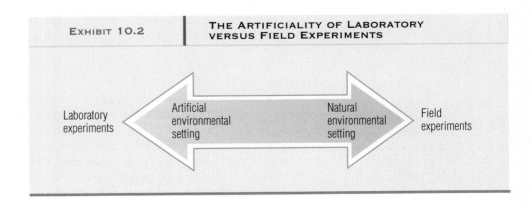

| EXHIBIT 10.2 | THE ARTIFICIALITY OF LABORATORY VERSUS FIELD EXPERIMENTS |

Laboratory experiments — Artificial environmental setting — Natural environmental setting — Field experiments

Generally, subjects know when they are participating in a laboratory experiment. In some situations only field studies are usable because it is not feasible to simulate such things as reactions to a new product by a retailer or a company's sales force. In field experiments, however, the researcher manipulates some variables but cannot control all the extraneous ones. One common hybrid of a laboratory experiment that simulates both a controlled purchasing environment and a test market that provides a natural testing of consumers' reactions is the **controlled store test.** The products are put into stores in a number of small cities or into selected supermarket chains. Product deliveries are made not through the traditional warehouse but by the research agency, so product information remains confidential. A study by News Marketing Canada (NMC) provides an example of a controlled store test. NMC evaluated how brand and category sales were affected by a sweepstakes offer advertised on ad pads that were placed next to a major household product that is sold across Canada by mass merchandisers, grocery stores, and drug outlets. For this study, a test panel of 20 mass-merchandiser outlets was divided into 10 test and 10 control stores. In these stores, all sales and promotion activity in this category were controlled during the 12-week test period. The study revealed that sweepstakes contests advertised via in-store ad pads can dramatically increase product sales for an advertised brand and its entire category.[11]

Controlled store tests offer secrecy, and sales movement and market share can be measured weekly, even daily if desired. However, national sales projections cannot be made; only benchmark sales data can be obtained because of the relatively small sample of stores and the limitations on the type of outlet where the product is tested.

controlled store test
A hybrid between a laboratory experiment and a test market; test products are sold in a small number of selected stores to actual customers.

ISSUES OF EXPERIMENTAL VALIDITY

Experiments are judged by two measures. The first, internal validity, indicates whether the independent variable was the sole cause of the change in the dependent variable. The other, external validity, indicates the extent to which the results of the experiment are applicable to the real world.[12]

Internal Validity

When choosing or evaluating experimental research designs, researchers must determine whether they have *internal validity* and *external validity*. The first has to do with the interpretation of the cause-and-effect relationship in the experiment. **Internal validity** refers to the question of whether the experimental treatment was the sole cause of observed changes in the dependent variable. If the observed results were influenced or confounded by extraneous factors, the researcher will have problems making valid conclusions about the relationship between the experimental treatment and the dependent variable. If the observed results can be unhesitatingly attributed to the experimental treatment, the experiment will be internally valid.

It is helpful to classify several types of extraneous variables that may jeopardize internal validity. The six major ones are *history, maturation, testing, instrumentation, selection,* and *mortality.*

internal validity
Validity determined by whether an experimental treatment was the sole cause of changes in a dependent variable or whether the experimental manipulation did what it was supposed to do.

History

Suppose a before-and-after experiment is being conducted to test a new packaging strategy for an imported Chinese toy. But if the Chinese engage in an anti-Canadian political action that gets considerable media coverage, this action may jeopardize the validity of the experiment because many Canadians may boycott this brand of toy. This is an example of a **history effect,** which refers to specific events in the external environment between the first and second measurements that are beyond the experimenter's control. History effect may also result from changes in

history effect
The loss of internal validity caused by specific events in the external environment, occurring between the first and second measurements, that are beyond the control of the experimenter.

the economic environment (e.g., labour strike). A common history effect occurs when competitors change their marketing strategies during a test marketing experiment.

A special case of the history effect is the **cohort effect,** which refers to a change in the dependent variable that occurs because members of one experimental group experienced different historical situations than members of other experimental groups. For example, two groups of managers used as subjects may be in different cohorts because one group experienced a different history and therefore might behave differently in a workplace experiment.

Maturation

People change over time; that is, they undergo a process of maturation. During the course of an experiment, subjects may mature or change in some way that will have an impact on the results. **Maturation effects** are effects on the results of an experiment caused by changes in experimental subjects over time. They are a function of time rather than of a specific event. For example, during a daylong experiment subjects may grow hungry, tired, or bored. In an experiment over a longer time span, maturation may influence internal validity because subjects grow older or more experienced or change in other ways that may influence the results. For example, suppose an experiment were designed to test the impact of a new compensation program on sales productivity. If this program were tested over a year's time, some of the salespeople probably would mature as a result of more selling experience or perhaps increased knowledge. Their sales productivity might improve because of their knowledge and experience rather than the compensation program.

Testing

Testing effects are also called *pre-testing effects* because the initial measurement or test alerts respondents to the nature of the experiment, causing a change in the validity of the experiment. Respondents may act differently than they would if no pre-test measures were taken. In a before-and-after study, taking a pre-test before the independent variable is manipulated may sensitize respondents when they are taking the test the second time. For example, students taking standardized achievement and intelligence tests for the second time usually do better than those taking the tests for the first time. The effect of testing may increase awareness of socially approved answers, increase attention to experimental conditions (that is, the subject may watch more closely), or make the subject more conscious than usual of the dimensions of a problem.

Instrumentation

Measuring the dependent variable in an experiment requires the use of a questionnaire or other form of measuring instrument. If the identical instrument is used more than once, a testing effect may occur. To avoid the effects of testing, an alternative form of the measuring instrument (for example, a questionnaire or test) may be given as the post-measurement. Although this may reduce the testing effect, it may result in an instrumentation effect because of the change in the measuring instrument.

A change in the wording of questions, a change in interviewers, or a change in other procedures used to measure the dependent variable causes an **instrumentation effect,** which may jeopardize internal validity. For example, if the same interviewers are used to ask questions for both before and after measurement, some problems may arise. With practice, interviewers may acquire increased skill in interviewing, or they may become bored and decide to reword the questionnaire in their own terms. To avoid this problem, new interviewers are hired, but different individuals are also a source of extraneous variation due to instrumentation variation. There are numerous other sources of instrument decay or variation.

Selection

The **selection effect** is a sample bias that results from differential selection of respondents for the comparison groups, or sample selection error, discussed earlier.

Mortality

If an experiment is conducted over a period of a few weeks or more, some sample bias may occur due to **mortality,** or **sample attrition.** Sample attrition occurs when some subjects withdraw from the experiment before it is completed. Mortality effects may occur if many subjects drop from one experimental treatment group and not from other treatment or control groups. Consider a sales training experiment investigating the effects of close supervision of salespeople (high pressure) versus low supervision (low pressure). The high-pressure condition may misleadingly appear superior if those subjects who completed the experiment did very well. If, however, the high-pressure condition caused more subjects to drop out than the other conditions, this apparent superiority may be due to a self-selection bias—perhaps only very determined and/or talented salespeople made it through the end of the experiment.

External Validity

The second type of validity involves the researcher's ability to *generalize* the results of an experiment to the marketplace or the external environment. **External validity** is the ability of an experiment to generalize beyond the data of the experiment to other subjects or groups in the population under study. In essence, determining external validity involves a sampling question: To what extent can the results of a simulated shopping experiment be transferred to real-world supermarket shopping? Will a test market in Thunder Bay, Ontario, be representative of a countrywide introduction of the product under study? Can one extrapolate the results from a tachistoscope to an in-store shopping situation? In other words, the experimental situation may be artificial and may not represent the true setting and conditions in which the investigated behaviour takes place. If the study lacks external validity, the researcher will have difficulty repeating the experiment with different subjects, settings, or time intervals.

If subjects in a shopping mall view a videotape that simulates an actual television program with a test commercial inserted along with other commercials, will the subjects view the commercial just as they would if it were being shown during a regular program? There probably will be some contamination, but the experiment may still be externally valid if the researcher knows how to adjust results from an artificial setting to the marketplace. Comparative norms may be established based on similar, previous studies so that the results can be projected beyond the experiment. If an experiment lacks internal validity, projecting results is not possible. Thus threats to internal validity may jeopardize external validity.

Trade-Offs Between Internal and External Validity

Naturalistic field experiments tend to have greater external validity than artificial laboratory experiments. One of the problems that face the marketing researcher is that often it is necessary to trade off internal validity for external validity because a laboratory experiment provides more control. A researcher who wishes to test advertising effectiveness via a split-cable experiment has the assurance that the advertisement will be viewed in an externally valid situation—that is, in the respondents' homes. However, the researcher has no assurance that some interruption (for example, a telephone call) will not have some influence that will reduce the internal validity of the experiment. Laboratory experiments with many controlled factors usually are high in internal validity, while field experiments generally have less internal validity, but greater external validity.

The design of an experiment may be compared to an architect's plans for a structure, whether a giant skyscraper or a modest home. The basic requirements for the structure are given to the architect by the prospective owner. It is the architect's task to fill these basic requirements; yet the architect has ample room for exercising ingenuity. Several different plans may be drawn up to meet all the basic requirements. Some may be more costly than others; of two plans with the same cost, one may offer potential advantages that the second does not.

There are various types of experimental designs. If only one variable is manipulated, the experiment has a **basic experimental design.** If the experimenter wishes to investigate several levels of the independent variable (for example, four price levels) or to investigate the interaction effects of two or more independent variables, the experiment requires a *complex,* or *statistical,* experimental design.

basic experimental design
An experimental design in which a single independent variable is manipulated to measure its effect on another single dependent variable.

Symbolism for Diagramming Experimental Designs

The work of Campbell and Stanley has helped many students master the subject of basic experimental designs.[13] The following symbols will be used in describing the various experimental designs:

X = exposure of a group to an experimental treatment

O = observation or measurement of the dependent variable; if more than one observation or measurement is taken, subscripts (that is, O_1, O_2, etc.) indicate temporal order[14]

$\boxed{R}$ = random assignment of test units; $\boxed{R}$ symbolizes that individuals selected as subjects for the experiment are randomly assigned to the experimental groups

The diagrams of experimental designs that follow assume a time flow from left to right. Our first example will make this clearer.

Three Examples of Quasi-Experimental Designs

Quasi-experimental designs do not qualify as true experimental designs because they do not adequately control for the problems associated with loss of external or internal validity.

quasi-experimental design
A research design that cannot be classified as a true experiment because it lacks adequate control of extraneous variables.

one-shot design
An after-only design in which a single measure is recorded after the treatment is administered.

One-Shot Design

The **one-shot design,** or *after-only design,* is one of the most commonly used designs in marketing. It is diagrammed as follows:

$$X \quad O_1$$

Suppose that during a very cold winter an automobile dealer finds herself with a large inventory of cars. She decides to experiment with a promotional scheme: offering a free trip to Whistler with every car sold. She experiments with the promotion (X = experimental treatment) and measures sales (O_1 = measurement of sales after the treatment is administered). The dealer is not really conducting a formal experiment; she is just "trying something out."

This one-shot design is a case study of a research project fraught with problems. Subjects or test units participate because of voluntary self-selection or arbitrary assignment, not because of random assignment. The study lacks any kind of comparison or any means of controlling extraneous influences. There should be a measure of what will happen when the test units have not been exposed to X to compare with the measures of when subjects have been exposed to X. Nevertheless, under certain circumstances, even though this design lacks internal validity, it is the only viable choice.

The nature of taste tests or product usage tests may dictate the use of this design. In a blind taste test for Agrinove, a Quebec-based dairy co-op, the new family of Grand Pré milks were favoured and eventually launched. The new milk product lasts at least six months without refrigeration and another 20 days once opened and refrigerated.[15]

One-Group Pre-test–Post-test Design

Suppose a real estate franchiser wishes to provide a training program for franchisees. If it measures subjects' knowledge of real estate selling before (O_1) they are exposed to the experimental treatment (X) and then measures real estate selling knowledge after (O_2) they are exposed to the treatment, the design will be as follows:

$$O_1 \quad X \quad O_2$$

In this example the trainer is likely to conclude that the difference between O_2 and O_1 ($O_2 - O_1$) is the measure of the influence of the experimental treatment. This **one-group pre-test–post-test design** offers a comparison of the same individuals before and after training. Although this is an improvement over the one-shot design, this research still has several weaknesses that may jeopardize internal validity. For example, if the time lapse between O_1 and O_2 was a period of several months, the trainees may have matured as a result of experience on the job (maturation effect). History effects may also influence this design. Perhaps some subjects dropped out of the training program (mortality effect). The effect of testing may also have confounded the experiment. For example, taking a test on real estate selling may have made subjects more aware of their lack of specific knowledge; either during the training sessions or on their own, they may have sought to learn subject material about which they realized they were ignorant.

If the second observation or measure (O_2) of salespersons' knowledge was not an identical test, the research may suffer from the instrumentation effect. If the researcher gave an identical test but had different graders for the before and after measurements, the data may not be directly comparable.

Although this design has a number of weaknesses, it is used frequently in marketing research. Remember, the cost of the research is a consideration in most business situations. While there will be some problems of internal validity, the researcher must always take into account questions of time and cost.

Static Group Design

In the **static group design** each subject is identified as a member of either an experimental group or a control group (for example, exposed or not exposed to a commercial). The experimental group is measured after being exposed to the experimental treatment, and the control group is measured without having been exposed to the experimental treatment:

$$\text{Experimental group: } X \quad O_1$$

$$\text{Control group: } \quad\quad O_2$$

The results of the static group design are computed by subtracting the observed results in the control group from those in the experimental group ($O_1 - O_2$).

A major weakness of this design is its lack of assurance that the groups were equal on variables of interest before the experimental group received the treatment. If the groups were selected arbitrarily by the investigator, or if entry into either group was voluntary, systematic differences between the groups could invalidate the conclusions about the effect of the treatment. For example, suppose a company that manufactures garbage compactors wishes to compare the attitudes of subjects who have used a garbage compactor for the first time with those of subjects who have not. If entry into the groups is voluntary, we might find that the group that receives the use of a garbage compactor might have had some reason for choosing that

one-group pre-test–post-test design
A quasi-experimental design in which the subjects in the experimental group are measured before and after the treatment is administered, but there is no control group.

static group design
An after-only design in which subjects in the experimental group are measured after being exposed to the experimental treatment and the control group is measured without having been exposed to the experimental treatment; no pre-measure is taken.

option (for example, atypical amounts of garbage or poor garbage-collection service). Sample attrition of experimental group members who do not like garbage compactors might also be a source of error.

Random assignment of subjects may minimize problems with group differences. If groups are established by the experimenter rather than existing as a function of some other causation, the static group design is referred to as an *after-only design with control group.*

On many occasions, an after-only design is the only possible option. This is particularly true when conducting use tests for new products or brands. Cautious interpretation and recognition of the design's shortcomings may make this necessary evil quite valuable. For example, Airwick Industries conducted use tests of Carpet Fresh, a rug cleaner and room deodorizer. Experiments with Carpet Fresh, which originally was conceived as a granular product to be sprinkled on the floor before vacuuming, indicated that people were afraid the granules would lodge under furniture. This research led to changing the texture of the product to a powdery form.

Three Better Experimental Designs

In a formal, scientific sense, the three designs just discussed are not true experimental designs. Subjects for the experiments were not selected from a common pool of subjects and randomly assigned to one group or another. In the following discussion of three basic experimental designs, the symbol R to the left of the diagram indicates that the first step in a true experimental design is the randomization of subject assignment.

Pre-test–Post-test Control Group Design (Before–After with Control)

The **pre-test–post-test control group design,** or *before–after with control group design,* is the classic experimental design:

$$\text{Experimental group: } \boxed{R} \;\; O_1 \;\; X \;\; O_2$$
$$\text{Control group: } \boxed{R} \;\; O_3 \;\;\;\;\; O_4$$

As the diagram indicates, the subjects in the experimental group are tested before and after being exposed to the treatment. The control group is tested at the same two times as the experimental group, but subjects are not exposed to the experimental treatment. This design has the advantages of the before–after design with the additional advantages gained by its having a control group. The effect of the experimental treatment equals

$$(O_2 - O_1) - (O_4 - O_3)$$

If there is brand awareness among 20 percent of the subjects ($O_1 = 20$ percent, $O_3 = 20$ percent) before an advertising treatment and then 35 percent awareness in the experimental group ($O_2 = 35$ percent) and 22 percent awareness in the control group ($O_4 = 22$ percent) after exposure to the treatment, the treatment effect equals 13 percent:

$$(.35 - .20) - (.22 - .20) = (.15) - (.02) = .13 \text{ or } 13\%$$

The effect of all extraneous variables is assumed to be the same on both the experimental and the control groups. For instance, since both groups receive the pre-test, no difference between them is expected for the pre-test effect. This assumption is also made for effects of other events between the before and after measurements (history), changes within the subjects that occur with the passage of time (maturation), testing effects, and instrumentation effects. In reality there will be some differences in the sources of extraneous variation. Nevertheless, in most cases assuming that the effect is approximately equal for both groups is reasonable.

However, a testing effect is possible when subjects are sensitized to the subject of the research. This is analogous to what occurs when people learn a new vocabulary word. Soon they discover that they notice it much more frequently in their reading. In an experiment the combination of being interviewed on a subject and receiving the experimental treatment might be a potential source of error. For example, a subject exposed to a certain advertising message in a split-cable experiment might say, "Ah, there is an ad about the product I was interviewed about yesterday!" The subject may pay more attention than normal to the advertisement and be more prone to change his or her attitude than in a situation with no interactive testing effects. This weakness in the before–after with control group design can be corrected (see the next two designs).

Testing the effectiveness of television commercials in movie theatres provides an example of the before–after with control group design. Subjects are selected for the experiments by being told that they are going to preview several new television shows. When they enter the theatre, they learn that a drawing for several types of products will be held, and they are asked to complete a product preference questionnaire (see Exhibit 10.3). Then a first drawing is held. Next, the television pilots and commercials are shown. Then the emcee announces additional prizes and a second drawing. Finally, subjects fill out the same questionnaire about prizes. The information from the first questionnaire is the before measurement, and that from the second questionnaire is the after measurement. The control group receives similar

EXHIBIT 10.3	PRODUCT PREFERENCE MEASURE IN AN EXPERIMENT

We are going to give away a series of prizes. If you are selected as one of the winners, which brand from each of the groups listed below would you truly want to win?

Special arrangements will be made for any product for which bulk, or one-time, delivery is not appropriate.

Indicate your answers by filling in the box like this: ■ [box is to be blacked in]

Do not "X," check, or circle the boxes please.

Cookies	Allergy Relief Products
(A 3-month supply, pick ONE.)	(A year's supply, pick ONE.)
NABISCO OREO □ (1)	ALLEREST □ (1)
NABISCO OREO DOUBLE STUFF □ (2)	BENADRYL □ (2)
NABISCO NUTTER BUTTER □ (3)	CONTAC □ (3)
NABISCO VANILLA CREMES □ (4)	TAVIST–D □ (4)
HYDROX CHOCOLATE □ (5)	DRISTAN □ (5)
HYDROX DOUBLES □ (6)	SUDAFED □ (6)
NABISCO COOKIE BREAK □ (7)	CHLOR–TRIMETON □ (7)
NABISCO CHIPS AHOY □ (8)	
KEEBLER E.L. FUDGE □ (9)	
KEEBLER FUDGE CREMES □ (10)	
KEEBLER FRENCH VANILLA CREMES □ (11)	

treatment except that on the day they view the pilot television shows, different (or no) television commercials are substituted for the experimental commercials.

Post-test–Only Control Group Design (After-Only with Control)

In some situations pre-test measurements are impossible. In other situations selection error is not anticipated to be a problem because the groups are known to be equal. The **post-test–only control group design,** or *after-only with control group design,* is diagrammed as follows:

$$\text{Experimental group: } \boxed{R} \quad X \quad O_1$$
$$\text{Control group: } \boxed{R} \qquad \quad O_2$$

The effect of the experimental treatment is equal to $O_2 - O_1$.

Suppose the manufacturer of an athlete's-foot remedy wishes to demonstrate by experimentation that its product is better than a competing brand. No pre-test measure about the effectiveness of the remedy is possible. The design is to randomly select subjects, perhaps students, who have contracted athlete's foot and randomly assign them to the experimental or the control group. With only the post-test measurement, the effects of testing and instrument variation are eliminated. Furthermore, researchers make the same assumptions about extraneous variables described above—that is, that they operate equally on both groups, as in the before–after with control group design.

Solomon Four-Group Design

By combining the pre-test–post-test (before–after) with control group and the post-test–only with control group designs, the **Solomon four-group design** provides a means for controlling the interactive testing effect as well as other sources of extraneous variation. In the following diagram the two Xs symbolize the same experimental treatment given to each experimental: group:

$$\text{Experimental group 1: } \boxed{R} \quad O_1 \quad X \quad O_2$$
$$\text{Control group 1: } \boxed{R} \quad O_3 \qquad \quad O_4$$
$$\text{Experimental group 2: } \boxed{R} \qquad \quad X \quad O_5$$
$$\text{Control group 2: } \boxed{R} \qquad \qquad \quad O_6$$

Although we will not go through the calculations, it is possible to isolate the effects of the experimental treatment and interactive testing in this design. Although this design allows for the isolation of the various effects, it is rarely used in marketing research because of the effort, time, and cost of implementing it. However, it points out that there are ways to isolate or control most sources of variation.

THE NATURE OF TEST MARKETING

Test marketing is an experimental procedure that provides an opportunity to test a new product or a new marketing plan under realistic market conditions to measure sales or profit potential. Cities like London, Ontario, or other small marketing areas are typical settings for field experiments where a new product is distributed and marketed.

The major advantage of test marketing is that no other form of research can beat the real world when it comes to testing actual purchasing behaviour and consumer acceptance of a product. The test marketing of Lighter Choices Menu items by McDonald's Canada, introduced at the beginning of the chapter, is one such example.

Functions of Test Marketing

Test marketing performs two useful functions for management. First, it offers the opportunity to estimate the outcomes of alternative courses of action. Estimates can be made about the optimal advertising expenditures, the need for product sampling, or how advertising and product sampling will interact. Researchers may be able to predict the sales effects of specific marketing variables, such as package design, price, or couponing, and select the best alternative action. Test marketing permits evaluation of the proposed national marketing mix.

A marketing manager for Life-Savers candies vividly portrays this function of experimentation in the marketplace:

> A market test may be likened to an orchestra rehearsal. The violinists have adjusted their strings, the trumpeters have tested their keys, the drummer has tightened his drums. Everything is ready to go. But all these instruments have not worked in unison. So a test market is like an orchestra rehearsal where you can practice with everything together before the big public performance.[16]

With test marketing, not only can a researcher evaluate the outcomes of alternative actions on a product's sales volume; he or she can also investigate the new product's impact on other items within the firm's product line. Test marketing allows a firm to determine whether a new product will cannibalize sales from already profitable company lines. For example, Nabisco has many cracker brands. A new cracker aimed at Saltine users may be a tremendous sales success, but a test market may show that the people who are actually buying it are snack cracker users and the new brand might take sales away from existing brands. Test marketing is the best way to establish market share relationships and to understand the problem of cannibalization.

The second useful function of test market experimentation is that it allows management to identify and correct any weaknesses in either the product or its marketing plan before committing the company to a national sales launch—by which time it normally will be too late to incorporate product modifications and improvements. Thus, if test market results fall short of management's expectations, advertising weights, package sizes, and so on may be adjusted.

For example, McDonald's test-marketed pizza for years in Canada and in the United States. In its first test market, it learned competitors' reactions and the problems associated with offering small, individual-portion pizzas. The product strategy was repositioned, and the product testing shifted to marketing a 14-inch pizza that was not available until late afternoon. The research then focused on how consumers reacted to these pizzas sold in experimental restaurants remodelled to include "Pizza Shoppes," in which employees assembled ingredients on ready-made dough. McDonald's decided to launch pizza nationally in Canada, but not in the United States, in 1992.[17]

Note that just because a product turns out to be a marketing failure does not mean that the test market is a failure; rather, it is a *research success*. Encountering problems in a local testing situation enables management to make adjustments in marketing strategy before national introduction. The managerial experience gained in test marketing, therefore, can be invaluable.

Test Marketing: A Lengthy and Costly Procedure

Test marketing is an expensive research procedure. Developing local distribution, arranging media coverage, and monitoring sales results take considerable effort. It should come as no surprise that this laborious process is costly. Test marketing a packaged-goods product typically costs million of dollars. As with other forms of marketing research, the value of the information must be compared with the costs of the research. However, if a company chooses to forgo test marketing, it runs the risk of losing millions of dollars. Anheuser-Busch's Catalina Blonde beer

DEEP-SIXED BY RECYCLING

When the Pepsi Sixpack, a half-dozen 710 mL fully resealable bottles bound together by a plastic ring, was test-marketed in Estrie, Quebec, consumer response levels were at or above any brand launch by Pepsi-Cola Canada Beverages since 1984. Pepsi claimed that a staggering 93 percent of repeat buyers and 82 percent of buyers said they would purchase the product again. Yet when the Sixpack was introduced to other Canadian provinces in the spring of 1997, it was met with condemnation from environmentalists and municipal officials.

Ontario municipalities are obligated by law to operate Blue Box (recycling) programs. Aluminum cans bring in up to $1,800 a tonne whereas a tonne of PET plastic (from which the Sixpack bottles were made) is worth less than $365. And because the Blue Box program was already operating at a loss, customers did not look favourably upon Pepsi's release of the Sixpack.

The timing of the Sixpack campaign added further problems. As Pepsi Sixpack billboards were going up, an organization called Corporations Supporting Recycling (of which Pepsi was a member) was launching its $1-million "Don't Trash Cans!" campaign. Needless to say, the obvious contradiction helped only to decrease sales of the Sixpack, which is no longer carried by retailers.[18]

(a "superlight" beer targeted at women), Frito-Lay's Max Snax, and Procter & Gamble's Pampers Rash Guard all failed in test markets. However, the mistakes would have been even more costly had the brands immediately been introduced nationally.

The appropriate time period for a test market varies depending on the research objectives. Sometimes, as in Procter & Gamble's testing of its new products Febreze, Dryel, and Fit Fruit & Vegetable Wash, the research takes several years. In other situations, as in Procter & Gamble's testing of Encaprin pain reliever (a product that ultimately failed in distribution), the time period may be shorter. The time required for test marketing also depends on the product; a package of chewing gum is consumed much sooner than a bottle of shampoo. The average length of test markets for grocery and drug packaged goods is ten months.

SELECTING TEST MARKETS: A SAMPLING PROBLEM

 Selecting test markets is for the most part a sampling problem. The researcher wishes to choose a sample of markets that is representative of the population of all cities and towns throughout Canada. Thus test market cities should represent the competitive situation, distribution channels, media usage patterns, product usage, and other relevant factors. Of course, there is no single ideal test market that is a perfect miniature of Canada. Nevertheless, the researcher must avoid cities that are not representative of the country. Regional or urban differences, atypical climates, unusual ethnic compositions, or different lifestyles may dramatically affect a marketing program.

Researchers who wish to select representative test markets have a more complex problem because it may be necessary to use three or four cities. Cities are selected as experimental units, and one or more additional cities may be required as control markets. Thus each of the experimental and control markets should be similar in population size, income, ethnic composition, and so on. Differences in these demographic factors and other characteristics among the experimental or control markets affect the test results. Because of the importance of having representative markets for comparisons, certain cities are used repeatedly for test-market operations.

Calgary, Edmonton, London, Kelowna, Nanaimo, and Winnipeg are all popular test markets, frequently used to test new products or elements of marketing plans because they are geographically isolated from other major cities. Here is how Dave Scholz, vice-president of consumer research firm Leger Marketing, describes Calgary as a test market:

> Marketers look to places where there is population growth and business growth, and both those criteria are available in Calgary. The city provides a well-educated, affluent demographic.[19]

Factors to Consider in Test Market Selection

Obtaining a representative test market requires considering many factors that may not be obvious to the inexperienced researcher. The following factors should be considered in the selection of a test market.

Population Size

The population should be large enough to provide reliable, projectable results, yet small enough to ensure that costs will not be prohibitive. Toronto is not a popular test market; its size makes it unacceptable.

Demographic Composition and Lifestyle Considerations

Ethnic backgrounds, incomes, age distributions, lifestyles, and so on within the market should be representative of the country. For example, test marketing in Quebec may not be representative of English Canada.

Competitive Situation

Competitive market shares, competitive advertising, and distribution patterns should be typical so that test markets will represent other geographic regions. If they are not representative, it will be difficult to project the test-market results to other markets.

Consider the firm that test-markets in one of its strongest markets. Its sales force has an easy time getting trade acceptance but might have difficulty in a market in which the firm is weak. That will influence the acceptance level, the cost of the sell-in (obtaining initial distribution), and the ultimate results of the test market. Hence, projecting the results of the test market into weaker markets becomes difficult. Selecting an area with an unrepresentative market potential may cause innumerable problems. Firms probably should not test Saskatoon berry pies in Saskatchewan.

Media Coverage and Efficiency

Local media (television spots, newspapers) will never exactly replicate national media. However, duplicating the national media plan or using one similar to it is important. Using newspapers' Sunday supplements as a substitute for magazine advertising does not duplicate the national plan, but may provide a rough estimate of the plan's impact. Ideally, a market should be represented by the major television networks, typical cable television programming, and newspaper coverage. Some magazines have regional editions or advertising inserts.

Media Isolation

Advertising in communities outside of the test market may contaminate the test market. Furthermore, advertising money is wasted when it reaches consumers who cannot buy the advertised product because they live outside the test area. Markets

As described in Chapter 1, Procter & Gamble used Canada as a test market for its battery-operated floor cleaning appliance, the Swiffer WetJet, a so-called wet cousin of the popular Swiffer Sweeper, before it was rolled out nationally in September of 2000. According to Christine Kotsopoulos, a public relations manager at Procter & Gamble Canada in Toronto, the reason for selecting Canada as a test market was Canadian consumers' enthusiastic response to the Swiffer Sweeper when it was introduced the year before. Procter & Gamble also launched the WetJet in Belgium a few weeks after its Canadian launch and assessed results from the two test markets before a worldwide rollout.

Heinz also tested its new products in Canada with its $50-million, teen-oriented ketchup campaign. The products were then rolled out worldwide with only minor creative tweaks. "The way teens approached ketchup isn't that different across geographies," said Casey Keller, VP for meal enhancement. "What they did with it wasn't that different." The primary adaptation Heinz and its agency, Leo Burnett, are making when the product moves into 75 countries is to customize the food teens are pouring the ketchup over, whether it be hot dogs, pasta, or hamburgers, depending on primary usage in the local market.

Testing internationally may be cheaper in many cases than testing in the home country and allows companies to test products or ads in relative secrecy, out of sight of less global competitors, which are better equipped to track competitive tests domestically.[20]

such as Winnipeg are highly desirable because advertising does not spill over into other areas.

Self-Contained Trading Area

Distributors should sell primarily or exclusively in the test market area. Shipments in and out of markets from chain warehouses can produce confusing shipping figures. Frito-Lay test-marketed Olean-based versions of Ruffles, Lay's, Doritos, and Tostitos under the Max name in Cedar Rapids, Iowa. However, large amounts of the chips were purchased by droves of consumers in markets far from the test site.[21] Publicity about the no-fat chips had retailers fielding telephone orders from as far away as California, Texas, and New Jersey. Had the company relied solely on shipment information, the plants it built for what became WOW! Chips would have been much larger than needed.

Overused Test Markets

If consumers or retailers become aware of the tests, they will react in a manner different from their norm. Thus it is not a good idea to establish one great test market. Consumers may display atypical reactions to new-product introductions once new-product displays at stores become the norm.

Loss of Secrecy

If a firm delays national introduction of a product to allow time for test marketing, a competitor may find out about the experiment and "read" the results of the test market. The firm, therefore, runs the risk of exposing a new product or its plans to competitors. If the competitor finds the product easy to imitate, it may beat the originating company to the national marketplace. While Clorox Super Detergent with Bleach remained in the test-market stage, Procter & Gamble introduced Tide with Bleach. Fab 1 Shot, a pouch laundry from Colgate-Palmolive, pre-empted Cheer Power Pouches by Procter & Gamble, but P&G wasn't sorry. Fab 1 Shot was

Some companies test-market overseas. Carewell Industries of Fairfield, New Jersey, tested its Dentax toothbrush in Singapore. While Singapore may not represent North America's demographic profile, it allows products to be tested relatively secretly and offers a low-cost environment for launching a new product.

not a commercial success. Although customers tried the new product, they stayed with the more traditional means of doing laundry over the long run.

Not all product introductions are test-marketed. Expensive durables, such as refrigerators, automobiles, and forklift trucks, rarely are test-marketed because of the prohibitive cost of producing a test unit. Many line extensions and me-too products that do not change consumers' usage habits are considered relatively safe bets for national or regional introductions without test marketing. For example, Swatch Olympic-themed watches were introduced without test marketing. Research studies conducted before making the decision to test-market may present findings that leave no doubt in management's minds that everything is right. Other considerations, such as the seasonality of the product, distribution strength, or experience with the product category, may also influence the test-marketing decision.

SUMMARY

Experimental research allows the investigator to control the research situation to evaluate causal relationships among variables. In an experiment, one variable (the independent variable) is manipulated to determine its effect on another (the dependent variable). The alternative manipulations of the independent variable are referred to as *experimental treatments*.

The choice of dependent variable is crucial because this determines the kind of answer given to the research problem. In some situations, deciding on an appropriate operational measure of the dependent variable is difficult.

For experiments, random sampling error is especially associated with selection of subjects and their assignment to the treatments. The best way to overcome this problem is by random assignment of subjects to groups and of groups to treatments.

Other errors may arise from using nonrepresentative populations (for example, college students) as sources of samples or from sample mortality or attrition, the withdrawal of subjects from the experiment before it is completed. In addition, marketing experiments often involve extraneous variables that may affect dependent variables and obscure the effects of independent variables. Experiments may also be affected by demand characteristics when experimenters inadvertently give cues to the desired responses. The guinea pig effect occurs when subjects modify their behaviour because they wish to cooperate with an experimenter.

4 Researchers can control extraneous variables by eliminating them or by holding them constant for all treatments. Some extraneous error may arise from the order of presentation. This can be controlled by counterbalancing the order. Blinding can be used, by keeping subjects ignorant of the treatment they are receiving. Sometimes the blinding is extended to the person who administers the experimental treatment. Finally, random assignment is an attempt to control extraneous variables by chance.

Two main types of marketing experiments are field experiments conducted in natural environments (such as test markets) and laboratory experiments conducted in artificial settings contrived for specific purposes.

5 Experiments are judged by two measures of validity. One is internal validity: whether the independent variable was the sole cause of the change in the dependent variable. Six types of extraneous variables may jeopardize internal validity: history, maturation, testing, instrumentation, selection, and mortality. The second type of validity is external validity, the extent to which the results are applicable to the real world. Field experiments are lower than laboratory experiments on internal validity, but higher on external validity.

6 Experimental designs fall into two groups. A basic design manipulates only one variable. A complex design isolates the effects of extraneous variables or uses more than one treatment (independent variable). Poor basic designs include the one-shot design, the one-group pre-test–post-test design, and the static group design. Better basic designs include the pre-test–post-test control group design, the post-test–only control group design, and the Solomon four-group design.

7 Test marketing is an experimental procedure that provides an opportunity to test a new product or marketing plan under realistic conditions to obtain a measure of sales or profit potential. Its major advantage as a research tool is that it closely approximates reality. Test marketing provides the opportunity to estimate the outcomes of alternative courses of action. It also allows marketers to identify and correct weaknesses in the product or its marketing plan before a full-scale sales launch. Test-market failures can be research successes if they point out the need for such adjustments.

Test marketing is an expensive research procedure; the value of the information gained from test marketing must be compared with the cost. It can also expose the new product to competitive reaction before the product is introduced. Test marketing generally occurs late in the product development process when a high probability of success is predicted.

The test market should allow enough time for consumers to use up the product and make a repeat purchase if they choose to do so. Too short a test period may overstate potential sales because many initial buyers may not repeat their purchases.

8 Selecting test markets is a sampling problem. The researcher wishes to use sample markets that are representative of the whole population. Several factors are important in test-market selection, including population size, demographics, lifestyles, competitive situation, media coverage and efficiency, media isolation, and a self-contained trading area. Researchers should also avoid overuse of particular markets, as people who are aware that a test is going on may alter their purchase behaviour patterns.

Key Terms and Concepts

experiment	control group	randomization
independent variable	dependent variable	matching
experimental treatments	test units	repeated measures
experimental group	random sampling error	constant error

demand characteristics
guinea pig effect
Hawthorne effect
blinding effect
double-blind design
constancy of conditions
debriefing
laboratory experiment
tachistoscope
field experiment

controlled store test
internal validity
history effect
cohort effect
maturation effect
testing effect
instrumentation effect
selection effect
mortality (sample attrition) effect
external validity

basic experimental design
quasi-experimental design
one-shot design
one-group pre-test–post-test design
static group design
pre-test–post-test control group
   design
post-test–only control group design
Solomon four-group design
test marketing

Questions for Review and Critical Thinking

1. Name some independent and dependent variables frequently studied in marketing.
2. A tissue manufacturer that has the fourth-largest market share plans to experiment with a 50-cents-off coupon during November. It plans to measure sales volume (as recorded by store scanners) for November to determine the effectiveness of the coupon. What is the independent variable? The dependent variable? Do you see any problems with the dependent variable?
3. What purpose does the random assignment of subjects serve?
4. In a test of a new coffee, three styrofoam cups labelled A, B, and C are placed before subjects. The subjects are instructed to taste the coffee from each cup. What problems might arise in this situation?
5. What are demand characteristics? Give some examples.
6. Do you think the guinea pig effect is a common occurrence in experiments? Why or why not?
7. How may experimenters control for extraneous variation?
8. Name the type of experiment described in each of the following situations. Evaluate the strengths and weaknesses of each design.
   a. A major petroleum corporation is considering phasing out its premium unleaded gasoline. It selects Vancouver, British Columbia, as an experimental market in which the product might be eliminated and decides to watch product line sales results.
   b. A soft-drink manufacturer puts the same brand of orange drink into two different containers with different designs. Two groups are given a package and asked about the drink's taste. A third group is given the orange drink in an unlabelled package and asked the same question.
   c. An advertising agency pre-tested a television commercial with a portable television set, simulating an actual television program with the test commercial inserted along with other commercials. This program was shown to a focus group, and a group discussion followed.
   d. A manufacturer of a new brand of cat food tested product sampling with a trial-size package versus no sampling and three price levels simultaneously to determine the best market penetration strategy.
9. Provide an example for each of the six major factors that influence internal validity.

10. Consider the following research project conducted by a company to investigate a self-contained heating and lighting source designed to be used during power failures. The product was given to the experimental subjects and they were asked to wait until dark, then turn off their heat and lights and test the product. A few days later, they were telephoned and interviewed about their opinions of the product. Discuss the external and internal validity of this experiment.
11. Name the type of experiment described in each of the following situations. Evaluate the strengths and weaknesses of each design.
   a. A major fast-food corporation is considering a drug-testing program for its counter workers. It selects its largest outlet in Toronto, implements the program, and measures the impact on productivity.
   b. A mass merchandiser conducts an experiment to determine whether a flexible work time program (allowing employees to choose their own work hours between 6 a.m. and 7 p.m.) is better than the traditional working hours (9 a.m. to 5 p.m.) for sales personnel. Each employee in the Calgary office is asked if he or she would like to be in the experimental or the control group. All employees in the Edmonton office remain on the traditional schedule.
12. Evaluate the ethical and research design implications of the following study.

   Sixty-six willing Australian drinkers helped a Federal Court judge decide that Tooheys didn't engage in misleading or deceptive advertising for its 2.2 beer. The beer contains 2.2 percent alcohol, compared to 6 percent for other beers.
   The volunteers were invited to a marathon drinking session after the Aboriginal Legal Service claimed Tooheys' advertising implied beer drinkers could imbibe as much 2.2 as desired without becoming legally intoxicated. Drunken driving laws prohibit anyone with a blood-alcohol level above 0.05 from getting behind the wheel.
   But the task wasn't easy; nor was it all fun. Some couldn't manage to drink in one hour the required 10 "middies," an Aussie term for a beer glass of 10 fluid ounces.
   Thirty-six participants could manage only nine glasses. Four threw up and were excluded; another

two couldn't manage the "minimum" nine glasses and had to be replaced.

Justice J. Beaumont observed that consuming enough 2.2 in an hour to reach the 0.05 level was "uncomfortable and therefore an unlikely process." Because none of the ads mentioned such extreme quantities, he ruled they couldn't be found misleading or deceptive.[22]

13. A nighttime cough relief formula contains alcohol. An alternative formulation contains no alcohol. During the experiment the subjects are asked to try the product in their homes. Alternative formulations are randomly assigned to subjects. No mention of alcohol is given in the instructions to subjects. Is this ethical?

14. A consumer goods marketer conducts an experiment to determine if a new, more ecological package will induce consumers to buy more of its brand than the existing package, which has several layers of packaging. The old package does slightly better than the ecological package. Is it socially responsible to stay with the old package?

15. What are the benefits of test marketing? When is test marketing likely to be conducted? When is it unlikely?

16. Which of the following products or marketing strategies are likely to be test-marketed? Why or why not?
    a. A computerized robot lawn mower
    b. A line of 500 gram servings of vegetarian dishes for senior citizens
    c. A forklift truck
    d. A new brand of eye drops especially for brown-eyed people
    e. A new, heavy-duty KitchenAid mixer
    f. An advertising campaign to get people to drink a cola drink in the morning

17. What measures should be used to project the results of test markets for the following?
    a. A new candy bar
    b. A new solar-powered radio built into sunglasses
    c. A toothpaste's new advertising campaign

Exploring the Internet

1. Go to www.apa.org/releases/ to find press releases about recent experiments. Identify experiments that relate to the methodological issues discussed in this chapter.

2. To learn more about experimental designs, visit William Trochim's Web site at www.socialresearch methods.net/.

CASE 10.1   THE IGA GROCERY STORE

At a family gathering, Dan Kessler, the manager of an IGA grocery store, got into conversation with his brother-in-law, who supervised a large number of data-entry workers at a public utility company. Kessler's brother-in-law mentioned that his company recently had begun programming background music into the data-entry workers' room. As a result, productivity had increased and the number of errors had decreased.

Kessler thought that playing music in a grocery store might have an impact on customers. Specifically, he thought that customers might stay in the store longer if slow, easy-to-listen-to music were played. After some serious thought, he decided he should hire a marketing researcher to design an experiment to test the influence of music tempo on shopper behaviour.

Questions
1. Operationalize the independent variable (that is, specify some way of measuring it).
2. What dependent variables do you think might be important in this study?
3. Develop a hypothesis for each of your dependent variables.

BBDO is a global advertising agency with 290 offices operating in 77 countries worldwide, including Canada.[1] In Canada, for example, BBDO Montreal was behind "Le Lait" advertising campaign in Quebec. BBDO has developed a measuring system to evaluate consumers' emotional responses to advertising.[2] Its Emotional Measurement System is a proprietary technique that uses photographs of actors' faces to help consumers choose their reactions to commercials. Researchers at BBDO believe that the process virtually eliminates the inherent bias in traditional copy testing. With the conventional system, consumers often underestimate their emotional responses because they feel silly putting them into words, and words are subject to varying interpretations. Thus traditional copy tests have tended to measure thoughts rather than feelings and, therefore, have failed to adequately measure emotional responses.

Rather than ask consumers to choose from a simple list or write in their own words, the agency has devised a deck of 53 photos—narrowed down from 1,800—representing what BBDO calls the "universe of emotions." Each features one of six actors with different expressions ranging from happy/playful to disgusted/revolted. The deck covers a total of 26 categories of emotions.

Here's how the system works. As with most copy testing, participants are shown a single commercial or group of spots and then are given a questionnaire to test whether they remembered brand names and copy points. At any point during this process, the researchers hand out the photos. Each person is asked not to write or speak about the spot but to quickly sort through the photos, setting aside any or all that reflect how he or she feels after viewing the commercial.

Innovative techniques such as the Emotional Measurement System have improved the measurement of marketing phenomena. This chapter discusses the basic measurement issues in marketing research. ■

What you will learn in this chapter

1 To know how a researcher might answer the question "What is to be measured?"

2 To define the term *operational definition*.

3 To distinguish among nominal, ordinal, interval, and ratio scales.

4 To understand the need for index or composite measures.

5 To define the three criteria for good measurement.

6 To discuss the various methods for determining reliability.

7 To discuss the various methods for assessing validity.

WHAT IS TO BE MEASURED?

An object, such as the edge of your textbook, can be measured with either side of a ruler (see Exhibit 11.1). Note that one side has inches and the other has centimetres. Thus the scale of measurement varies depending on whether the metric side or the standard side is used. Many measurement problems in marketing research are similar to this ruler with its alternative scales of measurement. Unfortunately, unlike the two edges of the ruler, many measurement scales used in marketing research are not directly comparable.

The first question the researcher must answer is "What is to be measured?" This is not as simple a question as it may at first seem. The definition of the problem, based on exploratory research or managerial judgment, indicates the concept to be investigated (for example, sales performance). However, a precise definition of the concept may require a description of how it will be measured—and frequently there is more than one way to measure a particular concept. For example, if we are conducting research to determine which factors influence a sales representative's performance, we might use a number of measures to indicate a salesperson's success, such as dollar or unit sales volume or share of accounts lost. Furthermore, true measurement of concepts requires a process of precisely assigning scores or numbers to the attributes of people or objects. The purpose of assigning numbers is to convey information about the variable being measured. Hence the key question becomes "On what basis will numbers or scores be assigned to the concept?"

Suppose the task is to measure the height of a boy named Michael. There are a number of ways to do this.

1. We can create five categories:
   (1)   Quite tall for his age
   (2)   Moderately tall for his age
   (3)   About average for his age
   (4)   Moderately short for his age
   (5)   Quite short for his age
   Then we can measure Michael by saying that, because he is moderately tall for his age, his height measurement is 2.

2. We can compare Michael to ten other neighbourhood children. We give the tallest child the rank of 1 and the shortest the rank of 11; Michael's height measurement using this procedure is 4 if he is fourth tallest among the 11 neighbourhood children.

3. We can use some conventional measuring unit such as centimetres and, measuring to the nearest centimetre, designate Michael's height as 137.

4. We can define two categories:
   (1)   A nice height
   (2)   A not-so-nice height
   By our personal standard, Michael's height is a nice height, so his height measurement is 1.[3]

In each measuring situation, a score has been assigned for Michael's height (2, 4, 137, and 1). In scientific marketing research, however, precision is the goal. These various scores have differing precision. The researcher must determine the best way to measure what is to be investigated.

On college campuses, girl or boy watching constitutes a measurement activity: What might be a 7 to one person may be a 9 to another. Precise measurement in marketing research requires a careful conceptual definition, an operational definition, and a system of consistent rules for assigning numbers or scores.

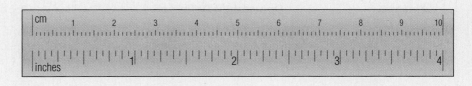

Concepts

concept
A generalized idea about a class of objects, attributes, occurrences, or processes.

Before the measurement process can occur, a marketing researcher must identify the concepts relevant to the problem. A **concept** (or construct) is a generalized idea about a class of objects, attributes, occurrences, or processes. Concepts such as *age, sex,* and *number of children* are relatively concrete properties, and they present few problems in definition or measurement. Other characteristics of individuals or properties of objects may be more abstract. Concepts such as *brand loyalty, personality, channel power,* and so on are more difficult to define and measure. For example, *brand loyalty* has been measured using the percentage of a person's purchases going to one brand in a given period of time, sequences of brand purchases, number of different brands purchased, amount of brand deliberation, and various cognitive measures, such as attitude toward a brand.

Operational Definitions

Concepts must be made operational in order to be measured. An operational definition gives meaning to a concept by specifying the activities or operations necessary to measure it.[4] For example, the concept of nutrition consciousness might be reflected when a shopper reads the nutritional information on a cereal package. Inspecting a nutritional label is not the same as being nutrition conscious, but it is a clue that a person *may* be nutrition conscious.

The operational definition specifies what the researcher must do to measure the concept under investigation. If we wish to measure consumer interest in a specific advertisement, we may operationally define interest as a certain increase in pupil dilation. Another operational definition of interest might rely on direct responses: what people *say* they are interested in. Each operational definition has advantages and disadvantages.

conceptual definition
A verbal explanation of the meaning of a concept. It defines what the concept is and what it is not.

operational definition
An explanation that gives meaning to a concept by specifying the activities or operations necessary to measure it.

An operational definition is like a manual of instructions or a recipe: Even the truth of a statement like "Gaston Gourmet likes key lime pie" depends on the recipe. Different instructions lead to different results.[5]

An operational definition tells the investigator, "Do such-and-such in so-and-so manner."[6] Exhibit 11.2 presents a **conceptual definition** and an **operational definition** from a study on media scepticism.

RULES OF MEASUREMENT

A *rule* is a guide that tells someone what to do. An example of a measurement rule might be "Assign the numerals 1 through 7 to individuals according to how brand loyal they are. If the individual is extremely brand loyal, assign a 7. If the individual is a total brand switcher with no brand loyalty, assign the numeral 1."

Operational definitions help the researcher specify the rules for assigning numbers. If the purpose of an advertising experiment is to increase the amount of time shoppers spend in a department store, for example, *shopping time* must be

EXHIBIT 11.2 | MEDIA SCEPTICISM: AN OPERATIONAL DEFINITION[7]

Concept	Conceptual Definition	Operational Definition
Media scepticism	Media scepticism is the degree to which individuals are sceptical of the reality presented in the mass media. Media scepticism varies across individuals, from those who are mildly sceptical and accept most of what they see and hear in the media to those who completely discount and disbelieve the facts, values, and portrayal of reality in the media.	Please tell me how true each statement is about the media. Is it very true, not very true, or not at all true? 1. The program was not very accurate in its portrayal of the problem. 2. Most of the story was staged for entertainment purposes. 3. The presentation was slanted and unfair. 4. I think the story was fair and unbiased. 5. I think important facts were purposely left out of the story. Individual items were scored on a 3-point scale with values from 1 to 3; higher scores represented greater scepticism. Media scepticism is defined as the sum of these five scores.

operationally defined. Once *shopping time* is defined as the interval between entering the door and receiving the receipt from the clerk, assignment of numbers via a stopwatch is facilitated. If a study on gasohol, a blend of ethyl alcohol and gasoline, is not concerned with a person's depth of experience, but classifies people as users or nonusers, it could assign a 1 for experience with gasohol and a 0 for no experience with gasohol.

The values assigned in the measuring process can be manipulated according to certain mathematical rules. The properties of the scale of numbers may allow the researcher to add, subtract, or multiply answers. In some cases there may be problems with the simple addition of the numbers, or other mathematical manipulations may not be permissible.

TYPES OF SCALES

scale
Any series of items that are arranged progressively according to value or magnitude; a series into which an item can be placed according to its quantification.

A **scale** may be defined as any series of items that are arranged progressively according to value or magnitude, into which an item can be placed according to its quantification.[8] In other words, a scale is a continuous spectrum or series of categories. The purpose of scaling is to represent, usually quantitatively, an item's, person's, or event's place in the spectrum.

Marketing researchers use many scales or number systems. It is traditional to classify scales of measurement on the basis of the mathematical comparisons that are allowable with them. The four types of scale are the nominal, ordinal, interval, and ratio scales.

Nominal Scale

nominal scale
A scale in which the numbers or letters assigned to objects serve as labels for identification or classification.

Number 12 on the Calgary Flames is Jarome Iginla; Todd Bertuzzi is number 44 on the Vancouver Canucks. These numbers nominally identify these superstars. A **nominal scale** is the simplest type of scale. The numbers or letters assigned to objects serve as labels for identification or classification. These are scales in name only. An example of a typical nominal scale in marketing research would be the coding of males as 1 and females as 2. As another example, the first drawing in Exhibit 11.3 depicts

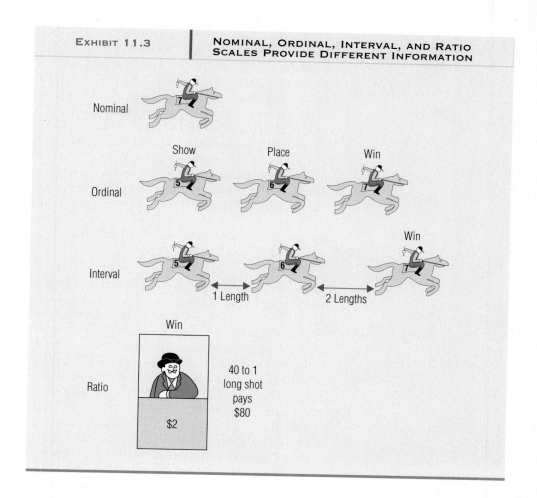

the number 7 on a horse's colours. This is merely a label to allow bettors and racing enthusiasts to identify the horse.

Ordinal Scale

ordinal scale
A scale that arranges objects or alternatives according to their magnitude in an ordered relationship.

If you've been to the racetrack, you know that when your horse finishes in the "show" position, it has come in third behind the "win" and the "place" horses (see the second drawing in Exhibit 11.3). An **ordinal scale** arranges objects or alternatives according to their magnitude in an ordered relationship. When respondents are asked to *rank order* their shopping centre preferences, they assign ordinal values to them. In our racehorse example, if we assign 1 to the win position, 2 to the place position, and 3 to the show position, we can say that 1 was before 2 and 2 was before 3. However, we cannot say anything about the degree of distance or the interval between the win and show horses or the show and place horses.

A typical ordinal scale in marketing asks respondents to rate brands, companies, and the like as excellent, good, fair, or poor. Researchers know excellent is higher than good, but they do not know by how much.

Interval Scale

interval scale
A scale that both arranges objects according to their magnitudes and distinguishes this ordered arrangement in units of equal intervals.

The third drawing in Exhibit 11.3 depicts a horse race in which the win horse is two lengths ahead of the place horse, which is one length ahead of the show horse. Not only is the order of finish known, but the distance between the horses is known. (The example assumes a standard measurement for the term *length*.) **Interval scales** not only indicate order, but they also measure order (or distance) in units of equal intervals.

The location of the zero point is arbitrary. In the Consumer Price Index, if the base year is 1993, the price level during 1993 will be set at 100. Although this is an equal-interval measurement scale, the zero point is arbitrary. The classic example of an interval scale is the Celsius temperature scale. If the temperature is 46°C, it cannot be said that it is twice as hot as 23°C, because 0°C represents not the lack of temperature, but a relative point on the Celsius scale (the freezing point of water). Due to the lack of an absolute zero point, an interval scale does not allow the conclusion that the number 36 is three times as great as the number 12, but only that the distance is three times as great. Likewise, when an interval scale is used to measure psychological attributes, the researcher can comment about the magnitude of differences or compare the average differences on the attributes that were measured, but cannot determine the actual strength of the attitude toward an object. However, the changes in concepts over time can be compared if the researcher continues to use the same scale in longitudinal research.

Ratio Scale

To be able to say that winning tickets pay 40 to 1 or that racehorse number 7 is twice as heavy as racehorse number 5, we need a ratio scale (see the fourth drawing in Exhibit 11.3). **Ratio scales** have absolute rather than relative quantities. For example, both money and weight are measured with ratio scales that possess absolute zeros and interval properties. The absolute zero represents a point on the scale at which there is an absence of the given attribute. If we hear that a person has zero ounces of gold, we understand the natural zero value for weight. In the measurement of temperature, the Kelvin scale (a ratio scale) begins at absolute zero, a point that corresponds to −273.16° on the Celsius scale (an interval scale). In distribution or logistical research it may be appropriate to think of physical attributes such as weight or distance as ratio scales in which the ratio of scale values is meaningful. For most behavioural marketing research, however, interval scales typically are the appropriate measurements. However, if a researcher wishes to construct ratios derived from the original scales, the scale of measurement must be ratio.

Mathematical and Statistical Analysis of Scales

The type of scale used in marketing research will determine the form of the statistical analysis. For example, certain operations, such as calculation of a mean (mathematical average), can be conducted only if the scale is of an interval or ratio nature; they are not permissible with nominal or ordinal scales.

Exhibit 11.4 shows the appropriate descriptive statistics for each type of scale. The most sophisticated form of statistical analysis for nominal scale data is counting. Because numbers in such a scale are merely labels for classification purposes, they have no quantitative meaning. The researcher tallies the frequency in each category and identifies which category contains the highest number of observations (individuals, objects, etc.). An ordinal scale provides data that may be rank ordered from lowest to highest. Observations may be associated with percentile ranks such as the median. Because all statistical analyses appropriate for lower-order scales are suitable for higher-order scales, an interval scale may be used as a nominal scale to uniquely classify or as an ordinal scale to preserve order. In addition, an interval scale's property of equal intervals allows researchers to compare differences among scale values and perform arithmetic operations such as addition and subtraction. Numbers may be changed, but the numerical operations must preserve order and relative magnitudes of differences. The mean and standard deviation may be calculated from true interval-scale data. A ratio scale has all the properties of nominal, ordinal, and interval scales. In addition, it allows researchers to compare absolute magnitudes because the scale has an absolute zero point. Using the actual quantities for arithmetic operations is permissible. Thus the ratios of scale values are meaningful.

Chapters 17 and 18 further explore the limitations scales impose on the mathematical analysis of data.

ratio scale
A scale that has absolute rather than relative quantities and an absolute zero where there is an absence of a given attribute.

TO THE POINT

When you can measure what you are talking about and express it in numbers, you know something about it.

WILLIAM THOMPSON, LORD KELVIN

EXHIBIT 11.4	DESCRIPTIVE STATISTICS FOR TYPES OF SCALES	
Type of Scale	**Numerical Operation**	**Descriptive Statistics**
Nominal	Counting	Frequency in each category Percentage in each category Mode
Ordinal	Rank ordering	Median Range Percentile ranking
Interval	Arithmetic operations that preserve order and relative magnitudes	Mean Standard deviation Variance
Ratio	Arithmetic operations on actual quantities	Geometric mean Coefficient of variation

Note: All statistics appropriate for lower-order scales (nominal being the lowest) are appropriate for higher-order scales (ratio being the highest).

INDEX MEASURES

attribute
A single characteristic or fundamental feature of an object, person, situation, or issue.

index (or composite) measure
A composite measure of several variables used to measure a single concept; a multi-item instrument.

So far we have focused on measuring a concept with a single question or observation. Measuring brand awareness, for example, might involve one question, such as "Are you aware of ———?" However, measuring more complex concepts may require more than one question because the concept has several attributes. An **attribute** is a single characteristic or fundamental feature of an object, person, situation, or issue.

Multi-item instruments for measuring a single concept with several attributes are called **index measures,** or **composite measures.** For example, one index of social class is based on three weighted variables: residence, occupation, and education. Measures of cognitive phenomena often are composite indexes of sets of variables or scales. Items are combined into composite measures. For example, a salesperson's morale may be measured by combining questions such as "How satisfied are you with your job? How satisfied are you with your territory? How satisfied are you in your personal life?" Measuring the same underlying concept using a variety of techniques is one method for increasing accuracy. Asking different questions to measure the same concept provides a more accurate cumulative measure than does a single-item estimate.

THREE CRITERIA FOR GOOD MEASUREMENT

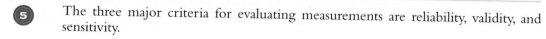

The three major criteria for evaluating measurements are reliability, validity, and sensitivity.

Reliability

reliability
The degree to which measures are free from random error and therefore yield consistent results.

A tailor measuring fabric with a tape measure obtains a "true" value of the fabric's length. If the tailor repeatedly measures the fabric and each time comes up with the same length, it is assumed that the tape measure is reliable. When the outcome of the measuring process is reproducible, the measuring instrument is reliable. Reliability applies to a measure when similar results are obtained over time and across situations. Broadly defined, **reliability** is the degree to which measures are free from random error and therefore yield consistent results. For example, ordinal measures are reliable if they consistently rank order items in the same manner; reliable interval measures consistently rank order and maintain the same distance between items. Imperfections in the measuring process that affect the assignment of scores or numbers in different ways each time a measure is taken, such as when a respondent misunderstands a question, cause low reliability. The actual choice among plausible responses may be governed by such transitory factors as mood, whim, or the context set by surrounding questions; measures are not always error-free and stable over time.

There are two dimensions underlying the concept of reliability: *repeatability* and *internal consistency*. Assessing the *repeatability* of a measure is the first aspect of gauging reliability. The **test-retest method** of determining reliability involves administering the same scale or measure to the same respondents at two separate times to test for stability. If the measure is stable over time, the test, administered under the same conditions each time, should obtain similar results. For example, suppose a researcher at one time attempts to measure buying intentions and finds that 12 percent of the population is willing to purchase a product. If the study is repeated a few weeks later under similar conditions and the researcher again finds that 12 percent of the population is willing to purchase the product, the measure appears to be reliable. The high stability correlation or consistency between the two measures at time 1 and time 2 indicates a high degree of reliability.

As an example at the individual (rather than the aggregate) level, assume that a person does not change his or her attitude about Alexander Keith's, a beer from Nova Scotia. If repeated measurements of that individual's attitude toward Alexander Keith's are taken with the same attitude scale, a reliable instrument will produce the same results each time the attitude is measured. When a measuring instrument produces unpredictable results from one testing to the next, the results are said to be unreliable because of error in measurement.

As another example, consider these remarks by a Gillette executive made about the reliability problems in measuring reactions to razor blades:

> There is a high degree of noise in our data, a considerable variability in results. It's a big mish mash, what we call the night sky in August. There are points all over the place. A man will give a blade a high score one day, but the next day he'll cut himself a lot and give the blade a terrible score. But on the third day, he'll give the same blade a good score. What you have to do is try to see some pattern in all this. There are some gaps in our knowledge.[9]

Measures of test–retest reliability pose two problems that are common to all longitudinal studies. First, the pre-measure, or first measure, may sensitize the respondents to their participation in a research project and subsequently influence the results of the second measure. Furthermore, if the time between measures is long, there may be an attitude change or other maturation of the subjects. Thus a reliable measure can indicate a low or a moderate correlation between the first and second administration, but this low correlation may be due to an attitude change over time rather than to a lack of reliability.

The second underlying dimension of reliability concerns the homogeneity of the measure. An attempt to measure an attitude may require asking several similar (but not identical) questions or presenting a battery of scale items. To measure the *internal consistency* of a multiple-item measure, scores on subsets of the items within the scale must be correlated.

The technique of splitting halves is a basic method of checking internal consistency when a measure contains a large number of items. In the **split-half method** the researcher may take the results obtained from one half of the scale items (for example, out of eight items, one half can be the odd-numbered items) and check them against the results from the other half (even-numbered items).

As you can imagine, in the split-half method, the correlation depends on how the items are split. You can have different correlations depending on the split of the items. A commonly used method that overcomes this problem is to calculate Cronbach's alpha (α). Cronbach's alpha (α) is mathematically equivalent to the average of all

test-retest method
Administering the same scale or measure to the same respondents at two separate points in time to test for stability.

split-half method
A method for assessing internal consistency by checking the results of one-half of a set of scaled items against the results from the other half.

possible random split-half correlations. As in the previous paragraph, assume that we calculated one correlation based on the split-half method where our two halves are items {1, 3, 5, 7} and items {2, 4, 6, 8}. We can calculate another split-half correlation for a different split: items {1, 2, 3, 4} and items {5, 6, 7, 8}. If we keep dividing our items into all possible halves and calculated split-half correlations and took the average of these correlations, this number corresponds to Cronbach's alpha (α). The mathematical calculation of Cronbach's alpha is different and shorter. A Cronbach's alpha (α) value closer to 1 indicates higher reliability.

equivalent-form method
A method that measures the correlation between alternative instruments, designed to be as equivalent as possible, administered to the same group of subjects.

The **equivalent-form method** is used when two alternative instruments are designed to be as equivalent as possible. The two measurement scales are administered to the same group of subjects. A high correlation between the two forms suggests that the scale is reliable. However, a low correspondence between the two instruments creates a problem. The researcher will be uncertain whether the measure has intrinsically low reliability or whether the particular equivalent form has failed to be similar to the other form. Both the equivalent-form and the split-half approaches to measuring reliability assume that the concept being measured is unidimensional; they measure homogeneity or inter-item consistency, rather than stability over time.

Reliability is a necessary condition for validity, but a reliable instrument may not be valid. For example, a purchase intention measurement technique may consistently indicate that 20 percent of those sampled are willing to purchase a new product. Whether the measure is valid depends on whether 20 percent of the population indeed purchases the product. A reliable but invalid instrument will yield consistently inaccurate results.

Validity

The purpose of measurement is to measure what we intend to measure. Achieving this obvious goal is not, however, as simple as it sounds. Consider the student who takes a test (measurement) in a statistics class and receives a poor grade. The student may say, "I really understood that material because I studied hard. The test measured my ability to do arithmetic and to memorize formulas rather than measuring my understanding of statistics." The student's complaint is that the test did not measure understanding of statistics, which was what the professor had intended to measure; it measured something else.

One method of measuring the intention to buy is the gift method. Respondents are told that a drawing will be held at some future period for a year's supply of a certain product. Respondents report which of several brands they would prefer to receive if they were to win. Do the respondents' reports of the brands they would prefer to win necessarily constitute a valid measure of the brands they will actually purchase in the marketplace if they do not win the contest? Could there be a systematic bias to identify brands they wish they could afford rather than the brands they would usually purchase? This is a question of **validity.**

validity
The ability of a scale to measure what was intended to be measured.

Another example of a validity question might involve a media researcher who wonders what it means when respondents indicate they have been *exposed* to a magazine. The researcher wants to know if the measure is valid. The question of validity expresses the researcher's concern with accurate measurement. Validity addresses the problem of whether a measure (for example, an attitude measure used in marketing) indeed measures what it is supposed to measure; if it does not, there will be problems.

Students should be able to empathize with the following validity problem. Consider the controversy about police officers using radar guns to clock speeders. A driver is clocked at 130 km/h in a 100 km/h zone, but the same radar gun aimed at a house registers 28 km/h. The error occurred because the radar gun had picked up impulses from the electrical system of the squad car's idling engine. The house wasn't speeding—and the test was not valid.

Establishing Validity

Researchers have attempted to assess validity in many ways. They attempt to provide some evidence of a measure's degree of validity by answering a variety of questions. Is there a consensus among my colleagues that my attitude scale measures what it is supposed to measure? Does my measure correlate with other measures of the same concept? Does the behaviour expected from my measure predict actual observed behaviour? The three basic approaches to establishing validity are face or content validity, criterion validity, and construct validity.

face (or content) validity
Professional agreement that a scale's content logically appears to accurately reflect what was intended to be measured.

Face, or **content, validity** refers to the subjective agreement among professionals that a scale logically appears to accurately reflect what it purports to measure. The content of the scale appears to be adequate. When it appears evident to experts that the measure provides adequate coverage of the concept, that measure has face validity. Clear, understandable questions such as "How many children do you have?" generally are agreed to have face validity. In scientific studies, however, researchers generally prefer stronger evidence because of the elusive nature of attitudes and other marketing phenomena. For example, the AC Nielsen television rating system is based on the PeopleMeter system, which mechanically records whether a sample household's television is turned on and records the channel selection. If one of the viewers leaves the room or falls asleep, the measure is not a valid measure of audience.

criterion validity
The ability of a measure to correlate with other standard measures of the same construct or established criterion.

Researchers who wish to establish **criterion validity** attempt to answer the question "Does my measure correlate with other measures of the same construct?" Consider the physical concept of *length*. Length can be measured with tape measures, calipers, odometers, and other variations of the ruler. If a new measure of length were developed (for example, through laser technology), finding that the new measure correlated with the other measures of length (the criteria) could provide some assurance that the new measure was valid. Criterion validity may be classified as either concurrent validity or predictive validity depending on the time sequence in which the new measurement scale and the criterion measure are correlated. If the new measure is taken at the same time as the criterion measure and is shown to be valid, then it has *concurrent validity. Predictive validity* is established when a new measure predicts a future event. The two measures differ only on the basis of a time dimension—that is, the criterion measure is separated in time from the predictor measure.

A practical example of predictive validity is illustrated by a commercial research firm's test of the relationship between a rough commercial's effectiveness (as determined, for example, by recall scores) and a finished commercial's effectiveness (also by recall scores). Ad agencies often test animatic rough, photomatic rough, or live-action rough commercials before developing actual finished commercials. One marketing research consulting firm suggests that this testing has high predictive validity. Rough commercial recall scores provide correct estimates of the final finished commercial recall scores more than 80 percent of the time.[11] While face (content) validity is a subjective evaluation, criterion validity provides a more rigorous empirical test.

construct validity
The ability of a measure to provide empirical evidence consistent with a theory based on the concepts.

Construct validity is established by the degree to which the measure confirms a network of related hypotheses generated from a theory based on the concepts. Construct validity is established during the statistical analysis of the data. Construct validity implies that the empirical evidence generated by a measure is consistent with the theoretical logic behind the concepts. In its simplest form, if the measure behaves the way it is supposed to in a pattern of intercorrelation with a variety of other variables, there is evidence of construct validity. For example, a consumer researcher developed a personality scale intended to measure several interpersonal response traits that management theorists previously had related to occupational preference. Testing the new scale against occupational preference would be a way to establish evidence of construct validity. This is a complex method of establishing validity and of less concern to the applied researcher than to the basic researcher.

Reliability versus Validity

Let us compare the concepts of reliability and validity. A tailor using a ruler may obtain a reliable measurement of length over time with a bent ruler. A bent ruler cannot provide perfect accuracy, however, and it is not a valid measure. Thus reliability, although necessary for validity, is not sufficient by itself. In marketing, a measure of a subject's physiological reaction to a package (for example, pupil dilation) may be highly reliable, but it will not necessarily constitute a valid measure of purchase intention.

The differences between reliability and validity can be illustrated by the archery targets in Exhibit 11.5. Suppose an expert archer from the Federation of Canadian Archers shoots an equal number of arrows using a century-old traditional bow and a modern Olympic recurve bow.[12] The arrows from the old bow (Target A) are considerably scattered, but those from the modern bow are closely clustered (Target B). The variability of the old bow compared with that of the new one indicates it is less reliable. Target B in the middle illustrates the concept of a systematic bias influencing validity. The modern bow is reliable (because it has little variance), but the archer's vision is hampered by glare from the sun. Although shots are consistent, the archer is unable to hit the bull's-eye. The shots on the far right target (Target C) are closely clustered and the archer is able to hit the bull's-eye, illustrating high reliability and validity.

Sensitivity

The sensitivity of a scale is an important measurement concept, particularly when *changes* in attitudes or other hypothetical constructs are under investigation. **Sensitivity** refers to an instrument's ability to accurately measure variability in stimuli or responses. A dichotomous response category, such as "agree or disagree," does

sensitivity
A measurement instrument's ability to accurately measure variability in stimuli or responses.

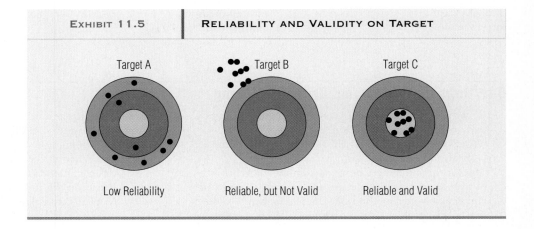

EXHIBIT 11.5 | RELIABILITY AND VALIDITY ON TARGET

Target A — Low Reliability
Target B — Reliable, but Not Valid
Target C — Reliable and Valid

not allow the recording of subtle attitude changes. A more sensitive measure with numerous categories on the scale may be needed. For example, adding "strongly agree," "mildly agree," "neither agree nor disagree," "mildly disagree," and "strongly disagree" will increase the scale's sensitivity.

The sensitivity of a scale based on a single question or single item can also be increased by adding questions or items. In other words, because index measures allow for a greater range of possible scores, they are more sensitive than single-item scales.

SUMMARY

  Marketing research problems often require the choice of an appropriate measuring system. The concept to be measured must be given an operational definition that specifies how it will be measured. There are four types of measuring scales. Nominal scales assign numbers or letters to objects only for identification or classification. Ordinal scales arrange objects or alternatives according to their magnitudes in an ordered relationship. Interval scales measure order (or distance) in units of equal intervals. Ratio scales are absolute scales, starting with absolute zeros at which there is a total absence of the attribute. The type of scale determines the form of statistical analysis to use.

 Index (composite) measures often are used to measure complex concepts with several attributes. Asking several questions may yield a more accurate measure than basing measurement on a single question.

 Measuring instruments are evaluated by reliability, validity, and sensitivity. *Reliability* refers to the measuring instrument's ability to provide consistent results in repeated uses. *Validity* refers to the degree to which the instrument measures the concept the researcher wants to measure. *Sensitivity* is the instrument's ability to accurately measure variability in stimuli or responses.

 Reliability may be tested using the test-retest method, the split-half method, or the equivalent-form method. The three basic approaches to evaluating validity are to establish content validity, to establish criterion validity, or to establish construct validity. The sensitivity of a scale can be increased by allowing for a greater range of possible scores.

Key Terms and Concepts

concept
operational definition
conceptual definition
scale
nominal scale
ordinal scale
interval scale

ratio scale
attribute
index (or composite) measure
reliability
test-retest method
split-half method
equivalent-form method

validity
face (or content) validity
criterion validity
construct validity
sensitivity

Questions for Review and Critical Thinking

1. What is the difference between a conceptual definition and an operational definition?
2. What descriptive statistics are allowable with nominal, ordinal, and interval scales?
3. Discuss the differences between validity and reliability.
4. What measurement problems might be associated with the PeopleMeter method of audience ratings? Would any special problem arise in rating children's programs?

5. Why might a researcher wish to use more than one question to measure satisfaction with a particular aspect of retail shopping?
6. Indicate whether the following measures use a nominal, ordinal, interval, or ratio scale:
   a. Prices on the stock market
   b. Marital status, classified as "married" or "never married"

c. Whether a respondent has ever been unemployed

d. Professorial rank: assistant professor, associate professor, or professor

e. Grades: A, B, C, D, or F

7. Comment on the validity and reliability of the following:

a. A respondent's report of an intention to subscribe to *Canadian Business* is highly reliable. A researcher believes this constitutes a valid measurement of dissatisfaction with the economic system and alienation from big business.

b. A general-interest magazine claimed that it was a better advertising medium than television programs with similar content. Research had indicated that for a soft drink and other test products, recall scores were higher for the magazine ads than for 30-second commercials.

c. A respondent's report of frequency of magazine reading consistently indicates that she regularly reads *Canadian House and Home* and *GardenWise* and never reads *Chatelaine*.

8. Define each of the following concepts, and then operationally define each one:

a. A good bowler

b. Television audience for *This Hour Has 22 Minutes*

c. Purchasing intention for a palm-sized computer

d. Consumer involvement with cars

e. A workaholic

f. Fast-food restaurant

9. Many Internet surveys want to know the demographic characteristics of their respondents and how technologically sophisticated they are. Create a conceptual definition of "technographics" and operationalize it.

10. Two academic researchers create a psychographic scale to measure travel behaviour. Without measuring reliability or validity of the measuring instrument, they submit an article to a scholarly publication for review. Comment on the ethics of this situation.

Exploring the Internet

1. The Office of Scale Research (OSR) is part of the Department of Marketing at Southern Illinois University at Carbondale. The OSR Web site provides a number of technical reports that deal with a wide variety of scaling issues. Go to www.siu.edu/departments/coba/osr/ and select an article from the reading list. What types of scales are listed?

2. A measure of procrastination can be found at www.queendom.com/tests/minitests/procrastination_short_access.html. Take this "test." Do you think this is a reliable and valid measure?

Campbell's Soup Company and *People* magazine hired Lieberman Research Incorporated to investigate the male food shopper. The following statement indicates the broad research objectives for the study:

While food shopping has been traditionally the responsibility of women, there is mounting evidence that food shopping is an activity in which men are becoming increasingly involved. Little is known about the characteristics of men who shop for food and men's food shopping habits. How large a role do men play in shopping for food?

What are the characteristics that differentiate men who shop for food items from men who do not shop for food? Are men's food shopping habits similar to or different from women's food shopping habits?

Questions
1. Suggest some conceptual definitions for the research variables to be studied.
2. Suggest some operational definitions for the research variables to be studied.

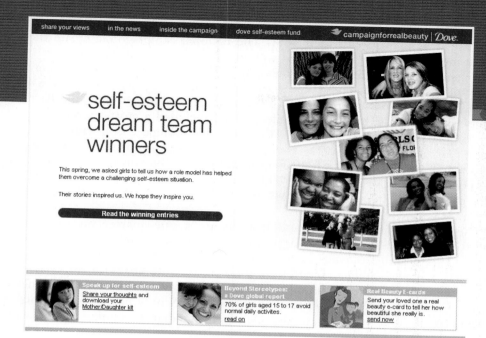

Eating disorders are quite deadly: the death rate is around 18 to 20 percent. In fact, for women between 15 and 24 years old, the annual death rate for anorexia is 12 times higher than the death rate due to all other causes combined.[1] Research suggests that body image, defined as one's feelings, attitudes, and perceptions toward one's body and physical appearance, and one's reliance on physical appearance as a source of self-esteem may be important indicators of potential eating disorders in females.[2] Body image dissatisfaction is consistently reported among girls as young as nine years old.[3] Research suggests that emphasizing and building self-esteem may prove to be an effective method for reducing eating disorders. However, repositioning a health and beauty product to help build self-esteem without increasing dissatisfaction with body image is a tricky and difficult task. But this is exactly what Unilever's Dove dared to do.[4]

A large multinational study commissioned by Dove in ten countries and involving 3,200 women between the ages of 18 and 64 revealed that only 2 percent of women chose "beautiful" to describe their looks. Interestingly, this finding held across different age groups. More importantly, the study found that 48 percent of the women agreed with the following statement: "When I feel less beautiful, I feel worse about myself in general," indicating the impact of physical appearance on self-esteem.[5]

In Dove's "Campaign for Real Beauty" designed by PHD Canada, a media management company, a massive LED billboard was erected on the busy Gardiner Expressway in Toronto in October 2004 featuring a zaftig woman wearing a slinky black dress. Consumers were asked to call 1-888-DOVE to cast their votes about whether the woman featured was fat or fabulous. In the following four weeks, the results were tracked and updated several times a day.

Online ads on yahoo.ca and huge billboards in Toronto, Montreal, Vancouver, and Calgary invited women to visit the Web site www.campaignforrealbeauty.ca. Inserts in major women's fashion

What you will learn in this chapter

1 To understand that an attitude is a hypothetical construct.

2 To understand the attitude-measuring process.

3 To discuss the differences among ranking, rating, sorting, and making choices to measure attitudes and preferences.

4 To discuss Likert scales, semantic differentials, and many other types of attitude scales.

5 To understand how to measure behavioural intentions.

6 To understand the issues involved in the decision to select a measurement scale.

magazines, such as *Flare, Canadian House and Home, Fashion,* and *Chatelaine,* again asked women to cast their votes. The national campaign *did* create the buzz it intended among the targeted women between the ages of 18 and 49.[6]

In January 2005, the Dove Self-Esteem Fund was launched and a body image Web site was created (www.realme.ca) in partnership with the National Eating Disorder Information Centre (www.nedic.ca). In August 2005, the Real Beauty photograph exhibit was unveiled, which included a cross-country tour that stopped in Toronto, Montreal, Winnipeg, and Calgary. A documentary, *Beauty Quest,* created with W Network, was broadcast, featuring a photographer's search for a subject. An online version of the exhibit was made available. The controversial TV commercials with women celebrating their curves and other promotional items, such as "My Beauty Rules" T-shirts, complemented the campaign.

The repositioning of the brand from being a one-quarter moisturizer soap to a high-quality product supporting a social cause helped Dove with its brand extensions as well, such as facial moisturizers and hair products. Dove has achieved higher recognition, more favourable attitudes, and sales. "We've experienced strong double-digit growth in every new category that we're in," says Mark Wakefield, marketing director. Ninety percent of people recognized the blue brand logo, just slightly fewer than recognize the Nike swoosh.

Investigating how to measure attitudes—an important construct in research and the marketing world—is the subject of this chapter. ■

MANAGERIAL IMPORTANCE OF ATTITUDES

Most marketing managers hold the intuitive belief that changing consumers' or prospects' attitudes toward a product is a major marketing goal. At the individual level this is a complicated issue; however, aggregate attitude change has been shown to be related to aggregate sales volume changes. Because modifying attitudes plays a pervasive role in marketing strategies, the measurement of attitudes is an important task. For example, Whiskas brand cat food had been sold in Europe by Mars' Pedigree Petfoods division for 30 years. Over time, as the brand faced increased competition from new premium brands, consumers had difficulty identifying with the brand. The attitude research conducted to determine how people felt about their cats and their food alternatives revealed that cat owners see their pets both as independent and as dependent fragile beings.[7] Cat owners held the attitude that cats wanted to enjoy their food but needed nutrition. This attitude research was directly channelled into managerial action. Whiskas marketers began positioning the product as having "Catisfaction" with ads featuring a purring kitty. The message: "Give cats what they like with the nutrition they need. If you do, they'll be so happy that they'll purr for you." This effort reversed the sales decline the brand had been experiencing.

ATTITUDES DEFINED

attitude
An enduring disposition to consistently respond in a given manner to various aspects of the world; composed of affective, cognitive, and behavioural components.

There are many definitions of *attitude.* **Attitude** usually is viewed as an enduring disposition to consistently respond in a given manner to various aspects of the world, including persons, events, and objects. One conception of attitude is reflected in this brief statement: "Sally loves shopping at Reitmans. She believes it's clean, is conveniently located, and has the lowest prices. She intends to shop there every Thursday." This short description has identified three components of attitudes: affective, cognitive, and behavioural. The affective component reflects an individual's general feelings or emotions toward an object. Statements such as "I love my Honda

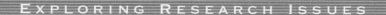

HYPOTHETICAL CONSTRUCT IS NEVER HAVING TO SAY YOU'RE SORRY—OR, LOVE IS A FOUR-LETTER WORD

Love is a four-letter word.[8] And a hypothetical construct—that is, a term that psychologists use to describe or explain consistent patterns of human behaviour. Love, hate, thirst, learning, intelligence—all of these are hypothetical constructs. They are hypothetical in that they do not exist as physical entities; therefore, they cannot be seen, heard, felt, or measured directly. There is no love centre in the brain that, if removed, would leave a person incapable of responding positively and affectionately toward other people and things. Love and hate are constructs in that we invent these terms to explain why, for instance, a young man spends all his time with one young woman while completely avoiding another. From a scientific point of view, we might be better off if we said that this young man's behaviour suggested that he had a relatively enduring, positive-approach attitude toward the first woman and a negative-avoidance attitude toward the second.

Civic," "I liked that book *Freakonomics,*" and "I hate cranberry juice" reflect the emotional character of attitudes. The way one feels about a product, an advertisement, or an object is usually tied to one's *beliefs* or *cognitions*. The cognitive component represents one's awareness of and knowledge about an object. One person might feel happy about the purchase of an automobile because she believes it "gets great gas mileage" or knows that the dealer is "the best in Montreal." The behavioural component includes buying intentions and behavioural expectations and reflects a predisposition to action.

Attitudes as Hypothetical Constructs

hypothetical construct
A variable that is not directly observable but is measurable through indirect indicators, such as verbal expression or overt behaviour.

Many variables that marketing researchers wish to investigate are psychological variables that cannot be directly observed. For example, someone may have an attitude toward a particular brand of shaving cream, but we cannot observe this attitude. To measure an attitude, we must infer it from the way an individual responds (by a verbal expression or overt behaviour) to some stimulus. The term **hypothetical construct** describes a variable that is not directly observable but is measurable through indirect indicators, such as verbal expression or overt behaviour.

THE ATTITUDE-MEASURING PROCESS

A remarkable variety of techniques have been devised to measure attitudes. This variety stems in part from lack of consensus about the exact definition of the concept. Furthermore, the affective, cognitive, and behavioural components of an attitude may be measured by different means. For example, sympathetic nervous system responses may be recorded using physiological measures to quantify affect, but they are not good measures of behavioural intentions. Direct verbal statements concerning affect, belief, or behaviour are used to measure behavioural intent. However, attitudes may also be measured indirectly using the qualitative exploratory techniques discussed in Chapter 5. Obtaining verbal statements from respondents generally requires that the respondents perform a task such as ranking, rating, sorting, or making choices. These will be discussed later in this chapter.

PHYSIOLOGICAL MEASURES OF ATTITUDES

Measures of galvanic skin response, blood pressure, and pupil dilations and other physiological measures may be used to assess the affective components of attitudes. These measures provide a means of assessing attitudes without verbally questioning the respondent. In general they can provide a gross measure of likes or dislikes, but they are not extremely sensitive to the different gradients of an attitude. Each of these measures is discussed elsewhere in the text.

ATTITUDE RATING SCALES

rating scale
A measurement task that requires respondents to estimate the magnitude of a characteristic or quality that a brand, store, or object possesses.

Using rating scales to measure attitudes is perhaps the most common practice in marketing research. **Rating scales** ask the respondent to estimate the magnitude of a characteristic or quality that an object possesses. A quantitative score, along a continuum that has been supplied to the respondent, is used to estimate the strength of the person's attitude or belief; in other words, the respondent indicates the position on one or more scales at which he or she would rate the object. This section discusses many rating scales designed to enable respondents to report the intensity of their attitudes.

Simple Attitude Scales

In its most basic form, attitude scaling requires that an individual agree or disagree with a statement or respond to a single question. For example, respondents in a political poll may be asked whether they agree or disagree with the statement "The prime minister should run for re-election." Or an individual might indicate whether he or she likes or dislikes jalapeño bean dip. This type of self-rating scale merely classifies respondents into one of two categories; thus it has only the properties of a nominal scale, and the types of mathematical analysis that may be used with this basic scale are limited.

Despite the disadvantages, simple attitude scaling may be used when questionnaires are extremely long, when respondents have little education, or for other specific reasons. A number of simplified scales are merely checklists: A respondent indicates past experience, preference, and the like merely by checking an item. In many cases the items are adjectives that describe a particular object.

Most attitude theorists believe that attitudes vary along continua. Early attitude researchers pioneered the view that the task of attitude scaling is to measure the distance from "good" to "bad," "low" to "high," "like" to "dislike," and so on. Thus the purpose of an attitude scale is to find an individual's position on the continuum. Simple scales do not allow for fine distinctions between attitudes. Several other scales have been developed for making more precise measurements.

Category Scales

The example just given is a rating scale that contains only two response categories: agree/disagree. Expanding the response categories provides the respondent with more flexibility in the rating task. Even more information is provided if the categories are ordered according to a particular descriptive or evaluative dimension. Consider the following question:

> **How often do you disagree with your spouse about how much to spend on various things?**
>
> ☐ **Never**   ☐ **Rarely**   ☐ **Sometimes**   ☐ **Often**   ☐ **Very often**

category scale
A rating scale that consists of several response categories, often providing respondents with alternatives to indicate positions on a continuum.

This **category scale** is a more sensitive measure than a scale that has only two response categories; it provides more information.

EXHIBIT 12.1 | SELECTED CATEGORY SCALES

Quality

Excellent	Good	Fair	Poor	
Very good	Fairly good	Neither good nor bad	Not very good	Not good at all
Well above average	Above average	Average	Below average	Well below average

Importance

Very important	Fairly important	Neutral	Not so important	Not at all important

Interest

Very interested		Somewhat interested	Not very interested

Satisfaction

Completely satisfied	Somewhat satisfied	Neither satisfied nor dissatisfied	Somewhat dissatisfied	Completely dissatisfied
Very satisfied	Quite satisfied	Somewhat satisfied	Not at all satisfied	

Frequency

All of the time	Very often	Often	Sometimes	Hardly ever
Very often	Often	Sometimes	Rarely	Never
All the time	Most of the time	Some of the time	Just now and then	

Truth

Very true	Somewhat true	Not very true	Not at all true
Definitely yes	Probably yes	Probably no	Definitely no

Uniqueness

Very different	Somewhat different	Slightly different	Not at all different

Question wording is an extremely important factor in the usefulness of these scales. Exhibit 12.1 shows some common wordings used in category scales. The issue of question wording is discussed in Chapter 13 and its appendix, Question Wording and Measurement Scales for Commonly Researched Topics.

Method of Summated Ratings: The Likert Scale

Likert scale
A measure of attitudes designed to allow respondents to rate how strongly they agree or disagree with carefully constructed statements, ranging from very positive to very negative attitudes toward some object; several scale items may be used to form a summated index.

Marketing researchers' adaptation of the method of summated ratings, developed by Likert, is an extremely popular means for measuring attitudes because it is simple to administer.[9] With the **Likert scale,** respondents indicate their attitudes by checking how strongly they agree or disagree with carefully constructed statements, ranging from very positive to very negative attitudes toward some object. Individuals generally choose from approximately five response alternatives—strongly agree, agree, uncertain, disagree, and strongly disagree—although the number of alternatives may range from three to nine.

Consider the following example from a study of food shopping behaviour:

In buying food for my family, price is no object.

Strongly disagree	Disagree	Uncertain	Agree	Strongly agree
(1)	(2)	(3)	(4)	(5)

1. My doctor's office staff takes a warm and personal interest in me.
2. My doctor's office staff is friendly and courteous.
3. My doctor's office staff is more interested in serving the doctor's needs than in serving my needs.
4. My doctor's office staff always acts in a professional manner.

To measure the attitude, researchers assign scores, or weights, to the alternative responses. In this example, weights of 5, 4, 3, 2, and 1 are assigned. (The weights, shown in parentheses, would not be printed on the questionnaire.) Strong agreement indicates the most favourable attitude on the statement, and a weight of 5 is assigned to this response. The statement given in this example is positive toward the attitude. If the statement given were negative toward the object (such as "I carefully budget my food expenditures"), the weights would be reversed and "strongly disagree" would be assigned a weight of 5. A single scale item on a summated scale is an ordinal scale.

A Likert scale may include several scale items to form an index. Each statement is assumed to represent an aspect of a common attitudinal domain. For example, Exhibit 12.2 shows the items in a Likert scale for measuring attitudes toward patients' interaction with the staff in a physician's office. The total score is the summation of the weights assigned to an individual's responses. Here the maximum possible score for the index would be 20 if a 5 were assigned to "strongly agree" responses for each of the positively worded statements and a 5 to "strongly disagree" responses for the negative statement. (Item 3 is negatively worded and therefore is reverse coded.)

In Likert's original procedure, a large number of statements are generated and an *item analysis* is performed. The purpose of the item analysis is to ensure that final items evoke a wide response and discriminate among those with positive and negative attitudes. Items that are poor because they lack clarity or elicit mixed response patterns are eliminated from the final statement list. However, many marketing researchers do not follow the exact procedure prescribed by Likert. Hence, a disadvantage of the Likert-type summated rating method is that it is difficult to know what a single summated score means. Many patterns of response to the various statements can produce the same total score. Thus identical total scores may reflect different *attitudes* because respondents endorsed different combinations of statements.

Semantic Differential

semantic differential
A measure of attitudes that consists of a series of 7-point rating scales that use bipolar adjectives to anchor the beginning and end of each scale.

The **semantic differential** is actually a series of attitude scales. This popular attitude measurement technique consists of presenting an identification of a product, brand, store, or other concept, followed by a series of 7-point bipolar rating scales. Bipolar adjectives, such as "good" and "bad," "modern" and "old-fashioned," or "clean" and "dirty," anchor the beginning and the end (or poles) of the scale. The subject makes repeated judgments about the concept under investigation on each of the scales. Exhibit 12.3 shows a series of scales to measure attitudes toward jazz saxophone recordings.

The scoring of the semantic differential can be illustrated using the scale bounded by the anchors "modern" and "old-fashioned." Respondents are instructed to check the place that indicates the nearest appropriate adjective. From left to right, the scale intervals are interpreted as "extremely modern," "very modern," "slightly modern," "both modern and old-fashioned," "slightly old-fashioned," "very old-fashioned," and "extremely old-fashioned":

Modern—:—:—:—:—:—:—Old-fashioned

The semantic differential technique originally was developed by Osgood and others as a method for measuring the meanings of objects or the "semantic space" of interpersonal experience.[11] Marketing researchers have found the semantic differential

Fast—:—:—:—:—:—:—Slow
Intellectual—:—:—:—:—:—:—Emotional
Contemporary—:—:—:—:—:—:—Traditional
Composed—:—:—:—:—:—:—Improvised
Flat—:—:—:—:—:—:—Sharp
Busy—:—:—:—:—:—:—Lazy
New—:—:—:—:—:—:—Old
Progressive—:—:—:—:—:—:—Regressive

versatile and have modified it for business applications. Replacing the bipolar adjectives with descriptive phrases is a frequent adaptation in image studies. For example, the phrases "aged a long time"/"not aged a long time," and "not watery looking"/"watery looking" were used in a beer brand image study. A bank study might use the phrases "low interest on savings" and "favourable interest on savings." These phrases are not polar opposites. Consumer researchers have found that respondents often are unwilling to use the extreme negative side of a scale. Research with industrial salespeople, for example, found that in rating their own performances, salespeople would not use the negative side of the scale. Hence, it was eliminated, and the anchor opposite the positive anchor showed "satisfactory" rather than "extremely poor" performance.

For scoring purposes, a weight is assigned to each position on the rating scale. Traditionally scores are 7, 6, 5, 4, 3, 2, 1, or +3, +2, +1, 0, −1, −2, −3. Many marketing researchers find it desirable to assume that the semantic differential provides interval data. This assumption, although widely accepted, has its critics, who argue that the data have only ordinal properties because the weights are arbitrary.

Exhibit 12.4 illustrates a typical **image profile** based on semantic differential data. Depending on whether the data are assumed to be interval or ordinal, the arithmetic mean or the median will be used to compare the profile of one product, brand, or store with that of a competing product, brand, or store.

Numerical Scales

Numerical scales have numbers, rather than semantic space or verbal descriptions, as response options to identify categories (response positions). For example, if the scale items have five response positions, the scale is called a 5-point numerical scale; with seven response positions, it is called a 7-point numerical scale; and so on.

Consider the following numerical scale:

Now that you've had your automobile for about 1 year, please tell us how satisfied you are with your Ford Fusion.

Extremely satisfied 7 6 5 4 3 2 1 Extremely dissatisfied

This numerical scale uses bipolar adjectives in the same manner as the semantic differential. In practice researchers have found that for educated populations a scale with numerical labels for intermediate points on the scale is as effective a measure as the true semantic differential.

Stapel Scale

The **Stapel scale** was originally developed in the 1950s to measure simultaneously the direction and intensity of an attitude. Modern versions of the scale, with a single adjective, are used as a substitute for the semantic differential when it is difficult

image profile
A graphic representation of semantic differential data for competing brands, products, or stores to highlight comparisons.

numerical scale
An attitude rating scale similar to a semantic differential except that it uses numbers, instead of verbal descriptions, as response options to identify response positions.

Stapel scale
A measure of attitudes that consists of a single adjective in the centre of an even number of numerical values.

EXHIBIT 12.4

IMAGE PROFILE OF COMMUTER AIRLINES
VERSUS MAJOR AIRLINES[13]

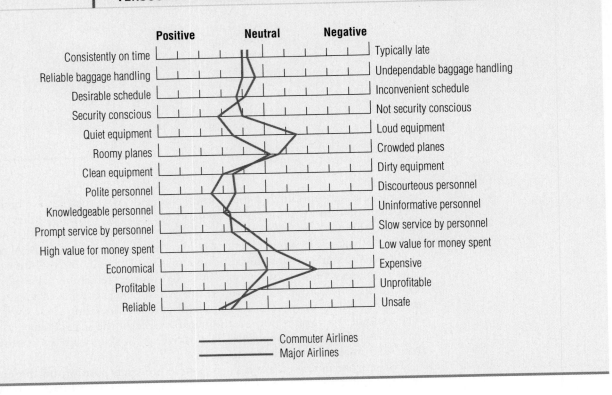

to create pairs of bipolar adjectives. The modified Stapel scale places a single adjective in the centre of an even number of numerical values (ranging, perhaps, from +3 to −3). It measures how close to or distant from the adjective a given stimulus is perceived to be. Exhibit 12.5 illustrates a Stapel scale item used in measurement of a retailer's store image.

The advantages and disadvantages of the Stapel scale are very similar to those of the semantic differential. However, the Stapel scale is markedly easier to administer, especially over the telephone. Because the Stapel scale does not require bipolar adjectives, it is easier to construct than the semantic differential. Research comparing the semantic differential with the Stapel scale indicates that results from the two techniques are largely the same.[14]

Constant-Sum Scale

Suppose Purolator wishes to determine the importance of the attributes of accurate invoicing, delivery as promised, and price to organizations that use its service in business-to-business marketing. Respondents might be asked to divide a constant sum to indicate the relative importance of the attributes. For example:

> **Divide 100 points among the following characteristics of a delivery service according to how important each characteristic is to you when selecting a delivery company.**
>
> **Accurate invoicing** _____
>
> **Delivery as promised** _____
>
> **Lower price** _____

EXHIBIT 12.5 | A STAPEL SCALE FOR MEASURING A STORE'S IMAGE[15]

The Bay

+3

+2

+1

Wide Selection

−1

−2

−3

Select a *plus* number for words that you think describe the store accurately. The more accurately you think the word describes the store, the larger the plus number you should choose. Select a *minus* number for words you think do not describe the store accurately. The less accurately you think the word describes the store, the larger the minus number you should choose. Therefore, you can select any number from +3 for words that you think are very accurate all the way to –3 for words that you think are very inaccurate.

constant-sum scale
A measure of attitudes in which respondents are asked to divide a constant sum to indicate the relative importance of attributes; respondents often sort cards, but the task may also be a rating task.

This **constant-sum scale** works best with respondents who have high educational levels. If respondents follow the instructions correctly, the results will approximate interval measures. As the number of stimuli increases, this technique becomes increasingly complex.

Brand preference may be measured using this technique. The approach, which is similar to the paired-comparison method, is as follows:

> **Divide 100 points among the following brands according to your preference for each brand:**
>
> **Brand A** _____
>
> **Brand B** _____
>
> **Brand C** _____

In this case, the constant–sum scale is a rating technique. However, with minor modifications it can be classified as a sorting technique.

Graphic Rating Scales

graphic rating scale
A measure of attitude that allows respondents to rate an object by choosing any point along a graphic continuum.

A **graphic rating scale** presents respondents with a graphic continuum. The respondents are allowed to choose any point on the continuum to indicate their attitude. Exhibit 12.6 shows a traditional graphic scale, ranging from one extreme position to the opposite position. Typically a respondent's score is determined by measuring the length (in millimetres) from one end of the graphic continuum to the point marked by the respondent. Many researchers believe that scoring in this manner strengthens the assumption that graphic rating scales of this type are interval scales. Alternatively, the researcher may divide the line into predetermined scoring categories (lengths) and record respondents' marks accordingly. In other words, the graphic rating scale has the advantage of allowing the researcher to choose any interval desired for scoring purposes. The disadvantage of the graphic rating scale is that there are no standard answers.

Graphic rating scales are not limited to straight lines as sources of visual communication. Picture response options or another type of graphic continuum may be used to enhance communication with respondents. A frequently used variation is the ladder scale, which also includes numerical options:

> **Here is a ladder scale. [Respondent is shown Exhibit 12.7.] It represents the "ladder of life." As you see, it is a ladder with 11 rungs numbered 0 to 10. Let's suppose the top of the ladder represents the best possible life for you as you describe it, and the bottom rung represents the worst possible life for you as you describe it.**
> **On which rung of the ladder do you feel your life is today?**
>
> **0 1 2 3 4 5 6 7 8 9 10**

Research to investigate children's attitudes has used happy face scales (see Exhibit 12.8). The children are asked to indicate which face shows how they feel about candy, a toy, or some other concept. Research with the happy face scale indicates that

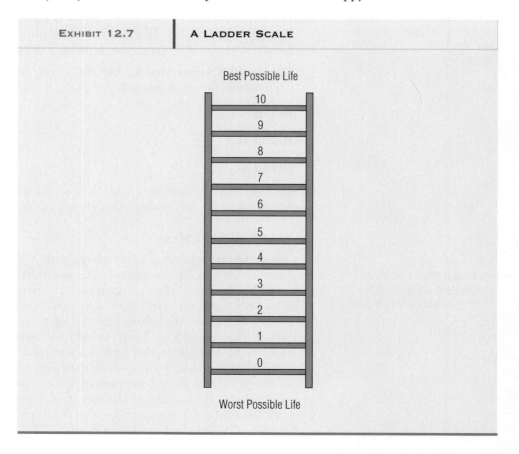

EXHIBIT 12.7	A LADDER SCALE

Best Possible Life

Worst Possible Life

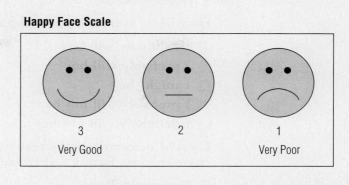

Happy Face Scale

| 3 | 2 | 1 |
| Very Good | | Very Poor |

children tend to choose the faces at the ends of the scale. Although this may be because children's attitudes fluctuate more widely than adults' or because they have stronger feelings both positively and negatively, the tendency to select the extremes is a disadvantage of the scale. Exhibit 12.9 summarizes the attitude-rating techniques discussed in this section.

MEASURING BEHAVIOURAL INTENTION

 The behavioural component of an attitude involves the behavioural expectations of an individual toward an attitudinal object. Typically this represents a buying intention, a tendency to seek additional information, or plans to visit a showroom.

EXHIBIT 12.9 | SUMMARY OF ADVANTAGES AND DISADVANTAGES OF RATING SCALES

Rating Measure	Subject Must	Advantages	Disadvantages
Category scale	Indicate a response category	Flexible, easy to respond to	Items may be ambiguous; with few categories, only gross distinctions can be made
Likert scale	Evaluate statements on a scale of agreement	Easiest scale to construct	Hard to judge what a single score means
Semantic differential and numerical scales	Choose points between bipolar adjectives on relevant dimensions	Easy to construct; norms exist for comparison, such as profile analysis	Bipolar adjectives must be found; data may be ordinal, not interval
Stapel scale	Choose points on a scale with a single adjective in the centre	Easier to construct than semantic differential, easy to administer	Endpoints are numerical, not verbal, labels
Constant-sum scale	Divide a constant sum among response alternatives	Approximates an interval measure	Difficult for respondents with low education levels
Graphic scale	Choose a point on a continuum	Visual impact, unlimited scale points	No standard answers
Graphic scale with picture response categories	Choose a visual picture	Visual impact, easy for poor readers	Hard to attach a verbal explanation to a response

Category scales for measuring the behavioural component of an attitude ask about a respondent's likelihood of purchase or intention to perform some future action, using questions like the following:

How likely is it that you will purchase a satellite radio?

☐ **I definitely will buy**
☐ **I probably will buy**
☐ **I might buy**
☐ **I probably will not buy**
☐ **I definitely will not buy**

I would recommend the real estate agent that helped me in my purchase to close family and friends.

☐ **Extremely likely**
☐ **Very likely**
☐ **Somewhat likely**
☐ **Likely, about a 50–50 chance**
☐ **Somewhat unlikely**
☐ **Very unlikely**
☐ **Extremely unlikely**

The wording of statements used in these scales often includes phrases such as "I would recommend," "I would write," or "I would buy" to indicate action tendencies.

A scale of subjective probabilities, ranging from 100 for "absolutely certain" to 0 for "absolutely no chance," may be used to measure expectations. Researchers have used the following subjective probability scale to estimate the chance that a job candidate will accept a sales position:

_____100%	**(Absolutely certain) I will accept**
_____90%	**(Almost sure) I will accept**
_____80%	**(Very big chance) I will accept**
_____70%	**(Big chance) I will accept**
_____60%	**(Not so big a chance) I will accept**
_____50%	**(About even) I will accept**
_____40%	**(Smaller chance) I will accept**
_____30%	**(Small chance) I will accept**
_____20%	**(Very small chance) I will accept**
_____10%	**(Almost certainly not) I will accept**
_____0	**(Certainly not) I will accept**

Behavioural Differential

behavioural differential
A rating scale instrument similar to a semantic differential, developed to measure the behavioural intentions of subjects toward future actions.

A general instrument, the **behavioural differential,** is used to measure the behavioural intentions of subjects toward an object or category of objects. As in the semantic differential, a description of the object to be judged is followed by a series of scales on which subjects indicate their behavioural intentions toward this object. For example, one item might be

RANKING

ranking

A measurement task that requires respondents to rank order a small number of stores, brands, or objects on the basis of overall preference or some characteristic of the stimulus.

A **ranking** task requires the respondent to rank order a small number of stores, brands, or objects on the basis of overall preference or some characteristic of the stimulus. An ordinal scale may be developed by asking respondents to rank order (from most preferred to least preferred) a set of objects or attributes. Respondents easily understand the task of rank ordering the importance of product attributes or arranging a set of brand names according to preference.

Paired Comparisons

paired comparison

A measurement technique that involves presenting the respondent with two objects and asking the respondent to pick the preferred object. More than two objects may be presented, but comparisons are made in pairs.

Consider a situation in which a chain saw manufacturer learned that a competitor had introduced a new lightweight (2.5 kg) chain saw. The manufacturer's lightest chain saw weighed 3.5 kg. Executives wondered if they needed to introduce a 2.5 kg chain saw into the product line. The research design chosen was a **paired comparison**. A 2.5 kg chain saw was designed and a prototype built. To control for colour preferences, the competitor's chain saw was painted the same colour as the 3.5 and 2.5 kg chain saws. Respondents were presented with two chain saws at a time and then asked to pick the one they preferred. Three pairs of comparisons were required to determine the most preferred chain saw.

The following question illustrates the typical format for asking about paired comparisons.

> **I would like to know your overall opinion of two brands of adhesive bandages. They are Elastoplast and Band-Aid. Overall, which of these two brands—Elastoplast or Band-Aid—do you think is the better one? Or are both the same?**
>
> **Elastoplast is better** _____
>
> **Band-Aid is better** _____
>
> **They are the same** _____

If researchers wish to compare four brands of pens on the basis of attractiveness or writing quality, six comparisons $[(n)(n - 1)/2]$ will be necessary.

Ranking objects with respect to one attribute is not difficult if only a few items, such as products or advertisements, are compared. As the number of items increases, the number of comparisons increases geometrically. If the number of comparisons is too large, respondents may become fatigued and no longer carefully discriminate among them.

SORTING

sorting

A measurement task that presents a respondent with several objects or product concepts and requires the respondent to arrange the objects into piles or classify the product concepts.

Sorting tasks require that respondents indicate their attitudes or beliefs by arranging items on the basis of perceived similarity or some other attribute. For instance, researchers at the BBDO advertising agency have consumers sort photographs of people to measure their perceptions of a brand's typical user. R. H. Bruskin Associates, a research company, uses a sorting technique called AIM (Association-Identification-Measurement), which consists of arranging cards from a deck of 52. Each card reflects an element from advertising for the brand name being studied. This omnibus service measures how well customers associate and identify these elements with a particular product, company, or advertising campaign.[16] The following condensed interviewer instructions illustrate how sorting is used in the AIM survey:

Thoroughly shuffle deck.

Hand respondent deck.

Ask respondent to sort cards into two piles:

> *Definitely Not Seen or Heard.*

> *Definitely or Possibly Seen or Heard.*

Set aside *Definitely Not Seen or Heard* **pile.**

Hand respondent the *Definitely or Possibly Seen or Heard* **pile.**

Have respondent identify the item on each card in *Definitely or Possibly Seen or Heard* **pile.**

Record on questionnaire.

A variant of the constant-sum technique uses physical counters (for example, poker chips or coins), to be divided among the items being tested. In an airline study of customer preferences, the following sorting technique could be used:

> **Here is a sheet that lists several airlines. Next to the name of each airline is a pocket. Here are 10 cards. I would like you to put these cards in the pockets next to the airlines you would prefer to fly on your next trip. Assume that all the airlines fly to wherever you would choose to travel. You can put as many cards as you want next to an airline, or you can put no cards next to an airline.**

	Cards
Air Canada	_____
Delta Airlines	_____
United Airlines	_____
Air France	_____
British Airways	_____

RANDOMIZED RESPONSE QUESTIONS

randomized response questions
A research procedure used for dealing with sensitive topics, in which a random procedure determines which of two questions a respondent will be asked to answer.

In special cases, such as when respondents are being asked to provide sensitive or embarrassing information in a survey, the researcher may use **randomized response questions**. To understand this procedure, it is helpful to consider a portion of a questionnaire from an Internal Revenue Service survey on income tax cheating in the United States:

> **In this section you will be asked some questions about different things you might have done when filling out your tax return. A flip of a coin will determine which questions you are to answer. All that we will know is your answer of either "yes" or "no"; we will not know which question you are answering. I'll show you how it works in a minute, but the important thing to know is that your answers**

are completely anonymous. Using special kinds of statistics we will *never* know what you do. So, we hope you will be completely honest with us. Only in this way will this survey be of help to us.

For example, let's flip the coin. (HAVE EXAMPLE CARD READY.) Let's say it comes up heads. Then you will respond to the "heads" statement: "I had scrambled eggs for breakfast this morning." If you did have scrambled eggs, you would say "yes." If you did not have scrambled eggs, you would say "no." Now, the coin could come up tails and you would respond to the "tails" question: "I had potatoes for dinner last night." You would say "yes" if you did and "no" if you didn't.

1. *Heads* Sometime in the past, I have failed to file a tax return when I think I should have.

   Tails I have lived in this community for over 5 years.
   Yes...1
   No...2

2. *Heads* Sometime in the past, I purposely listed more deductions than I was entitled to.

   Tails I voted in the last presidential election.
   Yes...1
   No...2

3. *Heads* Sometime in the past, I purposely failed to report some income on my tax return—even just a minor amount.

   Tails I own a car.
   Yes...1
   No...2

4. *Heads* On at least one occasion, I have added a dependant that I wasn't entitled to.

   Tails I have been to a movie within the last year.
   Yes...1
   No...2

5. *Heads* To the best of my knowledge, my tax return for [year] was filled out with absolute honesty.

   Tails I have eaten out in a restaurant within the last 6 months.
   Yes...1
   No...2

6. *Heads* I stretched the truth just a little in order to pay fewer taxes for [year].

   Tails Generally, I watch one hour or more of television each day.
   Yes...1
   No...2

This Is the End of the Interview.
Thank You Very Much for Your Cooperation.

The coin flipping randomly determines which of the two questions the respondent answers. Thus the interviewer does not know whether the sensitive question about income tax cheating or the meaningless question is being answered, because the responses ("yes" or "no") are identical for both questions.

The proportion of "yes" answers to the income tax question is calculated by a formula that includes previous estimates of the proportion of respondents who answer "yes" to the meaningless question and the probability (Pr) that the meaningless question is being answered:

$$Pr(\text{``yes'' answer}) = Pr(\text{``yes'' on question A}) + Pr(\text{``yes'' on question B})$$

$$= Pr(\text{question A is chosen}) \times Pr(\text{``yes'' on question A})$$

$$+ Pr(\text{question B is chosen}) \times Pr(\text{``yes'' on question B})$$

Although estimates are subject to error, the respondent remains anonymous, and response bias is thereby reduced.

The randomized response method originally was applied in personal interview surveys. However, randomized response questions in a slightly modified format have been successfully applied in other situations.

OTHER METHODS OF ATTITUDE MEASUREMENT

Attitudes, as hypothetical constructs, cannot be measured directly. Therefore, measurement of attitudes is to an extent subject to the imagination of the researcher. The traditional methods used for attitude measurement have been presented here, but several other techniques that are discussed in the published literature (for example, the Guttman scale) can be used when a situation dictates. Advanced students will seek out these techniques when the traditional measures do not apply to their research problems. With the growth of computer technology, techniques such as *multidimensional scaling* and *conjoint analysis* are used more frequently.

SELECTING A MEASUREMENT SCALE: SOME PRACTICAL DECISIONS

Now that we have looked at a number of attitude measurement scales, a natural question arises: "Which is most appropriate?" As in the selection of a basic research design, there is no single best answer for all research projects. The answer to this question is relative, and the choice of scale will depend on the nature of the attitudinal object to be measured, the manager's problem definition, and the backward and forward linkages to choices already made (for example, telephone survey versus mail survey). However, several questions will help focus the choice of a measurement scale:

1. Is a ranking, sorting, rating, or choice technique best?
2. Should a monadic or a comparative scale be used?
3. What type of category labels, if any, will be used for the rating scale?
4. How many scale categories or response positions are needed to accurately measure an attitude?
5. Should a balanced or unbalanced rating scale be chosen?
6. Should a scale that forces a choice among predetermined options be used?
7. Should a single measure or an index measure be used?

We will discuss each of these issues.

Is a Ranking, Sorting, Rating, or Choice Technique Best?

The answer to this question is determined largely by the problem definition and especially by the type of statistical analysis desired. For example, ranking provides only ordinal data, limiting the statistical techniques that may be used.

Should a Monadic or a Comparative Scale Be Used?

If the scale to be used is not a ratio scale, the researcher must decide whether to include a standard of comparison in the verbal portion of the scale. Consider the following rating scale:

Many rating scales have verbal labels. The scale shown in this humorous ad gives the reader a choice of appropriate category labels for ice cream pleasure.

Now that you've had your automobile for about 1 year, please tell us how satisfied you are with its engine power and pickup.

Completely satisfied	Very satisfied	Fairly well satisfied	Somewhat dissatisfied	Very dissatisfied

This is a **monadic rating scale**, because it asks about a single concept (the brand of automobile the individual actually purchased) in isolation. The respondent is not given a specific frame of reference. A **comparative rating scale** asks a respondent to rate a concept, such as a specific brand, in comparison with a benchmark—perhaps another similar concept, such as a competing brand—explicitly used as a frame of reference. In many cases the comparative rating scale presents an ideal situation as a reference point for comparison with the actual situation. For example:

Please indicate how the amount of authority in your present position compares with the amount of authority that would be ideal for this position.

Too much   About right   Too little

What Type of Category Labels, If Any, Will Be Used for the Rating Scale?

We have discussed verbal labels, numerical labels, and unlisted choices. Many rating scales have verbal labels for response categories because researchers believe that these help respondents better understand the response positions. The maturity and educational levels of the respondents will influence this decision. The semantic differential, with unlabelled response categories between two bipolar adjectives, and the numerical scale, with numbers to indicate scale positions, often are selected because the researcher wishes to assume interval-scale data.

How Many Scale Categories or Response Positions Are Needed to Accurately Measure an Attitude?

Should a category scale have four, five, or seven response positions or categories? Or should the researcher use a graphic scale with an infinite number of positions? The original developmental research on the semantic differential indicated that five to eight points is optimal. However, the researcher must determine the number of meaningful positions that is best for the specific project. This issue of identifying how many meaningful distinctions respondents can practically make is basically a matter of sensitivity, but at the operational rather than the conceptual level.

Should a Balanced or an Unbalanced Rating Scale Be Chosen?

balanced rating scale
A fixed-alternative rating scale with an equal number of positive and negative categories; a neutral point or point of indifference is at the centre of the scale.

The fixed-alternative format may be balanced or unbalanced. For example, the following question, which asks about parent–child decisions relating to television program watching, is a **balanced rating scale:**

Who decides which television programs your children watch?

Child decides all of the time.

Child decides most of the time.

Child and parent decide together.

Parent decides most of the time.

Parent decides all of the time.

This scale is balanced because a neutral point, or point of indifference, is at the centre of the scale.

unbalanced rating scale
A fixed-alternative rating scale that has more response categories piled up at one end and an unequal number of positive and negative categories.

Unbalanced rating scales may be used when responses are expected to be distributed at one end of the scale. Unbalanced scales, such as the following one, may eliminate this type of "end piling":

Satisfied

Neither satisfied nor dissatisfied

Quite dissatisfied

Very dissatisfied

The nature of the concept or the researcher's knowledge about attitudes toward the stimulus to be measured generally will determine the choice of a balanced or unbalanced scale.

Should a Scale That Forces a Choice Among Predetermined Options Be Used?

forced-choice rating scale
A fixed-alternative rating scale that requires respondents to choose one of the fixed alternatives.

non-forced-choice scale
A fixed-alternative rating scale that provides a "no opinion" category or that allows respondents to indicate that they cannot say which alternative is their choice.

In many situations a respondent has not formed an attitude toward the concept being studied and simply cannot provide an answer. If a **forced-choice rating scale** compels the respondent to answer, the response is merely a function of the question. If answers are not forced, the midpoint of the scale may be used by the respondent to indicate unawareness as well as indifference. If many respondents in the sample are expected to be unaware of the attitudinal object under investigation, this problem may be eliminated by using a **non-forced-choice scale** that provides a "no opinion" category. For example:

How does the Canadian Imperial Bank of Commerce compare with TD Canada Trust?

Canadian Imperial Bank of Commerce is better than TD Canada Trust.

Researchers face a number of attitude scaling decisions. One choice they must make is whether a balanced or an unbalanced scale should be used.

Canadian Imperial Bank of Commerce is about the same as TD Canada Trust.

Canadian Imperial Bank of Commerce is worse than TD Canada Trust.

Can't say.

Asking this type of question allows the investigator to separate respondents who cannot make an honest comparison from respondents who have had experience with both banks. The argument for forced choice is that people really do have attitudes, even if they are unfamiliar with the banks, and should be required to answer the question. Higher incidences of "no answer" are associated with forced-choice questions.

Should a Single Measure or an Index Measure Be Used?

How complex is the issue to be investigated? How many dimensions does the issue contain? Are individual attributes of the stimulus part of a holistic attitude, or are they seen as separate items? The researcher's conceptual definition will be helpful in making this choice.

The researcher has many scaling options. Generally, the choice is influenced by plans for the later stages of the research project. Again, problem definition becomes a determining factor influencing the research design.

SUMMARY

Attitude measurement is particularly important in marketing research. Attitudes are enduring dispositions to consistently respond in a given manner to various aspects of the world, including persons, events, and objects. Attitudes consist of three components: the affective, or the emotions or feelings involved; the cognitive, or awareness or knowledge; and the behavioural, or the predisposition to action. Attitudes are hypothetical constructs; that is, they are variables that are not directly observable, but must be measured indirectly.

Many methods for measuring attitudes have been developed, such as ranking, rating, sorting, and choice techniques.

One class of rating scales, category scales, provides several response categories to allow respondents to indicate the intensity of their attitudes. The simplest attitude scale calls for a "yes/no" or "agree/disagree" response to a single question. The Likert scale uses a series of statements with which subjects indicate agreement or disagreement. The responses are assigned weights that are summed to indicate the respondents' attitudes.

The semantic differential uses a series of attitude scales anchored by bipolar adjectives. The respondent indicates where his or her attitude falls between the polar attitudes. Variations on this method, such as numerical scales and the Stapel scale, are also used. The Stapel scale puts a single adjective in the centre of a range of numerical values from +3 to −3.

Graphic rating scales use continua on which respondents indicate their attitudes. Constant-sum scales require the respondent to divide a constant sum into parts, indicating the weights to be given to various attributes of the item being studied.

Several scales, such as the behavioural differential, have been developed to measure the behavioural component of attitude.

People often rank order their preferences. Thus ordinal scales that ask respondents to rank order a set of objects or attributes may be developed. In the paired-comparison technique, two alternatives are paired and respondents are asked to pick the preferred one. Sorting requires respondents to indicate their attitudes by arranging items into piles or categories.

The accuracy of answers to sensitive questions may be enhanced by using randomized response questions and calculations based on probability theory.

The researcher can choose among a number of attitude scales. Choosing among the alternatives requires considering several questions, each of which is generally answered by comparing the advantages of each alternative to the problem definition.

A monadic rating scale asks about a single concept. A comparative rating scale asks a respondent to rate a concept in comparison with a benchmark used as a frame of reference.

Scales may be balanced or unbalanced. Unbalanced scales prevent responses from piling up at one end. Forced-choice scales require the respondent to select an alternative; non-forced-choice scales allow the respondent to indicate an inability to select an alternative.

Key Terms and Concepts

attitude
hypothetical construct
rating scale
category scale
Likert scale
semantic differential
image profile
numerical scale

Stapel scale
constant-sum scale
graphic rating scale
behavioural differential
ranking
paired comparison
sorting
randomized response questions

monadic rating scale
comparative rating scale
balanced rating scale
unbalanced rating scale
forced-choice rating scale
non-forced-choice scale

Questions for Review and Critical Thinking

1. What is an attitude? Is there a consensus concerning its definition?
2. Distinguish between rating and ranking. Which is a better attitude measurement technique? Why?
3. In what type of situation would the choice technique be most appropriate?
4. In what type of situation would the sorting technique be most appropriate?
5. What advantages do numerical scales have over semantic differential scales?
6. Identify the issues a researcher should consider when choosing a measurement scale.

7. Name some situations in which a semantic differential might be useful.

8. Should a Likert scale ever be treated as though it had ordinal properties?

9. In each of the following identify the type of scale and evaluate it:

   a. An academic study on consumer behaviour:

   Most people who are important to me think I

   −3   **+3**

   | **Definitely should not buy** | **Definitely should buy** |

   [test brand] sometime during the next week.

   b. A psychographic statement:

   I shop a lot for specials.

Strongly agree	Moderately agree	Neutral	Moderately disagree	Strongly disagree
5	4	3	2	1

10. What problems might complicate an attempt to use attitude measures to predict specific behaviour?

11. If a Likert summated scale has ten scale items, do all ten items have to be phrased as either positive or negative statements, or can the scale contain a mix of positive and negative statements?

12. If a semantic differential has ten scale items, should all the positive adjectives be on the right and all the negative adjectives on the left?

13. A researcher wishes to compare two hotels on the following attributes:

    Convenience of location

    Friendly personnel

    Value for money

    a. Design a Likert scale to accomplish this task.

    b. Design a semantic differential scale to accomplish this task.

    c. Design a graphic rating scale to accomplish this task.

14. A researcher thinks many respondents will answer "don't know" or "can't say" if these options are printed on an attitude scale along with categories indicating level of agreement. The researcher does not print either "don't know" or "can't say" on the questionnaire because the resulting data would be more complicated to analyze and report. Is this proper?

Exploring the Internet

SRI International investigates consumers by asking questions about their attitudes and values. SRI has developed the VALS (value and lifestyle) scale to identify people's value and lifestyle types. It has a Web site so people can VALS-type themselves. To find out your VALS type, go to www.sric-bi.com/ and click on VALS Survey.

A marketing research company sent the attitude scales in Case Exhibit 12.1.1 to members of its consumer panel. Other questions on the questionnaire were about ownership and/or use of computers, consumer electronic devices, satellite TV ownership, cellular phones, and Internet activity.

Questions

1. What type of attitude scale appears in the case study?
2. Evaluate the list of statements. Do the statements appear to measure a single concept?
3. What do they appear to be measuring?

CASE EXHIBIT 12.1.1 | **ATTITUDE SCALE**

Below is a list of statements that may or may not be used to describe your attitudes toward technology and your lifestyle. Please indicate to what extent each statement describes your attitudes by placing an X in a box from 1 to 10, where 10 means that statement "Describes your attitudes completely" and a 1 means that statement "Does not describe your attitudes at all." (X ONE BOX ACROSS FOR EACH STATEMENT.)

	Does Not Describe Your Attitudes At All									Describes Your Attitudes Completely
	1	2	3	4	5	6	7	8	9	10
I like to impress people with my lifestyle.	☐	☐	☐	☐	☐	☐	☐	☐	☐	☐
Technology is important to me.	☐	☐	☐	☐	☐	☐	☐	☐	☐	☐
I am very competitive when it comes to my career.	☐	☐	☐	☐	☐	☐	☐	☐	☐	☐
Having fun is the whole point of life.	☐	☐	☐	☐	☐	☐	☐	☐	☐	☐
Family is important, but I have other interests that are just as important to me.	☐	☐	☐	☐	☐	☐	☐	☐	☐	☐
I am constantly looking for new ways to entertain myself.	☐	☐	☐	☐	☐	☐	☐	☐	☐	☐
Making a lot of money is important to me.	☐	☐	☐	☐	☐	☐	☐	☐	☐	☐
I spend most of my free time doing fun stuff with my friends.	☐	☐	☐	☐	☐	☐	☐	☐	☐	☐
I like to spend time learning about new technology products.	☐	☐	☐	☐	☐	☐	☐	☐	☐	☐
I like to show off my taste and style.	☐	☐	☐	☐	☐	☐	☐	☐	☐	☐
I like technology.	☐	☐	☐	☐	☐	☐	☐	☐	☐	☐
My family is by far the most important thing in my life.	☐	☐	☐	☐	☐	☐	☐	☐	☐	☐
I put a lot of time and energy into my career.	☐	☐	☐	☐	☐	☐	☐	☐	☐	☐
I am very likely to purchase new technology products or services.	☐	☐	☐	☐	☐	☐	☐	☐	☐	☐
I spend most of my free time working on improving myself.	☐	☐	☐	☐	☐	☐	☐	☐	☐	☐

How questions and answer options are worded can be very important in determining the type of answers that will be obtained from respondents. In the 1991 census, Statistics Canada had problems measuring "ethnic origin." Although respondents were provided with a checklist of 15 options (e.g., French, English), the option "Canadian" was not listed. Only 3 percent of the respondents wrote "Canadian" in the blank space provided. In response to the criticisms and the problems with the question, in the 1996 census, Statistics Canada did not provide a checklist, but a list of 24 example groups in which Canadian was listed fifth. The number of respondents who wrote "Canadian" jumped to 19 percent. However, there were concerns raised about the format of the questions and answers. One criticism was that the respondents were confused about their "ethnic background" as asked in the question and that being "Canadian" is related to self-identity, not ethnic origin. Statistics Canada tested the question "To which ethnic/cultural group did your ancestors belong?" without the example groups, but found that the question was not clear to respondents.[1]

Many experts in survey research believe that improving the wording of questions can contribute far more to accuracy than can improvements in sampling. Experiments have shown that the range of error due to vague questions or use of ambiguous words may be as high as 20 or 30 percentage points. Consider the following illustration of the critical importance of selecting the word with the right meaning in a survey conducted in the United States. The questions differ only in the use of the words *should, could,* and *might:*

Do you think anything *should* be done to make it easier for people to pay doctor or hospital bills?

Do you think anything *could* be done to make it easier for people to pay doctor or hospital bills?

Do you think anything *might* be done to make it easier for people to pay doctor or hospital bills?[2]

What you will learn in this chapter

1. To value the importance of proper wording of questions in questionnaire design.

2. How decisions about the data collection methods (mail, Internet, telephone, or personal interviews) will influence question format and questionnaire layout.

3. To understand the difference in the design and use of open-ended response questions and fixed-alternative questions.

4. To follow the guidelines that help prevent the most common mistakes in questionnaire design.

5. To discuss how the proper sequence of questions may improve a questionnaire.

6. How to plan and design a questionnaire layout.

7. How to pre-test and revise a questionnaire

8. The additional efforts required in designing questionnaires for global markets.

The results from the matched examples: 82 percent replied that something *should* be done, 77 percent that something *could* be done, and 63 percent that something *might* be done. A 19-percentage-point difference separated the two extremes *should* and *might*.

This chapter outlines a procedure for questionnaire design and illustrates that a little bit of research knowledge can be a dangerous thing. ■

A SURVEY IS ONLY AS GOOD AS THE QUESTIONS IT ASKS

 Each stage in the interdependent marketing research process is important. However, a marketing research survey is only as good as the questions it asks. The importance of question wording is easily overlooked, but questionnaire design is one of the most critical stages in the survey research process.

Business people who are inexperienced at marketing research frequently believe that constructing a questionnaire is a simple task. Amateur researchers find it quite easy to write short questionnaires in a matter of hours. Unfortunately, newcomers who naively believe that common sense and good grammar are all one needs to construct a questionnaire generally learn that their hasty efforts were inadequate.

Although common sense and good grammar are important in question writing, the art of questionnaire design requires far more. To assume that people will understand the questions is a common error. Respondents simply may not know what is being asked. They may be unaware of the product or topic of interest. They may confuse the subject with something else. The question may not mean the same thing to everyone interviewed. Finally, people may refuse to answer personal questions. Most of these problems can be minimized, however, if a skilled researcher composes the questionnaire.

QUESTIONNAIRE DESIGN: AN OVERVIEW OF THE MAJOR DECISIONS

Relevance and *accuracy* are the two basic criteria a questionnaire must meet if it is to fulfill a researcher's purposes. To achieve these ends, a researcher who is systematically planning a questionnaire's design will be required to make several decisions—typically, but not necessarily, in the following order:

1. What should be asked?
2. How should questions be phrased?
3. In what sequence should the questions be arranged?
4. What questionnaire layout will best serve the research objectives?
5. How should the questionnaire be pre-tested? Does the questionnaire need to be revised?

WHAT SHOULD BE ASKED?

 Certain decisions made during the early stages of the research process will influence the questionnaire design. The preceding chapters stressed the need to have a good problem definition and clear objectives for the study. The problem definition will indicate the type of information that must be collected to answer the manager's questions; different types of questions may be better at obtaining certain types of information than others. Furthermore, the communication medium used for data collection—that is, telephone interview, personal interview, or self-administered questionnaire—will have been determined. This decision is another forward linkage that influences the structure and content of the questionnaire. The specific questions to be asked will be a function of the previous decisions.

The latter stages of the research process will have an important impact on questionnaire wording. The questions that should be asked will, of course, take the form of data analysis into account. When designing the questionnaire, the researcher should consider the types of statistical analysis that will be conducted.

Questionnaire Relevancy

A questionnaire is *relevant* if no unnecessary information is collected and only the information needed to solve the marketing problem is obtained. Asking the wrong question or an irrelevant question is a common pitfall. If the marketing task is to pinpoint store image problems, questions asking for general information about clothing style preferences will be irrelevant. To ensure information relevance, the researcher must be specific about data needs and have a rationale for each item of information.

Many researchers, after conducting surveys, find that they omitted some important questions. Therefore, when planning the questionnaire design, researchers must think about possible omissions. Is information on the relevant demographic and psychographic variables being collected? Are there any questions that might clarify the answers to other questions? Will the results of the study provide the answer to the marketing manager's problem?

Questionnaire Accuracy

Once the researcher has decided what should be asked, the criterion of accuracy becomes the primary concern. *Accuracy* means that the information is reliable and valid. While experienced researchers generally believe that one should use simple, understandable, unbiased, unambiguous, and non-irritating words, no step-by-step procedure for ensuring accuracy in question writing can be generalized across projects. Obtaining accurate answers from respondents depends strongly on the researcher's ability to design a questionnaire that will facilitate recall and motivate respondents to cooperate. Respondents tend to be more cooperative when the subject of the research interests them. When questions are not lengthy, difficult to answer, or ego threatening, there is a higher probability of obtaining unbiased answers. Question wording and sequence also substantially influence accuracy. We will address these topics in this chapter.

There are many ways to phrase questions, and many standard question formats have been developed in previous research studies. This section presents a classification of question types and provides some helpful guidelines for writing questions.

Open-Ended Response versus Fixed-Alternative Questions

Two basic types of questions can be identified based on the amount of freedom respondents have in answering.

open-ended response question
A question that poses some problem and asks the respondent to answer in his or her own words.

Open-ended response questions pose some problem or topic and ask respondents to answer in their own words. If the question is asked in a personal interview, the interviewer may probe for more information. For example:

What names of local shoe stores can you think of offhand?

What comes to mind when you look at this advertisement?

In what way, if any, could this product be changed or improved? I'd like you to tell me anything you can think of, no matter how minor it seems.

What things do you like most about Canada Post's service?

Why do you buy more of your clothing in Bay stores than in other stores?

How can our stores better serve your needs?

Please tell me anything at all that you remember about the BMW commercial you saw last night.

Open-ended response questions are free-answer questions. They may be contrasted with **fixed-alternative questions**—sometimes called *closed questions*—which give respondents specific limited-alternative responses and ask them to choose the one closest to their own viewpoints. For example:

fixed-alternative question
A question in which the respondent is given specific, limited-alternative responses and asked to choose the one closest to his or her own viewpoint.

Did you use any commercial feed or supplement for livestock or poultry in 2001?

☐ Yes
☐ No

In which type of bookstore is it easier for you to shop—a regular bookstore or a bookstore on the Internet?

☐ **Regular bookstore**
☐ **Internet bookstore**

Open-ended response questions are most beneficial when the researcher is conducting exploratory research, especially when the range of responses is not known. Such questions can be used to learn which words and phrases people spontaneously give to the free-response question. Respondents are free to answer with whatever is uppermost in their minds. By obtaining free and uninhibited responses, the researcher may find some unanticipated reaction toward the product. Such responses will reflect the flavour of the language that people use in talking about products or services and thus may provide a source of new ideas for advertising copywriting. Also, open-ended response questions are valuable at the beginning of an interview. They are good first questions because they allow respondents to warm up to the questioning process.

WHAT A DIFFERENCE WORDS MAKE

Does advertising lower or raise prices?[3] The wording of the question influences the answer.

Consumer Attitude Toward Distribution
The consumer must pay more for goods because of advertising.

No	33
Yes	39
Doubtful	17
No answer	11

Consumer Attitude Toward Distribution
Advertising may cause the consumer to pay less for a product than if it were not advertised because it increases sales and makes it possible to cut the cost of production and marketing.

Yes	52
No	18
Doubtful	20
No answer	10

The cost of administering open-ended response questions is substantially higher than that of administering fixed-alternative questions because the job of editing, coding, and analyzing the data is quite extensive. As each respondent's answer is likely unique, there is some difficulty in categorizing and summarizing the answers. The process requires that an editor go over a sample of questions to classify the responses into some sort of scheme; then all the answers must be reviewed and coded according to the classification scheme.

Another potential disadvantage of the open-ended response question is the possibility that interviewer bias will influence the answer. While most interviewer instructions state that answers are to be recorded verbatim, rarely does even the best interviewer get every word spoken by the respondent. Interviewers have a tendency to take shortcuts in recording the answers. But changing even a few of the respondent's words may substantially influence the results; the final answer thus may reflect a combination of the respondent's and interviewer's ideas rather than the respondent's ideas alone.

Also, articulate individuals tend to give longer answers to open-ended response questions. Such respondents often are better educated and from higher income groups and therefore may not be representative of the entire population, and yet they may give a large share of the responses.

In contrast, fixed-alternative questions require less interviewer skill, take less time, and are easier for the respondent to answer. This is because answers to closed questions are classified into standardized groupings prior to data collection. Standardizing alternative responses to a question provides comparability of answers, which facilitates coding, tabulating, and ultimately interpreting the data.

Types of Fixed-Alternative Questions

Earlier in the chapter some examples of fixed-alternative questions were presented. We will now identify and categorize the various types.

The **simple-dichotomy,** or **dichotomous-alternative, question** requires the respondent to choose one of two alternatives. The answer can be a simple "yes" or "no" or a choice between "this" and "that." For example:

Did you make any long-distance calls last week?

☐ **Yes**   ☐ **No**

simple-dichotomy (dichotomous-alternative) question
A fixed-alternative question that requires the respondent to choose one of two alternatives.

Several types of questions provide the respondent with *multiple-choice alternatives*. The **determinant-choice question** requires the respondent to choose one—and only one—response from among several possible alternatives. For example:

Please give us some information about your flight. In which section of the aircraft did you sit?

☐ **First class**

☐ **Business class**

☐ **Coach class**

The **frequency-determination question** is a determinant-choice question that asks for an answer about the general frequency of occurrence. For example:

How frequently do you watch the Much Music channel?

☐ **Every day**

☐ **2–4 times a week**

☐ **Once a week**

☐ **Less than once a week**

☐ **Never**

Attitude rating scales, such as the Likert scale, semantic differential, Stapel scale, and so on, are also fixed-alternative questions. These were discussed in Chapter 12.

The **checklist question** allows the respondent to provide multiple answers to a single question. The respondent indicates past experience, preference, and the like merely by checking off items. In many cases the choices are adjectives that describe a particular object. A typical checklist question might ask the following:

Please check which of the following sources of information about investments you regularly use, if any.

☐ **Personal advice of your broker(s)**

☐ **Brokerage newsletters**

☐ **Brokerage research reports**

☐ **Investment advisory service(s)**

☐ **Conversations with other investors**

☐ **Web page(s)**

☐ **None of these**

☐ **Other (please specify)___**

A major problem in developing dichotomous or multiple-choice alternatives is the framing of the response alternatives. There should be no overlap among categories.

A questionnaire for a bowling alley used an adjective checklist question. Here is how people who bowl saw themselves: attractive (38 percent), romantic (43 percent), competitive (41 percent), and sports enthusiasts (30 percent). Here is how people in the general population saw themselves: attractive (28 percent), romantic (35 percent), competitive (33 percent), and sports enthusiasts (23 percent).[4]

Alternatives should be *mutually exclusive;* that is, only one dimension of an issue should be related to each alternative. The following listing of income groups illustrates a common error:

- ☐ **Under $15,000**
- ☐ **$15,000–30,000**
- ☐ **$30,000–55,000**
- ☐ **$55,000–70,000**
- ☐ **Over $70,000**

How many people with incomes of $30,000 will be in the second group, and how many will be in the third group? There is no way to determine the answer. Grouping alternatives without forethought about analysis is likely to diminish accuracy.

Few people relish being in the lowest category. Including a category lower than the lowest expected answers often helps to negate the potential bias caused by respondents' tendency to avoid an extreme category.

When a researcher is unaware of the potential responses to a question, fixed-alternative questions obviously cannot be used. If the researcher assumes what the responses will be but is in fact wrong, he or she will have no way of knowing the extent to which the assumption was incorrect.

Unanticipated alternatives emerge when respondents feel that closed answers do not adequately reflect their feelings. They may make comments to the interviewer or write additional answers on the questionnaire indicating that the exploratory research did not yield a complete array of responses. After the fact, little can be done to correct a closed question that does not provide enough alternatives; therefore, before writing a descriptive questionnaire, a researcher may find it valuable to spend time conducting exploratory research with open-ended response questions to identify the most likely alternatives. The researcher should strive to ensure that there are sufficient response choices to include almost all possible answers.

Respondents may check off obvious alternatives, such as price or durability, if they do not see the choice they would prefer. Also, a fixed-alternative question may tempt respondents to check an answer that is more prestigious or socially acceptable than the true answer. Rather than stating that they do not know why they chose a given product, they may select an alternative among those presented, or, as a matter of convenience, they may select a given alternative rather than think of the most correct response.

Most questionnaires mix open-ended and closed questions. As we have discussed, each form has certain benefits. In addition, a change of pace can eliminate respondent boredom and fatigue.

Phrasing Questions for Self-Administered, Telephone, and Personal Interview Surveys

The means of data collection (telephone interview, personal interview, self-administered questionnaire) will influence the question format and question phrasing. In general, questions for mail, Internet, and telephone surveys must be less complex than those used in personal interviews. Questionnaires for telephone and personal interviews should be written in a conversational style. Exhibit 13.1 illustrates how a question may be revised for a different medium.

Consider the following question from a personal interview:

There has been a lot of discussion about the potential health risks to non-smokers from tobacco smoke in public buildings, restaurants, and business offices. How serious a health threat to you personally is the inhaling of this second-hand smoke, often called *passive smoking:* Is it a very serious health threat, somewhat serious, not too serious, or not serious at all?

EXHIBIT 13.1 | REDUCING QUESTION COMPLEXITY BY PROVIDING FEWER RESPONSES⁵

Mail Form:

How satisfied are you with your community?

1. Very satisfied
2. Quite satisfied
3. Somewhat satisfied
4. Slightly satisfied
5. Neither satisfied nor dissatisfied
6. Slightly dissatisfied
7. Somewhat dissatisfied
8. Quite dissatisfied
9. Very dissatisfied

Revised for Telephone:

How satisfied are you with your community? Would you say you are very satisfied, somewhat satisfied, neither satisfied nor dissatisfied, somewhat dissatisfied, or very dissatisfied?

Very satisfied	1
Somewhat satisfied	2
Neither satisfied nor dissatisfied	3
Somewhat dissatisfied	4
Very dissatisfied	5

1. **Very serious**
2. **Somewhat serious**
3. **Not too serious**
4. **Not serious at all**
5. **(Don't know)**

You probably noticed that the last portion of the question was a listing of the four alternatives that serve as answers. This listing at the end is often used in interviews to remind the respondent of the alternatives, since they are not presented visually. The fifth alternative, "Don't know," is in parentheses because, although the interviewer knows it is an acceptable answer, it is not read; the researcher would prefer to "force" the respondent to choose from among the four listed alternatives.

The data collection technique also influences the layout of the questionnaire. Layout will be discussed later in the chapter.

THE ART OF ASKING QUESTIONS

No hard-and-fast rules determine how to develop a questionnaire. Fortunately, research experience has yielded some guidelines that help prevent the most common mistakes.

Avoid Complexity: Use Simple, Conversational Language

Words used in questionnaires should be readily understandable to all respondents. The researcher usually has the difficult task of adopting the conversational language of people at the lower education levels without talking down to better-educated respondents. Remember, not all people have the vocabulary of a college student.

Respondents can probably tell an interviewer whether they are married, single, divorced, separated, or widowed, but providing their *marital status* may present a problem. The technical jargon of top corporate executives should be avoided when surveying retailers or industrial users. "Brand image," "positioning," "marginal analysis," and other corporate language may not have the same meaning for or even be understood by a store owner-operator in a retail survey. The vocabulary used in the following question from an attitude survey on social problems probably would confuse many respondents:

> **When effluents from a paper mill can be drunk and exhaust from factory smokestacks can be breathed, then humankind will have done a good job in saving the environment. . . . Don't you agree that what we want is zero toxicity: no effluents?**

Besides being too long and confusing, this question is leading.

Avoid Leading and Loaded Questions

leading question
A question that suggests or implies certain answers.

Leading and loaded questions are a major source of bias in question wording. **Leading questions** suggest or imply certain answers. A study of the dry cleaning industry asked this question:

> **Many people are using dry cleaning less because of improved wash-and-wear clothes. How do you feel wash-and-wear clothes have affected your use of dry cleaning facilities in the past four years?**
>
> ☐ **Use less**　　☐ **No change**　　☐ **Use more**

The potential "bandwagon effect" implied in this question threatens the study's validity. *Partial mention of alternatives* is a variation of this phenomenon:

> **Do small imported cars, such as Volkswagens, get better gas mileage than small North American cars?**
>
> **How do you generally spend your free time, watching television or what?**

Merely mentioning an alternative may have a dramatic effect. The following question was asked in a research study for a court case (*Universal City* v. *Nintendo*, 1984).[6]

> **To the best of your knowledge, was "Donkey Kong" made with the approval or under the authority of the people who produced the *King Kong* movies?**

Eighteen percent of the respondents answered "yes." In contrast, 0 percent correctly answered the question **"As far as you know, who makes 'Donkey Kong'?"**

loaded question
A question that suggests a socially desirable answer or is emotionally charged.

Loaded questions suggest a socially desirable answer or are emotionally charged. Consider the following:

> **In light of today's farm crisis, it would be in the public's best interest to offer interest-free loans to farmers.**
>
> ☐ **Strongly agree**　　☐ **Agree**　　☐ **Disagree**　　☐ **Strongly disagree**

Answers might be different if the loaded portion of the statement, "farm crisis," were worded to suggest a problem of less magnitude than a crisis.

A television station produced the following 10-second spot asking for viewer feedback:

> **We are happy when you like programs on Channel 11. We are sad when you dislike programs on Channel 11. Write us and let us know what you think of our programming.**

Few people wish to make others sad. This question is likely to elicit only positive comments.

Certain answers to questions are more socially desirable than others. For example, a truthful answer to the following classification question might be painful:

> **Where did you rank academically in your high school graduating class?**
>
> ☐ **Top quarter**
> ☐ **2nd quarter**
> ☐ **3rd quarter**
> ☐ **4th quarter**

When taking personality or psychographic tests, respondents frequently can interpret which answers are most socially acceptable even if those answers do not portray their true feelings. For example, which are the socially desirable answers to the following questions on a self-confidence scale?

TOO GOOD A NAME!

The Arm & Hammer brand name has been used for a number of product line extensions—for example, heavy-duty laundry detergent, oven cleaner, and liquid detergent. Unfortunately, however, when the makers of Arm & Hammer baking soda launched Arm & Hammer spray deodorant and Arm & Hammer spray disinfectant, they did not fare well, even though marketing research studies indicated that consumers had expressed positive feelings about both products. What went wrong?

Researchers who investigated the product failures found that the Arm & Hammer name had such a strong consumer franchise that whenever it was associated with a new product or concept, consumer acceptance and buying intentions were always artificially high. When question wording included the socially desirable Arm & Hammer name, consumers were reluctant to reject it. The company had failed to realize how much response bias its name caused.

I feel capable of handling myself in most social situations.

☐ **Agree**   ☐ **Disagree**

I seldom fear my actions will cause others to have low opinions of me.

☐ **Agree**   ☐ **Disagree**

Invoking the status quo is a form of loading that results in bias because most people tend to resist change.[7] An experiment conducted in the early days of polling illustrates the unpopularity of change.[8] Comparable samples of respondents were simultaneously asked two questions about the presidential succession in the United States. One sample was asked: **"Would you favour or oppose adding a law to the Constitution preventing a president from succeeding himself more than once?"** The other sample was asked: **"Would you favour or oppose changing the Constitution in order to prevent a president from succeeding himself more than once?"** To the first question, 50 percent of the respondents answered in the negative; to the second question, 65 percent answered in the negative. Thus the U.S. public would rather add to than change the Constitution.

Asking respondents "how often" they use a product or visit a store leads them to generalize about their habits, because there usually is some variance in their behaviour. In generalizing, one is likely to portray one's *ideal* behaviour rather than one's *average* behaviour. For instance, brushing one's teeth after each meal may be ideal, but busy people may skip a brushing or two. An introductory **counterbiasing statement** or preamble to a question that reassures respondents that their "embarrassing" behaviour is not abnormal may yield truthful responses:

Some people have the time to brush three times daily; others do not. How often did you brush your teeth yesterday?

If a question embarrasses the respondent, it may elicit no answer or a biased response. This is particularly true with respect to personal or classification data such as income or education. The problem may be mitigated by introducing the section of the questionnaire with a statement such as

To help classify your answers, we'd like to ask you a few questions. Again, your answers will be kept in strict confidence.

counterbiasing statement
An introductory statement or preamble to a potentially embarrassing question that reduces a respondent's reluctance to answer by suggesting that certain behaviour is not unusual.

A question statement may be leading because it is phrased to reflect either the negative or the positive aspects of an issue. To control for this bias, the wording of attitudinal questions may be reversed for 50 percent of the sample. This **split-ballot technique** is used with the expectation that two alternative phrasings of the same question will yield a more accurate total response than will a single phrasing. For example, a study on small-car buying behaviour may send one-half of a sample of European-car purchasers a questionnaire in which they are asked to agree or disagree with the statement, **"Small North American cars are cheaper to maintain than small European cars."** The other half of the European-car owners may receive a questionnaire in which the statement reads **"Small European cars are cheaper to maintain than small North American cars."**

Avoid Ambiguity: Be as Specific as Possible

Items on questionnaires often are ambiguous because they are too general. Consider such indefinite words as *often, occasionally, regularly, frequently, many, good, fair,* and *poor.* Each of these words has many different meanings. For one person *frequent* reading of *Maclean's* magazine may be reading six or seven issues a year; for another it may be two issues a year. The word *fair* has a great variety of meanings; the same is true for many other indefinite words.

Questions such as the following one, used in a study measuring the reactions of consumers to a television boycott, should be interpreted with care:

Please indicate the statement that best describes your family's television viewing during the boycott of Channel 11.

☐ **We did *not* watch any television programs on Channel 11.**
☐ **We watched *hardly any* television programs on Channel 11.**
☐ **We *occasionally* watched television programs on Channel 11.**
☐ **We *frequently* watched television programs on Channel 11.**

Some marketing scholars have suggested that the rate of diffusion of an innovation is related to the perception of product attributes such as *divisibility,* which refers to the extent to which the innovation may be tried or tested on a limited scale.[9] An empirical attempt to test this theory using semantic differentials was a disaster. Pre-testing found that the bipolar adjectives *divisible–not divisible* were impossible for consumers to understand because they did not have the theory in mind as a frame of reference. A revision of the scale used these bipolar adjectives:

Testable — : — : — : — : — : — **Not testable**
(sample use   **(sample use**
possible)   **not possible)**

However, the question remained ambiguous because the meaning was still unclear.

A brewing industry study on point-of-purchase advertising (store displays) asked:

What degree of durability do you prefer in your point-of-purchase advertising?

☐ **Permanent (lasting more than 6 months)**
☐ **Semipermanent (lasting from 1 to 6 months)**
☐ **Temporary (lasting less than 1 month)**

Here the researchers clarified the terms *permanent, semipermanent,* and *temporary* by defining them for the respondent. However, the question remained somewhat ambiguous. Beer marketers often use a variety of point-of-purchase devices to serve different purposes—in this case, what is the purpose? Furthermore, analysis was difficult because respondents were merely asked to indicate a preference rather than a *degree* of preference. Thus the meaning of a question may not be clear because the frame of reference is inadequate for interpreting the context of the question.

A student research group asked this question:

What media do you rely on most?

- ☐ **Television**
- ☐ **Radio**
- ☐ **Internet**
- ☐ **Newspapers**

This question is ambiguous because it does not ask about the content of the media. "Rely on most" for what—news, sports, entertainment?

Avoid Double-Barrelled Items

double-barrelled question
A question that may induce bias because it covers two issues at once.

A question covering several issues at once is referred to as a **double-barrelled question** and should always be avoided. Making the mistake of asking two questions rather than one is easy—for example, **"Please indicate your degree of agreement with the following statement: 'Wholesalers and retailers are responsible for the high cost of meat.'"** Which intermediaries are responsible, the wholesalers or the retailers? When multiple questions are asked in one question, the results may be exceedingly difficult to interpret. For example, consider the following question from a magazine's survey entitled "How Do You Feel about Being a Woman?"

> **Between you and your husband, who does the housework (cleaning, cooking, dishwashing, laundry) over and above that done by any hired help?**
>
> - ☐ **I do all of it.**
> - ☐ **I do almost all of it.**
> - ☐ **I do over half of it.**
> - ☐ **We split the work fifty-fifty.**
> - ☐ **My husband does over half of it.**

The answers to this question do not tell us if the wife cooks and the husband washes the dishes.

A survey by a consumer-oriented library asked:

> **Are you satisfied with the present system of handling "closed-reserve" and "open-reserve" readings? (Are enough copies available? Are the required materials ordered promptly? Are the borrowing regulations adequate for students' use of materials?)**
>
> ☐ **Yes**   ☐ **No**

A respondent may feel torn between a "yes" to one part of the question and a "no" to another part. The answer to this question does not tell the researcher which problem or combination of problems concerns the library user.

Consider this comment about double-barrelled questions:

> Generally speaking, it is hard enough to get answers to one idea at a time without complicating the problem by asking what amounts to two questions at once. If two ideas are to be explored, they deserve at least two questions. Since question marks are not rationed, there is little excuse for the needless confusion that results [from] the double-barrelled question.[10]

Avoid Making Assumptions

Consider the following question:

Should The Bay continue its excellent gift-wrapping program?

☐ **Yes**   ☐ **No**

This question has a built-in assumption: that people believe the gift-wrapping program is excellent. By answering "yes," the respondent implies that the program is, in fact, excellent and that things are fine just as they are; by answering "no," he or she implies that the store should discontinue the gift wrapping. The researchers should not place the respondent in that sort of bind by including an implicit assumption in the question.

Another frequent mistake is assuming that the respondent had previously thought about an issue. For example, the following question may appear in a survey concerning Subway restaurants: **"Do you think Subway restaurants should consider changing their name?"** It is very unlikely that respondents had thought about this question before being asked it. Most respondents may answer the question even though they had no prior opinion concerning the name change. Research that induces people to express attitudes on subjects they do not ordinarily think about is meaningless.

Avoid Burdensome Questions That May Tax the Respondent's Memory

A simple fact of human life is that people forget. Researchers writing questions about past behaviour or events should recognize that certain questions may make serious demands on the respondent's memory. Writing questions about prior events requires a conscientious attempt to minimize the problems associated with forgetting.

In many situations respondents cannot recall the answer to a question. For example, a telephone survey conducted during the 24-hour period following the airing of the Stanley Cup Final game might establish whether the respondent watched the game and then ask: **"Do you recall any commercials on that program?"** If the answer is positive, the interviewer might ask: **"What brands were advertised?"** These two questions measure *unaided recall,* because they give the respondent no clue as to the brand of interest.

If the researcher suspects that the respondent may have forgotten the answer to a question, he or she may rewrite the question in an *aided-recall* format—that is, in a format that provides a clue to help jog the respondent's memory. For instance, the question about an advertised beer in an aided-recall format might be **"Do you recall whether there was a brand of beer advertised on that program?"** or **"I am going to read you a list of beer brand names. Can you pick out the name of the beer that was advertised on the program?"** While aided recall is not as strong a test of attention or memory as unaided recall, it is less taxing to the respondent's memory.

Telescoping and squishing are two additional consequences of respondents' forgetting the exact details of their behaviour. *Telescoping* occurs when respondents believe that past events happened more recently than they actually did. The opposite effect, *squishing,* occurs when respondents think that recent events took place longer ago than they really did. A solution to this problem may be to refer to a specific event that is memorable—for example, **"How often have you gone to a sporting event since the Grey Cup?"** Because forgetting tends to increase over time, the question may concern a recent period: **"How often did you watch TSN on cable television last week?"** (During the editing stage, the results can be transposed to the appropriate time period.)

In situations in which "I don't know" or "I can't recall" is a meaningful answer, simply including a "don't know" response category may solve the question writer's problem.

ONE OR TWO QUESTIONS?

A study, part of an ongoing series of research-on-research investigations conducted by Market Facts, Inc., was designed to establish an accurate means of measuring rate of purchase.[11] Like other studies, it involved demographically matched samples of households, with each sample receiving a different treatment. Self-administered questionnaires were mailed to female heads of households, and purchase data were obtained for the following products: all-purpose white glue, aspirin, and replacement automobile tires.

Two different ways of asking the purchase incidence questions were investigated. Alternative A was sent to one sample of 1,000 homes; Alternative B was sent to another sample of 1,000 homes. The samples were closely matched in age, income, geography, and city size. To the right is a sample pair of questions.

The table below lists the percentages of respondents who reported purchasing items in the past three months, as revealed by the two forms of the question.

Alternative A

Below are listed several products. Please X each product you or anyone in your household bought in the past three months.

Alternative B

Below are listed several products. Please X each product you or anyone in your household ever bought. For each product ever bought, X the box that best describes when the product was purchased most recently:

☐ **Within the past 3 months**
☐ **4–6 months ago**
☐ **7–12 months ago**
☐ **Over 12 months ago**

	PURCHASED WITHIN PAST 3 MONTHS		
	A: **One-Step** **Question (%)**	**B:** **Two-Step** **Question (%)**	**Percentage** **Point** **Difference**
White glue	46	32	+14
Aspirin	68	57	+11
Replacement auto tires	32	24	+8

WHAT IS THE BEST QUESTION SEQUENCE?

The order of questions, or the question sequence, may serve several functions for the researcher. If the opening questions are interesting, simple to comprehend, and easy to answer, respondents' cooperation and involvement can be maintained throughout the questionnaire. Asking easy-to-answer questions teaches respondents their role and builds their confidence; they know that this is a professional researcher and not another salesperson posing as one. If respondents' curiosity is not aroused at the outset, they can become disinterested and terminate the interview.

A mail survey among department store buyers drew an extremely poor return rate. A substantial improvement in response rate occurred, however, when researchers added some introductory questions seeking opinions on pending legislation of great importance to these buyers. Respondents completed all the questions, not only those in the opening section.

In their attempt to "warm up" respondents toward the questionnaire, student researchers frequently ask demographic or classificatory questions at the beginning. This generally is not advisable, because asking for personal information such as income level or education may embarrass or threaten respondents. It usually is better to ask potentially embarrassing questions at the middle or end of the questionnaire, after rapport has been established between respondent and interviewer.

Order bias can result from a particular answer's position in a set of answers or from the sequencing of questions. In political elections in which candidates lack high visibility, such as elections for school board trustees, the first name listed on the ballot may receive the highest percentage of votes. For this reason, it would be good practice to print several ballots so that each candidate's name appears in every possible position on the ballot.

Order bias can also distort survey results. For example, suppose a questionnaire's purpose is to measure levels of awareness of several charitable organizations. If Big Brothers Big Sisters of Canada is always mentioned first, the Canadian Red Cross second, and the Canadian Cancer Society third, Big Brothers Big Sisters of Canada may receive an artificially high awareness rating because respondents are prone to yea-saying (by indicating awareness of the first item in the list).

Asking specific questions before asking about broader issues is a common cause of order bias. For example, bias may arise if questions about a specific clothing store are asked prior to those concerning the general criteria for selecting a clothing store. Suppose a respondent indicates in the first portion of a questionnaire that she shops at a store where parking needs to be improved. Later in the questionnaire, to avoid appearing inconsistent, she may state that parking is less important than she really believes it is. Specific questions may thus influence the more general ones. Therefore, it is advisable to ask general questions before specific questions to obtain the freest of open-ended responses. This procedure, known as the **funnel technique**, allows the researcher to understand the respondent's frame of reference before asking more specific questions about the level of the respondent's information and the intensity of his or her opinions.

Consider how later answers might be biased by previous questions in this questionnaire on environmental pollution:

Circle the number on the following table that best expresses your feelings about the severity of each environmental problem:

Problem	Not a Problem				Very Severe Problem
Air pollution from automobile exhausts	1	2	3	4	5
Air pollution from open burning	1	2	3	4	5
Air pollution from industrial smoke	1	2	3	4	5
Air pollution from foul odours	1	2	3	4	5
Noise pollution from airplanes	1	2	3	4	5
Noise pollution from cars, trucks, motorcycles	1	2	3	4	5
Noise pollution from industry	1	2	3	4	5

Not surprisingly, researchers found that the responses to the air pollution questions were highly correlated—in fact, almost identical.

With attitude scales, there also may be an *anchoring effect*. The first concept measured tends to become a comparison point from which subsequent evaluations are made. Randomization of items on a questionnaire susceptible to the anchoring effect helps minimize order bias.

A related problem is bias caused by the order of alternatives on closed questions. To avoid this problem, the order of these choices should be rotated if producing alternative forms of the questionnaire is possible. However, marketing researchers rarely print alternative questionnaires to eliminate problems resulting from order bias. A more common practice is to pencil in Xs or check marks on printed questionnaires to indicate where the interviewer should start a series of repetitive questions. For example, the capitalized phrases in the following question provide instructions to the interviewer to "rotate" brands, starting with the one checked:

I would like to determine how likely you would be to buy certain brands of candy in the future. Let's start with (X'ED BRAND). (RECORD BELOW UNDER APPROPRIATE BRAND. REPEAT QUESTIONS FOR ALL REMAINING BRANDS.)

Start Here:	( ) Caramilk	(X) Coffee Crisp	( ) KitKat
Definitely would buy	−1	−1	−1
Probably would buy	−2	−2	−2
Might or might not buy	−3	−3	−3
Probably would not buy	−4	−4	−4
Definitely would not buy	−5	−5	−5

One advantage of Internet surveys is the ability to reduce order bias by having the computer randomly order questions and/or response alternatives. With complete randomization, question order is random and respondents see response alternatives in different random positions.

Asking a question that does not apply to the respondent or that the respondent is not qualified to answer may be irritating or cause a biased response because the respondent wishes to please the interviewer or to avoid embarrassment. Including a **filter question** minimizes the chance of asking questions that are inapplicable. Asking **"Where do you generally have cheque-cashing problems in Toronto?"** may elicit a response even though the respondent has had no cheque-cashing problems; he or she may wish to please the interviewer with an answer. A filter question such as **"Do you ever have a problem cashing a cheque in Toronto? — Yes — No"** would screen out the people who are not qualified to answer.

Another form of filter question, the **pivot question**, can be used to obtain income information and other data that respondents may be reluctant to provide. For example,

"Is your total family income over or under $50,000?" IF UNDER, ASK, "Is it over or under $25,000?" IF OVER, ASK, "Is it over or under $75,000?"

Under $25,000   **$50,001–$75,000**

$25,001–$50,000   **Over $75,000**

Exhibit 13.2 gives an example of a flowchart plan for a questionnaire. Structuring the order of the questions so that they are logical will help to ensure the respondent's cooperation and eliminate confusion or indecision. The researcher maintains legitimacy by making sure that the respondent can comprehend the relationship between a given question (or section of the questionnaire) and the overall purpose of the study. Furthermore, a logical order may aid the individual's memory. Transitional comments explaining the logic of the questionnaire may ensure that the respondent continues. Here are two examples:

We have been talking so far about general shopping habits in this city. Now I'd like you to compare two types of grocery stores—regular supermarkets (e.g., IGA) and grocery departments in wholesale club stores (e.g., Costco).

So that I can combine your answers with those of other farmers who are similar to you, I need some personal information about you. Your

---

filter question
A question that screens out respondents who are not qualified to answer a second question.

pivot question
A filter question used to determine which version of a second question will be asked.

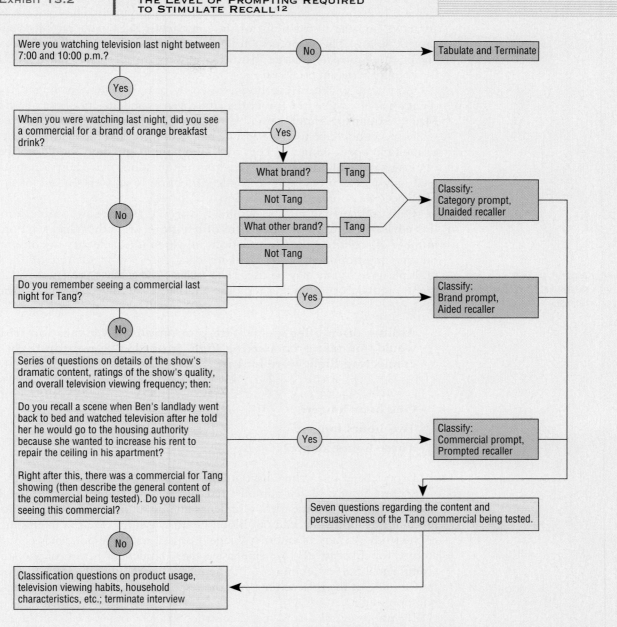

answers to these questions—as to all of the others you've answered—are confidential, and you will never be identified to anyone without your permission. Thanks for your help so far. If you'll answer the remaining questions, it will help me analyze all your answers.

WHAT IS THE BEST LAYOUT?

 Good layout and physical attractiveness are crucial in mail, Internet, and other self–administered questionnaires. For different reasons it is also important to have a good layout in questionnaires designed for personal and telephone interviews.

Traditional Questionnaires

Exhibit 13.3 shows a page from a telephone questionnaire. The layout is neat and attractive, and the instructions for the interviewer (all boldface capital letters) are easy to follow. The responses "It Depends," "Refused," and "Don't Know" are enclosed in a box to indicate that these answers are acceptable but responses from the 5-point scale are preferred.

Often rate of return can be increased by using money that might have been spent on an incentive to improve the attractiveness and quality of the questionnaire. Mail questionnaires should never be overcrowded. Margins should be of decent size, white space should be used to separate blocks of print, and the unavoidable columns of multiple boxes should be kept to a minimum. A question should not begin on one page and end on another page. Splitting questions may cause a respondent to read only part of a question, to pay less attention to answers on one of the pages, or to become confused.

Questionnaires should be designed to appear as short as possible. Sometimes it is advisable to use a booklet form of questionnaire rather than stapling a large number of pages together. In situations in which it is necessary to conserve space on the questionnaire or to facilitate data entry or tabulation of the data, a multiple-grid layout may be used. The **multiple-grid question** presents several similar questions and corresponding response alternatives arranged in a grid format. For example:

multiple-grid question
Several similar questions arranged in a grid format.

Airlines often offer special fare promotions. On a vacation trip would you take a connecting flight instead of a nonstop flight if the connecting flight were longer?

	Yes	No	Not sure
One hour longer?	☐	☐	☐
Two hours longer?	☐	☐	☐
Three hours longer?	☐	☐	☐

Experienced researchers have found that it pays to phrase the title of a questionnaire carefully. In self-administered and mail questionnaires a carefully constructed title may capture the respondent's interest, underline the importance of the research ("Nationwide Study of Blood Donors"), emphasize the interesting nature of the study ("Study of Internet Usage"), appeal to the respondent's ego ("Survey among Top Executives"), or emphasize the confidential nature of the study ("A Confidential Survey among . . . "). The researcher should take steps to ensure that the wording of the title will not bias the respondent in the same way that a leading question might.

By using several forms, special instructions, and other tricks of the trade, the researcher can design the questionnaire to facilitate the interviewer's job of following interconnected questions. Exhibits 13.4 and 13.5 illustrate portions of telephone and personal interview questionnaires. Note how the layout and easy-to-follow instructions for interviewers in Questions 1, 2, and 3 of Exhibit 13.4 help the interviewer follow the question sequence.

Instructions are often capitalized or printed in bold to alert the interviewer that it may be necessary to proceed in a certain way. For example, if a particular answer is given, the interviewer or respondent may be instructed to skip certain questions or go to a special sequence of questions.

Note that Questions 3 and 6 in Exhibit 13.5 instruct the interviewer to hand the respondent a card bearing a list of alternatives. Cards may help respondents grasp the intended meaning of the question and remember all the brand names or other items they are being asked about. Also, Questions 2, 3, and 5 in Exhibit 13.5 instruct the interviewer that rating of the banks will start with the bank that has been

EXHIBIT 13.3 | LAYOUT OF A PAGE FROM A TELEPHONE QUESTIONNAIRE

5. Now I'm going to read you some types of professions. For each one, please tell me whether you think the work that profession does, on balance, has a very positive impact on society, a somewhat positive impact, a somewhat negative impact, a very negative impact, or not much impact either way on society. First . . . **(START AT X'D ITEM. CONTINUE DOWN AND UP THE LIST UNTIL ALL ITEMS HAVE BEEN READ AND RATED.)**

| | | | | | | (DO NOT READ) | | |
Start Here	Very Positive Impact	Somewhat Positive Impact	Somewhat Negative Impact	Very Negative Impact	Not Much Impact	It Depends	Refused	Don't Know
[ ] Members of Parliament	1	2	3	4	5	0	X	Y (24)
[ ] Business executives	1	2	3	4	5	0	X	Y (25)
[ ] Physicians	1	2	3	4	5	0	X	Y (26)
[ ] Political pollsters—that is, people who conduct surveys for public officials or political candidates	1	2	3	4	5	0	X	Y (27)
[ ] Researchers in the media—that is, people in media such as television, newspapers, magazines, and radio, who conduct surveys about issues later reported in the media	1	2	3	4	5	0	X	Y (28)
[ ] Telemarketers—that is, people who sell products or services over the phone	1	2	3	4	5	0	X	Y (29)
[ ] Used car salesmen	1	2	3	4	5	0	X	Y (30)
[ ] Market researchers—that is, people who work for commercial research firms who conduct surveys to see what the public thinks about certain kinds of consumer products or services	1	2	3	4	5	0	X	Y (31)
[ ] Biomedical researchers	1	2	3	4	5	0	X	Y (32)
[ ] Public-opinion researchers—that is, people who work for commercial research firms who conduct surveys to see what the public thinks about important social issues	1	2	3	4	5	0	X	Y (33)
[ ] College and university professors	1	2	3	4	5	0	X	Y (34)
[ ] Lawyers	1	2	3	4	5	0	X	Y (35)
[ ] Members of the clergy	1	2	3	4	5	0	X	Y (36)
[ ] Journalists	1	2	3	4	5	0	X	Y (37)

EXHIBIT 13.4 | TELEPHONE QUESTIONNAIRE WITH SKIP QUESTIONS

1. Did you take the car you had checked to Canadian Tire for repairs?

__1 Yes   **(Skip to Q. 3)**   __2 No

2. **(If no, ask:)** Did you have the repair work done?

__1 Yes   __2 No

↓   ↓

1. Where was the repair work done? _____   1. Why didn't you have the car repaired?
_____   _____
                                                      _____
2. Why didn't you have the repair work done   _____
   at Canadian Tire? _____
_____
_____
_____

3. **(If yes to Q. 1, ask:)** How satisfied were you with the repair work? Were you . . .

__1 Very satisfied
__2 Somewhat satisfied
__3 Somewhat dissatisfied
__4 Very dissatisfied

(If somewhat or very dissatisfied:) In what way were you dissatisfied?
_____
_____
_____

4. **(Ask everyone:)** Do you ever buy gas at the 686 Queenston Road Canadian Tire gas station?

__1 Yes   __2 No **(Skip to Q. 6)**

5. **(If yes, ask:)** How often do you buy gas there?

__1 Always
__2 Almost always
__3 Most of the time
__4 Part of the time
__5 Hardly ever

6. Have you ever had your car washed there?

__1 Yes   __2 No

7. Have you ever had an oil change or lubrication done there?

__1 Yes   __2 No

checked in red pencil on the printed questionnaire. The name of the red-checked bank is not the same on every questionnaire. By rotating the order of the check marks, the researchers attempted to reduce order bias caused by respondents' tendency to react more favourably to the first set of questions. To facilitate coding, question responses should be pre-coded when possible, as in Exhibit 13.4.

Exhibit 13.6 illustrates a series of questions that includes a *skip question*. Either skip instructions or an arrow drawn pointing to the next question informs the respondent which question comes next.

EXHIBIT 13.5 | PERSONAL INTERVIEW QUESTIONNAIRE13

"Hello, my name is_____. I'm a Public Opinion Interviewer with Service Research Inc. We're making an opinion survey about banks and banking, and I'd like to ask you . . ."

1. What are the names of banks in your community you can think of offhand? (INTERVIEWER: List names in order mentioned.)

a. _____
b. _____
c. _____
d. _____
e. _____
f. _____
g. _____

2. Thinking now about the experiences you have had with the different banks here in Hamilton, have you ever talked to or done business with . . . (INTERVIEWER: Insert name of bank checked in red below.)

a. Are you personally acquainted with any of the employees or officers at _____?
b. (If YES) Who is that? _____
c. How long has it been since you have been inside? _____
(INTERVIEWER: Now go back and repeat 2–2c for all other banks listed.)

	(2) Talked		(2a and 2b) Know Employee Or Officer		(2c) Been in Bank in:				
	Yes	No	No	Name	Last Year	1–5	5-Plus	No	DK
Canadian Imperial Bank of Commerce	1	2	1	_____	1	2	3	4	5
TD Canada Trust	1	2	1	_____	1	2	3	4	5
National Bank of Canada	1	2	1	_____	1	2	3	4	5
Royal Bank	1	2	1	_____	1	2	3	4	5
Bank of Nova Scotia	1	2	1	_____	1	2	3	4	5

3. (HAND BANK RATING CARD) On this card there are a number of contrasting phrases or statements—for example, "Large" and "Small." We'd like to know how you rate (NAME OF BANK CHECKED IN RED BELOW) in terms of these statements or phrases. Just for example, let's use the terms "fast service" and "slow service." If you were to rate a bank #1 on this scale, it would mean you find their service "very fast." On the other hand, a 7 rating would indicate you feel their service is "very slow," whereas a 4 rating means you don't think of them as being either "very fast" or "very slow." Are you ready to go ahead? Good! Tell me then how you would rate (NAME OF BANK CHECKED IN RED) in terms of each of the phrases or statements on that card. How about (READ NEXT BANK NAME)? . . . (INTERVIEWER: Continue on until respondent has evaluated all five banks.)

	CIBC	TD Canada Trust	National Bank of Canada	Royal Bank	Bank of Nova Scotia
a. Service	____	____	____	____	____
b. Size	____	____	____	____	____
c. Business vs. Family	____	____	____	____	____
d. Friendliness	____	____	____	____	____
e. Big/Small Business	____	____	____	____	____
f. Rate of Growth	____	____	____	____	____
g. Modernness	____	____	____	____	____
h. Leadership	____	____	____	____	____
i. Loan Ease	____	____	____	____	____
j. Location	____	____	____	____	____
k. Hours	____	____	____	____	____
l. Ownership	____	____	____	____	____
m. Community Involvement	____	____	____	____	____

(continued)

EXHIBIT 13.5 | (CONTD.)

4. Suppose a friend of yours who has just moved to Hamilton asked you to recommend a bank. Which local bank would you recommend? Why would you recommend that particular bank?

CIBC	1
TD Canada Trust	2
National Bank of Canada	3
Royal Bank	4
Bank of Nova Scotia	5
Other (Specify) _____	
DK/Wouldn't	9

5. Which of the local banks do you think of as: (INTERVIEWER: Read red-checked item first, then read each of the other five.)

the newcomer's bank?

_____

the student's bank?

_____

the Personal Banker bank?

_____

the bank where most university faculty and staff bank?

_____

the bank most interested in this community?

_____

the most progressive bank?

_____

6. Which of these financial institutions, if any (HAND CARD 2), are you or any member of your immediate family who lives here in this home doing business with now?

Bank	1
Finance Company	2
Credit Union	3
None of these	4
DK/Not sure	5
(IF NONE, Skip to 19.)	

7. If a friend asked you to recommend a place where he or she could get a loan with which to buy a home, which financial institution would you probably recommend? (INTERVIEWER: Probe for specific name.) Why would you recommend (INSTITUTION NAMED)?

Would Recommend: _____

_____

Wouldn't	0
DK/Not Sure	9

Layout is extremely important when questionnaires are long or require the respondent to fill in a large amount of information. In many circumstances using headings or subtitles to indicate groups of questions will help the respondent grasp the scope or nature of the questions to be asked. Thus at a glance, the respondent can follow the logic of the questionnaire.

Internet Questionnaires

Layout is also an important issue for questionnaires appearing on the Internet. A questionnaire on a Web site should be easy to use, flow logically, and have a graphic

EXHIBIT 13.6 | EXAMPLE OF A SKIP QUESTION

1. If you had to buy a computer tomorrow, which of the following three types of computers do you think you would buy?

1 Desktop—Go to Q. 3
2 Laptop—Go to Q. 3
3 Palm-sized (PDA)

2. (If "Palm-sized" on Q. 1, ask): What brand of computer do you think you would buy?
3. What is your age?

look and overall feel that motivate the respondent to cooperate from start to finish. Many of the guidelines for layout of paper questionnaires apply to Internet questionnaires. There are, however, some important differences.

With *graphical user interface (GUI) software,* the researcher can exercise control over the background, colours, fonts, and other visual features displayed on the computer screen so as to create an attractive and easy-to-use interface between the computer user and the Internet survey. GUI software allows the researcher to design questionnaires in which respondents click on the appropriate answer rather than having to type answers or codes.

Researchers often use Web publishing software, such as WebSurveyor, Zoomerang, FrontPage, or Netscape Composer, to format a questionnaire so that they will know how it should appear online. However, several features of a respondent's computer may influence the appearance of an Internet questionnaire. For example, discrepancies between the designer's and the respondent's computer settings for screen configuration (e.g., 640 × 480 pixels versus 800 × 600 pixels) may result in questions not being fully visible on the respondent's screen, misaligned text, or other visual problems.[14] The possibility that the questionnaire the researcher/designer constructs on his or her computer may look different from the questionnaire that appears on the respondent's computer should always be considered when designing Internet surveys. One sophisticated remedy is to use the first few questions on an Internet survey to ask about operating system, browser software, and other computer configuration issues so that the questionnaire that is delivered is as compatible as possible with the respondent's computer. A simpler solution is to limit the horizontal width of the questions to 70 characters or less, to decrease the likelihood of wrap-around text.

Layout Issues

Even if the questionnaire designer's computer and the respondents' computers are compatible, there are several layout issues a Web questionnaire designer should consider. The first decision is whether the questionnaire will appear page by page, with individual questions on separate screens (Web pages), or on a scrolling basis, with the entire questionnaire appearing on a single Web page that the respondent scrolls from top to bottom. The *paging layout* (going from screen to screen) greatly facilitates skip patterns. Based on a respondent's answers to filter questions, the computer can automatically insert relevant questions on subsequent pages. If the entire questionnaire appears on one page (the *scrolling layout*), the display should advance smoothly, as if it were a piece of paper being moved up or down. The scrolling layout gives the respondent the ability to read any portion of the questionnaire at any time, but the absence of page boundaries can cause problems. For example, suppose a Likert scale consists of 15 statements in a grid-format layout, with the response categories **Strongly Agree, Agree, Disagree,** and **Strongly Disagree** at the beginning of the questionnaire. Once the respondent has scrolled down beyond the first few statements, he or she may not be able to see both the statements at the end of the list and the response categories at the top of the grid simultaneously. Thus avoiding the problems associated with splitting questions and response categories may be difficult with scrolling questionnaires.

When a scrolling questionnaire is long, category or section headings are helpful to respondents. It is also a good idea to provide links to the top and bottom parts of each section, so that users can navigate through the questionnaire without having to scroll through the entire document.[15]

Whether a Web survey is page-by-page or scrolling format, **push buttons** with labels should clearly describe the actions to be taken. For example, if the respondent is to go to the next page, a large arrow labelled "NEXT" might appear in colour at the bottom of the screen.

push button
In a dialogue box on an Internet questionnaire, a small outlined area, such as a rectangle or an arrow, that the respondent clicks on to select an option or perform a function, such as Submit.

Decisions must be made about the use of colour, graphics, animation, sound, and other special features that the Internet makes possible. One thing to remember is that, although sophisticated graphics are not a problem for people with very powerful computers, many respondents' computers are not powerful enough to deliver complex graphics at a satisfactory speed, if at all. A textured background, coloured headings, and small graphics can make a questionnaire more interesting and appealing, but they may present problems for respondents with older computers and/or low-bandwidth Internet connections.

With a paper questionnaire, the respondent knows how many questions he or she must answer. Because many Internet surveys offer no visual clues about the number of questions to be asked, it is important to provide a **status bar** or some other visual indicator of questionnaire length. For example, including a partially filled rectangular box as a visual symbol and a statement such as "The status bar at top right indicates approximately what portion of the survey you have completed" increases the likelihood that the respondent will finish the entire sequence of questions.

An Internet questionnaire uses windows known as dialogue boxes to display questions and record answers. Exhibit 13.7 portrays four common ways of displaying questions on a computer screen. Many Internet questionnaires require the respondent to activate his or her answer by clicking on the **radio button** for a response. Radio buttons work like push buttons on automobile radios: Clicking on an alternative response deactivates the first choice and replaces it with the new response. A **drop-down box**, such as the one shown in Exhibit 13.7, is a space-saving device that allows the researcher to provide a list of responses that are hidden from view until they are needed. A general statement, such as "Please select" or "Click here," is shown initially. Clicking on the downward-facing arrow makes the full range of choices appear. If the first choice in a list, such as "Strongly Agree," is shown while the other responses are kept hidden, the chance that response bias will occur is increased. Drop-down boxes may present a problem for individuals with minimal computer skills, as they may not know how to reveal hidden responses behind a drop-down menu or how to move from one option to another in a moving-bar menu.

Checklist questions may be followed by **check boxes**, several, none, or all of which may be checked by the respondent. **Open-ended boxes** are boxes in which respondents type their answers to open-ended questions. Open-ended boxes may be designed as *one-line text boxes* or *scrolling text boxes,* depending on the breadth of the expected answer. Of course, open-ended questions require that respondents have both the skill and the willingness to keyboard lengthy answers on the computer. Some open-ended boxes are designed so that respondents can enter numbers for frequency response, ranking, or rating questions. For example:

Below you will see a series of statements that might or might not describe how you feel about your career. Please rate each statement using a scale from 1 to 4, where 4 means "Totally Agree," 3 means "Somewhat Agree," 2 means "Somewhat Disagree," and 1 means "Totally Disagree."

Please enter your numeric answer in the box provided next to each statement. **Would you say that . . . ?**

A lack of business knowledge relevant to my field/ career could hurt my career advancement.

My career life is an important part of how I define myself.

Pop-up boxes are message boxes that can be used to highlight important information. For example, pop-up boxes may be used to provide a privacy statement, such as the following:

---

status bar
In an Internet questionnaire, a visual indicator that tells the respondent what portion of the survey he or she has completed.

radio button
In an Internet questionnaire, a circular icon, resembling a button, that activates one response choice and deactivates others when a respondent clicks on it.

drop-down box
In an Internet questionnaire, a space-spacing device that reveals responses when they are needed but otherwise hides them from view.

check box
In an Internet questionnaire, a small graphic box, next to an answer, that a respondent clicks on to choose that answer; typically, a check mark or an X appears in the box when the respondent clicks on it.

open-ended box
In an Internet questionnaire, a box where respondents can type in their own answers to open-ended questions.

pop-up boxes
In an Internet questionnaire, boxes that appear at selected points and contain information or instructions for respondents.

EXHIBIT 13.7 | ALTERNATIVE WAYS OF DISPLAYING INTERNET QUESTIONS

Radio button

Last month, did you purchase products or services over the Internet?

○ Yes

○ No

How familiar are you with Microsoft's X-box video game player?

Know Extremely Well	Know Fairly Well	Know a Little	Know Just Name	Never Heard of
○	○	○	○	○

Drop-down box, closed position

In which country or region do you currently reside?

| Click Here | ▼ |

Drop-down box, open position

In which country or region do you currently reside?

| Click Here | ▼ |

Click Here
United States
Asia/Pacific (excluding Hawaii)
Africa
Australia or New Zealand
Canada
Europe
Latin America, South America, or Mexico
Middle East
Other

Check box

From which location(s) do you access the Internet? Select all that apply.
☐ Home
☐ Work
☐ Other Location

Please indicate which of the following Web sites you have ever visited or used. (CHOOSE ALL THAT APPLY.)
☐ E*Trade's Web site
☐ Waterhouse's Web site
☐ Merrill Lynch's Web site
☐ Fidelity's Web site
☐ Schwab's Web site
☐ Powerstreet
☐ Yahoo! Finance
☐ Quicken.com
☐ Lycos Investing
☐ AOL's Personal Finance
☐ None of the above

Open-ended, one-line box

What company do you think is the most visible sponsor of sports?

Open-ended, scrolling text box

What can we do to improve our textbook?

IBM would like your help in making our Web site easier to use and more effective. Choose to complete the survey now or not at all.

| Complete | | No Thank You | | Privacy Statement |

Clicking on Privacy Statement opens the following pop-up box:

Survey Privacy Statement

This overall Privacy Statement verifies that IBM is a member of the TRUSTe program and is in compliance with TRUSTe principles. This survey is strictly for market research purposes. The information you provide will be used only to improve the overall content, navigation, and usability of ibm.com.

In some cases, respondents can learn more about how to use a particular scale or get a definition of a term by clicking on a link, which generates a pop-up box. One of the most common reasons for using pop-up boxes is *error trapping,* a topic discussed in the next section.

Chapter 12 described graphic rating scales, which present respondents with a graphic continuum. On the Internet, researchers can take advantage of scroll bars or other GUI software features to make these scales easy to use. For example, the graphic continuum may be drawn as a measuring rod with a plus sign on one end and a minus sign on the other. The respondent then moves a small rectangle back and forth between the two ends of the scale to scroll to any point on the continuum. Scoring, as discussed in Chapter 12, is in terms of some measure of the length (millimetres) from one end of the graphic continuum to the point marked by the respondent.

Finally, it is a good idea to include a customized thank-you page at the end of an Internet questionnaire, so that a brief thank-you note pops onto their screens when respondents click on the Submit push button.[16]

Software That Makes Questionnaires Interactive

Computer code can be written to make Internet questionnaires interactive and less prone to errors. The writing of software programs is beyond the scope of this discussion. However, several of the interactive functions that software makes possible should be mentioned here.

As discussed in Chapter 8, Internet software allows the branching off of questioning into two or more different lines, depending on a particular respondent's answer, and the skipping or filtering of questions. Questionnaire-writing software with Boolean skip and branching logic is readily available. Most of these programs have *hidden skip logic* so that respondents never see any evidence of skips. It is best if the questions the respondent sees flow in numerical sequence.[17] However, some programs number all potential questions in numerical order, and the respondent sees only the numbers on the questions he or she answers. Thus a respondent may answer questions 1 through 11 and then next see a question numbered 15 because of the skip logic.

Software can systematically or randomly manipulate the questions a respondent sees. **Variable piping software** allows variables, such as answers from previous questions, to be inserted into unfolding questions. Other software can randomly rotate the order of questions, blocks of questions, and response alternatives from respondent to respondent.

Researchers can use software to control the flow of a questionnaire. Respondents can be blocked from backing up, or they can be allowed to stop in mid-questionnaire and come back later to finish. A questionnaire can be designed so that if the respondent fails to answer a question or answers it with an incorrect

variable piping software
Software that allows variables to be inserted into an Internet questionnaire as a respondent is completing it.

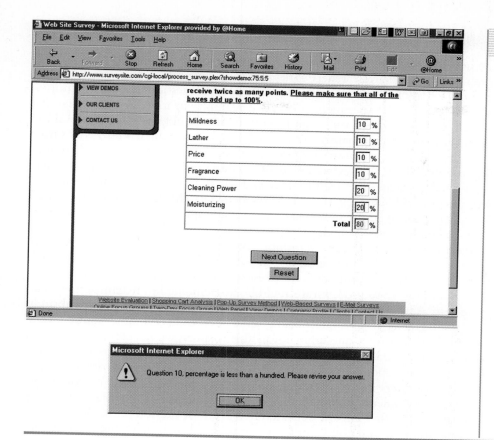

error trapping
Using software to control the flow of an Internet questionnaire—for example, to prevent respondents from backing up or failing to answer a question.

forced answering software
Software that prevents respondents from continuing with an Internet questionnaire if they fail to answer a question.

type of response, an immediate error message appears. This is called **error trapping**. With **forced answering software**, respondents cannot skip over questions as they do in mail surveys. The program will not let them continue if they fail to answer a question.[18] The software may insert a boldfaced error message on the question screen or insert a pop-up box instructing the respondent how to continue. For example, if a respondent does not answer a question and tries to proceed to another screen, a pop-up box might present the following message:

> **You cannot leave a question blank. On questions without a "Not sure" or "Decline to answer" option, please choose the response that best represents your opinions or experiences.**

The respondent must close the pop-up box and answer the question in order to proceed to the next screen.

Some respondents will leave the questionnaire Web site, prematurely terminating the survey. In many cases sending an e-mail message to these respondents at a later date, encouraging them to revisit the Web site, will persuade them to complete the questionnaire. Through the use of software and cookies, researchers can make sure that the respondent who revisits the Web site will be able to pick up at the point where he or she left off.

Once an Internet questionnaire has been designed, it is important to pre-test it to ensure that it works with Internet Explorer, Netscape, Firefox, Opera, AOL, WebTV, and other browsers. Some general-purpose programming languages, such as Java, do not always work with all browsers. Because different browsers have different peculiarities, a survey that works perfectly well with one may not function at all with another.[19]

Many novelists write, rewrite, revise, and rewrite again certain chapters, paragraphs, or even sentences. The researcher works in a similar world. Rarely does he or she write only a first draft of a questionnaire. Usually the questionnaire is tried out on a group, selected on a convenience basis that is similar in makeup to the one that ultimately will be sampled. Although the researcher should not select a group too divergent from the target market (for example, selecting business students as surrogates for business people), pre-testing does not require a statistical sample. The pre-testing process allows the researcher to determine whether respondents have any difficulty understanding the questionnaire and whether there are any ambiguous or biased questions. This process is exceedingly beneficial. Making a mistake with 25 or 50 subjects can avoid the potential disaster of administering an invalid questionnaire to several hundred individuals.

Getting respondents to add everything correctly is a problem. Notice how the questions in Exhibit 13.8 from a survey on secretarial support are designed to mitigate this problem. Pre-testing difficult questions such as these is essential.

What administrative procedures should be implemented to maximize the value of a pre-test? Administering a questionnaire exactly as planned in the actual study often is not possible; for example, mailing out a questionnaire might require several weeks. And pre-testing a questionnaire in this manner would provide important information on response rate, but it might not point out why questions were skipped or why respondents found certain questions ambiguous or confusing. Personal interviewers can record requests for additional explanation or comments that indicate respondents' difficulty with question sequence or other factors. This is the primary reason that interviewers are often used for pre-test work. Self-administered questionnaires are not reworded to be personal interviews, but interviewers are instructed to observe respondents and ask for their comments after they complete the questionnaire. When pre-testing personal or telephone interviews, interviewers may test alternative wordings and question sequences to determine which format best suits the intended respondents.

No matter how the pre-test is conducted, the researcher should remember that its purpose is to uncover any problems that the questionnaire may cause. Thus pre-tests typically are conducted to answer questions about the questionnaire such as the following:

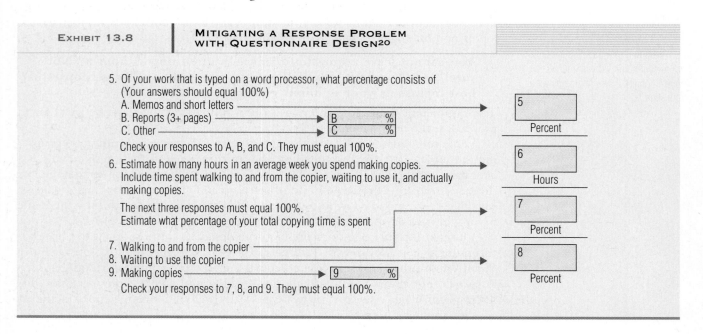

| EXHIBIT 13.8 | MITIGATING A RESPONSE PROBLEM WITH QUESTIONNAIRE DESIGN[20] |

5. Of your work that is typed on a word processor, what percentage consists of (Your answers should equal 100%)
A. Memos and short letters ⟶ 5 Percent
B. Reports (3+ pages) ⟶ B %
C. Other ⟶ C %
Check your responses to A, B, and C. They must equal 100%.

6. Estimate how many hours in an average week you spend making copies. ⟶ 6 Hours
Include time spent walking to and from the copier, waiting to use it, and actually making copies.

The next three responses must equal 100%.
Estimate what percentage of your total copying time is spent ⟶ 7 Percent

7. Walking to and from the copier ⟶ 8 Percent
8. Waiting to use the copier ⟶
9. Making copies ⟶ 9 %
Check your responses to 7, 8, and 9. They must equal 100%.

- Can the questionnaire format be followed by the interviewer?

- Does the questionnaire flow naturally and conversationally?

- Are the questions clear and easy to understand?

- Can respondents answer the questions easily?

- Which alternative forms of questions work best?

Pre-tests also provide means for testing the sampling procedure—to determine, for example, whether interviewers are following the sampling instructions properly and whether the procedure is efficient. Pre-tests also provide estimates of the response rates for mail surveys and the completion rates for telephone surveys.

Usually a questionnaire goes through several revisions. The exact number of revisions depends on the researcher's and client's judgment. The revision process usually ends when both agree that the desired information is being collected in an unbiased manner.

DESIGNING QUESTIONNAIRES FOR GLOBAL MARKETS

Now that marketing research is being conducted around the globe, researchers must take cultural factors into account when designing questionnaires. The most common problem involves translating a questionnaire into other languages. A questionnaire developed in one country may be difficult to translate because equivalent language concepts do not exist or because of differences in idiom and vernacular. For example, the concepts of uncles and aunts are not the same in Canada as in India. In India the words for *uncle* and *aunt* are different for the maternal and paternal sides of the family.[21] Although Spanish is spoken in both Mexico and Venezuela, one researcher found out that the Spanish translation of the English term *retail outlet* works in Mexico, but not in Venezuela. Venezuelans interpreted the translation to refer to an electrical outlet, an outlet of a river into an ocean, or the passageway into a patio.

back translation

Taking a questionnaire that has previously been translated into another language and having a second, independent translator translate it back to the original language.

International marketing researchers often have questionnaires back translated. **Back translation** is the process of taking a questionnaire that has previously been translated from one language to another and having it translated back again by a second, independent translator. The back translator is often a person whose native tongue is the language that will be used for the questionnaire. This process can reveal inconsistencies between the English version and the translation. For example, when a soft-drink company translated its slogan "Baby, it's cold inside" into Cantonese for research in Hong Kong, the result read "Small Mosquito, on the inside, it is very cold." In Hong Kong, *small mosquito* is a colloquial expression for a small child. Obviously the intended meaning of the advertising message had been lost in the translated questionnaire.[22] In another international marketing research project, "out of sight, out of mind" was back translated as "invisible things are insane."[23]

As indicated in Chapter 8, literacy influences the designs of self-administered questionnaires and interviews. Knowledge of the literacy rates in foreign countries, especially those that are just developing modern economies, is vital.

SUMMARY

Good questionnaire design is a key to obtaining accurate survey results. The specific questions to be asked will be a function of the type of information needed to answer the manager's questions and the communication medium of data collection. Relevance and accuracy are the basic criteria for judging questionnaire results. A questionnaire is *relevant* if no unnecessary information is collected and the information needed for solving the marketing problem is obtained. *Accuracy* means that the information is reliable and valid.

Knowing how each question should be phrased requires some knowledge of the different types of questions possible. Open-ended response questions pose some problem or question and ask the respondent to answer in his or her own words. Fixed-alternative questions require less interviewer skill, take less time, and are easier to answer. In fixed-alternative questions the respondent is given specific limited alternative responses and asked to choose the one closest to his or her viewpoint. Standardized responses are easier to code, tabulate, and interpret. Care must be taken to formulate the responses so that they do not overlap. Respondents whose answers do not fit any of the fixed alternatives may be forced to select alternatives that do not communicate what they really mean.

Open-ended response questions are especially useful in exploratory research or at the beginning of a questionnaire. They make a questionnaire more expensive to analyze because of the uniqueness of the answers. Also, interviewer bias can influence the responses to such questions.

Some guidelines for questionnaire construction have emerged from research experience. The language should be simple to allow for variations in educational level. Researchers should avoid leading or loaded questions, which suggest answers to the respondents, as well as questions that induce them to give socially desirable answers. Respondents have a bias against questions that suggest changes in the status quo. Their reluctance to answer personal questions can be reduced by explaining the need for the questions and by assuring respondents of the confidentiality of their replies. The researcher should carefully avoid ambiguity in questions. Another common problem is the double-barrelled question, which asks two questions at once.

Question sequence can be very important to the success of a survey. The opening questions should be designed to capture respondents' interest and keep them involved. Personal questions should be postponed to the middle or end of the questionnaire. General questions should precede specific ones. In a series of attitude scales the first response may be used as an anchor for comparison with the other responses. The order of alternatives on closed questions can affect the results. Filter questions are useful for avoiding unnecessary questions that do not apply to a particular respondent. Such questions may be put into a flowchart for personal or telephone interviewing.

The layout of a mail or other self-administered questionnaire can affect its response rate. An attractive questionnaire encourages a response, as does a carefully phrased title. Internet questionnaires present their own design issues. Decisions must be made about the use of colour, graphics, animation, sound, and other special layout effects that the Internet makes possible. Finally, pre-testing helps reveal errors while they can still be corrected easily.

International marketing researchers must take cultural factors into account when designing questionnaires. The most widespread problem involves translation into another language. International questionnaires are often back translated.

Key Terms and Concepts

open-ended response question
fixed-alternative question
simple-dichotomy (dichotomous-
    alternative) question
determinant-choice question
frequency-determination question
checklist question
leading question
loaded question
counterbiasing statement

split-ballot technique
double-barrelled question
order bias
funnel technique
filter question
pivot question
multiple-grid question
push button
status bar
radio button

drop-down box
check box
open-ended box
pop-up boxes
variable piping software
error trapping
forced answering software
back translation

Questions for Review and Critical Thinking

1. Evaluate and comment on the following questions, taken from several questionnaires:

   a. A university computer centre survey on SPSS usage:

   How often do you use SPSS statistical software? Please check one.

   ——Infrequently (once a semester)

   ——Occasionally (once a month)

   ——Frequently (once a week)

   ——All the time (daily)

   b. A survey of advertising agencies:

   Do you understand and like Advertising Standards Canada's code of advertising standards?

   ——Yes ——No

   c. A survey on a new, small electric car:

   Assuming 90 percent of your driving is in town, would you buy this type of car?

   ——Yes ——No

   If this type of *electric* car had the same initial cost as a current "Big 3" full-size, fully equipped car, but operated at one-half the cost over a five-year period, would you buy one?

   ——Yes ——No

   d. A student survey:

   Since the beginning of this semester, approximately what percentage of the time do you get to campus using each of the forms of transportation available to you per week?

   Walk ——

   Bicycle ——

   Public transportation ——

   Motor vehicle ——

   e. A survey of motorcycle dealers:

   Should the company continue its generous cooperative advertising program?

   f. A survey of media use by farmers:

   Thinking about *yesterday*, put an X in the box for *each* quarter-hour time period during which, so far as you can recall, you *personally* listened to *radio*. Do the same for *television*.

   If you did not watch TV any time yesterday, X here ☐

   If you did not listen to radio any time yesterday, X here ☐

   g. A government survey of gasoline retailers:

   Suppose the full-service pump selling price for regular gasoline is 94.9 cents per litre on the first day of the month. Suppose on the 10th of the month the price is raised to 97.9 cents per litre, and on the 25th of the month it is reduced to 92.4 cents per litre. In order to provide the required data you should list the accumulator reading on the full-service regular gasoline pump when the station opens on the 1st day, the 10th day, and the 25th day of the month and when the station closes on the last day of the month.

   h. A survey of the general public:

   In the next year, after accounting for inflation, do you think your real personal income will go up or down?

   1. **Up**

   2. **(Stay the same)**

   3. **Down**

   4. **(Don't know)**

   i. A survey of the general public:

   Some people say that companies should be required by law to label all chemicals and substances that the government states are potentially harmful. The label would tell what the chemical or substance is, what dangers it might pose, and what safety procedures should be used in handling the substance. Other people say that such laws would be too strict. They say the law should require labels on only those chemicals and substances that the companies themselves decide are potentially harmful. Such a law, they say, would be less costly for the companies and would permit them to exclude those chemicals and substances they consider to be trade secrets. Which of these views is closest to your own?

   1. **Require labels on all chemicals and substances that the government states are potentially harmful.**

   2. **(Don't know)**

   3. **Require labels on only those chemicals and substances that companies decide are potentially harmful.**

j. A survey of voters:

Since agriculture is vital to Canada's economy, how do you feel about the government's farm policies?

Strongly favour

Somewhat favour

Somewhat oppose

Strongly oppose

Unsure

2. The following question was asked of a sample of television viewers:

We are going to ask you to classify the type of fan you consider yourself to be for different sports and sports programs.

Diehard Fan: Watch games, follow up on scores and sports news many times a day

Avid Fan: Watch games, follow up on scores and sports news once a day

Casual Fan: Watch games, follow up on scores and sports news occasionally

Championship Fan: Watch games, follow up on scores and sports news only during championships or playoffs

Non-Fan: Never watch games or follow up on scores

Anti-Fan: Dislike, oppose, or object to a certain sport

Does this question do a good job of avoiding ambiguity?

3. How might the wording of a question about income influence respondents' answers?

4. What is the difference between a leading question and a loaded question?

5. Design one or more open-ended response questions to measure reactions to a magazine ad for a Xerox photocopier.

6. Design one or more questions to measure how a person who has just been shown a television commercial might describe the commercial.

7. Evaluate the layout of the filter question that follows:

Are you employed either full time or part time?

Mark (x) one.   ☐ Yes   ☐ No

If yes: How many hours per week are you usually employed? *Mark (x) one.*

☐ Less than 35   ☐ 35 or more

What is the postal code at your usual place of work?

_____

8. It has been said that surveys show that consumers hate advertising, but like specific ads. Comment.

9. Design a complete questionnaire to evaluate a new fast-food fried chicken restaurant.

10. Design a short but complete questionnaire to measure consumer satisfaction with an airline.

11. Develop a checklist of things to consider in questionnaire construction.

12. Design a complete personal interview questionnaire for a zoo that wishes to determine who visits the zoo and how they evaluate it.

13. Design a complete self-administered questionnaire for a bank to give to customers immediately after they open new accounts.

14. Design a questionnaire for your local Big Brothers Big Sisters of Canada organization to investigate awareness of and willingness to volunteer time to this organization.

15. Design a questionnaire for a bank located in a college town to investigate the potential for attracting college students as chequing account customers.

16. The Apple Assistance Centre is a hotline to solve problems for users of Macintosh computers and other Apple products. Design a short (postcard-size) consumer satisfaction/service quality questionnaire for the Apple Assistance Centre.

17. Visit the United Kingdom's Historic Royal Palaces Web site at www.hrp.org.uk/index2.htm. What type of questions might be asked in a survey to evaluate a visitor's experience at this Web site?

18. A client tells a researcher that she wants a questionnaire that evaluates the importance of 30 product characteristics and rates her brand and 10 competing brands on these characteristics. The researcher believes that this questionnaire will induce respondent fatigue because it will be far too long. Should the researcher do exactly what the client says or risk losing the business by suggesting a different approach?

19. A lobbying organization designs a short questionnaire about its political position. It also includes a membership solicitation with the questionnaire. Is this approach ethical?

20. A public figure who supports cost cutting in government asks the following question in a survey: **"Do you support a government campaign to eliminate waste in government?"** Is this question ethical?

Exploring the Internet

1. Visit Mister Poll at www.misterpoll.com, where you will find thousands of user-contributed polls on every imaginable topic from the controversial to the downright zany. What you find will depend on when you visit the site. However, you might find something such as a Movie Poll, where you pick your favourite film of the season. Evaluate the questions in the poll.

2. Visit Google at www.google.ca and conduct a search using the key phrase "Questionnaire Design." How many Web sites contain this phrase? Find an interesting Web site and report on your findings.

3. A language translator (English to Spanish, French to English, etc.) can be found at

   http://babelfish.altavista.com/.

Airfone®, currently operated by Verizon based in the United States, provides in-flight communications in Canada, the United States, and Mexico for major airlines, including Air Canada. The questionnaire presented in Case Exhibit 13.1.1 was sent to a sample of frequent airline fliers.[24]

Questions

1. Assuming that Airfone® wanted to learn about consumer perceptions of the ease of billing and quality of the phone service, evaluate the questionnaire below and identify if it would serve these information needs.

2. Can Airfone® also identify the most valuable airline partners with the information collected using the questionnaire below? Identify what other marketing-related uses Airfone® could use with the information collected.

CASE EXHIBIT 13.1.1	AIRFONE® QUESTIONNAIRE

If you have used the Airfone® service, please indicate your level of satisfaction with the Airfone service by circling the appropriate number below.

	Excellent 5	Good 4	Average 3	Fair 2	Poor 1
Airfone® service					
A1 Considering your Airfone® usage, how would you rate your overall experience?	5	4	3	2	1
A2 Availability of Airfone® on flights on which you've travelled	5	4	3	2	1
A3 Availability of operating instructions	5	4	3	2	1
A4 Understandability of operating instructions	5	4	3	2	1
A5 Length of time to obtain dial tone	5	4	3	2	1
A6 Ability to complete a call on the first attempt	5	4	3	2	1
A7 Transmission quality (static)	5	4	3	2	1
A8 Level of telephone background noise	5	4	3	2	1
A9 Calls fading	5	4	3	2	1
A10 Hearing the called party clearly	5	4	3	2	1
A11 Called party hearing you clearly	5	4	3	2	1
A12 Frequency of calls disconnected	5	4	3	2	1
A13 Convenience of computer voice messages	5	4	3	2	1
A14 Current price structure	5	4	3	2	1
A15 Flight attendant helpfulness, assistance, and knowledge of the Airfone® service	5	4	3	2	1
Billing					
B1 Accuracy of monthly charges	5	4	3	2	1
B2 Ease of understanding charges	5	4	3	2	1

The following questions concern your Airfone® usage, airline travel, preferred charge method, and a comparison of the Airfone® to cellular phones. Please answer as completely as possible.

1. In the past year, how often have you used the Airfone® service?

_____
(Enter # Times)

2. Have you used our Seatfone product?
   (Circle one answer)

   Yes ... 1
   No ... 2

3. Did you use the Airfone® service to make urgent business calls, nonurgent business calls, or personal calls?
   (Circle all that apply)

   Urgent business calls ... 1
   Nonurgent business calls ... 2
   Personal calls ... 3

4. Approximately how many airline round trips do you make annually?

   _____
   (Enter # Times)

5. Which airline do you most frequently travel on?

   _____
   (Enter Name of Airline)

6. Has the Airfone® service made your travel time productive and more beneficial to your completing business while in flight?
   (Circle one answer)
   If yes, please explain how _____

   Yes ... 1
   No ... 2

   _____
   _____

7. Considering the value of the Airfone® service, do you feel the cost of a call is comparable to the quality of service you've experienced?
   (Circle one answer)
   If no, please explain why _____

   Yes ... 1
   No ... 2

   _____
   _____

8. Given a choice of flights with the same schedule, destination, and cost, one with the Airfone® service, the other without, which flight would you choose to travel on? (Circle one answer)

   With Airfone ... 1
   Without Airfone ... 2

9. Which credit cards do you own? (Circle all that apply)
   1. American Express   3. Diners Club   5. MasterCard
   2. Discover   4. Visa

10. Which credit card have you used in the past to pay for the Airfone® service? (Circle all that apply)
    1. American Express   3. Diners Club   5. MasterCard
    2. Discover   4. Visa

11. Have you experienced problems activating the Airfone® Service with your card(s)?
    (Circle one answer)

    Yes ... 1
    No ... 2

12. Which card would you prefer to use to pay for the Airfone® service?
    (Circle all that apply)
    1. American Express   3. Diners Club   5. MasterCard
    2. Discover   4. Visa

13. Do you own a cellular phone or use a company-paid cellular phone?
    (Circle one answer)
    If yes, how does the quality of the Airfone® compare to that of the cellular phone? (Circle one answer)

    Yes ... 1
    No ... 2

    Airfone® is much higher quality than cellular ... 1
    Airfone® is somewhat higher quality than cellular ... 2
    Airfone® is about the same quality as cellular ... 3
    Airfone® is somewhat lower quality than cellular ... 4
    Airfone® is much lower quality than cellular ... 5

14. Have you ever seen any advertising for Airfone®?
    If yes, what did the advertising tell you about Airfone®?

    Yes ... 1
    No ... 2

    _____
    _____

(continued)

If yes, where have you seen Airfone® advertising? (Circle all that apply)

In-flight airline magazines	1
Posters or billboards	2
TV at airport	3
Newspapers	4
Business publications	5
Card located in the seatback pocket	6
Other	7

15. Are you aware of our Service Guarantee that provides credit when you are not satisfied with the quality of an Airfone® call?

Yes	1
No	2

If yes, how did you first become aware of it? (Circle one only)

In-flight airline magazines	1
Posters or billboards	2
TV at airport	3
Newspapers	4
Business publications	5
Card located in the seatback pocket	6
Flight attendant	7
Other	8

These next few questions are for classification purposes only.

16. What is your job classification? (Circle one answer)

Professional	1
Executive	2
Managerial	3
Administrative	4
Technical	5
Other	6

17. What is your age? (Circle one answer)

18–24	1
25–34	2
35–44	3
45–54	4
55–64	5
65 or over	6

18. What is your gender? (Circle one answer)

Male	1
Female	2

19. What is your annual individual income? (Circle one answer)

Under $20,000	1
$20,000–$39,999	2
$40,000–$59,999	3
$60,000–$79,999	4
$80,000–$99,999	5
$100,000–$149,999	6
$150,000+	7

20. What is your level of education? (Circle one answer)

Attended high school	1
High school graduate	2
Some college/university	3
College/university graduate	4
Postgraduate degree	5

21. Finally, what changes/improvements would you like to see in our service?

_____

_____

Thanks again for your assistance! Please return this completed survey in the enclosed preaddressed, postage-paid envelope.

QUESTION
WORDING AND
MEASUREMENT
SCALES FOR
COMMONLY
RESEARCHED
TOPICS

As Chapters 11, 12, and 13 explain, problem definitions and research objectives determine the nature of the questions to be asked. In most cases researchers construct custom questions for their specific projects. However, in many instances different research projects have some common research objectives. This appendix compiles question wordings and measurement scales frequently used by marketing researchers. It is by no means exhaustive. It does not repeat every question already discussed in the text. For example, it does not include the hundreds of possible semantic differential items or Likert scale items discussed in Chapter 12.

The purpose of this appendix is to provide a bank of questions and scales for easy reference. It can be used when marketing research objectives dictate investigation of commonly researched issues.

QUESTIONS ABOUT ADVERTISING

Awareness

Have you ever seen any advertising for (brand name)?

☐ Yes   ☐ No

Are you aware of (brand name)?

☐ Yes   ☐ No

If yes, how did you first become aware of (brand name)?

☐ In-flight airline magazine

☐ Poster or billboard at airport

☐ Television at airport

☐ Card in the seatback pocket

☐ Other (please specify)_____

Unaided Recall/Top of the Mind Recall

Can you tell me the names of any brands of (product category) for which you have seen or heard any advertising recently?

_____

_____

_____

(After reading a magazine or viewing a TV program with commercials) Please try to recall all the brands you saw advertised on/in (name of program or magazine). (DO NOT PROBE. WRITE BRAND NAMES IN ORDER MENTIONED BY RESPONDENT.)

(After establishing that the respondent watched a certain television program) Do you recall seeing a commercial for any (product category)? (IF YES) What brand of (product category) was advertised?

Aided Recall

(After establishing that the respondent watched a certain television program or read a certain magazine) Now, I'm going to read you a list of brands. Some of them were advertised on/in (name of program or magazine); others were not. Please tell me which ones you remember seeing, even if you mentioned them before.

Brand A (Advertised)

Brand B (Not advertised)

Brand C (Advertised)

Do you remember seeing a commercial for (specific brand name)?

Yes No

Recognition

(Show advertisement to respondent) Did you see or read any part of this advertisement?

☐ Yes   ☐ No

Message Communication/Playback (Sales Point Playback)

These questions require that the researcher first qualify awareness with a question such as **"Have you ever seen any advertising for (brand name)?"** The interviewer then asks message playback questions.

(If yes) What did the advertising tell you about (brand name or product category)?

_____

_____

Other than trying to sell you the product, what do you think was the main idea in the description you just read (commercial you just saw)?

_____

_____

What was the main thing it was trying to communicate about the product? What did the advertising for (brand name) say about the product?

_____

_____

What did you learn about (brand name) from this advertisement?

_____

_____

Attitude Toward the Advertisement

Please choose the statement below that best describes your feelings about the commercial you just saw.

☐ I liked it very much.

☐ I liked it.

☐ I neither liked nor disliked it.

☐ I disliked it.

☐ I disliked it very much.

Was there anything in the commercial you just saw that you found hard to believe?

☐ Yes ☐ No

What thoughts or feelings went through your mind as you watched the advertisement?

Attitude Toward Advertised Brand (Persuasion)

Based on what you've seen in this commercial, how interested would you be in trying the product?

☐ Extremely interested

☐ Very interested

☐ Somewhat interested

☐ Not very interested

☐ Not at all interested

The advertisement tried to increase your interest in (brand). How was your buying interest affected?

☐ Increased considerably

☐ Increased somewhat

☐ Not affected

☐ Decreased somewhat

☐ Decreased considerably

Based on what you've just seen in this commercial, how do you think (brand name) might compare to other brands you've seen or heard about?

☐ Better

☐ As good as

☐ Not as good as

Readership/Viewership

Have you ever read (seen) a copy of (advertising medium)?

☐ Yes ☐ No

How frequently do you (watch the evening news on channel X)?

☐ Every day

☐ 5–6 times a week

☐ 2–4 times a week

☐ Once a week

☐ Less than once a week

☐ Never

Several of the questions about products or brands in the following section are also used to assess attitudes toward advertised brands.

QUESTIONS ABOUT OWNERSHIP AND PRODUCT USAGE

Ownership

Do you own a (product category)?

☐ Yes ☐ No

Purchase Behaviour

Have you ever purchased a (product category or brand name)?

☐ Yes ☐ No

Regular Usage

Which brands of (product category) do you regularly use?

- ☐ Brand A
- ☐ Brand B
- ☐ Brand C
- ☐ Do not use _____

Which brands of (product category) have you used in the past month?

- ☐ Brand A
- ☐ Brand B
- ☐ Brand C
- ☐ Do not use _____

In an average month, how often do you buy (product category or brand name)?

Record Number of Times per Month _____

How frequently do you buy (product category or brand name)?

- ☐ Every day
- ☐ 5–6 times a week
- ☐ 2–4 times a week
- ☐ Once a week
- ☐ Less than once a week
- ☐ Never

Would you say you purchase (product category or brand name) more often than you did a year ago, about the same as a year ago, or less than a year ago?

- ☐ More often than a year ago
- ☐ About the same as a year ago
- ☐ Less than a year ago

QUESTIONS ABOUT GOODS AND SERVICES

Ease of Use

How easy do you find using (brand name)?

- ☐ Very easy
- ☐ Easy
- ☐ Neither easy nor difficult
- ☐ Difficult
- ☐ Very difficult

Uniqueness

How different is this brand from other brands of (product category)?

- ☐ Very different
- ☐ Somewhat different
- ☐ Slightly different
- ☐ Not at all different

How would you rate this product (brand name) on uniqueness?

- ☐ Extremely unique
- ☐ Very different
- ☐ Somewhat different
- ☐ Slightly different
- ☐ Not at all different

Please form several piles of cards so that statements that are similar to each other or say similar things are in the same pile. You may form as many piles as you like, and you may put as many or as few cards as you want in a pile. You can set aside any statements that you feel are unique or different and are not similar to any of the other statements.

Attribute Ratings/Importance of Characteristics

Measurement scales such as the semantic differential and Likert scales are frequently used to assess product attributes, especially when measuring brand image or store image. See Chapter 13.

How important is (specific attribute), as far as you are concerned?
- ☐ Very important
- ☐ Of some importance
- ☐ Of little importance
- ☐ Of absolutely no importance

We would like you to rate (brand name or product category) on several different characteristics. (For concept tests, add: Since you may not have used this product before, please base your answers on your impressions from what you've just read.)

Characteristic A
- ☐ Excellent
- ☐ Good
- ☐ Fair
- ☐ Poor

Interest

In general, how interested are you in trying a new brand of (product category)?
- ☐ Very interested
- ☐ Somewhat interested
- ☐ Not too interested
- ☐ Not at all interested

Like/Dislike

What do you like about (brand name)?

_____

_____

What do you dislike about (brand name)?

_____

_____

How do you like the taste of (brand name)?
- ☐ Like it very much
- ☐ Like it
- ☐ Neither like nor dislike it

☐ Dislike it

☐ Strongly dislike it

Preference

Which credit card do you prefer to use?

☐ American Express

☐ MasterCard

☐ Visa

☐ No preference

Expectations

How would you compare the way (company's) service was actually delivered with the way you had anticipated that (company) would provide the service?

☐ Much better than expected

☐ Somewhat better than expected

☐ About the same as expected

☐ Somewhat worse than expected

☐ Much worse than expected

Satisfaction

How satisfied were you with (brand name)?

☐ Very satisfied

☐ Somewhat satisfied

☐ Very dissatisfied

How satisfied were you with (brand name)?

☐ Very satisfied

☐ Very dissatisfied

☐ Somewhere in between

(If somewhere in between) On balance, would you describe yourself as leaning toward being more satisfied or more dissatisfied with (brand name) than with the brand you normally use?

☐ Satisfied

☐ Dissatisfied

Now that you have owned (brand name) for 6 months, please tell us how satisfied you are with it.

☐ Completely satisfied

☐ Very satisfied

☐ Fairly well satisfied

☐ Somewhat dissatisfied

☐ Very dissatisfied

Quality

How would you rate the quality of (brand name)?

☐ Excellent

☐ Good

☐ Fair

☐ Poor

Please indicate how the quality of (Brand A) compares with the quality of (Brand B).

☐ Better

☐ About the same

☐ Worse

Problems

Have you experienced problems with (company's) service?

☐ Yes   ☐ No

When attempting to contact (company's) representative, how much of a problem, if any, was each of the following:

Phones busy

☐ No problem at all   ☐ Slight problem   ☐ Somewhat of a problem

☐ Major problem

Put on hold too long or too often

☐ No problem   ☐ Slight problem   ☐ Somewhat of a problem

☐ Major problem

What are the major shortcomings of (brand name)? (PROBE: What other shortcomings are there?)

Benefits

Do you think (product concept) would have major benefits, minor benefits, or no benefits at all?

☐ Major benefits

☐ Minor benefits

☐ No benefits at all

Improvements

In what ways, if any, could (brand name) be changed or improved? We would like you to tell us anything you can think of, no matter how minor it seems.

_____

_____

Buying Intentions for Existing Products

Do you intend to buy a (brand name or product category) in the next month (3 months, year, etc.)?

☐ Yes   ☐ No

If a free (product category) were offered to you, which would you select?

☐ Brand A

☐ Brand B

☐ Brand C

☐ Do not use

Buying Intentions Based on Product Concept

(Respondent is shown a prototype or asked to read a concept statement.)
Now that you have read about (product concept), if this product were available at your local store, how likely would you be to buy it?

- [ ] Would definitely buy it
- [ ] Would probably buy it
- [ ] Might or might not buy it
- [ ] Would probably not buy it
- [ ] Would definitely not buy it

(Hand response card to respondent.) Which phrase on this card indicates how likely you would be to buy this product the next time you go shopping for a product of this type?

- [ ] Would definitely buy it
- [ ] Would probably buy it
- [ ] Might or might not buy it
- [ ] Would probably not buy it
- [ ] Would definitely not buy it

Now that you have read about (product concept), if this product were available at your local store for (price), how likely would you be to buy it?

- [ ] Would definitely buy it
- [ ] Would probably buy it
- [ ] Might or might not buy it
- [ ] Would probably not buy it
- [ ] Would definitely not buy it

How often, if ever, would you buy (product concept)?

- [ ] Once a week or more
- [ ] Once every 2 to 3 weeks
- [ ] Once a month/every 4 weeks
- [ ] Once every 2 to 3 months
- [ ] Once every 4 to 6 months
- [ ] Less than once a year
- [ ] Never

Based on your experience, would you recommend (company) to a friend who wanted to purchase (product concept)?

- [ ] Recommend that the friend buy from (company)
- [ ] Recommend that the friend not buy from (company)
- [ ] Offer no opinion either way

Reason for Buying Intention

Why do you say that you would (would not) buy (brand name)? (PROBE: What other reason do you have for feeling this way?)

QUESTIONS ABOUT DEMOGRAPHICS

Age

What is your age, please?

What year were you born?

Education

What is your level of education?

☐ Some high school or less
☐ Completed high school
☐ Some college
☐ Completed college
☐ Some graduate school
☐ Completed graduate school

What is the highest level of education you have obtained?

☐ Some high school or less
☐ High school graduate
☐ Some college
☐ College graduate
☐ Postgraduate school
☐ Completed graduate school

Marital Status

What is your marital status?

☐ Married
☐ Divorced/separated
☐ Widowed
☐ Never married/single

Children

Are there any children under the age of 6 living in your household?

☐ Yes   ☐ No

If yes, how many?

Income

Which group describes your annual family income?

☐ Under $20,000
☐ $20,000–$39,999
☐ $40,000–$59,999
☐ $60,000–$79,999
☐ $80,000–$99,999
☐ $100,000–$149,999
☐ $150,000 or more

Please check the box that describes your total household income before taxes in (year). Include income for yourself as well as for all other persons who live in your household.

☐ Less than $10,000	☐ $35,000–$39,999
☐ $10,000–$14,999	☐ $40,000–$49,999
☐ $15,000–$19,999	☐ $50,000–$59,999
☐ $20,000–$24,999	☐ $60,000–$74,999
☐ $25,000–$29,999	☐ $75,000 or more
☐ $30,000–$34,999	

Occupation

What is your occupation?

☐ Professional   ☐ Technical

☐ Executive   ☐ Labour

☐ Managerial   ☐ Secretarial

☐ Administrative   ☐ Clerical

☐ Sales   ☐ Other

What is your occupation?

☐ Homemaker   ☐ Clerical or service worker

☐ Professional/technical   ☐ Tradesperson/machine operator

☐ Upper management/executive   ☐ Labourer

☐ Middle management   ☐ Retired

☐ Sales/marketing   ☐ Student

SAMPLING DESIGNS
AND SAMPLING
PROCEDURES

What you will learn in this chapter

1. To define the terms sample, population, population element, and census.

2. To explain why a sample rather than a complete census may be taken.

3. To discuss the issues concerning the identification of the target population and the selection of a sampling frame.

4. To discuss common forms of sampling frames and sampling frame error.

5. To distinguish between random sampling and systematic (nonsampling) errors.

6. To explain the various types of systematic (nonsampling) errors that result from sample selection.

7. To discuss the advantages and disadvantages of the various types of probability and nonprobability samples.

8. To understand how to choose an appropriate sample design.

Sampling is intuitive and commonplace in our daily lives. We sample restaurants, books, university professors, and many other products or services. The inferences we draw from sampling may vary. For instance, every basketball player and fan believes that players are more likely to score after having seen them score a couple of shots.[1] Players who have hot hands can't seem to miss while those who have cold ones can't find the centre of the hoop. When psychologists interviewed team members of the Philadelphia 76ers, the players estimated they were about 25 percent more likely to make a shot after they had just made one than after a miss. Nine in ten basketball fans surveyed concurred that a player "has a better chance of making a shot after having just made his last two or three shots than he does after having just missed his last two or three shots." Believing in shooting streaks, players will feed a team-mate who has just made two or three shots in a row, and many coaches will bench the player who misses three in a row. When you're hot you're hot.

The only trouble is, it isn't true. When the psychologists studied detailed individual shooting records, they found that the 76ers—and the Boston Celtics, the New Jersey Nets, the New York Knicks, and Cornell University's men's and women's basketball players—were equally likely to score after a miss as after a basket. Fifty percent shooters average 50 percent after just missing three shots, and 50 percent after just making three shots.

Why, then, do players and fans alike believe that players are more likely to score after scoring and to miss after missing? In any series of 20 flips of a coin, there is a 50-50 chance of four heads in a row, and it is quite possible that one person out of five will have a streak of five or six. Players and fans notice these random streaks and so form the myth that when you're hot you're hot.

The same type of thing happens with investors who believe that a fund is more likely to perform well after a string of good years than after a string of bad years. Whether watching basketball, dining at restaurants, choosing stocks, flipping coins, or drawing a sample, random sequences often don't look random. In marketing research, sampling is a fundamental concept and the scientific process of sampling can be complex. This chapter explains important principles of sampling and focuses on how to determine the appropriate sample design in marketing research. ∎

SAMPLING TERMINOLOGY

sample
A subset, or some part, of a larger population.

population (universe)
Any complete group of entities that share some common set of characteristics.

population element
An individual member of a population.

census
An investigation of all the individual elements that make up a population.

The process of sampling involves using a small number of items or parts of the population to make conclusions about the whole population. A **sample** is a subset, or some part, of a larger population. The purpose of sampling is to enable one to estimate some unknown characteristic of the population.

We have defined sampling in terms of the population to be studied. A **population** or **universe** is any complete group—for example, of people, sales territories, stores, or college or university students—that shares some common set of characteristics. When a distinction is made between population and universe, it is made on the basis of whether the group is finite (a population) or infinite (a universe). The term **population element** refers to an individual member of the population. A **census** is an investigation of all the individual elements that make up the population—a total enumeration rather than a sample.

WHY SAMPLE?

At a wine-tasting party guests all recognize the impossibility of doing anything but sampling. However, in a scientific study in which the objective is to estimate an unknown population value, why should a sample rather than a complete census be taken?

Pragmatic Reasons

Applied marketing research projects usually have budget and time constraints. If Honda Canada wished to take a census of past purchasers' reactions to the company's recalls of defective models, millions of automobile buyers would have to be contacted. Some of these would be inaccessible (for example, out of the country), and it would be impossible to contact all these people within a short time period.

A researcher who wants to investigate a population with an extremely small number of population elements may elect to conduct a census rather than a sample because the cost, labour, and time drawbacks would be relatively insignificant. Thus a company that wants to assess salespersons' satisfaction with its computer networking system may have no pragmatic reason not to circulate a questionnaire to all 25 of its employees. In most situations, however, there are many practical reasons for sampling. Sampling cuts costs, reduces labour requirements, and gathers vital information quickly. These advantages may be sufficient in themselves for using a sample rather than a census, but there are other reasons.

Accurate and Reliable Results

Another major reason for sampling is that most properly selected samples give sufficiently accurate results. If the elements of a population are quite similar, only a small sample is necessary to accurately portray the characteristic of interest. Most of us have had blood samples taken from the finger, the arm, or another part of the body. The assumption is that the blood is sufficiently similar throughout the body that its characteristics can be determined on the basis of a sample. When the population elements are largely homogeneous, samples are highly representative of the population. Under these circumstances almost any sample is as good as another. Even when populations have considerable heterogeneity, however, large samples provide sufficiently precise data to make most decisions.

Exhibit 14.1 offers a simple demonstration of how sampling works. The four photographs show how one can take different-sized samples and produce very generalizable conclusions. The first photograph is finely screened and therefore is printed with thousands of dots of ink. Because of the fineness of detail, one might say that this photograph contains nearly all the detail, or information, that can be provided. The other photographs provide less detail. Photograph 2 consists of approximately 2,000 dots. The face is still very clear, but less so than in the first photograph; some detail is missing, but the face is still recognizable. Photograph 3 is made up of only 1,000 dots, constituting a sample that is only half as large as that in photograph 2; the face can still be recognized. In photograph 4 the sample is down to 250 dots, yet if you look at the picture at a distance, you can still make out a face and identify it as the same one shown in photograph 1. The 250-dot sample is still useful even though it contains only a small fraction of the number of dots in the other photographs. *Precision* has suffered, but *accuracy* has not.

Of course, samples are accurate only when researchers have taken care to properly draw representative samples. More will be said about this later in the chapter.

A sample may be more accurate than a census. Conducting a census of a large population introduces a greater likelihood of nonsampling errors. In a survey, mistakes may occur that are unrelated to the selection of people in the study; for example, a response may be coded incorrectly or entered into the wrong column. Interviewer mistakes, tabulation errors, and other nonsampling errors may increase during a census because of the increased volume of work. In a sample, however, increased accuracy is possible because the fieldwork and tabulation of the data can be more closely supervised than would be possible in a census. In a field survey, a small, well-trained, closely supervised group may do a more careful and accurate job of collecting information than a large group of non-professional interviewers who try to contact everyone. An interesting case in point is the use of samples by Statistics Canada to control the accuracy of the census. If the sample indicates a possible source of error, the census is redone.

PRACTICAL SAMPLING CONCEPTS

Researchers must make several decisions before taking a sample. Exhibit 14.2 (page 335) presents these decisions as a series of sequential stages, even though the order of the decisions does not always follow this sequence. These decisions are highly interrelated. The issues associated with each of these stages are discussed in this chapter and Chapters 15 and 16.

Defining the Target Population

Once the decision to sample has been made, the first question concerns identifying the target population. What is the relevant population? In many cases this is not a difficult question. Eligible voters may be clearly identifiable. Likewise, if a company's 106-person sales force is the population of concern, there are few definitional problems. In other cases the decision may be difficult. One survey concerning organizational buyer

EXHIBIT 14.1	A PHOTOGRAPHIC EXAMPLE OF HOW SAMPLING WORKS[2]

Photograph 1
Portrait of young man

Photograph 2
2,000 dots

Photograph 3
1,000 dots

Photograph 4
250 dots

behaviour incorrectly defined the population as purchasing agents whom sales representatives regularly contacted. Investigators discovered after the survey that industrial engineers within the customer companies had substantially affected buying decisions, but they rarely talked with the salespeople. Frequently the appropriate population element is the household rather than the individual member of the household. This presents some problems if household lists are not available.

At the outset of the sampling process, it is vital to carefully define the target population so that the proper sources from which the data are to be collected can

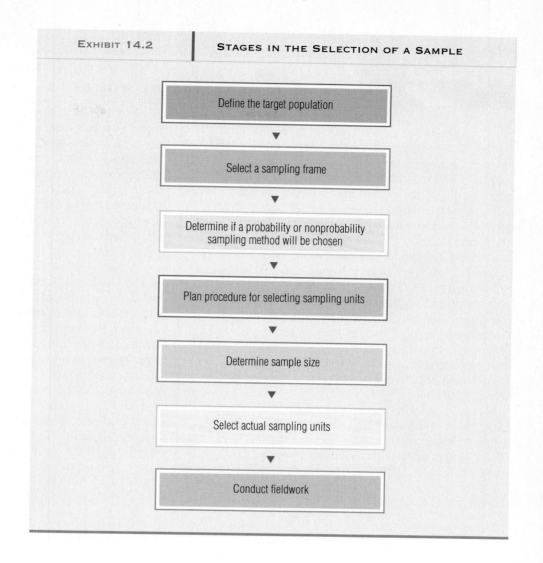

EXHIBIT 14.2 | STAGES IN THE SELECTION OF A SAMPLE

Define the target population

Select a sampling frame

Determine if a probability or nonprobability sampling method will be chosen

Plan procedure for selecting sampling units

Determine sample size

Select actual sampling units

Conduct fieldwork

be identified. Answering questions about the crucial characteristics of the population is the usual technique for defining the target population. Does the term *comic book reader* include children under six years of age who do not actually read the words? Does *all persons east of Lake Ontario* include only the people who live on the east coast of the lake or all people who live between Lake Ontario and the Atlantic ocean? The question "Whom do we want to talk to?" must be answered. It may be users, nonusers, recent adopters, or brand switchers. To implement the sample in the field, tangible characteristics should be used to define the population. A baby food manufacturer might define the population as all women still capable of bearing children. However, a more specific *operational definition* would be women between the ages of 12 and 50. While this definition by age may exclude a few women who are capable of childbearing and include some who are not, it is still more explicit and provides a manageable basis for the sample design

The Sampling Frame

In practice, the sample will be drawn from a list of population elements that often differs somewhat from the defined target population. A **sampling frame** is a list of elements from which the sample may be drawn. A simple example of a sampling frame would be a list of all members of the Canadian Medical Association. Generally it is not feasible to compile a list that does not exclude some members of the population.

sampling frame
A list of elements from which a sample may be drawn; also called working population.

WHAT WENT RIGHT?

YOU CAN LEARN A LOT FROM A FEW: GEORGE GALLUP'S NATION OF NUMBERS

In 1922 when he was still a college student, George Gallup, worked for the St. Louis newspaper, the *Post-Dispatch*. His job was to find out from readers what they liked and didn't like in the newspaper. At every door in a city of 55,000 homes, he would ask the same questions. Gallup, one hot day, knocked on one door too many, got the same answers one time too many, and decided: There's got to be a better way.

"A New Technique for Objective Methods for Measuring Reader Interest in Newspapers" was the title of Gallup's Ph.D. thesis. Working with the 200-year-old probability theories of Jakob Bernoulli, Gallup developed "sampling" techniques. You didn't have to talk to everybody, he said, as long as you randomly selected interviews according to a sampling plan that took into account whatever diversity was relevant in the universe of potential respondents—geographic, ethnic, economic.

Gallup published his work in the February 8, 1930, issue of the newspaper industry's trade journal, *Editor & Publisher*. He tried to explain what he was talking about and doing. "Suppose there are 7,000 white beans and 3,000 black beans well churned in a barrel," he said then, and again more than 52 years later in a conversation near his office in Princeton, New Jersey. "If you scoop out 100 of them, you'll get approximately 70 white beans and 30 black in your hand, and the range of your possible error can be computed mathematically. As long as the barrel contains many more beans than your handful, the proportion will remain within that margin of error 997 times out of 1,000."

In 1932, Gallup went to work for a new advertising agency, Young & Rubicam, where he developed a research department and procedures for evaluating the effectiveness of advertising. Gallup was in great demand. His methodology was valid not only for beans and newspaper readers, but for voters, too. As long as you understood the sampling universe—white, black, male, female, rich, poor, urban, rural—you could predict elections or calculate public attitudes on public questions by interviewing a relatively small number of people. In 1935, Gallup started syndicating weekly public opinion surveys to newspapers. Today the Gallup Organization conducts polls worldwide in over 20 countries, including Canada.

For example, if the student telephone directory is assumed to be a sampling frame of your university's student population, the sampling frame may exclude those students who registered late, those without phones, or those who have their telephones listed only under their roommates' or pets' names. The sampling frame is also called the *working population* because it provides the list for operational work. If a complete list of population elements is not available, materials such as maps or aerial photographs may be used as a sampling frame. The discrepancy between the definition of the population and the sampling frame is the first potential source of error associated with sample selection. We will discuss such errors later in the chapter.

Some firms, called *sampling services* or *list brokers,* specialize in providing lists or databases that include the names, addresses, phone numbers, and e-mail addresses of specific populations. Exhibit 14.3 shows a page from a mailing list company's offerings. Lists offered by companies such as this are compiled from subscriptions to professional journals, credit card applications, warranty card registrations, and a variety of other sources. One sampling service obtained its listing of households with children from an ice cream retailer who gave away free ice cream cones on children's birthdays. (The children filled out cards with their names, addresses, and birthdays, which the retailer then sold to the mailing list company.)

A valuable source of names is the Library and Archives Canada's Canadian City Directory Collection, which is the most complete collection of Canadian city directories in the country. The directories cover all provinces, regions, districts, cities, towns, and villages.[3] A reverse directory offers a different benefit. A **reverse directory** provides the same information contained in a telephone directory but arranges it differently.

reverse directory
A directory similar to a telephone directory except that listings are by city and street address or by phone number rather than alphabetically by last name.

EXHIBIT 14.3 | MAILING LIST DIRECTORY PAGE

Lists Available - Alphabetical

S.I.C. Code	List Title	Canadian Count		S.I.C. Code	List Title	Canadian Count
	A					
5122-02	Abdominal Supports	28		7313-03	Advertising-Radio	247
5085-23	Abrasives	277		7311-07	Advertising-Shoppers' Guides	4
6411-06	Accident & Health Insurance	9		5199-17	Advertising-Specialties	1648
8721-01	Accountants	6933		7313-05	Advertising-Television	102
8721-02	Accounting & Bookkeeping General Svc	2072		7319-02	Advertising-Transit & Transportation	38
5044-08	Accounting & Bookkeeping Machines/Supls	50		0721-03	Aerial Applicators (Service)	61
5044-01	Accounting & Bookkeeping Systems	1230		5191-04	Agricultural Chemicals	210
8711-02	Acoustical Consultants	91		8748-20	Agricultural Consultants	474
1742-02	Acoustical Contractors	433		5075-01	Air Cleaning & Purifying Equipment	342
1742-01	Acoustical Materials	210		5084-02	Air Compressors	717
8049-13	Acupuncture (Acupuncturists)	493			(See Compressors Air & Gas)	
5044-02	Adding & Calculating Machines/Supplies	648		1711-17	Air Conditioning Contractors & Systems	2667
5044-09	Addressing Machines & Supplies	29				
5169-12	Adhesives & Glues	4				
3579-02	Adhesives & Gluing Equipment	204				
6411-02	Adjusters	8357				
8322-07	Adoption Agencies	32				
7319-03	Advertising-Aerial	26				
7311-01	Advertising-Agencies & Counselors	2552				
7336-05	Advertising-Art Layout & Production Svc	101				
7331-05	Advertising-Direct Mail	540				
7311-03	Advertising-Directory & Guide	124				
7319-01	Advertising-Displays	571				
7319-11	Advertising-Indoor	63				
7311-05	Advertising-Motion Picture	11				
7311-06	Advertising-Newspaper	404				
7312-01	Advertising-Outdoor	297				
7311-08	Advertising-Periodical	78				

Listings may be by city and street address or by phone number, rather than alphabetically by last name. Such a directory is particularly useful when a retailer wishes to survey only a certain geographical area of a city or when census tracts are to be selected on the basis of income or another demographic criterion.

sampling frame error
An error that occurs when certain sample elements are not listed or are not accurately represented in a sampling frame.

A **sampling frame error** occurs when certain sample elements are excluded or when the entire population is not accurately represented in the sampling frame. As a result, the elements of the population excluded from the sampling frame have no chance of being included in the sample. Consider the use of the telephone directory as the sampling frame. Individuals who have opted to have their phone numbers unlisted will not have the chance to be included in the resulting sample.

Population elements can also be overrepresented in a sampling frame. A financial institution defined its population as all individuals who had savings accounts. However, when it drew a sample from the list of accounts rather than from the list of names of individuals, individuals who had multiple accounts were overrepresented in the sample.

Sampling Frames for International Marketing Research

The availability of sampling frames around the globe varies dramatically. Not every country's government conducts a census of population. In some countries telephone directories are incomplete, no voter registration lists exist, and accurate maps of urban areas are unobtainable.[4] However, in Taiwan, Japan, and other Asian countries, a researcher can build a sampling frame relatively easily because those governments

In countries with less well-developed economies, such as Sri Lanka, fewer than 5 percent of households may have telephones. Telephone directories cannot serve as sampling frames in such countries.

release some census information about individuals. If a family changes households, updated census information must be reported to a centralized government agency before communal services (water, gas, electricity, education, etc.) are made available.[5] This information is then easily accessible in the local *Inhabitants' Register.*

Sampling Units

During the actual sampling process, the elements of the population must be selected according to a certain procedure. The **sampling unit** is a single element or group of elements subject to selection in the sample. For example, if an airline wishes to sample passengers, it may take every 25th name on a complete list of passengers. In this case the sampling unit would be the same as the element. Alternatively, the airline could first select certain flights as the sampling unit, then select certain passengers on each flight. In this case the sampling unit would contain many elements.

If the target population has first been divided into units, such as airline flights, additional terminology must be used. The term **primary sampling units (PSU)** designates units selected in the first stage of sampling. Units selected in successive stages of sampling are called **secondary sampling units** or **tertiary sampling units** (if three stages are necessary). When there is no list of population elements, the sampling unit generally is something other than the population element. In a random digit dialling study, for example, the sampling unit will be telephone numbers.

sampling unit
A single element or group of elements subject to selection in the sample.

primary sampling unit (PSU)
A term used to designate a unit selected in the first stage of sampling.

secondary sampling unit
A term used to designate a unit selected in the second stage of sampling.

tertiary sampling unit
A term used to designate a unit selected in the third stage of sampling.

RANDOM SAMPLING AND NONSAMPLING ERRORS

⑤ To measure brand awareness and buying intentions among shoppers, an advertising agency sampled a small number of shoppers in grocery stores that used Shopper's Video, an in-store advertising network. Investigators expected this sample to be representative of the grocery-shopping population. However, if there is a difference between the value of a sample statistic of interest (for example, the average willingness-to-buy-the-advertised-brand score) and the value of the corresponding population parameter (again, willingness-to-buy score), a *statistical error* has occurred.

Chapter 7 classified two basic causes of differences between statistics and parameters: random sampling errors and systematic (nonsampling) errors.

An estimation made from a sample is not exactly the same as a census count. **Random sampling error** is the difference between the sample result and the result of a census conducted using identical procedures. Of course, the result of a census is unknown unless one is taken, which is rarely done. Other sources of error also can be present. Random sampling error occurs because of chance variation in the scientific selection of sampling units. The sampling units, even if properly selected according to sampling theory, may not perfectly represent the population, but generally they are reliable estimates. Our discussion on the process of randomization (a procedure designed to give everyone in the population an equal chance of being selected as a sample member) will show that, because random sampling errors follow chance variations, they tend to cancel one another out when averaged. This means that properly selected samples generally are good approximations of the population. There is almost always a slight difference between the true population value and the sample value—hence, a small random sampling error. Every once in a while an unusual sample is selected because too many atypical people were included in the sample and a large random sampling error occurred. The theories behind the concept of sample reliability and other basic statistical concepts are reviewed in detail in Chapter 15. At this point, simply recognize that *random sampling error* is a technical term that refers *only* to statistical fluctuations that occur because of chance variations in the elements selected for the sample.

Random sampling error is a function of sample size. As sample size increases, random sampling error decreases. Of course, the resources available will influence how large a sample may be taken. (The topic of sample size is covered in Chapter 15.) It is possible to estimate the random sampling error that may be expected with various sample sizes. Suppose a survey of approximately 1,000 people has been taken in Halifax to determine the feasibility of a new hockey franchise. Assume that 30 percent of the respondents favour the idea of a new professional sport in town. The researcher will know, based on the laws of probability, that 95 percent of the time a survey of slightly fewer than 900 people will produce results with an error of approximately plus or minus 3 percent. If the survey were conducted with only 325 people, the margin of error would increase to approximately plus or minus 5 percentage points. This example illustrates random sampling errors.

Systematic (nonsampling) errors result from nonsampling factors, primarily the nature of a study's design and the correctness of execution. These errors are *not* due to chance fluctuations. For example, highly educated respondents are more likely to cooperate with mail surveys than poorly educated ones, for whom filling out forms is a more difficult and intimidating task. Sample biases such as these account for a large portion of errors in marketing research. The term *sample bias* is somewhat unfortunate, because many forms of bias are not related to the selection of the sample.

⑥

We discussed nonsampling errors in Chapter 7. Errors due to sample selection problems, such as sampling frame errors, are systematic (nonsampling) errors and should not be classified as random sampling errors.

Less Than Perfectly Representative Samples

Random sampling errors and systematic errors associated with the sampling process may combine to yield a sample that is less than perfectly representative of the population. Exhibit 14.4 illustrates two nonsampling errors (sampling frame error and nonresponse error) related to sample design. The total population is represented by the area of the largest square. Sampling frame errors eliminate some potential respondents. Random sampling error (due exclusively to random, chance fluctuation) may cause an imbalance in the representativeness of the group. Additional errors will occur if individuals refuse to be interviewed or cannot be contacted. Such **nonresponse error** may

EXHIBIT 14.4 | ERRORS ASSOCIATED WITH SAMPLING[6]

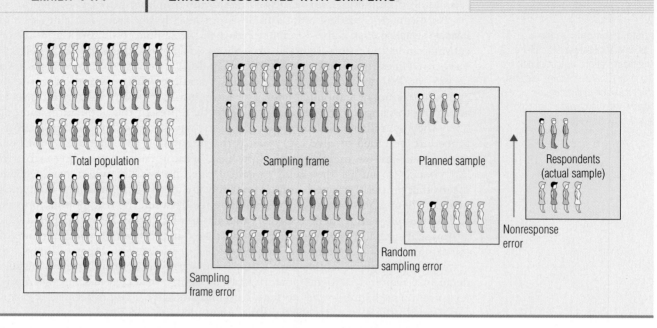

Total population

Sampling frame

Planned sample

Respondents (actual sample)

Sampling frame error

Random sampling error

Nonresponse error

also cause the sample to be less than perfectly representative. Thus the actual sample is drawn from a population different from (or smaller than) the ideal.

PROBABILITY VERSUS NONPROBABILITY SAMPLING

There are several alternative ways to take a sample. The main alternative sampling plans may be grouped into two categories: probability techniques and nonprobability techniques.

In **probability sampling** every element in the population has a *known, non-zero probability* of selection. The simple random sample, in which each member of the population has an equal probability of being selected, is the best-known probability sample.

In **nonprobability sampling** the probability of any particular member of the population being chosen is unknown. The selection of sampling units in nonprobability sampling is quite arbitrary, as researchers rely heavily on personal judgment. *There are no appropriate statistical techniques for measuring random sampling error from a nonprobability sample. Thus projecting the data beyond the sample is statistically inappropriate.* Nevertheless, there are occasions when nonprobability samples are best suited for the researcher's purpose.

We will now explore the various types of nonprobability and probability sampling. Although probability sampling is preferred, we will discuss nonprobability sampling first to illustrate some potential sources of error and other weaknesses in sampling.

probability sampling
A sampling technique in which every member of the population has a known, non-zero probability of selection.

nonprobability sampling
A sampling technique in which units of the sample are selected on the basis of personal judgment or convenience; the probability of any particular member of the population being chosen is unknown.

NONPROBABILITY SAMPLING

Convenience Sampling

convenience sampling
The sampling procedure of obtaining those people or units that are most conveniently available.

Convenience sampling (also called *haphazard* or *accidental sampling*) refers to sampling by obtaining the people or units that are most conveniently available. It may be convenient and economical to set up an interviewing booth from which to intercept consumers at a shopping centre. Just before elections, television stations often present person–on–the–street interviews that are presumed to reflect public opinion. (Of course, the television station generally warns that the survey was "unscientific and

purposive (judgment) sampling
A nonprobability sampling technique in which an experienced individual selects the sample based on personal judgment about some appropriate characteristic of the sample member.

snowball (referral) sampling
A sampling procedure in which initial respondents are selected by probability methods and additional respondents are obtained from information provided by the initial respondents.

random" [*sic*].) The college professor who uses his or her students has a captive sample—convenient, but perhaps unwilling and unrepresentative.

Researchers generally use convenience samples to obtain a large number of completed questionnaires quickly and economically. For example, many Internet surveys are conducted with volunteer respondents who, either intentionally or by happenstance, visit an organization's Web site. Although a large number of responses can be quickly obtained at a low cost, selecting all visitors to a Web site is clearly convenience sampling. Respondents may not be representative because of the haphazard manner by which many of them arrived at the Web site or because of self-selection bias. The user of research based on a convenience sample should remember that projecting the results beyond the specific sample is inappropriate. Convenience samples are best used for exploratory research when additional research will subsequently be conducted with a probability sample.

Purposive Sampling

Purposive, or **judgment**, **sampling** is a nonprobability sampling technique in which an experienced individual selects the sample based on his or her judgment about some appropriate characteristics required of the sample member. Researchers select samples that satisfy their specific purposes, even if they are not fully representative. The consumer price index (CPI) is based on a purposive sample of market-basket items, housing costs, and other selected goods and services expected to reflect a representative sample of items consumed by most Canadians.[7] Test market cities often are selected because they are viewed as typical cities whose demographic profiles closely match the national profile. A fashion manufacturer regularly selects a sample of key accounts that it believes are capable of providing the information needed to predict what will sell in the fall; the sample is selected to achieve a specific objective.

Purposive sampling often is used in attempts to forecast election results. People frequently wonder how a television network can predict the results of an election with only 2 percent of the votes reported. Political and sampling experts judge which small voting districts approximate overall returns from previous election years; then these *bellwether ridings* are selected as the sampling units. Of course, the assumption is that the past voting records of these districts are still representative of the political behaviour of its population.

Snowball Sampling

Snowball sampling refers to a variety of procedures in which initial respondents are selected by probability methods and additional respondents are obtained from information provided by the initial respondents. This technique, also called *referral sampling,* is used to locate members of rare populations by referrals. Suppose a manufacturer of sports equipment is considering marketing a mahogany croquet set for serious adult players. This market is certainly small. An extremely large sample would be necessary to find 100 serious adult croquet players. It would be much more economical to survey, say, 300 people and find 15 croquet players and ask them for the names of other players. Reduced sample sizes and costs are clear-cut advantages of snowball sampling. However, bias is likely to enter into the study because a person suggested by someone also in the sample has a higher probability of being similar to the first person. If there are major differences between those who are widely known by others and those who are not, this technique may present some serious problems. However, snowball sampling may be used to locate and recruit heavy users, such as consumers who buy more than 50 compact disks per year, for focus groups. As the focus group is not expected to be a generalized sample, snowball sampling may be very appropriate.

Quota Sampling

Suppose a firm wishes to investigate consumers who currently own digital versatile disk (DVD) players. The researchers may wish to ensure that each brand of DVD

quota sampling
A nonprobability sampling procedure that ensures that various subgroups of a population will be represented on pertinent characteristics to the exact extent that the investigator desires.

player is included proportionately in the sample. Strict probability sampling procedures would likely underrepresent certain brands and overrepresent other brands. If the selection process were left strictly to chance, some variation would be expected. The purpose of **quota sampling** is to ensure that the various subgroups in a population are represented on pertinent sample characteristics to the exact extent that the investigators desire. Stratified sampling, a probability sampling procedure, also has this objective, but it should not be confused with quota sampling. In quota sampling the interviewer has a quota to achieve. For example, an interviewer in a particular city may be assigned 100 interviews, 35 with owners of Sony DVD players, 30 with owners of Panasonic DVD players, 18 with owners of Samsung DVD players, and the rest with owners of other brands. The interviewer is responsible for finding enough people to meet the quota. Aggregating the various interview quotas yields a sample that represents the desired proportion of each subgroup.

Possible Sources of Bias

The logic of classifying the population by pertinent subgroups is essentially sound. However, because respondents are selected according to a convenience sampling procedure rather than on a probability basis (as in stratified sampling), the haphazard selection of subjects may introduce bias. For example, a professor hired some of his students to conduct a quota sample based on age. When analyzing the data, the professor discovered that almost all the people in the "under 25 years" category were university educated. Interviewers, being human, tend to prefer to interview people who are similar to themselves. Quota samples tend to include people who are easily found, willing to be interviewed, and middle class. Fieldworkers are given considerable leeway to exercise their judgment concerning selection of actual respondents. Interviewers often concentrate their interviewing in areas with heavy pedestrian traffic such as downtowns, shopping malls, and college or university campuses. Those who interview door-to-door learn quickly that quota requirements are difficult to meet by interviewing whoever happens to appear at the door; this tends to overrepresent less active people who are likely to stay at home. One interviewer related a story of working in an upper-middle-class neighbourhood. After a few blocks, it changed into a neighbourhood of mansions. Feeling that most of the would-be subjects were above his station, the interviewer skipped these houses because he felt uncomfortable knocking on doors that would be answered by servants.

Advantages of Quota Sampling

Speed of data collection, lower costs, and convenience are the major advantages of quota sampling over probability sampling. Although quota sampling has many problems, carefully supervised data collection may provide a representative sample of the various subgroups within a population. Quota sampling may be appropriate when the researcher knows that a certain demographic group is more likely to refuse to cooperate with a survey. For instance, if older men are more likely to refuse, a higher quota can be set for this group so that the proportion of each demographic category will be similar to the proportions in the population. A number of laboratory experiments also rely on quota sampling because it is difficult to find a sample of the general population willing to visit a laboratory to participate in an experiment.

PROBABILITY SAMPLING

All probability sampling techniques are based on chance selection procedures. Because the probability sampling process is random, the bias inherent in nonprobability sampling procedures is eliminated. Note that the term *random* refers to the procedure for selecting the sample; it does not describe the data in the sample. *Randomness* characterizes a procedure whose outcome cannot be predicted because it depends on chance. Randomness should not be thought of as unplanned or unscientific—it is the basis of all probability sampling techniques. This section will examine the various probability sampling methods.

Simple Random Sampling

simple random sampling
A sampling procedure that assures each element in the population of an equal chance of being included in the sample.

Simple random sampling is a sampling procedure that ensures that each element in the population will have an equal chance of being included in the sample. Drawing names from a hat and selecting the winning raffle ticket from a large drum are typical examples of simple random sampling. If the names or raffle tickets are thoroughly stirred, each person or ticket should have an equal chance of being selected. In contrast to other, more complex types of probability sampling, this process is simple because it requires only one stage of sample selection.

Although drawing names or numbers out of a fishbowl, using a spinner, rolling dice, or turning a roulette wheel may be an appropriate way to draw a sample from a small population, when populations consist of large numbers of elements, tables of random numbers (see Table A.1 in the Appendix) or computer-generated random numbers are used for sample selection.

Selecting a Simple Random Sample

Suppose a researcher is interested in selecting a simple random sample of all the Honda dealers in British Columbia, Alberta, Ontario, and Quebec. Each dealer's name is assigned a number from 1 to 105; then each number is written on a separate piece of paper, and all the slips are placed in a large drum. After the slips of paper have been thoroughly mixed, one is selected for each sampling unit. Thus, if the sample size is 35, the selection procedure must be repeated 34 times after the first slip has been selected. Mixing the slips after each selection will ensure that those at the bottom of the bowl will continue to have an equal chance of being selected in the sample.

To use a table of random numbers, a serial number is first assigned to each element of the population. Assuming the population is 99,999 or less, five-digit numbers may be selected from the table of random numbers merely by reading the numbers in any column or row, moving up, down, left, or right. A random starting point should be selected at the outset. For convenience, we will assume that we have randomly selected the first five digits in columns 1 through 5, row 1, of Table A.1 in the Appendix as our starting point. The first number in our sample would be 37751; moving down, the next numbers would be 50915, 99142, and so on.

The random digit dialling technique of sample selection requires that the researcher identify the exchange or exchanges of interest (the first three numbers) and then use a table of numbers to select the next four numbers.

Systematic Sampling

systematic sampling
A sampling procedure in which a starting point is selected by a random process and then every *n*th number on the list is selected.

Suppose a researcher wants to take a sample of 1,000 from a list of 200,000 names. With **systematic sampling**, every 200th name from the list would be drawn.

The procedure is extremely simple. A starting point is selected by a random process, then every *n*th number on the list is selected. To take a sample of consumers from a rural telephone directory that does not separate business from residential listings, every 23rd name might be selected as the *sampling interval*. In the process, it is possible that Tim Hortons would be selected. This unit is inappropriate because it is a business listing rather than a consumer listing, so the next eligible name would be selected as the sampling unit and the systematic process would continue.

While systematic sampling is not actually a random selection procedure, it does yield random results if the arrangement of the items in the list is random in character. The problem of *periodicity* occurs if a list has a systematic pattern—that is, if it is not random in character. Collecting retail sales information every seventh day would result in a distorted sample because there would be a systematic pattern of selecting sampling units—sales for only one day of the week (perhaps Monday) would be sampled. If the first 50 names on a list of contributors to a charity were extremely large donors, periodicity bias might occur in sampling every 200th name. Periodicity is rarely a problem for most sampling in marketing research, but researchers should be aware of the possibility.

Stratified Sampling

The usefulness of dividing the population into subgroups, or *strata,* whose members are more or less equal with respect to some characteristic was illustrated in our discussion of quota sampling. The first step is the same for both stratified and quota sampling: choosing strata on the basis of existing information—for example, classifying retail outlets based on annual sales volume. However, the process of selecting sampling units within the strata differs substantially. In **stratified sampling** a subsample is drawn using simple random sampling within each stratum. This is not true of quota sampling.

> **stratified sampling**
> A probability sampling procedure in which simple random subsamples that are more or less equal on some characteristic are drawn from within each stratum of the population.

The reason for taking a stratified sample is to obtain a more efficient sample than would be possible with simple random sampling. Suppose, for example, that urban and rural groups have widely different attitudes toward energy conservation, but members within each group hold very similar attitudes. Random sampling error will be reduced with the use of stratified sampling, because each group is internally homogeneous but there are comparative differences between groups. More technically, a smaller standard error may result from this stratified sampling because the groups will be adequately represented when strata are combined.

Another reason for selecting a stratified sample is to ensure that the sample will accurately reflect the population on the basis of the criterion or criteria used for stratification. This is a concern because occasionally simple random sampling yields a disproportionate number of one group or another and the sample ends up being less representative than it could be.

A researcher can select a stratified sample as follows. First, a variable (sometimes several variables) is identified as an efficient basis for stratification. A stratification variable must be a characteristic of the population elements known to be related to the dependent variable or other variables of interest. The variable chosen should increase homogeneity within each stratum and increase heterogeneity between strata. The stratification variable usually is a categorical variable or one easily converted into categories (that is, subgroups). For example, a pharmaceutical company interested in measuring how often physicians prescribe a certain drug might choose physicians' training as a basis for stratification. In this example the mutually exclusive strata are M.D.s (medical doctors) and O.D.s (osteopathic doctors).

Next, for each separate subgroup or stratum, a list of population elements must be obtained. (If such lists are not available, they can be costly to prepare, and if a complete listing is not available, a true stratified probability sample cannot be selected.) Using a table of random numbers or some other device, a *separate* simple random sample is then taken within each stratum. Of course, the researcher must determine how large a sample to draw for each stratum. This issue is discussed in the following section.

Proportional versus Disproportional Sampling

> **proportional stratified sample**
> A stratified sample in which the number of sampling units drawn from each stratum is in proportion to the population size of that stratum.

If the number of sampling units drawn from each stratum is in proportion to the relative population size of the stratum, the sample is a **proportional stratified sample.** Sometimes, however, a disproportional stratified sample will be selected to ensure an adequate number of sampling units in every stratum. Sampling more heavily in a given stratum than its relative population size warrants is not a problem if the primary purpose of the research is to estimate some characteristic separately for each stratum and if researchers are concerned about assessing the differences among strata. Consider, however, the percentages of retail outlets presented in Exhibit 14.5. A proportional sample would have the same percentages as in the population.

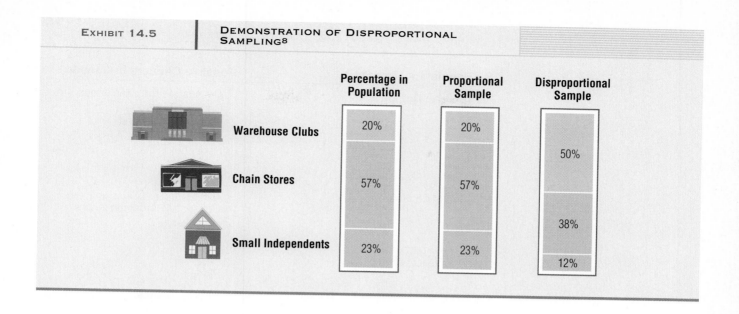

EXHIBIT 14.5 | **DEMONSTRATION OF DISPROPORTIONAL SAMPLING[8]**

	Percentage in Population	Proportional Sample	Disproportional Sample
Warehouse Clubs	20%	20%	50%
Chain Stores	57%	57%	38%
Small Independents	23%	23%	12%

disproportional stratified sample
A stratified sample in which the sample size for each stratum is allocated according to analytical considerations.

Although there is a small percentage of warehouse club stores, the average store size, in dollar volume, for the warehouse club store stratum is quite large and varies substantially from the average store size for the smaller independent stores. To avoid overrepresenting the chain stores and independent stores (with smaller sales volume) in the sample, a disproportional sample is taken. In a **disproportional stratified sample** the sample size for each stratum is not allocated in proportion to the population size, but is dictated by analytical considerations, such as variability in store sales volume. The logic behind this procedure relates to the general argument for sample size: as variability increases, sample size must increase to provide accurate estimates. Thus the strata that exhibit the greatest variability are sampled more heavily to increase sample efficiency—that is, produce smaller random sampling error. Complex formulas (beyond the scope of an introductory course in marketing research) have been developed to determine sample size for each stratum. A simplified rule of thumb for understanding the concept of optimal allocation is that the stratum sample size increases for strata of larger sizes with the greatest relative variability. Other complexities arise in determining population estimates. For example, when disproportional stratified sampling is used, the estimated mean for each stratum has to be weighed according to the number of elements in each stratum in order to calculate the total population mean.

Cluster Sampling

cluster sampling
An economically efficient sampling technique in which the primary sampling unit is not the individual element in the population but a large cluster of elements; clusters are selected randomly.

The purpose of **cluster sampling** is to sample economically while retaining the characteristics of a probability sample. Consider the researcher who must conduct 500 interviews with consumers scattered throughout Canada. Travel costs are likely to be enormous because the amount of time spent travelling will be substantially greater than the time spent in the interviewing process. If an aspirin marketer can assume the product will work as well in Toronto as it does in Montreal, or if a frozen pizza manufacturer assumes its product will taste the same in Vancouver as it does in Halifax, cluster sampling may be used.

In a cluster sample, the primary sampling unit is no longer the individual element in the population (for example, grocery stores) but a larger cluster of elements located in proximity to one another (for example, cities). The *area sample* is the most popular type of cluster sample. A grocery store researcher, for example, may randomly choose several geographic areas as primary sampling units and then interview all or a sample of grocery stores within the geographic clusters. Interviews are

EXHIBIT 14.6 | EXAMPLES OF CLUSTERS[9]

Population Element	Possible Clusters in Canada
Canadian adult population	Census Metropolitan Areas
	Census Tracts
	Dissemination Area
	Blocks
	Households
Graduating university students	Universities
Manufacturing firms	Cities
	Census Metropolitan Areas
	Localities
	Plants
Airline travellers	Airports
	Planes
Sports fans	Hockey Arenas
	Basketball Arenas
	Baseball Parks

confined to these clusters only. No interviews occur in other clusters. Cluster sampling is classified as a probability sampling technique because of either the random selection of clusters or the random selection of elements within each cluster.

Cluster samples frequently are used when lists of the sample population are not available. For example, when researchers investigating employees and self-employed workers for a downtown revitalization project found that a comprehensive list of these people was not available, they decided to take a cluster sample, selecting organizations (business and government) as the clusters. A sample of firms within the central business district was developed, using stratified probability sampling to identify clusters. Next, individual workers within the firms (clusters) were randomly selected and interviewed concerning the central business district. Some examples of clusters appear in Exhibit 14.6.

Ideally a cluster should be as heterogeneous as the population itself—a mirror image of the population. A problem may arise with cluster sampling if the characteristics and attitudes of the elements within the cluster are too similar. For example, geographic neighbourhoods tend to have residents of the same socioeconomic status. Students at a university tend to share similar beliefs. This problem may be mitigated by constructing clusters composed of diverse elements and by selecting a large number of sampled clusters.

Multistage Area Sampling

multistage area sampling
Sampling that involves using a combination of two or more probability sampling techniques.

So far we have described two-stage cluster sampling. **Multistage area sampling** involves two or more steps that combine some of the probability techniques already described. Typically geographic areas are randomly selected in progressively smaller (lower-population) units. For example, a political pollster investigating an election in Quebec might first choose cities within the province to ensure that the different areas are represented in the sample. In the second step, zones within the selected cities may be chosen. As a final step, the pollster may select blocks (or households) within the zones, and then interview all the blocks (or households) within the geographic area. Researchers may take as many steps as necessary to achieve a representative sample.

EXHIBIT 14.7 | AN ILLUSTRATION OF MULTISTAGE AREA SAMPLING

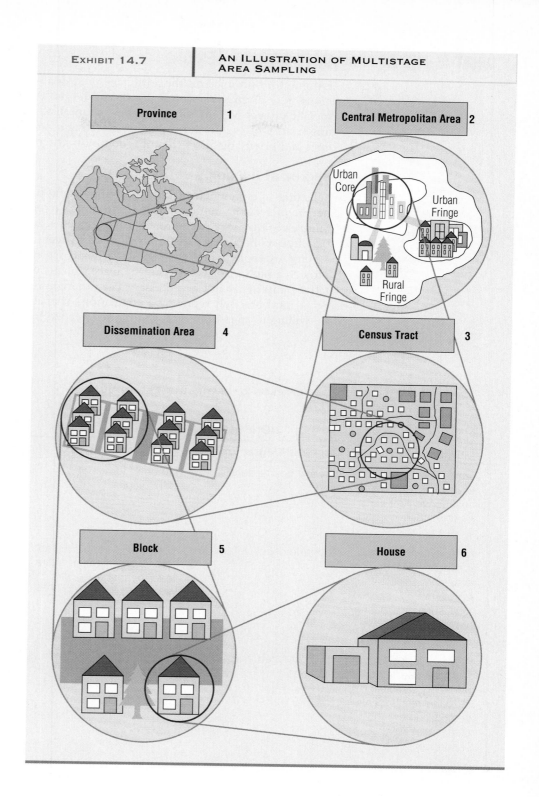

Exhibit 14.7 graphically portrays a multistage area sampling process. Progressively smaller geographic areas are chosen until a house is selected for interviewing.

Statistics Canada provides maps, population information, demographic characteristics for population statistics, and so on, by several small geographical areas; these may be useful in sampling. Census classifications of small geographic areas vary, depending on the extent of urbanization within the Central Metropolitan Area (CMA).

Exhibit 14.8 summarizes the advantages and disadvantages of each sampling technique. A researcher who must decide on the most appropriate sample design for a specific project will identify a number of sampling criteria and evaluate the relative importance of each criterion before selecting a sampling design. This section outlines and briefly discusses the most common criteria.

Degree of Accuracy

Selecting a representative sample is important to all researchers. However, the degree of accuracy required or the researcher's tolerance for sampling and nonsampling error may vary from project to project, especially when cost savings or another benefit may be a trade-off for a reduction in accuracy.

For example, when the sample is being selected for an exploratory research project, a high priority may not be placed on accuracy because a highly representative sample may not be necessary. For other, more conclusive projects, the sample result must precisely represent a population's characteristics, and the researcher must be willing to spend the time and money needed to achieve accuracy.

| EXHIBIT 14.8 | COMPARISON OF SAMPLING TECHNIQUES | | |

NONPROBABILITY SAMPLES

Description	Cost and Degree of Use	Advantages	Disadvantages
1. *Convenience:* The researcher uses the most convenient sample or economical sample units.	Very low cost, extensively used	No need for list of population	Unrepresentative samples likely; random sampling error estimates cannot be made; projecting data beyond sample is inappropriate
2. *Judgment:* An expert or experienced researcher selects the sample to fulfill a purpose, such as ensuring that all members have a certain characteristic.	Moderate cost, average use	Useful for certain types of forecasting; sample guaranteed to meet a specific objective	Bias due to expert's beliefs may make sample unrepresentative; projecting data beyond sample is inappropriate
3. *Snowball:* Initial respondents are selected by probability samples; additional respondents are obtained by referral from initial respondents.	Low cost, used in special situations	Useful in locating members of rare populations	High bias because sample units are not independent; projecting data beyond sample is inappropriate
4. *Quota:* The researcher classifies the population by pertinent properties, determines the desired proportion to sample from each class, and fixes quotas for each interviewer.	Moderate cost, very extensively used	Introduces some stratification of population; requires no list of population	Introduces bias in researcher's classification of subjects; non-random selection within classes means error from population cannot be estimated; projecting data beyond sample is inappropriate

EXHIBIT 14.8 | (CONTD.)

PROBABILITY SAMPLES

Description	Cost and Degree of Use	Advantages	Disadvantages
1. *Simple random:* The researcher assigns each member of the sampling frame a number, then selects sample units by random method.	High cost, moderately used in practice (most common in random digit dialling and with computerized sampling frames)	Only minimal advance knowledge of population needed; easy to analyze data and compute error	Requires sampling frame to work from; does not use knowledge of population that researcher may have; larger errors for same sampling size than in stratified sampling; respondents may be widely dispersed, hence cost may be higher
2. *Systematic:* The researcher uses natural ordering or the order of the sampling frame, selects an arbitrary starting point, then selects items at a preselected interval.	Moderate cost, moderately used	Simple to draw sample; easy to check	If sampling interval is related to periodic ordering of the population, may introduce increased variability
3. *Stratified:* The researcher divides the population into groups and randomly selects subsamples from each group. Variations include proportional, disproportional, and optimal allocation of subsample sizes.	High cost, moderately used	Ensures representation of all groups in sample; characteristics of each stratum can be estimated and comparisons made; reduces variability for same sample size	Requires accurate information on proportion in each stratum; if stratified lists are not already available, they can be costly to prepare
4. *Cluster:* The researcher selects sampling units at random, then does a complete observation of all units or draws a probability sample in the group.	Low cost, frequently used	If clusters geographically defined, yields lowest field cost; requires listing of all clusters, but of individuals only within clusters; can estimate characteristics of clusters as well as of population	Larger error for comparable size than with other probability samples; researcher must be able to assign population members to unique cluster or else duplication or omission of individuals will result
5. *Multistage:* Progressively smaller areas are selected in each stage by some combination of the first four techniques.	High cost, frequently used, especially in nationwide surveys	Depends on techniques combined	Depends on techniques combined

Resources

The cost associated with the different sampling techniques varies tremendously. If the researcher's financial and human resources are restricted, certain options will have to be eliminated. For a graduate student working on a master's thesis, conducting a national survey is almost always out of the question because of limited resources. Managers concerned with the cost of the research versus the value of the information often will opt to save money by using a nonprobability sampling design rather than make the decision to conduct no research at all.

Time

A researcher who needs to meet a deadline or complete a project quickly will be more likely to select a simple, less time-consuming sample design. A telephone survey that uses a sample based on random digit dialling takes considerably less time than a survey that uses an elaborate disproportional stratified sample.

Advance Knowledge of the Population

Advance knowledge of population characteristics, such as the availability of lists of population members, is an important criterion. In many cases, however, no list of population elements will be available to the researcher. This is especially true when the population element is defined by ownership of a particular product or brand, by experience in performing a specific job task, or on a qualitative dimension. A lack of adequate lists may automatically rule out systematic sampling, stratified sampling, or other sampling designs, or it may dictate that a preliminary study, such as a short telephone survey using random digit dialling, be conducted to generate information to build a sampling frame for the primary study. In many developing countries and in smaller Canadian towns, reverse directories are the exception rather than the rule; thus researchers planning sample designs will have to work around this limitation.

National versus Local Project

Geographic proximity of population elements will influence sample design. When population elements are unequally distributed geographically, a cluster sample may become much more attractive.

Need for Statistical Analysis

The need for statistical projections based on the sample often is a criterion. Nonprobability sampling techniques do not allow researchers to use statistical analysis to project data beyond their samples.

INTERNET SAMPLING IS UNIQUE

Internet surveys allow researchers to reach a large sample rapidly. This is both an advantage and a disadvantage. Sample size requirements can be met overnight or in some cases almost instantaneously. It is possible, for instance, for a researcher to release a survey during the morning in the Eastern Standard Time zone and have all sample size requirements met before anyone on the west coast wakes up. If rapid response rates are expected, the sample for an Internet survey should be metered out across all time zones. In addition, people in some populations are more likely to go online during the weekend than on a weekday. If the researcher can anticipate a day-of-the-week effect, the survey should be kept open long enough so that all sample units have the opportunity to participate in the research project.

A major disadvantage of Internet surveys is the lack of computer ownership and Internet access among certain segments of the population. A sample of Internet users is representative only of the Internet users. Historically, certain segments of the population, such as the older age groups, do not use the Internet regularly. Currently, regular Internet usage in Canada is comparatively high: In 2005 approximately 72 percent of the population used the Internet regularly, spending about 12 hours online per week.[10] Such high Internet usage means that researchers can turn to Internet sampling and expect the sample to be more representative of the general population compared to the past decade. Nevertheless, in general, when using Internet surveys, researchers should be keenly aware of potential sampling problems that can arise because some members of target populations do not have Internet access.

Web Site Visitors

As noted earlier, many Internet surveys are conducted with volunteer respondents who visit an organization's Web site intentionally or by happenstance. These *unrestricted samples* are clearly convenience samples. They may not be representative because of the haphazard manner by which many respondents arrived at a particular Web site or because of self-selection bias.

A better technique for sampling Web site visitors is to randomly select sampling units. SurveySite, a company that specializes in conducting Internet surveys, collects data by using its "pop-up survey" software. The software selects Web visitors at random and "pops up" a small javascript window asking the person if he or she wants to participate in an evaluation survey. If the person clicks "Yes," a new window containing the online survey opens up. The person can then browse the site at his or her own pace and switch to the survey at any time to express an opinion.[11]

Randomly selecting Web site visitors can cause a problem. It is possible to overrepresent frequent visitors to the site and thus represent site visits rather than visitors. There are several programming techniques and technologies (using cookies, registration data, or prescreening) that can help accomplish more representative sampling based on site traffic.[12] Details of these techniques are beyond the scope of this discussion.

This type of random sampling is most valuable if the target population is defined as visitors to a particular Web site. Evaluation and analysis of visitors' perceptions and experiences of the Web site would be a typical survey objective with this type of sample. Researchers who have broader interests may obtain Internet samples in a variety of other ways.

Panel Samples

Drawing a probability sample from an established consumer panel or other prerecruited membership panel is a popular, scientific, and effective method for creating a sample of Internet users. With the growing role of the Internet in marketing research, there has been a considerable increase in the number of panel providers. Exhibit 14.9 provides a list of Canadian and worldwide Internet survey panel providers.

Typically, sampling from a panel yields a high response rate because panel members have already agreed to cooperate with the research organization's e-mail or Internet surveys. Often panel members are compensated for their time with a sweepstake, a small cash incentive, or redeemable points. Further, because the panel has already supplied demographic characteristics and other information from previous questionnaires, researchers are able to select panellists based on product ownership, lifestyle, or other characteristics. A variety of sampling methods and data transformation techniques can be applied to ensure that sample results are representative of the general public or a targeted population. For instance, Harris Interactive Inc., an Internet survey research organization with panels in more than 125 countries, finds that two demographic groups are not fully accessible via Internet sampling: people ages 65 and older (a group that is rapidly growing) and those with annual incomes of less than $15,000. In contrast, 18- to 25-year-olds—a group that historically has been very hard to reach by traditional research methods—are now extremely easy to reach over the Internet.[13]

To ensure that survey results are representative, Harris Interactive uses a *propensity-weighting* scheme. The research company does parallel studies—by phone as well as over the Internet—to test the accuracy of its Internet data-gathering capabilities. Researchers look at the results of the telephone surveys and match those against the Internet-only survey results. Next, they use propensity weighting to adjust the results, taking into account the motivational and behavioural differences between

REDUCING SPAM

As the Internet grows, so does the amount of unsolicited bulk commercial e-mail, also know as "spam." In 2002, spam volume jumped 28 percent in North America alone, to 870 billion messages. Some estimates suggest that, by 2008, consumers may get more than 3,900 spam e-mails annually. Obviously, spam is costly for the recipients and hurts consumers' trust in the Internet. As a result, Internet-based data collection and Internet panels also are negatively affected.[14]

Discussions regarding prevention of spam have already started in the United States, Europe, Canada, and Australia. In 2003, Industry Canada, along with the Canadian Marketing Association, released a discussion paper that raised a number of serious questions regarding spam. Legislation is one alternative solution. In 2005, a special Task Force on Spam released a report that included a number of recommendations to address spam. The Task Force, which included the CMA, has introduced recommended "best practices."[15]

Recommended Best Practices

1. Marketing e-mail should be sent only to recipients who have consented to receive such information.
2. In all marketing e-mail, recipients must be provided with an obvious, clear, and efficient e-mail or Web-based means to opt out of receiving any further business and/or marketing e-mail messages from the organization.
3. The internal process used to obtain consent should be clear and transparent. Organizations should keep records of the type of consent obtained from recipients so that e-mail lists can be scrubbed prior to campaign broadcasts.
4. Every e-mail marketing communication should clearly identify the sender of the e-mail. The subject line and body text in the communication should accurately reflect the content, origin, and purpose of the communication.
5. Every e-mail should provide a link to the sender's privacy policy. The privacy policy should explain the intended use and disclosure of any personal information that might be gathered through "clickstream" means or other Web site monitoring techniques.
6. Marketers, list brokers, and list owners should take reasonable steps to ensure that the addresses on their e-mail lists were obtained with the proper consent.
7. Marketers should use a high degree of discretion and sensitivity in sending e-mail marketing to persons under the age of majority, in order to address the age, knowledge, sophistication, and maturity of this audience.
8a. Where the content of an e-mail is adult in nature the sender must—prior to sending the communication—verify that the recipient is of age to legally receive and view such content.
8b. All e-mail containing sexually explicit content should include the prefacing tag "SEXUALLY EXPLICIT" in the subject line.
9. Organizations should have in place a complaint-handling system that is fair, effective, confidential, and easy to use.
10. Organizations may disclose the e-mail addresses of existing customers to third-party affiliates or within a family of companies if
    - they have consent to do so;
    - they are using the addresses for purposes consistent with their collection (i.e., for marketing related to the original purchase or to provide services related to that purchase);
    - it is transparent to the recipients why they are receiving e-mail communications; and
    - there is an easy-to-use way to opt out of receiving further e-mail communications.

the online and offline populations. (How propensity weighting adjusts for the difference between the Internet population and the general population is beyond the scope of this discussion.)

Recruited Ad Hoc Samples

Another means of obtaining an Internet sample is to obtain or create a sampling frame of e-mail addresses on an *ad hoc* basis. Researchers may create the sampling frame offline or online. Databases containing e-mail addresses can be compiled from many sources, including customer/client lists, advertising banners on pop-up windows that recruit survey participants, online sweepstakes, and registration forms that must be

EXHIBIT 14.9 | CANADIAN INTERNET SURVEY PANEL PROVIDERS

Company Name	Internet Address
Consumer Link	http://canada.consumerlink.com
Canadian Viewpoint (through Survey Lion)	http://www.canview.com
comScore Networks	http://www.comscore.com
Decima Research	http://www.decima.com
Greenfield	http://www.greenfield.com
Harris Interactive	http://www.harrisinteractive.com/
Hotspex	http://www.hotspex.biz
Infopoll	http://www.infopoll.com
Ipsos Canada	http://www.ipsos.ca
Interactive Tracking Systems Inc.	http://itracks.ca
Lightspeed Consumer Panel	http://www.lightspeedpanel.com
Nooro Online Research	http://www.nooro.com
Open Venue e-research solutions	http://openvenue.com
Opinion Search Inc.	http://www.opinionsearch.com
Perseus Canada	http://www.perseuscanada.ca
Pollara	http://www.pollara.ca
Prophis eResearch	http://www.prophis.com
Survey Lion	http://www.surveylion.com
SurveySite	http://www.surveysite.com
Synovate	http://www.synovate.com
TNS Canadian Facts	http://www.tns-cf.com
Vision Critical	http://www.visioncritical.com

KidzEyes panellists have been prescreened and have given their permission to be surveyed online, in full compliance with the Children's Online Privacy Protection Act. It is very important that members of Internet samples opt in to receive e-mail about survey participation.

filled out in order to gain access to a particular Web site. Researchers may contact respondents by "snail mail" or by telephone to ask for their e-mail addresses and obtain permission for an Internet survey. Using offline techniques, such as random digit dialling and short telephone screening interviews, to recruit respondents can be a very practical way to get a representative sample for an Internet survey. For companies anticipating future Internet research, including e-mail addresses in their customer relationship databases (by inviting customers to provide that information on product registration cards, in telephone interactions, through on-site registration, etc.) can provide a valuable database for sample recruitment.[18]

Opt-in Lists

opt in
To give permission to receive selected e-mail, such as questionnaires, from a company with an Internet presence.

Survey Sampling International is a company that specializes in providing sampling frames and scientifically drawn samples. The company supplies samples to survey research agencies in Canada, the United States, Europe, Australia, and Japan and offers more than 3,500 lists of high-quality, targeted e-mail addresses of individuals who have given permission to receive e-mail messages related to a particular topic of interest. Survey Sampling International's database contains over 7 million names of Internet users who have **opted in** for limited participation. An important feature of Survey Sampling International's database is that the company has each individual confirm and reconfirm interest in communicating about a topic before the person's e-mail address is added to the company's database.[19]

By whatever technique the sampling frame is compiled, it is important *not* to send unauthorized e-mail to respondents. If individuals do not *opt in* to receive e-mail from a particular organization, they may consider unsolicited survey requests to be spam. A researcher cannot expect high response rates from individuals who have not agreed to be surveyed. Spamming is not tolerated by experienced Internet users, and it can easily backfire, creating a host of problems—the most extreme being complaints to the Internet service provider (ISP), which may shut down the survey site.

SUMMARY

Sampling is a procedure that uses a small number of units of a given population as a basis for drawing conclusions about the whole population. Sampling often is necessary because it would be practically impossible to conduct a census to measure characteristics of all units of a population. Samples also are needed in cases where measurement involves destruction of the measured unit.

The first problem in sampling is to define the target population. Incorrect or vague definition of this population is likely to produce misleading results. A sampling frame is a list of elements, or individual members, of the overall population from which the sample is drawn. A sampling unit is a single element or group of elements subject to selection in the sample.

There are two sources of discrepancy between the sample results and the population parameters. One, random sampling error, arises from chance variations of the sample from the population. Random sampling error is a function of sample size and may be estimated using the central-limit theorem, discussed in Chapter 15. Systematic, or nonsampling, error comes from sources such as sampling frame error, mistakes in recording responses, or nonresponses from persons who are not contacted or who refuse to participate.

The two major classes of sampling methods are probability and nonprobability techniques. Nonprobability techniques include convenience sampling, purposive sampling, quota sampling, and snowball sampling. They are convenient to use, but there are no statistical techniques with which to measure their random sampling error. Probability samples are based on chance selection procedures. These include simple random sampling, systematic sampling, stratified sampling, and cluster sampling. With these techniques, random sampling error can be accurately predicted.

A researcher who must determine the most appropriate sampling design for a specific project will identify a number of sampling criteria and evaluate the relative importance of each criterion before selecting a design. The most common criteria concern accuracy requirements, available resources, time constraints, knowledge availability, and analytical requirements.

Internet sampling presents some unique issues. Researchers must be aware that samples may be unrepresentative because not everyone has a computer or access to the Internet. Convenience samples drawn from Web site visitors can create problems. Drawing a probability sample from an established consumer panel or an ad hoc sampling frame whose members opt in can be effective.

Key Terms and Concepts

sample
population (universe)
population element
census
sampling frame
reverse directory
sampling frame error
sampling unit
primary sampling unit (PSU)
secondary sampling unit

tertiary sampling unit
random sampling error
systematic (nonsampling) error
nonresponse error
probability sampling
nonprobability sampling
convenience sampling
purposive (judgment) sampling
snowball (referral) sampling
quota sampling

simple random sampling
systematic sampling
stratified sampling
proportional stratified sample
disproportional stratified sample
cluster sampling
multistage area sampling
opt in

Questions for Review and Critical Thinking

1. If you decide whether you want to see a new movie or television program on the basis of the "coming attractions" or television commercial previews, are you using a sampling technique? A scientific sampling technique?
2. Name some possible sampling frames for the following:
   a. Electrical contractors
   b. Tennis players
   c. Dog owners
   d. Foreign-car owners
   e. Wig and hair goods retailers
   f. Minority-owned businesses
   g. Men over six feet tall
3. Describe the difference between a probability sample and a nonprobability sample.
4. In what types of situations is conducting a census more appropriate than sampling? When is sampling more appropriate than taking a census?
5. Comment on the following sampling designs:
   a. A citizen's group interested in generating public and financial support for a new university basketball arena prints a questionnaire in area newspapers. Readers return the questionnaires by mail.
   b. A department store that wishes to examine whether it is losing or gaining customers draws a sample from its list of credit card holders by selecting every 10th name.
   c. A motorcycle manufacturer decides to research consumer characteristics by sending 100 questionnaires to each of its dealers. The dealers will then use their sales records to track down buyers of this brand of motorcycle and distribute the questionnaires.
   d. An advertising executive suggests that advertising effectiveness be tested in the real world. A one-page ad is placed in a magazine. One-half of the space is used for the ad itself. On the other half, a short questionnaire requests that readers comment on the ad. An incentive will be given for the first 1,000 responses.
   e. A research company obtains a sample for a focus group through organized groups such as church groups, clubs, and schools. The organizations are paid for securing respondents; no individual is directly compensated.
   f. A researcher suggests replacing a consumer diary panel with a sample of customers who regularly shop at a supermarket that uses optical scanning equipment. The burden of recording purchases by humans will be replaced by computerized longitudinal data.
   g. A banner ad on a business-oriented Web site reads, "Are you a large company Sr. Executive? Qualified execs receive $50 for under 10 minutes of time. Take the survey now!" Is this an appropriate way to select a sample of business executives?
6. When would a researcher use a judgment, or purposive, sample?
7. A telephone interviewer asks, "I would like to ask you about race. Are you a First Nations member, Hispanic, Asian, or white?" After the respondent replies, the interviewer says, "We have conducted a large number of surveys with people of your background, and we do not need to question you further. Thank you for your cooperation." What type of sampling was used?
8. If researchers know that consumers in various geographic regions respond quite differently to a product category, such as tomato sauce, is area sampling appropriate? Why or why not?
9. What are the benefits of stratified sampling?
10. What geographic units within a metropolitan area are useful for sampling?
11. Marketers often are particularly interested in the subset of a market that contributes most to sales (for example, heavy beer drinkers or large-volume retailers). What type of sampling might be best to use with such a subset? Why?
12. Outline the step-by-step procedure you would use to select the following:
   a. A simple random sample of 150 students at your university
   b. A quota sample of 50 light users and 50 heavy users of beer in a shopping mall intercept study
   c. A stratified sample of 50 mechanical engineers, 40 electrical engineers, and 40 civil engineers from the subscriber list of an engineering journal
13. Selection for jury duty is supposed to be a totally random process. Comment on the following computer selection procedures, and determine if they are indeed random:
   a. A program instructs the computer to scan the list of names and pick names that were next to those from the last scan.
   b. Three-digit numbers are randomly generated to select jurors from a list of licensed drivers. If the weight information listed on the licence matches the random number, the person is selected.
   c. The juror source list is obtained by merging a list of eligible voters with a list of licensed drivers.
14. To ensure a good session, a company selects focus group members from a list of articulate participants instead of conducting random sampling. The client did not inquire about sample selection when it accepted the proposal. Is this ethical?

Exploring the Internet

1. Visit www.prb.org/ to find a Glossary of Population Terms compiled by the Population Reference Bureau.
2. Go to www.reversephonedirectory.com and put in your phone number. How accurate is this database?
3. Go to www.statcan.ca/english/freepub/92F0144XIB/92F0144XIB2001000.htm to learn more about census metropolitan areas and statistical area classification.
4. Use Google to search for ski resorts. At what URL can you find a sampling frame of Canadian ski resorts?

Charles Greenwood made a big move six months ago. He quit his job as director of retail marketing at one of the largest bank branches in New Brunswick to become marketing manager for Atlantic Canada Financing Corporation. It had been only 15 years since he received his bachelor's degree in marketing at the largest university in the province, but he was bright, personable, and ambitious. Now, after several months of orientation at Atlantic Canada Financing (Charles called it "Mickey Mouse"), he was beginning his own marketing operations, hiring Lauren Wilkie from a major university as his marketing research assistant.

Charles wanted to do an image study of each of the 13 branches of Atlantic Canada Financing located throughout the Atlantic provinces. The main branch and three others were located in downtown Fredericton and nearby suburbs. The other branches were located in Nova Scotia, Newfoundland, and Prince Edward Island. Their

architecture was designed to fit into the surroundings. One was located in a restored historical home, one was located next to a park, and another near a historic canal lock. All of them were designed to be compatible with the environment.

Charles asked Lauren to develop the sampling plan for the study. After some investigation, she learned that all the accounts were listed alphabetically in the main branch's computer. She thought that a list of names and addresses could be generated by taking a sample of 1,300. The computer would be programmed to randomly select every *n*th name. Since Atlantic Canada Financing Corporation had approximately 112,000 customers, every 86th name would be selected.

Questions
1. Evaluate Atlantic Canada's sampling plan.
2. What alternative sampling plans might be used?

15

DETERMINATION OF SAMPLE SIZE: A Review of Statistical Theory

What you will learn in this chapter

1 To discuss the purpose of inferential statistics by explaining the difference between population parameters and sample statistics.

2 To make data usable by organizing and summarizing them into frequency distributions, proportions, and measurements of central tendency.

3 To identify and calculate the various measures of central tendency and dispersion.

4 To identify the characteristics of the normal distribution.

5 To distinguish among population, sample, and sampling distributions and to identify the mean and standard deviation of each distribution.

6 To compute confidence interval estimates.

7 To understand the factors required for specifying sample size.

8 To estimate the sample size for a simple random sample when the characteristic of interest is a mean and when it is a proportion.

9 To understand which nonstatistical considerations influence the determination of sample size.

In late 2005 and early 2006, a common pattern was seen in the days leading up to the 39th Canadian federal election: A number of different poll results were published in newspapers and reported on the radio and TV. The results of one poll indicated 38 percent support for the Conservative Party of Canada. A second poll run by the same agency two months later showed 43 percent support for the Conservative Party, plus or minus 3.1 percentage points with 95 percent confidence level. This is an increase of 5 percentage points in two months. Assuming the same sample size and the same level of error for both polls, can we conclude that there was more support for the Conservative Party two months after the first poll?[1]

When making inferences based on results of marketing research, questions similar to the gain of a political party at the polls may be raised. For instance, when Ipsos Canada conducted a survey on behalf of Coast Capital Savings with a sample size of 800 Canadians between the ages of 19 and 55, it found that 58 percent of respondents are paying $6 to $20 in monthly service fees for financial transactions on their main chequing account. However, 50 percent of respondents perceived the profit that financial institutions make from service fees to be unfair whereas 40 percent perceived the profits to be fair. These results were reported with an error level of plus or minus 3.5 percentage points at 95 percent confidence level. This information could be quite useful for banks and financial institutions when they are planning changes to existing services or introduction of new service packages that would be more attractive to Canadians. Do the results statistically indicate that a majority of Canadians find service fees unfair?[2]

Based on the previous chapters in this text, you already know that there are different types of errors that could affect the findings in the studies above. When making inferences about the population, statistical theory allows us to quantify parts of the error and make sense of the findings. In addition to the decision of which sampling method to use, the determination of the appropriate sample size is a crucial element of marketing research. To formally identify the proper sample size, statistical theory is necessary. This chapter reviews some of the basic terminology of statistical analysis and explains how to determine sample size. ■

The first six sections of this chapter summarize key statistical concepts necessary for understanding the theory that underlies the derivation of sample size. These sections are intended for students who need to review the basic aspects of statistics theory. Even those students who received good grades in their elementary statistics classes probably will benefit from a quick review of the basic statistical concepts. Some students will prefer to just skim this material and proceed to page 377, where the discussion of the actual determination of sample size begins. Others need to study these sections carefully to acquire an understanding of statistics.

Descriptive and Inferential Statistics

Statistics Canada presents table after table of figures associated with numbers of births, number of employees in each province, and other data that the average person calls "statistics." These are descriptive statistics. Another type of statistics, inferential statistics, is used to make inferences about a whole population from a sample. For example, when a firm test-markets a new product in Winnipeg and Edmonton, it wishes to make an inference from these sample markets to predict what will happen throughout Canada. Thus there are two applications of statistics: (1) to describe characteristics of the population or sample and (2) to generalize from the sample to the population.

Sample Statistics and Population Parameters

The primary purpose of inferential statistics is to make a judgment about the population, or the collection of all elements about which one seeks information. The sample is a subset or relatively small fraction of the total number of elements in the population. It is useful to distinguish between the data computed in the sample and the data or variables in the population. The term **sample statistics** designates variables in the sample or measures computed from the sample data. The term **population parameters** designates variables or measured characteristics of the population. Sample statistics are used to make inferences about population parameters.[3] In our notation we will generally use Greek lowercase letters—for example, μ or σ—to denote population parameters and English letters, such as X or S, to denote sample statistics.

sample statistics
Variables in a sample or measures computed from sample data.

population parameters
Variables in a population or measured characteristics of the population.

Frequency Distributions

Suppose a telephone survey has been conducted for a financial institution. The data have been recorded on a large number of questionnaires. To make the data usable, this information must be organized and summarized. Constructing a *frequency table,* or **frequency distribution,** is one of the most common means of summarizing a set of data. The process begins with recording the number of times a particular value of a variable occurs. This is the frequency of that value. In our survey example Table 15.1 represents a frequency distribution of respondents' answers to a question that asked how much customers had deposited in their savings account.

Constructing a distribution of relative frequency, or a **percentage distribution**, is also quite simple. In Table 15.2 the frequency of each value in Table 15.1 has been divided by the total number of observations and the result multiplied by 100, to give a frequency distribution of percentages.

Probability is the long-run relative frequency with which an event will occur. Inferential statistics uses the concept of a probability distribution, which is conceptually the same as a percentage distribution except that the data are converted into probabilities (see Table 15.3).

frequency distribution
A set of data organized by summarizing the number of times a particular value of a variable occurs.

percentage distribution
A frequency distribution organized into a table (or graph) that summarizes percentage values associated with particular values of a variable.

probability
The long-run relative frequency with which an event will occur.

TABLE 15.1	FREQUENCY DISTRIBUTION OF DEPOSITS

Amount	Frequency (Number of People Who Hold Deposits in Each Range)
Under $3,000	499
$3,000–$4,999	530
$5,000–$9,999	562
$10,000–$14,999	718
$15,000 or more	811
	3,120

Proportions

proportion
The percentage of elements that meet some criterion.

When a frequency distribution portrays only a single characteristic in terms of a percentage of the total, it defines the **proportion** of occurrence. A proportion, such as the proportion of tenured professors at a university, indicates the percentage of population elements that successfully meet some standard concerning the particular characteristic. A proportion may be expressed as a percentage, a fraction, or a decimal value.

Measures of Central Tendency

On a typical day, a sales manager counts the number of sales calls each sales representative makes. He or she wishes to inspect the data to find the centre, or middle area, of the frequency distribution. Central tendency can be measured in three ways—the mean, median, or mode—each of which has a different meaning.

The Mean

mean
A measure of central tendency; the arithmetic average.

We all have been exposed to the average known as the **mean.** The mean is simply the arithmetic average, and it is a common measure of central tendency.

At this point it is appropriate to introduce the summation symbol, the capital Greek letter *sigma* (Σ). A typical use might look like this:

$$\sum_{i=1}^{n} X_i$$

which is a shorthand way to write the sum

$$X_1 + X_2 + X_3 + X_4 + X_5 + \cdots + X_n$$

TABLE 15.2	PERCENTAGE DISTRIBUTION OF DEPOSITS

Amount	Percent (Percentage of People Who Hold Deposits in Each Range)
Under $3,000	16
$3,000–$4,999	17
$5,000–$9,999	18
$10,000–$14,999	23
$15,000 or more	26
	100

TABLE 15.3	PROBABILITY DISTRIBUTION OF DEPOSITS

Amount	Probability
Under $3,000	.16
$3,000–$4,999	.17
$5,000–$9,999	.18
$10,000–$14,999	.23
$15,000 or more	.26
	1.00

Below the Σ is the initial value of an index, usually, $i, j,$ or k, and above it is the final value, in this case n, the number of observations. The shorthand expression says to replace i in the formula with the values from 1 to 8 and total the observations obtained. Without changing the basic formula, the initial and final index values may be replaced by other values to indicate different starting and stopping points.

Suppose a sales manager supervises the eight salespeople listed in Table 15.4. To express the sum of the salespeople's calls in Σ notation, we just number the salespeople (this number becomes the index number) and associate subscripted variables with their numbers of calls:

Index		Salesperson	Variable		Number of Calls
1	=	Mike	X_1	=	4
2	=	Patty	X_2	=	3
3	=	Billie	X_3	=	2
4	=	Bob	X_4	=	5
5	=	John	X_5	=	3
6	=	Frank	X_6	=	3
7	=	Chuck	X_7	=	1
8	=	Samantha	X_8	=	5

We then write an appropriate Σ formula and evaluate it:

$$\sum_{i=1}^{8} X_i = X_1 + X_2 + X_3 + X_4 + X_5 + X_6 + X_7 + X_8$$
$$= 4 + 3 + 2 + 5 + 3 + 3 + 1 + 5$$
$$= 26$$

TABLE 15.4	NUMBER OF SALES CALLS PER DAY BY SALESPEOPLE

Salesperson	Number of Sales Calls
Mike	4
Patty	3
Billie	2
Bob	5
John	3
Frank	3
Chuck	1
Samantha	5
Total	26

The formula for the arithmetic mean is

$$\text{Mean} = \frac{\sum_{i=1}^{n} X}{n} = \frac{26}{8} = 3.25$$

The sum $\sum_{i=1}^{n} X$ tells us to add all the Xs whose subscripts are between 1 and n inclusive, where n equals the number of observations. The formula shows that the mean number of sales calls in this example is 3.25.

Researchers generally wish to know the population mean, μ (lowercase Greek letter *mu*), which is calculated as follows:

$$\mu = \frac{\sum_{i=1}^{n} X}{N}$$

where

$$N = \text{number of all observations in the population}$$

Often we will not have enough data to calculate the population mean, μ, so we will calculate a sample mean, $\bar{X}$ (read "X bar"), with the following formula:

$$\bar{X} = \frac{\sum_{i=1}^{n} X}{n}$$

where

$$n = \text{number of observations made in the sample}$$

More likely than not, you already know how to calculate a mean. However, knowing how to distinguish among the symbols Σ, μ, and X is necessary to understand statistics.

In this introductory discussion of the summation sign (Σ), we have used very detailed notation that included the subscript for the initial index value (i) and the final index value (n). However, from this point on, references to Σ will not include the subscript for the initial index value (i) and the final index value (n) unless there is a unique reason to highlight these index values.

The Median

The next measure of central tendency, the **median**, is the midpoint of the distribution, or the 50th percentile. In other words, the median is the value below which half the values in the sample fall. In the sales manager example, 3 is the median because half the observations are greater than 3 and half are less than 3.

The Mode

In apparel *mode* refers to the most popular fashion. In statistics the **mode** is the measure of central tendency that identifies the value that occurs most often. In our example Patty, John, and Frank each made three sales calls. The value 3 occurs most often, and thus 3 is the mode. The mode is determined by listing each possible value and noting the number of times each value occurs.

Measures of Dispersion

The mean, median, and mode summarize the central tendency of frequency distributions. Knowing the tendency of observations to depart from the central tendency is also important. Calculating the dispersion (variability) of the data, or how the observations vary from the mean, is another way to summarize the data. Consider, for instance, the 12-month sales patterns of the two products shown in Table 15.5. Both have a mean monthly sales volume of 200 units, but the dispersion of observations for product B is much greater than that for product A. There are several measures of dispersion.

median
A measure of central tendency that is the midpoint; the value below which half the values in a distribution fall.

mode
A measure of central tendency; the value that occurs most often.

③

THE WELL-CHOSEN AVERAGE

When you read an announcement by a corporation executive or a business proprietor that the average pay of the people who work in his or her establishment is so much, the figure may mean something and it may not.[4] If the average is a median, you can learn something significant from it: half the employees make more than that; half make less. But if it is a mean (and believe us, it may be that if its nature is unspecified), you may be getting nothing more revealing than the average of one $450,000 income—the proprietor's—and the salaries of a crew of underpaid workers.

"Average annual pay of $57,000" may conceal both the $20,000 salaries and the owner's profits taken in the form of a whopping salary.

Let's take a longer look at that one. This table shows how many people get how much. The boss might like to express the situation as "average wage $57,000," using that deceptive mean. The mode, however, is more revealing: The most common rate of pay in this business is $20,000 a year. As usual, the median tells more about the situation than any other single figure does; half the people get more than $30,000 and half get less.

Number of People	Title	Salary
1	Proprietor	$450,000
1	President	150,000
2	Vice presidents	100,000
1	Controller	57,000 ← Mean (arithmetical average)
3	Directors	50,000
4	Managers	37,000
1	Supervisor	30,000 ← Median (the one in the middle; 12 above, 12 below)
12	Workers	20,000 ← Mode (occurs most frequently)

The Range

The range is the simplest measure of dispersion. It is the distance between the smallest and the largest values of a frequency distribution. Thus for product A the range is between 196 units and 202 units (6 units), whereas for product B the range is between 150 units and 261 units (111 units). The range does not take into account all the observations; it merely tells us about the extreme values of the distribution.

TABLE 15.5	SALES LEVELS FOR PRODUCTS A AND B (BOTH AVERAGE 200 UNITS)	
	Units Product A	**Units Product B**
January	196	150
February	198	160
March	199	176
April	200	181
May	200	192
June	200	200
July	200	201
August	201	202
September	201	213
October	201	224
November	202	240
December	202	261

EXHIBIT 15.1 | LOW DISPERSION VERSUS HIGH DISPERSION

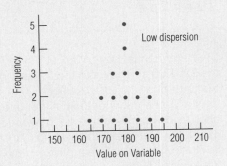

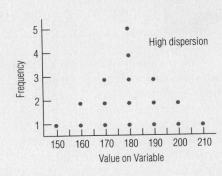

Just as people may be fat or skinny, distributions may be fat or skinny. For example, for product A the observations are close together and reasonably close to the mean. While we do not expect all observations to be exactly like the mean, in a skinny distribution they will lie a short distance from the mean, while in a fat distribution they will be spread out. Exhibit 15.1 illustrates this concept graphically with two frequency distributions that have identical modes, medians, and means but different degrees of dispersion.

The interquartile range is the range that encompasses the middle 50 percent of the observations—in other words, the range between the bottom quartile (lowest 25 percent) and the top quartile (highest 25 percent).

Deviation Scores

A method of calculating how far any observation is from the mean is to calculate individual deviation scores. To calculate a deviation from the mean, use the following formula:

$$d_i = X_i - \bar{X}$$

For the value of 150 units for product B for the month of January, the deviation score is -50; that is, $150 - 200 = -50$. If the deviation scores are large, we will have a fat distribution because the distribution exhibits a broad spread.

Why Use the Standard Deviation?

Statisticians have derived several quantitative indexes to reflect a distribution's spread, or variability. The *standard deviation* is perhaps the most valuable index of spread, or dispersion. Students often have difficulty understanding it. Learning about the standard deviation will be easier if we first look at several other measures of dispersion that may be used. Each of these has certain limitations that the standard deviation does not.

First is the average deviation. We compute the average deviation by calculating the deviation score of each observation value (that is, its difference from the mean), summing these scores, and then dividing by the sample size (*n*):

$$\text{Average deviation} = \frac{\Sigma(X_i - \bar{X})}{n}$$

While this measure of spread seems interesting, it is never used. The positive deviation scores are always cancelled out by the negative scores, leaving an average deviation value of zero. Hence, the average deviation is useless as a measure of spread.

One might correct for the disadvantage of the average deviation by computing the absolute values of the deviations. In other words, we ignore all the positive and negative signs and use only the absolute value of each deviation. The formula for the mean absolute deviation is

$$\text{Mean absolute deviation} = \frac{\Sigma |X_i - \bar{X}|}{n}$$

While this procedure eliminates the problem of always having a zero score for the deviation measure, there are some technical mathematical problems that make it less valuable than some other measures; it is mathematically intractable.

Variance   Another means of eliminating the sign problem caused by the negative deviations cancelling out the positive deviations is to square the deviation scores. The following formula gives the mean squared deviation:

$$\text{Mean squared deviation} = \frac{\Sigma(X_i - \bar{X})^2}{n}$$

This measure is useful for describing the sample variability. However, we typically wish to make an inference about a population from a sample, and so the divisor $n - 1$ is used rather than n in most pragmatic marketing research problems.[5] This new measure of spread, called the **variance**, has the formula

$$\text{Variance, } S^2 = \frac{\Sigma(X_i - \bar{X})^2}{n - 1}$$

The variance is a very good index of the degree of dispersion. The variance, S^2, will equal zero if and only if each and every observation in the distribution is the same as the mean. The variance will grow larger as the observations tend to differ increasingly from one another and from the mean.

Standard Deviation   While the variance is frequently used in statistics, it has one major drawback. The variance reflects a unit of measurement that has been squared. For instance, if measures of sales in a territory are made in dollars, the mean number will be reflected in dollars, but the variance will be in squared dollars. Because of this, statisticians often take the square root of the variance. Using the square root of the variance for a distribution, called the **standard deviation**, eliminates the drawback of having the measure of dispersion in squared units rather than in the original measurement units. The formula for the standard deviation is

$$S = \sqrt{S^2} = \sqrt{\frac{\Sigma(X_i - \bar{X})^2}{n - 1}}$$

Table 15.6 illustrates that the calculation of a standard deviation requires the researcher to first calculate the sample mean. In the example with eight salespeople's sales calls (Table 15.4), we calculated the sample mean as 3.25. Table 15.6 illustrates how to calculate the standard deviation for these data.

At this point we can return to thinking about the original purpose for measures of dispersion. We want to summarize the data from survey research and other forms of marketing research. Indexes of central tendency, such as the mean, help us interpret the data. In addition we wish to calculate a measure of variability that will give us a quantitative index of the dispersion of the distribution. We have looked at several measures of dispersion to arrive at two very adequate means of measuring dispersion: the variance and the standard deviation. The formula given is for the sample standard deviation, S.

The formula for the population standard deviation, σ, which is conceptually very similar, has not been given. Nevertheless, you should understand that σ measures

variance
A measure of variability or dispersion. Its square root is the standard deviation.

standard deviation
A quantitative index of a distribution's spread, or variability; the square root of the variance for a distribution.

	TABLE 15.6	CALCULATING A STANDARD DEVIATION: NUMBER OF SALES CALLS PER DAY BY SALESPERSONS	

X	$(X - \bar{X})$	$(X - \bar{X})^2$
4	$(4 - 3.25) = .75$	.5625
3	$(3 - 3.25) = -.25$	.0625
2	$(2 - 3.25) = -1.25$	1.5625
5	$(5 - 3.25) = 1.75$	3.0625
3	$(3 - 3.25) = -.25$	.0625
3	$(3 - 3.25) = -.25$	.0625
1	$(1 - 3.25) = -2.25$	5.0625
5	$(5 - 3.25) = 1.75$	3.0625
Σ^a	^{a}	13.5000

$$n = 8 \quad \bar{X} = 3.25$$

$$S = \sqrt{\frac{\Sigma(X - \bar{X})^2}{n - 1}} = \sqrt{\frac{13.5}{8 - 1}} = \sqrt{\frac{13.5}{7}} = \sqrt{1.9286} = 1.3887$$

^{a}The summation of this column is not used in the calculation of the standard deviation.

the dispersion in the population and S measures the dispersion in the sample. These concepts are crucial to understanding statistics. Remember, the student must learn the language of statistics to use it in a research project. If you do not understand the language at this point, review this material now.

THE NORMAL DISTRIBUTION

normal distribution
A symmetrical, bell-shaped distribution that describes the expected probability distribution of many chance occurrences.

standardized normal distribution
A purely theoretical probability distribution that reflects a specific normal curve for the standardized value, Z.

One of the most useful probability distributions in statistics is the **normal distribution**, also called the *normal curve*. This mathematical and theoretical distribution describes the expected distribution of sample means and many other chance occurrences. The normal curve is bell shaped, and almost all (99 percent) of its values are within ± 3 standard deviations from its mean. An example of a normal curve, the distribution of IQ scores, appears in Exhibit 15.2. In this example, 1 standard deviation for IQ equals 15. We can identify the proportion of the curve by measuring a score's distance (in this case, standard deviation) from the mean (100).

The **standardized normal distribution** is a specific normal curve that has several characteristics: (1) it is symmetrical about its mean; (2) the mean identifies the normal curve's highest point (the mode) and the vertical line about which this normal curve is symmetrical; (3) the normal curve has an infinite number of cases (it is a continuous distribution), and the area under the curve has a probability density equal to 1.0; (4) the standardized normal distribution has a mean of 0 and a standard deviation of 1. Exhibit 15.3 illustrates these properties. Table 15.7 is a summary version of the typical standardized normal table found at the end of most statistics textbooks. A more complex table of areas under the standardized normal distribution appears in Table A.2 in the appendix.

The standardized normal distribution is a purely theoretical probability distribution, but it is the most useful distribution in inferential statistics. Statisticians have spent a great deal of time and effort making it convenient for researchers to find the probability of any portion of the area under the standardized normal distribution. All we have to do is transform, or convert, the data from other observed normal distributions to the standardized normal curve. In other words, the standardized normal distribution is extremely valuable because we can translate, or transform, any normal variable, X, into the standardized value, Z. Exhibit 15.4 illustrates how to

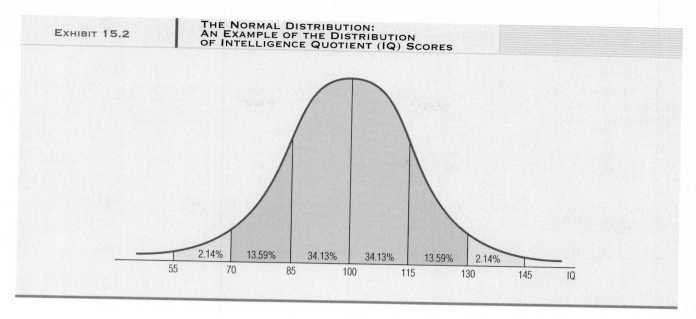

EXHIBIT 15.2 | THE NORMAL DISTRIBUTION: AN EXAMPLE OF THE DISTRIBUTION OF INTELLIGENCE QUOTIENT (IQ) SCORES

convert either a skinny distribution or a fat distribution into the standardized normal distribution. This ability to transform normal variables has many pragmatic implications for the marketing researcher. The standardized normal table in the back of most statistics and marketing research books allows us to evaluate the probability of the occurrence of many events without any difficulty.

Computing the standardized value, *Z*, of any measurement expressed in original units is simple: Subtract the mean from the value to be transformed and divide by the standard deviation (all expressed in original units). The formula for this procedure and its verbal statement follow. In the formula note that σ, the population standard deviation, is used for calculation.[6]

$$\text{Standardized value} = \frac{\text{Value to be transformed} - \text{Mean}}{\text{Standard deviation}}$$

$$Z = \frac{X - \mu}{\sigma}$$

EXHIBIT 15.3 | THE STANDARDIZED NORMAL DISTRIBUTION

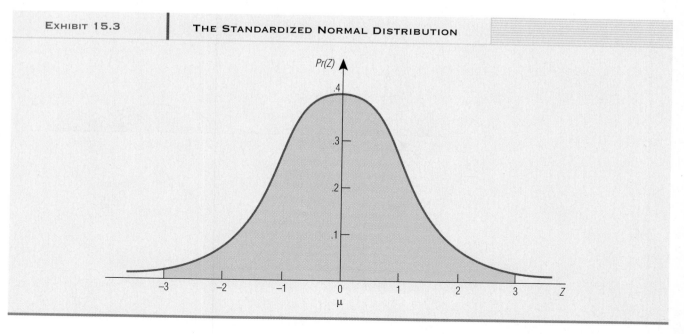

TABLE 15.7

THE STANDARDIZED NORMAL TABLE: AREA UNDER ONE-HALF OF THE NORMAL CURVE[a]

Z Standard Deviations from the Mean (Units)	Z STANDARD DEVIATIONS FROM THE MEAN (TENTHS OF UNITS)									
	.0	.1	.2	.3	.4	.5	.6	.7	.8	.9
0.0	.000	.040	.080	.118	.155	.192	.226	.258	.288	.315
1.0	.341	.364	.385	.403	.419	.433	.445	.455	.464	.471
2.0	.477	.482	.486	.489	.492	.494	.495	.496	.497	.498
3.0	.499	.499	.499	.499	.499	.499	.499	.499	.499	.499

[a] Area under the segment of the normal curve extending (in one direction) from the mean to the point indicated by each row-column combination. For example, the table shows that about 68 percent of normally distributed events can be expected to fall within 1.0 standard deviation on either side of the mean (.341 times 2). An interval of almost 2.0 standard deviations around the mean will include 95 percent of all cases.

where

$$\mu = \text{hypothesized or expected value of the mean}$$

Suppose that in the past a toy manufacturer has experienced mean sales, μ, of 9,000 units and a standard deviation, σ, of 500 units during September. The production manager wishes to know whether wholesalers will demand between 7,500 and 9,625 units during September of the upcoming year. Because no tables in the back of the textbook show the distribution for a mean of 9,000 and a standard deviation of 500, we must transform our distribution of toy sales, X, into the standardized form using our simple formula. The following computation shows that the probability (Pr) of obtaining sales in this range is equal to .893:

$$Z = \frac{X - \mu}{\sigma} = \frac{7,500 - 9,000}{500} = -3.00$$

EXHIBIT 15.4

LINEAR TRANSFORMATION OF ANY NORMAL VARIABLE INTO A STANDARDIZED NORMAL VARIABLE[7]

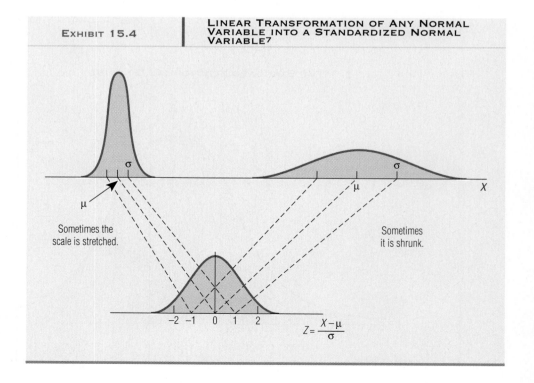

EXHIBIT 15.5 | STANDARDIZED DISTRIBUTION CURVE

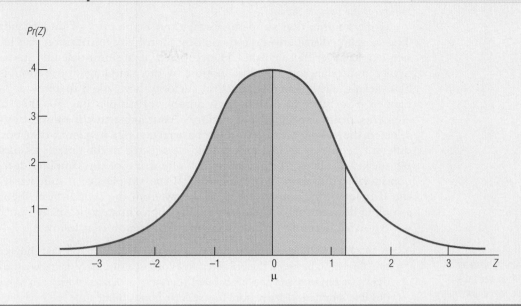

$$Z = \frac{X - \mu}{\sigma} = \frac{9,625 - 9,000}{500} = 1.25$$

Using Table 15.7 (or Table A.2 in the appendix), we find that

When $Z = -3.00$, the area under the curve (probability) equals .499.

When $Z = 1.25$, the area under the curve (probability) equals .394.

Thus the total area under the curve is .499 + .394 = .893. (The area under the curve corresponding to this computation is the shaded area in Exhibit 15.5.) The sales manager, therefore, knows there is a .893 probability that sales will be between 7,500 and 9,625.

At this point, it is appropriate to repeat that to understand statistics one must understand the language that statisticians use. Each concept discussed thus far is relatively simple, but a clear-cut command of this terminology is essential for understanding what we will discuss later on.

Now that we have covered certain basic terminology, we will outline the technique of statistical inference. However, before we do so, three additional types of distributions must be defined: population distribution, sample distribution, and sampling distribution.

POPULATION DISTRIBUTION, SAMPLE DISTRIBUTION, AND SAMPLING DISTRIBUTION

population distribution
A frequency distribution of the elements of a population.

sample distribution
A frequency distribution of a sample.

When conducting a research project or survey, the researcher's purpose is not to describe the sample of respondents, but to make an inference about the population. As defined previously, a population, or universe, is the total set, or collection, of potential units for observation. The sample is a smaller subset of this population.

A frequency distribution of the population elements is called a **population distribution**. The mean and standard deviation of the population distribution are represented by the Greek letters μ and σ. A frequency distribution of a sample is called a **sample distribution**. The sample mean is designated $\overline{X}$, and the sample standard deviation is designated S.

The concepts of population distribution and sample distribution are relatively simple. However, we must now introduce another distribution: the *sampling distribution of the sample mean.*

Understanding the sampling distribution is the crux of understanding statistics. The sampling distribution is a theoretical probability distribution that in actual practice would never be calculated. Hence, practical, business-oriented students have difficulty understanding why the notion of the sampling distribution is important. Statisticians, with their mathematical curiosity, have asked themselves, "What would happen if we were to draw a large number of samples (say, 50,000), each having *n* elements, from a specified population?" Assuming that the samples were randomly selected, the sample means, $\bar{X}$s, could be arranged in a frequency distribution. Because different people or sample units would be selected in the different samples, the sample means would not be exactly equal. The shape of the sampling distribution is of considerable importance to statisticians. If the sample size is sufficiently large and if the samples are randomly drawn, we know from the central-limit theorem that the sampling distribution of the mean will be approximately normally distributed.

A formal definition of the sampling distribution is as follows:

> A **sampling distribution** is a theoretical probability distribution that shows the functional relation between the possible values of some summary characteristic of *n* cases drawn at random and the probability (density) associated with each value over all possible samples of size *n* from a particular population.[8]

The sampling distribution's mean is called the *expected value* of the statistic. The expected value of the mean of the sampling distribution is equal to μ. The standard deviation of the sampling distribution of $\bar{X}$ is called the **standard error of the mean** $(S_{\bar{X}})$ and is approximately equal to

$$S_{\bar{X}} = \frac{\sigma}{\sqrt{n}}$$

To review, there are three important distributions that we must know about to make an inference about a population from a sample: the population distribution, the sample distribution, and the sampling distribution. They have the following characteristics:

	Mean	Standard Deviation
Population Distribution	μ	σ
Sample Distribution	$\bar{X}$	S
Sampling Distribution	$\mu_{\bar{X}} = \mu$	$S_{\bar{X}}$

We now have much of the information we need to understand the concept of statistical inference. To clarify why the sampling distribution has the characteristic just described, we will elaborate on two concepts: the standard error of the mean and the central-limit theorem. You may be wondering why the standard error of the mean, $S_{\bar{X}}$, is defined as $S_{\bar{X}} = \sigma/\sqrt{n}$. The reason is based on the notion that the variance or dispersion within the sampling distribution of the mean will be less if we have a larger sample size for independent samples. We can see intuitively that a larger sample size allows the researcher to be more confident that the sample mean is closer to the population mean. In actual practice the standard error of the mean is estimated using the sample's standard deviation. Thus $S_{\bar{X}}$ is estimated using $S/\sqrt{n}$.

Exhibit 15.6 shows the relationship among a population distribution, the sample distribution, and three sampling distributions for varying sample sizes. In part (a) the population distribution is not a normal distribution. In part (b) the sample distribution resembles the distribution of the population; however, there may be some differences. In part (c) each sampling distribution is normally distributed and has the

EXHIBIT 15.6 | SCHEMATIC OF THE THREE FUNDAMENTAL TYPES OF DISTRIBUTIONS[9]

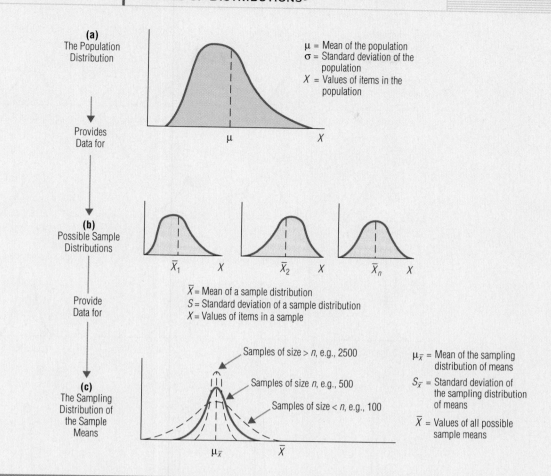

(a) The Population Distribution

Provides Data for

μ = Mean of the population
σ = Standard deviation of the population
X = Values of items in the population

(b) Possible Sample Distributions

Provide Data for

$\bar{X}$ = Mean of a sample distribution
S = Standard deviation of a sample distribution
X = Values of items in a sample

Samples of size > n, e.g., 2500
Samples of size n, e.g., 500
Samples of size < n, e.g., 100

(c) The Sampling Distribution of the Sample Means

$\mu_{\bar{x}}$ = Mean of the sampling distribution of means
$S_{\bar{x}}$ = Standard deviation of the sampling distribution of means
$\bar{X}$ = Values of all possible sample means

same mean. Note that as sample size increases, the spread of the sample means around μ decreases. Thus with a larger sample size we will have a skinnier sampling distribution.

CENTRAL-LIMIT THEOREM

central-limit theorem
The theory that, as sample size increases, the distribution of sample means of size n, randomly selected, approaches a normal distribution.

Finding that the means of random samples of a sufficiently large size will be approximately normal in form and that the mean of the sampling distribution will approach the population mean is very useful. Mathematically, this is the assertion of the **central-limit theorem**, which states: As the sample size, n, increases, the distribution of the mean, $\bar{X}$, of a random sample taken from practically any population approaches a normal distribution (with a mean, μ, and a standard deviation, $\sigma/\sqrt{n}$).[10] The central-limit theorem works regardless of the shape of the original population distribution (see Exhibit 15.7).

A simple example will demonstrate the central-limit theorem. Assume that a consumer researcher is interested in the number of dollars children spend on toys each month. Assume further that the population the consumer researcher is investigating consists of eight-year-old children in a certain school. In this example the population consists of only six individuals. (This is a simple and perhaps somewhat unrealistic example; nevertheless, assume that the population size is only six elements.) Table 15.8 shows the population distribution of toy expenditures. Alice, a

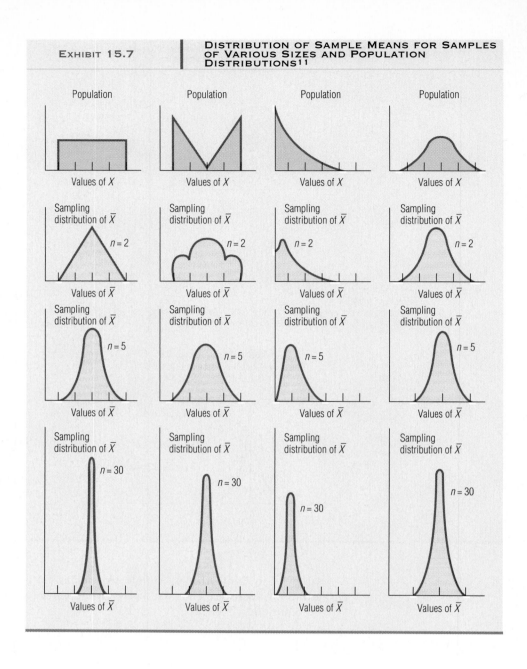

| EXHIBIT 15.7 | DISTRIBUTION OF SAMPLE MEANS FOR SAMPLES OF VARIOUS SIZES AND POPULATION DISTRIBUTIONS[11] |

| TABLE 15.8 | HYPOTHETICAL POPULATION DISTRIBUTION OF TOY EXPENDITURES |

Child	Toy Expenditures
Alice	$1.00
Becky	2.00
Noah	3.00
Tobin	4.00
George	5.00
Freddy	6.00

TABLE 15.9	CALCULATION OF POPULATION MEAN

X
$1.00
2.00
3.00
4.00
5.00
6.00
Σ$21.00

Calculations: $\mu = \dfrac{\Sigma X}{n} = \dfrac{21}{6} = 3.5 = \mu_{\bar{X}}$

relatively deprived child, has only $1 per month, whereas fat Freddy, the rich kid, has $6 to spend. The average expenditure on toys each month is $3.50, so the population mean, μ, equals 3.5 (see Table 15.9).

Now assume that we do not know everything about the population, and we wish to take a sample size of two, to be drawn randomly from the population of the six individuals. How many possible samples are there? The answer is 15, as follows:

1, 2				
1, 3	2, 3			
1, 4	2, 4	3, 4		
1, 5	2, 5	3, 5	4, 5	
1, 6	2, 6	3, 6	4, 6	5, 6

Table 15.10 lists the sample mean for each of the possible 15 samples and the frequency distribution of these sample means with their appropriate probabilities. These sample means comprise a sampling distribution of the mean, and the distribution is *approximately* normal. If we increased the sample size to three, four, or more, the distribution of sample means would more closely approximate a normal distribution. While this simple example is not a proof of the central-limit theorem, it should give you a better understanding of the nature of the sampling distribution of the mean.

This theoretical knowledge about distributions can be used to solve two practical marketing research problems: estimating parameters and determining sample size.

ESTIMATION OF PARAMETERS

A catalogue retailer, such as Lands' End, may rely on sampling and statistical estimation to prepare for Christmas orders. The company can expect that 28 days after mailing a catalogue, it will have received X percent of the orders it will get. With this information, it can tell within 5 percent how many ties it will sell by Christmas. Making a proper inference about population parameters is highly practical for a marketer that must have the inventory appropriate for a short selling season.

Suppose you are a product manager for Lactantia and you recently conducted a taste test to measure intention to buy a reformulated light cream cheese. The results of the research indicate that when the product was placed in 800 homes and a call-back was made two weeks later, 80 percent of the respondents said they would buy it: 76 percent of those who had not previously used low-fat cream cheese and 84 percent of those who had. How can you be sure there were no statistical errors in this estimate? How confident can you be of these figures?

Students often wonder whether statistics are really used in the business world. The two situations just described provide contemporary examples of the need for statistical estimation of parameters and the value of statistical techniques as managerial tools.

TABLE 15.10

ARITHMETIC MEANS OF SAMPLES AND FREQUENCY DISTRIBUTION OF SAMPLE MEANS

SAMPLE MEANS

Sample Probability	ΣX		$\overline{X}$
$1, $2	$3.00	$1.50	1/15
1, 3	4.00	2.00	1/15
1, 4	5.00	2.50	1/15
1, 5	6.00	3.00	1/15
1, 6	7.00	3.50	1/15
2, 3	5.00	2.50	1/15
2, 4	6.00	3.00	1/15
2, 5	7.00	3.50	1/15
2, 6	8.00	4.00	1/15
3, 4	7.00	3.50	1/15
3, 5	8.00	4.00	1/15
3, 6	9.00	4.50	1/15
4, 5	9.00	4.50	1/15
4, 6	10.00	5.00	1/15
5, 6	11.00	5.50	1/15

FREQUENCY DISTRIBUTION

Sample Mean	Frequency	Probability
$1.50	1	1/15
2.00	1	1/15
2.50	2	2/15
3.00	2	2/15
3.50	3	3/15
4.00	2	2/15
4.50	2	2/15
5.00	1	1/15
5.50	1	1/15

Point Estimates

Our goal in using statistics is to make an estimate about population parameters. The population mean, μ, and standard deviation, σ, are constants, but in most instances of marketing research they are unknown. To estimate population values, we are required to sample. As we have discussed, $\overline{X}$ and S are random variables that will vary from sample to sample with a certain probability (sampling) distribution.

Our previous example of statistical inference was somewhat unrealistic because the population had only six individuals. Consider the more realistic example of a prospective racquetball entrepreneur who wishes to estimate the average number of days players participate in this sport each week. When statistical inference is needed, the population mean, μ, is a constant but unknown parameter. To estimate the average number of playing days, we could take a sample of 300 racquetball players throughout the area where our entrepreneur is thinking of building club facilities. If the sample mean, $\overline{X}$, equals 2.6 days per week, we might use this figure as a **point estimate**. This single value, 2.6, would be the best estimate of the population mean. However, we would be extremely lucky if the sample estimate were exactly the same as the population value. A less risky alternative would be to calculate a confidence interval.

point estimate
An estimate of the population mean in the form of a single value, usually the sample mean.

Confidence Intervals

confidence interval estimate
A specified range of numbers within which a population mean is expected to lie; an estimate of the population mean based on the knowledge that it will be equal to the sample mean plus or minus a small sampling error.

If we specify a range of numbers, or interval, within which the population mean should lie, we can be more confident that our inference is correct. A **confidence interval estimate** is based on the knowledge that $\mu = \bar{X} \pm$ a small sampling error. After calculating an interval estimate, we can determine how probable it is that the population mean will fall within this range of statistical values. In the racquetball project the researcher, after setting up a confidence interval, would be able to make a statement such as "With 95 percent confidence, I think that the average number of days played per week is between 2.3 and 2.9." This information can be used to estimate market demand because the researcher has a certain confidence that the interval contains the value of the true population mean.

The crux of the problem for the researcher is to determine how much random sampling error to tolerate. In other words, what should the confidence interval be? How much of a gamble should be taken that μ will be included in the range? Do we need to be 80 percent, 90 percent, or 99 percent sure? The **confidence level** is a percentage or decimal that indicates the long-run probability that the results will be correct. Traditionally, researchers have used the 95 percent confidence level. While there is nothing magical about the 95 percent confidence level, it is useful to select this confidence level in our examples.

confidence level
A percentage or decimal value that tells how confident a researcher can be about being correct. It states the long-run percentage of confidence intervals that will include the true population mean.

As mentioned, the point estimate gives no information about the possible magnitude of random sampling error. The confidence interval gives the estimated value of the population parameter, plus or minus an estimate of the error. We can express the idea of the confidence interval as follows:

$$\mu = \bar{X} \pm \text{a small sampling error}$$

More formally, assuming that the researchers select a large sample (more than 30 observations), the small sampling error is given by

$$\text{Small sampling error} = Z_{c.l.}S_{\bar{X}}$$

where

$$Z_{c.l.} = \text{value of } Z, \text{ or standardized normal variable, at a specified}$$
$$\text{confidence level } (c.l.)$$
$$S_{\bar{X}} = \text{standard error of the mean}$$

The precision of our estimate is indicated by the value of $Z_{c.l.}S_{\bar{X}}$. It is useful to define the range of possible error, E, as follows:

$$E = Z_{c.l.}S_{\bar{X}}$$

Thus

$$\mu = \bar{X} \pm E$$

where

$$\bar{X} = \text{sample mean}$$
$$E = \text{range of sampling error}$$

or

$$\mu = \bar{X} \pm Z_{c.l.}S_{\bar{X}}$$

The confidence interval $\pm E$ is always stated as one-half of the total confidence interval.

The following step-by-step procedure can be used to calculate confidence intervals:

1. Calculate $\bar{X}$ from the sample.
2. Assuming σ is unknown, estimate the population standard deviation by finding S, the sample standard deviation.

3. Estimate the standard error of the mean, using the formula

$$S_{\bar{X}} = \frac{S}{\sqrt{n}}$$

4. Determine the Z-value associated with the desired confidence level. The confidence level should be divided by 2 to determine what percentage of the area under the curve to include on each side of the mean.

5. Calculate the confidence interval.

The following example shows how calculation of a confidence interval can be used in preparing a demographic profile, a useful tool for market segmentation. Suppose you plan to open a sporting goods store to cater to working women who golf. In a survey of your market area you find that the mean age ($\bar{X}$) of 100 women is 37.5 years, with a standard deviation (S) of 12.0 years. Knowing that it would be extremely coincidental if the point estimate from the sample were exactly the same as the population mean age (μ), you decide to construct a confidence interval around the sample mean using the steps just given:

1. $\bar{X} = 37.5$ years
2. $S = 12.0$ years
3. $S_{\bar{X}} = \frac{12}{\sqrt{100}} = 1.2$
4. Suppose you wish to be 95 percent confident—that is, assured that 95 times out of 100, the estimates from your sample will include the population parameter. Including 95 percent of the area requires that 47.5 percent (one-half of 95 percent) of the distribution on each side be included. From the Z-table (Table A.2 in the appendix), you find that .475 corresponds to the Z-value 1.96.
5. Substituting the values for $Z_{c.l.}$ and $S_{\bar{X}}$ into the confidence interval formula gives

$$\mu = 37.5 \pm (1.96)(1.2)$$
$$= 37.5 \pm 2.352$$

You can thus expect that μ is contained in the range from 35.148 to 39.852 years. Intervals constructed in this manner will contain the true value of μ 95 percent of the time.

Step 3 can be eliminated by entering S and n directly in the confidence interval formula:

$$\mu = \bar{X} \pm Z_{c.l.} \frac{S}{\sqrt{n}}$$

Remember that $S/\sqrt{n}$ represents the standard error of the mean, $S_{\bar{X}}$. Its use is based on the central-limit theorem.

If you wanted to increase the probability that the population mean will lie within the confidence interval, you could use the 99 percent confidence level, with a Z-value of 2.57. You may want to calculate the 99 percent confidence interval for the above example; you can expect that μ will be in the range between 34.416 and 40.584 years.

We have now examined the basic concepts of inferential statistics. You should understand that sample statistics such as the sample means, $\bar{X}s$, can provide good estimates of population parameters such as μ. You should also realize that there is a certain probability of being in error when you estimate a population parameter from sample statistics. In other words, there will be a random sampling error, which is the difference between the survey results and the results of surveying the entire population. If you have a firm understanding of these basic terms and ideas, which are the essence of statistics, the remaining statistics concepts will be relatively simple for you. Several ramifications of the simple ideas presented so far will permit you to make better decisions about populations based on surveys or experiments.

Random Error and Sample Size

When asked to evaluate a marketing research project, most people, even those with little marketing research training, begin by asking, "How big was the sample?" Intuitively we know that the larger the sample, the more accurate the research. This is in fact a statistical truth; random sampling error varies with samples of different sizes. In statistical terms, increasing the sample size decreases the width of the confidence interval at a given confidence level. When the standard deviation of the population is unknown, a confidence interval is calculated using the following formula:

$$\text{Confidence interval} = \bar{X} \pm Z \frac{S}{\sqrt{n}}$$

Observe that the equation for the plus or minus error factor in the confidence interval includes *n*, the sample size:

$$E = Z \frac{S}{\sqrt{n}}$$

If *n* increases, *E* is reduced. Exhibit 15.8 illustrates that the confidence interval (or magnitude of error) decreases as the sample size, *n*, increases.

We already noted that it is not necessary to take a census of all elements of the population to conduct an accurate study. The laws of probability give investigators sufficient confidence regarding the accuracy of data collected from a sample. Knowledge of the characteristics of the sampling distribution helps researchers make reasonably precise estimates.

Students familiar with the law of diminishing returns in economics will easily grasp the concept that increases in sample size reduce sampling error at a *decreasing rate*. For example, doubling a sample of 1,000 will reduce random sampling error by 1 percentage point, but doubling the sample from 2,000 to 4,000 will reduce random sampling error by only another 1/2 percentage point. More technically, random sampling error is inversely proportional to the square root of *n*. (Exhibit 15.8 gives an approximation of the relationship between sample size and error.) Thus the main issue becomes one of determining the optimal sample size.

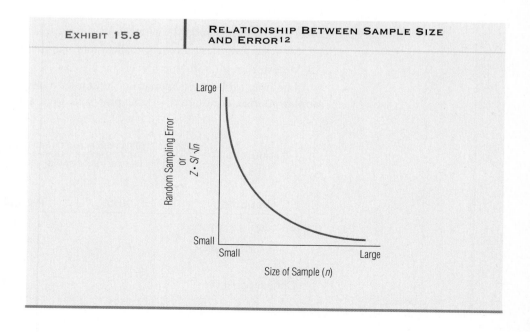

| EXHIBIT 15.8 | RELATIONSHIP BETWEEN SAMPLE SIZE AND ERROR[12] |

Factors in Determining Sample Size for Questions Involving Means

Three factors are required to specify sample size: (1) the variance, or heterogeneity, of the population; (2) the magnitude of acceptable error; and (3) the confidence level. Suppose a researcher wishes to find out whether nine-year-old boys are taller than four-year-old boys. Intuitively we know that even with a very small sample size, the correct information probably will be obtained. This is based on the fact that the determination of sample size depends on the research question and the variability within the sample.

The *variance,* or *heterogeneity,* of the population is the first necessary bit of information. In statistical terms, this refers to the *standard deviation* of the population. Only a small sample is required if the population is homogeneous. For example, predicting the average age of college students requires a smaller sample than predicting the average age of people who visit the zoo on a given Sunday afternoon. As *heterogeneity* increases, so must sample size. Thus, to test the effectiveness of an acne medicine, the sample must be large enough to cover the range of skin types.

The *magnitude of error,* or the confidence interval, is the second necessary bit of information. Defined in statistical terms as E, the magnitude of error indicates how precise the estimate must be. It indicates a certain precision level. From a managerial perspective, the importance of the decision in terms of profitability will influence the researcher's specifications of the range of error. If, for example, favourable results from a test market sample will result in the construction of a new plant and unfavourable results will dictate not marketing the product, the acceptable range of error probably will be small; the cost of an error would be too great to allow much room for random sampling errors. In other cases the estimate need not be extremely precise. Allowing an error of $\pm\$1,000$ in total family income instead of $E = \pm\$50$ may be acceptable in most market segmentation studies.

The third factor of concern is the *confidence level.* In our examples we will typically use the 95 percent confidence level. This, however, is an arbitrary decision based on convention; there is nothing sacred about the .05 chance level (that is, the probability of .05 of the true population parameter being incorrectly estimated). Exhibit 15.9 summarizes the information required to determine sample size.

Estimating Sample Size for Questions Involving Means

Once the preceding concepts are understood, determining the actual size for a simple random sample is quite easy. The researcher

1. Estimates the standard deviation of the population
2. Makes a judgment about the allowable magnitude of error
3. Determines a confidence level

The only problem is estimating the standard deviation of the population. Ideally, similar studies conducted in the past will give a basis for judging the standard

Exhibit 15.9	STATISTICAL INFORMATION NEEDED TO DETERMINE SAMPLE SIZE FOR QUESTIONS THAT INVOLVE MEANS	
Variable	**Symbol**	**Typical Source of Information**
Standard deviation	S	Pilot study or rule of thumb
Magnitude of error	E	Managerial judgment or calculation ($ZS_{\bar{X}}$)
Confidence level	$Z_{c.l.}$	Managerial judgment

deviation. In practice, researchers who lack prior information conduct a pilot study to estimate the population parameters so that another, larger sample, of the appropriate sample size, may be drawn. This procedure is called *sequential sampling* because researchers take an initial look at the pilot study results before deciding on a larger sample to provide more precise information.

A rule of thumb for estimating the value of the standard deviation is to expect it to be one-sixth of the range. If researchers conducting a study on television purchases expected the price paid to range from $100 to $700, a rule-of-thumb estimate for the standard deviation would be $100.

For the moment, assume that the standard deviation has been estimated in some preliminary work. If our concern is to estimate the mean of a particular population, the formula for sample size is

$$n = \left(\frac{ZS}{E}\right)^2$$

where

Z = standardized value that corresponds to the confidence level

S = sample standard deviation or estimate of the population standard deviation

E = acceptable magnitude of error, plus or minus error factor (range is one-half of the total confidence interval)[13]

Suppose a survey researcher studying annual expenditures on lipstick wishes to have a 95 percent confidence level ($Z = 1.96$) and a range of error (E) of less than $2. If the estimate of the standard deviation is $29, the sample size can be calculated as follows:

$$n = \left(\frac{ZS}{E}\right)^2 = \left(\frac{(1.96)\,(29)}{2}\right)^2 = \left(\frac{56.84}{2}\right)^2 = 28.42^2 = 808$$

If a range of error (E) of $4 is acceptable, sample size can be reduced:

$$n = \left(\frac{ZS}{E}\right)^2 = \left(\frac{(1.96)\,(29)}{4}\right)^2 = \left(\frac{56.84}{4}\right)^2 = 14.21^2 = 202$$

Thus doubling the range of acceptable error reduces sample size to approximately one-quarter of its original size. Stated conversely in a general sense, doubling sample size will reduce error by only approximately one-quarter.

The Influence of Population Size on Sample Size

The AC Nielsen Company estimates television ratings. Throughout the years it has been plagued with questions about how it is possible to rate 98-plus million American television homes with such a small sample (approximately 5,000 households). The answer to that question is that in most cases the size of the population does not have a major effect on the sample size. As we have indicated, the variance of the population has the largest effect on sample size. However, a finite correction factor may be needed to adjust a sample size that is more than 5 percent of a finite population. If the sample is large relative to the population, the foregoing procedures may overestimate sample size, and the researcher may need to adjust sample size. The finite correction factor is $\sqrt{(N - n)/(N - 1)}$, where N = population size and n = sample size.

Factors in Determining Sample Size for Proportions

Researchers frequently are concerned with determining sample size for problems that involve estimating population proportions or percentages. When the question involves the estimation of a proportion, the researcher requires some knowledge of the logic for determining a confidence interval around a sample proportion estimation (p) of the population proportion (π). For a confidence interval to be constructed around the sample proportion (p), an estimate of the standard error of the proportion (S_p) must be calculated and a confidence level specified.

The precision of the estimate is indicated by the value $Z_{c.l.}S_p$. Thus the plus or minus estimate of the population proportion is

$$\text{Confidence interval} = p \pm Z_{c.l.}S_p$$

If the researcher selects a 95 percent probability for the confidence interval, $Z_{c.l.}$ will equal 1.96 (see Table A.2 in the appendix).

The formula for S_p is

$$S_p = \sqrt{\frac{pq}{n}} \qquad \text{or} \qquad S_p = \sqrt{\frac{p(1-p)}{n}}$$

where

S_p = estimate of the standard error of the proportion
p = proportion of successes
$q = 1 - p$, or proportion of failures

Suppose that 20 percent of a sample of 1,200 television viewers recall seeing an advertisement. The proportion of successes (p) equals .2, and the proportion of failures (q) equals .8. To estimate the 95 percent confidence interval, we calculate

$$\begin{aligned}
\text{Confidence interval} &= p \pm Z_{c.l.}S_p \\
&= .2 \pm 1.96 S_p \\
&= .2 \pm 1.96 \sqrt{\frac{p(1-p)}{n}} \\
&= .2 \pm 1.96 \sqrt{\frac{(.2)(.8)}{1,200}} \\
&= .2 \pm 1.96(.0115) \\
&= .2 \pm .022
\end{aligned}$$

Thus the population proportion that sees an advertisement is estimated to be included in the interval between .178 and .222, or roughly between 18 and 22 percent, with a 95 percent confidence coefficient. Note that a similar calculation can be made for 90 percent confidence level easily.

To determine *sample size* for a proportion, the researcher must make a judgment about confidence level and the maximum allowance for random sampling error. Furthermore, the size of the proportion influences random sampling error; thus an estimate of the expected proportion of successes must be made, based on intuition or prior information. The formula is

$$n = \frac{Z_{c.l.}^2 pq}{E^2}$$

where

n = number of items in sample
$Z_{c.l.}^2$ = square of the confidence level in standard error units
p = estimated proportion of successes
$q = 1 - p$, or estimated proportion of failures
E^2 = square of the maximum allowance for error between the true proportion and the sample proportion, or $Z_{c.l.}S_p$ squared

Suppose a researcher believes that a simple random sample will show that 60 percent of the population (p) recognizes the name of an automobile dealership. The researcher wishes to estimate with 95 percent confidence ($Z_{c.l.} = 1.96$) that the allowance for sampling error is not greater than 3.5 percentage points (E). Substituting these values into the formula gives

$$n = \frac{(1.96)^2(.6)(.4)}{.035^2}$$
$$= \frac{(3.8416)(.24)}{.001225}$$
$$= \frac{.922}{.001225}$$
$$= 753$$

Calculating Sample Size for Sample Proportions

In practice, a number of tables have been constructed for determining sample size. Table 15.11 illustrates a sample size table for problems that involve sample proportions (p).

TABLE 15.11	SELECTED TABLES FOR DETERMINING SAMPLE SIZE WHEN THE CHARACTERISTIC OF INTEREST IS A PROPORTION[14]

SAMPLE SIZE FOR A 95 PERCENT CONFIDENCE LEVEL WHEN PARAMETER IN POPULATION IS ASSUMED TO BE OVER 70 PERCENT OR UNDER 30 PERCENT

Size of Population	Reliability			
	±1% Point	±2% Points	±3% Points	±5% Points
1,000	a	a	473	244
2,000	a	a	619	278
3,000	a	1,206	690	291
4,000	a	1,341	732	299
5,000	a	1,437	760	303
10,000	4,465	1,678	823	313
20,000	5,749	1,832	858	318
50,000	6,946	1,939	881	321
100,000	7,465	1,977	888	321
500,000 to ∞	7,939	2,009	895	322

SAMPLE SIZE FOR A 95 PERCENT CONFIDENCE LEVEL WHEN PARAMETER IN POPULATION IS ASSUMED TO BE OVER 85 PERCENT OR UNDER 15 PERCENT

Size of Population	Reliability			
	±1% Point	±2% Points	±3% Points	±5% Points
1,000	a	a	353	235
2,000	a	760	428	266
3,000	a	890	461	278
4,000	a	938	479	284
5,000	a	984	491	289
10,000	3,288	1,091	516	297
20,000	3,935	1,154	530	302
50,000	4,461	1,195	538	304
100,000	4,669	1,210	541	305
500,000 to ∞	4,850	1,222	544	306

[a]In these cases, more than 50 percent of the population is required in the sample. Since the normal approximation of the hypergeometric distribution is a poor approximation in such instances, no sample value is given.

TABLE 15.12

	ALLOWANCE FOR RANDOM SAMPLING ERROR (PLUS AND MINUS PERCENTAGE POINTS) AT 95 PERCENT CONFIDENCE LEVEL[15]						
	SAMPLE SIZE						
Response	**2,500**	**1,500**	**1,000**	**500**	**250**	**100**	**50**
10 (90)	1.2	1.5	2.0	3.0	4.0	6.0	8.0
20 (80)	1.6	2.0	2.5	4.0	5.0	8.0	11.0
30 (70)	1.8	2.5	3.0	4.0	6.0	9.0	13.0
40 (60)	2.0	2.5	3.0	4.0	6.0	10.0	14.0
50 (50)	2.0	2.5	3.0	4.0	6.0	10.0	14.0

The theoretical principles underlying calculation of sample sizes of proportions are similar to the concepts discussed in this chapter. Suppose we wish to take samples in two large cities, Toronto and Vancouver. We wish no more than 2 percentage points of error, and we will be satisfied with a 95 percent confidence level (see Table 15.11). If we assume all other things are equal, then in the Toronto market, where 15 percent of the consumers favour our product and 85 percent prefer competitors' brands, we need a sample of 1,222 to get results with only 2 percentage points of error. In the Vancouver market, however, where 30 percent of the consumers favour our brand and 70 percent prefer other brands (a less heterogeneous market), we need a sample size of 2,009 to get the same sample reliability.

Table 15.12 shows a sampling error table typical of those that accompany research proposals or reports. Most studies will estimate more than one parameter. Thus, in a survey of 100 people in which 50 percent agree with one statement and 10 percent with another, the sampling error is expected to be 10 and 6 percentage points of error, respectively.

Determining Sample Size on the Basis of Judgment

In the previous sections, we have discussed sample size selection based on reduction of sampling error. A closer look at the formula for sample size for questions involving means reveals that increasing the sample size does not result in equivalent reductions in error. To reduce the error by half, sample size would have to be increased by four times. This could be a large increase in costs. From a managerial perspective, the sample size selection may include other factors besides focusing on reduction of error.

Just as sample units may be selected to suit the convenience or judgment of the researcher, sample size may also be determined on the basis of managerial judgments. In practice, a few different methods can be used in determining the sample size. As a *rule of thumb,* the sample size used in previous studies similar to the one at hand may be adopted. For instance, similar past studies may have used a sample size of 100 and the inexperienced researcher may also use 100 to benefit from other researchers' judgments and to enable comparisons to past studies. The past studies may have reached 100 as the sample size based on sampling error reduction or subjective judgment.

Alternatively, the sample size determination may be based on the *statistical analysis* that will be employed. The number of subgroups that the researcher wants to compare is one factor that increases sample size requirements. For instance, the researcher may want to compare the percentage of households that would adopt a new water filtering system in Vancouver, Winnipeg, Calgary, and Regina. The researcher may collect data from 360 respondents for comparing these four groups, resulting in 90 respondents per group. This may enable the researcher to make inferences about the differences between the groups. However, if the researcher decides to make comparisons between three different income groups (less than $30,000, $30,000 to 50,000, more than $50,000) and three different age groups (under 30 years, 30 to 50 years, and over 50), the remaining sample size per group will become relatively small (e.g., 10 respondents per group if we assume equal distribution of the sample among groups). As a result, sampling error would be larger, preventing clear inferences about differences between groups. There is a judgmental rule of thumb for selecting minimum subgroup sample size: Each subgroup to be separately analyzed should have a minimum of 100 units in each category of the major breakdowns. With this procedure, the total sample size is computed by totalling the sample sizes necessary for these subgroups. Other types of analyses that the researcher intends to make can affect sample size requirements.

A common consideration in sample size determination is the *budget available* for the project. The marketing manager faced with a fixed budget may deduct other expenses in the project and determine the sample size he or she can get with the remaining funds. The resulting sample size may be too small for making scientific inferences or too large given the information needs for the project.

Finally, having a target sample size that may be determined with any of the above methods is not the end of story. Researchers still have to consider the number of contacts they have to make based on the expected response rates. For a telephone interview, only one in ten calls made may result in a completed interview.

Determining Sample Size for Stratified and Other Probability Samples

Stratified sampling involves drawing separate probability samples within the subgroups to make the sample more efficient. With a stratified sample the sample variances are expected to differ by strata. This makes the determination of sample size more complex. Increased complexity may also characterize the determination of sample size for cluster sampling and other probability sampling methods. The formulas are beyond the scope of this book. Students interested in these advanced sampling techniques should investigate advanced sampling textbooks.

A REMINDER ABOUT STATISTICS

Learning the terms and symbols defined in this chapter will provide you with the basics of the language of statisticians and researchers. As you learn more about the pragmatic use of statistics in marketing research, do not forget these concepts. The speller who forgets that *i* comes before *e* except after *c* will have trouble every time he or she must tackle the spelling of a word with the *ie* or *ei* combination. The same is true for the student who forgets the basics of the "foreign language" of statistics.

SUMMARY

1 Determination of sample size requires a knowledge of statistics. Statistics is the language of the researcher, and this chapter introduced its vocabulary. Descriptive statistics describe characteristics of a population or sample. Inferential statistics investigate samples to draw conclusions about entire populations.

2 A frequency distribution summarizes data by showing how frequently each response or classification occurs. A proportion indicates the percentage of group members that have a particular characteristic.

Three measures of central tendency are commonly used: the mean, or arithmetic average; the median, or halfway value; and the mode, or most frequently observed value. These three values may differ, and care must be taken to understand distortions that may arise from using the wrong measure of central tendency.

3 Measures of dispersion along with measures of central tendency can describe a distribution. The range is the difference between the largest and smallest values observed. The variance and standard deviation are the most useful measures of dispersion.

(4) The normal distribution fits many observed distributions. It is symmetrical about its mean, with equal mean, median, and mode. Almost the entire area of the normal distribution lies within plus or minus 3 standard deviations of the mean. Any normal distribution can easily be compared with the standardized normal, or Z, distribution, whose mean is 0 and standard deviation is 1. This allows easy evaluation of the probabilities of many occurrences.

(5) The techniques of statistical inference are based on the relationship among the population distribution, the sample distribution, and the sampling distribution. This relationship is expressed in the central-limit theorem.

(6) Estimating a population mean with a single value gives a point estimate. A range of numbers within which the researcher is confident that the population mean will lie is a confidence interval estimate. The confidence level is a percentage that indicates the long-run probability that the confidence interval estimate will be correct.

(7) The statistical determination of sample size requires knowledge of (1) the variance of the population, (2) the magnitude of acceptable error, and (3) the confidence level. Several computational formulas are available for determining sample size. Furthermore, a number of easy-to-use tables have been compiled to help researchers calculate sample size. The main reason a large sample size is desirable is that sample size is related to random sampling error. A smaller sample makes a larger error in estimates more likely.

(8) (9) Many research problems involve the estimation of proportions. Statistical techniques may be used to determine a confidence interval around a sample proportion. Calculation of sample size for a sample proportion is not difficult. However, most researchers use tables that indicate predetermined sample sizes.

Key Terms and Concepts

sample statistics	median	sample distribution
population parameters	mode	sampling distribution
frequency distribution	variance	standard error of the mean
percentage distribution	standard deviation	central-limit theorem
probability	normal distribution	point estimate
proportion	standardized normal distribution	confidence interval estimate
mean	population distribution	confidence level

Questions for Review and Critical Thinking

1. What is the difference between descriptive and inferential statistics?
2. The speed limits in 13 countries are as follows:

Country	Highway Kilometres per Hour
Italy	140
France	130
Hungary	120
Belgium	120
Portugal	120
Britain	112
Spain	100
Denmark	100
Netherlands	100
Greece	100
Japan	100
Norway	90
Turkey	90

Calculate the mean, median, and mode for these data.

3. Prepare a frequency distribution for the data in question 2.
4. Why is the standard deviation rather than the average deviation typically used?
5. Calculate the standard deviation for the data in question 2.
6. Draw three distributions that have the same mean value but different standard deviation values. Draw three distributions that have the same standard deviation value but different mean values.

7. A manufacturer of MP3 players surveyed 100 retail stores in each of the firm's sales regions. An analyst noticed that in the Atlantic region the average retail price was $165 (mean) and the standard deviation was $30. However, in the Pacific region the mean price was $170, with a standard deviation of $15. What do these statistics tell us about these two sales regions?

8. What is the sampling distribution? How does it differ from the sample distribution?

9. What would happen to the sampling distribution of the mean if we increased sample size from 5 to 25?

10. Suppose a fast-food restaurant wishes to estimate average sales volume for a new menu item. The restaurant has analyzed the sales of the item at a similar outlet and observed the following results:

$$\bar{X} = 500 \text{ (mean daily sales)}$$
$$S = 100 \text{ (standard deviation of sample)}$$
$$n = 25 \text{ (sample size)}$$

The restaurant manager wants to know into what range the mean daily sales should fall 95 percent of the time. Perform this calculation.

11. In the example on page 379 of research on lipstick, where $E = \$2$ and $S = \$29$, what sample size would we require if we desired a 99 percent confidence level?

12. Suppose you are planning to sample cat owners to determine the average number of cans of cat food they purchase monthly. The following standards have been set: a confidence level of 99 percent and an error of less than 5 units. Past research has indicated that the standard deviation should be 6 units. What is the required sample size?

13. In a survey of 500 people, 60 percent responded positively to an attitude question. Calculate a confidence interval at 95 percent to get an interval estimate for a proportion.

14. In a countrywide survey, a researcher expects that 30 percent of the population will agree with an attitude

statement. She wishes to have less than 2 percentage points of error and to be 95 percent confident. What sample size does she need?

15. To understand how sample size is conceptually related to random sampling error, costs, and nonsampling errors, graph these relationships.

16. Suppose you are a political analyst and wish to be extremely confident that you predict the outcome of a very close election. What should the sample size be for your poll? Are there any problems involved in determining the sample size for this election?

17. A researcher expects the population proportion of Montreal Canadiens fans in Montreal to be 80 percent. The researcher wishes to have an error of less than 5 percent and to be 95 percent confident of an estimate to be made from a mail survey. What sample size is required?

18. An automobile dealership plans to conduct a survey to determine what proportion of new-car buyers continue to have their cars serviced at the dealership after the warranty period ends. It estimates that 30 percent of customers do so. It wants the results of its survey to be accurate within 5 percent, and it wants to be 95 percent confident of the results. What sample size is necessary?

19. A local opera company wishes to take a sample of its subscribers to learn the average number of years people have been subscribing. The researcher expects the average number of years to be 12 and believes the standard deviation will be about 2 years (approximately one-sixth of the range). He wishes to be 95 percent confident of his estimate. What is the appropriate sample size?

20. Using the formula in this chapter, a researcher determines that at the 95 percent confidence level, a sample of 2,500 is required to satisfy a client's requirements. The researcher actually uses a sample of 1,200, however, because the client has specified a budget cap for the survey. What are the ethical considerations in this situation?

Exploring the Internet

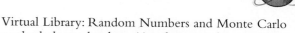

1. Go to www.dartmouth.edu/~chance/ to visit the Chance course. The Chance course is an innovative program to creatively teach introductory materials about probability and statistics. The Chance course is designed to enhance quantitative literacy. Numerous videos can be played online.

2. Go to Lycos at www.lycos.ca/. Enter "population sampling" into the search box and then click on the Go icon. How extensive is the list of sources?

3. A random number generator and other statistical information can be found at The World Wide Web

Virtual Library: Random Numbers and Monte Carlo methods, located at http://random.mat.sbg.ac.at/links.

4. The Platonic Realms Interactive Mathematics Encyclopedia is located at www.mathacademy.com. It provides many definitions of statistical and mathematical terms.

5. A Sample Size Calculator can be found at www.surveysystem.com/sscalc.htm.

6. Martindale's Calculators On-Line Center site at www.martindalecenter.com/Calculators.html is extremely valuable for researchers interested in statistical methods. Visit the site and report what you find.

CASE 15.1 PACIFIC SUN CORPORATION

Pacific Sun Corporation is a west coast wholesaler that markets leisure products from several manufacturers. The available products range from patio furniture to camping and marine gear. Pacific Sun has an 80-person sales force that sells to wholesalers in five provinces, which is divided into two sales regions. Case Exhibit 15.1.1 shows the names of a sample of 11 salespeople, some descriptive information about each person, and sales performance for each of the last two years.

Questions

1. Calculate a mean and a standard deviation for each variable.

2. Set a 95 percent confidence interval around the mean for each variable.
3. Calculate the median, mode, and range for each variable.
4. Organize the data for current sales into a frequency distribution with three classes: (a) under $500,000, (b) $500,001 to $999,999, and (c) $1,000,000 and over.
5. Organize the data for years of selling experience into a frequency distribution with two classes: (a) less than five years and (b) five or more years.
6. Convert the frequency distributions from question 5 to percentage distributions.

| CASE EXHIBIT 15.1.1 | PACIFIC SUN CORPORATION: SALESPERSON DATA | | | | |

| | | | | SALES | |
Region	Salesperson	Age	Years of Experience	Previous Year	Current Year
Atlantic	Desjardin	40	7	$ 412,744	$ 411,007
Atlantic	Gentry	60	12	1,491,024	1,726,630
Atlantic	La Forge	26	2	301,421	700,112
Atlantic	Miller	39	1	401,241	471,001
Atlantic	Barbieri	64	5	448,160	449,261
Pacific	Wu	51	2	518,897	519,412
Pacific	Fisk	34	1	846,222	713,333
Pacific	Kim	62	10	1,527,124	2,009,041
Pacific	Krieger	42	3	921,174	1,030,000
Pacific	Manzer	64	5	463,399	422,798
Pacific	Wang	27	2	548,011	422,001

DATA COLLECTION AND PREPARATION FOR DATA ANALYSIS

You have probably met and talked with a fieldworker of marketing research during one of your shopping trips. They are interviewers, usually women, who are located outside the shops and restaurants and who approach volunteers to participate in surveys, with questions ranging from how many beers you drink in a day to what you think of a certain line of clothing or your take on an advertising campaign by a large corporation. In marketing research, it's called "mall intercept." It is the art of going up to strangers, introducing yourself, and convincing prospects to participate in the research project. A high level of preparation is necessary to carry out marketing research projects from recruitment and training of interviewers to coding and entry of the data collected.

Consider PFI Research Inc. of Montreal, a marketing research company that conducts "mall intercept" studies. A project in 2003 involved interviewing 2,700 respondents from 12 cities and required 35 interviewers and 2 fulltime staff over 2 weeks just to coordinate the flights and hotel arrangements for the interviewers. Projects on this scale require careful planning of the data collection process, including the selection and training of fieldworkers.[1]

There are other steps on the path from developing a questionnaire to analyzing data; they include identifying different stages of data collection, selecting and training interviewers, coding and editing the data, and entering the data in a way to minimize errors. This chapter explores these steps and discusses quality control procedures. ■

What you will learn in this chapter

1. To discuss the job and training requirements of fieldworkers.

2. To understand how fieldworkers secure interviews.

3. To understand the major principles of asking questions in the field.

4. To discuss the activities involved in the management and supervision of fieldworkers.

5. To define and explain the terms *editing* and *coding*.

6. To code fixed-alternative and open-ended questions.

7. To define the term *code book*.

THE NATURE OF FIELDWORK

A personal interviewer administering a questionnaire door to door, a telephone interviewer calling from a central location, an observer counting pedestrians in a shopping mall, and others involved in the collection of data and the supervision of that process are all **fieldworkers.** The activities they perform vary substantially. The supervision of data collection for a mail survey differs from that for an observation study as much as the factory production process for cereal differs from that for a pair of ski boots. Nevertheless, just as quality control is basic to each production operation, there are some basic issues in fieldwork. For ease of presentation, this chapter focuses on the interviewing process conducted by personal interviewers. However, many of the issues apply to all fieldworkers, no matter what their specific settings.

WHO CONDUCTS THE FIELDWORK?

The actual data collection process is rarely carried out by the person who designs the research. However, the data-collecting stage is crucial, because the marketing research project is no better than the data collected in the field. Therefore, the marketing research administrator must select capable people and trust them to gather the data. An irony of marketing research is that highly educated and trained individuals design the research, but the people who gather the data typically have little research training or experience.

Much fieldwork is conducted by research suppliers that specialize in data collection. When a second party is subcontracted, the job of the study designer at the parent firm is not only to hire a research supplier but also to build in supervisory controls over the field service. In some cases a third-party firm is employed. For example, a company may contact a marketing research firm that in turn subcontracts the fieldwork to a **field interviewing service.**

There are a number of field interviewing services and full-service marketing research agencies that perform door-to-door surveys, central location telephone interviewing, and other forms of fieldwork for a fee. These agencies typically employ field supervisors who supervise and train interviewers, edit completed questionnaires in the field, and telephone or re-contact respondents to confirm that interviews have been conducted. Interviewers and other fieldworkers generally are paid hourly rates or per-interview fees. Often interviewers are part-time workers from a variety of backgrounds—homemakers, graduate students, and others.

In addition to the varying durations of training that the interviewers and data collection personnel should go through, there is almost always a **briefing session** on the particular project.

The objective of training is to ensure that the data collection instrument will be administered in a uniform fashion by all fieldworkers. The goal of training sessions is to ensure that each respondent is provided with common information. If the data are collected in a uniform manner from all respondents, the training session will have been a success.

More extensive training programs are likely to cover the following topics:

1. How to make initial contact with the respondent and secure the interview
2. How to ask survey questions
3. How to probe
4. How to record responses
5. How to terminate the interview

Typically, recruits record answers on a practice questionnaire during a simulated training interview.

POLLING THE DESIRED INDIVIDUAL IN POLITICAL ELECTIONS

To accurately predict election outcomes, political pollsters need to obtain representative samples.[2] Typically, to avoid interviewing too many respondents of the same age or gender, the pollster should not just interview the first person who answers the phone, because he or she is not always the individual who should be interviewed (a disproportionate number of younger males answer the phone). When the designated respondent—usually the eligible voter with the next birthday—is not home, the fieldworker should schedule a callback—an expensive and time-consuming practice that few media pollsters conduct.

Making Initial Contact and Securing the Interview

2 Making the initial contact is the first and the most important step in securing the interview or participation. Researchers must be trained to make appropriate opening remarks that will convince the respondent that his or her cooperation is important. Assurance that the information provided will remain anonymous and confidential will potentially increase participation. A letter of identification, communicating the name of the research agency or organization, and presentation of an ID card are all measures that would indicate that the study is a bona fide research project and not a sales call.

Asking the Questions

3 The five major rules in asking questions, listed below, are extremely useful in reducing interviewer bias as a source of considerable error in survey research.

1. Ask the questions exactly as they are worded in the questionnaire.
2. Read each question very slowly.

Conducting surveys in Canada requires attention to some important differences from the United States. One of every four Canadians speaks only French. This often means that interviewers should be bilingual, and data collection forms should be prepared in both English and French—especially if the research is conducted only in Quebec, where nine out of ten French-speaking Canadians reside.

Researchers for a bathroom cleaner kept hearing respondents refer to the surface of a tub or toilet as "shining." When interviewers probed to learn what respondents meant by "shine," they learned that shine was a synonym for clean and germ-free.

3. Ask the questions in the order in which they are presented in the questionnaire.
4. Ask every question specified in the questionnaire.
5. Repeat questions that are misunderstood or misinterpreted.[3]

Inexperienced interviewers and even professional interviewers may take shortcuts when the task becomes monotonous. However, even the slightest change in wording can distort the meaning of the question and inject some bias into a study. By reading the question, the interviewer may be reminded to concentrate on avoiding slight variations in tone of voice on particular words or phrases. Interviewers should refrain from supplying their own personal definitions and ad–libbing clarifications.

Often respondents volunteer information relevant to a question that is supposed to be asked at a later point in the interview. In this situation the response should be recorded under the question that deals specifically with that subject rather than skipping the question that was answered out of sequence. By asking every question, the interviewer can be sure that complete answers are recorded.

Probing

probing
The verbal prompts made by a fieldworker when the respondent must be motivated to communicate his or her answer or to enlarge on, clarify, or explain an answer.

Probing may be necessary when respondents give no answer, incomplete answers, or answers that require clarification. **Probing** may be needed for two types of situations. First, it is necessary when the respondent must be motivated to enlarge on, clarify, or explain his or her answer. It is the interviewer's job to probe for complete, unambiguous answers. The interviewer must encourage the respondent to clarify or expand on answers by providing a stimulus that will not suggest the interviewer's own ideas or attitudes. The ability to probe with neutral stimuli is the mark of an experienced interviewer. Second, probing may be necessary when the respondent begins to ramble or lose track of the question. In such cases the respondent must be led to focus on the specific content of the interview and to avoid irrelevant and unnecessary information.

The interviewer has several possible probing tactics to choose from, depending on the situation:

- *Repeating the question.* When the respondent remains completely silent, he or she may not have understood the question or decided how to answer it. Mere repetition may encourage the respondent to answer in such cases. For example, if

EXHIBIT 16.1 | COMMONLY USED PROBES AND THEIR ABBREVIATIONS[4]

Interviewer's Probe	Standard Abbreviation
Repeat question	(RQ)
Anything else?	(AE or Else?)
Any other reason?	(AO?)
Any others?	(Other?)
How do you mean?	(How mean?)
Could you tell me more about your thinking on that?	(Tell more)
Would you tell me what you have in mind?	(What in mind?)
What do you mean?	(What mean?)
Why do you feel that way?	(Why?)
Which would be closer to the way you feel?	(Which closer?)

the question is "What do you not like about this product?" and the respondent does not answer, the interviewer may probe: "Just to check, is there anything that you do not like about this product?"

- *Using a silent probe.* If the interviewer believes that the respondent has more to say, a silent probe—that is, an expectant pause or look—may motivate the respondent to gather his or her thoughts and give a complete response. However, the interviewer must be careful that this technique does not lead to an embarrassing silence.

- *Repeating the respondent's reply.* As the interviewer records the response, he or she may repeat the respondent's reply verbatim. This may stimulate the respondent to expand on the answer.

- *Asking a neutral question.* Asking a neutral question may specifically indicate the type of information that the interviewer is seeking. For example, if the interviewer believes that the respondent's motives should be clarified, he or she might ask, "Why do you feel that way?" If the interviewer feels that there is a need to clarify a word or phrase, he or she might say, "How do you mean_____?" Exhibit 16.1 lists some common interview probes and the standard abbreviations that are recorded on the questionnaire with the respondent's answers.

The purpose of asking questions as probes is to encourage responses. Such probes should be neutral and not leading. Probes may be general (such as "Anything else?") or they may be questions specifically designed by the interviewer to clarify a particular statement by the respondent.

Recording the Responses

Although the concept of recording an answer seems extremely simple, mistakes can occur in this phase of the research. Each fieldworker should use the same mechanics of recording. For example, the interviewer may not understand the importance of using a pencil rather than a pen. To the editor who must erase and rewrite illegible words, however, use of a pencil is extremely important.

The rules for recording responses to fixed-alternative questions vary with the specific questionnaire. The general rule, however, is to place a check mark in the box that correctly reflects the respondent's answer. All too often interviewers don't bother recording the answer to a filter question because they believe the subsequent answer will make the answer to the filter question obvious. However, editors and coders do not know how the respondent actually answered a question.

The general instruction for recording open-ended questions is to record the response verbatim, a task that is difficult for most people. Inexperienced interviewers should be given the opportunity to practise verbatim recording of answers before being sent into the field. Some suggestions for recording open-ended answers are as follows:

- Record responses during the interview.

- Use the respondent's own words.

- Do not summarize or paraphrase the respondent's answer.

- Include everything that pertains to the question objectives.

- Include all of your probes.[5]

Exhibit 16.2 shows an example of a completed questionnaire page. Note how the interviewer adds supplementary comments to the fixed-alternative questions and indicates probing questions by placing them in parentheses. The answers have been recorded without paraphrasing. The interviewer has resisted the temptation to conserve time and space by filtering comments. The RQ recorded in question A4a indicates a repeat question probe.

Terminating the Interview

The final aspect of training deals with instructing interviewers on how to close the interview. Fieldworkers should not close the interview before they have secured all pertinent information. Avoiding hasty departures is a matter of courtesy. Furthermore, it allows recording the spontaneous comments respondents offer after all formal questions have been asked. One of these comments may result in a new product idea or creative marketing campaign. The fieldworker should also answer any respondent questions concerning the nature and purpose of the study to the best of his or her ability.

The fieldworker may be required to re-interview the respondent at some future time. Thus the respondent should be left with a positive feeling about having cooperated in a worthwhile operation. Finally, it is extremely important to thank the respondent for his or her time and cooperation.

MANAGEMENT AND SUPERVISION OF THE FIELDWORK

 A proper research design will eliminate numerous sources of error, but careful execution of the fieldwork is necessary to produce results without substantial error. For these reasons fieldwork management and supervision are essential components of the marketing research process.

Project Briefing Session

There is always a need to inform fieldworkers about the individual project. This briefing session should cover the background of the sponsoring organization, sampling techniques, asking of questions, callback procedures, and other matters specific to the particular project.

If there are any special instructions—for example, about product trials or using video equipment or restricted interviewing times—these should also be covered during this training session. Instructions for handling certain key questions are always important.

EXHIBIT 16.2 | **EXAMPLE OF A COMPLETED QUESTIONNAIRE PAGE[6]**

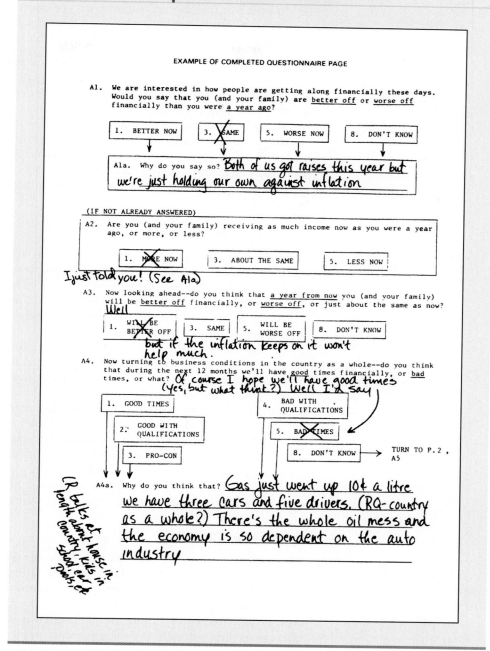

EXAMPLE OF COMPLETED QUESTIONNAIRE PAGE

The briefing session should also cover the sampling procedure. A number of research projects allow the fieldworker to be at least partially responsible for selecting the sample. In such situations the potential for selection bias exists. This is obvious in the case of quota sampling, but less obvious in other cases. For example, in probability sampling in which every nth house is selected, the fieldworker uses his or her discretion in identifying housing units. Avoiding selection bias may not be as simple as it sounds. For example, in an old, exclusive neighbourhood, a mansion's coach house or servants' quarters may have been converted into an apartment that should be identified as a housing unit. This type of dwelling and other unusual housing units (apartments with alley entrances only, summer cottages, or rooming houses) may be overlooked, giving rise to selection error. Considerable effort should be expended in training and supervisory control to minimize these errors.

Role of Fieldwork Supervision

Although briefing and training interviewers will minimize the probability of their interviewing the wrong households or asking biased questions, there is still considerable potential for errors in the field. Direct supervision of fieldwork (e.g., personal interviewers, telephone interviewers) is necessary to ensure that the techniques communicated in the training sessions are implemented in the field. This quality control process may also aid in identifying areas of future training. For example, if a telephone supervisor notices that interviewers are allowing the phone to ring more than eight times before considering the call a "no answer," the supervisor can instruct interviewers not to do so, as the person who eventually answers is likely to be annoyed.

Sampling Verification

A very important part of the supervision is to verify that data collection is conducted according to the sampling plan. For instance, an interviewer might be tempted to go to the household next door for an interview rather than record that the sampling unit was not at home, which would require a callback. Careful recording of the number of completed surveys will help ensure that the sampling procedure is being properly conducted.

Supervision can also identify whether the right people within the household or sampling unit are being contacted. One research project for a children's cereal required that several products be placed in the home and that children record their daily consumption and reactions to each cereal in a diary. Although the interviewers were supposed to contact the children to remind them to fill out the diaries, a field supervisor observed that in almost half the cases the mothers were filling out the diaries after the children left for school because their children had not done so. The novelty of the research project had worn off after a few days and the children had stopped keeping the diaries. Similar situations may occur with physicians, executives, and other busy people. The fieldworker may find it easier to interview a nurse, secretary, or other assistant rather than wait to speak with the right person.

Interviewer Cheating

interviewer cheating
The practice by fieldworkers of filling in fake answers or falsifying interviews.

Interviewer cheating in its most blatant form occurs when an interviewer falsifies interviews, merely filling in fake answers rather than contacting respondents. Although this situation does occur, it is not common if the job of selection has been properly accomplished. However, less obvious forms of interviewer cheating occur with greater frequency. Quota sampling often is seen as time consuming, and the interviewer may stretch the requirements a bit to obtain seemingly qualified respondents. Consider the fieldworker who must select only heavy users of a certain brand of hand lotion that the client says is used by 15 percent of the population. If the fieldworker finds that only 3 percent qualify as heavy users, he or she may be tempted to interview an occasional user to stretch the quota somewhat.

An interviewer may fake part of a questionnaire to make it acceptable to the field supervisor. In a survey on automobile satellite radio systems, suppose an interviewer is requested to ask for five reasons that consumers have purchased this product. If he or she finds that people typically give two or perhaps three reasons and even with extensive probing cannot think of five reasons, the interviewer might be tempted to cheat. Rather than have the supervisor think he or she was goofing off on the probing, the interviewer may fill in five reasons based on past interviews. In other cases the interviewer may cut corners to save time and energy.

Interviewers may fake answers when they find questions embarrassing or troublesome to ask because of sensitive subjects. Thus the interviewer may complete most of the questionnaire, but leave out a question or two because he or she found it troublesome or time consuming. For example, in a survey among physicians, an interviewer might find questions about artificial insemination donor programs embarrassing, skip these questions, and fill in the gaps later.

What appears to be interviewer cheating often is caused by improper training or fieldworkers' inexperience. A fieldworker who does not understand the instructions may skip or miss a portion of the questionnaire.

Verification by Re-interviewing

Supervision for quality control attempts to ensure that interviewers are following the sampling procedure and to detect falsification of interviews. Supervisors verify approximately 15 percent of the interviews by re-interviewing. Normally the interview is not repeated; rather, supervisors recontact respondents and ask about the length of the interview and their reactions to the interviewer; then they collect basic demographic data to check for interviewer cheating. Such **verification** does not detect the more subtle form of cheating in which only portions of the interview have been falsified. A validation check may simply point out that an interviewer contacted the proper household but interviewed the wrong individual in that household—which, of course, can be a serious error.

Fieldworkers should be aware of supervisory verification practices. Knowing that there may be a telephone or postcard validation check often reminds interviewers to be conscientious in their work. The interviewer who is conducting quota sampling and needs an upper-income South Asian male will be less tempted to interview a middle-income South Asian man and falsify the income data in this situation.

Certain information may allow for partial verification without recontacting the respondent. Computer-assisted telephone interviewers often do not know the phone number dialled by the computer or other basic information about the respondent. Thus answers to questions added to the end of the telephone interview to identify a respondent's area code, phone number, city, postal code, and so on may be used to verify the interview. The computer can also identify interviewers who cheat by recording every attempted call, the time intervals between calls, and the time required to conduct each completed interview.[7]

verification
Quality-control procedures in fieldwork intended to ensure that interviewers are following the sampling procedures and to determine whether interviewers are cheating.

EDITING

⑤

The goal of most research is to provide information. There is a difference between the raw data collected at the field and information. *Information* refers to a body of facts that are in a format suitable for decision making, whereas *data* are simply recorded measures of certain phenomena. The conversion of raw data into information requires that the data be edited and coded so that they may be transferred to a computer or other data storage medium. Let us first focus on editing.

Occasionally a fieldworker makes a mistake and records an improbable answer (for example, "birth year: 1843") or interviews an ineligible respondent (such as someone too young to qualify). Sometimes answers are contradictory, such as *no* to automobile ownership but *yes* to an expenditure on automobile insurance. These and other problems must be dealt with before the data can be coded. **Editing** is the process of checking and adjusting the data for omissions, legibility, and consistency and readying them for coding and storage.

Editing may be differentiated from **coding**, which is the assignment of numerical scores or classifying symbols to previously edited data. Careful editing makes the coding job easier. The purpose of editing is to ensure the completeness, consistency, and readability of the data to be transferred to storage. The editor's task is to check for errors and omissions on the questionnaires or other data collection forms. When

editing
The process of checking the completeness, consistency, and legibility of data and making the data ready for coding and transfer to storage.

coding
The process of assigning a numerical score or other character symbol to previously edited data.

the editor discovers a problem, he or she adjusts the data to make them more complete, consistent, or readable.

The editor may also have to reconstruct some data. For instance, a respondent may indicate weekly income rather than monthly income, as requested on the questionnaire. The editor must convert the information to monthly data without adding any extraneous information. The process of editing has been compared to the process of restoring a work of art. The editor should bring to light all the hidden values and extract all possible information from a questionnaire, while adding nothing extraneous.

The preliminary stage of editing, **field editing,** starts on the same day as the interview. The purpose of field editing is to catch technical omissions such as a blank page on the interview questionnaire, to check legibility of handwriting, and to clarify responses that are logically or conceptually inconsistent. Field editing as part of daily fieldwork supervision helps to deal with some questions by asking interviewers, who may be able to remember the interviews and correct the problems. In addition, the number of unanswered questions or incomplete responses can be reduced with rapid follow-up stimulated by a field edit. The daily field edit allows fieldworkers to recontact the respondent to fill in omissions before the situation changes. It may also indicate the need for further interviewer training if, for example, the interviewers did not correctly follow skip patterns or open-ended responses reflect a lack of probing.

Although simultaneous field editing is highly desirable, in many situations (particularly with mail questionnaires) early reviewing of the data is not always possible. **In-house editing** rigorously investigates the results of data collection. The research supplier or research department normally has a centralized office staff perform the editing and coding function.

For example, the Canadian Bureau of Broadcast Measurement measures radio audiences by having respondents record their listening behaviour—time and station—in diaries. After the diaries are returned by mail, in-house editors may perform usability edits in which they check that the postmark is after the last day of the survey week, verify the legibility of station call letters (station CXXX could look like CYYY), look for completeness of entries on each day of the week, and perform other editing activities. If the respondent's age or sex is not indicated, the respondent may be called to ensure that this information is included.

Editing for Consistency

The in-house editor's task is to adjust inconsistent or contradictory responses so that the answers will not be a problem for coders and keyboard operators. Suppose a telephone interviewer has been instructed to interview only people who are 21 years or older and living in Canada. If the editor's review of a questionnaire indicates that the respondent was only 17 years old, the editor's task is to eliminate this obviously incorrect sampling unit. In this example the job is to ensure that the sampling unit is consistent with the objectives of the study.

The editor also checks for adherence to the data collection framework. For example, a survey on out-shopping behaviour (shopping in towns other than the one in which the person resides) might have a question such as the following:

In which of the following towns do you shop for clothing? Please write in the clothing stores where you have shopped during the last month.

If a respondent lists a clothing store in town A but accidentally checks the box next to town B, this is an error. The answer must be changed to town A.

Editing requires checking for logically consistent responses. The in-house editor must determine if the answers a respondent gave to one question are consistent with those for other, related questions. Many surveys use filter questions or

field editing
Preliminary editing by a field supervisor on the same day as the interview to catch technical omissions, check legibility of handwriting, and clarify responses that are logically or conceptually inconsistent.

in-house editing
A rigorous editing job performed by a centralized office staff.

TO THE POINT

Excellence is to do a common thing in an uncommon way.
BOOKER T. WASHINGTON

skip questions that direct the sequence of questions according to the respondent's answers. In some cases the respondent will have been asked a sequence of questions that should not have been asked. The editor should adjust these answers, usually to "no answer" or "inapplicable," so that the responses will be consistent. In other cases illogical answers will signal potential recording errors. For example, a $50,000 valuation for a respondent's house may be inconsistent with the neighbourhood in which the house is located and the 45-year-old respondent's occupational listing as a physician. The editor must use good judgment in situations in which he or she finds it highly unlikely that the answers to two questions could both be correct.

Editing for Completeness

In some cases the respondent may have answered only the second portion of a two-part question. The following question creates a situation in which an in-house editor may have to adjust answers for completeness:

Does your organization have more than one mainframe computer installation?

☐ **Yes** ☐ **No**

If yes, how many?

If the respondent checked neither yes nor no but indicated three computer installations, the editor may use a coloured pencil to check Yes, to ensure that this item is not missing from the questionnaire.

item nonresponse
The technical term for an unanswered question on an otherwise complete questionnaire.

Item nonresponse is the technical term for an unanswered question on an otherwise complete questionnaire. Specific decision rules for handling this problem should be meticulously outlined in the editor's instructions. In many situations the decision rule is to do nothing with the unanswered question. The editor merely indicates an item nonresponse by providing a message instructing the coder to record "missing value" or "blank" as the response. However, when the relationship between two questions is important, such as that between a question about magazine readership and one on educational level, it may be necessary for the editor to insert a **plug value**. The decision rule may be to plug in an average or neutral value in each instance of missing data. Another decision rule may be to alternate the choice of the response categories used as plug values (for example, yes the first time, no the second time, yes the third time). Still another decision rule might be to randomly select an answer. For example, suppose a respondent has indicated as a first preference in brands of beer Budweiser, but has given Sleeman and Molson the same ranking. The editor may randomly select the number two and three brands so that data analysis may be performed as planned. The editor must decide whether an entire questionnaire is usable. When a questionnaire has too many missing answers, it may not be suitable for the planned data analysis. In such a situation the editor can record that a particular incomplete questionnaire has been dropped from the sample.

plug value
An answer that an editor "plugs in" to replace blanks or missing values so as to permit data analysis; choice of value is based on a predetermined decision rule.

Editing Questions Answered Out of Order

Another task an editor may face is rearranging the answers given to open-ended questions. For example, the respondent may have provided the answer to a subsequent question in his or her comments to an earlier open-ended question. Because the respondent already had clearly identified the answer, the interviewer may not have asked the subsequent question, wishing to avoid hearing "I already answered that earlier" and to maintain interview rapport. To make the responses appear in the same order as on other questionnaires, the editor may move certain answers to the section related to the skipped question.

Facilitating the Coding Process

While all of the previously described editing activities will help coders, several editing procedures are designed specifically to simplify the coding process. For example, the editor checks to make sure every circled response is clearly definable; a response that overlaps two numbers and could be either 3 or 4 must be judged. The editor edits missing information and determines if the answer is "don't know" (DK) or "not ascertained" (NA). These and other decisions by the editor should not be arbitrary, but rather based on a systematic procedure of applying fixed rules for making decisions.

Editing and Tabulating "Don't Know" Answers

In many situations, the respondent answers "don't know." On the surface, this response seems to indicate that the respondent is not familiar with the brand, product, or situation or is uncertain and has not formulated a clear-cut opinion. This *legitimate* "don't know" means the same as "no opinion." However, there may be reasons for this response other than the legitimate "don't know." The *reluctant* "don't know" is given when the respondent simply does not want to answer the question and wishes to stop the interviewer from asking more. For example, asking an individual who is not the head of the household about family income may elicit a "don't know" answer meaning "This is personal, and I really do not want to answer the question." If the individual does not understand the question, he or she may give a *confused* "I don't know" answer.

In some situations the editor can separate the legitimate "don't knows" ("no opinion") from the other "don't knows." The editor may try to identify the meaning of the "don't know" answer from other data provided on the questionnaire. For instance, the value of a home could be derived from a knowledge of the postal code and the average value of homes within that area.

The tabulation of "don't know" answers requires the editor to make a decision. One alternative is to record all "don't knows" as a separate category. This provides the actual response categories, but it may cause some problems with percentage calculation. Another alternative is to eliminate the "don't knows" from the percentage base. A third is to distribute the "don't know" answers among the other categories, usually proportionally. Although this is a simple procedure, it is criticized because it assumes that people who give "don't know" answers are the same as those who provide definite answers to a question on, say, income. In many situations this is not the case, and the "don't knows" are actually a highly homogeneous group.

Mechanics of Editing

Edited data frequently are written in with a coloured pencil. When space on the questionnaire permits, the original data usually are left in to permit a subsequent editor to identify the original concepts. In our experience, blue or green pencils have been used for editing and red pencils for coding.

Pitfalls of Editing

One possible problem in editing is subjectivity. To do a proper editing job, the editor must be intelligent, experienced, and *objective*. A *systematic procedure* for assessing the questionnaires should be developed by the research analyst so that the editor has clearly defined decision rules to follow.

Pre-testing Edit

Editing questionnaires during the pre-test stage can prove very valuable. For example, if respondents' answers to the open-ended questions were longer than anticipated, the fieldworkers, respondents, and analysts would benefit from a change to larger spaces for the answers. Answers will be more legible because the writers have enough space, answers will be more complete, and answers will be verbatim rather than summarized. Examining answers to pre-tests may identify poor instructions or inappropriate question wording on the questionnaire.

CODING

codes
Rules for interpreting, classifying, and recording data in the coding process; also, the actual numerical or other character symbols assigned to raw data.

data matrix
A rectangular arrangement of data in rows and columns.

The process of identifying and classifying each answer with a numerical score or other character symbol is called *coding*. Assigning numerical symbols permits the transfer of data from the questionnaires to the computer. **Codes** generally are considered to be numbered symbols; however, they are more broadly defined as rules for interpreting, classifying, and recording data. Codes allow data to be processed and analyzed using statistical software packages.

The Data Matrix

A **data matrix** is a rectangular arrangement of data in rows and columns. An accountant's spreadsheet, on traditional row and column accounting paper, is one example of a data matrix. Exhibit 16.3 illustrates a data matrix from a secondary data study investigating each province's (or territory's) population, average age, and automobile registrations (per 1,000 people). Each row in the matrix represents one province. In other words, the rows represent records for individual cases, reflecting the fundamental units of analysis.

Each column in Exhibit 16.3 represents a particular field. The columns correspond to variables that reflect data about each province. The first column contains an abbreviation of the province name. The second column shows the province's population in thousands. The third column contains the average age in the province. The fourth column gives the number of automobile registrations per 1,000 residents for each province. The intersection of a row and a column indicates where to enter a number or other code assigned to a particular province on a particular variable.

Years ago the data storage medium was the standard-sized 80-column punch card. Today an online computer terminal on which data-processing operators perform

EXHIBIT 16.3	A DATA MATRIX[8]			
		FIELDS		
	Province (Column 1)	**Population (thousands) (Column 2)**	**Average Age (Column 3)**	**Cars per 1,000 (Column 4)**
Alberta (Row 1)	AB	3256.8	35.3	660
British Columbia (Row 2)	BC	4254.5	30.1	534
Manitoba (Row 3)	MB	1177.6	32.2	523
New Brunswick (Row 4)	NB	752.0	25.6	588
.	.	.	.	.
.	.	.	.	.
.	.	.	.	.
.	.	.	.	.
Yukon (Row 13)	YT	31.0	28.1	771

EXHIBIT 16.4	CODING FOR AN ATTITUDE STATEMENT

Fixed-Alternative Question
In general, self-regulation by business itself is preferable to stricter control of business by the government.

1. Strongly agree
2. Mildly agree
3. Mildly disagree

4. Strongly disagree
8. Don't know
9. No answer

direct data entry is the most common input device for data storage, and punch cards are rarely used. Nevertheless, the terminology of direct data entry coding systems is based on that used in the traditional computer card system.

Code Construction

Exhibit 16.4 shows a typical survey question and its associated codes. When the question has a fixed-alternative (closed-ended) format, the number of categories that require codes is determined during the questionnaire design stage. The codes 8 and 9 conventionally are given to "don't know" (DK) and "no answer" (NA) responses, respectively. However, many computer programs recognize that a blank field or a certain character symbol, such as a period (.), indicates a missing value (no answer). The computer program that will be used should be considered when selecting codes for "no answer" responses.

There are two basic rules for code construction. First, the coding categories should be *exhaustive;* that is, coding categories should be provided for all subjects, objects, or responses. With a categorical variable such as sex, making categories exhaustive is not a problem. However, trouble may arise when the response represents a small number of subjects or when responses might be categorized into a class not typically found. For example, when questioned about automobile ownership, an antique car collector might mention that he drives a Packard Clipper. This may present a problem if separate categories have been developed for all possible makes of cars. Solving this problem frequently requires inclusion of an "other" code category to ensure that the categories are all-inclusive. For example, household size might be coded 1, 2, 3, 4, and 5 or more. The "5 or more" category assures all subjects of a place in a category.

Second, the coding categories should be *mutually exclusive* and *independent.* This means that there should be no overlap among the categories, to ensure that a subject or response can be placed in only one category.

When a questionnaire is highly structured, the categories may be pre-coded before the data are collected. Exhibit 16.5 presents a questionnaire for which the pre-coded response categories were determined before the start of data collection.

In many cases, such as when researchers are using open-ended response questions to explore an unfamiliar topic, a framework for classifying responses to questions cannot be established before data collection. This situation requires some careful thought concerning the determination of categories after the editing process has been completed. This is called *post-coding,* or simply *coding.*

Pre-coding Fixed-Alternative Questions

Exhibit 16.5 shows the last page of a questionnaire that asks several demographic questions to classify individuals' scores. Question 29 has three possible answers, and they are pre-coded 1, 2, 3. Question 30 asks a person to respond yes (1) or no (2) to the question "Are you the male or female head of the household?" The small slightly raised numbers to the left of the response boxes indicate the code for each

EXHIBIT 16.5 | PRE-CODING FIXED-ALTERNATIVE RESPONSES

29. Do you—or does anyone else in your immediate household—belong to a labour union?

$^1\square$ Yes, I personally belong to a labour union.
$^2\square$ Yes, another member of my household belongs to a labour union.
$^3\square$ No, no one in my household belongs to a labour union.

30. Are you the male or female head of the household—that is, the person whose income is the chief source of support of the household?

$^1\square$ Yes $^2\square$ No

31. Would you please check the appropriate combined yearly income (before income taxes and any other payroll deductions) from <u>all sources of all those</u> in your immediate household? (Please include income from salaries, investments, dividends, rents, royalties, bonuses, commissions, etc.) <u>Please remember that your individual answers will not be divulged.</u>

$^1\square$ Less than $4,000 $^7\square$ $8,000–$8,999 $^{13}\square$ $25,000–$29,999
$^2\square$ $4,000–$4,999 $^8\square$ $9,000–$9,999 $^{14}\square$ $30,000–$39,999
$^3\square$ $5,000–$5,999 $^9\square$ $10,000–$12,499 $^{15}\square$ $40,000–$49,999
$^4\square$ $6,000–$6,999 $^{10}\square$ $12,500–$14,999 $^{16}\square$ $50,000–$74,999
$^5\square$ $7,000–$7,499 $^{11}\square$ $15,000–$19,999 $^{17}\square$ $75,000–$99,999
$^6\square$ $7,500–$7,999 $^{12}\square$ $20,000–$24,999 $^{18}\square$ $100,000 or more

32a. Do you personally own corporate stocks?

$^1\square$ Yes $^2\square$ No

b. Do you own stocks in the corporation for which you work? $^1\square$ $^2\square$

Do you own them in a corporation for which you do not work?

(Please check as many as apply.)

Own <u>STOCK</u> in:

$^1\square$ Company for which I work $^2\square$ Other company

THANK YOU VERY MUCH FOR YOUR COOPERATION

If you would like to make any comments on any of the subjects covered in this study, please use the space below:

response and will be used by the keyboard operator when entering the data into the computer. For example, a field in the data matrix—say, column 32—will be assigned to the answer to question 30. If the respondent replies yes, a 1 will be entered. Question 31 will require a larger field because of the large number of possible answers.

The partial questionnaire in Exhibit 16.6 shows a pre-coded format for a telephone interview. In this situation the interviewer circles the coded numerical score as the answer to the question.

Pre-coding can be used if the researcher knows what the answer categories will be before data collection occurs. Once the questionnaire has been designed and the structured (or closed-form) answers identified, coding then becomes a routine

EXHIBIT 16.6 | PRE-CODED FORMAT FOR TELEPHONE INTERVIEW

Study #12345

Travel (Telephone Screening)

City:

Toronto

Hamilton

London

Sudbury

For office use only

Respondent #_____

Hello, I'm _____ from_____, a national survey research company.

We are conducting a study and would like to ask you a few questions.

A. Before we begin, do you—or any member of your family—work for . . .

    1 A travel agency 2 An advertising agency 3 A marketing research company

    (If "yes" to any of the above, terminate and tally on contact sheet)

B. By the way, have you been interviewed as part of a survey research study within the past month?

    1 Yes—(Terminate and tally on contact sheet)

    2 No—(Continue)

1. Have you yourself made any trips of over 100 kilometres within Canada in the past 3 months?

    1 Yes

    2 No—(Skip to Question 10)

2. Was the trip for business reasons (paid for by your firm), vacation, or personal reasons?

	Last Trip	Second Last Trip	Other Trips
Business	1	1	1
Vacation	2	2	2
Personal (excluding a vacation)	3	3	3

process; in fact, in some cases the predetermined responses are based on standardized classification schemes. A coding framework that standardizes occupation follows:

What is your occupation? (PROBE: What kind of work is that?)

01 Professional, technical, and kindred workers	07 Operatives and kindred workers
02 Farmers	08 Service workers
03 Managers, officials, and proprietors	09 Labourers, except farm and mine
04 Clerical and kindred workers	10 Retired, widow, widower
05 Sales workers	11 Student
06 Craftsmen, foremen, and kindred workers	12 Unemployed, on welfare, laid off
	13 Homemaker
	14 Other (specify)
	99 No occupation given

Computer-assisted telephone interviewing (CATI) and computer-interactive surveys require pre-coding. Changing the coding framework after the interviewing process has begun is extremely difficult because it requires changes in the computer programs.

Coding Open-Ended Questions

The usual reason for using open-ended questions is that the researcher has no clear hypotheses regarding the answers, which will be numerous and varied. The purpose of coding such questions is to reduce the large number of individual responses to a few general categories of answers that can be assigned numerical codes.

Similar answers should be placed in a general category and assigned the same code. For example, individuals asked why they were not purchasing a new microwaveable product might give the following answers:

- We don't buy frozen food very often.

- I like to prepare fresh food.

- Frozen foods are not as tasty as fresh foods.

- I don't like that freezer taste.

All of these answers could be categorized under "dislike frozen foods" and assigned the code 1. Code construction in these situations necessarily must reflect the judgment of the researcher.

A major objective in the code-building process is to accurately transfer the meanings from written responses to numeric codes. Experienced researchers recognize that the key idea in this process is that code building is based on thoughts, not just words. Exhibit 16.7 illustrates open-ended responses and preliminary open-ended codes generated for the question "Why does the chilli you just tasted taste closer to homemade?" During the coding procedure, the respondent's opinions are divided into mutually exclusive thought patterns. These separate divisions may consist of a single word, a phrase, or a number of phrases, but in each case represent only one thought. Each separate thought is coded once. When a thought is composed of more than one word or phrase, only the most specific word or phrase is coded.

Devising the Coding Scheme

A coding scheme should not be too elaborate. The coder's task is only to summarize the data. Table 16.1 shows a test tabulation of airport visitors' responses to a question that asked for comments about the Honolulu Airport. After the first pass at devising the coding scheme, the researcher must decide whether to revise it and whether the codes are appropriate for answering management's questions. A preliminary scheme with too many categories can always be collapsed or reduced later in the analysis. If initial coding is too abstract and only a few categories are established, revising the codes to more concrete statements will be difficult unless the raw data were recorded.

In the Honolulu Airport example, the preliminary tabulation contained too many codes, but it could be reduced to a smaller number of categories. For example, the heading *Friendly/Attractive Personnel* could include the responses *Friendly staff/people, Polite VIP/friendly/helpful,* and *Cute VIP.* Experienced coders group answers under generalized headings that are pertinent to the research question. It is important to make the codes consistent. Individual coders should give the same code to similar responses. The categories should be sufficiently unambiguous that coders will not classify items in different ways.

Coding open-ended questions is a very complex issue. Technical treatises on this subject may be referred to if complex problems develop.

EXHIBIT 16.7 | CODING OPEN-ENDED QUESTIONS ABOUT CHILLI[9]

You don't get that much meat in a can.	1. Don't get that much meat in a can
The beans are cooked just right.	2. Beans are cooked just right
It just (doesn't look) like any canned chilli I've had.	
I can see spices; I've never seen it in any canned chilli.	3. I can see spices
It is not too spicy,	4. Not too spicy
but it is tasty—savoury.	5. It is tasty
It's not (loaded with beans)—just enough beans.	6. Has just enough beans
It's moist—not too chewy.	7. Moist
	8. Not too chewy
Tastes (fresh).	9. Fresh taste
The canned stuff is too (soft). Too overcooked usually.	10. Canned is usually overcooked
It doesn't have a lot of filler and not too many beans.	11. Not a lot of filler
	12. Not too many beans
It's not too spicy. It's not too hot, it's mild.	13. Not too hot, it's mild
Has enough spice to make it tastier	14. Has enough spice
It seems to have a pretty good gravy. Some are watery.	15. Gravy not watery

Code Book

code book
A book that identifies each variable in a study and gives the variable's description, code name, and position in the data matrix.

Up to this point we have assumed that each code's position in the data matrix already has been determined. However, this plan generally is formed after the coding scheme has been designed for every question.

The **code book** gives each variable in the study and its location in the data matrix. With the code book the researcher can identify any variable's description, code name, and field. Exhibit 16.8 illustrates a portion of a code book from the telephone interview illustrated in Exhibit 16.6. Notice that the first few fields record the study number, city, and other information used for identification purposes. Researchers commonly identify individual respondents by giving each an identification number or questionnaire number. When each interview is identified with a number entered into each computer record, errors discovered in the tabulation process can be checked on the questionnaire to verify the answer. When there are several answers to a single question, the codes must be spread into several fields because of the possibility of multiple answers.

Editing and Coding Combined

Frequently the person coding the questionnaire performs certain editing functions, such as translating an occupational title provided by the respondent into a code for socioeconomic status. A question that asks for a description of the job or business

TABLE 16.1	OPEN-ENDED RESPONSES TO A SURVEY ABOUT THE HONOLULU AIRPORT[10]

	Number
Prices high: restaurant/coffee shop/snack bar	90
Dirty—filthy—smelly restrooms/airport	65
Very good/good/excellent/great	59
Need air-conditioning	52
Nice/beautiful	45
Gift shops expensive	32
Too warm/too hot	31
Friendly staff/people	25
Airport is awful/bad	23
Long walk between terminal/gates	21
Clean airport	17
Employees rude/unfriendly/poor attitude	16
More signs/maps in lobby/streets	16
Like it	15
Love gardens	11
Need video games/arcade	10
More change machines/different locations	8
More padded benches/comfortable waiting area	8
More security personnel including HPD	8
Replace shuttle with moving walkways	8
Complaint: flight delay	7
Cool place	7
Crowded	7
Provide free carts for carry-on bags	7
Baggage storage inconvenient/need in different locations	6
Floor plan confusing	6
Mailbox locations not clear/more needed	6
More restaurants and coffee shops/more variety	6
Need a place to nap	6
Polite VIP/friendly/helpful	6
Poor help in gift shops/rude/unfriendly	6
Slow baggage delivery/service	6
Very efficient/organized	6
Excellent food	5
Install chilled water drinking fountains	5
Love Hawaii	5
More TV sets	5
Noisy	5
People at sundries/camera rude	5
Shuttle drivers rude	5
Something to do for passengers with long waits	5
Airport too spread out	4
Better information for departing/arriving flights	4
Better parking for employees	4
Better shuttle service needed	4
Cute VIP	4

often is used to ensure that there will be no problem in classifying the responses. For example, respondents who indicate "salesperson" as their occupation might write their job description as "selling shoes in a shoe store" or "selling IBM super-computers to the defence department." Generally, coders are instructed to perform this type of editing function, seeking the help of a tabulation supervisor if questions arise.

| EXHIBIT 16.8 | | PORTION OF A CODE BOOK FROM A TRAVEL STUDY |

STUDY #12345
DECEMBER 2006
N = 743

Question Number	Field or Column Number	Description and Meaning of Code Values
—	1–5	Study number (12345)
—	6	City
		1. Toronto
		2. Hamilton
		3. London
		4. Sudbury
—	7–9	Interview number (3 digits on upper left-hand corner of questionnaire)
A	Not entered	Family, work for
		1. Travel agency
		2. Advertising agency
		3. Marketing research company
B	Not entered	Interviewed past month
		1. Yes
		2. No
1.	10	Travelled in past 3 months
		1. Yes
		2. No
2.	11	Purpose last trip
		1. Business
		2. Vacation
		3. Personal
	12	Purpose second last trip
		1. Business
		2. Vacation
		3. Personal
	13	Purpose other trips
		1. Business
		2. Vacation
		3. Personal

data entry
The activity of transferring data from a research project to computers.

optical scanning system
A data processing input device that reads material directly from mark sensed questionnaires.

Computerized Data Processing

Today, most of the data processing is completed using computers. The process of transferring data from a research project, such as answers to a survey questionnaire, to computers is referred to as **data entry.** In studies involving highly structured paper questionnaires, an **optical scanning system** may be used to read material directly into

Advanced scanner technology may be used for data entry. With modern scanning devices, store audits can be conducted more quickly and accurately than they were in the past, when data were recorded by hand.

the computer's memory from *mark sensed questionnaires.* This type of system requires that the computer can read the answers from a special sheet of paper devised for optical scanning.

With computer-assisted telephone interviewing or self-administered Internet questionnaires, responses can be automatically stored and tabulated as they are collected. Direct data capture substantially reduces clerical errors that occur during the editing and coding process. However, respondents may still make errors, and steps need to be taken to prevent such errors. For example, a respondent might click the Submit button at the end of a questionnaire two or more times until there is a response. The data capture software must be written so that respondents are prevented from submitting two or more identical questionnaires.

When data are not optically scanned or directly entered into the computer the moment they are collected, the data will be manually entered. Data entry workers, like anyone else, may make errors. To increase accuracy, the job is *verified* by a second data entry worker, who checks the accuracy of the data entered and corrects any errors. This process of verifying the data is never performed by the same person who entered the original data.

Recoding

recode
To use a computer to convert original codes used for raw data into codes that are more suitable for analysis.

In a number of situations it is easier to enter the raw data into the computer using the pre-coding on the questionnaire and then program the computer to **recode** certain raw data. This often occurs when a researcher measures attitudes with a series of both positive and negative statements. Reversing the order of the codes for the negative statements so that the statements' codes reflect the same order of magnitude as the positive statements' codes requires only a simple data transformation. For instance, if a seven-point scale for variable 1 (VAR1) is to be recoded, the following programming statement might be used to subtract the original code score from 8:

$$VAR1 = 8 - VAR1$$

Collapsing the number of categories or values of a variable or creating new variables also requires recoding. These topics, which are interrelated with data analysis, are discussed in Chapter 17.

Error Checking

The final stage in the coding process is error checking and verification, or *data cleaning,* to ensure that all codes are legitimate. For example, computer software can examine the entered data and identify coded values that lie outside the range of acceptable answers. For example, if "sex" is coded 1 for "male" and 2 for "female" and a 3 code is found, a mistake obviously has occurred and an adjustment must be made.

SUMMARY

The activities involved in collecting data in the field may be performed by the organization that needs the information, by research suppliers, or by third-party field service organizations. Proper execution of fieldwork is essential to produce research results without substantial error. New fieldworkers must be trained in opening the interview, asking the questions, probing for additional information, recording the responses, and terminating the interview. Experienced fieldworkers are briefed for each new project to familiarize them with its specific requirements. A particular concern of the briefing session is reminding fieldworkers to adhere closely to the prescribed sampling procedures.

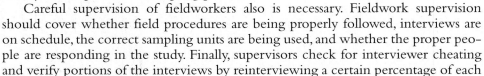

Careful supervision of fieldworkers also is necessary. Fieldwork supervision should cover whether field procedures are being properly followed, interviews are on schedule, the correct sampling units are being used, and whether the proper people are responding in the study. Finally, supervisors check for interviewer cheating and verify portions of the interviews by reinterviewing a certain percentage of each fieldworker's respondents.

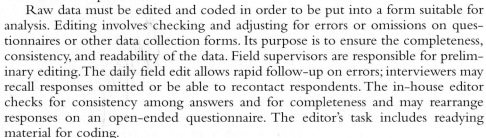

Raw data must be edited and coded in order to be put into a form suitable for analysis. Editing involves checking and adjusting for errors or omissions on questionnaires or other data collection forms. Its purpose is to ensure the completeness, consistency, and readability of the data. Field supervisors are responsible for preliminary editing. The daily field edit allows rapid follow-up on errors; interviewers may recall responses omitted or be able to recontact respondents. The in-house editor checks for consistency among answers and for completeness and may rearrange responses on an open-ended questionnaire. The editor's task includes readying material for coding.

Coding is the process of identifying and classifying each answer with a numerical score or other character symbol. It usually involves entering the data for computer storage. The coding categories should be exhaustive and provide for all possible responses. They should also be mutually exclusive and independent so that there is no overlap among categories. On highly structured questionnaires, the categories may be pre-coded. With open-ended questions, answers are post-coded. This means that the categories are assigned after the data have been collected, based on the researcher's judgment. It is better to assign too many categories than too few, and it is easier to collapse several categories into one than to increase the number of categories. A code book identifies each variable and the codes for responses.

Key Terms and Concepts

fieldworker	coding	direct data entry
field interviewing service	field editing	code book
briefing session	in-house editing	data entry
probing	item nonresponse	optical scanning system
interviewer cheating	plug value	recode
verification	codes	
editing	data matrix	

Questions for Review and Critical Thinking

1. What impact have changes in women's lifestyles had on fieldwork in the last 25 years?
2. What is the proper method for asking questions? What should the interviewer do if a question is misunderstood? If a respondent answers a question before encountering it in the questionnaire?
3. When should interviewers probe? Give some examples of how probing should be done.
4. How should respondents' answers to open-ended questions be recorded?
5. Why is it important to ensure that fieldworkers adhere to the sampling procedure specified for a project?
6. Contacting every individual in Canada is a major problem for Statistics Canada. List some other potential fieldwork problems that might arise in conducting the Census of Canada. What might be done to mitigate these problems?
7. A fieldworker asks respondents whether they will answer a few questions. However, the interviewer also observes the respondent's race and approximate age. Is this ethical?
8. Suppose respondents in a political survey were asked if they favoured or opposed the Canada Agricultural Trade Products Act. Edit the following open-ended answers:
   a. I don't know what it is, so I'll oppose it.
   b. Favourable, though I don't really know what it is.
   c. You caught me on that. I don't know, but from the sound of it I favour it.
9. What are the potential meanings of "don't know" responses in a political poll to evaluate two candidates for mayor?
10. Comment on the coding scheme for the following question: "In which of these groups did your total *family* income, from all sources, fall last year—2006—before taxes? Just tell me the code number." (Refer to the table.)

Response	Code
Under $9,999	01
$10,000 to $14,999	02
$15,000 to $24,999	03
$25,000 to $39,999	04
$40,000 to $54,999	05
$55,000 to $69,999	06
$70,000 to $89,999	07
$90,000 to $99,999	08
$100,000 to $124,999	09
$125,000 or over	10
Refused to answer	11
Don't know	98
No answer	99

11. Suppose information has been gathered about the occupations of several respondents. How would you classify the following respondents' answers in the occupational coding scheme discussed in this chapter: plumber, butcher, retail sales, X-ray technician, and veterinarian?
12. A researcher asks you to help build a coding scheme for types (not brands) of coffee found in supermarkets. These might be regular, instant, or decaffeinated. About how many codes might be needed?
13. A researcher asks, "What do you remember about advertising for Gillette Mach 3 razors?" How should the code book for this question be structured? What problems does it present?
14. Design a short questionnaire with fewer than five fixed-alternative questions to measure student satisfaction with your university bookstore. Interview five classmates, then arrange the database into a data matrix.
15. A researcher investigated attitudes toward her company and noticed that one individual answered all image questions at one end of a bipolar scale. Should she decline to use this questionnaire in the data analysis?

Exploring the Internet

1. Go to www.quirks.com and click on Directories. You will find a Directory of Telephone Interviewing Facilities and a Directory of Mall Interviewing Facilities. What other fieldwork organizations are shown?
2. The Web page of Consumer Contact (www.consumercontact.com/en/Frames.html) describes its coding of survey research data. Go to "Services" then "Data Processing" and review its data processing services.
3. The University of Michigan's Institute for Social Research (www.isr.umich.edu/index.html) houses the Survey Research Center. Go to the Center's Index of Projects and click on Surveys of Consumers. You can review the questionnaire and how the questionnaire is coded.
4. Search the Internet to learn what companies offer optical scanning systems and services.

A mail questionnaire that included a concept statement describing Nilla Wafer Sandwich Cookies, a proposed new product, was sent to members of a consumer panel. Exhibit 16.1.1 presents an excerpt from a questionnaire that a respondent filled out.

Questions

1. Does this questionnaire need editing? Explain why or why not.
2. Code each of the questions in Exhibit 16.1.1.

CASE EXHIBIT 16.1.1	RESPONDENT QUESTIONNAIRE (COMPLETED)

4a. Now that you have read the description for Nilla Wafer Sandwich Cookies, which statement best describes how likely you would be to buy Nilla Wafer Sandwich Cookies if it were being sold in the stores where you normally shop? ("X" ONE BOX)

Definitely would buy ☐
Probably would buy ☐
Might or might not buy ☐
Probably would not buy ☐
Definitely would not buy ☒

4b. Why do you feel that way about buying this product? (PLEASE BE AS SPECIFIC AS POSSIBLE)

I don't normally buy cookies—I bake them myself. I feel Nilla Wafers are
pretty bland and have only used them in recipes that require them.

5. Now, thinking of each different variety of Nilla Wafer Sandwich Cookies, please indicate how likely you would be to buy each variety if it were available in the stores where you normally shop? ("X" ONE BOX FOR EACH VARIETY)

	Definitely Would Buy	Probably Would Buy	Might or Might Not Buy	Probably Would Not Buy	Definitely Would Not Buy
Vanilla Cream	☒	☐	☐	☐	☐
Chocolate Fudge	☒	☐	☐	☐	☐
Peanut Butter	☒	☐	☐	☐	☐
Strawberry Jam	☒	☐	☐	☐	☐

6. Compared to other products now on the market, would you expect this new product to be . . . ? ("X" ONE BOX)

Very different . . . . ☐   Somewhat different . . . . ☒   Not at all different . . . . ☐

7. Overall, how believable is the description of this product? ("X" ONE BOX)

Very believable . . . . ☒   Somewhat believable . . . . ☐   Not at all believable . . . . ☐

8. Considering the price of this product, do you think this product would be . . . ? ("X" ONE BOX)

A very good value for the money ☐
A somewhat good value for the money ☐
An average value for the money ☐
A somewhat poor value for the money ☐
A very poor value for the money ☒

9. Considering the price of this product, do you think the price is . . . ? ("X" ONE BOX)

Very expensive ☐
Somewhat expensive ☒
About average ☐
Somewhat inexpensive ☐
Very inexpensive ☐

10. How often would you purchase this product? ("X" ONE BOX)

More than once a week	☐	Once a month	☐
Once a week	☐	Once every 2–3 months	☐
3 times a month	☐	Less than once every 3 months	☐
2 times a month	☐	Would not purchase	☒

Research in Practice: Principles of Good Interviewing

As an example from the field, the table below presents the principles of good interviewing followed by Yankelovich Partners, one of the top marketing research organizations.[11] These principles apply no matter what the nature of the specific assignment; they are universal and represent the essence of sound data collection for marketing research purposes. For clarity, they have been divided into two categories: (1) *the basics*—the interviewing point of view and (2) *required practices*—standard inquiry premises and procedures.

THE BASICS

1. *Have integrity and be honest.*

   This is the cornerstone of all professional inquiry, regardless of its purpose.

2. *Have patience and tact.*

   Interviewers ask for information from people they do not know. Thus all the rules of human relations that apply to inquiry situations—patience, tact, and courtesy—apply "in spades" to interviewing. Standard business conventions that control communications and contact are to be observed at all times.

3. *Pay attention to accuracy and detail.*

   To avoid inaccuracy and superficiality, do not record a response unless you fully understand it yourself. Probe for clarification and rich, full answers. Record responses verbatim: Never assume you know what a respondent is thinking or jump to conclusions as to what he or she might have said but did not.

4. *Exhibit a real interest in the inquiry at hand, but keep your own opinions to yourself.*

   Impartiality is imperative—if your opinions were wanted, you would be asked, not your respondent. You are an asker and a recorder of other people's opinions, not a contributor to the study data.

5. *Be a good listener.*

   Too many interviewers talk too much, wasting time when respondents could be supplying more pertinent facts or opinions on the study topic.

6. *Keep the inquiry and respondents' responses confidential.*

   Do not discuss the studies you are doing with relatives, friends, or associates; it is unacceptable to both the research agency and its clients. Above all, never quote one respondent's opinion to another—that is the greatest violation of privacy of all.

7. *Respect others' rights.*

   Marketing research depends on the goodwill of others to provide information. There is a happy medium path to pursue in obtaining this information. On the one hand is failure to get it all; on the other is unnecessary coercion. The middle road is one of clear explanation, friendliness, and courtesy, offered in an interested and persuasive way. Impress upon prospective respondents that their cooperation is important and valuable.

REQUIRED PRACTICES

1. Complete the number of interviews according to the sampling plan assigned to you.

   Both are calculated with the utmost precision so that when assignments are returned, the study will benefit from having available the amount and type of information originally specified.

2. Follow the directions provided.

Remember that there are many other interviewers working on the same study in other places. Lack of uniformity in procedure can only spell disaster for later analysis. Each direction has a purpose, even though it may not be completely evident to you.

3. Make every effort to keep schedules.

Schedules range from "hurry up" to "there should be plenty of time," but there is always a good reason, and you should be as responsive as possible. If you foresee problems, call and explain.

4. Keep control of each interview you do.

a. There is an established average length of an interview from the time you start to talk to the respondent to the time you finish. It represents a guideline, but some interviews will be shorter and some longer.

b. Always get the whole story from the respondent and write it all down in the respondent's own words. Also, remember to keep the interview focused on the subject at hand and not let it wander off into unnecessary small talk.

c. Avoid offending the respondent by being too talkative yourself.

5. Complete the questionnaires meticulously.

a. Follow exactly all instructions that appear directly on the questionnaire. Learn what these instructions direct you to do in advance.

b. Ask the questions in the order indicated in the directions. Much thought and effort go into determining the order of the questioning to avoid bias or to set the stage for subsequent questions.

c. Ask each question exactly as it is written. To ensure uniformity, do not rephrase a question.

d. Never leave a question blank. It will be difficult to tell whether you failed to ask it, whether the respondent could not answer it because of lack of knowledge or certainty, or whether the respondent refused to answer it for personal reasons. If none of the answer categories provided prove suitable, write in what the respondent said, in his or her own words.

e. Use all the props provided to aid both interviewers and respondents: show cards, pictures, descriptions, sheets of questions for the respondents to answer themselves, and so on. Keys to when and how to use them appear on the questionnaire at the point at which they are to be used.

6. Check over each questionnaire you have completed.

This is best done directly after it has been completed. If you find something you did wrong or omitted, correct it. Often you can call a respondent back, admit you missed something (or are unclear about a particular response), and then straighten out the difficulty.

7. Compare your sample execution and assigned quota with the total number of questionnaires you have completed.

Do not consider your assignment finished until you have done this.

8. Clear up any questions with the research agency.

If questions arise either at the start or during an assignment for which you can find no explanatory instructions, call the agency to get the matter clarified.

SPSS Instructions for Chapter 16

To follow these instructions, you will need to install SPSS 14.0 Student version included with your book and the data file available from the Web site. Before starting to analyze your own data, you may need to do one or more of the following procedures. This section explains preparation of the data file in a stepwise manner.

A. VIEWING THE DATA FILE: Data can be entered in Excel or other programs and opened in SPSS or directly entered in SPSS. For these instructions we will use an SPSS data file. Download the data file labelled "luxury.sav" from the following Web site: www.effectivemarketingresearch.nelson.com

Open the luxury data file in SPSS. The data is displayed in the DATA EDITOR either in data view or variable view. Most of the labelling and formatting changes can easily be made with the variable view.

DATA EDITOR: Data View

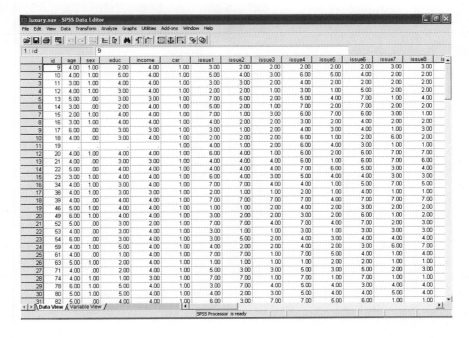

DATA EDITOR: Variable View

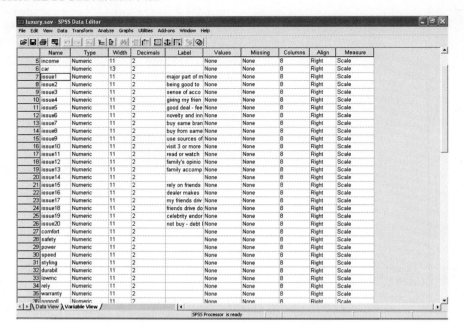

B. LABELLING A VARIABLE: For ease of reference in your analysis, it is best to label your variable and variable levels. Use the luxury.sav file for the following steps.

Step 1: If you are in *data view*, double clicking on the column of the variable you want to label will take you to *variable view*. In *variable view*, click on the cell under the "Label" column for your variable. Enter the variable name in this cell (e.g., Educ to be labelled "education").

LABELLING A VARIABLE

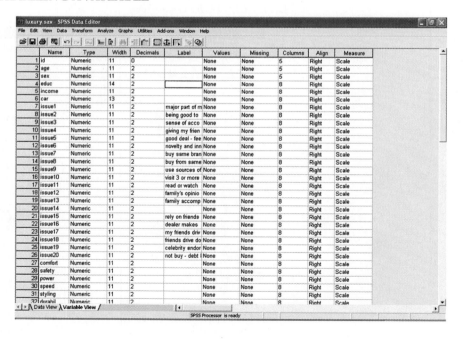

Step 2: Click on the cell under the "Values" column for your variable. A new window will appear. In this new window, enter the value of the variable in the "value" box and the label in the "value label" box. For example, "education" may have values of 1 to 5 and 1="less than high school," 2="high school grad," 3="some college," 4="college grad," 5="graduate degree." In this case, enter "1" in the value box and "less than high school" in the value label box. Make sure that you hit "add" button. Repeat for the rest of the "education" levels, 2 through 5.

ENTERING VALUE LABELS

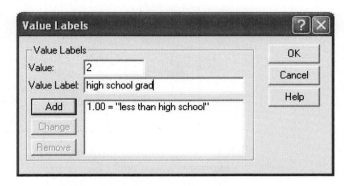

Step 3: Click on "OK" when you have labelled all the values of the variable.

Step 4: Click on the "DATA VIEW" at the bottom of the screen to return to your data display.

C. RECODING A VARIABLE

Step 1: Select the following menus/items: Transform > Recode > Into different variables.

Step 2: Once you get to the dialogue box, highlight the variable you want to recode and click on the arrow (▶). Then on the right enter the new name of the variable and click "change."

RECODE WINDOW

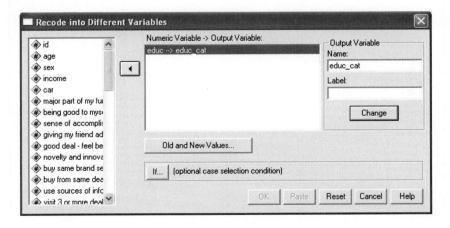

Step 3: Click on "old and new values." In the dialogue box that opens up, you can enter the old and new values in several ways. The simplest way is to specify one value at a time: enter the old value on the left, enter the new value on the right, and click "add." Do this for each value that you want recoded. The large box on the right shows the changes that you make.

RECODING INTO DIFFERENT VARIABLES

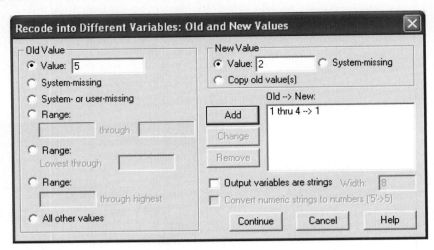

Alternatively, you could specify a range of old values (e.g., for education, 1 through 4) and then enter the new value corresponding to that range (e.g., 1). When you click "add," you will see "1 through 4—>1" appear in the box on the right.

Step 4: Finally, click "continue" and "OK." This will create a new variable (with the name you entered in step 2). Go to the data view and check the new variable you have created.

When Neopets.com, one of the most popular youth Web sites, asked kids which medium they would choose if they could have only one, 69 percent chose the Internet, while only 19 percent chose TV. Yet YTV research shows that 40 percent of Canadian tweens watch TV while surfing the net. YTV's studies further indicate that children between the ages of 9 and 10 spend nearly three hours per week on the Internet, while children aged 11 to 12 spend five hours, and tweens 13 to 14 spend eight hours. Nevertheless, TV hours still outnumber time spent on the Web. According to Nielsen Media Research, in 2003 and 2004, children aged 2 to 11 watched 17.3 hours of TV per week and youths aged 12 to 17 watched 16.8 hours.

Research also reveals that youths love to interact with others online. A 2005 Media Awareness Network study found 60 percent of Canadian tweens use instant messaging on a regular basis, while 40 percent choose instant messaging as their favourite online activity. MSN Canada is the leader in that market, being chosen by 95 percent of Canadian instant messaging users. These interesting findings illustrate the results of a typical descriptive analysis. This chapter explains how to perform descriptive analysis and basic hypothesis testing.[1] ∎

What you will learn in this chapter

1 To understand that analysis consists of summarizing, rearranging, ordering, or manipulating data.

2 To compute and explain the purposes of simple tabulations and cross-tabulations.

3 To use cross-tabulation procedures to discuss the relationship between two variables.

4 To discuss the nature of data transformations.

5 To explain how to summarize rank-order data.

6 To describe some computer software designed for descriptive analysis.

7 To define *hypothesis, null hypothesis, alternative hypothesis,* and *significance level.*

8 To discuss the steps in the hypothesis-testing procedure.

9 To describe the factors that influence the choice of statistical method to use for analysis.

THE NATURE OF DESCRIPTIVE ANALYSIS

In the context of marketing research, the term *analysis* is difficult to define because it refers to a variety of activities and processes. One form of analysis consists of summarizing large quantities of raw data so that the results can be interpreted. Categorizing, or separating out the components or relevant parts of the whole data set, is also a form of analysis for comprehending patterns in the data. Rearranging, ordering, or manipulating data may provide descriptive information that will answer questions posed in the problem definition. All forms of analysis attempt to portray data so that the results may be studied and interpreted in concise and meaningful ways.

descriptive analysis
The transformation of raw data into a form that will make them easy to understand and interpret; rearranging, ordering, and manipulating data to generate descriptive information.

Descriptive analysis refers to the transformation of raw data into a form that will make them easy to understand and interpret. Describing responses or observations typically is the first stage of analysis. Averages, frequency distributions, and percentage distributions are the most common ways to summarize data.

As the analysis progresses beyond the descriptive stage, researchers generally apply the tools of inferential statistics. Univariate analysis allows researchers to assess the statistical significance of various hypotheses about a single variable.

TABULATION

Tabulation refers to the orderly arrangement of data in a table or other summary format. Counting the numbers of different responses to a question and arranging them in a frequency distribution is a simple tabulation, or *marginal tabulation*. Simple tabulation of the responses or observations on a question-by-question or item-by-item basis provides the most basic—and in many cases the most useful—form of information for the researcher. It tells the researcher how frequently each response occurs. This starting point for analysis is to count responses or observations for each category or code assigned to a variable. Table 17.1 illustrates a **frequency table.** When this tabulation process is done by hand, it is called *tallying.* Today, this is rarely done and researchers use spreadsheet or statistical analysis software to complete tabluations.

frequency table
The arrangement of statistical data in a row-and-column format that exhibits the count of responses or observations for each category assigned to a variable.

Percentages

Whether data are tabulated by computer or by hand, percentages, cumulative percentages, and frequency distributions are useful. For example, consider Table 17.2. Most people find part B easier to interpret than part A because the percentages in part B are useful for comparing data for various time periods.

When a frequency distribution portrays only a single characteristic as a percentage of the total, the proportion of occurrence is defined. It may be expressed as a percentage, a fraction, or a decimal value.

When discussing percentages, researchers must be precise in their language. For example, the difference between 40 percent and 60 percent is not 20 percent, but 20 *percentage points,* or an increase of 50 percent.

TABLE 17.1	A FREQUENCY TABLE FOR A SIMPLE TABULATION

Do you shop at IGA?

Response	Frequency
Yes	330
No	120
Total	450

| TABLE 17.2 | AN ILLUSTRATION OF HOW PERCENTAGES AID IN THE INTERPRETATION OF FREQUENCY DISTRIBUTIONS AND CROSS-TABULATIONS[2] |

A: POPULATION BY YEAR AND SELECTED PROVINCES (IN THOUSANDS)

	2001	2005	Change
Alberta	3,056.7	3,256.8	200.1
British Columbia	4,078.4	4,254.5	176.1
New Brunswick	749.9	752.0	2.1
Ontario	11,897.6	12,541.4	643.8
Quebec	7,397.0	7,598.1	201.1

B: POPULATION BY YEAR AND SELECTED PROVINCES (IN THOUSANDS)

	2001	Percent of Population	2005	Percent of Population	Change	Percent Change
Alberta	3,056.7	9.85	3,256.8	10.1	200.1	+6.5
British Columbia	4,078.4	13.1	4,254.5	13.2	176.1	+4.3
New Brunswick	749.9	2.4	752.0	2.3	2.1	+0.3
Ontario	11,897.6	38.4	12,541.4	38.9	643.8	+5.4
Quebec	7,397.0	23.8	7,598.1	23.5	201.1	+2.7

Measures of Central Tendency

According to *Bride* magazine, $18,874 (US) is the average amount brides plan to spend on their weddings.[3] This is a measure of central tendency. Describing central tendencies of the distribution with the mean, median, or mode is another basic form of descriptive analysis. These measures are most useful when the purpose is to identify typical values of a variable or the most common characteristic of a group. If knowing the average or typical performance will satisfy the information need, the mean, median, or mode should be considered.

CROSS-TABULATION

cross-tabulation

Organizing data by groups, categories, or classes to facilitate comparisons; a joint frequency distribution of observations on two or more sets of variables.

Mere tabulation of data may answer many research questions; in fact, many studies do not go beyond examining simple tabulations of question-by-question responses to a survey. Although frequency counts, percentage distributions, and averages summarize considerable information, simple tabulation may not yield the full value of the research. Most data can be further organized in a variety of ways. For example, data from a survey that samples both men and women commonly are separated into groups or categories based on gender. Analyzing results by groups, categories, or classes is the technique of **cross-tabulation.** The purpose of categorization and cross-tabulation is to allow the inspection and comparison of differences among groups. This form of analysis also helps determine the type of relationship among variables. Since market segmentation is a major component of marketing strategy for many organizations, cross-tabulating the results of marketing research helps clarify the research findings as they pertain to market segments.

Two-Way (Contingency) Tables

two-way (contingency) table

The results of a cross-tabulation of two variables, such as answers to two survey questions.

Part A of Table 17.3 shows how the cross-tabulation of answers to two survey questions (or two variables) results in a **two-way (contingency) table.** The frequency counts for the question "Do you shop at IGA?" are presented as column totals. The total numbers of men and women in the sample are presented as row totals. These row and column totals often are called *marginals* because they appear in the table's margins.

TABLE 17.3 | POSSIBLE CROSS-TABULATIONS OF ONE QUESTION

(A) CROSS-TABULATION OF QUESTION "DO YOU SHOP AT IGA?" BY GENDER OF RESPONDENT

	Yes	No	Total
Men	150	75	225
Women	180	45	225
Total	330	120	450

(B) PERCENTAGE CROSS-TABULATION OF QUESTION "DO YOU SHOP AT IGA?" BY GENDER OF RESPONDENT, ROW PERCENTAGE

	Yes	No	Total (Base)
Men	66.7%	33.3%	100% (225)
Women	80.0%	20.0%	100% (225)

(C) PERCENTAGE CROSS-TABULATION OF QUESTION "DO YOU SHOP AT IGA?" BY GENDER OF RESPONDENT, COLUMN PERCENTAGE

	Yes	No
Men	45.5%	62.5%
Women	54.5%	37.5%
Total (Base)	100% (330)	100% (120)

Each of the four cells within part A represents a specific combination of the two variables. The cell that represents women who said they do not shop at IGA has a frequency count of 45.

The two-way table in part A is referred to as a *2 × 2 table* because it has two rows and two columns. Any cross-tabulation table may be classified according to the number of rows by the number of columns (*R* by *C*). Thus a 3 × 4 table has three rows and four columns.

Percentage Cross-Tabulations

When data from a survey are cross-tabulated, percentages help the researcher understand the nature of the relationship by allowing relative comparisons. The total number of respondents or observations may be used as a **base** for computing the percentage in each cell. When the objective of the research is to identify a relationship between answers to two questions (or two variables), one of the questions is commonly chosen to be the source of the base for determining percentages. For example, look at the data in parts A, B, and C of Table 17.3. Compare part B with part C. Selecting either the row percentages or the column percentages will emphasize a particular comparison or distribution. The nature of the problem the researcher wishes to answer will determine which marginal total will serve as a base for computing percentages.

Fortunately, a conventional rule determines the direction of percentages if the researcher has identified which variable is the independent variable and which is the dependent variable: The percentages should be computed *in the direction of the independent variable*. That is, the marginal total of the independent variable should be used as the base for computing the percentages. Although survey research does not

base
The number of respondents or observations (in a row or column) used as a basis for computing percentages.

TABLE 17.4	CROSS-TABULATION OF MARITAL STATUS, GENDER, AND RESPONSES TO THE QUESTION "DO YOU SHOP AT IGA?"			
	MARRIED		SINGLE	
	Men	**Women**	**Men**	**Women**
"Do you shop at IGA?"				
Yes	55%	80%	86%	80%
No	45%	20%	14%	20%

elaboration analysis
An analysis of the basic cross-tabulation for each level of a variable not previously considered, such as subgroups of the sample.

moderator variable
A third variable that, when introduced into an analysis, alters or has a contingent effect on the relationship between an independent variable and a dependent variable.

spurious relationship
An apparent relationship between two variables that is not authentic.

identify cause-and-effect relationships, one might argue that it would be logical to assume that a variable such as gender might predict shopping behaviour, in which case independent and dependent variables may be established so as to present the most useful information.

Elaboration and Refinement

The *Oxford Universal Dictionary* defines *analysis* as "the resolution of anything complex into its simplest elements." This suggests that once the researcher has examined the basic relationship between two variables, he or she may wish to investigate this relationship under a variety of different conditions. Typically a third variable is introduced into the analysis to elaborate and refine the researcher's understanding by specifying the conditions under which the relationship between the first two variables is strongest and weakest. In other words, a more elaborate analysis asks: "Will interpretation of the relationship be modified if other variables are simultaneously considered?"

Performing the basic cross-tabulation within various subgroups of the sample is a common form of **elaboration analysis.** The researcher breaks down the analysis for each level of another variable. For example, if the researcher has cross-tabulated shopping behaviour by gender (see Table 17.3) and wishes to investigate another variable (say, marital status) that may modify the original relationship, a more elaborate analysis may be conducted. Table 17.4 breaks down the responses to the question "Do you shop at IGA?" by gender and marital status. The data show that marital status does not change the original cross-tabulation relationship among women, but it does change that relationship among men. The analysis suggests that the original conclusion about the relationship between gender and shopping behaviour for women be retained; the data confirm the original interpretation. However, the refinements in analysis have pointed out a relationship among men that was not immediately discernible in the two-variable case: a higher percentage of single men than married men shop at IGA. The researcher can then conclude that marital status modifies the original relationship among men—that is, that there is an interaction effect.

In this situation marital status is a **moderator variable.** A moderator variable is a third variable that, when introduced into the analysis, alters or has a contingent effect on the relationship between an independent variable and a dependent variable.

In other situations the addition of a third variable to the analysis may lead us to reject the original conclusion about the relationship. When this occurs, the elaboration analysis will have indicated a **spurious relationship**—an apparent relationship between the original two variables that is not authentic. The example of a high correlation between high ice cream cone sales and drownings at the beach illustrates a spurious relationship.

How Many Cross-Tabulations?

Surveys may ask dozens of questions. Computer-assisted marketing researchers often indulge in "fishing expeditions," cross-tabulating every question on a survey with every other question. Thus every possible response becomes a possible explanatory variable.

All too often this activity provides reams of extra computer output, but no additional insight to management. The number of cross-tabulations should be determined early, when research objectives are stated.

DATA TRANSFORMATION

data transformation (data conversion)
The process of changing the original form of data to a format suitable to achieve the research objective.

Data transformation (also called **data conversion**) is the process of changing the data from their original form to a format suitable for performing a data analysis that will achieve research objectives. Researchers often modify the values of scalar data or create new variables. For example, many researchers believe that less response bias will result if interviewers ask respondents for their year of birth rather than their age, even though the objective of the data analysis is to investigate respondents' ages in years. This presents no problem for the research analyst, because a simple data transformation is possible. The raw data coded as birth year can easily be transformed to age by subtracting the birth year from the current year.

Collapsing or combining adjacent categories of a variable is a common form of data transformation used to reduce the number of categories. For example, Likert summated scales reflect combinations of scores (raw data) from the various attitude statements. The summative score for an attitude scale with three statements is calculated as follows:

$$\text{Summative score} = \text{Variable } 1 + \text{Variable } 2 + \text{Variable } 3$$

This calculation can be accomplished by simple arithmetic or by programming a computer with a data transformation equation that creates a new variable for the summative score.

CALCULATING RANK ORDER

Respondents often rank order brand preferences or other variables of interest to researchers. To summarize these data for all respondents, the analyst performs a data transformation by multiplying the frequency by the rank (score) to develop a new scale that represents the summarized rank orders.

For example, suppose a manager of a frequent-flier program had ten executives rank their preferences for "dream destinations" that would be prizes in a sales promotion contest. Table 17.5 shows how the executives ranked each of four locations: Hawaii, Paris, Greece, and Hong Kong. Table 17.6 tabulates the frequencies of these rankings. To calculate a summary rank ordering, the destination with the first (highest) preference was given the lowest number (1) and the least preferred destination

TABLE 17.5	INDIVIDUAL RANKINGS OF DREAM DESTINATIONS			
Executive	**Hawaii**	**Paris**	**Greece**	**Hong Kong**
1	1	2	4	3
2	1	3	4	2
3	2	1	3	4
4	2	4	3	1
5	2	1	3	4
6	3	4	1	2
7	2	3	1	4
8	1	4	2	3
9	4	3	2	1
10	2	1	3	4

TABLE 17.6	FREQUENCY TABLE OF DREAM DESTINATION RANKINGS			
	PREFERENCE RANKINGS			
Destination	**1st**	**2nd**	**3rd**	**4th**
Hawaii	3	5	1	1
Paris	3	1	3	3
Greece	2	2	4	2
Hong Kong	2	2	2	4

was assigned the highest number (4). The summarized rank orderings were obtained with the following calculations:

$$\text{Hawaii: } (3 \times 1) + (5 \times 2) + (1 \times 3) + (1 \times 4) = 20$$
$$\text{Paris: } (3 \times 1) + (1 \times 2) + (3 \times 3) + (3 \times 4) = 26$$
$$\text{Greece: } (2 \times 1) + (2 \times 2) + (4 \times 3) + (2 \times 4) = 26$$
$$\text{Hong Kong: } (2 \times 1) + (2 \times 2) + (2 \times 3) + (4 \times 4) = 28$$

The lowest total score indicates the first (highest) preference ranking. The results show the following rank ordering: (1) Hawaii, (2) Paris, (3) Greece, and (4) Hong Kong.

TABULAR AND GRAPHIC METHODS OF DISPLAYING DATA

The person who first said, "A picture is worth a thousand words" probably had graphic aids in mind. Used properly, graphic aids can clarify complex points or emphasize a message. Used improperly or sloppily, however, they can distract or even mislead. The key to effective use of graphic aids is to make them an integral part of the text. The graphics should always be interpreted in the text. This does not mean the writer should exhaustively explain an obvious chart or table, but it does mean that the text should point out the key elements of any graphic aid and relate them to the discussion in progress.

Tabular and graphic representations of the data may take a number of forms, ranging from a computer printout to an elaborate pictograph.

Tables

Tables are most useful for presenting numerical information, especially when several pieces of information have been gathered about each item discussed. The purpose of each table, however, is to facilitate the summarization and communication of the data's meaning. For example, Table 17.7 illustrates the relationships among education, income, and regional airline usage expenditures for vacation or pleasure trips. The shaded area emphasizes a key conclusion about market share. (To summarize the information in the shaded box: 32 percent of the population makes 78 percent of the expenditures.) This form of presentation simplifies interpretation.

Suppose an airline asks a question about customers' satisfaction with its baggage-handling service. In addition to showing the simple frequency for each category, most research analysts would cross-tabulate answers to the baggage-handling questions with several demographic variables such as gender, income, education, and age. Presenting multiple cross-tabulations individually in a separate table requires considerable space. Thus many research reports use a space-saving format with either *stubheads* for rows or *bannerheads* for columns, to allow the reader to view several cross-tabulations at the same time. Table 17.8 shows how several cross-tabulations can be presented in a single table by using stubheads.

TABLE 17.7

REGIONAL AIRLINE USAGE FOR VACATION/ PLEASURE BY INCOME AND EDUCATION CLASS

	Total	Under $20,000	$20,000– $39,000	$40,000– $59,000	$60,000 and Over
All consumers					
Expenditures (%)	100	10	7	16	67
Consumer units (%)	100	42	19	16	23
Index	100	26	36	100	291
Non–high school graduate					
Expenditures (%)	8	1	2	1	4
Consumer units (%)	35	21	6	4	4
Index	21	5	33	25	100
High school graduate					
Expenditures (%)	29	4	2	8	15
Consumer units (%)	30	11	6	6	7
Index	96	36	33	133	214
Attended/graduated college					
Expenditures (%)	63	5	3	7	48
Consumer units (%)	35	10	6	6	13
Index	180	50	50	116	369
				Percentage population = 32	Percentage expenditures =78

TABLE 17.8

A STUBHEAD FORMAT ALLOWING SEVERAL CROSS-TABULATIONS TO BE INCLUDED IN A SINGLE TABLE[4]

Confidence in Organized Religion

Question: I am going to read you a list of institutions in North American society. Would you tell me how much confidence you, yourself, have in each one—a great deal, quite a lot, some, or very little?

Organized Religion

	Great Deal	Quite a Lot	Some	Very Little	None	No Opinion	Number of Interviews
National	42%	24%	21%	11%	1%	1%	1,528
Gender							
Men	36	27	22	13	1	1	755
Women	48	21	20	9	1	1	773
Age							
Total under 30	39	26	24	10	1	*	320
18–24 years	38	28	24	9	1	*	138
25–29 years	40	23	23	13	1	*	182
30–49 years	38	25	23	12	1	1	593
Total 50 & older	50	21	18	10	*	1	608
50–64 years	48	23	18	10	*	1	302
65 and older	52	18	18	10	1	1	306

*Less than 1 percent.

EXHIBIT 17.1 | THE BASIC FORMS OF GRAPHIC PRESENTATION

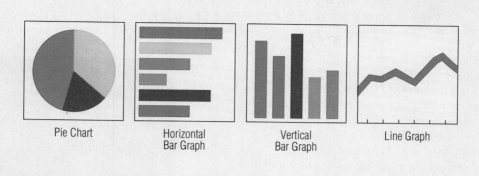

Pie Chart   Horizontal Bar Graph   Vertical Bar Graph   Line Graph

Charts and Graphs

Charts translate numerical information into visual form so that relationships may be easily grasped. Although a number of standardized forms exist for presenting data in charts or graphs, the researcher may use his or her creativity to increase the effectiveness of a particular presentation. Bar charts, pie charts, line charts, and other graphic forms of presentation create strong visual impressions. Exhibit 17.1 shows simple versions of a pie chart, horizontal bar graph, vertical bar graph, and line graph.

Pie Charts

One of the most useful kinds of charts is the *pie chart,* which shows the composition of some total quantity at a particular time. Each angle, or "slice," is proportional to its percentage of the whole and should be labelled with its description and percentage. The writer should not try to include too many small slices; about six slices is a typical maximum. Companies commonly use pie charts to show how revenues were used or the composition of their sales.

Line Graphs

Line graphs are useful for showing the relationship of one variable to another. The dependent variable generally is shown on the vertical axis and the independent variable on the horizontal axis. The most common independent variable for such charts is time, but it is by no means the only one. The line for each dependent variable should be in a different colour or pattern and should be clearly labelled. The researcher should not try to squeeze in too many variables; this can quickly lead to confusion rather than clarification.

Bar Charts

Bar charts show changes in the value of a dependent variable (plotted on the vertical axis) at discrete intervals of the independent variable (on the horizontal axis). A simple bar chart often presents the frequency of response to various questions. A multiple bar chart shows how multiple variables are related to the primary variable. In each case, each bar needs to be clearly identified with a different colour or pattern. The researcher should not use too many divisions or dependent variables. Too much detail obscures the essential advantage of charts, which is to make relationships easy to grasp.

FLORENCE NIGHTINGALE: INVENTOR OF THE PIE CHART

Florence Nightingale is remembered as a pioneering nurse and hospital reformer.[5] Less well known is her equally pioneering use of statistics to persuade people. In advocating medical reform Nightingale also promoted statistical description; she developed a uniform procedure for hospitals to report statistical information. She invented the pie chart, in which proportions are represented as wedges of a circular diagram, and she struggled to get the study of statistics introduced into higher education.

One of Nightingale's analyses compared the peacetime death rates of British soldiers and civilians. She discovered and showed that the soldiers, who lived in barracks under unhealthy conditions, were twice as likely to die as civilians of the same age and gender. She then used the soldiers' 2 percent death rate to persuade the Queen and the prime minister to establish a Royal Commission on the Health of the Army. It is just as criminal, she wrote, for the army to have a mortality of 20 per 1,000 "as it would be to take 1,100 men per annum out upon Salisbury Plain and shoot them."

COMPUTER PROGRAMS FOR ANALYSIS

The proliferation of computer technology within businesses and universities has greatly facilitated tabulation and statistical analysis. Commercial statistical packages eliminate the need to write a new program every time you want to tabulate and analyze data with a computer. SAS, Statistical Package for the Social Sciences (SPSS), and MINITAB are commonly used statistical packages. These user-friendly packages emphasize statistical calculations and hypothesis testing for varied types of data. They also provide programs for entering and editing data. Most of these packages contain sizable arrays of programs for descriptive analysis and univariate, bivariate, and multivariate statistical analysis. Several examples will be given in this section to illustrate how easy it is to use these statistical packages. In addition, spreadsheet packages, such as Microsoft Excel, also emphasize database management and allow a user to enter and edit data with minimal effort. They also incorporate some programs for descriptive analysis, graphic analysis, and limited statistical analysis. In Excel, statistical calculations can be performed using the Data Analysis and Paste Function menus shown in Exhibit 17.2. (Note: Depending on the version of Excel you have, you may have to "Add in" the statistical software applications. You will then find the enhanced functions by clicking on the Tools menu and then Data Analysis.)

Exhibit 17.3 shows an SPSS computer printout of descriptive statistics for two variables: EMP (number of employees working in a metropolitan area) and SALES

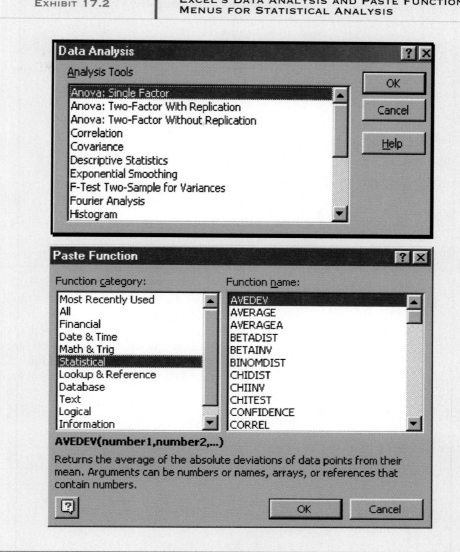

(sales volume in dollars in a metropolitan area) for ten metropolitan areas. The number of data elements (*N*), mean, standard deviation, and other descriptive statistics are displayed.

The frequency table in Exhibit 17.4 is output from the SPSS package showing the results of a question on a survey about a commercial respondents just saw. This

EXHIBIT 17.3 | **SPSS COMPUTER OUTPUT OF DESCRIPTIVE STATISTICS**

DESCRIPTIVE STATISTICS

	N	Minimum	Maximum	Mean	Std. Deviation
EMP	10	12,800	788,800	142,930	232,665
SALES	10	307,000	39,401,000	5,807,800	11,905,127
Valid N (listwise)	10				

EXHIBIT 17.4 | SPSS OUTPUT SHOWING FREQUENCIES[6]

Affect   Feelings about commercial you just saw

Value Label	Value	Frequency	Percent	Valid Percent	Cum. Percent
liked it very much	1.00	36	6.7	6.7	6.7
liked it	2.00	169	31.3	31.6	38.3
neither liked/disliked	3.00	191	35.4	35.7	74.0
disliked it	4.00	90	16.7	16.8	90.8
disliked it very much	5.00	49	9.1	9.2	100.0
		5	.9	Missing	
	Total	540	100.0	100.0	

Valid cases 535   Missing cases 5

SPSS output gives the absolute frequency of observations, the relative frequency as a percentage of all observations, the adjusted frequency as a percentage of the number of respondents who provided a recorded answer rather than answering "don't know" or leaving the question blank, and the cumulative percentage.

A histogram is similar to a bar chart. Exhibit 17.5 shows an SPSS histogram plot of purchase price data from a survey. Each bar indicates the number of purchases.

EXHIBIT 17.5 | SPSS HISTOGRAM OUTPUT[7]

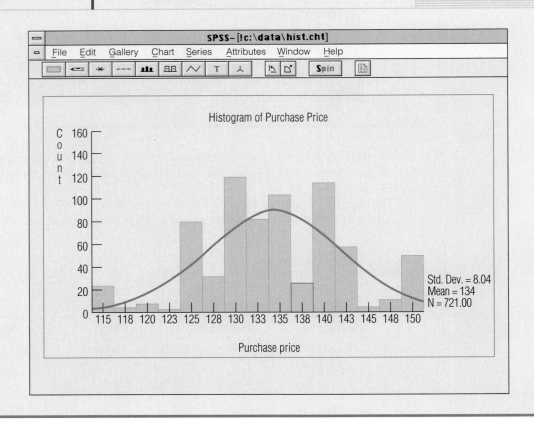

EXHIBIT 17.6 | SPSS CROSS-TABULATION OUTPUT[8]

Car Country of Origin * EDUC Crosstabulation

EDUC			1.00	2.00	3.00	4.00	5.00	Total
Car Country of Origin	American	Count	2	5	17	18	12	54
		% within Car Country of Origin	3.7%	9.3%	31.5%	33.3%	22.2%	100.0%
	European	Count		2	5	21	7	35
		% within Car Country of Origin		5.7%	14.3%	60.0%	20.0%	100.0%
	Japanese	Count		6	12	23	14	55
		% within Car Country of Origin		10.9%	21.8%	41.8%	25.5%	100.0%
Total		Count	2	13	34	62	33	144
		% within Car Country of Origin	1.4%	9.0%	23.6%	43.1%	22.9%	100.0%

Exhibit 17.6 shows an SPSS cross-tabulation of two variables, education (EDUC) and Car Country of Origin, with the row total used as a basis for percentages. (Note: The program identifies the number of respondents for whom data were not provided for both variables as missing observations.)

As you can see, statistical software programs are quite versatile, and they are extensively used in marketing research.

UNIVARIATE STATISTICS: STATING A HYPOTHESIS

What Is a Hypothesis?

hypothesis
An unproven proposition or supposition that tentatively explains certain facts or phenomena; a proposition that is empirically testable.

In marketing theory a **hypothesis** is an unproven proposition or supposition that tentatively explains certain facts or phenomena; it is a statement of assumption about the nature of the world. In its simplest form a hypothesis is a guess. A sales manager may hypothesize that the salespeople who are highest in product knowledge will be the most productive. An advertising manager may hypothesize that if consumers' attitudes toward a product change in a positive direction, there will be an increase in consumption of the product. Statistical techniques allow us to decide whether our theoretical hypothesis is confirmed by the empirical evidence.

Null and Alternative Hypotheses

null hypothesis
A statement about a status quo asserting that any change from what has been thought to be true will be due entirely to random sampling error.

Because scientists should be bold in conjecturing but extremely cautious in testing, statistical hypotheses generally are stated in a null form. A **null hypothesis** is a statement about a status quo. It is a conservative statement that communicates the notion that any change from what has been thought to be true or observed in the past will be due entirely to random error. In fact, the true purpose of setting up the null hypothesis is to provide an opportunity for nullifying it. For example, suppose academic researchers expect that highly dogmatic (that is, closed-minded) consumers will be less likely to try a new product than will less dogmatic consumers. The researchers would generally formulate a conservative null hypothesis. The null hypothesis in this case would be that there is *no difference* between high dogmatics

alternative hypothesis
A statement indicating the opposite of the null hypothesis.

and low dogmatics in their willingness to try an innovation. The **alternative hypothesis** would be that there *is* a difference between high dogmatics and low dogmatics. It states the opposite of the null hypothesis.

HYPOTHESIS TESTING

Generally we assign the symbol H_0 to the null hypothesis and the symbol H_1 to the alternative hypothesis. The purpose of hypothesis testing is to determine which of the two hypotheses is correct. The process of hypothesis testing is slightly more complicated than that of estimating parameters because the decision maker must choose between the two hypotheses. However, the student need not worry because the mathematical calculations are no more difficult than those we have already made.

The Hypothesis-Testing Procedure

The process of hypothesis testing goes as follows. First, we determine a statistical hypothesis. We then imagine what the sampling distribution of the mean would be if this hypothesis were a true statement of the nature of the population. Next, we take an actual sample and calculate the sample mean (or appropriate statistic, if we are not concerned about the mean). We know from our previous discussions of the sampling distribution of the mean that obtaining a sample value that is exactly the same as the population parameter is highly unlikely; we expect some small difference (although it may be large) between the sample mean and the population mean. We then must determine if the deviation between the obtained value of the sample mean and its expected value (based on the statistical hypothesis) would have occurred by chance alone—say, 5 times out of 100—if in fact the statistical hypothesis had been true. In other words, we ask this question: "Has the sample mean deviated substantially from the mean of the hypothesized sampling distribution by a value large enough for us to conclude that this large a deviation would be somewhat rare if the statistical hypothesis were true?" Suppose we observe that the sample value differs from the expected value. Before we can conclude that these results are improbable (or even probable), we must have some standard, or decision rule, for determining if in fact we should reject the null hypothesis and accept the alternative hypothesis. Statisticians define this decision criterion as the *significance level*.

significance level
The critical probability in choosing between the null and alternative hypotheses; the probability level that is too low to warrant support of the null hypothesis.

The **significance level** is the critical probability in choosing between the null hypothesis and the alternative hypothesis. The level of significance determines the probability level—say, .05 or .01—that is to be considered too low to warrant support of the null hypothesis. Assuming the null hypothesis being tested is true, if the probability of occurrence of the observed data is smaller than the significance level, then the data suggest that the null hypothesis should be rejected. In other words, there has been evidence to support contradiction of the null hypothesis, which is equivalent to supporting the alternative hypothesis.

In discussing confidence intervals (the set of acceptable hypotheses), statisticians use the term *confidence level,* or *confidence coefficient,* to refer to the level of probability associated with an interval estimate. However, when discussing hypothesis testing, statisticians change their terminology and call this the *significance level,* α (the Greek letter *alpha*).

An Example of Hypothesis Testing

An example should help to clarify the nature of hypothesis testing. Suppose the Buona Notte restaurant is concerned about its store image, one aspect of which is the friendliness of the service. In a personal interview customers are asked to indicate their perceptions of service on a 5-point scale, where 1 indicates "very unfriendly" service and 5 indicates "very friendly" service. The scale is assumed to be an interval scale, and experience has shown that the previous distribution of this attitudinal measurement assessing the service dimension was approximately normal.

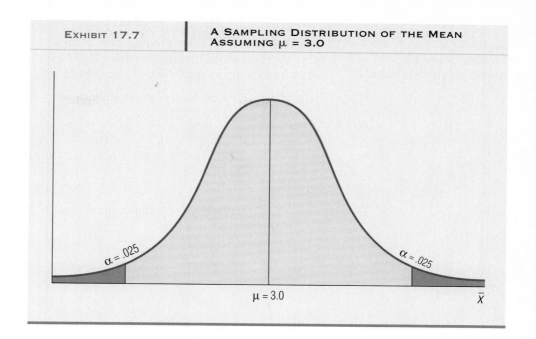

EXHIBIT 17.7 | A SAMPLING DISTRIBUTION OF THE MEAN ASSUMING μ = 3.0

$\alpha = .025$

$\alpha = .025$

$\mu = 3.0$

$\bar{X}$

Now, suppose the researcher entertains the hypothesis that customers feel the restaurant has neither friendly nor unfriendly service. The researcher formulates the null hypothesis that the mean is equal to 3.0:

$$H_0: \mu = 3.0$$

The alternative hypothesis is that the mean does not equal 3.0:

$$H_1: \mu \neq 3.0$$

Next, the researcher must decide on a region of rejection. Exhibit 17.7 shows a sampling distribution of the mean assuming the null hypothesis (that is, assuming $\mu = 3.0$). The darkly shaded area shows the region of rejection when $\alpha = .025$ in each tail of the curve. In other words, the *region of rejection* shows those values that are very unlikely to occur if the null hypothesis is true, but relatively probable if the alternative hypothesis is true. The values within the lighter area are called *acceptable at the 95 percent confidence level* (or 5 percent significance level, or .05 alpha level), and if we find that our sample mean lies within this region of acceptance, we conclude that the null hypothesis is true. More precisely, we fail to reject the null hypothesis. In other words, the range of acceptance (1) identifies those acceptable values that reflect a difference from the hypothesized mean in the null hypothesis and (2) shows the range within which any difference is so minuscule that we would conclude that this difference was due to random sampling error rather than to a false null hypothesis.

In our example, the Buona Notte restaurant hired research consultants who collected a sample of 225 interviews. The mean score on the 5-point scale equalled 3.78. (If σ is known, it is used in the analysis; however, this is rarely true and was not true in this case.[9]) The sample standard deviation was $S = 1.5$. Now we have enough information to test the hypothesis.

The researcher has decided that the decision rule will be to set the significance level at the .05 level. This means that in the long run the probability of making an erroneous decision when H_0 is true will be fewer than 5 times in 100 (.05). From the table of the standardized normal distribution, the researcher finds that the Z score of 1.96 represents a probability of .025 that a sample mean will lie above 1.96 standard errors from μ. Likewise, the table shows that about .025 of all sample means will fall below -1.96 standard errors from μ.

critical values
The values that lie exactly on the
boundary of the region of rejection.

The values that lie exactly on the boundary of the region of rejection are called the **critical values** of μ. Theoretically, the critical values are $Z = -1.96$ and $+1.96$. Now we must transform these critical Z-values to the sampling distribution of the mean for this image study. The critical values are

$$\text{Critical value—lower limit} = \mu - ZS_{\bar{X}} \text{ or } \mu - Z\frac{S}{\sqrt{n}}$$

$$= 3.0 - 1.96\left(\frac{1.5}{\sqrt{225}}\right)$$
$$= 3.0 - 1.96(.1)$$
$$= 3.0 - .196$$
$$= 2.804$$

$$\text{Critical value—upper limit} = \mu + ZS_{\bar{X}} \text{ or } \mu + Z\frac{S}{\sqrt{n}}$$

$$= 3.0 + 1.96\left(\frac{1.5}{\sqrt{225}}\right)$$
$$= 3.0 + 1.96(.1)$$
$$= 3.0 + .196$$
$$= 3.196$$

Based on the survey, $\bar{X} = 3.78$. In this case, the sample mean is contained in the region of rejection (see Exhibit 17.8). Since the sample mean is greater than the critical value, 3.196, the researcher says that the sample result is statistically significant beyond the .05 level. In other words, fewer than 5 of each 100 samples will show results that deviate this much from the hypothesized null hypothesis when in fact H_0 is actually true.

What does this mean to the management of the Buona Notte? The results indicate that customers believe the service is friendly. It is unlikely (probability of less than 5 in 100) that this result would occur because of random sampling error. This means that the restaurant should worry about factors other than the friendliness of the service personnel.

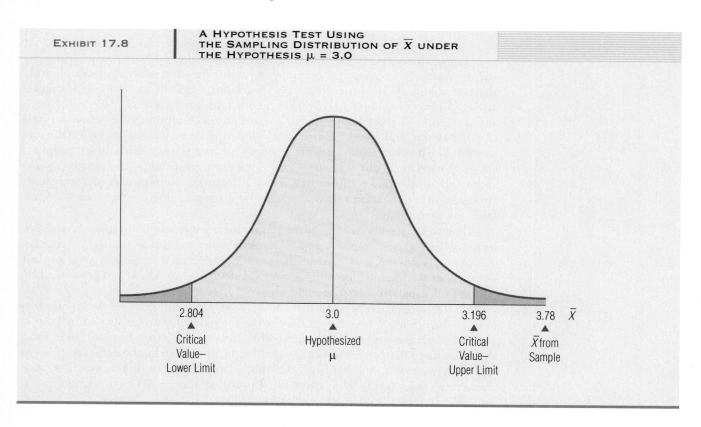

EXHIBIT 17.8

A HYPOTHESIS TEST USING THE SAMPLING DISTRIBUTION OF $\bar{X}$ UNDER THE HYPOTHESIS $\mu = 3.0$

2.804
Critical
Value–
Lower Limit

3.0
Hypothesized
μ

3.196
Critical
Value–
Upper Limit

3.78 $\bar{X}$
$\bar{X}$ from
Sample

An alternative way to test the hypothesis is to formulate the decision rule in terms of the Z-statistic. Using the following formula, we can calculate the observed value of the Z-statistic given a certain sample mean, $\bar{X}$:

$$Z_{obs} = \frac{\bar{X} - \mu}{S_{\bar{X}}}$$
$$= \frac{3.78 - \mu}{S_{\bar{X}}}$$
$$= \frac{3.78 - 3.0}{.1}$$
$$= \frac{.78}{.1}$$
$$= 7.8$$

In this case, the Z-value is 7.8 and we find that we have met the criterion of statistical significance at the .05 level. This result is statistically significant at the .000001 level.

THE CHI-SQUARE TEST FOR GOODNESS OF FIT

chi-square (χ^2) test
A hypothesis test that allows for investigation of statistical significance in the analysis of a frequency distribution.

Table 17.9 shows the responses to a survey to investigate awareness of a particular brand of automobile tire. This frequency distribution, or one-dimensional table from a sample of 100, suggests that the majority of the population (60 percent) is aware of the brand.

The **chi-square (χ^2)** test allows us to test for significance in the analysis of frequency distributions. Thus categorical data on variables such as gender, education, or dichotomous answers may be statistically analyzed. Suppose, for example, that we wish to test the null hypothesis that the number of consumers aware of a certain tire brand equals the number unaware of the brand. The logic inherent in the χ^2 test allows us to compare the observed frequencies (O_i) with the expected frequencies (E_i) based on our theoretical ideas about the population distribution or our presupposed proportions. In other words, the technique tests whether the data come from a certain probability distribution. It tests the "goodness of fit" of the observed distribution with the expected distribution.

Calculation of the chi-square statistic allows us to determine whether the difference between the observed frequency distribution and the expected frequency distribution can be attributed to sampling variation. The steps in this process are as follows:

1. Formulate the null hypothesis and determine the expected frequency of each answer.
2. Determine the appropriate significance level.
3. Calculate the χ^2 value, using the observed frequencies from the sample and the expected frequencies.
4. Make the statistical decision by comparing the calculated χ^2 value with the critical χ^2 value.

TABLE 17.9	ONE-WAY FREQUENCY TABLE FOR BRAND AWARENESS
Awareness of Tire Manufacturer's Brand	**Frequency**
Aware	60
Unaware	40
	100

To analyze the brand awareness data in Table 17.9, start with a null hypothesis that suggests that the number of respondents aware of the brand will equal the number of respondents unaware of it. Thus the expected probability of each answer (aware or unaware) is .5. In a sample of 100, 50 people would be expected to respond yes, or aware, and 50 would be expected to respond no, or unaware. After the researcher has determined that the chi-square test is appropriate at the .05 level of significance (or some other probability level), the chi-square statistic may be calculated.

To calculate the chi-square statistic, use the following formula:

$$\chi^2 = \sum \frac{(O_i - E_i)^2}{E_1}$$

where

χ^2 = chi-square statistic
O_i = observed frequency in the ith cell
E_i = expected frequency in the ith cell

Sum the squared differences:

$$\chi^2 = \frac{(O_1 - E_1)^2}{E_1} + \frac{(O_2 - E_2)^2}{E_2}$$

Thus we determine that the chi-square value equals 4:

$$\chi^2 = \frac{(60 - 50)^2}{50} + \frac{(40 - 50)^2}{50}$$
$$= 4$$

Table 17.10 shows the detailed calculation for this problem.

Like many other probability distributions, the χ^2 distribution is not a single probability curve, but a family of curves. These curves, although similar, vary according to the number of degrees of freedom ($k - 1$). Thus we must calculate the number of degrees of freedom. (*Degrees of freedom* refers to the number of observations that can be varied without changing the constraints or assumptions associated with a numerical system.) We do this as follows:

$$d.f. = k - 1$$

where

k = number of cells associated with column or row data[10]

In the brand awareness problem there are only two categorical responses. Thus the degrees of freedom equal 1 ($d.f. = 2 - 1 = 1$).

Now the computed chi-square value needs to be compared with the critical chi-square values associated with the .05 probability level with 1 degree of freedom. In Table 4 of the Appendix the critical chi-square value is 3.84. Since the calculated chi-square is larger than the tabular chi-square, the null hypothesis—that the observed values are comparable to the expected values—is rejected.[11]

TABLE 17.10	CALCULATING THE CHI-SQUARE STATISTIC				
Brand Awareness	Observed Frequency (O_i)	Expected Probability	Expected Frequency (E_i)	($O_i - E_i$)	$\frac{(O_i - E_i)^2}{E_i}$
Aware	60	.5	50	10	$\frac{100}{50} = 2.0$
Unaware	40	.5	50	−10	$\frac{100}{50} = 2.0$
Total	100	1.0	100	0	$\chi^2 = 4.0$

Now that we have looked at two statistical techniques for hypothesis testing, note that a number of descriptive and statistical techniques are available to assist the researcher in interpreting data. The choice of the method of analysis depends on (1) the number of variables, (2) the scale of measurement, and (3) the type of question to be answered.

Number of Variables

The number of variables to be simultaneously investigated is a primary consideration in the choice of statistical technique. A researcher who is interested only in the average number of times a prospective home buyer visits financial institutions to shop for interest rates concentrates on investigating only one variable at a time. The researcher conducts *univariate statistical analysis* when attempting to generalize from a sample about one variable at a time. Statistically describing the relationship between two variables at one time, such as the relationship between advertising expenditures and sales volume, requires *bivariate statistical analysis*. Tests of group differences and measuring the relationship (association) among variables are the subjects of Chapter 18.

Scale of Measurement

The scale of measurement on which the data are based or the type of measurement reflected in the data determines the permissible statistical techniques and appropriate empirical operations to perform. As we discussed earlier, testing a hypothesis about a mean requires interval-scaled or ratio-scaled data. We have also seen that the chi-square test can be used when the researcher employs a nominal scale to measure consumer awareness versus unawareness.

Exhibit 17.9 shows the appropriate descriptive statistics for each type of scale. It is important to remember that all statistics appropriate for lower-order scales (nominal is the lowest) are suitable for higher-order scales (ratio is the highest).

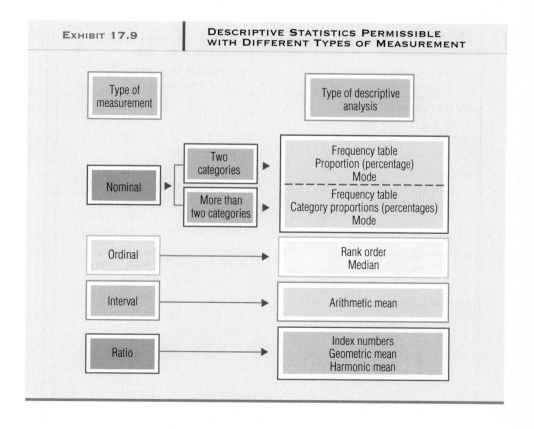

| EXHIBIT 17.9 | DESCRIPTIVE STATISTICS PERMISSIBLE WITH DIFFERENT TYPES OF MEASUREMENT |

The most sophisticated form of statistical analysis for nominal-scale data is counting. Because numbers are merely labels for classification purposes, they have no quantitative meaning. The researcher tallies the frequency in each category and identifies which category contains the highest number of observations (individuals, objects, etc.). An ordinal scale provides data that may be rank ordered from lowest to highest. For example, the ranking of brand preferences generally employs an ordinal scale. Observations may be associated with percentile ranks. With ordinal data, the median may be used as the average. Because all statistical analyses appropriate for lower-order scales are suitable for higher-order scales, an interval scale may be used as a nominal scale to uniquely classify or as an ordinal scale to preserve order. In addition, an interval scale's property of equal intervals allows researchers to compare differences among scale values and to perform arithmetic operations such as addition and subtraction. Numbers may be changed, but the numerical operations must preserve order and relative magnitudes of differences. The mean and standard deviation may be calculated from true interval-scale data. A ratio scale has all the properties of nominal, ordinal, and interval scales. In addition, it allows researchers to compare absolute magnitudes, because the scale has an absolute zero point. Using the actual quantities for arithmetic operations is permissible. Thus the ratios of scale values are meaningful.

Type of Question to Be Answered

The type of question the researcher is attempting to answer is a consideration in the choice of statistical technique. For example, we already illustrated a hypothesis test for a researcher who wants to determine whether the calculated mean value of a variable differs from the expected value. Marketing researchers frequently question whether a mean, a proportion, or a distribution differs from what was expected.

Two other frequently asked questions are (1) Are there differences between two (or more) groups and (2) Is there a relationship between two or more variables? These topics are discussed in the following chapter.

EXHIBIT 17.10	EXAMPLES OF SELECTING THE APPROPRIATE UNIVARIATE STATISTICAL METHOD	
Sample Marketing Problem	**Statistical Question to Be Asked**	**Possible Test of Statistical Significance**
Interval or Ratio Scales Compare actual vs. hypothetical values of average salary	Is the sample mean significantly different from the hypothesized population mean?	Z-test (if sample is large) t-test (if sample is small)
Ordinal Scales Compare actual evaluations and expected evaluations	Does the distribution of scores on a scale with the categories excellent, good, fair, and poor differ from the expected distribution?	chi-square test
Determine ordered preferences for all brands in a product class	Does a set of rank orderings in a sample differ from an expected or hypothetical rank ordering?	Kolmogorov-Smirnov test
Nominal Scales Identify gender of key executives	Is the number of female executives equal to the number of male executives?	chi-square test
Indicate percentage of key executives who are male	Is the proportion of male executives the same as the hypothesized proportion?	t-test of a proportion

Exhibit 17.10 provides guidelines for selecting the appropriate statistical method. Although you may be unfamiliar with most of them, the exhibit illustrates that a variety of statistical techniques exist and the proper one may be selected based on the research situation. A complete discussion of all the relevant techniques is beyond the scope of our discussion thus far. The important point is that the researcher should anticipate the method of statistical analysis before selecting the research design and before determining the type of data to collect. Once the data are collected, the research design will reflect the initial approach to analysis of the problem.

SUMMARY

①② Descriptive analysis refers to the transformation of raw data into an understandable form. Descriptive information is obtained by summarizing, categorizing, rearranging, and other forms of analysis. Tabulation refers to the orderly arrangement of data in a table or other summary format. Percentages, cumulative percentages, and frequency distributions are useful. The data may be described by measures of central tendency, such as the mean, median, or mode. Cross-tabulation shows how one variable relates to another to reveal differences between groups. Such cross-tabulations should be limited to categories related to the research problem and purpose. Putting the results into percentage form facilitates intergroup comparisons.

③ Performing the basic cross-tabulation within various subgroups of the sample is a common form of elaboration analysis. Elaboration analysis often identifies moderator variables or spurious relationships. A moderator variable is a third variable that, when introduced into the analysis, alters or has a contingent effect on the relationship between an independent variable and a dependent variable. A spurious relationship exists when adding a third variable to the analysis indicates that the relationship between the original two variables was not authentic.

④⑤ Data transformation is the process of changing data from their original form to a format that is more suitable for performing a data analysis. A data transformation is performed in order to summarize rank-order data. Rank scores are multiplied by their frequency of occurrence to develop a new scale that represents summarized rank orderings.

⑥ Tables and graphs help to simplify and clarify research data. Computer software greatly facilitates descriptive analysis. Many programs that enhance the construction of graphs and charts are available.

⑦ A hypothesis is a statement of assumption about the nature of the world. A null hypothesis is a statement about the status quo. An alternative hypothesis is a statement that indicates the opposite of the null hypothesis.

⑧ In hypothesis testing, a researcher states a null hypothesis about a population mean and then attempts to disprove it. The Z-test defines a region of rejection based on a significance level of the standardized normal distribution beyond which it is unlikely that the null hypothesis is true. If a sample mean is contained in the region of rejection, the null hypothesis is rejected.

⑨ The chi-square test allows testing of statistical significance in the analysis of frequency distributions: An observed distribution of categorical data from a sample may be compared with an expected distribution for goodness of fit.

A number of appropriate statistical techniques are available to assist the researcher in interpreting data. The choice of statistical analysis method depends on (1) the number of variables, (2) the scale of measurement, and (3) the type of question to be answered.

Key Terms and Concepts

descriptive analysis	elaboration analysis	null hypothesis
frequency table	moderator variable	alternative hypothesis
cross-tabulation	spurious relationship	significance level
two-way (contingency) table	data transformation (data conversion)	critical values
base	hypothesis	chi-square (χ^2) test

Questions for Review and Critical Thinking

1. A survey asked respondents to respond to the statement "My work is interesting." Interpret the frequency distribution in the following SPSS output.

My work is interesting.

Category Label	Code	Abs. Freq.	Rel. Freq. (Pct.)	Adj. Freq. (Pct.)	Cum. Freq. (Pct.)
Very true	1	650	23.9	62.4	62.4
Somewhat true	2	303	11.2	29.1	91.5
Not very true	3	61	2.2	5.9	97.3
Not at all true	4	28	1.0	2.7	100.0
	•	1,673	61.6	Missing	
	Total	2,715	100.0	100.0	
Valid cases	1,042	Missing cases	1,673		

2. Use the data in the following table to (a) prepare a frequency distribution of the respondents' ages and (b) cross-tabulate the respondents' genders with cola preference.

Individual	Gender	Age	Cola Preference	Weekly Purchases
John	M	19	Coke	2
Claudio	M	17	Pepsi	5
Bill	M	20	Pepsi	7
Marie	F	20	Coke	2
Pierre	M	18	Coke	4
Karen	F	16	Coke	4
Tom	M	17	Pepsi	8
Dawn	F	19	Pepsi	1

3. Data on the average size of a soda (in ounces) at all 30 hockey arenas are as follows: 14, 18, 20, 16, 16, 12, 14, 16, 14, 16, 16, 16, 14, 14, 16, 20, 12, 16, 20, 12, 16, 16, 24, 16, 16, 14, 14, 12, 14, 20. The results of an Excel Descriptive Statistics analysis of these data are shown below. Interpret the output.

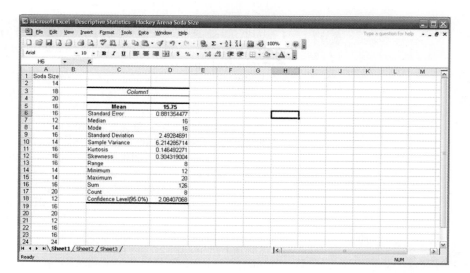

4. Interpret the following table giving the percentage of individuals on a low-fat or low-cholesterol diet by gender and age.

Age Group	Women	Men	Total
16–24	29%	13%	21%
25–34	43	25	34
35–44	46	28	37
45–54	54	32	43
55+	49	35	43

5. What types of scalar data (that is, nominal, ordinal, interval, or ratio) typically are used in cross-tabulation analysis?
6. It has been argued that analysis and interpretation of data are managerial arts. Comment.
7. Suppose that the data in the following tables show some of the results of a Revenue Canada survey of taxpayers. Analyze and interpret the data.

The last year you filed an income tax return, did you get any suggestions or information that was especially helpful to you in filing?

	Absolute Frequency	Rel. Freq. (Pct.)	Adj. Freq. (Pct.)
Yes	156	29.5	29.8
No	68	69.7	70.2
Don't know	1	.2	Missing
Not ascertained	1	.2	Missing
Blank	2	.4	Missing
	528	100.0	100.0

What kind of information was it?

	Absolute Frequency	Rel. Freq. (Pct.)	Adj. Freq. (Pct.)
Learned about RSP	8	1.5	5.4
Learned about another deduction	46	8.7	31.3
Obtained info. about forms to use	9	1.7	6.1
Received pamphlets/forms	40	7.6	27.2
Other	44	8.3	29.9
Don't know	6	1.1	Missing
Not ascertained	2	.4	Missing
Blank	373	70.6	Missing
	528	100.0	100.0

8. What is the purpose of a statistical hypothesis?
9. What is significance level? How does a researcher choose a significance level?
10. List the steps in the hypothesis-testing procedure.
11. After a bumper crop, a mushroom grower hypothesizes that mushrooms will remain at the wholesale average price of $1 per 500 g. State the null hypothesis and the alternative hypothesis.
12. Assume you have the following data: H_0: $\mu = 200$, $S = 30$, $n = 64$, and $\bar{X} = 218$. Conduct a two-tailed hypothesis test at the .05 significance level.
13. Assume you have the following data: H_0: $\mu = 2,450$, $S = 400$, $n = 100$, and $\bar{X} = 2,300$. Conduct a hypothesis test at the .01 significance level.
14. The answers to a researcher's question will be nominally scaled. What statistical test is appropriate to compare the sample data with the hypothesized population data?
15. What factors determine the choice of the appropriate statistical technique?
16. A researcher plans to ask employees whether they favour, oppose, or are indifferent to a change in the company retirement program. Formulate a null hypothesis for a chi-square test, and determine the expected frequencies for each answer.
17. A data-processing analyst for a research supplier finds that preliminary computer runs of survey results show that consumers love a client's new product. The employee buys a large block of the client's stock. Is this ethical?
18. A researcher finds that in a survey of 100 people, 15 respondents answer "don't know" to a question that has "yes" and "no" as alternatives. The researcher uses 85 as a base for calculating the percentage of respondents who answer "yes" or "no." Is this the correct choice?

Exploring the Internet

1. The Megapenny Project is located at

www.kokogiak.com/megapenny/.

Visit this site to get an insight into what large numbers mean.

2. The Data and Story Library is an online library of datafiles and stories that illustrate the use of basic statistics methods. The Web address is

http://lib.stat.cmu.edu/DASL/.

CASE 17.1   ST. LAWRENCE MOTORS

St. Lawrence Motors is an automobile dealership that regularly advertises in its local market area. It claims that a certain make and model of car averages 7.6 L per 100 km (highway and city kilometres combined) and mentions that this figure may vary with driving conditions. A local consumer group wishes to verify the advertising claim. To do so, it selects a sample of recent purchasers of this make and model of automobile. It asks them to drive their cars until two tanks of gasoline have been used up and to record the mileage. The group then calculates and records the litres per hundred kilometres for each car. The data in Case Exhibit 17.1.1 portray the results of the tests.

CASE EXHIBIT 17.1.1		FUEL ECONOMY REPORTS	
Buyer	**Litres per 100 km**	**Buyer**	**Litres per 100 km**
1	7.80	16	9.90
2	8.30	17	8.10
3	8.80	18	8.00
4	8.60	19	7.90
5	8.90	20	7.80
6	7.50	21	9.00
7	7.80	22	9.50
8	8.10	23	7.70
9	8.20	24	8.80
10	7.75	25	9.00
11	7.90	26	8.40
12	8.10	27	8.70
13	8.00	28	8.50
14	8.20	29	9.00
15	7.90	30	8.35

Questions

1. Formulate a statistical hypothesis appropriate for the consumer group's purpose.
2. Calculate the mean average kilometres per litre. Compute the sample variance and sample standard deviation.
3. Construct the appropriate statistical test for your hypothesis, using a .05 significance level.

CASE 17.2   DOWNY-Q QUILT

The research for Downy-Q is an example of a commercial test that was conducted when an advertising campaign for an established brand had run its course.[12] The revised campaign, "Fighting the Cold," emphasized that Downy-Q was an "extra-warm quilt"; previous research had demonstrated that extra warmth was an important and deliverable product quality. The commercial test was requested to measure the campaign's ability to generate purchase interest.

The marketing department had recommended this revised advertising campaign and was now anxious to know how effectively this commercial would perform. The test concluded that "Fighting the Cold" was a persuasive commercial. It also demonstrated that the new campaign would have greater appeal to specific market segments.

Method

Brand choices for the same individuals were obtained before and after viewing the commercial. The commercial was tested in 30-second, colour-moving, storyboard form in a theatre test. Invited viewers were shown programming with commercial inserts. Qualified respondents were women who had bought quilts in outlets that carried Downy-Q. The results are shown in Case Exhibits 17.2.1 through 17.2.4.

Question

Interpret the data in these tables. What recommendations and conclusions would you offer to Downy-Q management?

CASE EXHIBIT 17.2.1	SHIFTS IN BRAND CHOICE BEFORE AND AFTER SHOWING OF DOWNY-Q QUILT COMMERCIAL

Question: We are going to give away a series of prizes. If you are selected as one of the winners, which of the following would you truly want to win?

Brand Choice after Commercial	BRAND CHOICE BEFORE COMMERCIAL (%)	
	Downy-Q (n = 23)	Other Brand (n = 237)
Downy-Q	78	19
Other brand	22	81

CASE EXHIBIT 17.2.2	PRE/POST INCREMENT IN CHOICE OF DOWNY-Q

Question: We are going to give away a series of prizes. If you are selected as one of the winners, which of the following would you truly want to win? (Check list.)

Demographic Group	"FIGHTING THE COLD"		NORM: ALL QUILT COMMERCIALS	
	Base	Score	Average	Range
Total audience	(260)	+15	+10	6–19
By marital status				
Married	(130)	+17		
Not married	(130)	+12		
By age				
Under 35	(130)	+14		
35 and over	(130)	+15		
By employment status				
Not employed	(90)	+13		
Employed	(170)	+18		

CASE EXHIBIT 17.2.3	ADJECTIVE CHECKLIST FOR DOWNY-Q QUILT COMMERCIAL

Question: Which of these words do you feel come closest to describing the commercial you've just seen? (Check list.)

Adjective	"Fighting the Cold" (%)	Norm: All Quilt Commercials (%)
Positive		
Appealing	18	24
Clever	11	40
Convincing	20	14
Effective	19	23
Entertaining	5	24
Fast moving	12	21
Genuine	7	4

(continued)

Adjective	"Fighting the Cold" (%)	Norm: All Quilt Commercials (%)
Imaginative	7	21
Informative	24	18
Interesting	13	17
Original	7	20
Realistic	8	3
Unusual	3	8
Negative		
Amateurish	9	11
Bad Taste	4	4
Dull	33	20
Repetitious	17	16
Silly	8	19
Slow	8	7
Unbelievable	3	5
Unclear	3	2
Unimportant	14	14
Uninteresting	32	19

CASE EXHIBIT 17.2.4 | PRODUCT ATTRIBUTE CHECKLIST FOR DOWNY-Q

Question: Which of the following statements do you feel apply to Downy-Q? (Mark as many or as few as you feel apply.)

Attributes	"Fighting the Cold" (%)
Extra warm	56
Lightweight	48
Pretty designs	45
Durable fabrics	28
Nice fabrics	27
Good construction	27

To follow these instructions, you will need to install SPSS 14.0 Student version included with your book and the luxury2.sav data file available from the Web site: www. effectivemarketingresearch.nelson.com. This section explains basic descriptive analysis, cross-tabulation, and hypothesis testing.

A. CREATING FREQUENCY TABLES, FREQUENCY DISTRIBUTIONS, and DESCRIPTIVES

Step 1: Select the following menu items: Analyze > Descriptive Statistics > Frequencies.
Step 2: In the Frequencies dialogue box, highlight the variable(s) you want to display the frequencies for and click on the right arrow (▶).
Step 3: Make sure that "Display frequency tables" is checked.

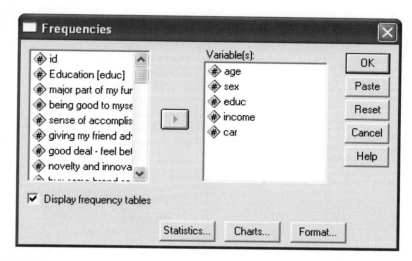

Step 4: CHARTS: If you want to display the frequencies on a graph, then click on the "charts . . ." button. Then select your chart type. Click "continue."
Step 5: DESCRIPTIVE MEASURES: If you want to display the central tendency and variability measures for the variable, then click on the "Statistics . . ." button. Next select the desired central tendency measures (mean, median, mode) and variability/dispersion measures (s.d., range, etc.). Click "continue."

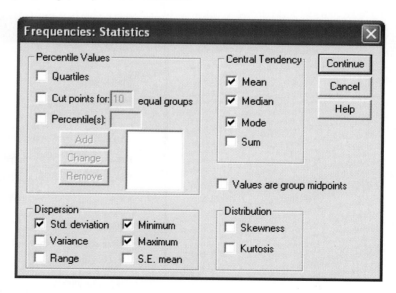

Step 6: Back in the Frequencies dialogue box, click OK.

B. CROSS-TABULATING TWO VARIABLES

Step 1: Make sure each variable has reasonably few levels. This is not a general requirement for crosstabs, but if you have small samples, then you may have empty cells or cells with too few people. If you have many levels of a variable, you can recode it into a new variable with fewer levels (see SPSS instructions for Chapter 16).

Step 2: Select the following menu items: Analyze > Descriptive Statistics > Crosstabs.

Step 3: In the Crosstabs dialogue box, highlight the variable you want in the rows of the crosstab and click on the right arrow for "rows." Then highlight the column variable and click on the right arrow for "columns."

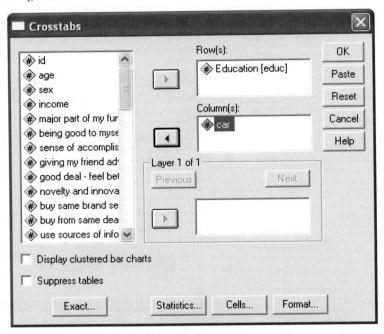

Step 4: Then click on the "Cells" button and in the Crosstabs dialogue box, make sure that "observed" is checked. Cell Display dialogue box will appear.

Step 5: Check "observed" in the Cell Display dialogue box. You can also check "expected"; however, this may result in crowded tables. Also, check either the "row" or "column" percentages, not both. Choose whichever you feel would be meaningful to

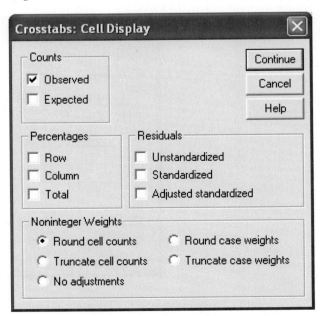

interpret. Click "continue." These are general suggestions—you can experiment with different cell displays.

Step 6: (OPTIONAL) You can also do chi-square test by clicking on the "Statistics . . ." button and checking "Chi-square" and "Continue." See Chapter 18 for discussion.

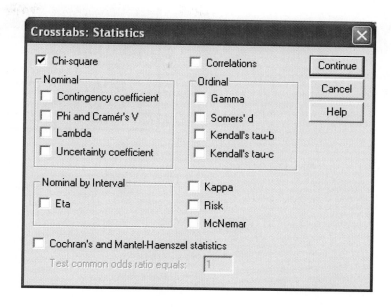

Step 7: Back in the crosstabs dialogue box, click OK.
Note that you can also create crosstabs with more than two variables.

C. HYPOTHESIS TESTING (Is μ = c?)

Step 1: Select the following menu items: Analyze > Compare Means > One Sample t-test.
Step 2: You will see the "One Sample t-test" dialogue box. Highlight the variables (interval/ratio scale) whose means you wish to compare and click on the right arrow for the "test variables."

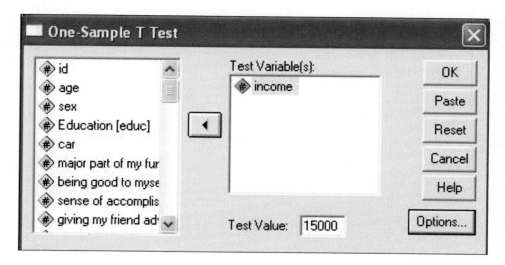

Step 3: Enter the value in the "Test Value" box. This is your null hypothesis. The default value is "0." You can change this value to correspond to your null hypothesis. For example, if you are interested in income variable and if you believe that the average income of the population will be $15,000, then you enter 15,000 in the "Test Value" box. Click "OK."

TIP. The default Confidence Interval is 95 percent. If you wish to change the confidence interval, you can do so by clicking on the "OPTIONS" button in the "One Sample t-test" dialogue box.

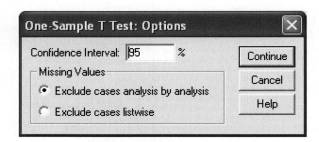

DIFFERENCES BETWEEN GROUPS AND RELATIONSHIPS AMONG VARIABLES

A survey conducted by the Canadian Internet Project provides interesting findings about Canadians' Internet use. Although older Canadians may be using the Internet more now, younger citizens are still much more likely to be Internet users than are older individuals. As age advances, the likelihood of using the Internet decreases. However, this finding also varies across Canada from a high of 92.4 percent of users in the 18- to 24-year-old category in Ontario to a low of 25 percent for the 65 and older category in Quebec. For marketers trying to reach the younger consumers in Ontario, the Internet is obviously a good route.

Internet use is also related to income level, high-income households having significantly more Internet users than lower-income households. The top of the range occurs in the highest income quartile ($80,000+ per year) in the Prairie region, which has Internet use of 96.2 percent; the lowest use is in Quebec in the lowest income quartile (less than $40,000 per year), where Internet use is 50.8 percent. Differences are also notable in the not-employed category across all regions. Within Ontario, Quebec, and the Prairie and Atlantic regions, there is a relatively low level of Internet use among those not employed (ranging from 47.6 percent in the Atlantic region to 68.8 percent in Ontario). In contrast, both British Columbia and Alberta have a much more robust level of Internet use for those not employed (85.7 percent in Alberta and 89.5 percent in British Columbia). Using the Internet to reach unemployed individuals in the Atlantic region would not be highly successsful, but it is likely to be more successful in British Columbia and Alberta.

English and French are the languages most used for Internet activities (making up a combined total of 95.1 percent of all users). Of these users, 76.9 percent predominantly use English and 15.9 percent use French as their primary language. A mere 2.3 percent reported using a combination of the two.[1]

Making comparisons such as the preceding ones involves bivariate analysis, the topic of this chapter. The purpose of descriptive

What you will learn in this chapter

1 To discuss reasons to conduct tests of differences.

2 To understand how the type of measurement scale influences the test of difference.

3 To calculate a chi-square test for a contingency table.

4 To understand the analysis of variance (ANOVA) tests for differences among three or more groups.

5 To give examples of marketing questions that may be answered by analyzing the associations among variables.

6 To discuss the concept of the simple correlation coefficient.

7 To understand that correlation does not mean causation.

8 To explain the concept of bivariate linear regression.

9 To discuss why multivariate regression is an important tool for analysis.

analysis is to summarize data. After summarizing the data, the researcher may wish to measure the association between variables or test the differences between groups of objects. This chapter goes beyond univariate statistics, in which the analysis focuses on one variable at a time, and into the realm of bivariate statistics, in which the researcher is concerned with scores on two variables. The chapter also includes a brief discussion of multiple regression, a form of multivariate analysis. ∎

DIFFERENCES BETWEEN GROUPS

test of differences
An investigation of a hypothesis stating that two (or more) groups differ with respect to measures on a variable.

One of the most frequently tested hypotheses states that two groups differ with respect to some behaviour, characteristic, or attitude. For example, in the classical experimental design, the researcher tests differences between subjects assigned to the experimental group and subjects assigned to the control group. The survey researcher may be interested in whether male and female consumers purchase a product with equal frequency. Such tests are bivariate **tests of differences.**

Often researchers are interested in testing differences in mean scores between groups or in comparing how two groups' scores are distributed across possible response categories. We will focus our attention on these issues.

Construction of contingency tables for chi-square analysis gives a procedure for comparing the distribution of one group with that of another group. This is a good starting point from which to discuss testing of differences.

Cross-Tabulation Tables: The Chi-Square Test for Goodness of Fit

cross-tabulation (contingency table)
A joint frequency distribution of observations on two or more sets of variables.

chi-square test for a contingency table
A test that statistically analyzes significance in a joint frequency distribution.

One of the simplest techniques for describing sets of relationships is the cross-tabulation. A **cross-tabulation**, or **contingency table**, is a joint frequency distribution of observations on two or more sets of variables. This generally means that tabulation of subgroups will be conducted for purposes of comparison. The chi-square distribution provides a means for testing the statistical significance of contingency tables. It allows us to test for differences in two groups' distributions across categories.

As mentioned in Chapter 17, the **chi-square test for a contingency table** involves comparing the observed frequencies (O_i) with the expected frequencies (E_i). It tests the goodness of fit of the observed distribution with the expected distribution.

Table 18.1 reproduces Table 17.9. This one-dimensional table suggests that the majority of the population (60 percent) is aware of the brand. However, if we analyze the data by subgroups based on gender of respondents, as in Table 18.2, we can see the logic of cross-classification procedures. Inspection of Table 18.2 suggests that most men are aware of the brand of tires, but most women are not. Thus from our simple analysis we conclude that there is a difference in brand awareness between men and women. (It might also be stated that brand awareness may be associated with gender of respondent.)

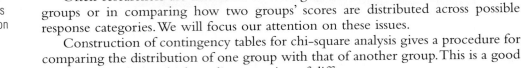

TABLE 18.1	ONE-WAY FREQUENCY TABLE FOR BRAND AWARENESS

Awareness of Tire Manufacturer's Brand	Frequency
Aware	60
Unaware	40
Total	100

TABLE 18.2	CONTINGENCY TABLE (CROSS-TABULATION) FOR BRAND AWARENESS BY GENDER		
Awareness of Tire Manufacturer's Brand	Men	Women	Total
Aware	50	10	60
Unaware	15	25	40
Total	65	35	100

So far we have not discussed the notion of statistical significance. Is the observed difference between men and women the result of chance variation due to random sampling? Is the discrepancy more than sampling variation? The chi-square test allows us to conduct tests for significance in the analysis of the $R \times C$ contingency table (where R = row and C = column). The formula for the chi-square statistic is the same as that for one-way frequency tables (see Chapter 17):

$$\chi^2 = \Sigma \frac{(O_i - E_i)^2}{E_i}$$

where

χ^2 = chi-square statistic
O_i = observed frequency in the ith cell
E_i = expected frequency in the ith cell

Again, as in the univariate chi-square test, a frequency count of data that nominally identify or categorically rank groups is acceptable for the chi-square test for a contingency table. Both variables in the contingency table will be categorical variables rather than interval- or ratio-scaled continuous variables.

We begin, as in all hypothesis-testing procedures, by formulating the null hypothesis and selecting the level of statistical significance for the particular problem. Suppose, for the preceding example, that we wish to test the null hypothesis that an equal number of men and women are aware of the brand and that the hypothesis test will be made at the .05 level of statistical significance.

In managerial terms the researchers ask whether men and women have different levels of brand awareness. Translated into a statistical question, the problem is "Is brand awareness independent of the respondent's gender?" Table 18.2 is a 2 × 2 ($R \times C$) contingency table that cross-classifies based on answers to the awareness question (rows) and the respondent's gender (columns).

To compute the chi-square value for the 2 × 2 contingency table (Table 18.2), the researcher must first identify an expected distribution for that table. Under the null hypothesis that men and women are equally aware of the tire brand, the same proportion of positive answers (60 percent) should come from both groups. In other words, the proportion of men aware of the brand would be the same as the proportion of women aware of it. Likewise, the proportion of men unaware of the brand would equal the proportion of women unaware.

There is an easy way to calculate the expected frequencies for the cells in a cross-tabulation. To compute an expected number for each cell, use the formula

$$E_{ij} = \frac{R_i C_j}{n}$$

where

R_i = total observed frequency in the ith row
C_j = total observed frequency in the jth column
n = sample size

TABLE 18.3	CALCULATION OF OBSERVED VERSUS EXPECTED FREQUENCIES FOR BRAND AWARENESS PROBLEM

Awareness of Tire Manufacturer's Brand	Men	Women	Total
Aware	50 (39)	10 (21)	60
Unaware	15 (26)	25 (14)	40
Total	65	35	100

Note: Expected frequencies are in parentheses. They were calculated as follows:

$$E_{11} = \frac{(60)(65)}{100} = 39 \quad E_{12} = \frac{(60)(35)}{100} = 21 \quad E_{21} = \frac{(40)(65)}{100} = 26 \quad E_{22} = \frac{(40)(35)}{100} = 14$$

A calculation of the expected values does not utilize the actual observed numbers of respondents in each individual cell; only the total column and total row values are used in this calculation. The expected cell frequencies are calculated as shown in Table 18.3.

To compute a chi-square statistic, use the same formula as before, but calculate degrees of freedom as the number of rows minus one $(R - 1)$ times the number of columns minus one $(C - 1)$:

$$\chi^2 = \Sigma \frac{(O_i - E_i)^2}{E_i}$$

with $(R - 1)(C - 1)$ degrees of freedom.

Table 18.3 shows the observed versus the expected frequencies for the brand awareness question. Using the data in Table 18.3, we calculate the chi-square statistic as follows:

$$\chi^2 = \frac{(50 - 39)^2}{39} + \frac{(10 - 21)^2}{21} + \frac{(15 - 26)^2}{26} + \frac{(25 - 14)^2}{14}$$
$$= 3.102 + 5.762 + 4.654 + 8.643$$
$$= 22.161$$

The number of degrees of freedom equals 1:

$$(R - 1)(C - 1) = (2 - 1)(2 - 1) = 1$$

From Table A.4 in the Appendix, we see that the critical value at the .05 probability level with 1 $d.f.$ is 3.84. Thus the null hypothesis is rejected. Brand awareness does not appear to be independent of the respondent's gender—in fact, the tabular value for the .001 level is 10.8, and the calculated value of 22.1 far exceeds this tabular value.

Proper use of the chi-square test requires that each expected cell frequency (E_{ij}) have a value of at least 5. If this sample size requirement is not met, the researcher should take a larger sample or combine (collapse) response categories.

Difference Between Two Groups When Comparing Means

Researchers often wish to test a hypothesis stating that the mean scores on some interval- or ratio-scaled variable will be significantly different for two independent samples or groups. The null hypothesis about differences between groups is normally stated as follows:

$$\mu_1 = \mu_2 \text{ or } \mu_1 - \mu_2 = 0$$

The question is whether the observed differences have occurred by chance alone. In most cases, comparisons are between two sample means $(\bar{X}_1 - \bar{X}_2)$. The formula utilized to test whether the differences are statistically significant depends on the knowledge of the value of the population standard deviation and the number of observations (sample size) in the groups. If either group is small (fewer than 30) and the population standard deviation is unknown, the researcher uses a *t*-test for difference of means. If the number of observations is large, the researcher uses a *Z*-test for difference of means to test the hypothesis.

Difference Between Two Groups When Comparing Proportions

What type of statistical comparison can be made when the observed statistics are proportions? Suppose a researcher wishes to test a hypothesis that wholesalers in western and eastern Canada differ in the proportion of sales they make to discount retailers. Testing the null hypothesis that the population proportion for group 1 (π_1) equals the population proportion for group 2 (π_2) is conceptually the same as the *t*-test or *Z*-test of two means. Again, sample size is the appropriate criterion for selecting either a *t*-test (small sample) or a *Z*-test (large sample).

The hypothesis, which is

$$H_0: \pi_1 = \pi_2$$

may be restated as

$$H_0: \pi_1 - \pi_2 = 0$$

The comparison between the observed sample proportions, p_1 and p_2, allows the researcher to ask whether the differences between two groups from random samples occurred due to chance alone.

Difference Among Three or More Groups When Comparing Means

When the means of more than two groups or populations are to be compared, one-way **analysis of variance (ANOVA)** is the appropriate statistical tool. Most ANOVA problems have a nominal variable as the independent variable and an interval- or ratio-scaled variable as the dependent variable. An example of an ANOVA problem would be to compare women who work full time outside the home, those who work part time outside the home, and those who work full time inside the home on the number of hours they spend shopping in grocery stores each week. Here there is one independent variable: working status. This variable is said to have three levels: full-time employment, part-time employment, and work only within the home. Because there are three groups (levels), we use an *F*-test to test for statistical significance instead of a *t*-test or a *Z*-test. The *F*-test will be explained in greater detail later in this chapter.

If we have three groups or levels of the independent variable, the null hypothesis is stated as follows:

$$\mu_1 = \mu_2 = \mu_3$$

The null hypothesis is that all the means are equal. In the grocery shopping example, we are concerned with the average number of hours of three different groups of women. As the term *analysis of variance* suggests, the problem requires comparing variances to make inferences about the means. The logic of this technique goes as follows: The variance among the means of the three groups will be large if these women differ significantly from one another in the number of hours spent shopping. By calculating the variance within the groups and the variance among the groups, we can determine if the means are significantly different.

analysis of variance (ANOVA)
Analysis involving the investigation of the effects of one treatment variable on an interval-scaled dependent variable; a hypothesis-testing technique to determine whether statistically significant differences on means occur among three or more groups.

RELATIONSHIPS AMONG VARIABLES

Many marketing questions deal with the association between two (or more) variables. Questions such as "Is sales productivity associated with pay incentives?", "Is socioeconomic status associated with the likelihood of purchasing a recreational

vehicle?", or "Does work status relate to attitudes toward the role of women in society?" can be answered by statistically investigating the relationships between the two variables in question.

In marketing, sales volume is often the dependent variable we wish to predict. The independent variables found to be associated with the dependent variable sales volume may be aspects of the marketing mix, such as price, number of salespeople, or amount of advertising, and/or uncontrollable variables, such as population or gross domestic product. For example, most managers would not be surprised to find that sales of baby strollers are associated with the number of babies born a few months prior to the sales period. In this case the dependent variable is the sales volume of baby strollers, and the independent variable is the number of babies born. The mathematical symbol X is commonly used for the independent variable, and Y typically denotes the dependent variable. It is appropriate to label dependent and independent variables only when it is assumed that the independent variable caused the dependent variable.

In many situations measures of differences, such as the chi-square test, provide information about whether two or more variables are associated. For example, a chi-square test between a measure of price consciousness and a measure of brand awareness provides some information about the independence or interrelationship of the two variables. Besides chi-square, statisticians have developed several other techniques as measures of association.

The type of measure used will influence the choice of the proper statistical **measure of association.** This chapter describes simple correlation (Pearson's product–moment correlation coefficient, r) and bivariate or simple regression. Both techniques require interval-scaled or ratio-scaled data.

Correlation Analysis

The most popular technique for indicating the relationship of one variable to another is simple correlation analysis. The **correlation coefficient** is a statistical measure of the covariation, or association, between two variables. The correlation coefficient, r, ranges from $+1.0$ to -1.0. If the value of r equals $+1.0$, there is a perfect positive linear (straight-line) relationship. If the value of r equals -1.0, there is a perfect negative linear relationship, or a perfect inverse relationship. No correlation is indicated if r equals 0. A correlation coefficient indicates both the magnitude of the linear relationship and the direction of that relationship. For example, if we find that $r = -.92$, we know we have a relatively strong inverse relationship—that is, the greater the value measured by variable X, the lower the value measured by variable Y.

measure of association
A general term that refers to a number of bivariate statistical techniques used to measure the strength of a relationship between two variables.

correlation coefficient
A statistical measure of the covariation, or association, between two variables.

The formula for calculating the correlation coefficient for two variables X and Y is as follows:

$$r_{xy} = r_{yx} = \frac{\Sigma(X_i - \bar{X})(Y_i - \bar{Y})}{\sqrt{\Sigma(X_i - \bar{X})^2 \Sigma(Y_i - \bar{Y})^2}}$$

where the symbols $\bar{X}$ and $\bar{Y}$ represent the sample averages of X and Y, respectively.

An alternative way to express the correlation formula is

$$r_{xy} = r_{yx} = \frac{\sigma_{xy}}{\sqrt{\sigma_x^2 \sigma_y^2}}$$

where

$$\sigma_x^2 = \text{variance of } X$$
$$\sigma_y^2 = \text{variance of } Y$$
$$\sigma_{xy} = \text{covariance of } X \text{ and } Y$$

with

$$\sigma_{xy} = \frac{\Sigma(X_i - \bar{X})(Y_i - \bar{Y})}{N}$$

If associated values of X_i and Y_i differ from their means in the same direction, their covariance will be positive. If the values of X_i and Y_i tend to deviate in opposite directions, their covariance will be negative.

The simple correlation coefficient actually is a standardized measure of covariance. In the formula the numerator represents covariance and the denominator is the square root of the product of the sample variances. Researchers find the correlation coefficient useful because they can compare two correlations without regard for the amount of variance exhibited by each variable separately.

Correlation and Causation

It is important to remember that correlation does not mean causation. No matter how highly correlated the rooster's crow is to the rising of the sun, the rooster does not cause the sun to rise. Consider the following common example that illustrates the difference between causation and correlation. The ice cream sales at a coastal city may correlate highly with the city's rate of deaths by drowning. However, concluding that ice cream consumption causes one to die by drowning would be ridiculous. Perhaps a third factor, a heat wave, may explain a hike in both the city's ice cream sales and the city's rate of drowning.

Coefficient of Determination

coefficient of determination (r^2)
A measure obtained by squaring the correlation coefficient; that proportion of the total variance of a variable that is accounted for by knowing the value of another variable.

If we wish to know the proportion of *variance* in Y that is explained by X (or vice versa), we can calculate the **coefficient of determination** by squaring the correlation coefficient:

$$r^2 = \frac{\text{Explained variance}}{\text{Total variance}}$$

The coefficient of determination, r^2, measures that part of the total variance of Y that is accounted for by knowing the value of X.

TABLE 18.4	**PEARSON PRODUCT-MOMENT CORRELATION MATRIX FOR SALESPERSON EXAMPLE**[a]									

Variables	S	JS	GE	SE	OD	VI	JT	RA	TP	WL
Performance (S)	1.00									
Job satisfaction (JS)	.45[b]	1.00								
Generalized self-esteem (GE)	.31[b]	.10	1.00							
Specific self-esteem (SE)	.61[b]	.28[b]	.36[b]	1.00						
Other-directedness (OD)	.05	−.03	−.44[b]	−.24[c]	1.00					
Verbal intelligence (VI)	−.36[b]	−.13	−.14	−.11	−.18[d]	1.00				
Job-related tension (JT)	−.48[b]	−.56[b]	−.32[b]	−.34[b]	.26[b]	−.02	1.00			
Role ambiguity (RA)	−.26[c]	−.24[c]	−.32[b]	−.39[b]	.38[b]	−.05	.44[b]	1.00		
Territory potential (TP)	.49[b]	.31[b]	.04	.29[b]	.09	−.09	−.38[b]	−.26[b]	1.00	
Work load (WL)	.45[b]	.11	.29[c]	.29[c]	−.04	−.12	−.27[c]	−.22[d]	.49[b]	1.00

[a] Numbers below the diagonal are for the sample; those above the diagonal are omitted.

[b] $p < .001$.

[c] $p < .01$.

[d] $p < .05$.

correlation matrix
The standard form for reporting correlational results.

Correlation Matrix

A **correlation matrix** is the standard form for reporting correlational results. It may be compared to a between–city mileage table, except that the research variables are substituted for cities and a coefficient of correlation is substituted for mileage. Table 18.4 shows a correlation matrix that relates some measures of sales force performance and job satisfaction to characteristics of the sales force, job attitudes from the Role Orientation Index, and territory work load.[2] You will encounter this type of matrix on many occasions. Note that the main diagonal consists of correlations of 1.00. This will always be the case when a variable is correlated with itself. The data in this example are from a survey of industrial salespeople selling steel and plastic strapping and seals used in shipping. Performance (S) was measured by identifying the salesperson's actual annual sales volume in dollars. Notice that the performance variable has a .45 correlation with the work-load variable (WL), which was measured by recording the number of accounts in the sales territory. Notice also that the salesperson's perception of job-related tension (JT) as measured on an attitude scale has a −.48 correlation with performance (S). Thus, when perceived job tension is high, performance is low. Of course, the correlation coefficients in these examples are moderate.

bivariate linear regression
A measure of linear association that investigates a straight-line relationship of the type $Y = \alpha + \beta X$, where Y is the dependent variable, X is the independent variable, and α and β are two parameters to be estimated.

Bivariate Linear Regression

Bivariate linear regression, also called simple linear regression, investigates a *straight-line relationship* of the type $Y = \alpha + \beta X$, where Y is the dependent variable, X is the independent variable, and α and β are two parameters to be estimated. The symbol α represents the Y intercept, and β is the slope coefficient. The slope β is the change in Y due to a corresponding change of one unit in X. The slope also may be thought of as *rise over run* (the rise in units on the Y-axis divided by the run in units along the X-axis).

Suppose a researcher is interested in forecasting sales for a construction distributor (wholesaler) in Winnipeg. Further, the distributor believes a reasonable association exists between sales and building permits issued by cities. Using bivariate

Dealer	Y Dealer's Sales Volume (thousands)	X Building Permits
1	77	86
2	79	93
3	80	95
4	83	104
5	101	139
6	117	180
7	129	165
8	120	147
9	97	119
10	106	132
11	99	126
12	121	156
13	103	129
14	86	96
15	99	108

TABLE 18.5 — RELATIONSHIP OF SALES POTENTIAL TO BUILDING PERMITS ISSUED

linear regression on the data in Table 18.5, the researcher will be able to estimate sales potential (Y) in various cities based on the number of building permits (X). To better illustrate the data in Table 18.5, we have plotted them on a scatter diagram (Exhibit 18.1). In the diagram the vertical axis indicates the value of the dependent variable, Y, and the horizontal axis indicates the value of the independent variable, X. Each single point in the diagram represents an observation of X and Y at a given point in time—that is, a paired value of X and Y. The relationship between X and Y could be "eyeballed"; that is, a straight line could be drawn through the points in the figure. However, this procedure is subject to human error: Two researchers might draw different lines to describe the same data.

The task of the researcher is to find the best means for fitting a straight line to the data. The least-squares method is a relatively simple mathematical technique for ensuring that the straight line will most closely represent the relationship between X and Y. The logic behind the least-squares technique goes as follows: No straight line can completely represent every dot in the scatter diagram; there will be a discrepancy between most of the actual scores (the dots) and the predicted score based on the regression line. Simply stated, any straight line drawn will generate errors. The least-squares method uses the criterion of attempting to make the least amount of total error in prediction of Y from X. More technically, the procedure used in the least-squares method generates a straight line that minimizes the sum of squared deviations of the actual values from this predicted regression line. With the symbol e representing the deviations of the dots from the line, the least-squares criterion is as follows:

$$\sum_{i=1}^{n} e_i^2 \text{ is minimum}$$

where

$e_i = Y_i - \hat{Y}_i$ (the residual)
Y_i = actual value of the dependent variable
$\hat{Y}_i$ = estimated value of the dependent variable ("Y hat")
n = number of observations
i = number of the particular observation

EXHIBIT 18.1 | SCATTER DIAGRAM AND EYEBALL FORECAST

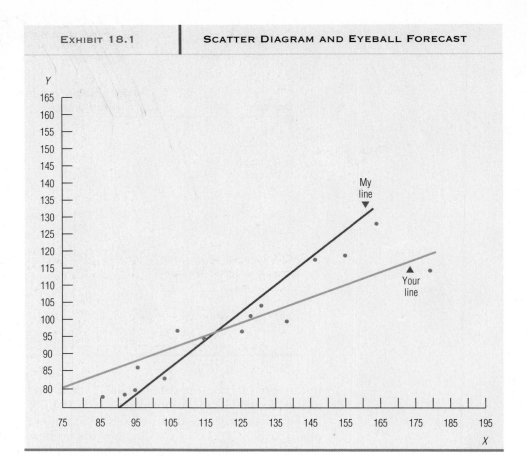

The general equation for a straight line is $Y = \alpha + \beta X$. A more appropriate estimating equation includes an allowance for error:

$$Y = \hat{\alpha} + \hat{\beta}X + e$$

The symbols $\hat{\alpha}$ and $\hat{\beta}$ are used when the equation is a regression estimate of the line. Thus, to compute the estimated values of α and β, we use the following formulas:

$$\hat{\beta} = \frac{n(\Sigma XY) - (\Sigma X)(\Sigma Y)}{n(\Sigma X^2) - (\Sigma X)^2}$$

and

$$\hat{\alpha} = \overline{Y} - \hat{\beta}\overline{X}$$

where

$\hat{\beta}$ = estimated slope of the line (the regression coefficient)
$\hat{\alpha}$ = estimated intercept of the Y-axis
Y = dependent variable
$\overline{Y}$ = mean of the dependent variable
X = independent variable
$\overline{X}$ = mean of the independent variable
n = number of observations

With simple arithmetic we can solve these equations for the data in Table 18.5; see Table 18.6. To estimate the relationship between the distributor's sales to a dealer and the number of building permits, we perform the following manipulations:

$$\hat{\beta} = \frac{n(\Sigma XY) - (\Sigma X)(\Sigma Y)}{n(\Sigma X^2) - (\Sigma X)^2}$$

$$= \frac{15(193,345) - 2,806,875}{15(245,759) - 3,515,625}$$

$$= \frac{2,900,175 - 2,806,875}{3,686,385 - 3,515,625}$$

$$= \frac{93,300}{170,760}$$

$$= .54638$$

$$\hat{\alpha} = \overline{Y} - \hat{\beta}\overline{X}$$

$$= 99.8 - .54638(125)$$

$$= 99.8 - 68.3$$

$$= 31.5$$

The formula $\hat{Y} = 31.5 + 0.546X$ is the regression equation used for the prediction of the dependent variable. Suppose the wholesaler is considering opening a new dealership in an area where the number of building permits equals 89. Sales in this area may be forecasted as

$$\hat{Y} = 31.5 + .546(X)$$

$$= 31.5 + .546(89)$$

$$= 31.5 + 48.6$$

$$= 80.1$$

TABLE 18.6		LEAST-SQUARES COMPUTATION			
	Y	**Y²**	**X**	**X²**	**XY**
1	77	5,929	86	7,396	6,622
2	79	6,241	93	8,649	7,347
3	80	6,400	95	9,025	7,600
4	83	6,889	104	10,816	8,632
5	101	10,201	139	19,321	14,039
6	117	13,689	180	32,400	21,060
7	129	16,641	165	27,225	21,285
8	120	14,400	147	21,609	17,640
9	97	9,409	119	14,161	11,543
10	106	11,236	132	17,424	13,992
11	99	9,801	126	15,876	12,474
12	121	14,641	156	24,336	18,876
13	103	10,609	129	16,641	13,287
14	86	7,396	96	9,216	8,256
15	99	9,801	108	11,664	10,692
	$\Sigma Y = 1,497$	$\Sigma Y^2 = 153,283$	$\Sigma X = 1,875$	$\Sigma X^2 = 245,759$	$\Sigma XY = 193,345$
	$\overline{Y} = 99.8$		$\overline{X} = 125$		

Thus the distributor may expect sales of 80.1 (or $80,100) in this new area.[3]

Calculation of the correlation coefficient gives an indication of how accurate the predictions are. In this example the correlation coefficient is $r = .9356$ and the coefficient of determination is $r^2 = .8754$.

Drawing a Regression Line

To draw a regression line on the scatter diagram, only two predicted values of Y need to be plotted.

$$\text{Dealer 7 (actual } Y \text{ value} = 129): \hat{Y}_7 = 31.5 + .546(165)$$
$$= 121.6$$
$$\text{Dealer 3 (actual } Y \text{ value} = 80): \hat{Y}_3 = 31.5 + .546(95)$$
$$= 83.4$$

Using the data for dealer 7 and dealer 3, we can draw a straight line connecting the points 121.6 and 83.4. Exhibit 18.2 shows the regression line.

To determine the error (residual) of any observation, the predicted value of Y is first calculated. The predicted value is then subtracted from the actual value. For example, the actual observation for dealer 3 is 80 (from Table 18.6), and the predicted value is 83.4; thus only a small margin of error, $e = -3.4$, is involved in this regression line:

$$e_i = Y_3 - \hat{Y}_3$$
$$= 80 - 83.4$$
$$= -3.4$$

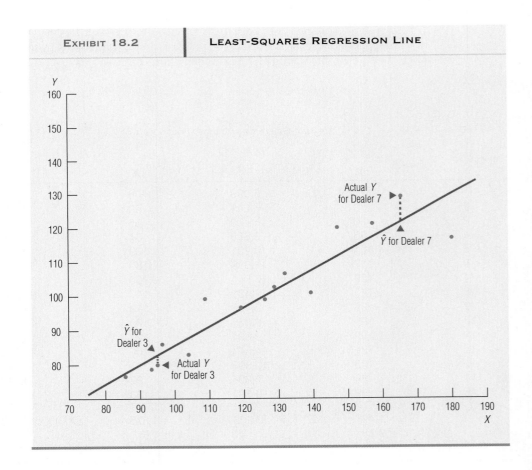

EXHIBIT 18.2 | LEAST-SQUARES REGRESSION LINE

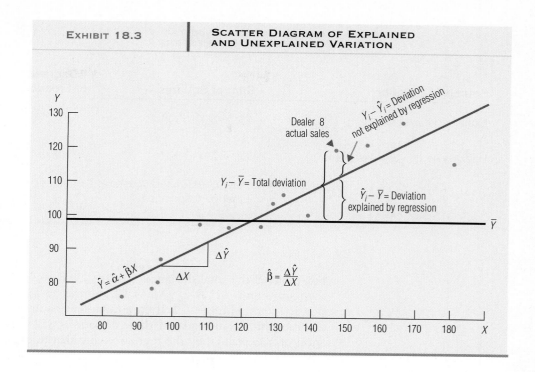

EXHIBIT 18.3	SCATTER DIAGRAM OF EXPLAINED AND UNEXPLAINED VARIATION

Test of Statistical Significance

Now that we have considered the error term, a more detailed look at explained and unexplained variation is possible. Exhibit 18.3 shows the fitted regression line. If a researcher wished to predict any dealer's sales volume (Y) without knowing the number of building permits (X), the best prediction would be the average sales volume ($\bar{Y}$) of all dealers. Suppose, for example, that a researcher wished to predict dealer 8's sales without knowing the value of X. The best estimate would be 99.8 ($\bar{Y} = 99.8$). Exhibit 18.3 shows that there would be a large error, because dealer 8's actual sales were 120. Once the regression line has been fitted, this error can be reduced. With the regression equation, dealer 8's sales are predicted to be 111.8, reducing the error from 20.2 ($Y_i - \bar{Y} = 120 - 99.8$) to 8.2 ($Y_i - \hat{Y} = 120 - 111.8$). Simply stated, error is reduced by using $Y_i - \hat{Y}_i$ rather than $Y_i - \bar{Y}$. The reduction in the error is the explained deviation due to the regression; the smaller number, 8.2, is the deviation not explained by the regression.

Thus the total deviation can be partitioned into two parts:

$$Y_i - \bar{Y} = (\hat{Y}_i - \bar{Y}) + (Y_i - \hat{Y}_i)$$

$$\begin{array}{c} \text{Total} \\ \text{deviation} \end{array} = \begin{array}{c} \text{Deviation} \\ \text{explained by} \\ \text{the regression} \end{array} + \begin{array}{c} \text{Deviation} \\ \text{unexplained by} \\ \text{the regression} \\ \text{(residual error)} \end{array}$$

where

$$\bar{Y} = \text{mean of the total group}$$
$$\hat{Y}_i = \text{value predicted with regression equation}$$
$$Y_i = \text{actual value}$$

TABLE 18.7   **ANALYSIS OF VARIANCE TABLE FOR BIVARIATE REGRESSION**

Source of Variation	Sum of Squares	Degrees of Freedom	Mean Square (Variance)
Explained by regression	$SS_r = \Sigma(\hat{Y}_i - \bar{Y})^2$	$k - 1$	$\dfrac{SS_r}{k-1}$
Unexplained by regression (error)	$SS_e = \Sigma(Y_i - \hat{Y}_i)^2$	$n - k$	$\dfrac{SS_e}{n-k}$

where k = number of estimated constants (variables)
n = number of observations

For dealer 8 the total deviation is $120 - 99.8 = 20.2$, the deviation explained by the regression is $111.8 - 99.8 = 12$, and the deviation unexplained by the regression is $120 - 111.8 = 8.2$. If these values are summed over all values of Y_i (that is, all observations) and squared, these deviations will provide an estimate of the variation of Y explained by the regression and that unexplained by the regression:

$$\Sigma(Y_i - \bar{Y})^2 = \Sigma(\hat{Y}_i - \bar{Y})^2 + \Sigma(Y_i - \hat{Y}_i)^2$$

$$\begin{array}{ccccc} \text{Total} & = & \text{Explained} & + & \text{Unexplained} \\ \text{variation} & & \text{variation} & & \text{variation} \\ & & & & \text{(residual)} \end{array}$$

We have thus partitioned the total sum of squares, SS_t, into two parts: the regression sum of squares, SS_r, and the error sum of squares, SS_e.

$$SS_t = SS_r + SS_e$$

F-test (regression)
A procedure to determine whether more variability is explained by the regression or unexplained by the regression.

An **F-test**, or an *analysis of variance,* can be applied to a regression to test the relative magnitudes of SS_r and SS_e with their appropriate degrees of freedom. Table 18.7 shows the technique for conducting the F-test.

For the example on sales forecasting, the analysis of variance summary table, which shows relative magnitudes of the mean square, is presented in Table 18.8. From Table A.6 in the appendix we find that the F-value of 91.3, with 1 degree of freedom in the numerator and 13 degrees of freedom in the denominator, exceeds the probability level of .01.

The *coefficient of determination, r^2,* reflects the proportion of variance explained by the regression line. The formula for calculating r^2 is

$$r^2 = \frac{SS_r}{SS_t} = 1 - \frac{SS_e}{SS_t}$$

TABLE 18.8   **ANALYSIS OF VARIANCE SUMMARY TABLE FOR REGRESSION OF SALES ON BUILDING PERMITS**

Source of Variation	Sum of Squares	Degrees of Freedom	Mean Square	F-Value
Explained by regression	3,389.49	1	3,398.49	91.30
Unexplained by regression (error)	483.91	13	37.22	
Total	3,882.40	14		

TO THE POINT

Forecasting is like trying to drive a car blindfolded and following directions given by a person who is looking out the back window.

ANONYMOUS

For our example r^2 is .875:

$$r^2 = \frac{3,398.49}{3,882.40} = .875$$

The coefficient of determination may be interpreted to mean that 87 percent of the variation in sales was explained by associating the variable with building permits.

MULTIPLE REGRESSION ANALYSIS

multiple regression analysis
An analysis of association in which the effects of two or more independent variables on a single, interval-scaled dependent variable are investigated simultaneously.

As we have seen, the investigation of one variable at a time is referred to as *univariate analysis* and the investigation of the relationship between two variables is called *bivariate analysis*. When problems are multidimensional and involve three or more variables, we use *multivariate statistical analysis*. Multivariate statistical methods allow us to consider the effects of more than one variable at the same time. For example, suppose a forecaster wishes to estimate oil consumption for the next five years. While consumption might be predicted by past oil consumption records alone, adding additional variables such as average number of kilometres driven per year, coal production, and nuclear plants under construction may give greater insight into the determinants of oil consumption. Multivariate analysis will be illustrated in our discussion of multiple regression analysis.

Multiple regression analysis is an extension of bivariate regression analysis that allows for simultaneous investigation of the effect of two or more independent variables on a single, interval-scaled dependent variable. In the previous section, we illustrated bivariate linear regression analysis with an example concerning a construction dealer's sales volume. In that example, variations in the dependent variable were attributed to changes in a single independent variable. Reality, however, suggests that several factors are likely to affect such a dependent variable. For example, sales volume might be hypothesized to depend not only on the number of building permits but also on price levels, amount of advertising, and income of consumers in the area. Thus the problem requires identification of a linear relationship with multiple regression analysis. The multiple regression equation is

$$Y = \alpha + \beta_1 X_1 + \beta_2 X_2 + \beta_3 X_3 + \ldots + \beta_n X_n$$

Another forecasting example is useful for illustrating multiple regression. Assume that a toy manufacturer wishes to forecast sales by sales territory. It is thought that competitors' sales, the presence or absence of a company salesperson in the territory (a binary variable), and grammar school enrollment are the independent variables that might explain the variation in sales. The data appear in Table 18.9. Following are the statistical results from multiple regression after mathematical computations have been made.

Regression equation: $Y = 102.18 + .387X_1 + 115.2X_2 + 6.73X_3$

Coefficient of multiple determination (R^2): .845
F-value: 14.6

The regression equation indicates that sales are positively related to X_1, X_2, and X_3. The coefficients (βs) show the effect on the dependent variable of a 1–unit increase in any of the independent variables. The value $\beta_2 = 115.2$ indicates that an increase of \$115,200 (000 included) in toy sales is expected with each additional unit of X_2. Thus it appears that adding a company salesperson will have a very positive effect on sales. Elementary school enrollments also may help predict sales. An increase of 1 unit of enrollment (1,000 students) indicates a sales increase of \$6,730 (000 included). A 1–unit increase in competitors' sales volume (X_1) in the territory adds little to the toy manufacturer's sales (\$387).

TABLE 18.9	DATA FOR A MULTIPLE REGRESSION PROBLEM		
Y Sales (000)	X_1 Competitors' Sales (000)	X_2 Salesperson (1) or Agent (0)	X_3 Elementary School Enrollment (000)
222	106	0	23
304	213	0	18
218	201	0	22
501	378	1	20
542	488	0	21
790	509	1	31
523	644	0	17
667	888	1	25
700	941	1	32
869	1,066	1	36
444	307	0	30
479	312	1	22

In multiple regression the coefficients β_1, β_2, and so on, are called *coefficients of partial regression*. Each independent variable is usually correlated with the other independent variables. The correlation between Y and X_1, with the correlation that X_1 and X_2 have in common with Y held constant, is the *partial correlation*. Because the partial correlation between sales and X_1 has been adjusted for the effect produced by variation in X_2 (and other independent variables), the correlation coefficient obtained from the bivariate regression will not be the same as the partial coefficient in the multiple regression. In other words, the original value of β is the simple bivariate regression coefficient. In multiple regression, the coefficient β_1 is defined as the partial regression coefficient for which the effects of other independent variables are held constant.

As in bivariate regression, the *coefficient of multiple determination,* or multiple index of determination, indicates the percentage of variation in Y explained by the variation in the independent variables. The value of $R^2 = .845$ in our example tells us that the variation in the independent variables accounted for 84.5 percent of the variance in the dependent variable. Typically, introducing additional independent variables into the regression equation explains more of the variation in Y than it is possible to explain with fewer variables. In other words, the amount of variation explained by two independent variables in the same equation is usually greater than the variation in Y explained by either one separately.

To test for statistical significance, an F-test is necessary to compare the different sources of variation. The F-test allows for testing of the relative magnitudes of the sum of squares due to the regression (SS_r) and the error sum of squares (SS_e), with their appropriate degrees of freedom:

$$F = \frac{(SS_r)/k}{(SS_e)/(n - k - 1)}$$

where

k = number of independent variables
n = number of observations

Table A.5 in the appendix shows the F-distributions for hypothesis testing at the .05 significance level. For our example the F-ratio equals 14.6. Degrees of freedom ($d.f.$) are calculated as follows:

$$d.f. \text{ for the numerator} = k$$
$$d.f. \text{ for the denominator} = n - k - 1$$

For this example,

$$d.f. \text{ (numerator)} = 3$$
$$d.f. \text{ (denominator)} = 12 - 3 - 1 = 8$$

Table A.5 indicates that an F-value of 4.07 or more is necessary to reject the null hypothesis at the .05 level of statistical significance. Thus it can be concluded that the estimated functional relationship is not due to chance or random variation; there does appear to be an association between the dependent and independent variables other than random variation in the data.

A continuous, interval-scaled dependent variable is required in multiple regression, as in bivariate regression. Interval scaling is also required for the independent variables; however, dummy variables, such as the binary variable in our example, may be used. A *dummy variable* is a variable that has two (or more) distinct levels that are coded as 0 and 1.

There are several other assumptions needed for multiple regression, all of which require advanced study. Several excellent technical books deal with this topic.[4] The availability of commercial computer programs allows the researcher to compute multiple regressions without a great deal of effort.

SUMMARY

① ② In many situations two variables are interrelated, or associated. Many bivariate statistical techniques can be used to measure this association. Researchers select the appropriate technique based on each variable's scale of measurement. Tests of difference investigate hypotheses stating that two (or more) groups differ with respect to a certain behaviour, characteristic, or attitude. Both the type of measurement and the number of groups to be compared influence researchers' choice of the type of statistical test of difference.

③ The chi-square statistic allows the researcher to test whether an observed sample distribution fits some given distribution. It can be used to analyze contingency with cross-tabulation tables. In this case, the test allows the researcher to determine whether two groups are independent. If they are not, the variables are interrelated.

④ Either a Z-test or a t-test for two independent samples is used to determine whether the means of two independent samples are significantly different. The t-test should be chosen over the Z-test if the population standard deviation is unknown and if the sample size is small (fewer than 30). Similarly, a t-test or Z-test for two independent samples may be used to determine whether two proportions are significantly different.

One-way analysis of variance (ANOVA) compares the means of samples from two or more populations to determine whether their differences are statistically significant.

⑤ Useful and practical marketing questions, such as whether age group or income level influence product purchases and whether men and women react differently to price promotions, can be answered using appropriate statistical techniques described in this chapter.

⑥ ⑦ Simple correlation is the measure of the relationship of one variable to another. The correlation coefficient (r) indicates the strength of the association of two variables and the direction of that association. Correlation does not prove causation, as variables other than those being measured may be involved. The coefficient of determination (r^2) measures the amount of the total variance in the dependent variable that is accounted for by knowing the value of the independent variable. The results of a correlation computation often are presented in a correlation matrix.

Bivariate linear regression investigates a straight-line relationship between one dependent variable and one independent variable. The regression can be done intuitively by plotting a scatter diagram of the X and Y points and drawing a line to fit the observed relationship. The least-squares method mathematically determines the best-fitting regression line for the observed data. The line determined by this method may be used to forecast values of the dependent variable given a value for the independent variable. The goodness of the line's fit may be evaluated by calculating the coefficient of determination.

Multiple regression analysis is an extension of bivariate regression analysis that allows for simultaneous investigation of the effect of two or more independent variables on a single, interval-scaled dependent variable.

Key Terms and Concepts

test of differences	analysis of variance (ANOVA)	correlation matrix
cross-tabulation (contingency table)	measure of association	bivariate linear regression
chi-square test for	correlation coefficient	F-test (regression)
a contingency table	coefficient of determination (r^2)	multiple regression analysis

Questions for Review and Critical Thinking

1. What tests of difference are appropriate in the following situations?
   a. Average campaign contributions of Liberals, Conservatives, and independents are to be compared.
   b. Advertising managers and brand managers have responded "yes," "no," or "not sure" to an attitude question. Their answers are to be compared.
   c. One-half of a sample received an incentive in a mail survey; the other half did not. A comparison of response rates is desired.
   d. A researcher believes that married men will push the grocery cart when grocery shopping with their wives.

2. What type of analysis should be used to analyze the following data on responses to the statement "Regulation is the best way to ensure safe products"?

	Managers	Blue-Collar Workers
Agree	58	66
Disagree	34	24
No opinion	8	10
Totals	100	100

3. A store manager's computer-generated list of all retail sales employees indicates that 70 percent are full-time employees, 20 percent are part-time employees, and 10 percent are laid-off employees. A sample of 50 employees from the list indicates that 40 are full-time employees, 6 are part-time employees, and 4 are laid-off employees. What statistical test should be used to determine whether the sample is representative of the population?

4. A sales force ($n = 67$) received some management-by-objectives training. The mean scores for salespeople's job performance are shown below. What type of data analysis is appropriate?

Skill	Before	After
Planning ability	4.84	5.43
Territory coverage	5.24	5.51
Activity reporting	5.37	5.42

5. The incomes of owners of garbage compactors were compared with those of nonowners. The average income in a sample of 200 was as follows:

	Owners	Nonowners
$\bar{X}$	4.6	3.5

Higher values represent higher levels of income. (Actual scaled average: less than $7,500 = 1; $7,501–$15,000 = 2; $15,001–$25,000 = 3; $25,001–$40,000 = 4; $40,001–$60,000 = 5; over $60,000 = 6.) Is a t-test appropriate?

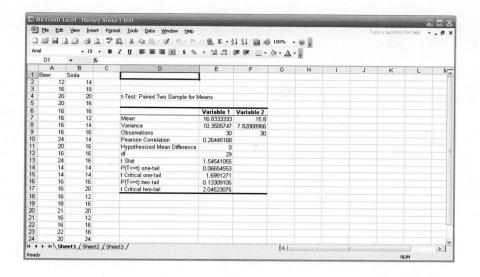

Spreadsheet contents:

	A	B	C	D	E	F
1	Beer	Soda				
2	12	14				
3	16	18				
4	20	20		t-Test: Paired Two Sample for Means		
5	20	16				
6	16	16			Variable 1	Variable 2
7	16	12		Mean	16.8333333	15.8
8	16	14		Variance	10.3505747	7.82068966
9	16	16		Observations	30	30
10	24	14		Pearson Correlation	0.26445168	
11	20	16		Hypothesized Mean Difference	0	
12	16	16		df	29	
13	24	16		t Stat	1.54541055	
14	14	14		P(T<=t) one-tail	0.06654553	
15	14	14		t Critical one-tail	1.6991271	
16	16	16		P(T<=t) two tail	0.13309106	
17	16	20		t Critical two-tail	2.04523076	
18	16	12				
19	18	16				
20	21	20				
21	16	12				
22	16	16				
23	22	16				
24	20	24				

6. An Excel Spreadsheet is reprinted above. Interpret the *t*-test results. Are they statistically significant?

7. The discussion in this chapter is limited to linear relationships. Try to diagram some nonlinear relationships that show *r* values of zero using the test methods shown in the text.

8. Comment on the following:
   a. Suppose John A. Macdonald answered a survey questionnaire and indicated he had not received a gradeschool diploma. The researcher found that Macdonald's educational score did not correlate highly with the expected variables. What was wrong?
   b. An international marketer has said, "When political instability increases, the price of quality increases." Is this a testable hypothesis?
   c. In 8 out of 11 years, when a racehorse won the Triple Crown (Kentucky Derby, Preakness, and Belmont Stakes), the stock market dropped.

9. A manufacturer of disposable washcloths/wipes told a retailer that sales for this product category closely correlated with sales of disposable diapers. The retailer thought he would check this out for his own sales-forecasting purposes. The researcher tells him, "Disposable washcloth/wipes sales can be predicted with knowledge of disposable diaper sales." Is this the right thing to say?

Exploring the Internet

1. SPSS is one of the most widely popular statistical software packages for social sciences. Visit and browse www.spss.com/ to find out marketing applications and uses of the software package.

2. Visit the homepage for the Minitab statistical software package: www.minitab.com/. The Web site provides information about product features, technical support, and trial versions for students.

3. Visit http://freestatistics.tk/. You will find a number of free downloadable or online statistical software packages. You will also find a number of teaching and learning tools on basic and more advanced statistics.

4. Visit http://StatCrunch.com. StatCrunch is a statistical data analysis package for the World Wide Web, developed by Dr. West from the University of South Carolina. It has the minimal requirement of a Java-capable Web browser to run most of the common statistical analyses.

5. Go to the Chance Web site at www.dartmouth.edu/~chance/ChanceLecture/AudioVideo.html and view the very interesting streaming video "Streaks in Sports."

In the design of advertisements, the characteristics of the users of a product category are important determinants of the design and delivery decisions of the advertisements. For instance, if the product is frequently purchased by men under age 35 who are seeking simple, functional aspects of the product, more effective advertisements may be designed communicating the functional aspects of the product.

Dr. Bianca Grohmann and Dr. H. Onur Bodur conducted a study with the purpose of understanding how college students vary in their product purchases and the aspects they seek in various product categories.[5] As a first step, they collected data about frequency of purchase, frequency of use, attitudes toward the product, and other relevant information regarding a variety of products and demographic information. Based on their first study, it appeared that certain products were purchased more often than others. The exhibit below, based on their first study involving 77 participants from the Montreal area, indicates whether participants frequently purchase a selection of products. A 9-point Likert-type scale with anchors "1 = Strongly Disagree" and "9 = Strongly Agree" was used to measure agreement to the following statement: "I frequently purchase ————."

FREQUENCY OF PURCHASES FOR MEN AND WOMEN

Product Category	Male		Female				
	Mean	Std. Dev.	Mean	Std. Dev.	t-Stats	DF	Significance
Alkaline Batteries	2.85	2.11	3.07	2.47	−0.411	75	0.683
Beer	4.21	3.25	6.61	2.95	−3.385	75	0.001
Laundry Detergent	6.58	2.75	3.84	3.15	3.974	75	<0.001
Video Games	4.82	2.76	7.89	2.03	−5.635	75	<0.001
Athletic Shoes	4.45	2.66	4.10	2.73	0.301	75	0.766
Toilet Paper	5.24	2.99	3.59	3.19	2.310	75	0.024
Dental Floss	6.48	2.81	3.68	2.83	4.319	75	<0.001

Questions

1. Which products are purchased more frequently by men?
2. Which products are purchased more frequently by women?
3. Based on the t-test results comparing men and women, what are some of the basic implications for companies marketing these products?

Despite the redesign of its Web site and online banking services, Canada Trust, a major Canadian bank, was not satisfied with the percentage of its clients using the Internet for their routine banking transactions. Only 51 percent of its clients used the bank's Web site for personal banking services. This number was up from 46 percent following Canada Trust's advertising campaign to increase customers' awareness about the online services. In a pilot study to understand why people liked online banking, Canada Trust sent out a mail survey to 300 randomly selected clients and received back 60 completed surveys. Canada Trust asked questions about how clients use the Internet, what they use for their Internet access, their type of Internet access, clients' online shopping behaviour, their beliefs about the Internet, and a set of demographic questions, such as age, income, and gender. Clients' beliefs about online banking are measured using a five-point Likert-type scale with end points "1 = Strongly Disagree" and "5 = Strongly Agree." Higher values indicate greater agreement with the statement. The results are shown in Case Exhibits 18.2.1 and Exhibit 18.2.2.

Questions

1. In Exhibit 18.2.1, results from a cross-tabulation between gender and whether the client uses the Internet for online banking are displayed. Exhibit 18.2.1 also presents the chi-square test results. Review these exhibits and interpret the findings.
2. Review the results presented in Exhibit 18.2.2. Explain whether there are any differences between the beliefs of customers who use online banking and those who do not.

GENDER AND USE OF INTERNET FOR BANKING CROSS-TABULATION

			Use Internet for Banking		
			No	Yes	Total
Gender	Male	Count	10	24	34
		% within Gender	29.4%	70.6%	100.0%
	Female	Count	20	6	26
		% within Gender	76.9%	23.1%	100.0%
Total		Count	30	30	60
		% within Gender	50.0%	50.0%	100.0%

CHI-SQUARE TESTS

	Value	df	Asymp. Sig. (2-sided)	Exact Sig. (2-sided)	Exact Sig. (1-sided)
Pearson Chi-Square	13.303(b)	1	.000		
Continuity Correction(a)	11.471	1	.001		
Likelihood Ratio	13.893	1	.000		
Fisher's Exact Test				.001	.000
Linear-by-Linear Association	13.081	1	.000		
N of Valid Cases	60				

a Computed only for a 2x2 table
b 0 cells (.0%) have expected count less than 5. The minimum expected count is 13.00.

GROUP STATISTICS

	Use Internet for Banking	N	Mean	Std. Deviation	Std. Error Mean
Online banking is easy to use	No	30	2.00	.910	.166
	Yes	30	1.33	.479	.088
Using the Internet for banking is not safe	No	30	3.20	1.186	.217
	Yes	30	2.53	1.383	.252
Online banking is convenient	No	30	1.73	.944	.172
	Yes	30	1.13	.346	.063
Online banking is enjoyable	No	30	3.27	.944	.172
	Yes	30	2.33	.959	.175
Online banking can be expensive	No	30	2.27	1.143	.209
	Yes	30	1.80	1.186	.217
Overall, the Internet is secure for purchases and financial transactions	No	30	3.27	1.143	.209
	Yes	30	2.53	1.332	.243

(continued)

INDEPENDENT SAMPLES TEST

		Levene's Test for Equality of Variances		t-test for Equality of Means						95% Confidence Interval of the Difference	
		F	Sig.	t	df	Sig. (2-tailed)	Mean Difference	Std. Error Difference		Lower	Upper
Online banking is easy to use	Equal variances assumed	3.766	.057	3.551	58	.001	.667	.188		.291	1.042
	Equal variances not assumed			3.551	43.957	.001	.667	.188		.288	1.045
Using the internet for banking is not safe	Equal variances assumed	3.646	.061	2.004	58	.050	.667	.333		.001	1.333
	Equal variances not assumed			2.004	56.684	.050	.667	.333		.000	1.333
Online banking is convenient	Equal variances assumed	28.186	.000	3.268	58	.002	.600	.184		.232	.968
	Equal variances not assumed			3.268	36.636	.002	.600	.184		.228	.972
Online banking is enjoyable	Equal variances assumed	.003	.955	3.798	58	.000	.933	.246		.441	1.425
	Equal variances not assumed			3.798	57.987	.000	.933	.246		.441	1.425
Online banking can be expensive	Equal variances assumed	.003	.957	1.552	58	.126	.467	.301		−.135	1.069
	Equal variances not assumed			1.552	57.919	.126	.467	.301		−.135	1.069
Overall, the Internet is secure for purchases and financial transactions	Equal variances assumed	1.840	.180	2.289	58	.026	.733	.320		.092	1.375
	Equal variances not assumed			2.289	56.686	.026	.733	.320		.092	1.375

SPSS Instructions for Chapter 18

To follow these instructions, you will need to install SPSS 14.0 Student version included with your book and the *luxury2.sav* data file available from the Web site: www.effectivemarketingresearch.nelson.com

This section explains using SPSS for calculating bivariate correlations, testing differences, and regression analysis.

A. COMPARING MEANS OF TWO GROUPS (IS $\mu_1 = \mu_2$?)

Step 1: Select the following menu items: Analyze > Compare Means > Independent Samples *t*-test.

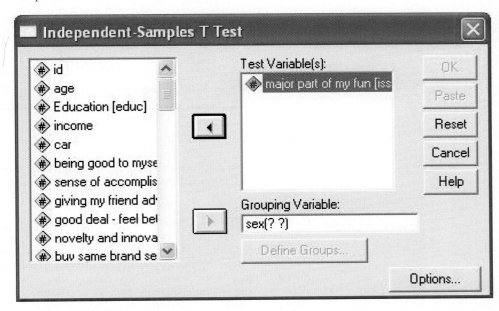

Step 2: Highlight the variables (interval/ratio scale) whose means you wish to compare and click on the right arrow for the "test variables."

Step 3: Highlight the grouping or segmentation variable. This should be an ordinal or nominal scale variable with only two values. Click on the right arrow for "grouping variable." Click on the "define groups" button. In the Define Groups dialogue box that opens up, click on "Use specified values" and then enter the values corresponding to your two groups in the boxes "Group 1" and "Group 2." For example, if your grouping variable is SEX, and you have coded Male as "1" and Female as "0", enter values 0 and 1 and corresponding labels "female" and "male" respectively. Click "Continue."

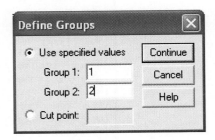

Step 4: Back in the Independent Samples dialogue box, click OK.
Note that you can enter more than one "test variable" before clicking OK. But you cannot enter more than one "grouping variable."

B. CALCULATING CORRELATIONS

Step 1: Select the following menu items: Analyze > Correlate > Bivariate Correlations.
Step 2: In the Bivariate Correlations dialogue box, highlight the variable(s) you want to calculate the correlations for and click on the right arrow (▶).

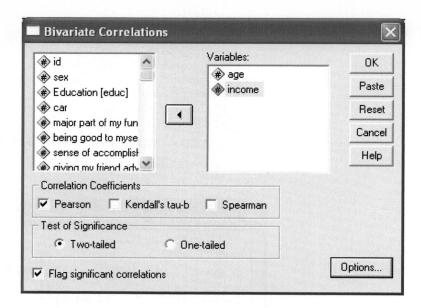

Step 3: By default, you will see that the "Pearson" Correlations coefficient will be calculated. Click other options if necessary.

Step 4: By default, it will apply a two-tailed significance test. Click "One–tailed" if necessary.

Step 5: By default, it will flag significant correlations with stars (★). Uncheck if you prefer otherwise.

C. REGRESSION ANALYSIS

Step 1: Select the following menu items: Analyze > Regression > Linear.

Step 2: In the "Linear Regression" dialogue box, highlight the dependent variable of interest and click on the right arrow (▶) next to "Dependent" box on the top.

Step 3: Highlight the independent variable(s) you want to use and click on the right arrow (▶) next to "Independents" box.

Step 4: You do not need additional options for basic analysis. However, you can explore Statistics, Plots, Save, and Options dialogue boxes.

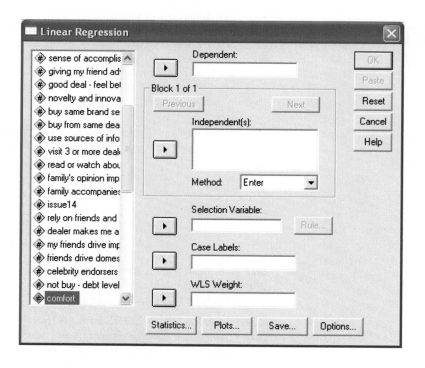

COMMUNICATING
RESEARCH RESULTS:
Research Report,
Oral Presentation,
and Research
Follow-Up

The marketing research project is not complete until the findings are presented to the client, whether the client is internal or external to the company. Although it may seem a mere formality, the communication of the research results is one of the most important stages in the marketing research process. No matter how well the project was designed, how carefully the data were obtained and analyzed, and how much time and effort were spent, the project is only as successful as the effectiveness of the communication to the clients.

As one expert from the marketing research industry notes, the success of marketing research departments or companies today depends on staff that have strong writing and oral presentation skills in addition to a wide array of research skills.[1]

What does the marketing research report mean to the clients? A research project conducted with 155 marketing managers from firms with sales volumes of at least $1 billion annually explored the most important determinants of clients' satisfaction with the marketing research services they received. The average overall satisfaction reported by the marketing research clients was 5.70 on a 7-point scale, with 7 indicating complete satisfaction—these findings were similar to those of previous studies. The results revealed that marketing research clients consider product quality (as opposed to cost management, timeliness of the project, or service quality) to be the most important aspect of a research project. The product, of course, is the tangible research report that the clients receive and on which they base their decisions. Interestingly, only 46 percent of the clients that participated in the study were completely satisfied with their research firm's performance in one critical aspect of the research report quality: "Whether the analysis of the results was useful." This finding can be related to a mismatch between the problem definition and the conclusions of the report, a poor interpretation of the research findings, or simply ineffective communication. The importance of communicating the research results to the clients is further amplified by

What you will learn in this chapter

1 To explain how the research report is the crucial means for communicating the whole research project.

2 To discuss the format and the components of the research report.

3 To discuss the importance of using graphics in research reporting.

4 To explain how tables and charts are useful for presenting numerical information and how to interpret their various components.

5 To identify the various types of research charts.

6 To discuss how an oral presentation may be the most efficient means of supplementing the written report.

7 To understand the importance of research follow-up.

the fact that repeat business and establishment of a long-term relationship with the clients depend on their overall satisfaction with the marketing research service.[2]

In this chapter, we explain how research reports, oral presentations, and follow-up conversations can be used to better communicate research results.[3] ■

COMMUNICATING THE RESEARCH RESULTS

Communicating the research report is one of the most important stages of the marketing research project. It is extremely optimistic to assume that the communication of the research project will be smooth and effortless. For starters, when communicating the completed marketing research project, the writer or the presenter of the report and the audience (i.e., the manager of the company or the organization that will make the decision based on the information provided) each has individual fields of experience. These overlap to some extent; otherwise no communication would be possible. Nevertheless, there is much experience that is not common to both parties. The terminology and approach used by the writer or the presenter of the report may make sense to her based on her field of experience. However, the manager may decode the message provided by the report differently, based on his own fields of experience. The communication of the marketing research report is successful only if both parties share enough common experience for it to be encoded, transmitted, and decoded with roughly the same meaning.

In the research setting, there is a communicator (the researcher) who has spent a great deal of time studying a problem. The researcher has looked at secondary sources, gathered primary data, used statistical techniques to analyze the data, and reached conclusions. When the report on the project is written, all this "baggage" will affect its contents. A researcher may assume that the reader has a lot of background information on the project and produce pages and pages of unexplained tables, assuming the reader will unearth from them the same patterns that the researcher has observed. The report may contain technical terms such as *parameter, F-distribution, hypothesis test, correlations,* and *eigenvalue,* on the assumption that the reader will understand them. Another researcher may assume that the reader does not have a lot of background information and may go overboard explaining everything in the report in terms that are too simple. Although the researcher's intent is to ensure that the reader will not get lost, he or she may insult the reader in the process.

Usually when readers receive a report, they have not thought much about the project. They may not know anything about statistics and most likely have many other responsibilities. If the report cannot be understood quickly, they may put it on a stack of things to do someday.

Simply delivering a report to its audience is not sufficient to ensure that it gets attention. The report needs to be written so as to draw on the common experience of the researcher and the reader. And it is the writer's responsibility to make sure that it does so—not the reader's. Unless a report is really crucial, a busy reader will not spend time and effort struggling through an inadequate or difficult-to-read document.

THE RESEARCH REPORT

research report
An oral presentation or written statement of research results, strategic recommendations, and/or other conclusions to a specific audience.

A **research report** is an oral, written, or digital statement whose purpose is to communicate the purpose of the report, the research questions, methodology, research results, strategic recommendations, and/or other conclusions to management or other specific audiences. In this chapter we will focus on the final *written* report and the *presentation* that an extensive research project requires. However, remember that the final report may vary in its specificity depending on the extent and complexity of the project. For

Never use a long word where a diminutive one will do.

instance, for a small project, a shorter written report focusing on the results may be all that is needed. For more complex projects, written reports at different stages of the project followed by a comprehensive final written report may be more appropriate. In addition, given the reliance of marketing research companies and client companies on the Internet, the report may be made available to the company on the Internet. Most of the detailed technical materials may be posted on an organization's intranet.

The chapter's emphasis on the final report should not be taken to mean that other communications, such as progress reports during the course of the project, are any less important to the project's eventual success. The chapter's suggestions can be easily adapted to apply to shorter, less formal reports as well as reports using other hybrid modes of communication.

ORGANIZATION OF THE WRITTEN RESEARCH REPORT

report format
The makeup or arrangement of parts necessary to a good research report.

Although every research report is custom-made for the project it represents, some conventions of **report format** are universal. They represent a consensus about the parts necessary for a good research report and how they should be ordered. This consensus is not a law, however. Every book on report writing suggests the use of its own unique format, and every report writer has to pick and choose the section and order that will work best for the project at hand. Many companies and universities also have in-house report formats or writing guides for writers to follow. The format presented below serves as a starting point from which a writer can shape his or her own appropriate format.

1. Title page (sometimes preceded by a title fly page)
2. Letter of transmittal
3. Table of contents (and lists of figures and tables)
4. Executive summary
   - (a) Objectives
   - (b) Results
   - (c) Conclusions
   - (d) Recommendations
5. Introduction
6. Research objectives
7. Methodology
8. Results
9. Conclusions and recommendations
10. Limitations
11. Appendix
    - (a) Data collection forms
    - (b) Detailed calculations
    - (c) General tables
    - (d) Bibliography
    - (e) Other support material

Tailoring the Format to the Written Research Project

The format of a research report may need to be adjusted for two reasons: (1) to obtain the proper level of formality and (2) to decrease the complexity of the report. The format given here is for the most formal type of report, such as one for a large project done within an organization or one done by a research agency for a client company. This type of report is usually bound in a permanent cover and may be hundreds of pages long.

In less formal reports, each part is shorter and some parts are omitted. The situation may be compared to the way people's clothing varies according to the formality of the occasion. The most formal report is dressed, so to speak, in a tuxedo or long evening gown. It includes the full assortment of prefatory parts—title page, letters of transmittal, and table of contents. Like changing into an everyday business suit, dropping down to the next level of formality involves eliminating parts of the prefatory material that are not needed in this situation and reducing the complexity of the report body. In general, as the report moves down through the sport coat and slacks and then blue jeans stages, more prefatory parts are dropped and the complexity and length of the report body are reduced.

How does the researcher decide on the appropriate level of formality? The general rule is to include all the parts needed for effective communication in the particular circumstances—and no more. This depends on how far up in management the report is expected to go and how routine the matter is. A researcher's immediate supervisor does not need a 100-page, full report on a routine project. A longer written report may be less likely to be read and gather dust. A parsimonious, clear communication is preferred. However, the board of directors does not want a one-page report on a big project that backs a major expansion program. The full report to top management may later be stripped of some of the prefatory parts (and thus reduced in formality) for wider circulation within the company.

The Components of the Written Research Report

Title Page

The *title page* should state the title of the report, for whom the report was prepared (the client), by whom it was prepared (the name of the research firm), and the date of release or presentation. The title should give a brief but complete indication of the purpose of the research project. Addresses and titles of the preparer and recipient may also be included. On confidential reports, a list of the people to whom the report should be circulated may be supplied. For the most formal reports, a title fly page should precede the title page; only the title appears on this page.

Letter of Transmittal

The *letter of transmittal* is included in relatively formal and very formal reports. Its purpose is to release or deliver the report to the recipient. It also serves to establish some rapport between the reader and the writer. This is the one part of the formal report in which a personal or even slightly informal tone should be used. The transmittal should not dive into the report findings except in the broadest terms. The letter may comment generally on findings and matters of interest regarding the research. A closing section may be added to express the writer's personal interest in the project just completed and in doing additional, related work.

Table of Contents

A *table of contents* is essential to any report more than a few pages long. It should list the divisions and subdivisions of the report with page references. The table of contents is based on the final outline of the report, but it should include only the first-level subdivisions. For short reports it is sufficient to include only the main divisions. The table of contents should be followed by a list of tables, figures, and other supplementary materials.

Executive Summary

The *executive summary* briefly explains the objectives of the research project, what aspects of the problem were considered, what the key findings were, and what should be done. It is a vital part of the report. Studies have indicated that nearly all managers read a report's executive summary, while only a minority read the rest of the report. Thus the writer's only chance to produce an impact may be in the executive summary.

The summary should be written only after the rest of the report has been completed. It represents the essence of the report. This is a difficult section to write, because it has to be short, yet still communicate the objectives and the findings of the report. The writer must carefully consider what is important enough to be included in the one-page (at most two pages) executive summary. Several pages of the full report may have to be condensed into one summarizing sentence. Different parts of the report may be condensed more than others; the number of words in the executive summary need not be in proportion to the length of the section being discussed. The executive summary should be written to be self-sufficient; in fact, the summary is often detached from the report and circulated by itself.

The executive summary contains four elements. First, it states the objectives of the report, including the most important background information and the specific purposes of the project. Second, it presents the methodology and the major results. Next come the conclusions. These are opinions based on the results and constitute an interpretation of the results. Finally come recommendations, or suggestions for action, based on the conclusions. In many cases managers prefer not to have recommendations included in the report or executive summary. Whether recommendations are to be included should be clear from the particular context of the report.

Introduction

The **introduction section** presents the general context and the background factors that made the project necessary. It explains why the project was done, what it aimed to discover, and what decisions it aimed to aid. The *relevant* background comes next. Enough background should be included to explain why the project was worth doing, but unessential historical factors should be omitted. Including unessential facts and information is a common mistake in written reports. The question of how much is enough should be answered by referring to the needs of the audience. A government report that will be widely circulated requires more background than a company's internal report on customer satisfaction.

Research Objectives

This part of the project should clearly explain exactly what the project tried to discover. First, it should state the problem and then list relevant research questions as they were stated in the research proposal. Each research objective presented here should have a corresponding entry in the results section later in the report. In that sense, the **research objectives** clearly set the expectations for what the project should deliver in later sections of the report.

Research Methodology

This part of the report should address four topics and may be represented by subheadings:

1. *Research design.* Was the study exploratory, descriptive, or causal? Did the data come from primary or secondary sources? Were results collected by survey, observation, or experiment? A copy of the survey questionnaire or observation form should be included in the appendix. Why was this particular design suited to the study?

introduction section
The part of the research report that discusses background information and the overall purpose of the research.

research objectives
The part of the research report that clearly explains the research problem and the relevant research questions that the research aims to answer.

research methodology
The section of the report that explains the research design, sampling procedures, and other technical and methodological procedures that were employed to collect the data.

2. *Sample design.* What was the target population? What sampling frame was used? What sample units were used? How were they selected? How large was the sample? What was the response rate? Detailed computations to support these explanations should be saved for the appendix.

3. *Data collection and fieldwork.* How many and what types of fieldworkers were used? What training and supervision did they receive? Was the work verified? This section is important for establishing the degree of accuracy of the results.

4. *Analysis.* This section should outline the general statistical methods used in the study, but the information presented here should not overlap with what is presented in the results section.

One of the challenges in writing this section is to explain technical procedures in a manner appropriate for the audience. The material in this section may be supplemented with more detailed explanations in the appendix or a glossary of technical terms.

Results

results section
The part of the body of a report that presents the findings of the project. It includes tables, charts, and an organized narrative.

The **results section** should make up the bulk of the report and should present, in some logical order, those findings of the project that bear on the objectives. The results should be organized as a continuous narrative, designed to be convincing but not to oversell the project. Summary tables and charts should be used to aid the discussion. One tool that could be used as a visual aid in this section is a chart of dependent and independent variables studied in the project and expected relationships (e.g., positive, negative) between these variables. This chart can be overlaid with the observed relationships from the project. Such charts and tables may serve as points of reference to the data being discussed and free the prose from excessive facts and figures. Any figures, tables, or other supplementary material used in this section should clearly be explained in the report and should help interpretation of the findings. Comprehensive or detailed charts, however, should be saved for the appendix.

Conclusions and Recommendations

conclusions and recommendations
The part of the report that provides opinions based on the results and suggestions for action.

As mentioned earlier, conclusions are opinions based on the results, and recommendations are suggestions for action. The **conclusions and recommendations** should be presented in this section in more detail than in the executive summary, and the text should include justification as needed.

Limitations

limitations
The part of the research report that indicates the shortcomings of the research.

By this time, you have learned in this textbook that there is no perfect research. Therefore, your written project should also indicate the **limitations**. If problems arose with nonresponse error or sampling procedures, these should be discussed. However, the discussion of limitations should avoid overemphasizing the weaknesses; its aim should be to provide a realistic basis for assessing the results.

Appendix

The *appendix* presents the "too . . ." material. Any material that is too technical or too detailed to go in the body should appear in the appendix. This includes materials of interest only to some readers or subsidiary materials not directly related to the objectives. Some examples of appendix materials are data collection forms, detailed calculations, discussions of highly technical questions, detailed or comprehensive tables of results, and a bibliography (if appropriate). This section may also include a letter of authorization for the research project. Since the advent of company intranets, much appendix material is posted on internal Web pages.

Including all of the sections above and putting together the full written report is a task that requires the writer's attention to detail. The most important issue when writing the final written report is to remember the *raison d'être* of the research: to answer research questions in order to help in making decisions. The written report

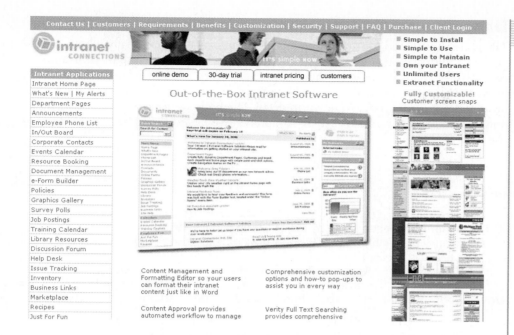

Information technology is changing how marketing research knowledge is communicated. Many organizations post research reports on their private intranets so that the information is available to executives around the world.

communicates these research questions in the research objectives section. The results, the conclusions, and the recommendations should be tightly related to the research objectives stated earlier in the report to accomplish the goals of the research project.

EFFECTIVE USE OF GRAPHIC AIDS

graphic aids
Pictures or diagrams used to clarify complex points or emphasize a message.

Recall our quote in Chapter 17: "A picture is worth a thousand words." If used properly, a written research report may communicate complex and hard-to-visualize messages clearly by using **graphic aids**. The length of the written report can be significantly reduced. In today's marketing research environment, the implicit expectation is an efficient use of graphic aids. However, if graphic aids are not prepared properly, such as providing too much detail in one graph, omitting descriptors or legends, or avoiding interpretation in the text, graphic aids can confuse, distract, and even mislead the audience.

Today, software packages such as Microsoft PowerPoint for presentations and Microsoft Word, Microsoft Excel, or SPSS for creating tables, charts, and graphs increase the ease with which graphic aids can be used in written reports and oral presentations. One of the key factors in the effective use of graphic aids is to make sure that they are *always* discussed and interpreted in the text. A table or chart included in the written report without any discussion will not motivate the reader to examine the graphic aid. This does not mean that the writer should exhaustively explain an obvious chart or table, but it *does* mean that the text should point out the key elements of any graphic aid and relate them to the discussion in progress. Another key point is to remember that various types of graphic aids can be used in the written report for more efficient delivery of information than words can provide, and the writer should explore different graphic aids to deliver the message. The following discussion briefly covers the most common graphic aids: tables and charts. The reader interested in other types of graphic material should consult more specialized sources.

Tables

Tables are most useful for presenting numerical information, especially when several pieces of information have been gathered about each item discussed. For example, consider how hard it would be to follow all the information in Table 19.1 if it were presented in narrative form. Using tables allows a writer to point out significant features without getting bogged down in detail. The body of the report should include only relatively short summary tables; comprehensive tables should be reserved for an appendix.

TABLE 19.1 | **PARTS OF A TABLE**

Table number ⟶   Title ⟶

No. 768. Consumer Price Index (CPI), by Major Groups: 1980–1999

[1982–84 = 100. Represents annual averages of monthly figures. Reflects buying patterns of all urban consumers. Minus sign (−) indicates decrease. See text, this section]

Year	All items	Com- modi- ties	Energy	Food	Shelter	Apparel and upkeep	Trans- porta- tion	Medi- cal care	Fuel oil	Elec- tricity	Utility (piped) gas	Tele- phone services
1980	82.4	86.0	86.0	86.8	81.0	90.9	83.1	74.9	87.7	75.8	65.7	77.7
1985	107.6	105.4	101.6	105.6	109.8	105.0	106.4	113.5	94.6	108.9	104.8	111.7
1986	109.6	104.4	88.2	109.0	115.8	105.9	102.3	122.0	74.1	110.4	99.7	117.2
1987	113.6	107.7	88.6	113.5	121.3	110.6	105.4	130.1	75.8	110.0	95.1	116.5
1988	118.3	111.5	89.3	118.2	127.1	115.4	108.7	138.6	75.8	111.5	94.5	116.0
1989	124.0	116.7	94.3	125.1	132.8	118.6	114.1	149.3	80.3	114.7	97.1	117.2
1990	130.7	122.8	102.1	132.4	140.0	124.1	120.5	162.8	98.6	117.4	97.3	117.7
1991	136.2	126.6	102.5	136.3	146.3	128.7	123.8	177.0	92.4	121.8	98.5	119.7
1992	140.3	129.1	103.0	137.9	151.2	131.9	126.5	190.1	88.0	124.2	100.3	120.4
1993	144.5	131.5	104.2	140.9	155.7	133.7	130.4	201.4	87.2	126.7	106.5	121.2
1994	148.2	133.8	104.6	144.3	160.5	133.4	134.3	211.0	85.6	126.7	108.5	123.1
1995	152.4	136.4	105.2	148.4	165.7	132.0	139.1	220.5	84.8	129.6	102.9	124.0
1996	156.9	139.9	110.1	153.3	171.0	131.7	143.0	228.2	97.0	131.8	107.2	125.9
1997	160.5	141.8	111.5	157.3	176.3	132.9	144.3	234.6	96.9	132.5	114.6	127.7
1998	163.0	141.9	102.9	160.7	182.1	133.0	141.6	242.1	84.8	127.4	112.4	100.7
1999	166.6	144.4	106.6	164.1	187.3	131.3	144.4	250.6	86.6	126.5	113.0	100.1
PERCENT CHANGE[1]												
1980	13.5	12.3	30.9	8.6	17.6	7.1	17.9	11.0	39.0	15.5	19.2	2.5
1985	3.6	2.1	0.7	2.3	5.6	2.8	2.6	6.3	−4.0	3.4	−0.7	3.9
1986	1.9	−0.9	−13.2	3.2	5.5	0.9	−3.9	7.5	−21.7	1.4	−4.9	4.9
1987	3.6	3.2	0.5	4.1	4.7	4.4	3.0	6.6	2.3	−0.4	−4.6	−0.6
1988	4.1	3.5	0.8	4.1	4.8	4.3	3.1	6.5	—	1.4	−0.6	−0.4
1989	4.8	4.7	5.6	5.8	4.5	2.8	5.0	7.7	5.9	2.9	2.8	1.0
1990	5.4	5.2	8.3	5.8	5.4	4.6	5.6	9.0	22.8	2.4	0.2	0.4
1991	4.2	3.1	0.4	2.9	4.5	3.7	2.7	8.7	−6.3	3.7	1.2	1.7
1992	3.0	2.0	0.5	1.2	3.3	2.5	2.2	7.4	−4.8	2.0	1.8	0.6
1993	3.0	1.9	1.2	2.2	3.0	1.4	3.1	5.9	−0.9	2.0	6.2	0.7
1994	2.6	1.7	0.4	2.4	3.1	−0.2	3.0	4.8	−1.9	0.0	1.9	1.6
1995	2.8	1.9	0.6	2.8	3.2	−1.0	3.6	4.5	−0.9	2.3	−5.2	0.7
1996	3.0	2.6	4.7	3.3	3.2	−0.2	2.8	3.5	14.4	1.7	4.2	1.5
1997	2.3	1.4	1.3	2.6	3.1	0.9	0.9	2.8	−0.1	0.5	6.9	1.4
1998	1.6	0.1	−7.7	2.2	3.3	0.1	−1.9	3.2	−12.5	−3.8	−1.9	—
1999	2.2	1.8	3.6	2.1	2.9	−1.3	2.0	3.5	2.1	−0.7	0.5	−0.6

Stubheads ⟵   Bannerheads ⟶   Footnotes ⟵

— Represents zero.   [1]Change from prior year.

Source: Bureau of Labor Statistics, *Monthly Labor Review and Handbook of Labor Statistics*, periodic.

⟶ Source

TABLE 19.2 — REPORTING FORMAT FOR A TYPICAL CROSS-TABULATION FROM A SURVEY[4]

Which subjects did your household argue about in the past 12 months?

	AGE			
	Under 35 Years	35–49 Years	50–64 Years	65 Years or More
Argued about something	79%	80%	58%	37%
Money	54	45	25	12
Children	33	43	24	6
Household chores	35	35	17	8
Diets/health	22	25	21	16
Job decisions	28	20	8	3
In-laws	24	15	10	4
Sex	20	19	7	4
Where to live	24	9	9	7
Vacations	12	12	10	6
Politics	8	6	7	4
Religion	10	6	4	3
Did not argue about anything	21	20	42	63

Each table should include the following:

1. *Table number.* This allows for simple reference from the text to the table. If the text includes many tables, a list of tables should be included just after the table of contents.

2. *Title.* The title should indicate the contents of the table and be complete enough to be intelligible without referring to the text. The table number and title are generally placed at the top because the table is read from the top down.

3. *Stubheads and bannerheads.* The stubheads contain the captions for the rows of the table, and the bannerheads (or boxheads) contain those for the columns.

4. *Footnotes.* Any explanations or qualifications for particular table entries or sections should be given in footnotes.

5. *Source notes.* If a table is based on material from one or more secondary sources rather than on new data generated by the project, the sources should be acknowledged, usually below the table.

Table 19.2 illustrates a typical table from a survey research report; it cross-tabulates demographics with survey responses. Table 19.3 shows how data from a statistical test might be reported in table form.

TABLE 19.3 — REPORTING FORMAT FOR A TYPICAL STATISTICAL TEST[5]

Will investors be more cautious about buying stock in companies with questionable advertising?

	Business	Advertising Management
Yes	57%	46%
No	27	35
Not sure	16	19
	$n = 177$	$n = 154$

$$\chi^2 = c4.933 \qquad d.f. = 2 \qquad p < .08$$

Suppose an airline asks a question about customers' satisfaction with its baggage-handling service. In addition to showing the simple frequency for each category, most research analysts would cross-tabulate answers to the baggage-handling questions with several demographic variables such as gender, income, education, and age. To present multiple cross-tabulations individually in separate tables requires considerable space. Thus many research reports use a space-saving format, with either stubheads for rows or bannerheads for columns, to allow the reader to view several cross-tabulations at the same time.

Charts

Charts translate numerical information into visual form so that relationships may be easily grasped. The accuracy of the numbers is reduced to gain this advantage. Each chart should include the following:

1. *Figure number.* Charts (and other illustrative material) should be numbered in a separate series from tables. The numbers allow for easy reference from the text. If there are many charts, a list of them should be included after the table of contents.

2. *Title.* The title should describe the contents of the chart and be independent of the text explanation. The number and title may be placed at the top or bottom of the chart.

3. *Explanatory legends.* Enough explanation should be put on the chart to spare the reader a need to look at the accompanying text. Such explanations should include labels for axes, scale numbers, and a key to the various quantities being graphed.

4. *Source and footnotes.* Any secondary sources for the data should be acknowledged. Footnotes may be used to explain items, although they are less common for charts than for tables.

Charts are subject to distortion, whether unintentional or deliberate. Exhibit 19.1 shows how altering the scale changes the reader's impression of the data. A particularly severe kind of distortion comes from treating unequal intervals as if they were equal; this generally results from a deliberate attempt to distort data. Exhibit 19.2 shows this type of distortion; someone has attempted to make the rise on the chart more dramatic by compressing the portion in which the data show little real change.

Another common way of introducing distortion is to begin the vertical scale at some value larger than zero. Exhibit 19.3 shows how this exaggerates the amount of change in the period covered. This kind of broken scale is often used in published reports of stock price movements. In this case it is assumed that the reader is interested

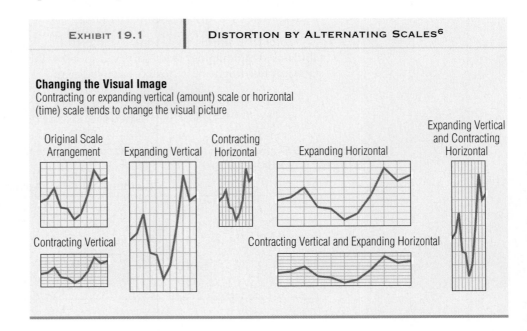

EXHIBIT 19.1 | DISTORTION BY ALTERNATING SCALES[6]

Changing the Visual Image
Contracting or expanding vertical (amount) scale or horizontal (time) scale tends to change the visual picture

Original Scale Arrangement

Expanding Vertical

Contracting Horizontal

Expanding Horizontal

Expanding Vertical and Contracting Horizontal

Contracting Vertical

Contracting Vertical and Expanding Horizontal

EXHIBIT 19.2

DISTORTION FROM TREATING UNEQUAL TIME INTERVALS AS EQUAL[7]

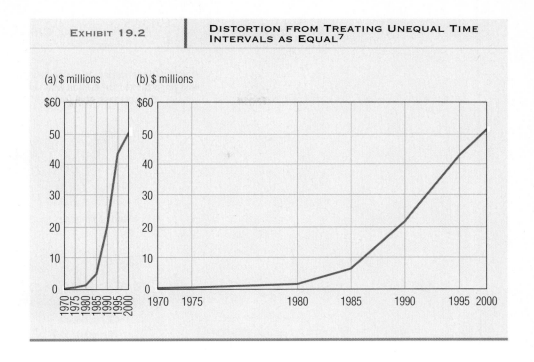

(a) $ millions   (b) $ millions

EXHIBIT 19.3

DISTORTION OF CHART FROM BROKEN VERTICAL SCALES[8]

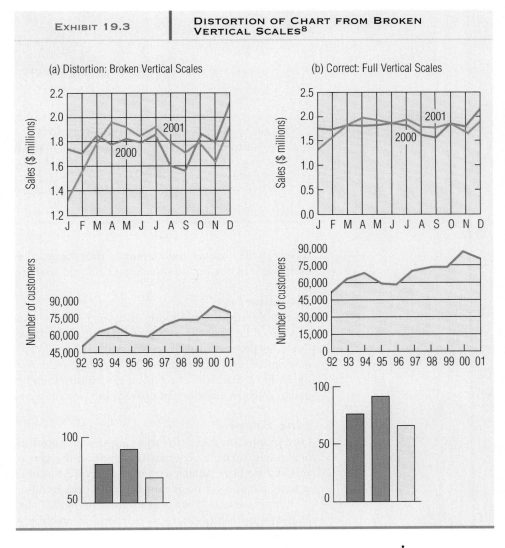

(a) Distortion: Broken Vertical Scales   (b) Correct: Full Vertical Scales

EXHIBIT 19.4 | SERIES OF PIE CHARTS[9]

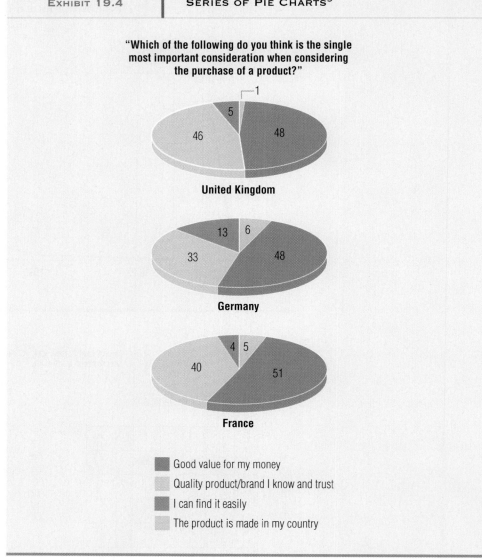

"Which of the following do you think is the single most important consideration when considering the purchase of a product?"

1

5

46

48

United Kingdom

13   6

33

48

Germany

4   5

40

51

France

Good value for my money

Quality product/brand I know and trust

I can find it easily

The product is made in my country

mostly in the changes and is aware of the exaggeration. For most research reports, how-ever, this will not be the case. Graphs should start at zero on the vertical axis.

Pie Charts

One of the most useful kinds of charts is the pie chart, which shows the composition of some total quantity at a particular time. As shown in Exhibit 19.4, each angle, or "slice," is proportional to its percentage of the whole and should be labelled with its description and percentage. The writer should not try to include too many small slices; about six slices is a typical maximum. Pie charts are commonly used by com-panies to show how revenues were used or the composition of their sales.

Line Graphs

Line graphs are useful for showing the relationship of one variable to another. The dependent variable generally is shown on the vertical axis and the independent vari-able on the horizontal axis. The most common independent variable for such charts is time, but it is by no means the only one. Exhibit 19.5 depicts a *simple line graph*.

Other variations are also useful. The *multiple line graph* (Exhibit 19.6) shows the relationship of more than one dependent variable to the independent variable. The

EXHIBIT 19.5 | SIMPLE LINE GRAPH[10]

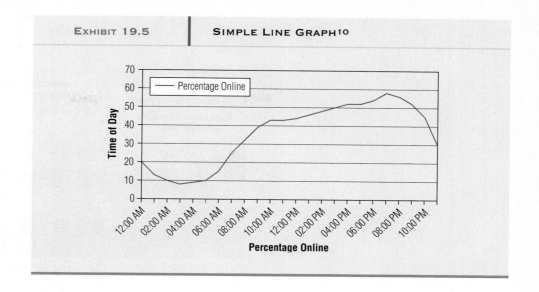

EXHIBIT 19.6 | MULTIPLE LINE GRAPH[11]

Annual Percent Change in Consumer Price Indexes: 1980 to 1999

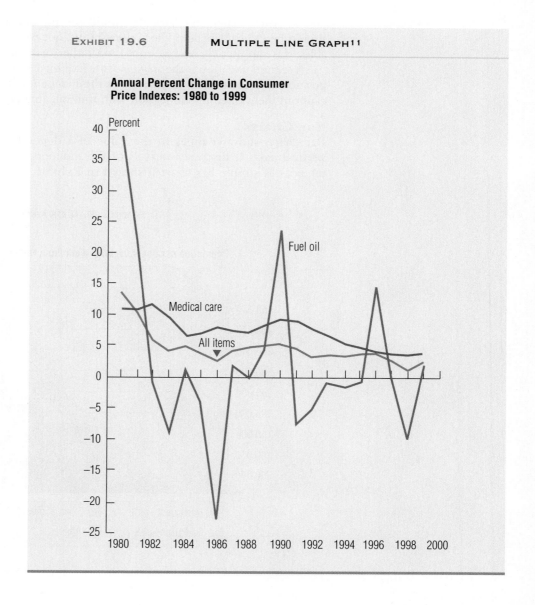

EXHIBIT 19.7 | STRATUM CHART

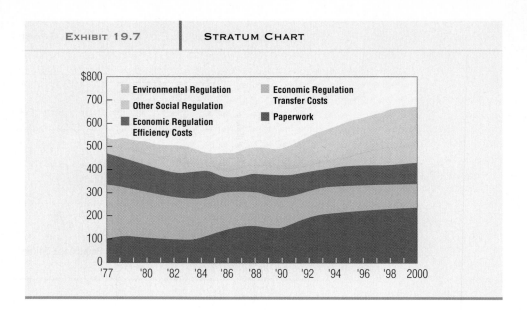

line for each dependent variable should be in a different colour or pattern and should be clearly labelled. The writer should not try to squeeze in too many variables; this can quickly lead to confusion rather than clarification.

A second variation is the *stratum chart* (Exhibit 19.7), which shows how the composition of a total quantity changes as the independent variable changes. The same cautions mentioned in connection with multiple line graphs apply to stratum charts.

Bar Charts

Bar charts show changes in the value of a dependent variable (plotted on the vertical axis) at discrete intervals of the independent variable (on the horizontal axis). A simple bar chart is shown in Exhibit 19.8. A common variant is the

EXHIBIT 19.8 | SIMPLE BAR CHART[12]

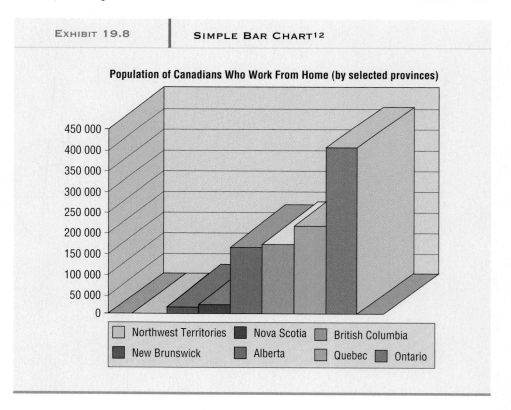

EXHIBIT 19.9 | SUBDIVIDED BAR CHART[13]

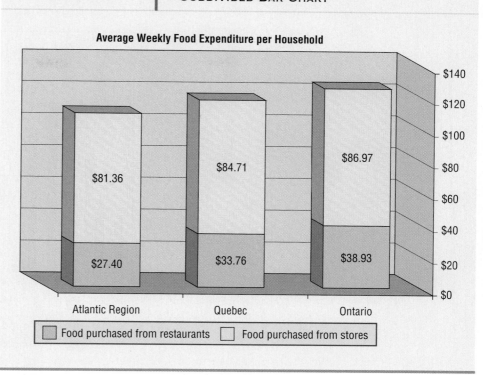

Average Weekly Food Expenditure per Household

subdivided bar chart (see Exhibit 19.9). It is much like a stratum chart, showing the composition of the whole quantity. The *multiple bar chart* (see Exhibit 19.10) shows how multiple variables are related to the primary variable. In each of these cases, each bar needs to be clearly identified with a different colour or pattern. The writer should not use too many divisions or dependent variables. Too much detail obscures the essential advantage of charts, which is to make relationships easy to grasp.

THE ORAL PRESENTATION

oral presentation
A spoken summary of the major findings, conclusions, and recommendations, given to clients or line managers to provide them with the opportunity to clarify any ambiguous issues by asking questions.

Although the final written report communicates all the details of the project, the oral presentation is very important in communicating the conclusions and recommendations of the research. The purpose of an **oral presentation** is to highlight the most important findings of a research project and provide clients or line managers with the opportunity to clarify any ambiguous issues by asking questions.

The oral presentation may be as simple as a short conference with a manager at the client organization's location or as formal as a report to the board of directors. The key to effective presentation in either situation is preparation.

A few steps can be taken in the preparation for an oral presentation:

1. Communication specialists often suggest that a person preparing an oral presentation begin at the end.[14] In other words, while preparing a presentation, a researcher should think about what he or she wants the client to know when it has been completed.

2. The overall flow of the presentation can be printed in the form of an outline or slide notes to be handed out to the audience. The outline may cover the most important parts of the presentation and also provide some blank space for taking notes. Software packages, such as Microsoft PowerPoint, have options to create such outlines (see Exploring the Internet at the end of chapter for more PowerPoint tips).

EXHIBIT 19.10 | MULTIPLE BAR CHART[15]

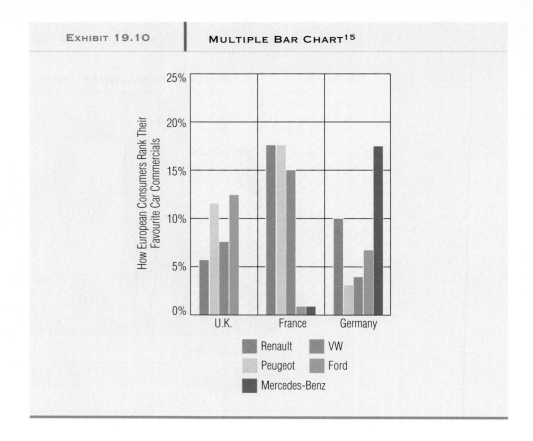

3. It is very important to have practice runs of the presentation and to pay attention to the time constraints of the presentation. This will enable revision of slides that are too complicated or too long to communicate. Avoid crowded slides (see Exploring Research Issues).

4. Try to anticipate some typical questions that may come from the audience, such as type and sample of some of the questions used in the survey, additional findings that are of secondary importance, etc. Preparing additional back-up slides for such questions not only prepares you for the presentation, but it also helps understanding the perspective of the audience.

5. Include graphic and visual aids to communicate your messages and to sustain interest in the presentation. Given the technological luxuries of today, this may include audio or video files that can be incorporated into the slide, Web sites that provide examples for your points, or animated bubbles that explain parts of your slide.

Note that in most cases, it may be impossible to include all the information regarding the research project during an oral presentation. Therefore, the presenter must pay careful attention to selection of the most useful findings from the project. The researcher should select the three or four most important findings for emphasis and rely on the written report for a full summary.

In addition, most audiences (e.g., time-pressed managers) will not have the time to go over the final written report from cover to cover. The oral presentation itself may serve as the best, if not the only, exposure some members of the audience may have to the project outcomes.

The researcher needs to be ready to defend the results of the research. This is not the same as being defensive; rather, it means being prepared to deal in a confident, competent manner with the questions that arise. Remember that even the most reliable and valid research project is worthless if the managers who must act on its results are not convinced of its importance.

NOAH'S LAW OF PRESENTATIONS

Whether you are using a PowerPoint presentation or transparencies, one issue that should be addressed is the amount of material to provide on each slide. During oral presentations of research reports, many presenters use slides that viewers in the back row cannot read.[16] In fact, some presenters use slides that viewers in the front row cannot read.

All viewers would be much happier if all presenters were to follow Noah's Law of Presentations. Noah's Law says: Never, ever, under any circumstances whatsoever, put more than 40 words on a slide. A number counts as a word. Noah's Law is called Noah's Law because when God made it rain for 40 days and 40 nights, He flooded the whole world, and no presenter should attempt that with one slide.

Note that, in Noah's Law, 40 is the absolute upper limit. Twenty is a good average. Seven is even better. If seven words look lonely, presenters can always MAKE THE LETTERS BIGGER.

Advertising legend David Ogilvy was a devout follower of Noah's Law. He thought so highly of it that he invented and enforced Ogilvy's Corollary. Ogilvy's Corollary says: Never put anything on a slide (or a chart) that you don't intend to read out loud to your audience word for word. He reasoned that when one message comes in on the visual channel while another comes in on the auditory channel, the audience will probably neglect one message or the other.

As with written reports, a key to effective oral presentation is adapting to the audience. Delivering an hour-long formal speech when a 10-minute discussion is called for (or vice versa) will reflect poorly on both the presenter and the report.

The principles of good speechmaking apply to a research presentation. Lecturing or reading to the audience is sure to impede communication at any level of formality. The presenter should refrain from reading prepared text word for word. By relying on brief notes, familiarity with the subject, and as much rehearsal as the occasion calls for, the presenter will foster better communication. He or she should avoid research jargon and use short, familiar words. The presenter should maintain eye contact with the audience and repeat the main points. Because the audience cannot go back and replay what the speaker has said, an oral presentation often is organized around a standard format: "Tell them what you are going to tell them, tell them, and tell them what you just told them."

As mentioned above, graphic and other visual aids can be as useful in an oral presentation as in a written one. Presenters can choose from a variety of media. Whatever medium is chosen, each visual aid should be designed to convey a simple, attention-getting message that supports a point on which the audience should focus its thinking. As they do in written presentations, presenters should interpret graphics for the audience. The best slides are easy to read and interpret. Large typeface, multiple colours, bullets that highlight, and other artistic devices can enhance the readability of charts.

In today's digital society, overhead transparencies are almost extinct. However, preparing a set of simple, black and white transparencies as a back-up may be a safe strategy to avoid technical problems that cannot be fixed quickly.

Using gestures during presentations can also help convey the message and make presentations more interesting. Here are some tips on how to gesture:[17]

■ Open up your arms to embrace your audience. Keep your arms between your waist and shoulders.

■ Drop your arms to your sides when not using them.

■ Avoid quick and jerky gestures; they make you appear nervous. Hold gestures longer than you would in normal conversation.

Oral presentations can be enhanced with computer-generated graphics. Presentation software, such as Microsoft's PowerPoint, allows a researcher to select background design, colour, bullets that highlight, and other graphic effects that make communication of the message more effective. It is a good idea to use simple attractive graphics and to avoid overwhelming the audience with flashiness.

- Vary gestures. Switch from hand to hand and at other times use both hands or no hands.
- Don't overuse gestures.

REPORTS ON THE INTERNET

Many clients want numerous employees to have access to research findings. One easy way to share data is to make executive summaries and reports available on a company intranet. Today, common software packages, such as Microsoft PowerPoint, will publish your presentations for the Web and facilitate posting your slides.

A company can use information technology on the Internet to design questionnaires, administer surveys, analyze data, and share the results in a presentation-ready format. Real-time data capture allows for beginning-to-end reporting. A number of companies offer fully Web-based research management systems. The best example is the WebSurveyor software, which provides an online solution for capturing and reporting research findings.

THE RESEARCH FOLLOW-UP

research follow-up
Recontacting decision makers and/or clients after they have had a chance to read over a research report, in order to determine whether additional information or clarification is necessary.

Research reports and oral presentations should communicate research findings so that managers can make business decisions. In many cases the manager who receives the research report is unable to interpret the information and draw conclusions relevant to managerial decisions. For this reason, effective researchers do not treat the report as the end of the research process. They conduct a **research follow-up**, in which they recontact decision makers and/or clients after the latter have had a chance to read over the report. The purpose is to determine whether the researchers need to provide additional information or clarify issues of concern to management. Just as marketing research may help an organization learn about its customers' satisfaction, the research follow-up can help marketing research staffers ensure the satisfaction of their customers, marketing management.

SUMMARY

Report preparation is the final stage of the research project. It is an important stage because the project can guide management decisions only if the ideas are effectively communicated. The theory of communications emphasizes that the writer (communicator) must tailor the report (message) so that it will be understood by the manager (audience), who has a different field of experience. A research report is an oral or written presentation of research findings directed to a specific audience to accomplish a particular purpose.

(2) There is a consensus that the format for a research report should include certain prefatory parts, the body of the report, and appended parts. The report format should be varied to suit the level of formality of the particular situation.

The prefatory parts of a formal report include a title page, letters of transmittal and authorization, a table of contents, and a summary. The summary is the part of a report most often read and should include a brief statement of the objectives, results, conclusions, and (depending on the research situation) recommendations. The report body includes an introduction that gives the background and objectives, a statement of methodology, and a discussion of the results, their limitations, and appropriate conclusions and recommendations. The appendix includes various materials too specialized to appear in the body of the report.

(3) (4) (5) Effective use of graphic aids enhances a presentation. Tables present large amounts of numerical information in a concise manner. Charts present numerical data in a way that highlights their relationships. Pie charts, line graphs, and bar charts are useful forms of charts and all have variants for special purposes.

(6) Most research projects are reported on orally as well as in writing, so the researcher needs to prepare an oral presentation. The presentation should defend the results without being defensive. The presentation must be tailored to the situation and the audience. Here, too, graphic aids are useful supplements.

(7) The research follow-up involves recontacting decision makers after the report has been submitted to determine whether the researchers need to provide further information or clarify any issues of concern to management.

Key Terms and Concepts

research report
report format
introduction section
research objectives

research methodology
results section
conclusions and recommendations
limitations

graphic aids
oral presentation
research follow-up

Questions for Review and Critical Thinking

1. Why is it important to think of the research report from a communications perspective?
2. As a manager, what degree of formality would you want from your research department?
3. What types of tables might be used to describe some of the various statistical tests discussed in previous chapters?
4. What do you believe will be the impact of computer graphics on the research report writing format?

5. Go to your library and find some research reports. How do they meet the standards set forth in this chapter?
6. How does the oral presentation of research differ from the written research report?
7. What rules should be followed when preparing slides or computer-generated presentations?
 8. What ethical concerns arise when you prepare (or read) a report?

Exploring the Internet

1. Go to Burke Interactive's Digital Dashboard demo at http://report.burke.com_demo/Tour/Index.asp. Take a tour and view the demo. Evaluate the format of the online research report.
2. Go to www.websurveyor.com/analyze-and-share-results.asp and explore how to share results online.
3. Go to www.presentersuniversity.com/ to identify assistance you can get to enhance your presentations.
4. Go to http://office.microsoft.com/ to explore training on using PowerPoint software and recent templates.

5. Go to *American Demographics* magazine's home page at http://adage.com/americandemographics/.
   a. Browse a back issue of *American Demographics*. Find a story that appears to be a summary of research reports.
   b. What research reports are available in the magazine's Marketing and Research catalogue?

VALUES AND THE AUTOMOBILE MARKET

In the last decade, the luxury car segment became one of the most competitive in the automobile market. Many North American consumers who purchase luxury cars prefer imports from Germany and Japan.

A marketing vice-president with General Motors once commented, "Import-committed buyers have been frustrating to us." This type of thinking has led industry analysts to argue that to successfully compete in the luxury car segment, carmakers need to develop a better understanding of the consumers so that they can better segment the market and better position their products via more effective advertising. Insight into the foreign-domestic luxury car choice may result from examining owners' personal values in addition to their evaluations of car attributes, because luxury cars, like many other conspicuously consumed luxury products, may be purchased mainly for value-expressive reasons.

Industry analysts believe it would be important to assess whether personal values of consumers could be used to explain ownership of North American, German, and Japanese luxury cars. Further, they believe they should also assess whether knowledge of owners' personal values provides any additional information useful in explaining ownership of North American, German, and Japanese luxury cars beyond that obtained from their evaluations of the cars' attributes.

Personal values are likely to provide insights into reasons for ownership of luxury cars for at least two reasons. First, North Americans have always had a very personal relationship with their cars and have used them as symbols of their self-concept. For instance, people who value a sense of accomplishment are quite likely to desire a luxury car that they feel is an appropriate symbol of their achievement, whereas people who value fun, enjoyment, and excitement are likely to desire a luxury car that they perceive as fun and exciting to drive. An advertiser trying to persuade the former segment to purchase a luxury car should position the car as a status symbol that will help its owners demonstrate their accomplishments to others. Similarly, an advertiser trying to persuade the latter segment to purchase a luxury car should position the car as a fun and exciting car to drive. In other words, effective advertising shows consumers how purchasing a given product will help them achieve their valued state, because brands tied to values will be perceived more favourably than brands that deliver more mundane benefits.

Second, when a market is overcrowded with competing brands offering very similar options — as is the case with the luxury car market — consumers are quite likely to choose between brands on the basis of value-expressive considerations.

METHOD

Data were collected via a mail survey sent to 498 consumers chosen at random from a list obtained from a syndicated research company located in an affluent county in a southern U.S. state. The list contained names of people who had purchased either a luxury North American car (Cadillac or Lincoln Mercury), a luxury German car (Mercedes or BMW), or a luxury Japanese car (Infiniti or Lexus) within the last year. A cover letter explained that the survey was part of an academic research project. People were asked to return the questionnaires anonymously to a university address (a postage-paid envelope was provided with each survey). Beyond an appeal to help the researchers, respondents were not offered any other incentive to complete the surveys. Of the 498 questionnaires originally sent, 17 were returned by the post office as undeliverable. One-hundred fifty-five completed surveys were received, for a response rate of 32.2 percent.

Having a luxury car is a major part of my fun and excitement.[a] (Issue 1)

Owning a luxury car is a part of "being good to myself." (Issue 2)

When I was able to buy my first luxury car, I felt a sense of accomplishment. (Issue 3)

I enjoy giving my friends advice about luxury cars. (Issue 4)

Getting a good deal when I buy a luxury car makes me feel better about myself. (Issue 5)

I seek novelty and I am willing to try new innovations in cars. (Issue 6)

I tend to buy the same brand of car several times in a row. (Issue 7)

I tend to buy from the same dealer several times in a row. (Issue 8)

I usually use sources of information such as *Consumer Reports* in deciding on a car. (Issue 9)

I usually visit three or more dealerships before I buy a car. (Issue 10)

I would read a brochure or watch a video about defensive driving. (Issue 11)

When buying a new luxury car, my family's opinion is very important to me. (Issue 12)

My family usually accompanies me when I am shopping for a new luxury car. (Issue 13)

I usually rely upon ads and salespersons for information on cars. (Issue 14)

I usually rely upon friends and acquaintances for information on cars. (Issue 15)

When shopping for a car, it is important that the car dealer make me feel at ease. (Issue 16)

Most of my friends drive luxury import cars. (Issue 17)

Most of my friends drive luxury domestic cars. (Issue 18)

I think celebrity endorsers in ads influence people's choices of luxury cars. (Issue 19)

I would not buy a luxury car if I felt that my debt level is higher than usual. (Issue 20)

[a]Note: Subjects' responses were measured with 1 as "strongly agree" and 7 as "strongly disagree."

The Survey Instrument

The survey included questions on (1) various issues that people consider when purchasing new cars, (2) importance of car attributes, (3) importance of different values, and (4) demographics (sex, age, education, and family income). Questions relating to the issues that people consider when purchasing new cars were developed through initial interviews with consumers and were measured with a 7-point Likert scale with end anchors of "strongly agree" and "strongly disagree." (See Case Exhibit 1.) A list of 12 car attributes was developed from the initial interviews with consumers and by consulting *Consumer Reports*. (See Case Exhibit 2.) The importance of each attribute was measured with a 7-point numerical scale with end points labelled "very important" and "very unimportant." The List of Values (LOV) scale in Case Exhibit 3 was used to measure the importance of values. Respondents were asked to rate each of the eight values (fun–enjoyment and excitement were combined into one value) on a 7-point numerical scale with end points labelled "very important" and "very unimportant."

| CASE EXHIBIT 2 | CAR ATTRIBUTES |

Attribute	Code	Attribute	Code
Comfort	Comfort	Low maintenance cost	Lomc
Safety	Safety	Reliability	Rely
Power	Power	Warranty	Warrant
Speed	Speed	Nonpolluting	Nonpol
Styling	Styling	High gas mileage	Gasmle
Durability	Durabil	Speed of repairs	Repairs

Value	Code	Value	Code
Fun-Enjoyment-Excitement	Fun	Sense of Accomplishment	Accomp
Sense of belonging	Belong	Warm relationship	Warm
Being well respected	Respect	Security	Security
Self-fulfillment	Selfful	Self-respect	Selfres

The Sample

Of the 155 respondents in the sample, 58 (37.4 percent) owned a North American luxury car, 38 (24.5 percent) owned a European luxury car, and 59 (38.1 percent) owned a Japanese luxury car. The majority of the sample consisted of older (85 percent were 35 years of age or above), more educated (64 percent were college graduates), and economically well-off (87.2 percent earned $65,000 U.S. or more) consumers.

THE CODE BOOK

Case Exhibit 4 lists the SPSS variable names and identifies codes for these variables. (Note that this data set is also available in Microsoft Excel.)

ADDITIONAL INFORMATION

Several of the questions will require the use of a computerized database. Your instructor will provide information about obtaining the VALUES data set if the material is part of the case assignment.

Questions
1. Is the sampling method adequate? Is the attitude measuring scale sound? Explain.
2. Using the computerized database (luxury3.sav) with a statistical software package (e.g., SPSS), explore whether there is a relationship between
   a. "car" owned and "sex"
   b. "car" owned and "age"
   c. "car" owned and "income"

ID—Identification number

AGE (categories are 2 = 35 years and under, 3 = 36–45 yrs, 4 = 46–55 yrs, 5 = 56–65 yrs, 6 = 65 + yrs)

SEX (1 = male, 0 = female)

EDUC—Education (1 = Less than high school, 2 = High school grad, 3 = Some college, 4 = College grad, 5 = Graduate degree)

INCOME (1 = less than $35,000, 2 = $35–50,000, 3 = $50–65,000, 4 = $65,000+)

CAR—Type of luxury car (North American car, European car, Japanese car)

ISSUES—The sequence of issues listed in Case Exhibit 1. (Strongly agree = 1; strongly disagree = 7)

ATTRIBUTES—The sequence of car attributes listed in Case Exhibit 2. (Very important to you = 1; very unimportant to you = 7)

VALUES—The sequence of values listed in Case Exhibit 3. (Very important = 1; very unimportant = 7)

3. Using the computerized database (luxury3.sav) with a statistical software package (e.g., SPSS), answer the following questions:
   a. In general, do consumers visit three or more dealers?
   b. In general, do consumers buy from the same dealer several times in a row?
   c. In general, do consumers rely on friends and acquaintances for information on cars?
   d. In general, do consumers rely on ads and salespeople for information on cars?
4. Using the computerized database (luxury3.sav) with a statistical software package (e.g., SPSS), explain whether the following attributes are more important to women than men when shopping for luxury cars:
   a. high gas mileage
   b. durability of the car
   c. comfort
   d. styling
   e. safety
   What is the null and alternative hypotheses for each of the tests in a to e?
5. Using the computerized database (luxury3.sav) with a statistical software package (e.g. SPSS), calculate the means of the three automotive groups (North American, Japanese, European) for the values variables. Do any of the values variables show significant differences between North American, Japanese, and European car owners?
6. Are there any significant differences on importance of attributes between North American, Japanese, and European car owners?
7. Write a short statement interpreting the results of this research.

Advanced Questions
8. Are any of the value scale items highly correlated?
9. Should multivariate analysis be used to understand the data? Explain.

APPENDIX

STATISTICAL TABLES

TABLE A.1		RANDOM DIGITS							
37751	04998	66038	63480	98442	22245	83538	62351	74514	90497
50915	64152	82981	15796	27102	71635	34470	13608	26360	76285
99142	35021	01032	57907	80545	54112	15150	36856	03247	40392
70720	10033	25191	62358	03784	74377	88150	25567	87457	49512
18460	64947	32958	08752	96366	89092	23597	74308	00881	88976
65763	41133	60950	35372	06782	81451	78764	52645	19841	50083
83769	52570	60133	25211	87384	90182	84990	26400	39128	97043
58900	78420	98579	33665	10718	39342	46346	14401	13503	46525
54746	71115	78219	64314	11227	41702	54517	87676	14078	45317
56819	27340	07200	52663	57864	85159	15460	97564	29637	27742
34990	62122	38223	28526	37006	22774	46026	15981	87291	56946
02269	22795	87593	81830	95383	67823	20196	54850	46779	64519
43042	53600	45738	00261	31100	67239	02004	70698	53597	62617
92565	12211	06868	87786	59576	61382	33972	13161	47208	96604
67424	32620	60841	86848	85000	04835	48576	33884	10101	84129
04015	77148	09535	10743	97871	55919	45274	38304	93125	91847
85226	19763	46105	25289	26714	73253	85922	21785	42624	92741
03360	07457	75131	41209	50451	23472	07438	08375	29312	62264
72460	99682	27970	25632	34096	17656	12736	27476	21938	67305
66960	55780	71778	52629	51692	71442	36130	70425	39874	62035
14824	95631	00697	65462	24815	13930	02938	54619	28909	53950
34001	05618	41900	23303	19928	60755	61404	56947	91441	19299
77718	83830	29781	72917	10840	74182	08293	62588	99625	22088
60930	05091	35726	07414	49211	69586	20226	08274	28167	65279
94180	62151	08112	26646	07617	42954	22521	09395	43561	45692
81073	85543	47650	93830	07377	87995	35084	39386	93141	88309
18467	39689	60801	46828	38670	88243	89042	78452	08032	72566
60643	59399	79740	17295	50094	66436	92677	68345	24025	36489
73372	61697	85728	90779	13235	83114	70728	32093	74306	08325
18395	18482	83245	54942	51905	09534	70839	91073	42193	81199
07261	28720	71244	05064	84873	68020	39037	68981	00670	86291
61679	81529	83725	33269	45958	74265	87460	60525	42539	25605
11815	48679	00556	96871	39835	83055	84949	11681	51687	55896
99007	35050	86440	44280	20320	97527	28138	01088	49037	85430
06446	65608	79291	16624	06135	30622	56133	33998	32308	29434

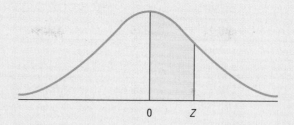

z	.00	.01	.02	.03	.04	.05	.06	.07	.08	.09
0.0	.0000	.0040	.0080	.0120	.0160	.0199	.0239	.0279	.0319	.0359
0.1	.0398	.0438	.0478	.0517	.0557	.0596	.0636	.0675	.0714	.0753
0.2	.0793	.0832	.0871	.0910	.0948	.0987	.1026	.1064	.1103	.1141
0.3	.1179	.1217	.1255	.1293	.1331	.1368	.1406	.1443	.1480	.1517
0.4	.1554	.1591	.1628	.1664	.1700	.1736	.1772	.1808	.1844	.1879
0.5	.1915	.1950	.1985	.2019	.2054	.2088	.2123	.2157	.2190	.2224
0.6	.2257	.2291	.2324	.2357	.2389	.2422	.2454	.2486	.2518	.2549
0.7	.2580	.2612	.2642	.2673	.2704	.2734	.2764	.2794	.2823	.2852
0.8	.2881	.2910	.2939	.2967	.2995	.3023	.3051	.3078	.3106	.3133
0.9	.3159	.3186	.3212	.3238	.3264	.3289	.3315	.3340	.3365	.3389
1.0	.3413	.3438	.3461	.3485	.3508	.3531	.3554	.3577	.3599	.3621
1.1	.3643	.3665	.3686	.3708	.3729	.3749	.3770	.3790	.3810	.3830
1.2	.3849	.3869	.3888	.3907	.3925	.3944	.3962	.3980	.3997	.4015
1.3	.4032	.4049	.4066	.4082	.4099	.4115	.4131	.4147	.4162	.4177
1.4	.4192	.4207	.4222	.4236	.4251	.4265	.4279	.4292	.4306	.4319
1.5	.4332	.4345	.4357	.4370	.4382	.4394	.4406	.4418	.4429	.4441
1.6	.4452	.4463	.4474	.4484	.4495	.4505	.4515	.4525	.4535	.4545
1.7	.4554	.4564	.4573	.4582	.4591	.4599	.4608	.4616	.4625	.4633
1.8	.4641	.4649	.4656	.4664	.4671	.4678	.4686	.4693	.4699	.4706
1.9	.4713	.4719	.4726	.4732	.4738	.4744	.4750	.4756	.4761	.4767
2.0	.4772	.4778	.4783	.4788	.4793	.4798	.4803	.4808	.4812	.4817
2.1	.4821	.4826	.4830	.4834	.4838	.4842	.4846	.4850	.4854	.4857
2.2	.4861	.4864	.4868	.4871	.4875	.4878	.4881	.4884	.4887	.4890
2.3	.4893	.4896	.4898	.4901	.4904	.4906	.4909	.4911	.4913	.4916
2.4	.4918	.4920	.4922	.4925	.4927	.4929	.4931	.4932	.4934	.4936
2.5	.4938	.4940	.4941	.4943	.4945	.4946	.4948	.4949	.4951	.4952
2.6	.4953	.4955	.4956	.4957	.4959	.4960	.4961	.4962	.4963	.4964
2.7	.4965	.4966	.4967	.4968	.4969	.4970	.4971	.4972	.4973	.4974
2.8	.4974	.4975	.4976	.4977	.4977	.4978	.4979	.4979	.4980	.4981
2.9	.4981	.4982	.4982	.4983	.4984	.4984	.4985	.4985	.4986	.4986
3.0	.49865	.4987	.4987	.4988	.4988	.4989	.4989	.4989	.4990	.4990
4.0	.49997									

DISTRIBUTION OF *t* FOR GIVEN PROBABILITY LEVELS

	LEVEL OF SIGNIFICANCE FOR ONE-TAILED TEST					
	.10	.05	.025	.01	.005	.0005
	LEVEL OF SIGNIFICANCE FOR TWO-TAILED TEST					
d.f.	.20	.10	.05	.02	.01	.001
1	3.078	6.314	12.706	31.821	63.657	636.619
2	1.886	2.920	4.303	6.965	9.925	31.598
3	1.638	2.353	3.182	4.541	5.841	12.941
4	1.533	2.132	2.776	3.747	4.604	8.610
5	1.476	2.015	2.571	3.365	4.032	6.859
6	1.440	1.943	2.447	3.143	3.707	5.959
7	1.415	1.895	2.365	2.998	3.499	5.405
8	1.397	1.860	2.306	2.896	3.355	5.041
9	1.383	1.833	2.262	2.821	3.250	4.781
10	1.372	1.812	2.228	2.764	3.169	4.587
11	1.363	1.796	2.201	2.718	3.106	4.437
12	1.356	1.782	2.179	2.681	3.055	4.318
13	1.350	1.771	2.160	2.650	3.012	4.221
14	1.345	1.761	2.145	2.624	2.977	4.140
15	1.341	1.753	2.131	2.602	2.947	4.073
16	1.337	1.746	2.120	2.583	2.921	4.015
17	1.333	1.740	2.110	2.567	2.898	3.965
18	1.330	1.734	2.101	2.552	2.878	3.922
19	1.328	1.729	2.093	2.539	2.861	3.883
20	1.325	1.725	2.086	2.528	2.845	3.850
21	1.323	1.721	2.080	2.518	2.831	3.819
22	1.321	1.717	2.074	2.508	2.819	3.792
23	1.319	1.714	2.069	2.500	2.807	3.767
24	1.318	1.711	2.064	2.492	2.797	3.745
25	1.316	1.708	2.060	2.485	2.787	3.725
26	1.315	1.706	2.056	2.479	2.779	3.707
27	1.314	1.703	2.052	2.473	2.771	3.690
28	1.313	1.701	2.048	2.467	2.763	3.674
29	1.311	1.699	2.045	2.462	2.756	3.659
30	1.310	1.697	2.042	2.457	2.750	3.646
40	1.303	1.684	2.021	2.423	2.704	3.551
60	1.296	1.671	2.000	2.390	2.660	3.460
120	1.289	1.658	1.980	2.358	2.617	3.373
∞	1.282	1.645	1.960	2.326	2.576	3.291

Source: Abridged from Table III of R. A. Fisher and F. Yates, *Statistical Tables for Biological, Agricultural, and Medical Research*, published by Longman Group, Ltd., London (previously published by Oliver & Boyd, Ltd., Edinburgh). Reproduced with the permission of Pearson Education Ltd.

CHI-SQUARE DISTRIBUTION

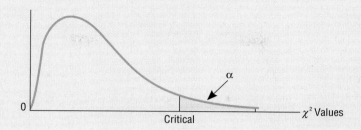

Degrees of Freedom (d.f.)	AREA IN SHADED RIGHT TAIL (α)		
	.10	.05	.01
1	2.706	3.841	6.635
2	4.605	5.991	9.210
3	6.251	7.815	11.345
4	7.779	9.488	13.277
5	9.236	11.070	15.086
6	10.645	12.592	16.812
7	12.017	14.067	18.475
8	13.362	15.507	20.090
9	14.684	16.919	21.666
10	15.987	18.307	23.209
11	17.275	19.675	24.725
12	18.549	21.026	26.217
13	19.812	22.362	27.688
14	21.064	23.685	29.141
15	22.307	24.996	30.578
16	23.542	26.296	32.000
17	24.769	27.587	33.409
18	25.989	28.869	34.805
19	27.204	30.144	36.191
20	28.412	31.410	37.566
21	29.615	32.671	38.932
22	30.813	33.924	40.289
23	32.007	35.172	41.638
24	33.196	36.415	42.980
25	34.382	37.652	44.314
26	35.563	38.885	45.642
27	36.741	40.113	46.963
28	37.916	41.337	48.278
29	39.087	42.557	49.588
30	40.256	43.773	50.892

Example of how to use this table: In a chi-square distribution with 6 degrees of freedom (*d.f.*), the area to the right of a critical value of 12.592—i.e., the α area—is .05.

Source: Abridged from Table IV of R. A. Fisher and F. Yates, *Statistical Tables for Biological, Agricultural, and Medical Research,* published by Longman Group, Ltd., London (previously published by Oliver & Boyd, Ltd., Edinburgh). Reproduced with the permission of Pearson Education Ltd.

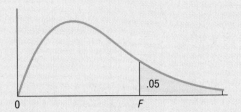

v_1 = DEGREES OF FREEDOM FOR NUMERATOR

v_2 = DEGREES OF FREEDOM FOR DENOMINATOR

	1	2	3	4	5	6	7	8	9	10	12	15	20	24	30	40	60	120	∞
1	161	200	216	225	230	234	237	239	241	242	244	246	248	249	250	251	252	253	254
2	18.5	19.0	19.2	19.2	19.3	19.3	19.4	19.4	19.4	19.4	19.4	19.4	19.5	19.5	19.5	19.5	19.5	19.5	19.5
3	10.1	9.55	9.28	9.12	9.01	8.94	8.89	8.85	8.81	8.79	8.74	8.70	8.66	8.64	8.62	8.59	8.57	8.55	8.53
4	7.71	6.94	6.59	6.39	6.26	6.16	6.09	6.04	6.00	5.96	5.91	5.86	5.80	5.77	5.75	5.72	5.69	5.66	5.63
5	6.61	5.79	5.41	5.19	5.05	4.95	4.88	4.82	4.77	4.74	4.68	4.62	4.56	4.53	4.50	4.46	4.43	4.40	4.37
6	5.99	5.14	4.76	4.53	4.39	4.28	4.21	4.15	4.10	4.06	4.00	3.94	3.87	3.84	3.81	3.77	3.74	3.70	3.67
7	5.59	4.74	4.35	4.12	3.97	3.87	3.79	3.73	3.68	3.64	3.57	3.51	3.44	3.41	3.38	3.34	3.30	3.27	3.23
8	5.32	4.46	4.07	3.84	3.69	3.58	3.50	3.44	3.39	3.35	3.28	3.22	3.15	3.12	3.08	3.04	3.01	2.97	2.93
9	5.12	4.26	3.86	3.63	3.48	3.37	3.29	3.23	3.18	3.14	3.07	3.01	2.94	2.90	2.86	2.83	2.79	2.75	2.71
10	4.96	4.10	3.71	3.48	3.33	3.22	3.14	3.07	3.02	2.98	2.91	2.85	2.77	2.74	2.70	2.66	2.62	2.58	2.54
11	4.84	3.98	3.59	3.36	3.20	3.09	3.01	2.95	2.90	2.85	2.79	2.72	2.65	2.61	2.57	2.53	2.49	2.45	2.40
12	4.75	3.89	3.49	3.26	3.11	3.00	2.91	2.85	2.80	2.75	2.69	2.62	2.54	2.51	2.47	2.43	2.38	2.34	2.30
13	4.67	3.81	3.41	3.18	3.03	2.92	2.83	2.77	2.71	2.67	2.60	2.53	2.46	2.42	2.38	2.34	2.30	2.25	2.21
14	4.60	3.74	3.34	3.11	2.96	2.85	2.76	2.70	2.65	2.60	2.53	2.46	2.39	2.35	2.31	2.27	2.22	2.18	2.13
15	4.54	3.68	3.29	3.06	2.90	2.79	2.71	2.64	2.59	2.54	2.48	2.40	2.33	2.29	2.25	2.20	2.16	2.11	2.07
16	4.49	3.63	3.24	3.01	2.85	2.74	2.66	2.59	2.54	2.49	2.42	2.35	2.28	2.24	2.19	2.15	2.11	2.06	2.01
17	4.45	3.59	3.20	2.96	2.81	2.70	2.61	2.55	2.49	2.45	2.38	2.31	2.23	2.19	2.15	2.10	2.06	2.01	1.96
18	4.41	3.55	3.16	2.93	2.77	2.66	2.58	2.51	2.46	2.41	2.34	2.27	2.19	2.15	2.11	2.06	2.02	1.97	1.92
19	4.38	3.52	3.13	2.90	2.74	2.63	2.54	2.48	2.42	2.38	2.31	2.23	2.16	2.11	2.07	2.03	1.98	1.93	1.88
20	4.35	3.49	3.10	2.87	2.71	2.60	2.51	2.45	2.39	2.35	2.28	2.20	2.12	2.08	2.04	1.99	1.95	1.90	1.84
21	4.32	3.47	3.07	2.84	2.68	2.57	2.49	2.42	2.37	2.32	2.25	2.18	2.10	2.05	2.01	1.96	1.92	1.87	1.81
22	4.30	3.44	3.05	2.82	2.66	2.55	2.46	2.40	2.34	2.30	2.23	2.15	2.07	2.03	1.98	1.94	1.89	1.84	1.78
23	4.28	3.42	3.03	2.80	2.64	2.53	2.44	2.37	2.32	2.27	2.20	2.13	2.05	2.01	1.96	1.91	1.86	1.81	1.76
24	4.26	3.40	3.01	2.78	2.62	2.51	2.42	2.36	2.30	2.25	2.18	2.11	2.03	1.98	1.94	1.89	1.84	1.79	1.73
25	4.24	3.39	2.99	2.76	2.60	2.49	2.40	2.34	2.28	2.24	2.16	2.09	2.01	1.96	1.92	1.87	1.82	1.77	1.71
30	4.17	3.32	2.92	2.69	2.53	2.42	2.33	2.27	2.21	2.16	2.09	2.01	1.93	1.89	1.84	1.79	1.74	1.68	1.62
40	4.08	3.23	2.84	2.61	2.45	2.34	2.25	2.18	2.12	2.08	2.00	1.92	1.84	1.79	1.74	1.69	1.64	1.58	1.51
60	4.00	3.15	2.76	2.53	2.37	2.25	2.17	2.10	2.04	1.99	1.92	1.84	1.75	1.70	1.65	1.59	1.53	1.47	1.39
120	3.92	3.07	2.68	2.45	2.29	2.18	2.09	2.02	1.96	1.91	1.83	1.75	1.66	1.61	1.55	1.50	1.43	1.35	1.25
∞	3.84	3.00	2.60	2.37	2.21	2.10	2.01	1.94	1.88	1.83	1.75	1.67	1.57	1.52	1.46	1.39	1.32	1.22	1.00

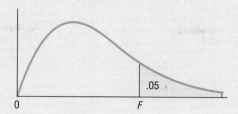

v_1 = DEGREES OF FREEDOM FOR NUMERATOR

	1	2	3	4	5	6	7	8	9	10	12	15	20	24	30	40	60	120	∞
1	4,052	5,000	5,403	5,625	5,764	5,859	5,928	5,982	6,023	6,056	6,106	6,157	6,209	6,235	6,261	6,287	6,313	6,339	6,366
2	98.5	99.0	99.2	99.2	99.3	99.3	99.4	99.4	99.4	99.4	99.4	99.4	99.4	99.5	99.5	99.5	99.5	99.5	99.5
3	34.1	30.8	29.5	28.7	28.2	27.9	27.7	27.5	27.3	27.2	27.1	26.9	26.7	26.6	26.5	26.4	26.3	26.2	26.1
4	21.2	18.0	16.7	16.0	15.5	15.2	15.0	14.8	14.7	14.5	14.4	14.2	14.0	13.9	13.8	13.7	13.7	13.6	13.5
5	16.3	13.3	12.1	11.4	11.0	10.7	10.5	10.3	10.2	10.1	9.89	9.72	9.55	9.47	9.38	9.29	9.20	9.11	9.02
6	13.7	10.9	9.78	9.15	8.75	8.47	8.26	8.10	7.98	7.87	7.72	7.56	7.40	7.31	7.23	7.14	7.06	6.97	6.88
7	12.2	9.55	8.45	7.85	7.46	7.19	6.99	6.84	6.72	6.62	6.47	6.31	6.16	6.07	5.99	5.91	5.82	5.74	5.65
8	11.3	8.65	7.59	7.01	6.63	6.37	6.18	6.03	5.91	5.81	5.67	5.52	5.36	5.28	5.20	5.12	5.03	4.95	4.86
9	10.6	8.02	6.99	6.42	6.06	5.80	5.61	5.47	5.35	5.26	5.11	4.96	4.81	4.73	4.65	4.57	4.48	4.40	4.31
10	10.0	7.56	6.55	5.99	5.64	5.39	5.20	5.06	4.94	4.85	4.71	4.56	4.41	4.33	4.25	4.17	4.08	4.00	3.91
11	9.65	7.21	6.22	5.67	5.32	5.07	4.89	4.74	4.63	4.54	4.40	4.25	4.10	4.02	3.94	3.86	3.78	3.69	3.60
12	9.33	6.93	5.95	5.41	5.06	4.82	4.64	4.50	4.39	4.30	4.16	4.01	3.86	3.78	3.70	3.62	3.54	3.45	3.36
13	9.07	6.70	5.74	5.21	4.86	4.62	4.44	4.30	4.19	4.10	3.96	3.82	3.66	3.59	3.51	3.43	3.34	3.25	3.17
14	8.86	6.51	5.56	5.04	4.70	4.46	4.28	4.14	4.03	3.94	3.80	3.66	3.51	3.43	3.35	3.27	3.18	3.09	3.00
15	8.68	6.36	5.42	4.89	4.56	4.32	4.14	4.00	3.89	3.80	3.67	3.52	3.37	3.29	3.21	3.13	3.05	2.96	2.87
16	8.53	6.23	5.29	4.77	4.44	4.20	4.03	3.89	3.78	3.69	3.55	3.41	3.26	3.18	3.10	3.02	2.93	2.84	2.75
17	8.40	6.11	5.19	4.67	4.34	4.10	3.93	3.79	3.68	3.59	3.46	3.31	3.16	3.08	3.00	2.92	2.83	2.75	2.65
18	8.29	6.01	5.09	4.58	4.25	4.01	3.84	3.71	3.60	3.51	3.37	3.23	3.08	3.00	2.92	2.84	2.75	2.66	2.57
19	8.19	5.93	5.01	4.50	4.17	3.94	3.77	3.63	3.52	3.43	3.30	3.15	3.00	2.92	2.84	2.76	2.67	2.58	2.49
20	8.10	5.85	4.94	4.43	4.10	3.87	3.70	3.56	3.46	3.37	3.23	3.09	2.94	2.86	2.78	2.69	2.61	2.52	2.42
21	8.02	5.78	4.87	4.37	4.04	3.81	3.64	3.51	3.40	3.31	3.17	3.03	2.88	2.80	2.72	2.64	2.55	2.46	2.36
22	7.96	5.72	4.82	4.31	3.99	3.76	3.59	3.45	3.35	3.26	3.12	2.98	2.83	2.75	2.67	2.58	2.50	2.40	2.31
23	7.88	5.66	4.76	4.26	3.94	3.71	3.54	3.41	3.30	3.21	3.07	2.93	2.78	2.70	2.62	2.54	2.45	2.35	2.26
24	7.82	5.61	4.72	4.22	3.90	3.67	3.50	3.36	3.26	3.17	3.03	2.89	2.74	2.66	2.58	2.49	2.40	2.31	2.21
25	7.77	5.57	4.68	4.18	3.86	3.63	3.46	3.32	3.22	3.13	2.99	2.85	2.70	2.62	2.53	2.45	2.36	2.27	2.17
30	7.58	5.39	4.51	4.02	3.70	3.47	3.30	3.17	3.07	2.98	2.84	2.70	2.55	2.47	2.39	2.30	2.21	2.11	2.01
40	7.31	5.18	4.31	3.83	3.51	3.29	3.12	2.99	2.89	2.80	2.66	2.52	2.37	2.29	2.20	2.11	2.02	1.92	1.80
60	7.08	4.98	4.13	3.65	3.34	3.12	2.95	2.82	2.72	2.63	2.50	2.35	2.20	2.12	2.03	1.94	1.84	1.73	1.60
120	6.85	4.79	3.95	3.48	3.17	2.96	2.79	2.66	2.56	2.47	2.34	2.19	2.03	1.95	1.86	1.76	1.66	1.53	1.38
∞	6.63	4.61	3.78	3.32	3.02	2.80	2.64	2.51	2.41	2.32	2.18	2.04	1.88	1.79	1.70	1.59	1.47	1.32	1.00

v_2 = DEGREES OF FREEDOM FOR DENOMINATOR

CRITICAL VALUES OF THE PEARSON CORRELATION COEFFICIENT

	LEVEL OF SIGNIFICANCE FOR ONE-TAILED TEST			
	.05	.025	.01	.005
	LEVEL OF SIGNIFICANCE FOR TWO-TAILED TEST			
d.f.	.10	.05	.02	.01
1	.988	.997	.9995	.9999
2	.900	.950	.980	.990
3	.805	.878	.934	.959
4	.729	.811	.882	.917
5	.669	.754	.833	.874
6	.622	.707	.789	.834
7	.582	.666	.750	.798
8	.549	.632	.716	.765
9	.521	.602	.685	.735
10	.497	.576	.658	.708
11	.576	.553	.634	.684
12	.458	.532	.612	.661
13	.441	.514	.592	.641
14	.426	.497	.574	.623
15	.412	.482	.558	.606
16	.400	.468	.542	.590
17	.389	.456	.528	.575
18	.378	.444	.516	.561
19	.369	.433	.503	.549
20	.360	.423	.492	.537
21	.352	.413	.482	.526
22	.344	.404	.472	.515
23	.337	.396	.462	.505
24	.330	.388	.453	.496
25	.323	.381	.445	.487
26	.317	.374	.437	.479
27	.311	.367	.430	.471
28	.306	.361	.423	.463
29	.301	.355	.416	.486
30	.296	.349	.409	.449
35	.275	.325	.381	.418
40	.257	.304	.358	.393
45	.243	.288	.338	.372
50	.231	.273	.322	.354
60	.211	.250	.295	.325
70	.195	.232	.274	.303
80	.183	.217	.256	.283
90	.173	.205	.242	.267
100	.164	.195	.230	.254

Source: Abridged from Table IV of R. A. Fisher and F. Yates, *Statistical Tables for Biological, Agricultural, and Medical Research*, published by Longman Group, Ltd., London (previously published by Oliver & Boyd, Ltd., Edinburgh). Reproduced with the permission of Pearson Education Ltd.

Greek Letters

α (alpha)   level of significance or probability of a Type I error

β (beta)   probability of a Type II error or slope of the regression line

μ (mu)   population mean

ρ (rho)   population Pearson correlation coefficient

Σ (summation)   take the sum of

π (pi)   population proportion

σ (sigma)   population standard deviation

χ^2 chi-square statistic

English Letters

$d.f.$ number of degrees of freedom

F F-statistic

n sample size

p sample proportion

$\Pr(\ )$ probability of the outcome in the parentheses

r sample Pearson correlation coefficient

r^2 coefficient of determination (squared correlation coefficient)

R^2 coefficient of determination (multiple regression)

S sample standard deviation (inferential statistics)

$S_{\overline{X}}$ estimated standard error of the mean

S_p estimated standard error of the proportion

S^2 sample variance (inferential statistics)

t t-statistic

X variable or any unspecified observation

$\overline{X}$ sample mean

Y any unspecified observation on a second variable, usually the dependent variable

$\hat{Y}$ predicted score

Z standardized score (descriptive statistics) or Z-statistic

A

acquiescence bias A category of response bias that results because some individuals tend to agree with all questions or to concur with a particular position.

administrative error An error caused by the improper administration or execution of the research task.

advocacy research Research undertaken to support a specific claim in a legal action.

alternative hypothesis A statement indicating the opposite of the null hypothesis.

analysis of variance (ANOVA) Analysis involving the investigation of the effects of one treatment variable on an interval-scaled dependent variable; a hypothesis-testing technique to determine whether statistically significant differences on means occur among three or more groups.

applied research Research conducted when a decision must be made about a real-life problem.

at-home scanning system A system that allows consumer panellists to perform their own scanning after taking home products, using hand-held wands that read UPC symbols.

attitude An enduring disposition to consistently respond in a given manner to various aspects of the world; composed of affective, cognitive, and behavioural components.

attribute A single characteristic or fundamental feature of an object, person, situation, or issue.

auspices bias Bias in the responses of subjects caused by their being influenced by the organization conducting the study.

B

back translation Taking a questionnaire that has previously been translated into another language and having a second, independent translator translate it back to the original language.

balanced rating scale A fixed-alternative rating scale with an equal number of positive and negative categories; a neutral point or point of indifference is at the centre of the scale.

base The number of respondents or observations (in a row or column) used as a basis for computing percentages.

basic experimental design An experimental design in which a single independent variable is manipulated to measure its effect on another single dependent variable.

basic (pure) research Research conducted to expand the limits of knowledge, to verify the acceptability of a given theory, or to learn more about a certain concept.

behavioural differential A rating scale instrument similar to a semantic differential, developed to measure the behavioural intentions of subjects toward future actions.

bivariate linear regression A measure of linear association that investigates a straight-line relationship of the type $Y = \alpha + \beta X$, where X is the independent variable and α and β are two constants to be estimated.

blinding effect A technique used to control subjects' knowledge of whether or not they have been given a particular experimental treatment.

briefing session A training session to ensure that each interviewer is provided with common information to a particular project.

C

callback An attempt to recontact individuals selected for a sample who were not available initially.

case study method The exploratory research technique that intensively investigates one or a few situations similar to the problem situation.

categorical variable A variable that has a limited number of distinct values.

category scale A rating scale that consists of several response categories, often providing respondents with alternatives to indicate positions on a continuum.

causal research Research conducted to identify cause-and-effect relationships among variables.

census An investigation of all the individual elements that make up a population.

central-limit theorem The theory that, as sample size increases, the distribution of sample means of size n, randomly selected, approaches a normal distribution.

central location interviewing Telephone interviews conducted from a central location using WATS lines at fixed charges.

check box In an Internet questionnaire, a small graphic box, next to an answer, that a respondent clicks on to choose that answer; typically, a check mark or an X appears in the box when the respondent clicks on it.

checklist question A fixed-alternative question that allows the respondent to provide multiple answers to a single question by checking off items.

chi-square (χ^2) test A hypothesis test that allows for investigation of statistical significance in the analysis of a frequency distribution.

chi-square test for a contingency table A test that statistically analyzes significance in a joint frequency distribution.

client Term often used by the research department to refer to line management for whom services are being performed.

cluster sampling An economically efficient sampling technique in which the primary sampling unit is not the individual element in the population but a large cluster of elements; clusters are selected randomly.

code book A book that identifies each variable in a study and gives the variable's description, code name, and position in the data matrix.

code of ethics A set of guidelines that states the standards and operating procedures for ethical practices by researchers.

codes Rules for interpreting, classifying, and recording data in the coding process; also, the actual numerical or other character symbols assigned to raw data.

coding The process of assigning a numerical score or other character symbol to previously edited data.

coefficient of determination (r^2) A measure obtained by squaring the correlation coefficient; that proportion of the total variance of a variable that is accounted for by knowing the value of another variable.

cohort effect A change in the dependent variable that occurs because members of one experimental group experienced different historical situations than members of other experimental groups.

comparative rating scale Any measure of attitudes that asks respondents to rate a concept in comparison with a benchmark explicitly used as a frame of reference.

computer-assisted telephone interview (CATI) Technology that allows answers to telephone interviews to be entered directly into a computer for processing.

concept A generalized idea about a class of objects, attributes, occurrences, or processes.

concept testing Any exploratory research procedure that tests some sort of stimulus as a proxy for an idea about a new, revised, or repositioned product, service, or strategy.

conceptual definition A verbal explanation of the meaning of a concept. It defines what the concept is and what it is not.

conclusions and recommendations The part of the report that provides opinions based on the results and suggestions for action.

conclusions and report preparation stage The stage in which the researcher interprets information and draws conclusions to be communicated to decision makers.

confidence interval estimate A specified range of numbers within which a population mean is expected to lie; an estimate of the population mean based on the knowledge that it will be equal to the sample mean plus or minus a small sampling error.

confidence level A percentage or decimal value that tells how confident a researcher can be about being correct. It states the long-run percentage of confidence intervals that will include the true population mean.

constancy of conditions A situation in which subjects in experimental groups and control groups are exposed to situations identical except for differing conditions of the independent variable.

constant error An error that occurs in the same experimental condition every time the basic experiment is repeated; a systematic bias.

constant-sum scale A measure of attitudes in which respondents are asked to divide a constant sum to indicate the relative importance of attributes; respondents often sort cards, but the task may also be a rating task.

construct validity The ability of a measure to provide empirical evidence consistent with a theory based on the concepts.

consumer panel A longitudinal survey of the same sample of individuals or households to record their attitudes, behaviour, or purchasing habits over time.

content analysis The systematic observation and quantitative description of the manifest content of communication.

continuous variable A variable that has an infinite number of possible values.

contrived observation Observation in which the investigator creates an artificial environment in order to test a hypothesis.

control group The group of subjects exposed to the control condition in an experiment—that is, not exposed to the experimental treatment.

controlled store test A hybrid between a laboratory experiment and a test market; test products are sold in a small number of selected stores to actual customers.

convenience sampling The sampling procedure of obtaining those people or units that are most conveniently available.

correlation coefficient A statistical measure of the covariation, or association, between two variables.

correlation matrix The standard form for reporting correlational results.

counterbiasing statement An introductory statement or preamble to a potentially embarrassing question

that reduces a respondent's reluctance to answer by suggesting that certain behaviour is not unusual.

cover letter Letter that accompanies a questionnaire to induce the reader to complete and return the questionnaire.

criterion validity The ability of a measure to correlate with other standard measures of the same construct or established criterion.

critical values The values that lie exactly on the boundary of the region of rejection.

cross-checks The comparison of data from one source with data from another source to determine the similarity of independent projects.

cross-functional teams Teams composed of individuals from various organizational departments such as engineering, production, finance, and marketing who share a common purpose.

cross-sectional study A study in which various segments of a population are sampled and data are collected at a single moment in time.

cross-tabulation (contingency table) Organizing data by groups, categories, or classes to facilitate comparisons; a joint frequency distribution of observations on two or more sets of variables.

custom research A marketing research study designed for an individual client and tailored to the client's unique needs.

D

data conversion The process of changing the original form of the data to a format suitable to achieve the research objective, also called data transformation.

data entry The activity of transferring data from a research project to computers.

data gathering stage The stage in which the researcher collects the data.

data matrix A rectangular arrangement of data in rows and columns.

data mining The use of powerful computers to dig through volumes of data to discover patterns about an organization's customers and products. It is a broad term that applies to many different forms of analysis.

data processing and analysis stage The stage in which the researcher performs several interrelated procedures to convert the data into a format that will answer management's questions.

data processing error A category of administrative error that occurs because of incorrect data entry, incorrect computer programming, or other procedural errors during data analysis.

data transformation (data conversion) The process of changing the original form of data to a format suitable to achieve the research objective.

database marketing The use of customer databases to promote one-to-one relationships with customers and create precisely targeted promotions.

debriefing The process of providing subjects with all pertinent facts about the nature and purpose of an experiment after its completion.

decision makers' objectives Managerial goals expressed in measurable terms.

decision making The process used to resolve a problem or to choose from alternative opportunities.

demand characteristics Experimental design procedures or situational aspects of an experiment that provide unintentional hints about the experimenter's hypothesis to subjects.

dependent variable The criterion or standard by which the results of an experiment are judged; a variable expected to be dependent on the experimenter's manipulation of the independent variable.

depth interviews A relatively unstructured, extensive interview in which the interviewer asks many questions and probes for in-depth answers.

descriptive analysis The transformation of raw data into a form that will make them easy to understand and interpret; rearranging, ordering, and manipulating data to generate descriptive information.

descriptive research Research designed to describe characteristics of a population or phenomenon.

determinant-choice question A fixed-alternative question that requires the respondent to choose one response from among multiple alternatives.

dialogue box A window that opens on a computer screen to prompt the user to enter information.

direct data entry The use of an online computer terminal as an input device for data storage.

direct observation A straightforward attempt to observe and record what naturally occurs; the investigator does not create an artificial situation.

director of marketing research The person who plans, executes, and controls the marketing research function.

discussion guide A document prepared by the focus group moderator that contains remarks about the nature of the group and outlines the topics or questions to be addressed.

disguised question An indirect question that assumes the purpose of the study must be hidden from the respondent.

disproportional stratified sample A stratified sample in which the sample size for each stratum is allocated according to analytical considerations.

door-to-door interview Personal interview conducted at respondents' doorsteps in an effort to increase the participation rate in the survey.

double-barrelled question A question that may induce bias because it covers two issues at once.

double-blind design A technique in which neither the subjects nor the experimenter knows which are the experimental and which the controlled conditions.

drop-down box In an Internet questionnaire, a space-spacing device that reveals responses when they are needed but otherwise hides them from view.

drop-off method A survey method that requires the interviewer to travel to the respondent's location to drop off questionnaires that will be picked up later.

E

editing The process of checking the completeness, consistency, and legibility of data and making the data ready for coding and transfer to storage.

elaboration analysis An analysis of the basic cross-tabulation for each level of a variable not previously considered, such as subgroups of the sample.

e-mail survey Surveys distributed through electronic mail.

environmental scanning Information gathering and fact-finding that is designed to detect indications of environmental changes in their initial stages of development.

equivalent-form method A method that measures the correlation between alternative instruments, designed to be as equivalent as possible, administered to the same group of subjects.

error trapping Using software to control the flow of an Internet questionnaire—for example, to prevent respondents from backing up or failing to answer a question.

experience survey An exploratory research technique in which individuals who are knowledgeable about a particular research problem are questioned.

experiment A research method in which conditions are controlled so that one or more independent variables can be manipulated to test a hypothesis about a dependent variable. Experimentation allows evaluation of causal relationships among variables while all other variables are eliminated or controlled.

experimental group The group of subjects exposed to the experimental treatment.

experimental treatments Alternative manipulations of the independent variable being investigated.

exploratory research Initial research conducted to clarify and define a problem.

external data Data created, recorded, or generated by an entity other than the researcher's organization.

external validity The ability of an experiment to generalize beyond the experiment data to other subjects or groups in the population under study.

extremity bias A category of response bias that results because some individuals tend to use extremes when responding to questions.

eye-tracking monitor A mechanical device used to observe eye movements. Some eye monitors use infrared light beams to measure unconscious eye movements.

F

face (or content) validity Professional agreement that a scale's content logically appears to accurately reflect what was intended to be measured.

fax survey A survey that uses fax machines as a way for respondents to receive and return questionnaires.

field editing Preliminary editing by a field supervisor on the same day as the interview to catch technical omissions, check legibility of handwriting, and clarify responses that are logically or conceptually inconsistent.

field experiment An experiment conducted in a natural setting, where complete control of extraneous variables is not possible.

field interviewing service A research supplier that specializes in gathering data.

fieldworker An individual who is responsible for gathering data in the field.

filter question A question that screens out respondents who are not qualified to answer a second question.

fixed-alternative question A question in which the respondent is given specific, limited-alternative responses and asked to choose the one closest to his or her own viewpoint.

focus group interview An unstructured, free-flowing interview with a small group of people.

forced answering software Software that prevents respondents from continuing with an Internet questionnaire if they fail to answer a question.

forced-choice rating scale A fixed-alternative rating scale that requires respondents to choose one of the fixed alternatives.

frequency distribution A set of data organized by summarizing the number of times a particular value of a variable occurs.

frequency table The arrangement of statistical data in a row-and-column format that exhibits the count of responses or observations for each category assigned to a variable.

frequency-determination question A fixed-alternative question that asks for an answer about general frequency of occurrence.

F-test (regression) A procedure to determine whether more variability is explained by the regression or unexplained by the regression.

funnel technique Asking general questions before specific questions in order to obtain unbiased responses.

G

graphic aids Pictures or diagrams used to clarify complex points or emphasize a message.

graphic rating scale A measure of attitude that allows respondents to rate an object by choosing any point along a graphic continuum.

guinea pig effect An effect on the results of an experiment caused by subjects changing their normal behaviour or attitudes in order to cooperate with an experimenter.

H

Hawthorne effect An unintended effect on the results of a research experiment caused by the subjects knowing that they are participants.

hidden observation Observation in which the subject is unaware that observation is taking place.

history effect The loss of internal validity caused by specific events in the external environment, occurring between the first and second measurements, that are beyond the control of the experimenter.

hypothesis An unproven proposition or supposition that tentatively explains certain facts or phenomena; a proposition that is empirically testable.

hypothetical construct A variable that is not directly observable but is measurable through indirect indicators, such as verbal expression or overt behaviour.

I

iceberg principle The idea that the dangerous part of many marketing problems is neither visible to nor understood by marketing managers.

image profile A graphic representation of semantic differential data for competing brands, products, or stores to highlight comparisons.

independent variable A variable that is expected to influence a dependent variable.

index (or composite) measure A composite measure of several variables used to measure a single concept; a multi-item instrument.

index of retail saturation A calculation that describes the relationship between retail demand and supply.

informed consent Notion that the individual understands the reason for the research and waives his or her right to privacy when he or she agrees to participate in the research study.

in-house editing A rigorous editing job performed by a centralized office staff.

instrumentation effect An effect on the results of an experiment caused by a change in the wording of questions, a change in interviewers, or other changes in procedures used to measure the dependent variable.

internal and proprietary data Secondary data that originate inside the organization.

internal validity Validity determined by whether an experimental treatment was the sole cause of changes in a dependent variable or whether the experimental manipulation did what it was supposed to do.

Internet survey A self-administered questionnaire posted on a Web site.

interval scale A scale that both arranges objects according to their magnitudes and distinguishes this ordered arrangement in units of equal intervals.

interviewer bias A response bias that occurs because the presence of the interviewer influences respondents' answers.

interviewer cheating The practice by fieldworkers of filling in fake answers or falsifying interviews.

interviewer error Mistakes made by interviewers failing to record survey responses correctly.

introduction The part of the research report that discusses background information and the overall purpose of the research.

item nonresponse Failure of a respondent to provide an answer to a survey question.

J

judgment (purposive) sampling
A nonprobability sampling technique in which an experienced individual selects the sample based on personal judgment about some appropriate characteristic of the sample member.

L

laboratory experiment An experiment conducted in a laboratory or other artificial setting to obtain almost complete control over the research setting.

leading question A question that suggests or implies certain answers.

Likert scale A measure of attitudes designed to allow respondents to rate how strongly they agree or disagree with carefully constructed statements, ranging from very positive to very negative attitudes toward some object; several scale items may be used to form a summated index.

limitations The part of the research report that indicates the shortcomings of the research.

loaded question A question that suggests a socially desirable answer or is emotionally charged.

longitudinal study A survey of respondents at different times, thus allowing analysis of response continuity and changes over time.

M

mail survey A self-administered questionnaire sent to respondents through the mail.

mall intercept interview Personal interview conducted in a shopping mall.

manager of customer quality research A research staff person who specializes in conducting surveys to measure consumer's satisfaction with product quality.

market tracking The observation and analysis of trends in industry volume and brand share over time.

marketing concept The most central idea in marketing thinking, which calls on managers to be consumer-oriented, to stress long-run profitability rather than sales volume, and to adopt a cross-functional perspective.

marketing research The systematic and objective process of generating information to aid in making marketing decisions.

matching A procedure for the assignment of subjects to groups that ensures each group of respondents is matched on the basis of pertinent characteristics.

maturation effect An effect on the results of an experiment caused by experimental subjects maturing or changing over time.

mean A measure of central tendency; the arithmetic average.

measure of association A general term that refers to a number of bivariate statistical techniques used to measure the strength of a relationship between two variables.

median A measure of central tendency that is the midpoint; the value below which half the values in a distribution fall.

mixed-mode survey Study that employs any combination of survey methods.

mode A measure of central tendency; the value that occurs most often.

model building The use of secondary data to help specify relationships between two or more variables. Model building can involve the development of descriptive or predictive equations.

moderator The person who leads a focus group discussion.

moderator variable A third variable that, when introduced into an analysis, alters or has a contingent effect on the relationship between an independent variable and a dependent variable.

monadic rating scale Any measure of attitudes that asks respondents about a single concept in isolation.

mortality (sample attrition) effect A sample bias that results from the withdrawal of some subjects from the experiment before it is completed.

multiple-grid question Several similar questions arranged in a grid format.

multiple regression analysis An analysis of association in which the effects of two or more independent variables on a single, interval-scaled dependent variable are investigated simultaneously.

multistage area sampling Sampling that involves using a combination of two or more probability sampling techniques.

N

neural network A form of artificial intelligence in which a computer is programmed to mimic the way that human brains process information.

no contact A person who is not at home or who is otherwise inaccessible on the first and second contact.

nominal scale A scale in which the numbers or letters assigned to objects serve as labels for identification or classification.

non-forced-choice scale A fixed-alternative rating scale that provides a "no opinion" category or that allows respondents to indicate that they cannot say which alternative is their choice.

nonprobability sampling A sampling technique in which units of the sample are selected on the basis of personal judgment or convenience; the probability of any particular member of the population being chosen is unknown.

nonrespondent A person who is not contacted or who refuses to cooperate in the research.

nonresponse error The statistical differences between a survey that includes only those who responded and a perfect survey that would also include those who failed to respond.

normal distribution A symmetrical, bell-shaped distribution that describes the expected probability distribution of many chance occurrences.

null hypothesis A statement about a status quo asserting that any change from what has been thought to be true will be due entirely to random sampling error.

numerical scale An attitude rating scale similar to a semantic differential except that it uses numbers, instead of verbal descriptions, as response options to identify response positions.

O

observation The systematic process of recording the behavioural patterns of people, objects, and occurrences as they are witnessed.

observer bias A distortion of measurement resulting from the cognitive behaviour or actions of a witnessing observer.

one-group pre-test–post-test design A quasi-experimental design in which the subjects in the experimental group are measured before and after the treatment is administered, but there is no control group.

one-shot design An after-only design in which a single measure is recorded after the treatment is administered.

online focus group A focus group whose members use Internet technology to carry on their discussion.

open-ended box In an Internet questionnaire, a box where respondents can type in their own answers to open-ended questions.

open-ended response question A question that poses some problem and asks the respondent to answer in his or her own words.

operational definition An explanation that gives meaning to a concept by specifying the activities or operations necessary to measure it.

opt in To give permission to receive selected e-mail, such as questionnaires, from a company with an Internet presence.

optical scanning system A data processing input device that reads material directly from mark sensed questionnaires.

oral presentation A spoken summary of the major findings, conclusions, and recommendations, given to clients or line managers to provide them with the opportunity to clarify any ambiguous issues by asking questions.

order bias Bias caused by the influence of earlier questions in a questionnaire or by an answer's position in a set of answers.

ordinal scale A scale that arranges objects or alternatives according to their magnitude in an ordered relationship.

P

paired comparison A measurement technique that involves presenting the respondent with two objects and asking the respondent to pick the preferred object. More than two objects may be presented, but comparisons are made in pairs.

percentage distribution A frequency distribution organized into a table (or graph) that summarizes percentage values associated with particular values of a variable.

performance-monitoring research Research that regularly provides feedback for evaluation and control of marketing activity.

personal interview Face-to-face communication in which an interviewer asks a respondent to answer questions.

picture frustration A version of the TAT that uses a cartoon drawing for which the respondent suggests dialogue the characters might engage in.

pilot study A collective term for any small-scale exploratory research project that uses sampling but does not apply rigorous standards.

pivot question A filter question used to determine which version of a second question will be asked.

plug value An answer that an editor "plugs in" to replace blanks or missing values so as to permit data analysis; choice of value is based on a predetermined decision rule.

point estimate An estimate of the population mean in the form of a single value, usually the sample mean.

population (universe) Any complete group of entities that share some common set of characteristics.

population distribution A frequency distribution of the elements of a population.

population element An individual member of a population.

population parameters Variables in a population or measured characteristics of the population.

pop-up boxes In an Internet questionnaire, boxes that appear at selected points and contain information or instructions for respondents.

post-test–only control group design An after-only design in which the experimental group is tested after exposure to the treatment and the control group is tested at the same time without having been exposed to the treatment; no pre-measure is taken. Random assignment of subjects and treatment occurs.

pre-testing Screening procedure that involves a trial run with a group of respondents to iron out fundamental problems in the survey design.

pre-test–post-test control group design A true experimental design in which the experimental group is tested before and after exposure to the treatment and the control group is tested at the same two times without being exposed to the experimental treatment.

primary sampling unit (PSU) A term used to designate a unit selected in the first stage of sampling.

probability The long-run relative frequency with which an event will occur.

probability sampling A sampling technique in which every member of the population has a known, non-zero probability of selection.

probing A method used in personal interviews in which the interviewer asks the respondent for clarification of answers to standardized questions.

problem definition stage The stage in which management seeks to identify a clear-cut statement of the problem or opportunity.

problem or opportunity formulation The crucial first stage in the research process—determining the problem to be solved or the opportunity to be studied and the objectives of the research.

program strategy The overall plan to conduct a series of marketing research projects; a planning activity that places each marketing project in the context of the company's marketing plan.

projective technique An indirect means of questioning that enables a respondent to project beliefs and feelings onto a third party, an inanimate object, or a task situation.

proportion The percentage of elements that meet some criterion.

proportional stratified sample A stratified sample in which the number of sampling units drawn from each stratum is in proportion to the population size of that stratum.

pseudo-research Activities that appear to be research but are conducted for the purposes of organizational politics rather than objective gathering of information.

psychogalvanometer A device that measures galvanic skin response, a measure of involuntary changes in the electrical resistance of the skin.

pupilometer A mechanical device used to observe and record changes in the diameter of a subject's pupils.

push button In a dialogue box on an Internet questionnaire, a small outlined area, such as a rectangle or an arrow, that the respondent clicks on to select an option or perform a function, such as Submit.

push technology Internet information technology that automatically delivers content to the researcher's or manager's desktop.

Q

quasi-experimental design A research design that cannot be classified as a true experiment because it lacks adequate control of extraneous variables.

quota sampling A nonprobability sampling procedure that ensures that various subgroups of a population will be represented on pertinent characteristics to the exact extent that the investigator desires.

R

radio button In an Internet questionnaire, a circular icon, resembling a button, that activates one response choice and deactivates others when a respondent clicks on it.

random digit dialling Use of telephone exchanges and a table of random numbers to contact respondents with unlisted phone numbers.

random sampling error The difference between sample result and the result of a census conducted using identical procedures; a statistical fluctuation that occurs because of chance variations in the elements selected for a sample.

randomization A procedure in which the assignment of subjects and treatments to groups is based on chance.

randomized response questions A research procedure used for dealing with sensitive topics, in which a random procedure determines which of two questions a respondent will be asked to answer.

ranking A measurement task that requires respondents to rank order a small number of stores, brands, or objects on the basis of overall preference or some characteristic of the stimulus.

rating A measurement task that requires respondents to estimate the magnitude of a characteristic or quality that a brand, store, or object possesses.

ratio scale A scale that has absolute rather than relative quantities and an absolute zero where there is an absence of a given attribute.

recode To use a computer to convert original codes used for raw data into codes that are more suitable for analysis.

refusal A person who is unwilling to participate in a research project.

relationship marketing The idea that a major goal of marketing is the building of long-term relationships with the parties that contribute to an organization's success.

reliability The degree to which measures are free from random error and therefore yield consistent results.

repeated measures Experimental technique in which the same subjects are exposed to all experimental treatments to eliminate any problems due to subject differences.

report format The makeup or arrangement of parts necessary to a good research report.

research design A master plan that specifies the methods and procedures for collecting and analyzing needed information.

research design stage The stage in which the researcher determines a framework for the research plan of action by selecting a basic research method.

research follow-up Recontacting decision makers and/or clients after they have had a chance to read over a research report, in order to determine whether additional information or clarification is necessary.

research generalist A person who can serve as a communication link between management and the research specialist because he or she understands the needs of both parties.

research methodology The section of the written report that explains the research design, sampling procedures, and other technical and methodological procedures that were employed to collect the data.

research objectives The part of the research report that clearly explains the research problem and the relevant research questions that the research aims to answer.

research proposal A written statement of the research design that includes a statement explaining the purpose of the study and a detailed, systematic outline of procedures associated with a particular research methodology.

research report An oral presentation or written statement of research results, strategic recommendations, and/or other conclusions to a specific audience.

research sophistication A stage in which managers have considerable experience in the proper use of research techniques.

research supplier A commercial marketing research service that conducts marketing research for clients. The marketing research supplier may be thought of as a marketing research consulting company.

respondent The person who verbally answers an interviewer's questions or provides answers to written questions.

respondent error A category of sample bias resulting from some respondent action or inaction such as nonresponse or response bias.

response bias A bias that occurs when respondents either consciously or unconsciously tend to answer questions with a certain slant that misrepresents the truth.

response latency The amount of time it takes to make a choice between two alternatives; used as a measure of the strength of preference.

response rate The number of questionnaires returned or completed divided by the number of eligible people who were asked to participate in the survey.

results section The part of the body of a report that presents the findings of the project. It includes tables, charts, and an organized narrative.

reverse directory A directory similar to a telephone directory except that listings are by city and street address or by phone number rather than alphabetically by last name.

role-playing technique A projective technique that requires the subject to act out someone else's behaviour in a particular setting.

S

sample A subset, or some part, of a larger population.

sample bias A persistent tendency for the results of a sample to deviate in one direction from the true value of the population parameter.

sample distribution A frequency distribution of a sample.

sample selection error An administrative error caused by improper sample design or sampling procedure execution.

sample statistics Variables in a sample or measures computed from sample data.

sample survey A more formal term for a survey.

sampling distribution A theoretical probability distribution of sample means for all possible samples of a certain size drawn from a particular population.

sampling frame A list of elements from which a sample may be drawn; also called working population.

sampling frame error An error that occurs when certain sample elements are not listed or are not accurately represented in a sampling frame.

sampling stage The stage in which the researcher determines who is to be sampled, how large a sample is needed, and how sampling units will be selected.

sampling unit A single element or group of elements subject to selection in the sample.

scale Any series of items that are arranged progressively according to value or magnitude; a series into which an item can be placed according to its quantification.

scanner-based consumer panel A type of consumer panel in which participants' purchasing habits are recorded with a laser scanner rather than a purchase diary.

scientific method The techniques and procedures used to recognize and understand marketing phenomena.

secondary data Data that have been previously collected for some purpose other than the one at hand.

secondary sampling unit A term used to designate a unit selected in the second stage of sampling.

selection effect A sampling bias that results from differential selection of respondents for the comparison groups.

self-administered questionnaire Survey in which the respondent takes the responsibility for reading and answering the questions.

self-selection bias A bias that occurs because people who feel strongly about a subject are more likely to respond to survey questions than people who feel indifferent about it.

semantic differential A measure of attitudes that consists of a series of 7-point rating scales that use bipolar adjectives to anchor the beginning and end of each scale.

sensitivity A measurement instrument's ability to accurately measure variability in stimuli or responses.

sentence completion method A projective technique in which respondents are required to complete a number of partial sentences with the first word or phrase that comes to mind.

significance level The critical probability in choosing between the null and alternative hypotheses; the probability level that is too low to warrant support of the null hypothesis.

simple-dichotomy (dichotomous-alternative) question A fixed-alternative question that requires the respondent to choose one of two alternatives.

simple random sampling A sampling procedure that assures each element in the population of an equal chance of being included in the sample.

single-source data Diverse types of data offered by a single company. The data are usually integrated on the basis of a common variable such as geographic area or store.

site analysis techniques Techniques that use secondary data to select the best location for retail or wholesale operations.

situation analysis A preliminary investigation or informal gathering of background information to familiarize researchers or managers with the decision area.

snowball sampling A sampling procedure in which initial respondents are selected by probability methods and additional respondents are obtained from information provided by the initial respondents.

social desirability bias Bias in responses caused by respondents' desire, either conscious or unconscious, to gain prestige or appear in a different social role.

societal norms Codes of behaviour adopted by a group that suggest what a member of the group ought to do under given circumstances.

Solomon four-group design A true experimental design that combines the pre-test–post-test with control group design and the post-test–only with control group design, thereby providing a means for controlling the interactive testing effect and other sources of extraneous variation.

sorting A measurement task that presents a respondent with several objects or product concepts and requires the respondent to arrange the objects into piles or classify the product concepts.

split-ballot technique Using two alternative phrasings of the same questions for respective halves of a sample to elicit a more accurate total response than would a single phrasing.

split-half method A method for assessing internal consistency by checking the results of one-half of a set of scaled items against the results from the other half.

spurious relationship An apparent relationship between two variables that is not authentic.

standard deviation A quantitative index of a distribution's spread, or variability; the square root of the variance for a distribution.

standard error of the mean The standard deviation of the sampling distribution.

standardized normal distribution A purely theoretical probability distribution that reflects a specific normal curve for the standardized value, Z.

standardized research service A research organization that has developed a unique methodology for investigating a specialty area, such as advertising effectiveness.

Stapel scale A measure of attitudes that consists of a single adjective in the centre of an even number of numerical values.

static group design An after-only design in which subjects in the experimental group are measured after being exposed to the experimental treatment and the control group is measured without having been exposed to the experimental treatment; no pre-measure is taken.

status bar In an Internet questionnaire, a visual indicator that tells the respondent what portion of the survey he or she has completed.

stratified sampling A probability sampling procedure in which simple random subsamples that are more or less equal on some characteristic are drawn from within each stratum of the population.

streaming media Multimedia content, such as audio or video, that can be accessed on the Internet without being downloaded first.

structured question A question that imposes a limit on the number of allowable responses.

survey A method of collecting primary data in which information is gathered by communicating with a representative sample of people.

syndicated service A marketing research supplier that provides standardized information for many clients.

systematic error Error resulting from some imperfect aspect of the research design that causes respondent error or from a mistake in the execution of the research.

systematic sampling A sampling procedure in which a starting point is selected by a random process and then every nth number on the list is selected.

T

tachistoscope A device that controls the amount of time a subject is exposed to a visual image.

telephone interview Personal interview conducted by telephone, the mainstay of commercial survey research.

television monitoring Computerized mechanical observation used to obtain television ratings.

tertiary sampling unit A term used to designate a unit selected in the third stage of sampling.

test marketing A scientific testing and controlled experimental procedure that provides an opportunity to measure sales or profit potential for a new product or to test a new marketing plan under realistic marketing conditions.

test of differences An investigation of a hypothesis stating that two (or more) groups differ with respect to measures on a variable.

test-retest method Administering the same scale or measure to the same respondents at two separate points in time to test for stability.

test units Subjects or entities whose responses to experimental treatments are observed or measured.

testing effect In a before-and-after study, the effect of pre-testing, which may sensitize subjects when taking a test for the second time, thus affecting internal validity.

thematic apperception test (TAT) A projective technique that presents a series of pictures to research subjects and asks them to provide a description of or a story about the pictures.

third-person technique A projective technique in which the respondent is asked why a third person does what he or she does or what he or she thinks about a product. The respondent is expected to transfer his or her attitudes to the third person.

total quality management A business philosophy that focuses on integrating customer-driven quality throughout an organization with continuous improvement of product quality and service.

tracking study A type of longitudinal study that uses successive samples to compare trends and identify changes in variables such as consumer satisfaction, brand image, or advertising awareness.

two-way (contingency) table The results of a cross-tabulation of two variables, such as answers to two survey questions.

U

unbalanced rating scale A fixed-alternative rating scale that has more response categories piled up at one end and an unequal number of positive and negative categories.

undisguised question A straightforward question that assumes the respondent is willing to answer.

unstructured question A question that does not restrict the respondents' answers.

V

validity The ability of a scale to measure what was intended to be measured.

variable Anything that may assume different numerical or categorical values.

variable piping software Software that allows variables to be inserted into an Internet questionnaire as a respondent is completing it.

variance A measure of variability or dispersion. Its square root is the standard deviation.

verification Quality-control procedures in fieldwork intended to ensure that interviewers are following the sampling procedures and to determine whether interviewers are cheating.

visible observation Observation in which the observer's presence is known to the subject.

voice pitch analysis A physiological measurement technique that records abnormal frequencies in the voice that are supposed to reflect emotional reactions to various stimuli.

W

welcome screen The first Web page in an Internet survey, which introduces the survey and requests that the respondent enter a password or PIN.

word association test A projective technique in which the subject is presented with a list of words, one at a time, and asked to respond with the first word that comes to mind.

CHAPTER 1

1. Adapted from Rebecca Harris, "Zwak Attack," *Marketing Magazine,* February 21, 2005.

2. McCain Foods Limited, http://www.mccain.com.

3. McCain Foods Limited, http://www.zwakpack.com.

4. "Bell Canada Launches New Wireless Service Dedicated to Country's Youth," *Canada NewsWire,* July 25, 2005.

5. Michelle Keyo, "Web Site of the Week: Jelly Belly: Using Sampling to Build a Customer Database," *Inc. Online,* http://www.inc.com, December 9, 1996.

6. Brian Sternthal and Alice M. Tybout, "Segmentation and Targeting," in Dawn Iacobucci, *Kellogg on Marketing* (New York: John Wiley and Sons, 2001), p. 21.

7. American Marketing Association, *Report of the Committee on Definitions of Marketing Research,* 1987.

8. Adapted from the definition of research in American Marketing Association, Committee on Definitions, *Marketing Definition: A Glossary of Marketing Terms* (Chicago: American Marketing Association, 1960), p. 17; and from American Marketing Association, *Report of the Committee on Definitions of Marketing Research,* 1987. The official AMA definition is as follows: "Marketing research is the function which links the consumer, customer, and public to the marketer through information—information used to identify and define marketing opportunities and problems; generate, refine, and evaluate marketing actions; monitor marketing performance; and improve understanding of marketing as a process. Marketing research specifies the information required to address these issues; designs the method for collecting the information; manages and implements the data collection process; analyzes the results; and communicates the findings and their implications."

9. AMA Web site: www.marketingpower.org.

10. Adapted from "Radio Ads Promote Swim Safety," *Marketing Magazine,* August 16 2005.

11. For discussions on this issue, see George Day, "The Capabilities of Market-Driven Organizations," *Journal of Marketing,* October 1994, pp. 37–52; John C. Narver and Stanley F. Slater, "The Effect of Marketing Orientation on Business Profitability," *Journal of Marketing,* October 1990, pp. 20–35; A. K. Kohli and B. J. Jaworski, "Marketing Orientation: The Construct, Research Proposition, and Managerial Implications," *Journal of Marketing,* 1990 (2), 1–18; Bernard J. Jaworski and Ajay K. Kohli, "Market Orientation: Antecedents and Consequences," *Journal of Marketing,* July 1993, pp. 53–70; Stanley F. Slater and John C. Narver, "Does Competitive Environment Moderate the Market Orientation-Performance Relationship?" *Journal of Marketing,* January 1994, pp. 46–55; Gary L. Frankwick, James C. Ward, Michael D. Hutt, and Peter H. Reingen, "Evolving Patterns of Organizational Beliefs in the Formation of Strategy," *Journal of Marketing,* April 1994, pp. 96–110; and James M. Sinkula, William E. Baker, and Thomas Noordewier, "A Framework for Market-Based Organizational Learning: Linking Values, Knowledge, and Behavior," *Journal of the Academy of Marketing Science,* Fall 1997, pp. 305–318.

12. Adapted from Barb Grant, "Getting the Right Balance," *Marketing Magazine,* September 22, 2003, p. 21.

13. "Burger King Opens Customer Hot Line," *Marketing News,* May 28, 1990, p. 7.

14. Stephanie Thompson, "EZ Being Green: Kids' Line Is Latest Heinz Innovation," *Advertising Age,* July 10, 2000, pp. 3, 5; Greg Farrell, "What's Green, Easy to Squirt? Ketchup," *USA Today,* July 10, 2000, p. 2b; and Kristen Hays, "Heinz Gooses an Old Flavor with a New Color," *Marketing News,* July 31, 2000, p. 24.

15. Adapted from "'Shrek' Wants U.S. Kids to Choose the Ooze," *Marketing Magazine,* April 6, 2001.

16. Adapted from Jon Berry, "The Art of Rubbermaid," *Adweek,* March 16, 1992, p. 24.

17. Courtesy of General Electric Corporation.

18. "Recent Survey Concludes Quebec Residents Are Least Likely to Forget a Loved One's Birthday," Canada Post Print Press Release, http://www.canadapost.ca/business/corporate/about/newsroom/pr/.

19. For a detailed discussion of marketing strategy and tactics, see William G. Zikmund and Michael d'Amico, *Marketing* (Cincinnati: South-Western, 2001), Chapter 2.

20. Adapted from Michelle Halpern, "*Chatelaine* Targets Gamer Moms," *Marketing Magazine,* July 20, 2005.

21. *Maclean's* Media Kit.

22. David Churchill, "Cabin Pressures," *Management Today,* October 1, 1994, p. 96. Copyright 1994, Management Publications Ltd. (U.K.).

23. Lee Oliver, "Appetite for Resurrection," *Profit,* November 2003.

24. N. Carroll Mohn, "Pricing Research for Decision Making," *Marketing Research,* Winter 1995, pp. 11–12.

25. Adapted from Paul Hunt, "The Price Is Right," *Marketing Magazine,* October 21, 2002.

26. Adam Froman, "Real Time Research," *Marketing Magazine,* June 7, 2004.

27. Adapted from Eve Lazarus, "Graphic Car Crash Spots Depicts Dangers of Drunk Driving," *Marketing Magazine,* July 26, 2005.

28. Adapted from Wayne Mouland, "Those Who Use Them, Use Them a Lot," *Marketing Magazine,* February 10, 2003.

29. Canadian Press, "Awareness of Federal Agency Drops after Ad Campaign," *Canadian Press,* August 1, 2005. © The Canadian Press.

30. Gary Hilson, "Walking in the Customer's Shoes," *Computing Canada,* May 10, 2002.

31. Ipsos Canada, http://www.ipsos.ca/offices.cfm.

32. "You Say Tomato, I Say Tomahto," *Express Magazine,* Spring 1992, p. 19.

33. Statistics Canada, "Quarterly Retail Commodity Survey," *The Daily,* July 14, 2006; Statistics Canada, "Quarterly Retail Commodity Survey," *The Daily,* July 15, 2005.

34. Information from Ben & Jerry's Web page at http://www.benjerry.com; LearNet's Video *Ben & Jerry's;* and a press release from Ben & Jerry's, February 20, 1997.

CHAPTER 2

1. This section is based on Richard Draft, *Management* (Hinsdale, IL: Dryden Press, 1994), pp. 252–255; and John R. Schermerhorn Jr., James G. Hunt, and Richard N. Osborn, *Managing Organizational Behavior* (New York: John Wiley and Sons, 1991), pp. 364–366.

2. Agricultural, Food and Rural Development, Alberta Government, "Consumer Trends in Organic Food," http://www1.agric.gov.ab.ca/$department/deptdocs.nsf/all/sis8434.

3. "Outdoor Cooks Want Better, Bigger and More Expensive," *Propane Canada,* March/April 2003.

4. comScore Media Metrix Canada, May 2005.

5. Michelle Halpern, "Yellow Pages Changing to Meet Consumer Demand," *Marketing Magazine,* June 15, 2005.

6. Paul E. Green, Donald S. Tull, and Gerald Albaum, *Research for Marketing Decisions* (Upper Saddle River, NJ: Prentice-Hall, 1988), pp. 105–107.

7. A. Einstein and L. Infeld, *The Evolution of Physics* (New York: Simon and Schuster, 1942), p. 95.

8. Pre-tests of full-blown surveys and experiments also are considered pilot studies. These smaller versions of the formal studies generally are used to refine techniques rather than to define a problem or clarify a hypothesis.

9. Adapted from David Brown, "DDB Working to Stop Crime in Toronto," *Marketing Magazine,* August 4, 2005.

10. Pasquale A. Pellegrini, "How Canada Counts Its Viewers," *Broadcasting & Cable,* September 5, 2005, and www.arbitron.com.

11. Adapted from Chris Powell, "Net Loss," *Marketing,* May 17-May 24, 2004, pp. 11-12.

12. Willard I. Zangwill, "Manager's Journal: When Customer Research Is a Lousy Idea." Reprinted from the *Wall Street Journal* March 8, 1993, p. A12. © 1993/2000 Dow Jones & Company. All rights reserved.

13. Adapted from John Harding, "Recent Studies Demonstrate Radio's Efficacy as a Brand Building Medium," *Marketing Magazine,* September 19, 2006.

14. Adapted from Chris Daniels, "Turning Browsers into Buyers," *Marketing Magazine,* March 18, 2002.

15. Adapted from Rebecca Harris, "Waking up to Fair Trade," *Marketing Magazine,* June 14, 2004.

CHAPTER 3

1. Ralph W. Giacobbe and Madhay N. Segal, "A Comparative Analysis of Ethical Perceptions in Marketing Research: U.S.A. vs. Canada," *Journal of Business Ethics,* October 2000, p. 229.

2. "Nine in Ten Canadians Support Market and Survey Research," MRIA Press Release, April 11, 2005 (www.mria-arim.ca/).

3. Giacobbe and Segal, "A Comparative Analysis of Ethical Perceptions in Marketing Research: U.S.A. vs. Canada."

4. James B. Stuart, R. J. Reynolds Tobacco Company, personal communication.

5. www.mbarecherche.com.

6. Vincent P. Barabba, "Market Research Technique—What, Why, Who, Where, When, and How?" *Harvard Business Review,* June 14, 1989.

7. Thomas C. Kinnear and Ann Root, Eds., *1994 Survey of Marketing Research* (Chicago: American Marketing Association, 1995).

8. Stuart, personal communication.

9. Sara Dobson, "Cara's Winning Combo," *Marketing Magazine,* October 28 2002.

10. Dudley M. Ruch, "Getting the Lowdown on the Role of Marketing Research in the Corporation," *Advertising Age,* October 18, 1982, p. M25. Used with permission. Copyright 1982 © Crain Communications.

11. John Aulino, "Will the Real Market Research Manager Stand Up?" *Marketing Review,* April 1975, p. 12.

12. Adler and Mayer, *Managing the Marketing Research Function,* p. 32; and Stewart Smith, "Research and Pseudo-research in Marketing," *Harvard Business Review,* March-April 1974, p. 76.

13. Adapted from John G. Keane, "Some Observations on Marketing Research in Top Management Decision Making," *Journal of Marketing,* October 1969, p. 13.

14. Ipsos Canada, http://www.ipsos.ca/prod/syndicated.

15. AC Nielsen Canada, http://www.acnielsen.ca.

16. AC Nielsen Canada, http://www.bases.com and http://www.acnielsen.ca.

17. Leger Marketing, http://www.legermarketing.com/eng/services.asp.

18. "Top 20 Canadian Marketing Communications Services Companies," *Marketing Magazine,* June 21, 2004. Reprinted with permission.

19. Leo Bogart, "The Researcher's Dilemma," *Journal of Marketing,* January 1962, pp. 6-11.

20. "AMA Adopts New Code of Ethics," *Marketing News,* September 11, 1987, pp. 1, 10. Reprinted with permission of the American Marketing Association.

21. Marketing Research and Intelligence Association, http://www.mria-arim.ca/.

22. Canadian Marketing Association, "Code of Ethics and Standards of Practice," http://www.the-cma.org/regulatory/codeofethics.cfm. Reprinted with permission of the Canadian Marketing Association.

23. Marketing Research and Intelligence Association, http://www.mria-arim.ca/.

24. Adapted from Stan Sutter, "Flying into a Privacy Storm," *Marketing Magazine,* July 30 2001.

25. AOL Canada, Privacy Policy, http://canada.aol.com/portal/misc/PrivacyPolicy.adp.

26. "Consumer Demand, Not New Laws, Will Protect Web Privacy," *USA Today,* July 7, 1998, p. 12A.

27. Rick Bruner, "eTRUST Pitches Its Seal of Approval," *Advertising Age,* June 9, 1997.

28. "Consumer Demand, Not New Laws, Will Protect Web Privacy." *USA Today,* July 7, 1998, p. 12A.

29. Cathy Loblaw, "The Whole World Is Watching," *Marketing News,* August 6, 2001.

30. Advisory Panel on Research Ethics (PRE), Government Canada. http://www.pre.ethics.gc.ca/english/aboutus/aboutus.cfm.

31. Marketing Research and Intelligence Association, http://www.mria-arim.ca/STANDARDS/CODE2005.asp. The Ten Core Principles of MRIA's Code of Conduct have been reprinted with permission of the Marketing Research and Intelligence Association.

CHAPTER 4

1. Robert F. Mager, *Preparing Instructional Objectives* (Belmont, CA: David S. Lake, Publishers, 1984). Copyright © 1984 by David S. Lake Publishers, Belmont, CA 94002.

2. Adapted from Charles Ramond, *The Art of Using Science in Marketing* (New York: Harper & Row, 1974), p. 17. Copyright © 1974 by Charles Ramond.

3. Deborah E. Rosen, J. E. Schroeder, and E. F. Purinton, "Marketing High Tech Products: Lessons in Consumer Focus From the Marketplace," *Academy of Marketing Science Review,* 1998.

4. Russell L. Ackoff, *Scientific Method* (New York: John Wiley and Sons, 1962), p. 71.

5. Randall G. Chapman, "Problem Definition in Marketing Research Studies," *Journal of Marketing Research,* Spring 1989, pp. 51-59; also, Yoo S. Yang, Robert P. Leone, and Dala L. Alden, "A Market Expansion Ability Approach to Identify Potential Exporters," *Journal of Marketing,* January 1992, p. 88.

6. Robert Ferber, Donald F. Blankertz, and Sidney Hollander, Jr., *Marketing Research* (New York: Ronald Press, 1964), p. 157. Reprinted with permission from John Wiley and Sons.

7. Patrick Coyne, "The ACD Conference on Interactive Media," *Communication Arts,* January/February 1995, pp. 135-140. Reprinted with permission of *Communication Arts,* © 2006 Coyne & Blanchard, Inc. All rights reserved.

8. Martin Weinberger, "Seven Perspectives on Consumer Research," *Marketing Research: A Magazine of Management and Applications,* December 1989, pp. 9-17.

9. Chapman, "Problem Definition in Marketing Research Studies."

10. Fictitious research proposal, does not reflect communication with Revenue Canada.

11. Space restrictions do not permit the inclusion of a complete research proposal. Often entire questionnaires appear as exhibits in proposals. Students interested in additional information on writing research proposals should review Chapter 19 on writing the research report.

CHAPTER 5

1. Reprinted with permission from Jeff Green, "The PT Cruiser's Storied History," *BrandWeek,* October 16, 2000, pp. M68-M70. © 1998-1999 VNUBusiness Media Inc. Used with permission.

2. Adapted from "Cassies Awards: Packaged Goods Other," *Marketing Magazine,* November 18, 2002.

3. David Schwartz, *Concept Testing: How to Test New Product Ideas before You Go to Market* (New York: AMACOM, 1987), p. 57.

4. Glen L. Urban and John R. Hauser, *Design and Marketing of New Products* (Englewood Cliffs, NJ: Prentice-Hall, 1980). © 1980 Prentice-Hall, Inc.

5. Gary Hamel and C. K. Prahalad, "Corporate Imagination and Expeditionary Marketing," *Harvard Business Review,* July–August 1991, p. 85.

6. Excerpt from Ray Burch, "Marketing Research: Why It Works, Why It Doesn't Work," speech to the Chicago Chapter of the American Marketing Association, 1973. Reprinted with the permission of the Chicago Chapter of the American Marketing Association.

7. Adapted from Michael A. Hitt, R. Duane Ireland, and Robert E. Huskisson, *Strategic Management: Competitiveness and Globalization Concepts* (St. Paul, MN: West Publishing, 1995), p. 82.

8. Adapted from "Recommended Reading: Birks' Rebuilding Blueprint," *Marketing Magazine,* December 2, 2002.

9. Adapted from Chris Daniels, "Giving It Away," *Marketing Magazine,* August 15, 2005.

10. Adapted from Angela Scardillo, "Making Milk Cool," *Marketing Magazine,* August 11, 2003.

11. John M. Hess, "Group Interviewing," in *New Science of Planning,* R.L. King, Ed. (Chicago: American Marketing Association, 1968), p. 194.

12. Adapted from David Walker, "Rubbermaid Tries Its Hand at Bristles and Wood," *ADWEEK'S Marketing Week,* March 5, 1990, pp. 20–21. Adapted with permission of *ADWEEK'S Marketing Week.*

13. Betsy D. Gelb and Michael P. Eriksen, "Market Research May Help Prevent Cancer," *Marketing Research,* September 1991, p. 46. Published by the American Marketing Association. Reprinted by permission.

14. Real, http://www.realnetworks.com/getstarted/index.html, downloaded June 30, 2001.

15. Pollara, http://www.pollara.ca/news/Fs_focus.htm.

16. Nicholas Negroponte, "Being Anonymous," *Wired,* October 1998, p. 216.

17. Casey Sweet, "Anatomy of an Online Focus Group," *Quirks Marketing Research Review,* December 1999, Article Number 0548.

18. Kate Maddox, "Virtual Panels Add Real Insights for Marketers," *Advertising Age,* June 29, 1998, p. 34.

19. Jon Rubin, "Online Marketing Research Comes of Age," *BrandWeek,* October 30, 2000, p. 28.

20. Corus Entertainment, http://www.corusmedia.com/ytv/research/index.asp#ARCHIVE and Media Digest," *Marketing Magazine,* September 13, 1999, p. 13.

21. Derek Drewry, "Lying in Their Beer," *Canadian Business,* March 1996, p. 21. Adapted with permission of the author.

22. Contemporary researchers are in the process of creating new projective techniques. See Jennifer E. Chang, "Tapping the Untapped Consumer: Personally Relevant Elicited Projectives (PREP)," paper presented at the Association for Consumer Research Conference, Salt Lake City, October 2000; Daniel H. Pink, "Metaphor Marketing: Harvard Business School Professor Jerry Zaltman," *FC,* No. 14, p. 214; Gwendolyn Catchings-Castello, "The ZMET Alternative," *Marketing Research,* Summer 2000, p. 8; and Jerry Zaltman's Web page, http://www.hbs.edu/units/marketing/zmet.

23. Harold H. Kassarjian, "Projective Methods," in *Handbook of Marketing Research,* Robert Ferber, Ed. Copyright 1974, McGraw-Hill. Adapted with the permission of McGraw-Hill Book Company.

24. James McNeal, *The Kids Market: Myths and Realities* (Ithaca, NY: Paramount Market Publishers, 1999), p. 245.

25. From Donald F. Cox, Ed., *Risk Taking and Information Handling in Consumer Behavior* (Boston: Division of Research, Harvard Business School, © 1967), pp. 65–66. Reprinted by permission.

26. Philip Kotler, "Behavioral Models for Analyzing Buyers," *Journal of Marketing* (October 1965), pp. 37–45.

27. Ronald Alsop, "Advertisers Put Consumers on the Couch," *Wall Street Journal,* May 13, 1988, p. 19.

28. Adapted from Eve Lazarus, "Gag Factor," *Marketing Magazine,* June 21, 2004.

29. William G. Zikmund and William J. Lundstrom, *A Collection of Outstanding Cases in Marketing Management* (St. Paul, MN: West Publishing, 1979). All rights reserved.

30. Adapted with permission from Mike Hoffman, "Hocus-Pocus Focus," *Inc.,* July 1998, p. 90.

CHAPTER 6

1. Statistics Canada, http://www40.statcan.ca/l01/cst01/demo02.htm.

2. Eve Lazarus, "The New Mainstream," *Marketing Magazine,* October 24, 2005, and Statistics Canada, http://www.statcan.ca/.

3. The idea for Exhibit 6.1 came from Robert W. Joselyn, *Designing the Marketing Research Project* (New York: Petrocelli/Charter, 1977).

4. NPD Group, http://www.npdcanada.com/dynamic/releases/press_050302.html.

5. The Coca-Cola Company: 2005 Annual Review, www.coca-cola.com, accessed on September 7, 2006.

6. Bette Harrison, "Retro Activity as Generation Y Plumbs Parents' Culture; the Kids Claim Birdies and Bowling, with a Twist," *Atlanta Constitution,* October 27, 1998, p. F1.

7. Lee Fleming, "Digital Delivery: Pushing Content to the Desktop," *Digital Information Group,* January 31, 1997.

8. "How Smart Agents Will Change Selling," *Forbes ASAP,* August 28, 1995, p. 95.

9. Nortel, http://www.nortelnetworks.com/.

10. "Datawatch," *Advertising Age,* January 18, 1993, p. I-12.

11. Statistics Canada, "Arts, Entertainment and Recreation: Spectator Sports," http://www40.statcan.ca/l01/cst01/serv21.htm.

12. This section is based on Michael Levy and Barton Weitz, *Retail Management* (Homewood, IL: Richard D. Irwin © 1992), pp. 357–358.

13. Based on information on DataMind's home page at http://www.datamindcorp.com.

14. Srikumar S. Rao, "Technology: The Hot Zone," *Forbes,* November 18, 1996.

15. John Foley, "Squeezing More Value From Data," *InformationWeek,* December 9, 1996.

16. Adapted from Marlene Milczarek, "Database Diamond Mining," *Marketing Magazine,* August 13, 2001.

17. IBM Business Intelligence Data Mining Product Discovery, http://www.ibm.com.

18. Todd Wasserman, Gerry Khermouch, and Jeff Green, "Mining Everyone's Business," *Brandweek,* February 28, 2000, p. 34; and Ira Sager, "Big Blue Wants to Mine Your Data," *Business Week,* June 3, 1996.

19. Based on information on DataMind's home page at http://www.datamindcorp.com.

20. Excerpt reprinted with permission from Janet Novack, "The Data Miners," *Forbes,* February 12, 1996. Reprinted by permission of Forbes Magazine. © 2002 Forbes Inc.

21. Adapted from "Media Digest: Broadcast Data Sources," *Marketing Magazine,* September 24, 2001.

22. Bill Gates, *The Road Ahead* (New York: Viking Penguin, 1995), p. 138.

23. "New Cluster System Shows Values," *Direct Marketing News,* September 2004 and http://www.dmn.ca.

CHAPTER 7

1. Reprinted with permission from Sara Eckel and Alison Stein Wellner, "For Wannabe Chefs, Pictures Speak Louder than Words," *American Demographics,* March 2001, p. S15. Copyright © 2001 by Crain Communications, Inc.

2. David Todd, "Special Report: Youth Marketing: Dentyne Ice Locks Lips with Youth Target," *Strategy: The Canadian Marketing Report,* May 8, 2000, p. B14, http://www.strategymag.com/articles/20000508/youth-dentyneice.asp, downloaded January 28, 2001.

3. Adapted from "Recommended Reading: Research's Long Reach," *Marketing Magazine,* March 27, 2000.

4. The popularity of marketing research has affected the willingness of respondents to participate in surveys. People are increasingly refusing to participate.

5. Evalu8.org, http://www.evalu8.org/staticpage?page=review&siteid=2407.

6. Paul B. Sheatsley, "Survey Design," in *Handbook of Marketing Research,* Robert Ferber, Ed. (New York: McGraw-Hill, 1974), pp. 2–66.

7. Peter Tuckel and Harry O'Neill, "The Vanishing Respondent in Telephone Surveys," a paper presented at the 56th annual conference of the American Association of Public Opinion Research (AAPOR) in Montreal on May 17–20, 2001.

8. David Bosworth, "Levi's Probes Buyer Loyalty: Canadian Division Leads Relationship Marketing Test," *Strategy Magazine,* September 15, 1997.

9, 10. Health Action Network Society, http://hans.org/news?item=11, CNW Group, http://www.newswire.ca/en/releases/archive/March2005/16/c5220.html, and Catelli, http://catelli.com/whats_new/press_releases.htm#release.

11. Douglas Aircraft, *Consumer Research* (undated), p. 13.

12. Health Action Network Society and CNW Group.

13. Reprinted with permission from Christy Marshall, "Here's the Word on Surveys About Burger Favorites," *Advertising Age,* March 21, 1983. Copyright © 1983 by Crain Communications, Inc.

14. For an interesting study of extremity bias, see Hans Baumgartner and Jan-Benedict E. M. Steekamp, "Response Styles in Marketing Research: A Cross-National Investigation," *Journal of Marketing Research,* May 2001, pp. 143–156.

15. See Robert J. Lavidge, "Seven Tested Ways to Abuse and Misuse Strategic Advertising Research," *Marketing Research: A Magazine of Management and Applications,* March 1990, p. 43; "VCR/VDP Market Products and Important Research Questions," *Marketing News,* January 6, 1984, p. 7. Lavidge says: "Suppose a researcher asks purchasing intention questions for an inexpensive nondurable product using answer categories as follows: 'Definitely will buy,' 'Probably will buy,' 'May or may not buy,' 'Probably will not buy,' and 'Definitely will not buy.' Based on past experience the researchers may estimate that about 80 percent of the 'definitely will buy' respondents plus 30 percent of the 'probably will buy' category will actually buy the product if it becomes available on the market."

16. The term *questionnaire* technically refers only to mail and self-administered surveys, and the term *interview schedule* is used for interviews by telephone or face-to-face. However, we will use *questionnaire* to refer to all three forms of communications in this book.

17. "Outdoor cooks want better, bigger & more expensive," *Propane Canada,* March/April 2003, pp. 8, 25.

18. Janice Castro, "Making It Better," *Time,* November 13, 1989, pp. 78–81; and David A. Gavin, "Competing on the Eight Dimensions of Quality," *Harvard Business Review,* November–December 1987, pp. 101–108.

19. Castro, "Making It Better."

20. *Profiles in Quality: Blueprints for Action from 50 Leading Companies* (Boston: Allyn and Bacon, 1991), p. 113.

21. Adapted with permission from Barbara Buell, "The Effect of Expecting to Evaluate on Quality and Satisfaction Evaluations," *Stanford Business,* Vol. 68, No. 3 (May 2000). The research was based on Chezy Ofir and Itamar Simonson, *GSB Research Paper #1608,* Stanford University Graduate School of Business, July 1999.

22. Don Mills, "Success Through Teamwork: Clairol Canada Has Recently Undergone a Number of Developments That Revolutionized the Firm Resulting in Leading Edge Haircolouring Techniques and Products," *Cosmetics,* November 1993, p. 29.

23. Mills, "Success Through Teamwork."

CHAPTER 8

1. Jeff Green, "The PT Cruiser's Storied History," *BrandWeek,* October 16, 2000, pp. M68–M70.

2. Donald T. Warwick and Charles A. Lininger, *The Sample Survey: Theory and Practice* (New York: McGraw-Hill, 1975), p. 2.

3. L. C. Lockley, "Notes on the History of Marketing Research," *Journal of Marketing,* April 1950, p. 733.

4. Bell Canada, http://www.bell.ca/shop/en_CA_QC/439.details.

5. Lesley Young, "Hanging Up on Telemarketing," Marketing News, August 25, 2003.

6. National Do Not Call Registry, https://www.donotcall.gov/.

7. Canadian Marketing Association, "Canadian Marketing Association Welcomes Legislation to Create National Do-Not-Call Service," December 13, 2004. CMA News Release (http://www.the-cma.org/newsroom/).

8. "CRTC Extends Telemarketing Regs.," *Marketing News,* March 12, 2001.

9. David W. Stark, NFO CFgroup, "Privacy: Stop Talking About It and Do It" at http://www.pmrs-aprm.com/SpecialStandards/PDF/StarkPaper.pdf.

10. Marketing Research and Intelligence, "MRIA Committees: Response Rate Committee," http://www.mria-arim.ca/COMMITTEES/Response.asp.

11. Peter Tuckel and Harry O'Neill, "The Vanishing Respondent in Telephone Surveys," a paper presented at the 56th annual conference of the American Association of Public Opinion Research (AAPOR) in Montreal on May 17–20, 2001.

12. Peter Tuckel and Trish Shukers, "The Answering Machine Dilemma," *Marketing Research,* Fall 1997, pp. 5–9.

13. P. S. Tuckel and B. M. Finberg, "The Answering Machine Poses Many Questions for Telephone Survey Research," *Public Opinion Quarterly,* Summer 1991.

14. Don A. Dillman, *Mail and Internet Surveys: The Tailored Design Method* (New York: John Wiley and Sons, 2000), p. 173.

15. David R., Schaefer and Don A. Dillman, "Development of a Standard E-Mail Methodology: Results of an Experiment," *Public Opinion Quarterly,* Vol. 62, No. 3 (Fall 1998), p. 378.

16. Don A. Dillman, *Mail and Internet Surveys: The Tailored Design Method* (New York: John Wiley & Sons, 2000), p. 162. Reprinted with permission of John Wiley & Sons, Inc.

17. For an interesting article dealing with this issue, see Michael Geurts and David Whitlark, "A Little Inducement Goes a Long Way," *Marketing Research: A Magazine of Management and Applications,* Summer 1994, pp. 13–15.

18. Schaefer and Dillman, "Development of a Standard E-Mail Methodology."

19. Press release, "PepsiCo Foods International to Introduce Lay's Potato Chips to Consumers Worldwide," *PRNewswire,* November 30, 1995.

20. Lewis C. Winters, "International Psychographics," *Marketing Research: A Magazine of Management and Application,* September 1992, p. 48.

21. For a complete discussion of fax surveys, see the excellent article by John P. Dickson and Douglas L. Maclachlan, "Fax Surveys: Return Patterns and Comparison with Mail Surveys," *Journal of Marketing Research,* February 1996, pp. 108–113.

22. Itracks, http://www.itracks.com/Pages/02_Services/Default.aspx.

23. Dillman, *Mail and Internet Surveys,* pp. 369–372.

24. http://www.websurveyor.com/learn_howto.asp, downloaded May 14, 2001.

25. Neil Postman, *Technopoly: The Surrender of Culture to Technology* (New York: Vintage Books, 1993), pp. 6–15; and James P. Ronda, "Thomas Moran and the Eastern Railroads," *The Gilcrease Journal,* Spring/Summer 1997, p. 38.

26. DMS Research, http://www.dmsdallas.com/cust_research/videval.html, downloaded April 23, 2001.

27. "Recent Research Confirms Online Surveys Are a Viable Means of Reaching General Population," Digital Marketing Services, Inc., September 17, 1998, http://www.dmsdallas.com/press_room.html, downloaded April 24, 2001.

28. "Real-Time and Online Research Is Paying Off," *Direct Marketing,* May 2000, p. 58. Copyright © 2000 Hoke Communications, Inc.

29. For an interesting empirical study, see Ishmael P. Akaah and Edward A. Riordan, "The Incidence of Unethical Practices in Marketing Research: An Empirical Investigation," *Journal of the Academy of Marketing Sciences,* Spring 1990, pp. 143-152.

CHAPTER 9

1. Adapted from Astrid Van Den Broek, "Germ Warfare: Producers Are Cleaning up with New Hygiene-driven Products," *Marketing Magazine,* November 29, 1999.

2. Kendra Parker, "How Do You Like Your Beef?" *American Demographics,* January 2000, p. D50.

3. Adapted from Norma Ramage, "Mark's Super Brand Ambition," *Marketing Magazine,* March 29, 2004.

4. Claire Selltiz, Lawrence S. Wrightsman, and Stuart W. Cook, *Research Methods in Social Relations* (New York: Holt, Rinehart and Winston, 1976), p. 251.

5. Joshua Macht, "The New Market Research," *Inc.,* July 1998, pp. 92-93.

6. Nancy M. Henley, *Body Politics: Power, Sex, and Nonverbal Communication* (New York: Simon & Schuster, 1977), p. 181.

7. Adapted with permission from Erik Larson's "Attention Shoppers: Don't Look Now, but You Are Being Tailed." Copyright © 1993 by Erik Larson. First appeared in *Smithsonian Magazine.* Reprinted by permission of the author.

8. Howard B. Waitzkin, "Information Giving and Medical Care," *Journal of Health and Social Behavior,* Vol. 26 (1985), pp. 81-101.

9. Angus Campbell, Philip E. Converse, and Willard L. Rodgers, *The Quality of American Life* (New York: Russell Sage Foundation, 1976), p. 112. Although weather conditions did not correlate with perceived quality of life, the comfort variable did show a relationship with the index of well-being. This association might be confounded by the fact that ventilation and/or air conditioning equipment is less common in less affluent homes. Income was previously found to correlate with quality of life.

10. Bill Abrams, *The Observational Research Handbook* (Chicago: NTC Business Books, 2000), p 14.

11. Abrams, *The Observational Research Handbook,* pp. 2, 105.

12. Adapted from Mark David Campbell, "No More Duck Blinds," *Marketing Magazine,* September 27, 1999.

13. Reprinted with permission from the April 30, 1980, issue of *Advertising Age.* Copyright © 1980 by Crain Communications, Inc.

14. William Rathje and Cullen Murphy, "Garbage Demographics," *American Demographics,* May 1992, pp. 50-53.

15. Witold Rybczynski, "We Are What We Throw Away," *New York Times Book Review,* July 5, 1992, pp. 5-6.

16. AC Nielsen, http://www.acnielsen.com, downloaded July 5, 2001.

17. "Broadcast Data Sources," *Marketing Magazine,* September 24, 2001.

18. Justin Martin, "Ignore Your Customer," *Fortune,* May 1, 1995, p. 126.

19. BBM, www.bbm.ca.

20. Marketing Research Association, http://www.mra-net.org/docs/resources/technology/buzzwords.cfm, downloaded April 24, 2001.

21. "Canadian Consumers Shopping at Retail Stores Share Same Demographic and Geographic Profile as those Browsing e-Retail Web Sites," comScore Press Release, Toronto, Canada, September 18, 2000.

22. "Live, Simultaneous Study of Stimulus, Response Is Physiological Measurement's Great Virtue," *Marketing News,* May 15, 1981, pp. 1, 20.

23. Herbert B. Krugman's statement as quoted in "Live, Simultaneous Study of Stimulus, Response Is Physiological Measurement's Greatest Virtue," p. 1.

24. Adapted from Karl Moore, "Maybe It Is Like Brain Surgery," *Marketing Magazine,* April 25, 2005.

25. Edmund L. Andrews, "Delving into the Consumer Unconscious," *New York Times,* July 22, 1990, p. F-9. Copyright © 1990 by the New York Times Company. Reprinted by permission.

CHAPTER 10

1. Samson Okalow, "Exploiting Atkins," *Strategy Magazine,* February 9, 2004.

2. Astrid Van Den Broek, "The Research Behind the McLaunch," *Strategy Magazine,* July 15, 2002.

3. Bob Burgdorfer, "McDonald's Shares Jump on Sales Rise," *National Post,* June 7, 2003, p. FP.9.

4. Samson Okalow, "McDonald's: Adapt or Die," *Strategy Magazine,* November 2004.

5. Vernon Ellingstad and Norman W. Heimstra, *Methods in the Study of Human Behavior* (Monterey, CA: Brooks/Cole, 1974), pp. 61-62.

6. Barry F. Anderson, *The Psychological Experiment: An Introduction to the Scientific Method* (Belmont, CA: Brooks/Cole, 1971), p. 28.

7. M. Venkatesan and Robert J. Holloway, *An Introduction to Marketing Experimentation: Methods, Applications and Problems* (New York: Free Press, 1971), p. 14.

8. See F. J. Roethlisberger and W. J. Dickson, *Management and the Worker* (Cambridge, MA: Harvard University Press, 1939).

9. Alice M. Tybout and Gerald Zaltman, "Ethics in Marketing Research: Their Practical Relevance," *Journal of Marketing Research,* November 1974, pp. 357-368.

10. Herbert C. Kelman, "Human Use of Human Subjects: The Problem of Deception in Social Psychological Experiments," *Psychological Bulletin,* January 1967, pp. 1-11. Reprinted by permission.

11. Adapted from Wayne Mouland, "Sweeping up Additional Sales," *Marketing Magazine,* October 6, 2003.

12. This section is based on Donald T. Campbell and Julian C. Stanley, *Experimental and Quasi-Experimental Designs for Research* (Chicago: Rand McNally, 1963), pp. 5-9.

13. Campbell and Stanley, *Experimental and Quasi-Experimental Designs for Research,* p. 9.

14. The term *observation* is used in the most general way. Although most marketing experiments will use some other form of measurement rather than direct observation of some dependent variable, the terminology used by Campbell and Stanley is used here because of its traditional nature.

15. Adapted from Danny Kucharsky, "Agrinove Milks Dairy Shelf-life Line," *Marketing Magazine,* August 19, 2002.

16. *Market Testing Consumer Products* (New York: National Industrial Conference Board, 1967), p. 13.

17. "McPizza Soon in All Outlets," *The Ottawa Citizen,* March 19, 1992, p. D6.

18. Adapted from David Menzies, "Has Pepsi Canned the SixPack?" *Marketing Magazine,* April 6, 1998, p. 12.

19. Norma Ramage, "Testing, Testing 1-2-3," *Marketing Magazine,* July 18-July 25, 2005, p. 6.

20. Chris Powell, "Sink or Swim?" *Marketing Magazine,* October 30, 2000; Jack Neff, "Test It in Paris, France, Launch It in Paris, Texas: IBM, Heinz, Mars, and Others Find It's a Small World for Ad and Product Intros," *Advertising Age,* May 31, 1999, p. 28.

21. Judann Pollack, "Price Issues Dog Frito Olean Tests," *Advertising Age,* November 25, 1996, p. 4.

22. Ronald E. Frank and William F. Massy, "Shelf Positions and Space Effects on Sales," *Journal of Marketing Research,* February 1970, pp. 59-66.

CHAPTER 11

1. Adbrand.net, http://www.adbrands.net/us/bbdo_us.htm?gclid=CMKFqbeth4ICFSa6Pgod0mOIDA.

2. Reprinted with permission from Gary Levin, "Emotion Guides BBDO's Ad Tests," *Advertising Age,* January 29, 1990, p. 12. Copyright © 1990 Crain Communications, Inc. All rights reserved.

3. Sarah M. Dinham, *Exploring Statistics: An Introduction for Psychology and Education* (Monterey, CA: Brooks/Cole, 1976), p. 3.

4. This definition is adapted from Fred N. Kerlinger, *Foundations of Behavioral Research* (New York: Holt, Rinehart and Winston, 1973), p. 31.

5. Barry F. Anderson, *The Psychology Experiment* (Monterey, CA: Brooks/Cole, 1971), p. 26.

6. Kerlinger, *Foundations of Behavioral Research,* p. 41.

7. Adapted from Michael D. Cozzens and Noshir S. Contractor, "The Effect of Conflicting Information on Media Skepticism," *Communications Research,* August 1987, pp. 437-451.

8. Benjamin B. Wolman, Ed., *Dictionary of Behavioral Science* (New York: Van Nostrand Reinhold, 1973), p. 333.

9. Chris Wells, "The War of the Razors," *Esquire,* February 1980, p. 3.

10. Cathy Lynn Grossman, "Passenger-Jet Designers Ponder Pie-in-the-Sky Idea," *USA Today,* April 18, 1995, p. 3D.

11. Burke Marketing Research, "Rough Commercial Recall Testing," Cincinnati, OH; undated.

12. Based on: Keith K. Cox and Ben M. Enis, *The Marketing Research Process* (Pacific Palisades, CA: Goodyear, 1972), pp. 353-355; and Fred N. Kerlinger, *Foundations of Behavioral Research,* 3rd ed. (Ft. Worth: Holt, Rinehart and Wilson, 1986).

CHAPTER 12

1. Carolyn Cavanaugh, "What We Know About Eating Disorders: Facts and Statistics," in *Eating Disorders: A Reference Sourcebook,* Raymond Lemberg and Leigh Cohn, Eds. (Phoenix, AZ: Oryx Press, 1999); National Eating Disorder Information Centre, Toronto, Ontario, www. nedic.ca; and "The Real Truth About Beauty: A Global Report," www. dove.ca.

2. Josée L. Jarry, Amy Kossert, and Karen Ip, "Do Women With Low Self-Esteem Use Appearance to Feel Better?" National Eating Disorder Information Centre, Toronto, Ontario, www.nedic.ca.

3. L. M. Irving, "Promoting Size Acceptance in Elementary School Children: The EDAP Puppet Program," *Eating Disorders,* 8, pp. 221-232; A. B. Moreno and M. H. Thelen, "Eating Behaviour in Junior High School Females," *Adolescence,* 30 (1995), pp. 171-177; and www.dove.ca.

4. Natalia Williams, "Dove: Brand Beautiful," *Strategy Magazine,* November 2005.

5. Nancy Etcoff, Susie Orbach, Jennifer Scott, and Heidi D'Agostino, "The Real Truth about Beauty: A Global Report," September 2004, www.campaignforrealbeauty.ca.

6. Natalia Williams, "De*con*struct*ed: The Plans," *Strategy Magazine,* April 2005.

7. Karen Nickel Anhalt, "Whiskas Campaign Recruits a Tiny Tiger," *Advertising Age International,* October 19, 1998, p. 41.

8. *Psychology Today: An Introduction* (Del Mar, CA: CRM Books, 1970), p. 613.

9. Rensis Likert, "A Technique for the Measurement of Attitudes," *Archives of Psychology,* 19 (1931), pp. 44-53.

10. Stephen W. Brown and Teresa A. Swarts, "A Gap Analysis of Professional Service Quality," *Journal of Marketing,* April 1989, p. 95.

11. Charles Osgood, George Suci, and Percy Tannenbaum, *The Measurement of Meaning* (Urbana: University of Illinois Press, 1957). Seven-point scales were used in the original work; however, subsequent researchers have modified the scale to have five points, nine points, and so on.

12. Joel Huber and Morris B. Holbrook, "Using Attribute Ratings for Product Positioning: Some Distinctions Among Compositional Approaches," *Journal of Marketing Research,* November 1979, p. 510, American Marketing Association.

13. J. Richard Jones and Sheila I. Cocke, "A Performance Evaluation of Commuter Airlines: The Passengers' View," *Proceedings: Transportation Research Forum,* Vol. 22 (1981), p. 524. Reprinted with permission.

14. Dennis Menezes and Norbert F. Elbert, "Alternative Semantic Scaling Formats for Measuring Store Image: An Evaluation," *Journal of Marketing Research,* February 1979, pp. 80-87.

15. Based on: Menezes and Elbert, "Alternate Semantic Scaling Formats for Measuring Store Image: An Evaluation." Reprinted by permission of the American Marketing Association.

16. A.I.M. technique, R. H. Bruskin and Associates; Cornelius Dubois, "The Card-Sorting or Psychophysical Interview," *Public Opinion Quarterly,* volume 13, pp. 619-628, Copyright 1950 Princeton University Press.

17. This material was created by Ajay Sukhdial, Oklahoma State University; Damon Aiken, Butler University; and Lynn Kahle, University of Oregon. Additional details can be found in "Are You Old School? A Scale for Measuring Sports Fans' Old-School Orientation," *Journal of Advertising Research,* Vol. 42, 2002. The data have been modified for this case study project.

CHAPTER 13

1. Lynda Hurst, "The Politics of People Counting," *Toronto Star,* January 22, 2000.

2. Stanley L. Payne, *The Art of Asking Questions* (Princeton, NJ: Princeton University Press, 1951), pp. 8-9. The reader who wants a more detailed account of question wording is referred to this classic book on that topic.

3. Stephen A. Greyser and Raymond A. Bauer, "Americans and Advertising," *Public Opinion Quarterly,* Vol. 30 (Spring 1966), pp. 69-78.

4. "USA Snapshots," *USA TODAY,* February 26, 1998, p. C1.

5. Don A. Dillman, *Mail and Telephone Surveys: The Total Design Method* (New York: John Wiley & Sons, 1978), p. 209. Reprinted with permission.

6. Fred W. Morgan, "Judicial Standards for Survey Research: An Update and Guidelines," *Journal of Marketing,* January 1990, pp. 59-70.

7. Payne, *The Art of Asking Questions,* p. 185.

8. Charles W. Roll, Jr., and Albert H. Cantril, *Polls: Their Use and Misuse in Politics* (New York: Basic Books, 1972), pp. 106-107.

9. Other product attributes are relative advantage, compatibility, complexity, and communicability.

10. Payne, *The Art of Asking Questions,* pp. 102-103.

11. From Omar J. Bendikas, "One-Step Questionnaire May Overstate Response: Two-Step Questionnaires Hike Involvement, Accuracy," *Marketing News,* May 18, 1979, p. 9. Reprinted with permission.

12. "General Foods Corporation: Tang Instant Breakfast Drink (B)," © 1978 F. Stewart DeBruicker and Harvey N. Singer, The Wharton School, University of Pennsylvania. Reprinted with permission.

13. Reprinted with permission from the Council of American Survey Research, http://www.casro.org.

14. Research Services, Inc. of Denver, CO and the United Bank of Boulder, CO.

15. Don A. Dillman, *Mail and Internet Surveys: The Tailored Design Method* (New York: John Wiley and Sons, 2000), pp. 357-361.

16. Sarah J. Young and Craig M. Ross, "Web Questionnaires: A Glimpse of Survey Research in the Future," *Parks & Recreation,* Vol. 35, No. 6 (June 2000), p. 30.

17. Decisions Analyst, Inc., http://www.decisionanalyst.com/online/surtech.htm, downloaded February 6, 2001.

18. Decisions Analyst, Inc., http://www.decisionanalyst.com/online/surtech.htm.

19. Matt Michel, "Controversy Redux," *CASRO Journal,* http://www.decisionanalyst.com/publ_art/contredux.htm, downloaded February 8, 2001.

20. Adapted by permission from IBM Management Staff Booklet for Systems Design, 1975 (Z140-3008-2 U/M 001). Courtesy, IBM Archives.

21. Philip R. Cateora, *International Marketing* (Homewood, IL: Richard D. Irwin, 1990), pp. 387-389.

22. Cateora, *International Marketing,* pp. 387-389.

23. Subhash C. Jain, *International Marketing* (Boston: PWS Kent, 1990), p. 338.

24. GTE Airfone, authorization for limited use granted by GTE Airfone, Inc.

CHAPTER 14

1. From David G. Meyers, *Exploring Psychology* (New York: Worth Publishers, 1990), p. 471.

2. Adapted from A. D. Fletcher and T. A. Bowers, *Fundamentals of Advertising Research* 4/e. Wadsworth Publishing Company, 1991. pp. 60-61.

3. Library and Archives Canada, http://www.collectionscanada.ca/collectionsp-bin/colldisp/l=0/c=41.

4. Phillip R. Cateora, *International Marketing* (Homewood, IL: Irwin, 1990), pp. 384-385.

5. Sabra E. Brock, "Marketing Research in Asia: Problems, Opportunities, and Lessons," *Marketing Research,* September 1989, p. 47.

6. Adapted from Keith K. Cox and Ben M. Enis, *The Marketing Research Process* (Pacific Palisades, CA: Goodyear, 1972); and Danny N. Bellenger and Barnet A. Greenberg, *Marketing Research: A Management Information Approach* (Homewood, IL: Richard D. Irwin, 1978), pp. 154–155.

7. Statistics Canada, http://www.statcan.ca/english/edu/tfeature/cpi.htm.

8. This is a hypothetical example.

9. Statistics Canada Cat. No. 92F0146GIE, Dissemination Areas Reference Maps, 2001 Census, Reference Guide.

10. "Internet Adoption Slowing – But Dependence On It Continues To Grow," Ipsos Canada Press Release, March 29, 2006 (http://www.ipsos-na.com/news/).

11. SurveySite, http://www.surveysite.com.

12. "Frequently Asked Questions about Conducting Online Research: New Methodologies for Traditional Techniques," Council of American Survey Research Organizations, http://www.casro.org/faq.cfm, February 8, 2001.

13. Gloria Mellinger, "Harris Interactive Inc.," *World Opinion Research Profiles,* July 18, 2000.

14. Adapted from John Gustavson, "Can the Spam," *Marketing Magazine,* April 7, 2003.

15. Industry Canada's "Recommended Best Practices for Email Marketing," Task Force on Spam, Working Group on Validating Commercial Email, May 2005. http://e-com.ic.gc.ca/epic/internet/inecic-ceac.nsf/en/h_gv00348e.html. Reproduced with the permission of the Minister of Public Works and Government Services, 2006.

16. "Internet Adoption Slowing – But Dependence On It Continues To Grow."

17. Adapted from Andrea Zoe Aster, "Consumer Research Goes Online," *Marketing Magazine,* June 7, 2004.

18. "Frequently Asked Questions about Conducting Online Research: New Methodologies for Traditional Techniques."

19. SSI, http://www.ssisamples.com, January 3, 2001.

CHAPTER 15

1. Peter McKnight, "Understanding a Poll's Margin of Error," *The Vancouver Sun,* June 3, 2006, p. C.5.

2. Catherine Dawson, "Service Fee Opinion Survey," Ipsos Canada Press Release, January 17, 2005 (http://www.ipsos-na.com/news/pressrelease.cfm?id=2522#).

3. Most of the statistical material in this book assumes that the population parameters are unknown, which is the typical situation in most applied research projects.

4. Darrell Huff and Irving Geis, *How to Lie with Statistics* (New York: W. W. Norton, 1954), p. 33.

5. The reasons for this are related to the concept of degrees of freedom, which will be explained later. At this point, disregard the intuitive notion of division by *n,* because it produces a biased estimate of the population variance.

6. In practice, most survey researchers will not use this exact formula. A modification of the formula, $Z = (X - \mu)/S$, using the sample standard deviation in an adjusted form, is frequently used.

7. Thomas H. Wonnacott and Ronald J. Wonnacott, *Introductory Statistics* (New York: John Wiley & Sons, 1969), p. 70. Reprinted with permission.

8. William L. Hayes, *Statistics* (New York: Holt, Rinehart and Winston, 1963), p. 193.

9. Adapted from D. H. Sanders, A. F. Murphy, and R. J. Eng, *Statistics: A Fresh Approach* (New York: McGraw-Hill, 1980), p. 123.

10. Thomas H. Wonnacott and Ronald J. Wonnacott, *Introductory Statistics,* 2nd ed. (New York: John Wiley & Sons, 1972), p. 125.

11. Ernest Kurnow, Gerald J. Glasser, and Frederick R. Ottman, *Statistics for Business Decisions* (Homewood, IL: Richard D. Irwin, 1959), pp. 182–183.

12. Fred N. Kerlinger, *Foundations of Behavioral Research* (New York: Holt, Rinehart & Winston, 1986), p. 117.

13. Note that the derivation of this formula is (1) $E = ZS_{\bar{X}}$, (2) $E = ZS\sqrt{n}$, (3) $\sqrt{n}ZS/E$, (4) $n = (ZS/E)^2$.

14. Nan Lin, *Foundations of Social Research* (New York: McGraw-Hill, 1976), p. 447. Copyright © 1976 by Nan Lin. Used with permission.

15. Lin, *Foundations of Social Research.*

CHAPTER 16

1. PFI Research Inc., http://www.pfi-research.com/?n=intrcpts.

2. "Horse Race: All Polls Are Not Created Equal," *U.S. News & World Report,* September 28, 1992.

3. *Interviewer's Manual,* rev. ed. (Ann Arbor, MI: Survey Research Center, Institute for Social Research, University of Michigan, 1976), p. 11.

4. *Interviewer's Manual,* p. 16.

5. *Interviewer's Manual,* pp. 11–13. Reprinted by permission.

6. *Interviewer's Manual,* p. 26. Reprinted by permission.

7. Alan Dutka, *AMA Handbook for Customer Satisfaction* (Lincolnwood, IL: NTC Business Books, 1993), p. 108.

8. Statistics Canada, http://www12.statcan.ca/english/census01/home/index.cfm.

9. Walker Research, "Coding Open Ends Based on Thoughts," *The Marketing Researcher,* December 1979, pp. 1–3.

10. Reprinted with permission of the State of Hawaii, Department of Transportation.

11. This section is adapted from Yankelovich, Skelly and White, Inc., *Interviewing Handbook for Senior Council Interviewers.*

CHAPTER 17

1. Adapted from Michelle Halpern, "Child's Play," *Marketing Magazine,* August 29, 2005.

2. Statistics Canada, www.statcan.ca.

3. Becky Ebenkamp, "For Whom the Bell Tolls," *BrandWeek,* May 7, 2001, p. 22.

4. From "Confidence in Church/Organized Religion," *The Gallup Report 238,* July 1985, p. 4.

5. Adapted from David G. Meyers, *Exploring Psychology* (New York: Worth Publishers, 1990), p. 464.

6. SPSS Inc.

7. From *Real Stats Real Easy: SPSS for Windows.* Copyright © 1992, SPSS, Inc.

8. SPSS Inc.

9. Technically the *t*-distribution should be used when the population variance is unknown and the standard deviation is estimated from sample data. However, with large samples it is convenient to use the *Z*-distribution, because the *t*-distribution approximates the *Z*-distribution.

10. The reader with an extensive statistics background will recognize that there are a few rare cases in which the degrees of freedom do not equal *k* - 1. However, these cases will rarely be encountered by readers of this level of book, and to present them would only confuse the discussion here.

11. An example of how to use the chi-square table is given in Table A.4 of the appendix.

12. Reprinted with permission from Melvin Prince, *Consumer Research for Management Decisions* (New York: John Wiley and Sons, 1982), pp. 163–166.

CHAPTER 18

1. Charles Zamaria, André H. Caron, and Fred Fletcher, "Canada Online: A Comparative Analysis of Internet Users and Non-users in Canada and the World: Behaviour, Attitudes and Trends 2004," Canadian Internet Project, October 2005. "The Canadian Internet Project is a research initiative funded by the Canadian Media Research Consortium, under the direction of Professor Charles Zamaria (Ryerson University) and Dr. Fred Fletcher (York University) in partnership with the following parties: Bell Canada, the Government of Canada, Telefilm Canada and the Ontario Media Development Corporation."

2. See Richard P. Bagozzi, "Salesforce Performance and Satisfaction as a Function of Individual Difference, Interpersonal and Situational Factors," *Journal of Marketing Research,* November 1978, pp. 517-531.

3. This is a point estimate. A confidence interval can be calculated for this sales estimate; however, the topic is beyond the scope of this book.

4. For discussions of multivariate analysis, see Joseph F. Hair Jr., Rolph E. Anderson, Ronald L. Tatham, and Bernie J. Grablowsky, *Multivariate Data Analysis with Readings,* 3rd ed. (New York: Macmillan, 1994).

5. H. Onur Bodur and Bianca Grohmann, "Goal-Oriented Ad Design: An Investigation of Message Type and Consumption Goal Congruence," ASAC 2004 Conference, Quebec City, QC.

CHAPTER 19

1. Michael R. Malone, "Home Grown," *Marketing Research,* Winter 1996, p. 12.

2. Linda I. Nowak and Judith H. Washburn, "Antecedents to Client Satisfaction in Business Services," *The Journal of Services Marketing,* Vol.12, No. 6, p. 441.

3. This chapter was revised by H. Onur Bodur based on the original work written by John Bush, Oklahoma State University. It originally appeared in William G. Zikmund, *Business Research Methods* (Hinsdale, IL: Dryden Press, 1984).

4. "Americans and Their Money," the fourth national survey from *Money* magazine, 1986, p. 49.

5. Report to the Federal Trade Commission on the Effects of the STP "Public Notice" Advertising Campaign, June 1979.

6. Adapted with permission from Mary Eleanor Spear, *Practical Charting Techniques* (New York: McGraw-Hill, 1969), p. 56.

7. Adapted with permission from Spear, *Practical Charting Techniques,* p. 57.

8. Adapted with permission from Spear, *Practical Charting Techniques,* pp. 58-59.

9. "A Series of Pie Charts," *Advertising Age International,* April 27, 1992, pp. 1-26. Reprinted with permission. Copyright © 1992 Crain Communications, Inc.

10. This is a hypothetical example.

11. Statistical Abstract of the United States, http://www.census.gov/prod/2001pubs/statab/sec15.pdf.

12. http://www40.statcan.ca/l01/cst01/labor40a.htm, Statistics Canada census 2001.

13. Statistics Canada, Income Statistics Division, Catalogue No. 62-554-XIE. Last modified: 2005-01-11. www.statcan.ca.

14. *Advertising Age International,* April 27, 1992, pp. 1-26. Reprinted with permission. Copyright © 1992 Crain Communications, Inc.

15. "A Speech Tip," *Communication Briefings,* Vol. 14, No. 2, p. 3. Reprinted with permission from *Communication Briefings,* Briefings Publishing Group, www.briefings.com.

16. Adapted with permission from William D. Wells, University of Minnesota, "Noah's Law of Overhead Transparencies," *ACR Newsletter,* June 1993, p. 10. Reprinted with permission from the Association for Consumer Research.

17. "How to Gesture When Speaking," *Communication Briefings,* Vol. 14, No. 11, p. 4. Reprinted with permission from *Communication Briefings,* Briefings Publishing Group, www.briefings.com.

STATISTICAL TABLES

Table A.1: *A Million Random Digits with 100,000 Normal Deviates* (New York: Free Press, 1955). Copyright © The Rand Corporation.

Table A.2: Chaiho Kim, *Statistical Analysis for Induction and Decision.* Copyright © 1973 by The Dryden Press, a division of South-Western Publishing.

Table A.3: Abridged from Table III of R. A. Fisher and F. Yates, *Statistical Tables for Biological, Agricultural, and Medical Research,* published by Longman Group, Ltd., London (previously published by Oliver & Boyd, Ltd., Edinburgh). Reproduced with the permission of Pearson Education Limited.

Table A.4: Abridged from Table IV of R. A. Fisher and F. Yates, *Statistical Tables for Biological, Agricultural, and Medical Research,* published by Longman Group, Ltd., London (previously published by Oliver & Boyd, Ltd., Edinburgh). Reproduced with the permission of Pearson Education Limited.

Table A.5: Maxine Merrington and Catherine M. Thompson, "Tables of the Percentage Points of the Inverted *F*-Distribution." *Biometrika,* Vol. 33, 1943, pp. 73-78. Reprinted with the permission of the Biometrika Trustees.

Table A.6: Maxine Merrington and Catherine M. Thompson, "Tables of the Percentage Points of the Inverted *F*-Distribution," *Biometrika,* Vol. 33, 1943, pp. 73-78. Reprinted with the permission of the Biometrika Trustees.

Table A.7: Abridged from Table IV of R. A. Fisher and F. Yates, *Statistical Tables for Biological, Agricultural, and Medical Research,* published by Longman Group, Ltd., London (previously published by Oliver & Boyd, Ltd., Edinburgh). Reproduced with the permission of Pearson Education Limited.

sample, 332
sample attrition effect, 506
sample bias, 151, 509
sample distribution, 369–370, 509
sample selection errors, 157–158, 225, 509
sample size, 377–383
   definition of, 36
   by judgment, 382–383
   and means, 378–379
   and population size, 379
   probability sampling, 383
   and proportions, 379–382
   and random error, 377
   stratified sampling, 382
sample statistics, 359, 509
sample surveys. *See* surveys
sampling, 35–36
   design, 348–350
   frame, 335–338, 509
   Internet, 350–355
   interval, 343
   nonprobability, 339–342
   probability, 340, 342–347
   proportional, 344–345
   random, 338–340
   reasons for, 332–333
   services, 336
   target population in, 333–335
   terminology, 331
   units, 338, 509
sampling distribution, 370, 509
sampling frame error, 337, 509
Samsonite Corp., 188
Saskatchewan, 116
scale of measurement, 435–436
scales, 252–255
   definition of, 509
   interval, 253–254
   mathematical analysis of, 254
   nominal, 252–253
   ordinal, 253
   ratio, 254
   sensitivity of, 259–260
   statistical analysis of, 254
scanner-based consumer panels, 215, 509
scanner-based research, 214–215
Scantel Research, 17
scientific method, 4, 509
Scott's Directories, 140
scrolling layout, 307
scrolling test boxes, 308
seafood products, concept statements for, 90
Sears Canada Inc., 13
secondary data research, 117–118
   advantages of, 117
   definition of, 509
   disadvantages of, 117–118
   in exploratory research, 30, 92–93
   objectives, 120–128
      customer relationship management (CRM), 127–128
      database marketing, 127–128

data mining, 125–127
   fact-finding, 120–122
   model building, 123–125
sources of data, 128–134
   corporate directories, 142
   distribution channels of information, 129–133
   external data, 128–129
   global, 134–135
   indexes, 139–140
   industry data, 142
   integrated data, 134
   internal and proprietary data, 128
   international sources, 142–143
   market data, 141
   reference guides, 139–140, 142
   statistical data, 140–141
   See also research
secondary sampling units, 338, 509
selection effect, 234, 509
self-administered questionnaires, 181–188
   definition of, 509
   e-mail surveys, 190
   fax surveys, 189–190
   Internet surveys, 191–195
   kiosk interactive surveys, 195
   mail surveys, 181–188
   phrasing questions in, 291–292
   See also surveys
self-selection bias, 153, 509
semantic differential scale, 268–269, 509
sensitivity, 259–260, 509
sentence completion method, 104, 509
sequence discovery, 127
Shake'n Bake food products, 149
Sharpe Blackmore Euro RSCG, 54
shopping centre sampling, 175–176
significance level, 430, 509
simple-dichotomy questions, 289, 509
simple random sampling, 343, 509
single-source data, 134, 509
site analysis, 124–125, 509
situation analysis, 74, 509
Small Business Profiles, 141
smart agents, 121–122
smokeless cigarettes, marketing of, 22
snack foods, 120
snowball sampling, 341, 509
social desirability bias, 156, 509
societal norms, 55, 509
Solomon four-group design, 239, 509
Sony Corp., 71–72
sorting, 275–276, 509
spam, 352
split-ballot technique, 295, 509
split-half method, 256–257, 510
sponsorship, 186
SportChek, 15
spurious relationship, 421, 510
staff function, 45
standard deviation, 364–365, 510
Standard Directory of International Advertisers & Agencies, 142

standard error of the mean, 370–371, 510
standardized normal distribution, 366–368, 510
standardized research services, 53, 510
Stapel scale, 269–270, 510
static group design, 236–237, 510
Statistical Abstract of the United States, 142
statistical analysis, 254
statistical errors, 338
Statistical Yearbook, 142
statistics, 364
   central-limit theorem, 371–373
   descriptive, 359
   estimation of parameters, 373–376
   frequency distributions, 359–360
   inferential, 359
   measures of central tendency, 360–362
      mean, 360–362
      median, 362
      mode, 362
   measures of dispersion, 363–365
      deviation scores, 364
      range, 363–364
      standard deviation, 364–365
   normal distribution, 366–369
   population distribution, 369
   proportions, 360
   sample distribution, 369–370
   sample size, 377–383
   sampling distribution, 370
   standard error of the mean, 370–371
Statistics Canada, 116, 131, 140
status bar, 307, 308, 510
Steelcase, 214
stratified sampling, 344, 382, 510
stratum charts, 483–484
streaming media, 101, 510
structured questions, 159, 510
subdivided bar charts, 484
Subway, 221
Sun-Rype Products Ltd., 5–6
Survey Lion, 353
Survey of Buying Power: Canadian Data, 141
surveys, 148–150
   administrative errors in, 157–158
   advantages of, 149–150, 197
   classification of, 159–162
      structured and disguised questions, 159
      temporal classification, 160–162
   definition of, 510
   disadvantages of, 197
   errors in, 150–151
   ethical issues in, 198
   interviews in. *See* interviews
   in marketing research, 33–34
   objectives of, 148–149
   pre-testing, 196
   respondent errors in, 151–157